Aphrodite's Island

ALSO BY ANNE SALMOND

Hui: A Study of Maori Ceremonial Gatherings
Eruera: Teachings of a Maori Elder
Amiria: The Life Story of a Maori Woman
Two Worlds: First Meetings between Maori and Europeans, 1642–1772
Between Worlds: Early Meetings Between Maori and Europeans, 1773–1815
The Trial of the Cannibal Dog: Captain Cook in the South Seas

Aphrodite's Island

The European Discovery of Tahiti

ANNE SALMOND

University of California Press | *Berkeley Los Angeles London*

University of California Press, one of the most distinguished university presses in the
United States, enriches lives around the world by advancing scholarship in the humanities,
social sciences, and natural sciences. Its activities are supported by the UC Press Foundation
and by philanthropic contributions from individuals and institutions. For more information,
visit www.ucpress.edu.

University of California Press
Berkeley and Los Angeles, California

University of California Press, Ltd.
London, England

First published in New Zealand and Australia by Penguin Group (NZ), 2009
First University of California Press edition published in 2010

1 3 5 7 9 10 8 6 4 2

Designed and typeset by Pindar NZ
Printed in Australia by McPherson's Printing Group

Cataloging-in-Publication Data for this title is on file with the Library of Congress

ISBN 978-0-520-26114-3 (cloth : alk. paper)

Contents

List of Illustrations

Colour Plates

List of Maps

A Note to Readers

LOST SOURCES ON TAHITI

There are four irreplaceable manuscripts or groups of manuscripts relating to Tahiti's early history which have been lost, each of which may still survive somewhere in the world. If these can be located, they will be a treasured addition to the known heritage of the island.

The first of these is an account of Tahitian cosmology by Tupaia, recorded by Joseph Banks in 1769 and loaned to Joseph Correa de Serra, who returned the last page to him from Paris in April 1805. This may be somewhere among Banks's papers.

The second is Máximo Rodríguez's account of Tahitian customs and his vocabulary of Tahitian, written during his visit to the island during 1774–75 and presented to the Viceroy of Peru, Manuel de Amat, who may have sent it to the archives in Madrid or Lima.

The third is John Muggeridge Orsmond's manuscript history of Tahiti, presented by Orsmond to Commandant Lavaud, the representative of the French Republic in Tahiti, in 1848 for publication.

The fourth is the collection of John Orsmond's original manuscripts on Tahitian life, language and customs, upon which Teuira Henry based her book *Ancient Tahiti*. These were left to her literary legatees, Ed Ahne and Henry Orsmond Walker. Anyone knowing the whereabouts of these manuscripts is asked to contact the author, who will alert interested colleagues in Tahiti and elsewhere, and gratefully acknowledge the discovery.

Acknowledgements

One of the joys of writing this book – apart from the sheer delight of visiting Tahiti and its people – has been the pleasure of shared endeavour. I would like to thank my colleagues in the 'Cross-cultural Voyaging' project: Mercedes Camino (now a Professor at the University of Lancaster in the United Kingdom), whose re-examination of Spanish voyaging in the Pacific casts new light on the colonial history of Spain; Amiria Salmond, Fellow at Gonville and Caius College and Senior Curator at the Museum of Archaeology and Anthropology at the University of Cambridge (and my daughter), whose insights into the exchanges between islands and explorers and the artefacts collected during the voyages illuminated this research from the beginning;[1] and all those who assisted in our researches – Carl Hogsden, who worked with Amiria in Cambridge to build the KIWA voyaging database; Billie Lythberg, who collaborated with them, making innumerable meticulous entries in KIWA; Gwyn Fox, who transcribed and translated the documents in Spanish; Isabel Ollivier in Paris, who produced elegant translations of the documents in French; Christine Hemming, who located documents from the voyages in archives throughout France; Meredith Filihia, who scoured archives around Australia and transcribed a number of crucial documents; Ian Johnson, for processing endless accounts; and Kori Netana, who ordered documents and books, organised trips and meetings, paid invoices, kept everyone in touch with each other and dealt with crises with inexhaustible good humour. Heartfelt thanks, too, to my husband Jeremy, who handled the logistics of various research excursions, getting us to and from remote and difficult locations, taking innumerable photographs and sharing the delights of discovery.

Without these people, there would have been no research, no book, and much less enjoyment during the process of investigation. I am grateful to the Royal Society of New Zealand and the Marsden Fund for making possible the investigations that led to this book; and to Dr John Hood, then the Vice-Chancellor of The University of Auckland, for approving the leave that allowed me to write in relative tranquillity. It is also a pleasure to thank Jenny Newell and Joan Druett, who meticulously checked the manuscript and made many helpful suggestions; and to acknowledge Amiria's colleagues and collaborators in the Pasifika Styles project at the Museum of Anthropology and Archaeology, particularly Rosanna Raymond and the Māori and Pacific artists whose works they assembled in Cambridge for that brilliant, unforgettable exhibition.

The sources (oral and written) upon which this work is based are scattered across the world, and many people helped me to locate them. I am indebted to the Centre for Cross-cultural Research and colleagues at the Australian National University, particularly Benjamin Penny, Bronwen Douglas, Margaret Jolly and Mark Mosko, for their warm welcome during a visit in 2004; Richard Unger for an invitation to take part in the conference 'Spain's Legacy in the Pacific' in San Diego, where I met many leading Spanish scholars; and Glyn Williams, Nigel Rigby and Margarette Lincoln for their generous support during a research stay at the National Maritime Museum in Greenwich as a Caird Short-term Fellow. I am also indebted to Martyn Lyons for his invitation to deliver a Special Lecture at the International Congress for Historical Sciences in Sydney in 2005; Elfriede Hermann for inviting me to participate in a conference in Honolulu sponsored by the University of Göttingen and the Honolulu Academy of Arts in 2006; and Roy Bridges and the Council of the Hakluyt Society for asking me to deliver the Hakluyt Lecture in London in 2007. These invitations made it possible for me to visit these places, meet many Pacific and voyaging experts, and collect documents from local archives. I am also deeply grateful to friends and colleagues at the University of Cambridge, including Dame Marilyn Strathern, Stephen Hugh-Jones, Nicholas Thomas, Alan Macfarlane, and Ann Taylor and Michael Kelly, for their hospitality and kindness during research visits to the United Kingdom to locate documents from the British voyages. I would also like to thank Elizabeth Taylor, and Padre Maroni from the Franciscan order in Rome, for their assistance in tracking down biographical information on the Franciscan Fathers who travelled to Tahiti from Peru.

One serendipitous spin-off from the Cross-cultural Voyaging project has been a collaboration with Professor Serge Tcherkézoff of the CREDO Research Institute in Marseilles, supported by the French Embassy in Wellington, New Zealand and the French government. I would like to thank the former French Ambassador, Jean-Michel Marlaud, for his warm goodwill, and Marleen van Roosmalen and Typhaine Biard-Hamon of the embassy for their guidance. With their assistance, a joint research project was established that allowed Serge and myself to organise a memorable workshop in Paris in 2005 between the Cross-cultural Voyaging team and French researchers; to work together as Pacific scholars, exchanging visits to each other's countries, gathering and translating documents from the early European voyages to Polynesia, and to return some of these documents to the islanders whose ancestors participated in those first world-shifting encounters. Serge's insights into life in Polynesia are an ongoing source of inspiration, grounded as they are in his long field experience, deep knowledge, and abiding love of the Pacific. During visits to CREDO, Serge and his colleagues at the Institute, including Ann di Piazza and Erik Pearthree, Paul van der Grijp and Françoise Douaire-Marsaudon, Isabelle Merle and Deborah Pope, offered hospitality and many new ideas – a pleasurable entrée to intellectual life in France. I would also like to thank the French government's Pacific Fund for supporting our project; Isabel Ollivier for her hospitality in Paris; and the École des Haute Études in Paris, which appointed me a Visiting Professor in 2006.

Finally and perhaps above all, I would like to give thanks to those people in Tahiti who gave their time and expertise so generously to this project. In particular I am indebted to Bruno Saura of the Université de Polynésie Française for his exceptional generosity in going through the manuscript line by line, checking the detail of Tahitian names, genealogies, references and oral histories; and the Académie Tahitienne Fare Vana'a for checking a number of matters. Their kindness and expertise have ensured that this book is free of many errors that would otherwise mar its pages. I am also grateful to Robert and Denise Koenig for their hospitality and expert knowledge of French Polynesia; Mark Eddowes for sharing his insights as an archaeologist and scholar of Tahitian oral history; Raanui Daunassans for welcoming us to the old Pomare home in Pape'ete; and Francis and Jacquie Mortimer for their kindness. During a visit to Tahiti in 2006, Ari'ihau and Karine Tuheiava, Romy Tavaeari'i, Matorai Pani and their comrades in Na Papa e Va'u at Taputapuatea in Ra'iatea welcomed me and colleagues from the Māori Heritage Council to the Society Islands, sharing with us their love of Tahitian language, history and traditions, and their passion for taking care of that great voyaging *marae* for future generations. I will never forget the warmth of their flower-decked welcome; our workshops on the beach; Romy's explanations of the different structures on Taputapuatea; our visit by boat to Te Ava Mo'a; and the evening parties, with their feasts, music and laughter. I hope that the French government will ensure that their dream to have Taputapuatea honoured as a World Heritage Site is soon realised.

After a lifetime of studying Māori culture and tradition in New Zealand, it has been a marvellous privilege to learn more about Tahiti and the Society Islands, that Hawaiki (homeland) of Māori people. In the words of the Māori elders who first led me into the world of the ancestors:

Whakarongo! Whakarongo! Whakarongo!	Listen! Listen! Listen!
Ki te tangi a te manu e karanga nei	To the cry of the bird calling
Tui, tui, tuituiā!	Bind, join, be one!
Tuia i runga, tuia i raro,	Bind above, bind below,
Tuia i roto, tuia i waho,	Bind within, bind without,
Tuia i te here tangata	Tie the knot of humankind
Ka rongo te pō, ka rongo te pō	The night hears, the night hears
Tuia i te kāwai tangata i heke mai	Bind the lines of people coming down
I Hawaiki nui, i Hawaiki roa,	From great Hawaiki, from long Hawaiki
I Hawaiki pāmamao	From Hawaiki far away
I hono ki te wairua, ki te whai ao	Bind to the spirit, to the daylight
Ki te Ao Mārama!	To the World of Light!

Aphrodite's Island

For five days, it had been raining. Sharp gusts buffeted the two ships as they beat against contrary winds, heading north-westward across the Pacific. Squalls drove torrents of rain and seawater above and below decks, making everything wet and miserable. The sea was grey and the sky was grey, hanging low over the mastheads. As Louis de Bougainville, the diplomat and soldier who commanded the French expedition, wrote despondently in his journal: 'This South Sea is not favourable to us; almost always calm or rain and head wind . . . This is the worst weather in the world, night and day.'[1]

Since leaving Rio de Janeiro the *Boudeuse* and *Étoile* had been at sea for almost five months, and conditions on board were dismal. Clothing and hammocks were sodden, the drinking water stank and the bread was rotting in the barrels. Bougainville and his men were on a voyage of discovery, looking for new lands in the South Sea, perhaps Davis's Land or the fabled Southern Continent, rumoured to be rich in gold, silver and spices. When they stopped at Rio the *Boudeuse*, a frigate with a crew of 220 men and limited cargo space, had taken on provisions for only three months; and they had obtained little fresh food during their passage through the Strait of Magellan. In the Tuamotu Islands, Bougainville had not dared risk a landing on those dangerous atolls. Scurvy was appearing among the sailors, with twenty cases on board the storeship *Étoile* among her crew of just 120 men; and its symptoms of bowed limbs, swollen gums, stinking breath and livid ulcers were lowering everyone's spirits.

At last, on 2 April 1768, the sky cleared, and when the sun came out two high peaks of land appeared on the horizon. Bougainville and his men were overjoyed, because these peaks were unmarked on their charts and the land looked green and alluring. The winds were still contrary, forcing the ships to tack for two days before they could approach the eastern shoreline of the larger island, where the coast rose up in a jagged amphitheatre of volcanic peaks with deep valleys, glinting waterfalls tumbling down the cliffs and a strip of shoreline glowing green in the sunlight, covered with coconut palms, trees and scattered, palm-thatched houses. After long months at sea and endless tropical storms, Tahiti looked like Paradise – irresistible and enticing; and they thought that it was a new discovery. In fact, Captain Samuel Wallis in the *Dolphin* had visited the island just nine months earlier, claiming it for Britain, but news of his landfall had not yet reached Europe.[2]

On shore, the local warriors were on the alert. When he left the island, Captain Wallis had told the islanders that he would return, and they must have thought that these were his vessels. As the two ships headed towards the coast a large sailing canoe approached them, the crew paddling to increase its speed. It was manned by twelve strapping men, almost naked, and as this canoe came alongside the *Boudeuse*, a man with tall, bristling hair stood and presented the strangers with a plantain branch, a small pig and some bananas in a ritual of welcome, tying them onto a rope that a French sailor threw overboard. As soon as the strangers accepted these offerings, a hundred or more canoes crowded around the ships, their crews handing up gifts of fruit and plantain branches; Bougainville handed over woollen caps and several knives in return, and these people left in high good humour. When another canoe came out, manned by ten paddlers and carrying a man and a fine-looking, pale-skinned young girl, it could not keep up with the frigate and dropped back to the storeship, where the sailors threw the paddlers a mooring rope. The male passenger, a tall, robust fellow, seized the rope and with remarkable agility hauled himself across to the *Étoile*, climbing the rigging chains up to the deck where he presented a plantain branch to her captain; and that night he slept on board the vessel.

During these first encounters no women ventured on board the ships, although several girls came out in the canoes. After dark the land twinkled with small flares placed at intervals along the shoreline, and Bougainville ordered his men to fire some rockets in reply before tacking away from the island. Sailing back towards the south-east coast the next morning, they saw a village surrounded by fruit trees where a spectacular waterfall tumbled into the ocean. Gazing at this glorious spot, Bougainville sent the boats to look for an anchorage, but to his dismay the sea floor was too rocky. As night fell they tacked out to sea again, and the next morning, 6 April, returned to the coast where they found an anchorage inside the reef at Hitia'a, where a river ran out to the ocean. As the *Boudeuse* led the way into the lagoon, canoes packed with young women flocked around the ship, their crews gesturing and calling out '*Taio!*' or 'Friend!'.

As each canoe came alongside, elderly men and women stripped the girls of their bark-cloth garments. Finally, one beautiful young girl climbed on board, and in his official account of the voyage, Bougainville described what happened:

> The men . . . pressed us to choose a woman, and to come on shore with her; and their gestures denoted in what manner we should form an acquaintance with her. It was very difficult, amidst such a sight, to keep at their work four hundred young French sailors, who had seen no women for six months.
>
> In spite of all our precautions, a young girl came on board, and placed herself upon the quarter-deck, near one of the hatch-ways, which was open, in order to give air to those who were heaving at the capstern [sic] below it. The girl carelessly dropt a cloth, which covered her, and appeared to the eyes of all beholders, such as Venus shewed herself to the Phrygian shepherd, having indeed the celestial form of that goddess. Both sailors and soldiers endeavoured to come to the hatch-way; and the capstern was never hove with more alacrity than on this occasion.
>
> At last our cares succeeded in keeping these bewitched fellows in order, though it was no less difficult to keep the command of ourselves.[3]

As the young woman dropped her bark-cloth garments, the commander was irresistibly reminded of Venus, the goddess of love, known to the Greeks as Aphrodite. Painting and sculpture in eighteenth-century Europe were dominated by neo-classical themes, and the goddess of love was often depicted draped in robes, naked or bare-breasted. Fesche, a junior officer on board the *Boudeuse*, also invoked the gods of antiquity on this occasion – in his case, Cupid or Eros, Aphrodite's messenger and companion: 'This veil I say, is soon lifted, more promptly it is true by the Indian divinity herself than by them, she was following the customs of her country, a practice that alas the corruption of our ways has destroyed among us. What brush could depict the marvels we discover when that troublesome veil happily falls – an enchanting grove no doubt planted by that god himself?'[4] Fesche was right in supposing that the girl was following a local custom, for in Tahiti people stripped to the waist in the presence of gods and high chiefs, and a high-ranking stranger was often greeted by a young girl swathed in layers of bark cloth who slowly turned around, unwinding the bark cloth from her body until she stood naked – a ritual presentation with no necessary implication of sexual availability. The sailors did not understand this, however, and they crowded around the girl, fondling her longingly; and after a while she left the ship looking distressed and offended.

Captivated by this display, Bougainville named the island *'Nouvelle Cythère'* after the Greek island Cythera, where the young goddess Aphrodite had first been washed ashore. In Europe at this time, this gorgeous, capricious deity was a celebrated symbol of sexual desire, along with her male companion Eros. Like Bougainville, Commerson the expedition's naturalist and several of the officers on board were educated men, steeped in the classics, and Greek and Roman mythology gave them a means of grasping these exotic experiences. Later, in a rhapsodic account that was widely circulated in Europe, Commerson described Tahiti as an island of Love, with glorious, beguiling women:

> Born under the most beautiful of skies, fed on the fruits of a land that is fertile and requires no cultivation, ruled by the fathers of families rather than by kings, they know no other Gods than Love. Every day is dedicated to it, the entire island is its temple, every woman is its altar, every man its priest. And what sort of women? you will ask. The rivals of Georgian women in beauty, and the sisters of the unclothed Graces.[5]

From this time onwards, Polynesian women became mythical figures, associated with ideas of a Golden Age of innocent desire and sexual freedom.[6]

One can still catch glimpses of the Arcadian visions that inspired Bougainville and his companions in many Utopian writings or paintings and images from this period in Europe. At the Louvre in Paris, for instance, a 1717 painting by Watteau called 'Pilgrimage to Cythera' shows a group of elegantly dressed people landing on a beach, a flock of Cupids flying overhead as they arrive at the island of Venus; while at the National Art Gallery in Canberra or the Honolulu Academy of Arts in Hawai'i, a French wallpaper titled 'Savages of the Pacific Ocean' (1804) depicts the inhabitants of the South Sea Islands. In the section of the wallpaper depicting Tahiti, three girls in white robes dance gaily on a grassy meadow beneath fruit and palm trees, accompanied by musicians playing on flutes and drums, evoking the three Graces, the companions of the goddess Aphrodite. (*See Plate 5.*)

As the author of the original caption to this section of the wallpaper remarked: 'M. de Bougainville . . . made such a seductive description of [Tahiti] that one is tempted, at times, to detect the Romantic hand of a poet in the explorer's reports, . . . particularly on the merits of the women whose games depict those of Paphos and Cythera in Greek antiquity.'[7] In fact, such mythic allusions still colour the images used to promote the

Pacific Islands to tourists – brown-skinned, long-haired young women decked in bright flowers who smile or beckon – Aphrodite and her nymphs in Polynesian guise, the quintessential South Sea Island maiden.

Although Bougainville's experiences in Tahiti were shaped by the classics, his recourse to Greek mythology was not entirely far-fetched, because in places the myths of Aphrodite are reminiscent of Tahitian ancestral stories. According to Hesiod, for instance, at the beginning of the world the Sky god Ouranos and his wife Gaia, the Earth, lay for aeons locked in an embrace so close that their children were crushed between them. Finally, in frustration, their son Kronos lopped off his father's genitals with a sickle and threw them backwards into the ocean. As the sea swept them away, white foam gathered about them and in it grew a maiden. She was carried on the waves to Cythera and thence to Cyprus where she stepped ashore as the beautiful white-skinned goddess Aphrodite, immortalised by Botticelli in his famous painting *The Birth of Venus* which hangs in the Uffizi Gallery in Florence:

> 'As for the genitals, slashed away by the sickle of steel,
> Their impetus carried them out from shore to the tide of the sea.
> For years the waters swirled them about, as white foam kept oozing
> From out the immortal flesh. Within it there grew up a maiden
> Who drifted first to holy Cythera, then on to Cyprus
> There she emerged from the sea as a modest and beautiful goddess
> Around whose slim-ankled feet arose all the flowers of springtime.
> Gods and mortals alike call her Aphrodite, the Foam-born,
> Or else Cytherea, to honor the island where first she was seen.
> Eros walked by her side, and fair Desire came after
> As she joined the race of the gods. These are the honors she holds;
> Giggling whispers of girls, the smiling deceptions they practice,
> As well as the honeyed delights and all the allurements of passion.'[8]

As the anthropologist Marshall Sahlins has insisted – drawing a contrast between 'the mythopraxis of Polynesian peoples and . . . the utilitarianism of our own historical consciousness'[9] – Polynesian myths played a powerful role in shaping these early encounters. However, as the references to Cythera, Aphrodite and Venus during this and later voyages to Tahiti demonstrate, the European explorers also saw the islanders through a haze of their own enchantments. Although Europe discovered Tahiti during the Age of Reason, fantasy was far from dead, and the worlds that came together in these meetings were as much imaginative as real.

I

Thunder in 'Opoa

How can we grasp the Pacific visions that shaped these first, strange encounters? If one looks at those extraordinary images of the earth taken from outer space, Tahiti appears as a speck of land, set in the midst of the world's largest ocean. Around it swirls the Pacific, a vast expanse of water covering more than a third of the earth's surface. In the origin stories in Tahiti there is a sense of cosmic loneliness, of floating adrift in the void. According to the priests in the old schools of learning, when the world began there was only one god, Ta'aroa, alone, with no parents, in utter darkness:

> Ta'aroa was his name
> He stood in the void
> No land, no sky
> No sea, no men
> Ta'aroa called, but nothing replied to him
> And alone existing he changed himself into the universe
> His pivots and axes
> His rocks and bases
> Ta'aroa is the sand
> That is how he himself is called
> Ta'aroa is brightness, the day or intelligence
> Ta'aroa is the centre, is in everything, the principle of all
> Ta'aroa is the seed, the propagator
> Ta'aroa is the basis or the foundation
> Ta'aroa is the incorruptible
> Ta'aroa is the strength
> Who creates the earth of the universe
> Which is only the body or shell of Ta'aroa
> He is the source of life for all things.[1]

Alone in the abyss, the feathered god lay in his shell. One day he came out and stood there, calling, but no one answered. Ta'aroa went back into his shell and stayed there for aeons, and when he came out again he changed one part of his body into Rumia, the multi-layered dome of the sky, above the world that was now forming.[2] Other parts he transformed into Tetumu, the Rock of Foundation (an *ata* – shadow or incarnation – of his own phallus), and the Earth, Papa-fenua. Ta'aroa looked down at the Earth and said, 'Here are Ta'aroa's genitals. Cast your eyes upon my Tumu. Stand up and gaze upon them. Insert them.'[3] He came down to Papa, entering the Earth in a valley at 'Opoa in Havai'i (now Ra'iatea), one of the most sacred places in the Society Islands. Where his foot struck the ground, a *marae* named Vaeara'i (separate the sky) was later built. When he entered the earth, there was thunder at 'Opoa.[4]

Now Ta'aroa created Tu, the god of artisans, and Atea (Space) who bore him a son named Tane, the god of peace and beauty. When Ta'aroa shook his red and yellow feathers, some of these fell on the Earth and became trees and plants; and when he created other gods they found themselves trapped in the darkness between Earth and Sky, chafing at their captivity. Cramped and frustrated, they tried to separate Earth and Sky, attacking the great octopus that held them tightly together (another *ata* or incarnation of Ta'aroa), first with incantations and then by chopping its tentacles, but they clung to each other so tightly that every effort was futile. It was only when the god Tane propped up the dome of the sky on star pillars, thrusting Earth and Sky apart, that light entered the world, creating Te Ao, the realm of people. Water rushed in, rocks formed, forests sprang up and the skies grew, and the octopus's tentacles fell into the sea and became Tupua'i in the Austral Islands. Tane set the ten heavens in order and went to live in the highest sky, where the Milky Way or Te Vai-ora-o-Tane (the living water of Tane) flowed. A great blue shark (also an *ata* of Ta'aroa) swam in the Water of Life, and over it flew red birds, the messengers of Tane.[5] Atea slept with another god and gave birth to the shooting stars, the moon, the sun, comets and constellations; and as the star gods were born, they sailed across the sky in their voyaging canoes, and new stars were created.[6]

After Tane had set up the ten domed skies, each above the last, Ta'aroa changed himself into land, the homeland Havai'i – his backbone became the mountain ridges, his ribs the slopes, and his flesh the soil. Next he changed himself into the first god-house, with his backbone as its ridge-pole and his ribs as its supports; and finally into the first sacred canoe with his backbone as the keel, floating on the water.[7] In each district Ta'aroa made a mountain, a cape and a *marae* or stone temple, and set a star above it, ordering the universe.[8] After his union with Papa, the Earth, she bore Hina, a Janus-headed goddess who beat bark cloth for the gods and later flew to the moon; and later Ta'aroa slept incestuously with Hina, his *ata* (or incarnation), on this occasion being a breadfruit branch that hung above her, and she bore the great god 'Oro.[9]

'Oro was the god of fertility and war, controlling the main portals between the Po, the dark void inhabited by gods and spirits, and the Ao, the bright world of people. After 'Oro's birth, his father Ta'aroa looked around and saw that although the Po, the realm of the gods, was now full of life, the Ao, the realm of people, was still empty. He conjured up Ti'i, the first man, and Ti'i slept with Hina, the moon goddess, and the world of light began to fill with human beings who brought with them trouble, mockery and wisdom. These children of Ti'i and Hina became the leading family in the Society Islands, wearers of the red and yellow feather girdles of high chiefs, descended from the gods in darkness.[10]

Although Havai'i, the birthplace of land, gods and people, had been created, the great ocean in which it floated was still largely empty. Other islands now began to form. First the islands of Borabora and Ra'iatea emerged,[11] and eventually the island of Tahiti took shape when a section of Ra'iatea turned into a shark that swam off to the south-east, leaving the small islands of Me'eti'a and Te Ti'aroa as droppings in its wake. At the time of early contact Tahitians spoke of their island as a great fish, with its head at Tai'arapu ('disturbed sea', from the way the fish thrashed about in the ocean) in the south; its left pectoral fin in the east at Hitia'a (where Bougainville landed); its right pectoral fin in the west at Papara; and its tail at the north-west point of the island in Fa'a'a. The shark kept swimming in the sea until the god Tafa'i, the red-headed grandson of Hina, struck it with his sacred axe, creating the Taravao isthmus that divides the island into Tahiti-nui, its large northern part, and Tahiti-iti, the smaller southern peninsula.[12] Afterwards the sea god Ruahatu swam round the island, cutting passages through the reefs and placing the stones for the coastal *marae* or stone temples as portals between the Po, the world of the gods and darkness, and the Ao, the everyday world of people and light, so that people could communicate with their ancestors.[13] When he arrived at Papara, Ruahatu carved a passage through the reef and placed the stones for a great *marae* named Mahaiatea, which he dedicated to Ta'aroa.[14]

In this vast, watery world, many of the founding ancestors were voyagers and explorers. First Tane, the god of peace and beauty, sailed through the skies in his canoe, putting them in order, while the demi-gods Maui and Ru sailed around the earth, raising islands out of the ocean. After cutting the sinews of the fish, Tahiti, Tafa'i navigated his sacred canoe the 'Rainbow' around the archipelago, pulling the islets of Te Ti'aroa and the Tuamotu up out of the water; while the trickster god Hiro, the god of thieves, built the first *pahi* (a long-distance canoe with high planked sides) and set off in search of feathers for the first *maro 'ura* (red feather girdle), discovering many islands.[15] These ancestors were revered as gods, and navigation became a sacred pursuit in the islands. Their feats were celebrated in voyaging chants passed down through the generations, like Homer's *The Iliad* and *The Odyssey* and Virgil's *The Aeneid*.[16]

Like Odysseus, Tafa'i visited many exotic locations. These included the land of the dead, guarded by Uhi, a blind old woman. Although Uhi tried to catch Tafa'i with her magical hook he escaped, and impressed by his cunning, she promised to help him rescue his father if he restored her sight. He did this by throwing two unripe coconuts into her eye sockets, and as a reward she gave him her two daughters to sleep with – Venus, the evening star (Te 'uraiopena) and Venus, the morning star (Te 'uraiti'ahotu, also known as Tau'ura-nui). Tau'ura-nui was kind to Tafa'i, showing him where his father Hema was trapped in the underworld, huddled in a cave filled with excrement. Hema was naked and blind, and his eyes had been taken to light the house where Ta'aroa's daughters were weaving their fine mats. After rescuing his father, Tafa'i retrieved Hema's eyes, tricking Ta'aroa's daughters into handing them over.[17] In Tahiti, Tafa'i's adventures in the land of the dead were greatly celebrated, especially during the rituals of mourning and those to install a new *ari'i rahi* or high chief on the island.

And as in ancient Greece, the time of the gods in Tahiti ran directly into the time of people. The high chiefs were the lineal descendants of the gods, and from the first settlement of the island to the first arrival of Europeans, the genealogical experts reckoned forty generations of high chiefs in Tahiti.[18] These *ari'i rahi* were the 'living faces' of the gods in the everyday world of light, and in their presence men and women stripped to the waist. They 'flew' or were carried on the shoulders of men; and were spoken of as gods themselves – their houses were called the Clouds of Heaven, their voices Thunder, their torches Lightning, and their sacred canoes the *Rainbow* after Tafa'i's sacred vessel.[19]

In the spectacular landscapes of the Society Islands with their high, sharp-edged mountains and deep caves and valleys, at the time of first European arrival the gods were still present. At Ra'iatea, for instance, the great Foundation Rock Tumu-nui stood in darkness in the extinct crater of Te Mehani'ura, where the entrance to Te Po or the realm of the gods was located,[20] while Rohutu-no'ano'a, the perfumed, flowering paradise for chiefs and *'arioi*, floated above the great volcano.[21] On the mountain plateau, a cliff called the Stone of Life led to Rohutu-no'ano'a.[22] The area around the sacred site at Cape Matahira-i-te-ra'i in 'Opoa, where *marae* Taputapuatea now stands, is still known as Te Po, because in this place the gods are in residence. The first of the high chiefs built a *marae* or stone temple there, bringing order out of chaos, and dedicated it to Ta'aroa. At each *marae*, Te Po (the world of darkness, death and the gods) entered Te Ao (the world of light, life and people), and a star stood above the *marae*, fixing it in the cosmos.

For many generations the chiefs on the island were devoted to Tane, the god of peace and beauty who presided over an era of harmony which people later remembered with nostalgia. In the generations before the first Europeans arrived, however, the worship of 'Oro spread across the archipelago, bringing with it fighting and human sacrifices. The sacrifices were dedicated to him in his role as the god of war, while his worship as the god of fertility featured sexually explicit displays and dancing. 'Oro's descendant, the trickster god Hiro, built a *marae* at Cape Matahira-i-te-ra'i in 'Opoa in honour of the god of life and death, naming it Taputapuatea or 'Sacrifices from afar'.[23] At this *marae*, a drum named Ta'imoana was made, which boomed out ominously each time a human sacrifice was offered.[24] Near the beach Hiro erected Te Papatea-o-Ru'ea, the white rock of investiture where his descendants, the paramount chiefs of Ra'iatea, were invested with the *maro 'ura* (red feather girdle). The image of the god for this *marae* – fashioned from fine sennit, shaped like a man about three feet high and covered with red and yellow feathers – also wore a red feather girdle, and thus it was known as 'Oro-maro-'ura ('Oro of the red feather girdle, the insignia of high chiefs in the Society Islands).[25]

During this period, *marae* became fearful places. They were dark, shaded by groves of sacred trees – the *tamanu*, *miro* and especially the *aito* or casuarina.[26] People spoke of these places as the jawbones of the gods, biting the spirits who passed into the dark underworld where they were consumed by the gods; while the stone uprights on their pavements were called their *niho* or teeth. Vai'otaha *marae* on Borabora, for instance, with its yellow feather girdle, was spoken of as the upper jawbone of the god; Mata'ire'a *marae* on Huahine with its black feather girdle was his lower jawbone; while Taputapuatea *marae* on Ra'iatea with its red feather girdle was his throat, swallowing spirits into the darkness.[27] As the high priests of Tahiti and Mo'orea explained to an early missionary, John Orsmond, these sacred places were treated with utmost reverence and awe:

> *Marae* were the sanctity and glory of the land, they were the pride of the people of these islands. A place of dread and of great silence was the *marae*. A person's

errand must be to pray there, but for no other purpose. When people approached a place where stood a *marae*, they gave it a wide berth, they lowered their clothes from their shoulders down to their waists, and carried low their burdens in their hands, until they got out of sight of it.

Terrible were the *marae* of the royal line; their ancestral and national *marae*! They were places of stupendous silence, terrifying and awe-inspiring; places of pain to the priest, to the owners, and to all the people. It was dark and shadowy among the great trees of those *marae*; and the most sacred of all was the *miro* that was the sanctifier. That was the basis of the ordinances; It was the basis of royalty; It awakened the gods; It fixed the red feather girdle of the high chiefs.[28]

As the cult of 'Oro spread, Taputapuatea became the centre of a far-flung voyaging network. When they set out on a journey, 'Oro's followers swore an oath not to turn back before reaching their destination.[29] In their sacred canoes, they carried images of the god and stones from Taputapuatea throughout the Society Islands, south to the Cook Islands (where the voyaging ancestor Tangi'ia built a *marae* called Taputapuatea, upon which the paramount chief was invested with a *maro kura* or red feather girdle);[30] and east to the Australs, where other *marae* called Taputapuatea were established. It seems that the followers of 'Oro also travelled to more distant islands, because there are places called Taputapuatea in New Zealand and Kapukapuakea in Hawai'i.[31] An alliance called Ti'ahauatea was forged between the followers of 'Oro, dividing these far-flung islands between those of Te Aouri (the world of darkness) to the east of Ra'iatea, where the ocean was called Moana-a-Marama (the Sea of the Moon) and those of Te Aotea (the world of light) to the west, where the sea was called Moana-urifa (the rank-smelling Sea).[32] As they used to chant:

Na nia Te Ao Uri	The dark land above
Na raro Te Ao Tea	The light land below
E to roa te manu e	Surrounded by birds
E hi'o i te hiti o te ra.	At the flash of sunrise.[33]

Priests from these islands periodically gathered at Taputapuatea in Ra'iatea, bearing offerings to 'Oro.[34] According to an early European visitor to the island:

[To Taputapuatea] human victims, ready slain, were sent to be offered on the altar of Oro, the god of war, whose principal image was worshipped here . . . Opoa was also the residence of the kings of this island, who, besides the prerogatives of royalty, enjoyed divine honors, and were in fact living idols among the dead ones, being deified at the time of their accession to political supremacy here. These sovereigns (who always took the name of Tamatoa) were wont to receive presents from the kings and chiefs of adjacent and distant islands, whose gods were also considered tributary to the Oro of Raiatea.[35]

Among the followers of 'Oro were the 'arioi, a society of orators, priests, navigators, travelling performers, warriors and famed lovers. These men and women were dedicated to 'Oro, each grade having its distinctive tattoos and special garments.[36] Like the god, the 'arioi had power over life and death, and they were greatly venerated. According to the missionary John Orsmond, who collected accounts from former 'arioi during the early nineteenth century: 'The 'arioi were a company of fine bodied people, and separate . . . Let not the ceremony of the 'arioi be defiled. They were adorned with scented oil, flowers, scarlet dyed cloth. Their bed places must not be trodden on. They were sacred.'[37] Each district in Tahiti had its own 'arioi lodge carrying the title of its head 'arioi (the avae parae or 'black leg'), an impressive individual who wore a red loincloth (and was thus sometimes referred to as the 'arioi maro 'ura), and had legs tattooed from thigh to heel. During 'arioi ceremonies the 'black legs' sat in state on a high stool or platform, receiving and distributing lavish gifts of cloth and pigs and watching the dances and skits of their junior colleagues. According to Orsmond, there were both male and female 'arioi lodges in the Society Islands, each with their own 'black leg'.[38] And although the 'arioi were privileged, they were forbidden to have children; unless their babies were killed at birth, they lost their sacred status.

While their own fertility was thus constrained, the dances, skits and songs of the younger 'arioi were often intensely erotic, galvanising the power of the gods to enhance the fertility of plants, animals and people.[39] Some of the 'arioi were dancers, musicians, singers, actors or artists who tattooed or painted on bark cloth; others were navigators, chiefs, priests and specialists in ancestral lore. Although their rituals were often stately and dignified, their skits and mimes could be hilarious, ridiculing those in power. Only good-looking men and women could become 'arioi, and most of them were high-born. They wore elegant bark-cloth garments decorated with colours and patterns, wore garlands of flowers, and oiled their bodies and hair with scented oil; and if they coveted the fine bark cloth that someone else was wearing, they simply took it. When groups of 'arioi (or mareva) travelled on their journeys,[40] they were showered with gifts and feasts, but still they seized bark-cloth garments, pigs, fruit, vegetables and other objects for their pleasure. They played a crucial role in all life-cycle rituals, particularly those for high-ranking people – at birth, marriage and funerals. In welcoming an important visitor to a district, a young female *'arioi* with a large quantity of bark cloth wound around her body walked towards the guest and slowly twirled around, unwinding the bark cloth until she stood there nude, laying the bark cloth as a gift before him.

When the *'arioi* sailed on their expeditions, a fleet of canoes with flying feather streamers and small circular sails at the tops of their masts gathered

Young 'arioi *girl presents bark-cloth*

under 'Oro's protection. Before setting off they carried out rituals, sacrificing pigs, plantains and other fruits to the gods. At sea they were led by the sacred canoe carrying 'Oro's image, and gifts for the gods and high chiefs of the islands they intended to visit. Another canoe carried a temporary *marae* for 'Oro's two brothers, 'Oro-tetefa and Uru-tetefa, the gods of the *'arioi* society.[41] Upon approaching an island the *'arioi* performers, decked with flowers, feathers and perfumed bark-cloth garments, sang and danced on the canoe platforms, led by a senior *'arioi*. The missionary Ellis gave a vivid description of the arrival of an *'arioi* flotilla:

> [They] advanced towards the land, with their streamers floating in the wind, their drums and flutes sounding, and the Areois, attended by their chief, who acted as their prompter, appeared on a stage erected for the purpose, with their wild distortions of person, antic gestures, painted bodies, and vociferated songs, mingling with the sound of the drum and the flute, the dashing of the sea, and the rolling and breaking of the surf . . . the whole . . . presented a ludicrous imposing spectacle.[42]

On this occasion the fleet had come to honour 'Oro-i-te-te'amo'e, 'Oro the god of fertility and life, and they were greeted with joy and merriment. When the *'arioi* travelled en masse to the ceremonies at Taputapuatea to honour 'Oro-taua, 'Oro the god of war, however, the atmosphere was sombre and frightening. Their canoes, paddled by naked men, carried the priests and images of their gods. Sacred drums and shell trumpets lay under the platforms in the bows, and pairs of dead men and fish (including cavally fish, sharks and turtles) on the stages as offerings for 'Oro. When the canoes beached by the *marae*, wailing conch trumpets sounded, and the heads and genitals of their most high-ranking victims were tightly bound with the multi-coloured plaited sennit of the god, destroying the *mana* (ancestral power) and fertility of their lineages and districts.[43] Some of these corpses were hung up in the sacred trees, while others were used as canoe rollers. When the great drums boomed, announcing the offering of human sacrifices to 'Oro, the people in the district were filled with dread, hushing their children, silencing their animals and putting out the fires. There was thunder in 'Opoa.[44]

The great *marae* of Taputapuatea still stands on Cape Matahira-i-te-ra'i on the beach at 'Opoa, opposite the sacred pass known as Te Ava-mo'a. Around the *marae*, a sandy flat known as Te Po (the realm of the gods) is bordered by the sea to the north, a mountain inland to the east, and a small hill to the south, brought there from Mo'orea by ancestral power. The site is dominated by the ruins of the main *ahu* or stone platform – a narrow rectangular edifice of tumbled rocks 140 feet long faced by huge upright slabs, with shrubs and a large tree growing on it. In front of the *ahu* stand a few low uprights at which the chiefs used to kneel, to which their genealogies were tied. Most of the sacred trees that once shaded *marae* Taputapuatea have been chopped down and it now stands in bright daylight, no longer linked to the world of the gods (the Po) by darkness. Te Papa-ua-mea-o-Ru'ea, the white rock of investiture where the high chiefs of the Tamatoa lineage were once hailed, still stands by the sea at Hauviri, the family *marae* of the Tamatoa by the beach; and the western boundary of Te Po, the district around the *marae*, is marked by a stone known as Tu'ia.[45] As the black leg *'arioi* from 'Opoa used to chant, proclaiming the landmarks of their district:

> The mountain above at 'Opoa is Te A'e-tapu
> The assembly ground is Mata-ti'i-tahua-roa
> The seaward point is Mata-hira-i-te-ra'i
> The sacred pool is Vaitiare
> The marae is Taputapuatea, the home of 'Oro
> The harbour outside is Te Ava Mo'a
> The high chief is Tamatoa
> The *'arioi* houses are Na-nu'u, Fare-'ohe, Fare-mei'a and Tairoiro
> The chief *'arioi* is Te-ra-manini.[46]

Today there are new signs of life at Taputapuatea; and navigators from far-flung islands are arriving there again, retracing the star paths of their ancestors. At Manaha, a small stone shrine where 'Oro's *fare atua* (god-house) once stood, shell necklaces have been draped over a fan-shaped stone upright, and anchor stones and rocks brought by navigators from distant islands are scattered before it. Platforms for sacrificial offerings have been rebuilt and piled with heaps of yams and bananas, while a small stone god daubed with red ochre stands at a shrine at the foot of the main *ahu*.

In 2007 a group from New Zealand, Hawai'i, the Cook Islands and Australia, invited by Na Papa e Va'u, a group of 'Opoa people dedicated to protecting this sacred *marae*, visited Taputapuatea. Romy Tavaeari'i, the main orator, welcomed our party; and there were workshops and celebrations, including a visit by the French Minister for Overseas Territories who stood on its stone pavement, garlanded with flowers, promising French Government support for placing Taputapuatea on the World Heritage List. Later a group of 'Opoa people escorted their visitors along the coast to Fa'aroa Bay, where voyaging canoes were once built; and out to the sacred pass, Te Ava-mo'a, where dolphins played around our boat. Afterwards, Romy recited the names of various parts of the *marae*, telling stories about them. Taputapuatea is still a place of great power, echoing with memories of the high priests in their red loincloths and towering feathered helmets, the royal chiefs with their red feather girdles, the thundering drums and conch-shell trumpets, and the sacrifices dedicated to 'Oro.

The Glorious Children of Tetumu

In writings about global exploration, European voyagers are often portrayed as the harbingers of history, 'discovering' indigenous people who lived in a timeless, myth-ridden, ahistorical haze. As in Europe, however, in Tahiti, the early eighteenth century was a turbulent, volatile era, dominated by leaders whose ambitions led to battles, conquests and migrations. During those first, world-shaking encounters the Tahitians were also influenced by recent historical events, including the introduction of the worship of 'Oro to their island.[1]

According to the oral traditions, when 'Oro's followers first tried to take his cult from Taputapuatea to Tahiti the expedition was attacked; and 'Oro picked up the canoe, raised it into the clouds and carried it back to 'Opoa.[2] In about 1720 when the head *'arioi* at Taputapuatea, Teramanini, was on his deathbed, he decided to try again. Summoning his friend Mahi, he sent him as an envoy to Tahiti. Three times Mahi visited Tahiti by canoe, and three times he returned to Ra'iatea without having received a welcome. Finally he landed near the Taravao peninsula in southern Tahiti, where a young woman named Tau'ura (the morning star, Venus) took pity on Mahi and led him to her father Huaatua, who adopted him as his *taio* or bond friend, feasting him and showering him with presents. In Tahiti, a *taio* friendship amounted to a partial merging of identities. Gifts, names and genealogies were exchanged, along with obligations to support each other and rights to share each other's possessions (including a *taio*'s wife if she was willing).

Mahi did not have enough wealth with him to repay his friend's generosity, however, so he sailed back to Taputapuatea to fetch offerings for his *taio*. By this time the high priest Teramanini had died, but at Mahi's request Tamatoa I, the high chief of Ra'iatea,[3] ordered a sacred canoe called *Hotu* to be loaded with treasures which are listed in the traditions – a shell trumpet, a fly whisk, rolls of fine cloth, a wooden pillow, a coconut-shell water bottle, fine mats, a cloth beater, capes, girdles and a feather headdress. In a final gesture, Tamatoa I ceremonially exchanged names with Mahi, sharing his *mana* (ancestral prestige and power) with him; and when Mahi returned with these gifts (including Tamatoa's name), the *'arioi* cult became established in Huaatua's home district.[4] A party of *'arioi* accompanied Mahi from Ra'iatea in the sacred canoe, and as they travelled around Tahiti from district to district, the sound of their drums and flutes and the sight of their dancing attracted many people. After presenting rich gifts to his bond friend, Mahi established *'arioi* lodges in districts around the island.[5]

The first 'Oro *marae* in Tahiti – which later played a prominent role during early Spanish visits to the island – was *marae* Vai'otaha (water of the frigate bird), sited on the beach at Tautira in southern Tahiti at the mouth of a glorious valley. The name of this *marae* was changed to Taputapuatea when it was consecrated to 'Oro.[6] Its god, 'Oro-rahi-to'o-toa (Great 'Oro of the Toa log), was a *toa* log about six feet long, bound in sacred sennit and decorated with red, yellow and black feathers. After this, another *marae*, 'Utu-'ai-mahurau – which featured during Captain Cook's visits – was built for 'Oro on a small coastal point in the district of Pa'ea, and its image of 'Oro, decorated with feathers from the Tai'arapu god, was called 'Oro-hu'a-manu ('Oro of the bird-feathered body).[7] As the worship of 'Oro spread across the island, other *marae* began to follow the new god, taking the name Taputapuatea, which was also given to any sacred canoe or god-house in which the god's image was placed, and many of the chiefs joined the *'arioi* society.

At about the same time, rumours arrived in Tahiti that strange craft had been seen in the Tuamotu archipelago. Three of these weird vessels, which had no outriggers, had been sighted off the northern atolls of Tikei and Takaroa, and one had run aground on the windward side of Takapoto. Most of the crew of this vessel left the island in small boats, although five stayed behind while the other two craft sailed past Manihi, Apataki, Tikei and Rangiroa before landing at Makatea, where the beings on board mysteriously killed some of the inhabitants with their weapons. Sharp pieces of a very hard substance had been collected from the wreck at Takapoto, some of which made their way to Tahiti. These stories referred to Roggeveen's Dutch West India Company expedition, which was searching for the fabled Southern Continent; and treasures brought from the wreck of the *Afrikaansche Galei* (1722) gave the Tahitians their first knowledge of iron and nails.[8]

During the years that followed, the far-flung devotees of 'Oro continued to meet periodically for ceremonies at 'Opoa. The alliance was fragile, however, and eventually the peace was broken. During one of the great gatherings at Taputapuatea a chief from Ao-uri quarrelled with Pa'oa-tea, the high priest of Ao-tea, and killed him. When the leading chief of Ao-tea heard that his high priest had been mudered, he flew into a rage and struck down Pa'oa-'uri, the high priest of Ao-'uri. As Pa'oa-'uri lay insensible, the people of Ao-tea fled from the *marae* in their canoes, leaving the high priests and their sacred drum Ta'imoana behind them. In their haste they left the island through Te Ava-rua, the *noa* (profane, ordinary) passage through the reef instead of the sacred passage Te Ava-mo'a, a terrible omen.[9] After this time, it is said, only Ra'iatea and Tahiti continued to exchange the rites for 'Oro, alternately at 'Opoa in Ra'iatea and at Tautira in the south of Tahiti.[10]

The shattering of this alliance was still fresh in people's memories when the early Europeans arrived in the islands. When the missionary John Williams landed at Rarotonga in the Cook Islands in 1823, for instance, the local people accosted a Raiatean sailor who had come with him, demanding what his people had done with Ta'imoana, the great drum they had sent to Taputapuatea, and why they had killed Pa'oa-'uri and Pa'oa-tea?[11] Indeed, echoes of this great quarrel still resound around Polynesia. As recently as 1995, canoes from a number of islands sailed to Ra'iatea in an attempt to heal this ancient *hara* or wrongdoing. Ben Finney, an anthropologist who along with the Hawaiian artist-scholar Herb Kane and the Micronesian navigator Mau Piailug helped to inspire the renaissance of Polynesian voyaging, describes how as the fleet of canoes gathered and entered the reef at dawn through the sacred pass, Te Ava-mo'a, a Māori elder, chanted an incantation recalling the murder of Pa'oa-tea and the flight of his ancestors from this *marae*; and a Tahitian standing in a canoe chanted in reply that the *ra'a* or sacred restriction was now lifted. As a group of trumpeters blew their conch shells, a Tahitian orator standing in the shallow waters of the lagoon called out to the visitors, welcoming them and their ancestors back to Taputapuatea.[12]

Once the alliance between 'Oro's followers was broken, life in the Society Islands became increasingly violent, with bloody battles and feuds between different islands and districts.[13] According to oral histories, infanticide and the human sacrifice associated with 'Oro's worship also became more common. In about 1750 when war broke out on the west coast of Tahiti between the districts of Atehuru and Papara, the Papara warriors were defeated. Refugees from Papara fled to Ra'iatea, among them Te'e'eva, the aristocratic first-born daughter of the high chief of Papara, and her nephew Fa'anounou. They took shelter at 'Opoa, where this high-born woman married Ari'ima'o (Shark Chief), the eldest son of

Tamatoa I, the sacred chief of the island, and gave birth to a son named Mau'a.[14] In about 1760 when warriors from the neighbouring island of Borabora invaded Ra'iatea, they killed her husband, and according to some accounts their young son Mau'a was taken to Taputapuatea, invested with the *maro 'ura* or red feather girdle and hailed as the paramount chief of Ra'iatea.[15] At Te'e'eva's request the priests also made an image of 'Oro and a new red feather girdle known as Te Ra'i-puatata (the Sky of Red Blossoms)[16] which they gave to her nephew to carry secretly to her family in the Papara district back in Tahiti, preparing a safe haven for the young high chief. Accompanied by a priest from Taputapuatea named Tupaia, her nephew took the sacred canoe and carried 'Oro to Papara, where he quietly placed the god and the red feather girdle in their family *marae*.[17]

Described by George Forster as 'an extraordinary genius',[18] Tupaia was a leading *'arioi* priest and navigator, born at Ha'amanino Harbour on Ra'iatea in about 1725. It is likely that Tupaia and Mau'a were kinsmen, because leading priests were invariably recruited from high chiefly families; and the histories of these two men are closely entangled. After delivering the god and the red feather girdle to Papara, Tupaia returned to Ra'iatea. In about 1763 when the Borabora forces under Puni, their elderly warrior chief, attacked the island again, the two armies clashed out at sea; and as the great war canoes with their high sterns and prows lined up in the 'net of war' formation and paddled furiously towards each other, their crews yelling and shell trumpets blaring, the warriors whirled their slings and hurled rocks at their opponents. When the canoes collided there was desperate hand-to-hand fighting with clubs and spears. The Ra'iatea warriors had almost defeated their assailants when their former friends and allies from the island of Taha'a, which sits within the same reef, betrayed them, arriving to join the Borabora fleet and routing the exhausted defenders with great slaughter.[19] During this battle, Tupaia was wounded by a stingray barb wielded as a weapon by the enemy *rauti*, an orator and warrior who exhorted the troops in battle.[20] He escaped to the mountains, and hid there while his wounds healed, taking the name Tupaia (beaten) so that he would never forget this bitter debacle.[21]

After their victory the Borabora warriors rampaged through the island, killing women and children and destroying gardens, trees, canoes and houses. In their fury they attacked Taputapuatea, pulling down the god-houses on the sacred *marae*, wrecking the platform and hacking down the trees that sheltered the altar. Distraught at this desecration, a priest named Vaita went into a trance, and announced that a new kind of people were coming to the islands:

> The glorious children of Tetumu
> will come and see this forest at Taputapuatea.
> Their body is different, our body is different
> We are one species only from Tetumu.
>
> And this land will be taken by them
> The old rules will be destroyed
> And sacred birds of the land and the sea
> Will also arrive here, will come and lament
> Over that which this lopped tree has to teach
> They are coming up on a canoe without an outrigger.[22]

According to Vaita's prophecy, although the bodies of these new people would be different from those of the Society Islanders, they would come from the same ancestral source, Tetumu. In their wake they would bring defeat and destruction, the loss of land and the demise of the old rules. Unimpressed by this ominous prediction, however, the Borabora warriors continued their rampage across the island.

For a time his father's people kept Mau'a in hiding, but there was no safe haven on the island. The young *ari'i* was forced to flee to his mother's family in Tahiti, where he took the name Mau'a (wasted) as a bitter reminder of his exile. As soon as his wounds healed, Tupaia joined the former high chief in the Papara district. They took refuge with Amo, the son of Te'e'eva's younger brother and now the high chief of Papara, with whom Mau'a was living.[23] In return for his protection, they threw in their lot with Amo and his wife Purea,[24] a formidable, ambitious high-born woman; and Tupaia became Amo and Purea's chief strategist and advisor.[25] When he brought the red feather girdle and the image of 'Oro from Taputapuatea out of hiding, Tupaia became the high priest of Papara, a leading priest of 'Oro in Tahiti, and soon, Purea's lover. During 1765, reports arrived from the Tuamotu about the arrival of two more weird vessels whose crews had killed more of their people, garbled tales that referred to two British ships commanded by John Byron, which had visited Tepoto, Napuka, Takaroa, Takapoto (where they found the carved head of a Dutch longboat's rudder, some iron tools and brass from the wreck of the *Afrikaansche Galei*) and Rangiroa.[26]

Tupaia the high priest navigator and Mau'a (or Mau'arua) the young high chief from Ra'iatea were both ambitious, adventurous men, and no doubt these rumours about 'canoes without outriggers' sparked their curiosity. In later years Tupaia would sail with Captain Cook, piloting the *Endeavour* through the Society Islands and visiting New Zealand,

Australia and Batavia; while Mau'a would sail with Lieutenant Gayangos (acting commander of the Spanish ship *Águila*) to Lima, Peru, where he took up permanent residence.[27] Now that they were both in exile in Papara, however, Tupaia and Mau'a joined forces with Amo and Purea, who planned to install their infant son, Teri'irere, as the paramount chief of Tahiti. With the support of the Papara people they began to build a huge new *marae* at Mahaiatea, the largest in the Society Islands.[28] Five to ten human sacrifices from each district were offered to the war god, and buried beneath the cornerstones of its tiered stone platform.[29]

When the great new *marae* was completed, Purea and Amo intended to send heralds to summon the chiefs of the surrounding islands to Mahaiatea, where Tupaia would invest their son with Te Ra'i-puatata (the red feather girdle from Taputapuatea) along with the yellow feather girdle of his Teva ancestors, installing him as the paramount chief (or *ari'i maro 'ura*) of Tahiti. Once Teri'irere's paramount status was recognised, Tupaia hoped that with the help of his warriors he could free Ra'iatea from the Borabora invaders. In this audacious plan lay the seeds of disaster for the Papara leaders, however, because among the other chiefs, hostile alliances were forming. This was the state of affairs on Tahiti when the first Europeans burst into their cosmos, changing their lives forever.

The Dolphin *off Mo'orea*

At daylight on 19 June 1767, when a fleet of canoes paddled out from the south-east coast of Tahiti, the fog was so thick on the ocean that the reef was invisible, although the breakers boomed on the rocks in warning. The fleet was led by several large canoes with high prows and sterns, decorated with feather streamers and carrying *'arioi* priests on their platforms. These men, who wore red bark-cloth garments, carried plantain branches (*ta'ata mei'a roa* or 'man long-banana' – symbols of human bodies, used instead of human sacrifices to propitiate the gods).[30] In their canoes, they carried bales of white and red bark cloth as offerings in case these were needed.

The previous day, canoes had arrived from the nearby island of Me'eti'a to warn them that a strange apparition was approaching their island: a high, massive object with lights on its sides, moving across the ocean. Several small craft dropped from its sides had approached Me'eti'a, crewed by beings who might have been ancestors, or gods, or even people, before it moved off towards the southern coast of Tahiti. Some thought that this might be a floating island, just as Tahiti itself had once been, driven by ancestral power.[31] Others remembered Vaita's prophecy about a canoe without an outrigger, and wondered whether it might be this awesome vessel.

At about 10 a.m. when the fog began to lift, these people were amazed to find a great floating hulk, its high sides decorated in red and yellow ('Oro's sacred colours), out at sea off the south coast of the island. They paddled towards it, yelling and hooting, and stopping at a distance to confer while the beings on board waved and held up beads and other objects. Finally one of the canoes paddled towards it, its crew holding up plantain branches while a priest made a long speech before throwing his branch into the ocean. The islanders regarded the sea as a great *marae*, sacred to all, and this was a sign of peaceful intentions. By this time 150 or more canoes crowded with at least 800 warriors were circling around this strange spectre, buzzing with speculation. If this was a great canoe, they noted, it had no outriggers to keep it upright in the water. Perhaps the weird beings on board were indeed 'the glorious offspring of Tetumu,' and Vaita's prophecy had been vindicated.

On board the Royal Naval frigate *Dolphin*, this first encounter was equally fraught with mythic speculation. As the ship's master, George Robertson, noted when they first sighted the high mountains of Tahiti, many of the sailors thought that at last they had discovered the Unknown Southern Continent:

> This made us all rejoice and fild us with the greatest hopes Imaginable, we now lookt upon our selves as relived from all our distresses as we was almost Certain of finding all sorts of refreshments on this great Body of Land . . . We now suposed we saw the long wishd for Southern Continent, which has been often talkd of, but neaver before seen by any Europeans.[32]

For centuries, European nations – Spain, the Netherlands, France and Britain – had vied to discover the legendary land-mass, and this geopolitical contest had inspired a number of exploratory voyages. In fact, this was the second time that the *Dolphin* had sailed on such a mission. In 1764 Lord Egmont, First Lord of the Admiralty, had despatched Commodore John Byron on the *Dolphin*, accompanied by a smaller frigate the *Tamar*, to search for Terra Australis Incognita in the South Atlantic. Byron had also been ordered to take possession of the Falkland Islands as a British base controlling access to the Pacific, and he sailed first to the West Falklands where he conducted a survey and claimed sovereignty over the islands. When he reached the Straits of Magellan, Byron handed over his charts to a British ship for delivery to Lord Egmont. In the Straits a French ship was sighted which he later discovered was commanded by Louis de Bougainville, who had in fact forestalled him by claiming the Falkland Islands nine months earlier for France and establishing a French colony on East Falkland.

After leaving South America, Byron's ships sailed west into the Pacific and through the northern Tuamotu Islands where they visited the atolls of Tepoto, Napuka, Takaroa and Takapoto. At Tepoto and Napuka local warriors had threatened the landing party, while at Takaroa they attacked, wounding several men before the sailors opened fire, killing five or six islanders. At Takapoto, where Roggeveen's ship had been wrecked, an old man with a long white beard held up a green bough, sang a song and threw the bough towards the strangers before accepting their gifts. As they sailed towards the atoll of Rangiroa, Byron wrote in his journal:

> For a day or two before we made [the northern Tuamotu] till this day we had entirely lost that great [south-westerly] Swell & for some time before we first made the Land we saw vast Flocks of Birds which we observed towards Evening always flew away to the southward. This is a convincing proof to me that there is Land that way, & had not the Winds failed me in the higher Latitudes, I make no doubt but I should have fell in with it, & in all probability made the discovery of the Southern Continent.[33]

Despite these signs of land, Byron did not discover any large land-mass in this stretch of ocean. He crossed the Pacific in record time, missing Tahiti and making few other discoveries, and returned home in May 1766 to report that almost certainly he and his men had located Terra Australis.

Galvanised by this news, Lord Egmont began to plan another voyage in search of the elusive continent, this time to the South Sea, with the enthusiastic support of George III, the young monarch who shared Egmont's passion for exploration and discovery. Once again the *Dolphin* was chosen as the expedition's main vessel. The Spanish government, which had

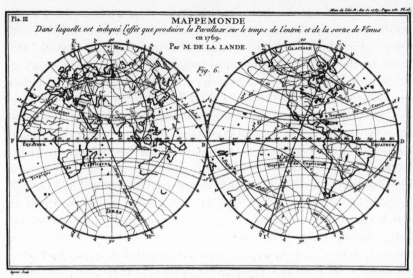

The Coastline of Terra Australis Incognita

acquired an illicit summary of Byron's visits to the Falklands and the South Sea, was much alarmed by these developments, and the King of Spain ordered the Prince of Masserano, the Spanish ambassador to the Court of St James, to lodge a protest about Byron's voyage. The Prince was frustrated by his reception, however, reporting that when he asked the Duke of Richmond why the *Dolphin* had been sent on a voyage to the Falklands and the Pacific, the Duke 'replied in a bantering tone that they had been out looking for giants'. When Masserano retorted that all the countries in that region belonged to Spain and no one might settle in them, and Richmond asked quizzically whether the whole world was Spain's, the Prince had replied, 'As to that portion, yes!', adding that the Spanish government could not look with indifference on English ships going to the South Sea.[34] After this conversation, Masserano concluded (quite rightly) that the British government was set upon challenging Spanish rights in the Pacific Ocean.

The Spanish government based their claims to the South Sea (as the Pacific was called at this time) on an ancient treaty, the Treaty of Tordesillas, which divided the world into those territories claimed by Spain and those claimed by Portugal. Under this and the later Treaty of Zaragoza (1529), a line had been drawn around the globe west of the Cape Verde Islands across South America and through the Pacific east of the Moluccas. One half of the globe west of the Cape Verde Islands was allocated to Spain, while the other half 'belonged' to Portugal. Other European nations including the Netherlands, Britain and France contested these agreements, which excluded them from the gold and silver mines in South America among other riches, and there had been incursions into the Pacific which the Spanish bitterly resented. Determined not to cede a base in the Falklands to Britain or France, the Spanish government protested about British and French activities in the region. Resolved neither to abandon the small British outpost at Port Egmont (established in the West Falklands the year after Byron's visit) nor the search for Terra Australis, Egmont decided to send another expedition to the Southern Ocean, but his Cabinet colleagues, reluctant to risk another war with France and Spain, forced him to hand in his resignation.

Undaunted and with the King's support, before leaving office Lord Egmont signed Secret Instructions for Captain Samuel Wallis, ordering him to take command of the *Dolphin*, and lead an expedition to reinforce the British colony in West Falkland and to search in the South Sea for the Southern Continent. Captain Wallis was instructed to sail west from South America as far south as possible, looking for Terra Australis until he reached the longitude of New Zealand, a coastline partly charted by the Dutch explorer Abel Tasman more than a century earlier. A storeship, the *Prince Frederick*, would accompany him and drop off supplies in the Falklands, while Philip Carteret, Byron's first lieutenant, was appointed to command the *Dolphin*'s consort ship, the *Swallow*. The captains were instructed to get their ships ready for sea as a matter of urgency.[35] Their destination was so deeply cloaked in mystery that Wallis did not even tell Carteret, captain of his consort ship, where they were going. His own officers were sworn to secrecy by the Treasurer of the Navy, while the sailors on board the *Dolphin* had to swear a similar oath in front of a judge of the Navy.[36]

Samuel Wallis, who succeeded Byron as the *Dolphin*'s commander, was a genial Cornishman who had joined the Navy as a boy, earning his commission as a lieutenant during the Seven Years' War. His third command, the sixty-gun *Prince of Orange*, had taken part in the siege of Quebec at the same time that James Cook, then a master in the Navy, was charting the St Lawrence River. After the fall of Quebec, Wallis returned to Britain and served on the Home Station patrolling the coastline, a mundane task, and this new command was an exhilarating opportunity to win fame and glory. The *Dolphin*, a frigate 113 feet long with twenty-four guns, was only the third ship in the Navy to have been sheathed with copper to protect the hull from marine growth and worms. After her voyage around the world with Byron the ship arrived in fine condition back in Deptford, where she was refitted and loaded with plentiful provisions for 150 men during a year at sea and supplies for the boatswains, gunners and carpenters.

Captain Samuel Wallis

Captain Wallis recruited a youthful, talented crew for this voyage, along with some experienced men. William Clarke, his first lieutenant, had long served in the Navy, although he was ill during the voyage and much disliked by the crew for his irascible, querulous behaviour. Tobias Furneaux, the second lieutenant who had won his commission in battle, was related to Wallis by marriage; while the ship's master George Robertson, a well-educated man who wrote a vivid, exciting journal of the voyage, loathed the first lieutenant (calling him 'Mr Knowall' and 'Old Growl'). There was also John Gore, an American-born master's mate from Byron's voyage on the *Dolphin*, unflappable and a mad-keen huntsman; and four other former *Dolphin*s including the ship's cooper and gunner. They were accompanied by the surgeon John Hutchinson, a capable doctor who did his utmost to protect the men from the ravages of scurvy; the purser John

Harrison, a good-humoured man and gifted mathematician and astronomer; Benjamin Butler, the master's mate, who produced an excellent chart
of Matavai Bay;[37] and four sailors including Richard Pickersgill (18) and
Robert Molyneux (20), who along with Furneaux and Gore later sailed
with James Cook on his Pacific voyages.

Philip Carteret, the *Swallow*'s commander, had a difficult time preparing his ship for this voyage. The pay scales for a sloop were lower than
those for a frigate, and Carteret was forced to sail with a scratch crew
of seventy-eight, short of the ship's official complement of ninety. The
Swallow was twenty years old, in poor repair and with only fourteen guns,
no trade goods and inadequate supplies on board, and a reputation for
being slow and clumsy to handle. Although Carteret worked furiously
to get the sloop ready for sea, most of his requests for improvements
were turned down by the dockyard. Nevertheless, obedient to his orders,
Carteret sailed with Wallis from Plymouth, accompanied by the storeship,
while reports from French and Spanish spies flew to Paris and Madrid,
warning that this new British expedition posed a serious threat to their
governments' territorial interests in the Falklands, South America and
the Pacific.

At Madeira when Wallis finally showed Carteret a copy of his Secret
Instructions, Carteret was appalled to find that his little sloop was expected
to accompany the *Dolphin* around the world, and fired off a furious protest.
Unmoved, Wallis said that he could not change the Admiralty's orders.
The ships sailed in company to Port Famine at the eastern entrance to the
Strait of Magellan, where they took on supplies from the storeship before
it left for West Falkland. Carteret, who had navigated through the Strait
before, sailed ahead to guide the *Dolphin* through this difficult passage,
but the *Swallow* was so slow and awkward that it took three frustrating
months to reach the western exit. As soon as they caught sight of the open
sea the *Dolphin* set her topsails and studding sails in a gale and flew away
from her consort, heading north-west into the Pacific; and they did not see
each other again for the rest of the voyage.

Over the next two months the lookouts saw no signs of land, and by the
time they reached the central Tuamotu Islands there was little fresh food
and water left on board the *Dolphin*. Despite the surgeon's best efforts,
many of the crew were ill with scurvy (caused by a lack of vitamin C),
while Samuel Wallis and his first lieutenant William Clarke were afflicted
by bilious disorders which were probably also scurvy-related. In the
Tuamotu archipelago, where the ship visited six small atolls in succession
(Pinaki, Nukutaveke, Vairaatea, Paraoa, Manuhangi and Nengonengo),
the second lieutenant, Tobias Furneaux, and the master's mate, John Gore,

took the boats ashore, claiming sovereignty over each atoll on which they landed, collecting small amounts of fresh food and water and looking for signs of the Unknown Southern Continent. On Nukutaveke they discovered heaps of turtle shell, rocks brought from elsewhere and big canoes under construction, signs suggesting trade with a larger population, perhaps the inhabitants of Terra Australis. When they landed, the islanders fled in five double canoes, each about thirty feet long, which Robertson described in some detail.[38] At Pukarunga and Paraoa, however, the warriors stood and resisted the strangers, who drove them off by firing muskets overhead and nine-pound cannons.

On 18 June 1767 the ship approached Me'eti'a, the most easterly of the Society Islands, where they attempted a landing. Some local warriors seized the buoy rope of the cutter and tried to weigh the grapnel, falling back only when a musket was fired in their faces. At this time Me'eti'a was under the sway of Vehiatua I, the elderly *ari'i* or high chief of Tahiti-iti (southern Tahiti),[39] who sent expeditions there three or four times a year, bringing back pearls, pearl shell, stools, wooden pillows, mats, cloth, oil and pigs from Me'eti'a and Ana'a. When the *Dolphin* headed off in the direction of Tahiti, the islanders sent fast canoes ahead to warn the southern chiefs that this strange apparition was heading in their direction. By this time Wallis and Clarke were so ill that they could hardly stand, while many of the crew were suffering from the symptoms of advanced scurvy – weakness, nervousness and depression; a desperate yearning for land; and in the more severe cases rotting gums, teeth loose or falling out, stinking, wheezing breath, stiffened limbs covered with purple-black ulcers, and scummy green urine.[40] It was difficult to work the ship, and that afternoon when the sailors sighted a high mountain to the south-west and a lofty range of mountains further south, it seemed like a sign of salvation.

As the steersman headed the ship towards the distant mountain peak, Furneaux and Gore climbed up to the masthead to look out for shoals. At 10 p.m. the *Dolphin* lay to, and early the next morning they set sail again in bright moonlight, still heading towards the mountain. At 9 a.m. when they ran into thick fog, the sailors listened anxiously as breakers thumped on a nearby reef, hidden in the mist. When the fog lifted soon afterwards, there was a moment of mutual astonishment – the crew found their ship surrounded by about a hundred canoes, the islanders yelling, hooting and making a deafening uproar as they gazed at the first Europeans that they had ever encountered.

Behind the canoes lay a glorious coastline, the south-east end of Tahiti – high, jagged mountains covered in forest to the summits; the lower slopes with grassland and gardens; while waterfalls tumbled down to the coastal flats where scattered houses stood surrounded by groves of coconut and fruit trees and gardens. On board the canoes, after gazing at this weird apparition the warriors held a hasty consultation. According to their descendants:

> They were struck with astonishment at so extraordinary an appearance, and various were their conjectures respecting it; some supposed that it was a floa-ting island; this opinion seemed to prevail, and was strengthened by a tradition they have among them, that Otaheite Eete [Tahiti-iti], the smallest part of the island, was formerly driven from its situation in some distant part of the sea, by a tremendous gale of wind, and striking against the east end of Otaheite Arahye [Tahiti-rahi], coalesced with it. But on the nearer approach of the ship they were induced to alter their opinion, but could not account for such an amazing phenomenon, which filled them with wonder and fear.[41]

Eventually one of their leaders stood up, made a speech and threw a plantain branch into the ocean as a gesture of welcome; and after a fur-ther pause, a fine-looking young man climbed up the ship's mizzen chains, jumping from the shrouds onto the wooden awning that shaded the quarterdeck. When the sailors handed up some trinkets to him, trying to persuade him to come down, he just stood there, staring and laughing while the men in the canoes made more speeches and threw more plantain branches onto the deck of the *Dolphin*. Once these ceremonies were over, this young man climbed down from the awning, shook hands with some of the crew and accepted some gifts, while other warriors scrambled on board the vessel.

The sailors, who were longing for fresh food, tried to show that they were eager to barter for live animals. Holding up cloth, knives, beads and ribbons, they grunted like pigs, crowed like cocks and pointed ashore in an effort to show what they wanted. Mystified by this bizarre performance, the islanders grunted, crowed and pointed in return. Finally, in frustration the sailors led some of these people to the animal pens and showed them pigs, chickens and turkeys. Although the warriors indicated that they had pigs and chickens ashore, they were amazed by the turkeys, and when they saw the sheep and goats they dived overboard in terror. When they climbed back on board, Wallis gave these warriors some beads and nails as a sign of friendship. Delighted, they began to grab at everything made of iron on board including the stanchions and ring-balls on deck, and seemed astonished that they could not break them.

The Tahitians had known about iron since the wreck of the *Afrikaansche Galei* in the Tuamotu forty-five years earlier, but iron from that vessel was scarce and almost impossible to procure. The people in the canoes now began to clamour for nails or other iron goods, and when they were refused they 'began to be a Little surly'. As more canoes crowded around the *Dolphin*, their crews hooting and shouting, Wallis ordered a nine-pound shot to be fired. As the cannon flashed and roared, the warriors leaped off the ship and swam to their canoes, for in Tahiti, thunder and lightning were a sign of 'Oro's power. As he jumped overboard, one of these men, who had been standing next to Henry Ibbot, had the presence of mind to snatch the gold-laced hat off the midshipman's head, swimming rapidly away and waving the hat triumphantly in the air from a safe distance. An audacious theft was greatly admired in Tahiti, demonstrating that the thief was protected by Hiro, the trickster god; although unsuccessful thefts were harshly avenged, the offender being summarily killed or his property confiscated.[42] Ignoring this defiant gesture, Wallis ordered his men to set sail, heading the *Dolphin* along the south-west coast to search for a safe harbour.

Off the west side of Taravao the cutter was lowered, and John Gore took an armed crew to sound Teaua'a Bay (or Port Phaeton). As the cutter approached the reef it was surrounded by canoes, and when the sailors waved these people off, aiming their muskets in a warning gesture, the warriors just laughed, aiming their paddles back at the strangers in derision. Seeing more canoes flocking out, Wallis ordered a nine-pounder to be fired to recall the cutter; and Gore headed back to the ship, chased by the canoes. None of these craft had sails, and the cutter easily outran them until it was intercepted by several sailing canoes whose crews whirled their slings and pelted the sailors with stones. As these missiles hit several of his men, Gore fired his musket loaded with buckshot at the leading warrior, wounding him in the right shoulder, while his companions jumped overboard in consternation, diving underwater for safety.

When the cutter's crew returned on board, Wallis saw a large canoe flying towards them. Thinking that this might be an envoy from the sovereign of 'Terra Australis', he decided to wait for this vessel. When it came alongside a man stood up, made a short speech and threw a plantain branch onto the ship's deck, and in reply one of the officers made a speech, tossing a plantain branch back into the canoe. During these exchanges the sailors amused themselves by throwing nails and beads overboard, and watched the crew of this canoe diving to catch these objects in the water, swimming underwater like fish. Afterwards the man who had stolen Ibbot's gold-laced hat approached in another canoe, putting on the hat in triumphant mockery, but the *Dolphin* set sail before he could reach her. As the ship sailed up the west coast of Tahiti towards Papara, thousands of men, women and children stood along the shoreline, gazing in amazement. That night Robertson, still convinced that this was the Unknown Southern Continent, wrote in his journal:

> We saw the whole coast full of Canoes, and the country hade the most Beautiful appearance its posable to Imagin, from the shore side one two and three miles Back . . . a fine Leavel country appears to be all laid out in plantations, and the regular built Houses seems to be without number, with Great Numbers of Cocoa Nut Trees and several other trees . . . all allong the Coast. There is beautiful valeys between the Mountains – from the foot of the Mountains half way up the Country appears to be all fine pasture land – from that to the very tops of the Mountains is all full of tall Trees.[43]

The next morning at daybreak, 20 June, as the *Dolphin* headed up the east coast of Tahiti, William Clarke, the irascible first lieutenant, read the Articles of War to the crew. Even he was overjoyed by the sight of this beautiful island: 'Sailing along the Pleasant't shore I ever saw, Hills, Valleys & Lawns, in appearance all well Cultivated, & many Houses all along the Shore.'[44] Several big canoes headed down the coast towards them, sailing about one-and-a-quarter times faster than the *Dolphin* under full sail (that is, about 15 knots compared with the *Dolphin*'s 12 knots). At about 4 p.m. they passed the Papeno'o Valley, which Robertson described as fine and pleasant with a large river, many gardens and long houses and a large population. As the ship rounded the northern end of Tahiti, more sailing canoes flew ahead to warn the local people. Crossing a wide, curving bay, the master saw white water, the sign of a good anchoring ground, and thought that they might shelter there in the morning. This was Matavai Bay, soon to become the favourite British port in Tahiti. It was probably then, off the northern point, that the *Dolphin*'s crew began to realise that Tahiti was an island and not part of Terra Australis Incognita.

During this passage Captain Wallis and Lieutenant Clarke were so ill that they were confined to their cabins, while thirty of the crew were at death's door. That evening, many of the other sailors were in high spirits, eager to land on this beautiful island and confident that they would obtain plentiful supplies and fresh food in the morning. Others were despondent, predicting that they would have to fight their way ashore; while a few, intimidated by the signs of a large, well-organised population, argued that a landing would be impossible and it would be better to run to Tinian for refreshments. As Robertson observed wryly, it was just as well that these men were not in command of the ship, because Tinian was 4346 miles away from Tahiti.

At dawn the next day, 21 June, the barge and cutter were sent to sound the coastline south-east of Matavai Bay, off the Ha'apape district. The timing was unpropitious, however. As it happened, this was the day of the winter solstice in Tahiti, when the gods were farewelled to the Po, the dark world of the spirits.[45] During these rituals, the ocean was under a strict ritual prohibition, and canoes were forbidden to go to sea; and at Ha'apape there was a famous school of learning where chiefly children (including the ancestor-god Hiro) had long been taught astronomy, the creation accounts, genealogies and kin group histories.[46] On shore, the priests watched the *Dolphin*'s arrival with foreboding. When a large fleet of canoes was sent out to prevent them from landing, and surrounded the boats, Robertson took the barge in close to the cutter to protect Gore and his men so that they could carry on with their soundings. Every time the boats headed towards the shore, however, the crews of the canoes seemed enraged, waving them back. Gore found good anchoring ground about two miles offshore and ten miles south-east from Te Auroa (now Point Venus), and guided the ship towards this location. As the anchor chains rattled down into the ocean, the *Dolphin* was surrounded by a fleet of about a hundred canoes, their crews bringing out fat pigs, chickens, coconuts and fruit which they gave to the strangers, receiving nails, pieces of iron hoop, beads and trinkets in return. Some of these men seemed wary, even hostile, refusing to hand over their goods until they had nails or toys in their hands, and several of them struck the sailors. Wallis had given his men strict orders not to harm any of these people and, although the sailors were resentful, they reluctantly put up with this treatment. By this time there were several thousand people standing on the beach, and about two hundred canoes paddling between the boats and the shore.

After dinner when the barge and the cutter were sent back towards the land to look for a watering place, they were chased by double sailing canoes, their crews hooting and yelling. Again the master tried to protect the cutter so that Gore could carry on with his soundings, but the big canoes sailed so close to the barge that this proved to be impossible. When the boats headed back towards the ship, the people on the beaches yelled and the warriors in the canoes hooted in unison; and at that moment one of the large canoes tacked away and headed straight for the cutter, ramming her at high speed and carrying away her mizzen boom and tearing the sail. While the cutter's crew were fending off the warriors with bayonets and picks, three more large canoes sailed rapidly towards the barge. Four tall warriors armed with paddles and clubs jumped on the prow of their canoe, ready to board the barge; and when they ignored a musket shot fired in warning, Robertson ordered the sergeant and one of the marines to fire. One of these warriors was shot dead and the other was wounded in the thigh, and both of these men fell into the water. As the canoes dropped back, the men on board held their paddles in front of their faces while the crew of the first canoe hauled their companions out of the water. They tried to help the dead man to stand, and then to sit, baffled by what had happened to him, but finally they laid him down in the hull of the canoe, supporting the wounded man while they set sail.

When he returned to the *Dolphin* Robertson found that the islanders were trying to take nails and other trade items without giving up their own goods, but as soon as a musket or a spyglass was pointed at them, they gave the nails back or meekly handed over fruit, pigs or chickens. Some of these people indicated that the strangers had killed two of their warriors, crying out 'Bon bon!', hitting their chests and foreheads, and then lying back motionless, eyes fixed, in their canoes. During this barter, the sailors exchanged a twenty-penny (or three-inch) nail for a twenty-pound pig; a ten-penny (or two-and-a-quarter-inch) nail for a roasting pig;[47] and six-pence or a string of beads for a chicken or a quantity of fruit – breadfruit, coconuts, plantains, bananas, mangoes and *vi* or Tahitian apples.

In his Secret Instructions, Wallis had been ordered to establish friendly relationships with the inhabitants of the various places he visited, 'invit-ing them to Trade, and shewing them every kind of Civility and Regard; taking care however if they are numerous not to be surprised by them, but to be always upon your guard against any Accidents'.[48] Anxious to avoid further bloodshed, the following morning Wallis sent Gore ashore with the barge and cutter manned with armed sailors to fetch fresh water from the Papeno'o River, giving the master's mate nails, hatchets and other trade items to barter with the islanders. As canoes crowded around the ship, their crews exchanged fruit, chickens and pigs for nails, knives and beads, obtaining enough fresh pork to give every man in the ship's company a pound a day for the next two days. On shore, the surf ran so high that the boats could not land at the watering place, where thousands of people seemed to beckon them ashore (although in fact, in Tahiti, this was a gesture of dismissal). Some of the islanders were still willing to barter, and swam out with water in large bamboos and calabashes, swimming and diving with impressive agility.

After dinner when Gore took the boats back to the Papeno'o River, where he tried to persuade the islanders to fill the water casks, the Tahitians took six of these casks ashore but returned only four of them. In an attempt to intimidate these people, the crews of the boats pointed their muskets and musketoons at them, but the islanders only laughed, thinking themselves safe at such a distance. Gore ordered one of his men to fire a musketoon (a large, bell-mouthed firearm) into the water, but as soon as they realised that no one was hurt, these people laughed again and returned to the beach, this time bringing a number of beautiful young girls with them, some quite dark, others copper-skinned, and some almost white in colour.

As these young women performed many 'droll, wanton' tricks, exposing themselves to the strangers, the sailors watched avidly. Although the British understood these performances as sexual enticement, in fact they were acts of derision. As Sydney Parkinson, the artist on board the *Endeavour*, later noted, during contests between teams of women in Tahiti the victors would advance on their rivals, stamping their feet, twisting their mouths awry, straddling their legs, lifting up their garments and exposing their genitals while chanting in a disagreeable tone.[49] This display of female power was intended to humiliate those at whom it was directed; and when men were taunted in this way it was even more demeaning, because the *noa* (unrestricted) power of women was inimical to the *ra'a* (restricted, sacred) power of men, destroying their *mana* or ancestral power.[50] Oblivious to these cosmological implications, the sailors responded in kind, exposing themselves to the women, but did not attempt a landing. As the boats put off, the women yelled loudly, pelting the strangers with bananas and Tahitian apples.

That night Wallis and his first lieutenant William Clarke were still confined to their cabins. The ship's water was running out, and at supper Robertson urged Wallis to return to the river at Matavai Bay, where the beach was protected by a low point (Te Auroa, now Point Venus) and his men could land to collect water without wetting their muskets. Clarke disagreed, arguing that they should land by the Papeno'o River under cover of the ship's guns. Matavai Bay was more sheltered, however, and in those days the Tuauru River ran along the shores of the bay just behind the beach, forming pools of fresh water where the sailors could fill the barrels. Following Robertson's advice, Wallis decided to return to Matavai Bay, and at daylight the next morning the barge and the cutter went ahead of the ship, taking soundings. As they rounded Point Venus and entered the bay, a large fleet of canoes swarmed out from a canoe harbour at Pira'e (a small bay with a stone pier marked on Benjamin Butler's coloured chart at the west end of Matavai Bay),[51] chasing the boats as their crews made a deafening uproar.

Certain that the boats were about to be attacked, Furneaux kept the ship so close to the cutter that no one on board saw Robertson's signal when his leadsman reported a sounding of just three fathoms. A minute later the *Dolphin* struck Te To'a-o-Hiro Shoal (named after Hiro, the god of thieves, and now called Dolphin Bank), grinding on the rocks as it grounded. To the warriors in the canoes and the spectators on the beaches, this must have seemed a spectacular demonstration of Hiro's power. As the ship spun in the wind, striking on the coral and damaging the upper masts, there was consternation on board. Followed by the first lieutenant, Wallis ran up from his cabin, ordering the decks to be cleared and the stream cable and anchor lowered to heave the ship off the coral.

When Robertson came on board soon afterwards, asking Captain Wallis for further orders, Lieutenant Clarke growled that this was all his fault, and that he should stay out of the way and keep quiet. In the Navy, although masters had once been responsible for navigating and handling the ships, by the mid-eighteenth century that role had been largely taken over by the lieutenants. Robertson, seeing the ship facing out to sea with a land breeze on her beam, ignored him and suggested to Wallis that the sails might be turned to the wind. No sooner had Wallis agreed than Clarke grabbed a rope to haul in one of the sails, but the sailors watched impassively and did nothing to help the first lieutenant. At that instant, the sails filled with the wind and the ship began to move off the shoal, to general rejoicing. As Robertson noted later: 'This gave great joy to all onbd but to me in particular.'[52]

Although the warriors in the canoes seemed delighted by the strangers' misfortune, they made no attempt to attack while the ship was vulnerable. In a fury, Clarke now ordered Gore to take the barge to sound off the shore of Point Venus, sending the cutter away on another duty. When Robertson asked which boat he should use for the soundings, Clarke told him to take the jolly-boat, as it drew the least water and there was less risk of him wrecking it on the coral. Infuriated by this jibe, Robertson was tempted to complain to Wallis but held his peace, knowing that his captain was ill and should not be up on deck. He armed himself with his pistols and broadsword, and taking the jolly-boat with five unarmed small lads and two marines with their muskets, set off to sound 'Port Royal Bay' in this tiny craft, surrounded by two hundred canoes.

As soon as the boats left the *Dolphin*, Clarke ordered the sails to be set and took the ship about three miles offshore, leaving the barge, the cutter and the jolly-boat behind. As the ship sailed away, the canoes crowded around the jolly-boat and threatened its young crew, one old man vehemently urging his companions to attack; although when Robertson ordered the two marines to aim their muskets at this man, he held up his paddle and ordered his canoe to drop back immediately. Robertson found a fine anchorage just a cable's length from the beach, where he rewarded his crew with a dram of old rum each; and they bravely declared that 'there was no Danger to be feard from the Natives'.[53] The moment that the jolly-boat headed back towards the ship, however, the canoes surrounded it again, intent upon attacking. As soon as one of the warriors hurled a stone at them from his slingshot, Robertson shot him with his pistol and one of the marines fired his musket, but despite these signs of distress the barge did not come to their assistance.

Fortunately, Captain Wallis, who had been watching the boats from his cabin window, now took control, ordering the ship to stand towards the shore and telling Lieutenant Clarke to fire several shots at the barge to warn them of the jolly-boat's predicament. Although the barge ignored this signal, the roar of the great guns and the firing of a musket frightened the warriors in the canoes and they immediately dispersed. Wallis sent the armed cutter to rescue the jolly-boat, and when it reached them Robertson ordered the midshipmen in charge to board the jolly-boat, and taking command of the cutter he guided the ship in to her new anchorage. Once the *Dolphin* was safely at anchor, Wallis divided the crew into four watches, each man armed with a pistol and cutlass. All of the great guns were loaded, some with round shot and some with grape shot, musketoons were fixed in each of the boats and all of the small arms primed and loaded. It was a fine, calm evening, and although they heard no canoes passing in the night, the sailors saw a great number of lights on a long reef at the south-west point of the bay, Utuha'iha'i Point, where the people later told them that they had been fishing with torches.

In fact, however, this was the site of Taraho'i, the main *marae* of the Pare-'Arue district, where the tomb of the Pomare dynasty now stands. The occupants of this strange floating object had proved to be hostile, killing one warrior and wounding another with supernatural power. The chiefs of the north-eastern districts had summoned their allies, and that night the priests went to the *marae* where they sent spirit messengers to the ancestor gods, asking whether or not an attack was likely to be successful.[54] The answer must have been positive, for at daylight on 24 June warriors in canoes approached the *Dolphin* and tried to weigh the stream anchor, retreating only when they were fired at with muskets. Soon afterwards at 6 a.m., when Wallis ordered the ship to be warped into Matavai Bay, the boats were lowered, each carrying an anchor, and as the anchors were taken ahead of the ship and lowered to the ocean floor, the sailors hauled the *Dolphin* along, chanting as they heaved on the capstan. By now about three hundred canoes flocked around the ship, their crews bartering pigs, chickens and fruit for beads, knives, nails and trinkets and watching this strange performance.

At 8 a.m. several very large double canoes approached the *Dolphin*, carrying loads of round stones and manned by burly warriors. When these men began to distribute stones to the crews of the other canoes, Wallis ordered Furneaux to put the fourth watch on alert. By now about five hundred canoes were crowding around the *Dolphin*, carrying several thousand warriors and flying bark-cloth banners (the flags of the gods of each district).[55] About two hours later a fleet of *'arioi* canoes approached the frigate, each carrying a number of young girls on their high platforms, and at a signal these girls lined up and for about a quarter of an hour 'made all the Gestures & Wanton tricks they could invent' while their male companions sang in hoarse voices and played on flutes, drums and conch trumpets. These people seemed merry and friendly, smiling and laughing as the sailors crowded onto the gangway and the forecastle, enraptured by the girls' 'lascivious' antics. Once again, although these gestures were hostile and challenging, the sailors mistook them for erotic enticement. As Wilkinson, one of the sailors, remarked in his journal:

> The woman was Derected by the Men to Stand in the Prow of their Canoes & Expose their Bodys Naked to our View as our men is in good Health & Spirits and begin to feel the Good Effect of the fresh Pork we Thank God for it. It is Not to be wondred that their Attention Should be Drawn to A Sight so uncommon to them Especially as their woman are so well Proportisnd.[56]

In ancient Polynesia, however, acts of genital exposure opened a pathway to Te Po, the realm of the ancestor gods, channelling their power. In times of peace, the *'arioi* might expose themselves to invoke the generative force of the ancestors, enhancing the fertility of plants, animals and people; while in times of war, the power of female gods could be directed against enemy warriors, attacking their *mana*. As soon as the sailors were all up on deck, gaping at this performance, a large double canoe approached the *Dolphin*. A man sitting on its wooden awning handed up a bunch of red and yellow feathers to one of the sailors, indicating that he should hand this to his captain. Thinking that this was a gesture of welcome, Wallis held a few trinkets out of the gallery window in return. In fact, however, this was an invitation to battle. As soon as Wallis accepted the bunch of feathers the man (who must have been a high priest of 'Oro) tossed a red bark-cloth cloak around his shoulders and threw the branch of a coconut tree high in the air; and in that instant three hundred war canoes paddled in a line at high speed towards the *Dolphin*,[57] the warriors whirling their slings and hurling stones (many weighing two or three pounds each) at the stupefied sailors. (*See Plate 4.*)

As the barrage of rocks struck his men, Wallis ordered the sentries to fire their muskets, but this had little effect on the infuriated warriors. Two quarterdeck guns loaded with small shot were fired into the canoes, making their crews pause, but before long they resumed whirling their slingshots. When the ship's drums sounded, the sailors ran to the great guns, firing a ragged volley into the fleet of canoes and at other canoes that were boarding warriors from the beaches, watched by thousands of people. As the cannon balls struck the canoes, sending out a lethal spray of splinters, their crews jumped overboard in terror, hanging on to floating remnants or sinking into the bloodstained water. The rest of the canoes fled, and when at last the great guns stopped firing they gathered in two groups, one offshore about a mile from the ship and the other closer to the beach (almost certainly the fleets of two different districts), thinking themselves safe at that distance.

After another pause, the great canoe that signalled the first attack began to rally the offshore group of canoes, hoisting white streamers as a signal; and when they renewed their attack Wallis's men fired two cannons loaded with round and grape shot at this craft, cutting it in two. Thinking that the great canoe belonged to the 'King of the Island', the sailors admired the courage of the men in four or five small canoes who paddled towards it under heavy fire, picking up the dead and wounded from the water. In fact this was probably the 'Rainbow', the sacred canoe that carried a leading priest and the image of 'Oro into battle.[58] The crews of the small canoes towed the two shattered halves of this great canoe to the reef, where they carried the dead and dying ashore. At another signal, the inshore fleet of about three hundred canoes paddled furiously towards the *Dolphin*. This time the sailors waited until these canoes were only 400 yards away before firing a three-pounder loaded with seventy musket balls into their midst, scything across the canoes and killing many more warriors. As the canoes fled in terror, they were pursued by two round shot. That night Robertson wrote in his journal:

> All the Bay and tops of the Hills round was full of Men, Women and Children to behould the onset, and I dare say in great hopes of sheering all our nails and Toys, besides the pleasure of calling our great Canoe their own, and having all of us at their mercy.
>
> How terrible must they be shocked, to see their nearest and dearest of friends Dead, and toar to peces in such a manner as I am certain they neaver beheald before – to Attempt to say what these poor Ignorant creatures thought of us, would be taking more upon me than I am able to perform. Some of my mess-mates thought they would now look upon us as Demi Gods, come to punish them for some of their past transgrations.[59]

During this battle when the *Dolphin*'s guns fired a hail of round, grape and musket balls into the canoes, this seemed an overwhelming display of ancestral power. According to James Cover, a missionary who lived on Tahiti in 1797–98, as they fled from the *Dolphin* the people cried 'E Atua haere mai – it's the god that's come';[60] while William Ellis, another early missionary, reported that the people called guns *pupuhi*, to blow repeatedly; cannons *pupuhi fenua*, because they blew across the land; and cannon and musket balls *ofa 'i*, or stones. The islanders saw the first Europeans who visited Tahiti as terrifying beings who blew into their weapons, making them thunder and flash and hurl stones that killed many people.[61]

After the last barrage, the great sea battle was over. As the canoes fled from Matavai Bay, the onlookers ran from the hills and beaches. Afterwards, the sailors mounted two three-pounders loaded with musket balls on the *Dolphin*'s forecastle, and musketoons on each of the boats, to guard against further surprises. By noon not a single canoe could be seen in the bay and only about ten people on shore, while the sea looked like a millpond. That afternoon the sailors carried on sounding in calm, fine weather. At dusk a fragrant, spicy scent came out to the ship, blown by the land breeze as a woman's body floated past the *Dolphin*'s cutwater, killed by a shot through her belly.

Matavai Bay

3

Purea, 'Queen' of Tahiti

At dawn on 25 June 1767, the morning after the great sea battle, Matavai Bay was deserted. People had been gathering from all over the island to see these astonishing strangers, however, and after a while they drifted back to the harbour. The Tuauru River ran behind the black sandy beach, forming a pool where the water barrels could be filled; and Wallis decided to take the ship further into the bay and anchor the *Dolphin* with her broadside covering this watering place. That afternoon a few canoes paddled

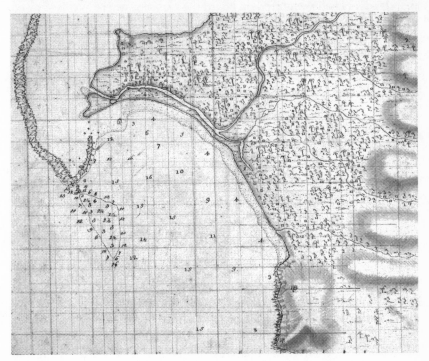

Plan of Matavai Bay

out to the ship, plantain branches set up in their bows (a sign that they were in the presence of ancestor gods) while their crews carried others as signs of peace. As Robertson noted: 'We this day behaved very haughty to them, and only sufferd two or three to come allong side at one time . . . The poor creatures used a great deal of ceremony.'[1]

Upon approaching the *Dolphin*, each of the paddlers in these canoes held up their plantain branches. One man stood up and made a speech, pointing to his bough and putting his body into various postures, while his companions looked up at the sky before throwing their plantain branches into the ocean as a gesture of propitiation. If the sailors looked surly these men forced a smile, holding up a green bough and offering the things that they had brought to barter. At the same time, however, they expected fair treatment. When William Welsh, a twenty-year-old sailor who had been struck on the head by a rock during the attack, took two chickens from one of these men and refused to give him anything in return, the islander shook his fist and yelled loudly, pointing at Welsh and abusing him. Wallis was determined to maintain discipline, and when one of the midshipmen told him what Welsh had done, he ordered the sailor to be given a flogging of two dozen lashes, which was carried out immediately. Some of the islanders finally ventured on board the *Dolphin*, where Wallis showed them a bag of grape shot and a cannon ball, trying to indicate with gestures the damage that these could do and ordering one of his men to fire a pistol ball into the hull of a canoe as a further demonstration. When the shot struck the hull these men all leaped into the water, but they came back on board as soon as they realised that no one had been wounded.

After dinner Wallis ordered Furneaux to take the barge, cutter and launch with a crew of armed men to take possession of the island, while the rest of his men stood on guard by their cannons. In a light drizzle, Furneaux set off with twelve marines and their sergeant, eighteen armed seamen, a mate and three midshipmen; and when this party landed on the beach, the islanders offered no opposition. The mate, Robert Molyneux, was left in charge of the boats, keeping them afloat in shallow water in case Furneaux's men had to beat a hasty retreat. The marines in their scarlet coats lined up beside the Tuauru River and went through their drill, watched by a curious crowd of Tahitians; and Furneaux turned a sod on the beach, reading out a document Wallis had given him that claimed Tahiti by right of conquest for His Most Sacred Majesty King George III of Great Britain, France and Ireland. During this ceremony he named Tahiti 'King George's Island' after the British monarch; Matavai Bay 'Port Royal'; and Mo'orea 'The Duke of York's Island'. Afterwards the men toasted the King with grog, celebrating their discovery.

In his Secret Instructions, Wallis had been ordered to acquire land for British trading posts at any places he might discover, but only with the consent of the inhabitants (if any):

> You are . . . to endeavour to make Purchases and with the consent of the Inhabitants take possession of convenient Situations – in the Country in the Name of the King of Great Britain; But if no Inhabitants are found on the Land or Islands so discovered, you are, in such Case, to take possession of such Lands or Islands for His Majesty by setting up proper Marks & Inscriptions as first Discoverers and Possessors.[2]

Because Wallis had failed to befriend the Tahitians, however, he decided to claim the island by right of conquest. When the ceremony was over, about five hundred people approached the Tuauru River, each man crouching, holding up a plantain branch and making submissive gestures towards the strangers; and when Lieutenant Furneaux beckoned to their leaders, three old men waded across the river, each holding a small pig and a plantain branch.[3] One of these elders, a man with a long white beard, crawled on his hands and knees towards the lieutenant, abasing himself. He spoke for a while and then laid down his pig, placing a plantain branch upon it as a peace offering. Later, they learned that this old man, 'Faa' (Fa'a), was a leading elder from the Matavai district. Making a speech in reply, Furneaux ordered a sailor to take up the gifts and handed nails and trinkets to the old man. He indicated that they wanted fresh water, and when Fa'a gestured that they could take as much as they liked, the sailors rolled two casks across the beach and filled them. The marines raised a pole by the river, hoisting a red pennant as a sign that the island now belonged to King George, and more islanders crossed the river, laying down their plantain branches, pigs and some fruit. Furneaux ordered all of these gifts to be loaded in the boats, shaking hands with Fa'a and leaving toys, hatchets, nails and two billhooks (or pruning knives) behind on the beach as return gifts. At 4 p.m. the landing party got into the boats and rowed back to the *Dolphin*.

As the sailors departed, a group of islanders crossed the river and stood on the beach, each man carrying a plantain branch and gazing uneasily at the red pennant on the pole, unsure of its purpose and power. Eventually two old men approached the flagstaff, crawling on their hands and knees and stopping at every eight or ten paces, speaking seriously and gazing up at the red pennant before kneeling and laying their plantain boughs beneath it. Several hundred other men followed, also on their hands and knees, holding up plantain branches and kneeling as they laid these at the foot of the staff; and when a breeze caught the pennant, snapping it in the wind over their heads, they jumped up and ran away in terror. At dusk that evening, Fa'a and another elder ceremoniously approached the pole, carrying two large pigs and some chickens. Placing their plantain branches at its foot, they took the pigs and chickens and tied these to the pole. After making long speeches, they picked up the pigs, put them in a canoe loaded with plantain branches and paddled out to the ship, stopping at intervals and making more speeches before approaching the *Dolphin*, where they threw their plantain boughs in the ocean. According to Ibbot, one of the sailors: 'The[ir] countenances and manner . . . was something very remarkable, there being so confus'd a mixture of dread fear & surprise in Ym that I dare say they thought us supernatural.'[4]

Alongside the ship, the old men gestured to the sailors to pull up the pigs on a rope, refusing to accept any return gifts but talking earnestly and pointing back at the pennant. Through their spyglasses, the officers could see two men on the beach throwing stones at the flag and stopping other people from laying down plantain branches beneath it. As soon as the two elders landed back on the beach, they went to the pole, lowered the red pennant, carefully folded it up and carried it away with them. That night the sailors heard conches, drums and flutes playing as fires flared up on the hillside.

According to Tahitian histories, Amo, the high chief of Papara, and his ex-wife Purea were both present on this occasion. Amo (also known as Tevahitua-i-Patea), a dignified aristocrat and a former black leg *'arioi*, traced his descent from the senior line of the Teva clan, which dominated eight districts stretching from Tai'arapu in the south of Tahiti to Puna'aui'a in the north. His father Tu-i-te-ra'i had been the *ari'i* (high chief) of the Teva-i-tai people with his headquarters at Papara, a district halfway down the west coast; while his mother was a chieftainess from Ha'apape, the district in which Matavai Bay was located. From his mother, Amo had inherited a seat on Farero'i *marae* near Point Venus, and he was at home in this district. His ex-wife Purea (formally known as Tevahine-'ai-roro-atua-i-Ahurai), also a leading *'arioi*, was an intelligent, forceful woman. The first-born in her family, this 'Great Woman' was descended from some of the most powerful lineages on the island. Her mother had been the high chieftainess of Ahurai, the main *marae* in the Fa'a'a district just north of Puna'aui'a; and her younger brother was now the high chief of that district. Purea's marriage with Amo was over, however. When she had decided to keep their son Teri'irere alive rather than to kill him at birth as *'arioi* custom dictated, she and Amo both lost their sacred status as black leg *'arioi*.[5] Amo had been so angry with her that he left her, although they remained close political allies. Having inherited the *mana* and kin titles of both parents,[6] Teri'irere was arguably the most aristocratic young man on the island, and they were fiercely ambitious for their son. With the support of Tupaia, the high priest-navigator from Taputapuatea and now Purea's lover, and other high-born exiles from Ra'iatea, Purea and Amo had begun to build a great *marae* at Papara which they called Mahaiatea. Here they intended to invest Teri'irere with their family titles and sacred feather girdles, and install him as the paramount chief of the island.

According to the oral traditions, on this occasion Amo sent Fa'a, the elder who first approached the British, to discover their intentions. When the strangers erected a red pennant in the bay, this was a puzzling portent. On the one hand, if a party was tired of fighting in Tahiti, they sent a messenger with a *manu faiti* or emblem of peace, a reed with a bunch of red feathers and a small red flag tied to one end of a staff, and a sheet of bark cloth (red on one side and white on the other) tied to the other.[7] On the other hand, when a new high chief was born a herald carried a *vane* or red flag around his district; and when he was about to be installed, his flag was carried around the island. If this was ritually received in a district it was a mark of acceptance and support, but if the *vane* was torn up this was a declaration of war.[8] And if a high chief decided to reserve a particular fishing ground or part of the reef for a time, he might announce this *rahui* or restriction by erecting a bark-cloth banner on a pole.[9] When the strangers in their scarlet garments ceremoniously hoisted a red pennant on a pole on the beach, this might have been a declaration of peace; but under the circumstances it seemed more likely they were asserting their *mana* over the island (as indeed the British intended); and when the elders presented ritual gifts to their enemies and carried the red flag away, they were in turn upholding their own *mana* over the strangers. When the red pennant was delivered to Purea, Amo and Tupaia, they decided to deploy the power of this talisman against the invaders.

At daybreak the next morning, 26 June, Lieutenant Furneaux and his men returned to the watering place where Fa'a was waiting. The old man summoned a few people who carried fruit and chickens to the river-bank, but at 7.30 a.m. the sailors on board the *Dolphin* noticed a fleet of large canoes approaching from the south-west side of the bay, hugging the coast, as thousands of warriors ran swiftly around the point towards the Tuauru River. When Amo's men appeared over 'One Tree Hill' (as Wallis named Tahara'a Hill, after the red-flowering tree on its summit), armed with spears, they were led by a young man who proudly carried the *Dolphin*'s red pennant flying from a pole, while hundreds of other warriors crept through the bushes and the woods around the watering place. Wallis sent the jolly-boat to warn Furneaux, but he had already seen the warriors approaching and embarked his men in the boats, pointing their guns at these men in warning and telling Fa'a to order them to stay at a distance.

As soon as they realised that they had been detected the warriors yelled loudly, crossing the river and seizing the casks from the watering place. Fleets of canoes from the east and the west pulled into Matavai Bay, took more warriors on board and paddled slowly towards the *Dolphin* as a huge crowd of men, women and children sat on One Tree Hill, watching these manoeuvres with rapt attention. Alert to the danger, Wallis ordered his men to their stations and a round shot was fired over the canoes. When the warriors ignored this signal, cannons loaded with grape shot, round shot and double-headed shot were fired into the two fleets of canoes which turned and fled, and then the sailors fired into the woods where many of the warriors were hiding. As thousands of people ran towards One Tree Hill, Wallis commanded his men to lower their guns and fire a broadside among them. According to one of Amo's descendants, several of these cannon balls knocked down a swathe of trees and landed in front of Purea and Amo, throwing dirt in their faces.[10] Bowing to this demonstration of superior power, Purea and Amo fled with their companions, vowing to make peace with the strangers. Tupaia also fled, carrying the *Dolphin*'s red pennant away to Mahaiatea where he placed it with the other sacred relics held at the great *marae* – the yellow feather girdle of the Tevas, the feathered image of 'Oro and Te Ra'i-puatata, and the red feather girdle that Tupaia had brought from Ra'iatea.

As soon as the bay was deserted, Wallis sent the boats ashore carrying armed men and carpenters with their axes to destroy the canoes that were lined up along the beach. They smashed about eighty of these craft, two of which were ornately carved, fifty feet long and able to carry thirty or more men; and collected the pigs, chickens and fruit that the islanders had brought to barter. Upon returning to the *Dolphin* the sailors were given a dinner with fruit and fresh pork broth, lifting their morale. As Robertson noted with satisfaction:

> This day the Capt. gave orders, to let every man in the ship have as many cocoa nuts, and oyther fruit as they thought proper to Eate, likeway orderd Hogs and Pigs to be killd to make broath for all hands – in short all hand now lived so well that they began to revive their sunk spirits, and the most of the sick began to crawl upon deck.[11]

Later that afternoon, a group of men, women and children silently approached the watering place where they laid down six large bales of white cloth, eight large hogs, four pigs, a dozen chickens, fruit, green boughs, and two fine dogs with their forefeet tied over their backs on the beach as a peace offering.[12] One of these men stood in the sea up to his waist, carrying a child and gazing out at the ship. Furneaux took the boats back to the beach, and pretended to head towards their canoes as if he was about to destroy them. Greatly afraid, the people gestured at the peace offering and brought down a beautiful fan as another gift, its ribs made of mother-of-pearl and the fan of feathers. Accepting the fan, Furneaux ordered the sailors to take the pigs, chickens and fruit but released the two dogs, which scampered away, and left the bales of bark cloth on the beach. Although the islanders pointed at the bark cloth, urging him to take it, Furneaux ignored them, ordering his men to lay down hatchets, billhooks, nails and trinkets in exchange for these items.

When the sailors loaded the water casks in the boats and returned to the ship, the people on shore seemed uneasy, gesturing towards the ship with green branches, so Wallis sent two armed boats back to pick up the bark cloth. As soon as they landed and took up the cloth, the islanders looked intensely relieved and brought down more pigs and fruit. In the Society Islands, bark cloth was prized as a ceremonial gift that helped to contain *tapu* or ancestral power. Some old men also led a number of beautiful young girls down to the beach where they made them stand in a line, indicating with graphic gestures how the sailors should treat them. Laughing, the sailors responded with lewd gestures of their own, exposing themselves to the girls; and according to the *Dolphin*'s master, Robertson, 'the poor young Girls seemed a little afraid, but soon after turned better acquanted'.[13] Many of these girls were in their early teens, and it was a terrifying prospect to be handed over to the strangers, whether they were ancestors, conquering *'arioi*, or some weird kind of being.[14] Worse still, many of the sailors were suffering from scurvy, with ulcerated limbs, protruding gums and stinking breath; and after months at sea they were also filthy – not an alluring prospect.

In Tahiti, however, *'arioi* warriors were sexually voracious, and it seems that these girls had been offered to the British sailors as part of the peace-making exchanges. That night on board the *Dolphin*, the men were in high spirits. As Robertson remarked:

All the sailors swore that they neaver saw handsomer made women in their lives, and declard they would all to a man, live on two thirds allowance, rather than lose so fine an opportunity of geting a Girl apiece – this piece of news made all our men madly fond of the shore, even the sick which hade been on the Doctor's list for some weeks before, now declard they would be happy if they were permited to go ashore, and at the same time said a Young Girl would make an Excelent Nurse . . . we past this Night very merry.[15]

Most of the crew were in their twenties or younger, and unmarried. Back in Britain, where seamen brought prostitutes on to the ships in port, or met them in inns and brothels, men often took whores out in the open, on bridges or in parks, while in brothels and below decks in port, orgiastic sex was not uncommon; and the sexual displays they had seen in Matavai Bay must have reminded them of these practices. In Britain at this time, too, sex was often spoken of in aggressive terms, and women as property to be owned or taken;[16] while women who exposed themselves were regarded as harlots. In Tahiti, however, although sex was also a powerful force, it was associated with the fertility of the ancestors and the fecundity of local resources. As Tcherkézoff has argued, throughout Polynesia young girls (who were virgin or had not yet had children) might be presented to the gods or their representatives in the Ao or world of light – chiefs, 'arioi, or in this case, visiting Europeans.[17] When they were offered to victorious warriors, this was a gesture of reconciliation – children might be born from the union, binding the lineages together. The sailors, understanding none of these subtleties, however, simply revelled in the thought of having sex with these beautiful young women.

This act of submission was a turning point. The next morning when Fa'a came down to meet the landing party he berated some men who had gathered on the beach, pointing at the slings and piles of stones left behind by the warriors. Furneaux shook hands and embraced the elder, indicating that although the islanders could bring their trade goods to the opposite side of the river, only Fa'a was allowed to carry these across to the British – an arrangement that angered those chiefs who outranked the elder. Captain Wallis had appointed the ship's gunner, William Harrison, to handle the trade for the *Dolphin*, an arrangement that equally irritated his shipmates. Although the 'Season of Scarcity' was approaching (which lasted from May to November after the end of the breadfruit harvest),[18] vast quantities of pigs, chickens and breadfruit were bartered that day. On the advice of the ship's surgeon, Wallis ordered pork broth to be boiled with wheat and chunks of breadfruit, plantain and bananas for every meal, and the scurvy sufferers quickly began to recover. That afternoon some islanders crept down to the beach on their hands and knees, launched one of the double canoes and paddled away to the south as fast as they could go. The sailors let them leave, feeling that the Tahitians had been sufficiently punished for their temerity.

On 28 June, Wallis, Clarke and the purser John Harrison were so ill that they stayed in their cabins. Harrison was an excellent mathematician and astronomer, and with his help Wallis had hoped to observe the satellites of Jupiter, but because the purser was confined to his bed this proved to be impossible. Over the next few days when the sailors went ashore, Furneaux and Gore were vigilant, and the islanders seemed chastened and friendly. On 1 July the surgeon John Hutchinson went to select a site for the sick tent, which was pitched on an islet in the middle of the river to prevent the sick men from wandering, guarded by two midshipmen, four marines, and three dogs from the ship, which bit some of the Tahitians. Although there were numerous Polynesian dogs in the bay, they were a species that did not bark and were very docile, the islanders often carrying them in their arms. That afternoon while Hutchinson was walking by the river, a wild duck flew over his head and he fired his musket, killing it stone dead, and its body fell amongst the local people. They brought it to him, trembling, and when another flock flew overhead he shot three more ducks on the wing, further intimidating the Tahitians.

Although Amo, the high chief of Papara, stayed away from the strangers throughout this visit, his wife Purea (or 'Oberea', as the British called her) soon appeared at the watering place. On 3 July, Henry Ibbot, one of the midshipmen, noted the arrival of this tall and stately woman, who seemed to have considerable authority over the local people: 'Petty coat interest here as well as in other parts, is the most prevailing, the principal person hereabout being a Woman, whom we stiled the Queen, she was the stoutest woman I ever saw there, & had a very commanding aspect, but not Handsome being on ye decline, she liv'd at a House, which we call'd the large House.'[19] Impressed by her demeanour and the respect that she was shown, the sailors quickly dubbed Purea 'the Queen' of Tahiti.

The morning after Purea's visit to the watering place, the sailors caught a large female shark about twelve-and-a-half feet long, which they stabbed and shot through the head. They decided to tow the shark ashore and left it on the beach, rowing off some distance to watch the islanders' reactions. To the islanders this must have seemed a powerful omen, because in Tahiti sharks were *ata* or the incarnation of ancestor gods,[20] and Amo's people, the Teva, had been founded by a shark god. Many generations earlier when a woman named Hotutu married a chief of Puna'aui'a, she bore him a son called Teri'i-te-moana-rau. Having inherited the titles of both parents, the boy's rank was exalted, and his father set off in his canoe to fetch red feathers from the Tuamotu Islands to make him a *maro 'ura* or red feather girdle. During his absence, however, a shark god, taking a human form, came to visit Hotutu and stayed with her for a time. They became lovers, but one day when Hotutu's pet dog came up to her and affectionately licked her face, the shark god flew into a jealous rage. Exclaiming, 'You have been untrue to your husband with me, so you may be untrue to me with the dog!', he decided to leave Hotutu. Before turning himself back into a shark and swimming away, he uttered a prophecy: 'You will bear me a child; if a girl, she will belong to you and take your name; but if a boy, you are to call him Teva; rain and wind will accompany his birth, and . . . rain and wind will always foretell his coming. He is of the race of the *Ari'i rahi* (high chiefs) and you are to build him a *Marae* which you are to call Mataoa and there he is to wear the *Maro tea* (the yellow feather girdle).' As the shark god had predicted, after his departure Hotutu bore him a child, a boy named Teva who was installed as a high chief with the yellow feather girdle.[21] The Teva clans sang a chant celebrating their ancestor:

> I am a bird, a Teva
> A Teva in the rain, a Teva in the shade,
> The little shade of 'Oro with the yellow body.
> Let the heralds sing,
> Papara produces warriors,
> For Oropa'a, for Fenua-'ura (One Tree Hill, with its red soil),
> For Orion's belt
> Of the summer solstice,
> Papara of the trade wind and rippling sea
> Papara that fosters young women
> Papara veiled in white mist![22]

Amo was Teva's direct descendant, and before the birth of his son Teri'irere, he had held the yellow feather girdle with its associated titles. In Tahiti, when a son was born to an *ari'i* or high chief, however, his *mana* or ancestral power immediately passed to the child, although the transfer was not formally ratified until the boy was installed with these titles and the girdle at a leading *marae*.

At the time of the *Dolphin*'s arrival, Amo and Purea were planning to invest Teri'irere with the insignia of the shark god and other sacred regalia at Mahaiatea *marae*, and given these associations, it is not surprising that the islanders greeted the shark in a ceremonial fashion.[23] They walked up to its body, stopping about twenty yards away and then slowly stepping forward again. Two men went off to fetch plantain branches, and when they returned they walked slowly to the head of the shark, laying down these branches before stepping back and speaking for a time, gazing at it earnestly. The ritual lasted for about an hour, but when they finally realised that the shark was dead, one of these men put his foot on the tail of the shark and yanked, while another put his fingers into the shot-holes. When the men in the boats gestured to them to take the shark away, they cut it into large pieces and carried these off, finding twenty baby sharks in its belly (a propitious sign of fertility).

On 6 July when Wallis was at last well enough to leave the *Dolphin*, he and Robertson went in the barge on a tour of the coast. During this excursion they saw two very large canoes about fifty feet long, and a stone pyramid on the north-west point (Point Utuha'iha'i) with seven steps, each step about two feet high and faced with round stones, with some large images carved out of trees standing nearby. This was Taraho'i, the principal *marae* of the Pare-'Arue district, Purea and Amo's main rivals, with its stepped *ahu* or altar and *ti'i* or sexually explicit carved figures where ancestor spirits (the guardians of fertility) came to rest during the ritual ceremonies.[24] Returning to the ship for dinner, Robertson saw that the trading party had obtained little fresh food that day, and he soon found out why. As he wrote that night in his journal:

> I was toud by one of the Young Gentlemen that a new sort of trade took up most of their attention that day, but it might be more properly called the old trade, he says a Dear Irish boy one of our Marins was the first that began the trade, for which he got a very severe cobing [or thrashing] from the Liberty men for not beginning in a more decent manner, in some house or at the back of some bush or tree, Padys Excuse was the fear of losing the Honour of having the first.[25]

In fact this was not a new trade at all, because according to evidence in the journals, these sexual exchanges had begun several days earlier. Because the senior officers were so ill during the *Dolphin*'s visit to Matavai Bay, discipline on shore was lax; and when some girls appeared at the watering place, offering pearl earrings and other items for European goods, the sailors took advantage of the fact that of their officers, only Lieutenant Furneaux was fit, and he could not be everywhere at once. One or two at a time, the sailors began to wander into the woods where they gave nails for sex with these girls, some of whom were only ten or eleven years old. As we have seen, on the island young virgins might be presented to ancestor gods or visiting high chiefs, and nails were regarded as treasures, invaluable for woodworking and fish-hooks.[26] This soon developed into a kind of barter, the local men bringing girls to the watering place where they demanded a small nail for an unattractive girl and a large nail for a great beauty, although the high-ranking women refused to have anything

to do with the strangers. Very likely Robertson and the other petty officers turned a blind eye to these transactions, or joined in themselves. Now
that Wallis was aware of what was going on, he formally asked the ship's
surgeon whether any of his men had venereal diseases, and Hutchinson
swore on his honour that 'no man on board was infected with any sort
of disorder, that they could communicate to the Natives of this beautiful
Island'.[27] The sailors had been having a marvellous time on shore, and no
one wanted to be responsible for spoiling these delectable exchanges.

Despite Hutchinson's assurances, however, upon their arrival at the
island at least ten of the sailors were infected with venereal diseases,
'three very bad with Damn'd Inveterate Poxes and Claps; the Rest has but
Trifiling Complaints, mostly of the same Kind'.[28] In fact, it is likely that
many more of the crew had venereal disorders; although syphilis can be
asymptomatic but still infectious for up to four years, this was unknown
to medical science in the eighteenth century. Many of the local girls were
infected with these new diseases, and some became pregnant. As Francis
Wilkinson, one of the sailors, remarked:

> The Women were far from being Coy. For when A Man Found a Girl to
> his Mind, which he might Easily Do Amongst so many, there was not much
> Ceremony on Either Side, and I believe whoever comes here after will find
> Evident Proofs that they are not the First Discoverys. The men are so far from
> having Objaction to an Intercourse of this Kind that they Brought down their
> Women & Recommend them to us with the Greatest Eagerness, which makes
> me Imagine they want a Breed of English Men Amongst them.[29]

As news of these illnesses began to spread, the people were filled with
foreboding. In Tahiti, illness was inflicted by the gods, the guardians of
health and fertility; a bad sign at a time when the ceremony to farewell the
gods from the island was imminent.

On 8 July a great fleet of large 'arioi canoes appeared in Matavai Bay,
decked with red, yellow, white and blue banners. These were heavily
loaded, carrying food and gifts to Taraho'i marae for the ritual that heralded the departure of the gods and the 'arioi, and the beginning of the
Season of Scarcity. According to Pomare II,[30] in preparation for this ceremony the priests would set themselves apart from their families and fast,
tying their girdles tightly around their waists to heighten their communication with the gods – for in Tahiti, emotions and thought originated in
the belly where the mind-heart was located. The marae attendants made
a special white bark cloth to offer to the gods, renewed the carved posts
that stood on the marae, and set up long rods upon which the gods could

alight while the priests refurbished the 'Rainbow', the sacred canoe that carried the *to'o* or image of 'Oro. The people collected lavish supplies of food for the feasts that followed the main ritual, and when everything was prepared the *ari'i rahi* (high chief) sent a messenger around his district, announcing that the gods were coming:

> The gods above, the gods below,
> The gods of the ocean, the gods of the land,
> The gods within, the gods without,
> They will all come to this ritual,
> It is sacred and holy!

Such ceremonies invariably began at dusk. Sacred drums thundered, and as night fell all of the lights in the district were extinguished. People stayed inside their houses, tying up the mouths of their pigs, dogs and poultry and hushing their children; and while the ceremonies were under way they did not light their fires, walk about, or paddle their canoes. The chiefs bared their bodies to the waist and weeded the *marae*, removing all the moss and plants while the *marae* attendants renewed its sacred paraphernalia; and when the stone temple had been cleansed the hungry, shivering priests approached the *marae* in a solemn procession. As the *ti'i* or images of the messenger spirits were set up at the *marae* and their spirits were despatched, the priests chanted to summon the gods from the Po (the dark world of ancestors and spirits):

> The *marae* is restored, it is weeded and handsome.
> The carved ornaments are renewed
> The altars are renewed
> The home of the gods is renewed.
> The gods will all come, and gather in the darkness.

Over the next few days as each god whistled through the air and landed at the *marae*, the high priest announced his arrival. At the height of the ritual, the priests carried the images of the main gods in procession to the *marae* for the *pa'i-atua* rite (literally 'wrapping the gods'), led by the high priest and chanting 'Ho, ho, ho!' to summon the gods. At the *marae*, the high priest took the *to'o* or image of the leading god and stripped off its bark-cloth wrapping and red and yellow feathers, releasing its *mana* or ancestral power. In their turn, the other priests stripped the *to'o* of the lesser gods, anointing the wooden staffs inside them with oil, offering new red or yellow feathers to the leading god and in return receiving old feathers from his body, recharging their gods with *mana* and *tapu* (ancestral presence). When all of the images had been oiled, re-wrapped, re-bound and re-decorated, allowing them to be possessed by the ancestors and renewing their *ora* or life force,[31] a sacred fire was lit; pigs and dogs were killed, singed over the flames and placed on the altar as an offering to the gods, along with plantain shoots or *ta'ata-o-mei'a roa* (man long-banana) instead of human sacrifices. Finally, the gods were farewelled back to the Po, the priests imploring them to return again in summer bringing prodigal supplies of fish and good crops from the breadfruit trees, along with other resources. At the end of this ritual, the priests chanted, freeing the participants from their sacred restrictions:

> Let *tapu* [sacredness] stay here, so that we can become *noa* [freed from ritual restriction].
> You remain sacred, o god, and let the priests hold the sacredness of the high chief and the congregation
> We will now retire to use our hands and become *noa* [ordinary]
> We will do domestic work
> Wear flowers, paint ourselves with yellow *mati*
> Blow fire, curse, hit each other, practise black magic
> Put on unconsecrated clothes, eat pork, cavally fish, shark, bananas
> And drink '*ava* [an intoxicating drink],
> Do not be angry at us for this, o god!
> You stay here in this sacred place
> Turn your face to the Po
> Do not look upon the deeds of men.[32]

As on this occasion, the '*arioi* flocked to these rituals. During the feasts after the main ceremony they danced, performed hilarious skits, and chanted sagas celebrating the creation of the world and the exploits of heroes such as Maui, Hiro and 'Oro, illustrating their words with graphic actions. According to John Orsmond, they also engaged in orgiastic sex: 'There were scores and scores and scores of men and only five or six or seven women. No payment, just copulation, copulation to climax, one after another. They were subject neither to restraint or shame. Right there in front of husbands and wives.'[33] These acts of public intercourse were carried out by young '*arioi*, especially the initiates, arousing 'Oro, Ta'aroa and the other male gods to make love with their female counterparts, ensuring the fertility of land, sea and people and encouraging the gods to return after the Season of Scarcity.

The young girls who performed public sex on these occasions were known as *taiato* (which the missionaries later translated as 'whores').[34] This translation was based on an error, however, because these girls were dedicated to the gods and their performances were ceremonial in nature, bringing health, well-being and fertility to people, plants and animals on the island. On this occasion, assuming the British sailors to be associated with the gods, the *'arioi* included them in their revelry. Later, however, the islanders would complain that the English had corrupted their women by offering iron for sex. As Wilson, one of the early London Missionary Society missionaries noted: 'They lay the charge wholly at our door, and say that Englishmen are ashamed of nothing, and that we have led them to public acts of indecency never before practised among themselves. Iron here, more precious than gold, bears down every barrier of restraint; honesty and modesty yield to the force of temptation.'[35] This was fair comment, because during the *Dolphin*'s visit some women began to trade sex for nails on their own account. On 9 July, the day after the *'arioi* canoes arrived, Robertson and two of the midshipmen went ashore where they were accosted by three lovely young girls (probably visiting *'arioi*) who smiled at them seductively, making signals with their hands to indicate the length of the nails for which they were willing to barter. According to the master:

> I desired one of them to Explain the meaning of the Signal . . . Another repeated the same Signal, which was this, she held up her right hand and first finger of the right hand streight, then laid hould of her right wrist with the left hand, and heald the Right hand and first finger up streight and smiled, then crooked all her fingers and kept playing with them and Laughed very hearty, which set my young friends a Laughing as hearty as the Young Girl.
>
> This made me insist on their Explaining the Sign, and they told me the Young Girls only wanted a Long Nail each, but they neaver before saw them make a sign for one longer nor their fingers, but they supposed the Young Girls thought I carried longer nails nor the rest becaus I was drest in a different manner.[36]

At the same time, nails were also being bartered for fresh food and firewood. The next day, some sailors who were sent to fell trees for firewood punched a nail into the trunk of each tree they wished to harvest; but when an old man collected one of these nails, a tall, powerful man came up and took it from him, provoking vehement protests from the elder. When Purea, 'a fine, well-looking woman of the dark Mustee colour', appeared on the scene, the bystanders told her what had happened; and after the old man explained his grievance, she spoke angrily to the younger man (who may have been another visiting *'arioi*, since they often seized goods from ordinary people) and he immediately handed over the nail and walked away, looking abashed and frightened.

Later that day, two young men came on board the *Dolphin* to dine with Captain Wallis. One was the son of Fa'a, the Matavai elder, and the other was a young chief about thirty years old whom the sailors nicknamed 'Jonathan'. As he sat at the dining table in the Great Cabin, Jonathan looked at the chairs and inspected the plates, knives and forks, and when the meal was served he sat down and waited politely until food was offered to him. When a feast was placed on the table – broth made from two fat chickens, two roasted chickens, a roasted pig, roasted yams, plantains, bananas, soft bread, and a pudding and pie made with Tahitian apples or *vi*, the young chief ate heartily, watching to see how the British used their cutlery and imitating them carefully. He tasted the wine and grog but did not seem to like spirits, drinking water instead, and when he saw the men wipe their mouths with their handkerchiefs before he drank, he wanted to do likewise. Robertson offered him a corner of the tablecloth, which affronted Lieutenant Clarke (whom Robertson now dubbed 'Old Growl') who spoke angrily, making Jonathan uneasy.

To comfort the young chief, Robertson now wiped his own mouth with a corner of the tablecloth, which made him laugh; and Jonathan offered to bring Clarke a fine young woman to cheer him up. After dinner the officers showed him a looking glass. He was astonished at first, but then used it while he plucked the hairs of his beard with tweezers. When they showed him the miniature of a beautiful, well-dressed young English lady the young chief was enchanted, hugging and kissing the picture in raptures. They assured him that if he came to their island, he could have a young woman like this to sleep with, and he seemed overjoyed at the prospect. When he went ashore Jonathan was met by a large crowd who seemed eager to hear about his adventures. The next morning he came out again in a canoe, paddled by four men and bringing two very beautiful young women for Lieutenant Clarke. Clarke was not there, but the sailors gladly gave these women a guided tour of the vessel.

On 12 July, Purea came out to visit Captain Wallis. Although he was very ill, Wallis invited 'the Queen' into his cabin and greeted her warmly, presenting her with a long blue cloak tied with ribbons, a looking glass, some beads and many other gifts. Concerned about the state of his health, Purea invited Wallis to visit her at the large house, and he promised to go the next morning. That afternoon John Harrison, the gunner, escorted Purea back to the chief's house on the western side of the bay where she was staying (also marked on Butler's chart), which he described as 'prodigiously large' and closed in with latticework.[37] The same afternoon Robertson walked to some houses at the foot of One Tree Hill where he saw some large wooden *ti'i* (images in which ancestor spirits resided, placed there to protect the owners of these places, the fertility of their lineage and the resources of their district),[38] one of which was adorned with five human figures with prominent genitals, both women and men, standing on each other's heads. When the master began to handle these images, looking to see how the islanders would react, they remained impassive. When he tried to get one of them to touch an image, they refused; and even when he poked at a *ti'i* with his broadsword and cut a piece from it they all walked away, although they did not seem angry. Evidently these people had decided that it was too risky to confront the British, no matter what the provocation. When he returned to the ship Robertson found that 'Jonathan' had arrived on another visit, bringing two large roasted pigs and some fruit. The sailors asked the young chief about the girls he had brought to the ship the previous day, and he said they were at home crying, but if their boyfriends on the *Dolphin* wanted to sleep with them on shore, they would be happy.

The next morning Captain Wallis kept his promise and went ashore to visit Purea. On the beach, she instructed some of her people to take Wallis, Lieutenant Clarke and the purser John Harrison and the other sick men in their arms, and carry them across the river. They were followed by the captain's guard of honour, a party of marines wearing their scarlet coats

Purea greets Captain Wallis

('Oro's sacred colour) and high sugar-loaf hats, marching with bayonets
fixed to their muskets. A huge crowd of people followed the procession,
but when Purea waved them away they quickly dispersed.

Upon approaching the chief's house Wallis noticed some walled marae
nearby handsomely paved with round stones, with little sheds inside their
enclosures and images of men, women, pigs and dogs carved on the posts
around them (probably also *ti'i* or ancestor figures). The chief's house
was large, 327 feet long by 42 feet wide, and a crowd was waiting there to
greet them. Indicating that these were her relatives, Purea made each of
them kiss Wallis's hand in greeting. When they entered the house, she got
her visitors to sit down and summoned some young girls, four of whom
gently rolled down the captain's stockings, took off his shoes and coat and
began to massage his limbs. When the surgeon John Hutchinson removed
his wig, the islanders gasped in astonishment. Clarke, Harrison the purser,
Hutchinson and all of the sick men were given massages, which they
declared to be very beneficial. After about half an hour Purea ordered
some bundles of bark cloth to be brought so that she could wrap Wallis
and his companions in this fabric. Wrapping up a high-ranking guest in
bark cloth was a way of containing their *mana* or ancestral power while
binding them into the donor's kin group.[39] Although Wallis hesitated to
remove his uniform, he did not want to offend Purea and reluctantly
agreed. When they left the chief's house she ordered a large pregnant sow
to be taken to the boat, and when Wallis walked back she went with him,
lifting him carefully over every creek and hollow.

During Wallis's visit to Purea, 'Jonathan' had arrived at the *Dolphin*
with Fa'a, who showed the young chief great respect. Robertson and
Furneaux, who had stayed on board, decided to dress this young man in
European style, with shoes, breeches, shirt and coat. Jonathan walked up
and down the deck, preening himself, and after dinner when he went back
to the beach he summoned some servants who carried him ashore, so that
he did not wet his fine garments. People crowded around him, greatly
admiring this curious costume, but this was the last time that the British
saw him. Robertson thought that his people, afraid that he might join the
strangers on their great vessel, had sent Jonathan away; but it is equally
likely that he and his companions had returned to their own district. Now
that the farewell to the gods and its feasts were over, it was customary for
the *'arioi* to withdraw to their homes to mourn the absence of the gods;
and the visiting priests returned to their own *marae* to implore the ancestors to return with a bountiful harvest in the summer.[40]

The following day Wallis sent a gift of six hatchets, six billhooks and
other valuable objects to Purea, thanking her for her hospitality. When

John Harrison, the gunner and one of Purea's favourites, arrived with these gifts at the chief's house, he found Purea presiding over a feast for about a thousand people. She was feeding the principal chiefs with her own hands, giving them puddings made of shredded chicken and Tahitian apples before being fed by her own attendants. Purea seemed delighted with Wallis's gifts and sent him more pigs, chickens and fruit. That afternoon an old woman dressed in red bark cloth arrived at the riverside, accompanied by a young man carrying a plantain branch. He made a long speech before laying down the branch, and guided the old lady and two large pigs across the river. Looking intently at the sailors, this old woman wept loudly, crying so bitterly that she could hardly stand, and explaining that the British had killed her husband and three sons. Ordering the young man to hand over the hogs, she departed. In Tahiti, when a warrior was killed in battle his family approached the man responsible, the bereaved daughters danced before the victor and adopted him in place of the dead man, giving him their father's name and obliging him to support them;[41] and this seems to have been another version of this ritual. That night the British saw plumes of smoke rising from Taraho'i *marae*, perhaps from the ovens for the feast that ended all major ceremonies. The gods had been farewelled; and for many of the local people, no doubt this seemed a proper time for their powerful visitors – who might be gods themselves – to leave the island.

Two days later, 16 July, Wallis sent Furneaux with all the boats and sixty armed men to explore the western coast of the island. Marching about six miles along the coast, Furneaux and his men saw a dense population with large houses and gardens. These people seemed to have plenty of chickens, pigs and vegetables but were not willing to trade them to the strangers – not surprisingly, for these provisions would be needed during the Season of Scarcity. A few days later, Wallis was once again confined to his cabin and Furneaux, 'a Gentele Agreeable well behaved Good man, and very humain to all the Ship's company', also fell ill.[42] The crew was despondent, because the first lieutenant William Clarke had recovered and was now in command, quarrelling with everyone on board except for the gunner. The sailors had become obsessed with bartering nails for sex, ruining the trade for food, and discipline had become shaky. Since their arrival at Matavai Bay there had been several floggings, and now one of the marines was given twenty-four lashes for mutinous behaviour.

On 18 July, Purea visited the ship again, bringing more large pigs, and the following day Pickersgill and the sergeant of marines (another of the 'Queen's favourites) walked through the woods to the *'arioi* house where Purea, dressed in red bark cloth, the insignia of a black leg *'arioi*,[43] was

The Great 'Arioi House, by Captain Wallis

hosting a lavish feast for about five hundred people. No doubt she hoped to win support for her son's installation with these displays of chiefly generosity. She invited Pickersgill to join her under a little shelter that protected the earth ovens; and when the meal was served, her guests gathered around Purea, who sat on a fine mat with two beautiful young women standing beside her. As the food was delivered, these young women put it in dishes and gave it to the servants who took it to their guests, beginning with the highest-ranking people. These chiefs seemed very solemn, taking a small portion out of their dishes and setting it aside as an offering to the gods before eating; and they all ate in silence. When three new meat dishes were placed before the 'Queen' she invited Pickersgill and the sergeant to share them, but realising that this was her own meal, they refused. The two young women now fed her, taking it in turns, each one putting her hand in a bowl of fresh water before taking up some meat and putting it in Purea's mouth, and washing that hand in another bowl of water. As a 'Great Woman' she was so *ra'a* or sacred that she could not touch food, and these young women had to wash their hands each time they touched her. After the meal Purea made a speech to these people, and then left with Pickersgill and the sergeant to visit the *Dolphin*, accompanied by six of her leading men.

That afternoon when Purea arrived at the ship, Wallis was so ill that he could not entertain her in the Great Cabin. She had brought another large gift of food, and the captain ordered her to be given gifts in return. Although her companions ate and drank heartily in the gunroom, Purea did not eat or drink, preserving her *ra'a* (or ancestral power). There were many food restrictions in Tahiti, and because most women were *noa* (ordinary, unrestricted), they were not normally permitted to eat food prepared by men (except for their own male servants), nor did they usually eat with men. As a Great Woman, however, Purea was highly *tapu* (sacred) and exempt from this prohibition.[44] She looked around the ship curiously, visiting the galley where a pig and two chickens were roasting on a spit and carefully inspecting the cook's two bright coppers. When Purea was shown geese and turkeys she was not very interested, but she examined the ship's rigging with rapt attention. On this occasion, Robertson vividly described the 'Queen'. About forty-five years old, she was

> [a] strong well made Woman about five foot ten Inches high, and very plainly drest without eather Shoes Stockings or head dress, and no kind of Jewels or trinkets about her, but the Serjent says She hade very large Pearls in Each Ear, when he first saw her. Her Cloaths was Different from the Rest, but wore after the same manner. Her under garments was white, which I shall call her Skirt, her petecoat was White and Yellow, and her Gown was Red.[45] She appeared very cheerful and merry all the time she was Onboard.[46]

At sunset that evening Wallis ordered the barge to take him ashore, inviting the 'Queen' and her two head men to accompany him. When they landed, hundreds of people were waiting on the beach, gathering around Purea and listening raptly as she made a long speech, talking about the ship and introducing Wallis and his officers as its leaders. That day the *Dolphin* was lavishly provisioned, obtaining forty-eight pigs, four dozen chickens and huge quantities of fruit from the local people. There had been a good harvest that year, but the Season of Scarcity was now under way and the local food supplies were being depleted.

The next day Wallis was so ill that once again he was confined to his cabin. In his absence, the carpenter came to Robertson, reporting in alarm that every cleat in the ship had been drawn and his supplies of nails had been plundered. When the boatswain made his report, he added that most of the hammock nails had also been drawn, and about two-thirds of the men were sleeping on deck because they had no nails to sling their hammocks. So many of the spike nails (long nails four inches or longer that held the planks to the ship's frame) had been prised from the hull to barter for sex that the timbers were no longer secure, putting the ship at risk; and to make matters worse, the gunner reported that the trade for fresh food was being ruined. Robertson immediately stopped the 'liberty men' from going ashore, saying that until he knew who had stolen the nails, no one could leave the ship unless they were on duty. When these offences were reported to the captain, Wallis cancelled all shore leave until the offenders had been identified and punished. That night in the galley, while the men were preparing their food, there was a great deal of angry talk, the sailors accusing each other. Standing nearby in the dark, Robertson realised that in fact almost all of the crew had been involved in the thefts. Some of the sailors said they would rather take a flogging than be confined to the ship, and they decided to conduct a trial. A jury was appointed and deliberated before convicting six of the sailors for giving large spike nails for sex instead of the hammock nails, pricing their shipmates off the market. Two of these men cleared themselves by arguing that they had got double value for the spike nails, but later that night there was a scuffle below decks and more angry yelling.

The following morning no shore leave was granted. When Robertson reminded the crew that no one could go ashore until the guilty parties had been identified, three of the sailors named a scapegoat, Francis Pinkney, accusing him of drawing the belaying cleat from the main sheet, essential for controlling the sail. Pinkney, a twenty-five-year-old Welsh seaman who had already been flogged for theft, was an inveterate sufferer from venereal diseases; and as Robertson remarked unsympathetically, 'a proper object to make an Example off'.[47] When his sea chest was searched, a collection of fish-hooks and large shells was discovered which could only have been obtained in exchange for iron. Wallis was informed of the theft, and ordered Pinkney to run the 'gauntlet' three times. His shipmates stood around the deck, each holding knotted rope or 'nettles', and when Robertson asked Pinkney whether any other men were involved in the thefts he said 'No!', so the men struck him very lightly on his first circuit. On the second round, however, Pinkney began to name some of his shipmates and got a much harder drubbing; so Robertson excused him from his third time around the gauntlet.

Although the *Dolphin*'s sailors had put their own survival at risk by bartering nails for sex, the Tahitians were delighted by these new treasures. According to later oral accounts, some of the nails were made into fish-hooks while others were offered to the gods at their *marae*, or planted in their gardens to see whether they would grow.[48]

On 22 July when Purea visited the *Dolphin* again, bringing more pigs and chickens, Wallis, who was feeling a little better, invited her to share his breakfast in the Great Cabin. On this occasion she was accompanied by her 'principal companion', the high priest Tupaia. When bread and butter was served he stood and made a long speech, looking all around the cabin, then went to the quarter-galley to look at the sun, speaking earnestly. When the sailors tried to show Tupaia how to spread butter on his bread with a knife he misunderstood them, picking up a little of the butter with his fingers and throwing it down as an offering to the ancestors. Annoyed, Clarke snatched the butter away and ordered a clean plate, which upset the priest and made the 'Queen' look very grave. Neither of them would eat anything, so Wallis tried to restore their good humour by giving Purea more presents. After breakfast they took a tour of the ship, visiting the cabins and giving Purea anything she fancied – a looking glass, a ruffled shirt and a wine glass. Back in the captain's cabin, she asked to conclude a formal alliance with Wallis by getting him to write on a piece of paper, but his hand was so shaky from his illness that he had to excuse himself.

Purea was fascinated by all the things she saw, and by these strange visitors. Curious to know whether or not Robertson was tattooed, she asked to look at his body. When he stripped, she seemed astonished at the colour of his skin and the hair on his chest, feeling his thighs and arms and testing the muscles, and when he flexed his leg and arm, she cried out in surprise, getting Tupaia to feel the muscles as well. When she tried to lift Robertson up, he prevented her and then lifted her in the air with one arm. As the master remarked complacently:

> This seemd to pleas her greatly and She Eyed me all round and began to be very merry and cheerful, and, if I am not mistaken by her Majesty's behaviour afterwards, this is the way the Ladys here try the men, before they Admit them to be their Lovers.[49]

When Purea went ashore again, Captain Wallis, Robertson and several of the officers accompanied her. Crowds of people were waiting, and as they landed she took Wallis and the officers by the hand, introducing them to the leading people. She invited them to sit down, and taking off their hats, tied bunches of feathers onto them. Purea also put strings of knotted hair around their necks, which she indicated were made from her own hair; presented them with fine mats; and placed a very large pregnant sow in the boat with a quantity of fruit.

With this ritual, Purea was taking Wallis and his officers as ceremonial friends or *taio*. In Tahiti, bunches of red feathers were used to summon the gods (because Ta'aroa, the god who created the cosmos, was covered with red and yellow feathers; and red- and yellow-feathered birds were his messengers);[50] while pregnant sows were associated with 'Oro. After the god 'Oro cast off his first wife, his two sisters had searched the islands for a woman beautiful enough for him to marry. At last they found Vairaumati, an incomparably lovely high-born young woman from Borabora whose face was fair as the moon, who lived near Vai'otaha *marae*, and persuaded her to mate with their brother. 'Oro came down on a rainbow, they made love, and that night he returned into the sky on the rainbow. After they had slept together in this way during three days and nights, 'Oro's brothers 'Oro-tetefa and Uru-tetefa (the other sons of Hina, the moon goddess) came down the rainbow to visit him. When they discovered that 'Oro had no gifts to offer his new wife's family, his brothers transformed themselves into a bunch of red feathers and a pregnant sow. That night the sow had a litter: one piglet for the gods, one for the red girdle of the *'arioi*, and others for the guests, for the household and feasting; and 'Oro was so pleased with his brothers' gesture that he appointed them the gods of the *'arioi*.[51] In Tahiti, each pig had its own name and *varua* or spirit, and the *'arioi* pig was a sacred animal, decorated with a red bark-cloth girdle.[52] Fine mats were also prestigious gifts, presented at marriages and when ceremonial friends were adopted; while the hair of chiefs was imbued with the power of their ancestors. Braided hair embodied genealogies, and the bonds that linked people together. With these gifts, Purea was tying Wallis and the British into her lineage.

After receiving these gifts, however, Wallis told Purea that he would soon be leaving the island. She was devastated; because she must have been hoping that her new friends would help her and her allies to install Teri'irere as paramount chief of the island. She urged Wallis to stay for twenty more days, and when he replied that he could only stay for seven more days, she sat down on the beach and cried bitterly. Wallis was still very weak, and when he returned to the ship Purea invited Robertson and the midshipman to accompany her to the *'arioi* house instead. They set out arm in arm and upon their arrival Purea made a long speech, and then sat her guests on a fine mat before making another speech to the assembled gathering. While the feast was being prepared Robertson went to look around outside, where a young man asked if he could look at his broadsword. Purea gestured that he should give it to him, and as soon as the master handed it over, the young man began to caper about, swinging the sword in the air. When Robertson took the sword away from him in annoyance, slashing at a nearby plantain tree and cutting it right through, prompting the young man to run away in terror, Purea and her companions laughed heartily.

Purea now called for a roll of bark cloth and, cutting up some of the cloth, made a poncho or *tiputa* for Robertson, putting it over his head. Although an old lady tried to persuade the master to stay for dinner, pointing at two beautiful young women and offering them to him and

Purea farewells Captain Wallis

the midshipman, they were under strict orders to return to the ship, and eventually Purea accompanied them back to the watering place. On their way, however, they stopped at a house where two very beautiful young girls were sitting, and when Robertson began to flirt, holding up his arm to theirs and comparing the colour of their skins, Purea spoke sharply to one of these girls, who looked startled. Trying to comfort her, the master held her in his arms, but Purea pulled him away and looked fiercely at the young woman, who seemed terrified. Purea now led Robertson back to the boats, and waited there until he was rowed away to the *Dolphin*.

The following day Wallis sent Purea a lavish gift of two turkeys, two geese, three guinea hens, a pregnant cat, some china, glass, bottles, two iron pots, knives, scissors and spoons, shirts, needles and thread, cloth, ribbons, peas and sixteen different sorts of garden seeds, sealing their alliance. At the same time the gunner gave his friend Fa'a a present of an iron pot, some hatchets and billhooks and some cloth, and took two marines ashore with shovels to plant a garden for Purea, leaving the shovels with her. According to Wallis, Fa'a's son, who had visited the ship on a number of occasions, seemed eager to sail with them when they left the island. That evening when Robertson, who had been looking through the *Nautical Almanac*, realised that there would be an eclipse of the sun in two days' time, he asked the captain whether an observation should be attempted. Wallis gave his approval, and the master fitted a dark glass from a sextant to the ship's large telescope for the purpose.

In preparation for his departure, on 25 July Captain Wallis despatched John Gore, the master's mate, with an armed party ashore to explore the Tuauru Valley and bring back a report on the soil, vegetation and minerals inland. After Wallis had gone ashore, Robertson, John Harrison the purser (an excellent astronomer and mathematician) and George Pinnock, one of the midshipmen, lowered the barge, intending to observe the eclipse of the sun. Taking advantage of the captain's absence, however, Lieutenant Clarke ordered Robertson to take the jolly-boat instead, delaying their departure. By the time they arrived at the northern point they were already a little late, so Pinnock took an altitude of the sun to fix the time while Harrison looked at the sun through his spyglass. The eclipse had begun, but it was a fine, clear day and they had an excellent view of the event. When it was almost over Wallis arrived and looked through the telescope, timing the end of the eclipse with some precision. Shortly afterwards when Purea approached with one of her chiefs (probably Tupaia), Robertson showed them the sun through the dark glass. They seemed greatly afraid, because in Tahiti an eclipse was a portent of war, showing the anger of the gods who were 'eating' the heavenly body.[53] When the master pointed the telescope at some people about five miles away and they found that they could clearly see their friends, Purea and her companion were astounded. Remembering that some of his men were exploring the river valley, Wallis invited Purea back to the ship for dinner, supposing that if anything happened on shore, he could detain the chiefs as hostages until his men had safely returned. As was her custom, Purea would not eat or drink on board, but her companions ate heartily and greatly enjoyed their meals.

Back at the ship that evening Gore reported that his party of four midshipmen, the sergeant and twelve marines and twenty-four armed seamen had followed the Tuauru River some miles inland, guided by the old man Fa'a. The valley was densely inhabited, with irrigation channels cut into the hillsides to water the gardens and fruit trees. The soil was rich and black and the gardens nicely fenced, with breadfruit and Tahitian apple trees planted in neat rows along the hillsides. They found no metal around the river or in the creeks, but discovered a number of springs. When they climbed into the hills, their companions helped them up the steeper slopes. Higher up they had a wonderful view of the ship and could see many villages on the hillsides and in adjacent valleys, indicating a dense population. Gore planted peach, plum and cherry stones with garden seeds in likely places, along with cuttings from lime, lemon and orange trees. In the afternoon their companions cooked them a meal of pork and chicken with breadfruit, and they parted in great friendship. As soon as his men were safely back on the beach, Captain Wallis sent Purea and her companions ashore in the boats. She was still trying to persuade him to stay longer, and was desolate to find that he was determined to leave the island.

The next morning Purea made a brief visit to the ship, bringing out a gift of pigs and chickens. That day the sailors traded for 'curiosities' (artefacts made by the local people), bartering goods for pearls, fish-hooks and lines, stone tools and bows and arrows that they hoped to sell for a profit back in England. During their stay at Tahiti, Wallis acquired a collection of conch shells, flutes, fishing nets, tattooing instruments, breadfruit pounders, breastplates and bark cloth, some of which (especially the breastplates and bark cloth) were given to him as ceremonial gifts; and upon his return he presented these to the Admiralty, along with a small canoe from Nukutaveke that is now held in the British Museum.[54] Also upon his arrival back in London, Wallis handed over the objects that Purea had given him to Queen Charlotte– the tufts of red feathers used to communicate with the ancestor gods, the fine mats, and the plaited string of Purea's hair that bound Wallis into her lineage, along with a hundred pearls, pearl fish-hooks and other treasures – a gift to the Queen of England from Purea, the Queen of Tahiti.[55]

By this time many chiefs had arrived at Matavai Bay, including some whom the British had not seen before; and these strangers watched intently as the sailors filled the remaining water barrels, collected wood, and got the ship ready for her voyage. Some of these people seemed hostile and ready to challenge the British, and the marines pointed muskets at them to keep them at a distance. After dinner Purea returned to the ship with Fa'a, begging Wallis to stay ten days longer. When he replied that the *Dolphin* must sail the next morning, she wept bitterly and asked when he would return; and Wallis made signs to demonstrate that he would return in fifty days' time, which seemed to console her. At nightfall Purea did not want to leave the ship, lying down on the arms' chest, weeping for a long time and asking if she could sleep on board, but at last she returned ashore with Fa'a.

At daylight on 27 July 1767 the *Dolphin* was unmoored, and the barge and cutter went ashore to fill the last water casks. The beach was so crowded that they almost decided not to land, but Purea appeared and ordered the people back to the other side of the river, allowing the sailors to come ashore. Fa'a and his son were nowhere to be seen, and in the event, the young man did not sail with the strangers. Although Purea brought gifts of pigs and fruit and asked to be taken out to the ship, the officer had orders to allow no one in the boats and he refused. A double canoe was launched, taking her out to the *Dolphin*, accompanied by about sixteen other canoes which carried 'Many familys of Jolly fatt well made people, and mutch fairer nor any that we ever saw before'.[56] These were aristocratic families from other districts, and in one of these vessels, which Robertson was told came from the south, they saw a dignified old man with a long, grey beard and a white turban who seemed to be highly respected. This may have been Vehiatua I, the white-haired and bearded old chief of southern Tahiti, and Purea and Amo's inveterate enemy. When his canoe touched Purea's, he ordered his paddlers to pull away and spoke some words which Robertson wrote down on a piece of paper, but it blew overboard.

As Purea climbed on board to weep over her friends, a breeze sprang up, the sails were set and the anchors raised; and Wallis sent her back to her canoe. She embraced her friends affectionately, crying, and boarded her canoe, which was tied to the gunroom port. There she sat weeping while they gave her many gifts, but as Robertson remarked: 'This Great freindly Woman took no manner of notice of what she got from us, but Shaked hands with all that she could come near. She wept and cryd, in my oppinion with as mutch tenderness and Affection as any Wife or Mother could do, at the parting with their Husbands or children.'[57] At 10 a.m. a

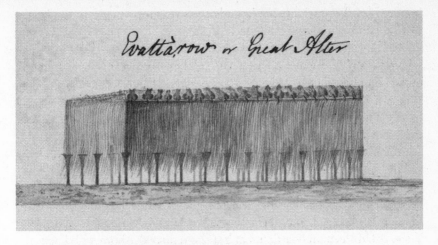

Te Raʻi-puatata, sketched by William Bligh

strong breeze filled the sails, her canoe was untied from the port, and the *Dolphin* sailed away from the island.

Although Purea was devastated by Wallis's departure, she, along with Amo and Tupaia, was determined to carry on with Teriʻirere's installation. As the construction of the great new *marae* of Mahaiatea continued, the builders spoke in hushed tones, cooked on sacred fires, and stayed away from their womenfolk. Chiefs from the other districts arrived with human sacrifices which were buried beneath the cornerstones, and red and yellow feathers to renew the two feather girdles with which Teriʻirere would be invested. In Tahiti only one high chief at a time could wear the *maro ʻura* or red feather girdle, however; and when Teriʻirere was invested with Te Raʻi-puatata, this would be a momentous occasion. For each investiture, a new section was added to the *maro*, made of fine strands of *roʻa* bark backed with banyan cloth into which new red and yellow feathers were inserted and stitched on with a needle of human bone. As the cloth was stretched onto pegs for this purpose, a human sacrifice was offered; a second when the new section was sewn on; and a third when the *maro ʻura* was taken off the pegs. At each step in its making thunder crashed and lightning flashed in the sky, a sign of 'Oro's presence.[58] In the case of Teriʻirere's *maro ʻura*, however, something unprecedented happened. Although Wallis and his men had left the island, Amo, Purea and Tupaia still hoped to draw upon the power of the British to support his installation. In order to achieve this, the upper end of the red pennant from the *Dolphin* was stitched to the *maro ʻura* from Taputapuatea, joining the *mana* of the strangers to the *mana* of 'Oro. Clearly they intended that Teriʻirere would be a new kind of leader, wielding new kinds of sacred power.

Happy Island of Cythera

When the *Dolphin* sailed away from Tahiti, the mood on board was buoyant. The sailors were rested, fit and in high good humour, convinced that they had made an important discovery. Like Byron's crew, they hoped that they would be rewarded with double pay at the end of the voyage. To their puzzlement, however, Wallis did not head further south in search of Terra Australis, although many were sure that they had seen the mountains of the fabled continent in that direction. Instead the ship sailed west. As Robertson grumbled: 'This Orders Griefd me Greatly and several of our Young Gentlemen. We hoped to have our cureosity Gratefied, with a Sight of the Southern Continent.'[1]

Now that Wallis had decided to head for home, he took his ship swiftly across the Pacific. After brief visits to Niuatoputapu in the Tongan archipelago and Tinian in the Ladrones, the *Dolphin* crossed the China Sea to Batavia and back to England via the Cape of Good Hope and St Helena. Having sailed around the world, his men were filled with pride in their splendid voyage; and the ship's barber, Rogers Richardson, composed a ballad that he presented to Captain Wallis on behalf of his shipmates.[2] Wallis cherished this tribute, placing it carefully in his journal along with a short list of Tahitian words, some sketches of ships and island profiles, and an ink sketch showing the construction of Purea's *'arioi* house. As they approached the coastline of England, Wallis reminded his men about the oath of secrecy they had taken, cautioning them not to reveal any details of the lands they had discovered. On 19 May 1768 when the *Dolphin* anchored in the Downs, Captain Wallis hastened to London to make his report to the Admiralty.

Despite their vow of silence, the men flocked to the inns and taverns to celebrate their homecoming; and the news soon leaked out that they had found a marvellous island in the Pacific with high volcanic mountains, waterfalls, a tropical climate and beautiful, amorous women. In the taverns, the *Dolphin*s used to sing a song about Tahiti, or King George's Island as they called it:

> Then we plow'd the South Ocean, such land to discover
> As amongst other nations has made such a pother.
> We found it, my boys, and with joy be it told,
> For beauty such islands you ne'er did behold.
> We've the pleasure ourselves the tidings to bring
> As may welcome us home to our country and King.
>
> For wood, water, fruit, and provision well stor'd
> Such an isle as King George's the world can't afford.
> For to each of these islands great Wallis gave name,
> Which will e'er be recorded in annals of fame.
> We'd the fortune to find them, and homeward to bring
> These tidings as a tribute to country and King.[3]

A poetic version of their adventures had a wider circulation when Richardson's ballad was published in *The Gentleman's Magazine*,[4] and soon afterwards when a Spanish spy procured a journal of Wallis's voyage, including a description of Tahiti, this was despatched to the Spanish ambassador in London.[5] Fearful of incursions into their territories, the Spanish government warned the Viceroy of Peru, Manuel de Amat, that the British were trying to establish an outpost in the South Sea; but in fact their allies the French had already sent two ships into the South Pacific that were also searching for Terra Australis. These vessels were commanded by Louis-Antoine de Bougainville, whose ships Byron had encountered in the Strait of Magellan just two years earlier.

Louis-Antoine de Bougainville was a witty, charming courtier, mathematician and soldier who had recently established a French colony in the Falkland Islands.[6] His family belonged to the *noblesse de robe*, a lower echelon in the French nobility, and he and his brother Jean-Pierre had been tutored in mathematics, astronomy, the sciences, the classics, and the history of European exploration and discovery. After joining the Black Musketeers, a corps of dragoons in the French Army, in 1754 Louis was posted to London as a junior diplomat. During the following year he published a study in calculus and was elected a Fellow of the Royal Society in London, where he heard a great deal about the search for Terra Australis.

In 1756 when war broke out again between France and Britain, Louis de

Louis de Bougainville

Bougainville was appointed as aide-de-camp to the Marquis de Montcalm, the commander of the French forces in Canada. He fought alongside Iroquois warriors who adopted him as their clansman, but their customs in battle made him doubt the praises heaped by *philosophes* such as Jean-Jacques Rousseau upon the lives of 'savages'. In his letters Bougainville often used classical parallels to describe his experiences in Canada, referring to the Pyrrhic dances, Pygmalion's statue, the pythoness on the tripod, the Spartans and the Helots.[7] During this campaign, Samuel Wallis commanded one of the ships in the British force while a thirty-year-old ship's master, James Cook, was busily charting the St Lawrence River for the attack on Quebec, where Bougainville was in charge of a troop of French soldiers. During the final battle Cook was on the *Pembroke*, one of the blockading ships, and Bougainville led his men in desperate fighting, but was eventually forced to surrender.

After giving his parole, Bougainville was released by the British and returned to Paris where he began to look for new challenges. His brother Jean-Pierre, by now a noted classical scholar, had written books on ancient voyages of discovery, and with his friends among the scientists and *philosophes*, they discussed scientific exploration and the Southern Continent.

In his famous *Discourse* on human inequality, Jean-Jacques Rousseau had bemoaned the inaccuracy of many travel accounts, exclaiming:

> I am amazed that in an Age, in which Men so much affect useful and polite Learning, there does not start up two Men perfectly united, and rich, one in Money, the other in Genius, both Lovers of Glory, and studious of Immortality, one of whom should be willing to sacrifice twenty thousand Crowns of his Fortune, and the other ten Years of his Life to make such a serious Voyage round the world, as would recommend their Names to the present and future Generations; not to confine themselves to Plants and Stones, but for once study Men and Manners.[8]

Charles de Brosses, whom they also knew, had been even more specific, suggesting in his famous work on Terra Australis that the first explorers of this great continent should be brave and humane, and accompanied by cartographers, astronomers, botanists, painters, and others who might win the admiration of savages – doctors, surgeons, even musicians.[9] Jean-Pierre, a sickly, frail man, was eager to win immortality for his brother, and soon they were planning a French voyage of discovery to the Pacific. During his posting in London, Louis-Antoine had become aware of the scale of British geopolitical ambitions, and as a patriot he was eager to ensure that France would be the first European country to discover Terra Australis and its people. Bougainville saw the Falkland Islands as a perfect base for such an expedition, and in 1763 he submitted a plan for the colonisation of the Falklands and a voyage of discovery across the Pacific to his patron the Duc de Choiseul, the most powerful politician in France. The Seven Years' War had almost bankrupted the French Government, however, and Spain also had claims to the Falklands; and Choiseul hesitated to support this proposal.

It was not until Bougainville set up a private company to finance the colony, asking the King of France to pay only for the ships, crews, equipment and munitions, and promising to keep his plans strictly secret until they had sailed, that Choiseul and the King decided that a French colony should be established in the Falklands. Bougainville's two ships sailed in September 1763; and during the voyage he learned a great deal about ship-handling and navigation. A small French colony was established on East Falkland, and after a quick voyage to France, Bougainville brought back more colonists to reinforce the settlement. In February 1765 during an expedition to the Strait of Magellan he met John Byron's ships, en route to the Pacific.

During his next visit to France, Bougainville was told that the Spanish had found out about the Falklands venture and were deeply affronted. Reluctant to risk further hostilities with Spain, the French government decided to surrender the new colony, and Bougainville was despatched to Madrid to negotiate the terms of a handover. In May 1766 he had an audience with Carlos III during which they reached an amicable settlement, including a promise that Spain would refund Bougainville's costs in setting up the French outpost on the Falklands. By now French spies had procured a copy of a log of Byron's voyage and a map that showed the *Dolphin*'s track around the world,[10] warning their government that yet another British expedition to the South Sea led by Samuel Wallis was being planned with Byron's assistance.

Bougainville's diplomatic efforts in Madrid earned him grateful recognition from the French government, and when he returned he found that they were at last willing to sponsor his voyage of Pacific exploration. Two ships had been chosen: a brand-new frigate the *Boudeuse*, 125 feet long and with a crew of 220; and the storeship the *Étoile* from his Falklands voyages with its crew of 120. Choiseul agreed that many of the officers and men from Bougainville's former voyages could be appointed to this expedition, which, like Wallis's, was planned and conducted in the utmost secrecy. Choiseul proposed that after sailing to the Falklands to hand over his colony to the Spanish, Bougainville should take his two ships westward across the southern Pacific to look for the Unknown Southern Continent. Choiseul also decided that if Terra Australis was discovered by France, it should be properly explored and documented, and a contingent of scientists was selected by the Académie des Sciences for the voyage.[11]

As commander of the expedition, Bougainville was supported by Nicholas Duclos-Guyot, the captain of the *Boudeuse* (or 'Tutera', as the Tahitians called him), an experienced officer who had sailed with Bougainville on a number of occasions. Because he was a commoner, Duclos-Guyot was given only a temporary commission, although Bougainville regarded him as his mentor at sea, writing to his naval superiors: 'This officer is assuredly one of the best in Europe and few could claim such extensive periods of service both in peace and in war-time.'[12] The junior officers on the frigate were all high-born young men who had fought in the Seven Years' War, mostly in Canada. Charles-Félix-Pierre Fesche, who wrote a fascinating journal of the voyage, joined as a volunteer. He had sailed with Bougainville on his two previous journeys to the Falklands, and claimed to be a distant relative of the Bonaparte family.

Among the civilians on board the *Boudeuse*, the clerk Louis-Antoine Starot de Saint-Germain, a sharp-tongued colonial administrator who had been appointed to the expedition against his will, was quick to complain about shipboard conditions. The *Boudeuse* also carried an aristocratic passenger, the Prince of Nassau or Charles-Nicolas-Othon d'Orange et de Nassau-Siegen, a young army officer who, like Bougainville, had found himself bored and aimless in Paris at the end of the Seven Years' War. After fighting duels and conducting several notorious affairs, he had met Bougainville at a dinner and decided to join the expedition. The Prince of Nassau was a witty, good-humoured man who savoured the delights of Tahiti with a connoisseur's appreciation. Most of the crew of the *Boudeuse* were French, although there were also foreigners and black slaves on board the vessel.

The *Étoile*, the storeship, was small but sturdy. Her commander, François Chesnard de la Giraudais, was the most experienced officer on the expedition. Like many of the crew, he served in the Navy during the Seven Years' War, and after the war sailed with Bougainville on his first two voyages to the Falklands. His second-in-command, Jean-Louis Caro, was an officer from the French East India Company who wrote a practical, down-to-earth journal of the voyage. The storeship's surgeon, François Vivez, had also gone to sea as a very small boy. He was principled but judgemental, devoted to his duties, and wrote a detailed and vivid account of their adventures.

The party of scientists was accommodated on the *Étoile*, rather than on board the frigate with Bougainville. None of them was an aristocrat, which probably explains this arrangement. They included Charles Routier de Romainville, an engineer-cartographer, and Pierre-Antoine Véron, the expedition's astronomer, a brilliant young man from a poor family. His patron Lalande, the Astronomer Royal, who had been in charge of France's efforts for observing the 1769 Transit of Venus, had drafted a map of the world that summarised current geographical knowledge, including a speculative coastline of Terra Australis. Gentle, shy and devoted to his work, Véron made the astronomical observations that fixed the ships' positions and located the places they visited during the voyage.

Perhaps the best known of the *Étoile*'s scientific party, however, was Philibert Commerson, the naturalist and an ardent admirer of Rousseau's theories about the innocence of savages. Commerson had studied medicine, zoology and botany; and when Bougainville met him to discuss the expedition, he seemed eager but nervous, insisting that his valet should accompany him on the voyage. Perhaps because he suffered from persistent ill health, Commerson was often bad-tempered, and he had a difficult time on the *Étoile*, describing the ship as 'that hellish den where hatred, insubordination, bad faith, brigandage, cruelty and all kinds of disorders reign'.[13] The real reason for his unpopularity, however, was that his valet,

Philibert Commerson

Jean Baret, was in fact a woman in disguise and his lover; and when this was discovered, his shipmates resented the deception. Jean Baret had worked for Commerson after his wife died, looking after his infant son; and after they became lovers she accompanied him on board the *Étoile*, dressed as a man, staying close to him, helping to collect and sort his specimens, and managing to hide her sex from their shipmates for most of the voyage.[14]

The *Boudeuse* sailed from the Loire on 15 November 1766, arriving at Montevideo two months later, where Bougainville finalised the arrangements for handing over the French colony in the Falklands to the Spanish. When the *Boudeuse* sailed to the Falklands the ship was accompanied by two Spanish frigates, and the handover was peacefully accomplished. In the meantime, the *Étoile* had sailed directly for South America, arriving in Montevideo after a two-month crossing. The weather had been rough, causing considerable damage to the storeship; and some of the scientists, who had not previously been to sea, quickly repented of their decision to join the voyage. As Commerson lamented:

> I am tempted to compare a ship to a mousetrap: everyone who walks onto the gangway sees his little strip of bacon, but once the sails are unfurled, the trap is sprung, the mouse is caught. Nothing can be done and one can only gnaw at the bars.[15]

The *Étoile* carried on to Rio, anchoring there on 13 June; and when the *Boudeuse* arrived at Rio a week later Bougainville, who had been waiting for the storeship in the Falklands and feared that she had been wrecked, was delighted to see her safely at anchor. The Portuguese authorities were suspicious and unhelpful, however, so the ships returned to Montevideo for provisioning and repairs, where the Spanish governor was friendly and hospitable. The *Étoile* suffered further damage in a collision with another ship in Montevideo Harbour, and it was not until 14 November 1767 that they set sail for the Strait of Magellan. The weather in the Strait was foul, and as snow piled on the decks Bougainville remarked: 'I do believe this is the worst climate in the world.'[16] It took them more than two months to navigate through this frozen labyrinth of rocks, islands and winding channels, although Wallis's expedition had taken a month longer.

After two long months of sailing across a wide, empty ocean, on 22 March 1768 they finally sighted land – Akiaki, a small atoll in the eastern Tuamotu, where about thirty warriors armed with spears threatened them from the beaches. Amazed to find people so far from South America, Bougainville exclaimed: 'Who will tell me how they have been transported to this place and what links them to other human beings? Have Deucalion's . . . stones been flung as far as this isolated lump of earth?'[17] Here he was referring to Prometheus's son Deucalion who, during his flight from a great flood to the summit of Mount Parnassus, hurled stones that turned into men when they hit the ground. The surf was running so high on the reef around Akiaki that a landing was impossible, so they carried on past Vahitahi (another new discovery) and Hao, where they saw five or six canoes with lateen sails and some people. Bougainville mused: 'What is this island? Did Quiros see it? It is very much like a great island . . . drowned in its centre that he describes, but the latitudes do not tally.' In fact, when the Spanish explorer had visited Hao in 1606, the people embraced the strangers and welcomed them to their island.

Sailing through the Tuamotu Islands was nerve-wracking, because the coral atolls and reefs were almost invisible, especially at night, and Bougainville dubbed this the 'Dangerous Archipelago'. During this passage the ships were hit by rough weather and the sailors began to suffer from scurvy. At last, in the morning of 2 April, two high islands appeared on the horizon, Me'eti'a and Tahiti, both recently 'discovered' by Wallis. By now shipboard conditions were dreadful, as Vivez, the surgeon on board the *Étoile*, recounted:

Twenty clear cases of scurvy and the rest of the crew weakened and spiritless, having lived for four months on nothing but salt meat, a bottle of stinking and

rotting water, brandy rationed, one meal only with wine, the biscuit beginning
to go bad, the refreshments for the sick very scarce and our food at the officers'
mess not much more appealing.[18]

The men were longing for fresh food, and these islands with their
high, green mountains and luxuriant coastlines looked entrancing. They
decided to head for the larger island but contrary winds forced them to
tack away, and the next evening as the ships approached the eastern coast
of Tahiti, they were overjoyed to see a line of small fires glowing along
the beach, suggesting a large population.[19] On 4 April in the morning as
the *Boudeuse* and the *Étoile* sailed in towards the Taravao isthmus with
favourable winds, two small outrigger canoes came out to meet them, one
crewed by two men and the other with a man and two boys on board, followed by more than a hundred canoes bringing out unarmed men (many
of them with long beards) and young boys, until by 4 p.m. 'the sea was
covered with canoes'.[20]

The leading canoe was manned by twelve male paddlers who wore
narrow coconut-fibre belts and genital pouches made of bark cloth,[21] led
by a man with bristling, spiky hair who presented a sucking pig and a
plantain branch to the strangers. No women were present during this first
encounter, and none of the islanders carried arms. In 'arioi rituals at sea,
the paddlers stripped almost naked, and the *Boudeuse* and the *Étoile* were
being given a ceremonial welcome. In early April the breadfruit were plentiful, the Season of Plenty was at its height, and the 'arioi had assembled,
entertaining the people with dancing, music and skits, and competing in
wrestling, boxing and archery. Bougainville presented this man with a cap
and some handkerchiefs, and the crews of the canoes began to barter with
the sailors, placing coconuts, *vi* or Tahitian apples, bunches of bananas
and other fruit in baskets that were lowered down the sides of the ships
and in return receiving woollen caps, handkerchiefs, several knives and
other small items.

That afternoon a double canoe with ten paddlers approached the
Boudeuse, bringing out a lovely light-skinned, bare-breasted girl about
sixteen years old who wore a white bark-cloth loincloth and a turban, the
first female they had seen; accompanied by a man wearing three or four
ponchos of white bark cloth who held up a plantain branch in greeting. As
the surgeon Vivez noted, the girl wore a loincloth 'around her waist and
the rest quite naked and white, one could say better than in Europe or at
least equal for that age. At this charming sight, we were soon wishing for
an early stop, our imagination worked a great deal from that time to know
whether this beauty belonged to the country. How could such charming

people be so far from Europe and how is it that in this island they are so white whereas all we had seen in the other islands since the time of our departure were different?'[22] This young woman had stripped her clothes down to the waist, a sign that she was in the presence of ra'a or ancestral power. The frigate was sailing too fast for their canoe, however, so they headed for the *Étoile* instead, followed by about twenty other canoes. The man in the double canoe, who seemed to have some authority over the others, stood on the prows of the canoe, and when a sailor on board the *Étoile* threw him a mooring rope he grabbed it and, displaying 'incredible strength', hauled his canoe to the ship and climbed up the rigging chains. On board the ship he offered his plantain branch to the tallest of the ship's officers, the second lieutenant La Fontaine, who introduced him to the captain. Presenting his branch to La Giraudais he said, '*Taio*' or 'Friend' and with gestures invited him and his companions to come ashore where they would be given food and drink.

This was Ahutoru, a ceremonial friend of Reti, the chief of Hitia'a on the east coast of Tahiti-nui, and the first Tahitian to sail on a European vessel. When Ahutoru seemed to ask if the strangers came from the sun, the French answered in the affirmative. Because of La Fontaine's height, Ahutoru thought that the second lieutenant must be an *ari'i* or high chief (because, in Tahiti, *ari'i* were often exceptionally tall) and presented him with his bark-cloth garments. In return the officer gave him a shirt, a pair of trousers, a vest and a hat, which Ahutoru put on with great pleasure, for headdresses were a mark of status in the Society Islands. When the French gave him a mirror he was not surprised to see himself, but seemed startled by the reflection of someone standing behind him.

Ahutoru found the *Étoile* fascinating, staring around in amazement and examining everything. When he asked whether the strangers had women with them, he seemed astonished when they replied that they had none. Ahutoru decided to spend the night on the ship, sending the other canoes away; and when prayers were held he knelt like the others. When the sailors shouted, 'God save the King!' he joined in heartily; and at mess that evening he sat on the floor with the sailors, eating soup from their mess tins, sniffing everything before he ate it. He seemed to know what muskets were for, because when a sailor pointed one at him he shouted, 'Poux poux!' (*Pu, pu!*) and shuddered, looking pale and frightened. At supper with the officers, Ahutoru drank water but refused wine and stew, liking the taste of neither. He asked for different kinds of food, tasting each until he found that dried jam was his favourite. After the meal, as the ships tacked off the southern coast, the line of small lights flared up again along the shore, looking 'like oil burning in some kind of vase' (perhaps

candlenuts lit in coconut shells);[23] and the officers fired off rockets in
response, Ahutoru watched in alarm. In Tahiti comets were thought to
be the fiery spirits of the gods,[24] warning of momentous events; and these
rockets must have seemed an ominous signal. That night he slept below on
a pile of sails, going up frequently to look at the stars as the *Étoile* tacked
off the coast, so he could tell where the ship was heading.

On 5 April as the ships headed up the east coast of Tahiti, the island
looked enchanting, with its green meadows, groves of trees, deep valleys,
woods and coastal plains backed by high mountains. When they sighted
a village set beside a waterfall that tumbled down from the mountains,
shaded by groves of fruit trees, Bougainville longed to anchor at this
idyllic spot, but to his dismay, the lagoon had too many coral outcrops.
Canoes flocked out to the ships, some with open-work carving on their
sterns, where their crews bartered fruit, a live parakeet, a cock, a pigeon,
two flutes, fish-hooks, stone chisels, bark cloth and shells for nails and
earrings. One of these canoes brought out two white-skinned young girls
about thirteen or fourteen years old, and the men on board kept asking
whether the strangers had brought women with them. As Caro noted:
'Our boarder [Ahutoru] seems to desire one greatly, he looks at everyone
to see if he could not find a woman.'[25] During this encounter, however,
none of the journal writers comments upon the islanders' reactions to the
black slaves on board, although this was the first time that black people
had visited the island.

The following day the boats found a gap in the reef where four coral
islets lay in the blue lagoon, opposite a village sited on a plain beside a river
that flowed down from the mountains. This was Hitia'a, the main centre
for the worship of 'Oro on the east coast of Tahiti-nui. During gatherings
at its great *'arioi* house, the chief *'arioi* of Hitia'a used to chant:

> From Vai-o-Va'u to 'Ea'ea, Hitia'a is the land
> The mountains above are Te Vaitohi, Mauru and Tahoutira,
> The assembly ground is Te 'Iri'iri
> The seaward point is Pape-he'e
> The rivers are Manini-haorea and Maha-te-ao
> The *marae* are Hitia'a and Taputapuatea . . .
> Te Ri'itua is the chief
> The *'arioi* house is Pereue,
> The *'arioi* warrior is Maro-'ura,
> The school is Maha-te-ao
> Hitia'a is a land of riddles.[26]

As the boats rowed in through a gap in the reef, canoes flocked around the ships, their crews crying out '*Taio!*' or 'Friend!' Some of these canoes carried beautiful young women; and as they came alongside, the men and old women stripped them naked, offering them to the French sailors with graphic gestures, although the girls themselves seemed uneasy and frightened. As Bougainville reflected, this might have been 'because nature has every where embellished their sex with a natural timidity; or because even in those countries, where the ease of the golden age is still in use, women seem least to desire what they most wish for.'[27] More likely, however, these girls were repelled by the strangers, particularly the sailors in the advanced stages of scurvy with their twisted limbs and blackened ulcers, and the black slaves on the ships whose appearance, as Commerson later remarked, the Tahitians found unattractive.[28]

Soon another beautiful, white-skinned young woman, wearing bark cloth and accompanied by an old man and several other women, climbed on board the *Boudeuse*. When she reached the quarterdeck she gracefully dropped her bark-cloth garments and stood there naked, the image of a Polynesian Venus. According to Fesche, 'several Frenchmen, who were gourmets, and to whom an enforced fast of several months had given a ravenous appetite, look, admire, touch. Soon the veil that hid the charms which a regrettable modesty no doubt requires to be hidden, this veil I say, is soon lifted, more promptly by the Indian divinity than by them, she was following the customs of her country.'[29] Any further liberties would have been a serious breach of discipline, however; and although the old man who accompanied her urged the officers to make love to this girl they demurred, and she left the vessel looking disconcerted and offended.[30]

This young woman must have been an '*arioi* bringing a ritual offering of bark cloth, a customary way of greeting the gods or their avatars in the Ao, the world of light. During Wallis's visit, leading '*arioi* (particularly Purea and Amo) had forged close relationships with the British sailors, who exhibited strange, destructive powers; and many people thought that the *Dolphin* was a great canoe belonging to 'Oro. After hearing about the shootings during that visit, the Hitia'a people had no wish to challenge this new group of powerful strangers. Rather, they treated them with awe, trying to propitiate them with gifts and recruit them as allies. At the same time, they were intensely curious, and when the cook from the *Boudeuse*, inflamed by the girl's performance, managed to sneak onto one of the visiting canoes, its crew took the hapless Frenchman ashore where a crowd of people surrounded him, stripping him naked and examining every inch of his body. After satisfying their curiosity they gave him back his clothes and presented him with the girl, demanding that he have sex with her, but

he was too terrified to comply. As Bougainville reported: 'All their persuasive arguments had no effect; they were obliged to bring the poor cook on
board, who told me, that I might reprimand him as much as I pleased, but
that I could never frighten him so much, as he had just now been frightened on shore.'[31]

The ships anchored off Hitia'a at two o'clock that afternoon, where
the Prince of Nassau penned a rhapsodic description of the island and its
people:

> The country is as beautiful as it could be, forests, fertile vales, streams and gar-
> dens make up a charming setting in which the inhabitants have located their
> houses . . . These people belong to a superb race, the men are usually 5 feet six
> inches to six feet tall. We even saw one who was 6 feet 4 inches. They all are
> handsome and well built, they have very long hair which they rub with coconut
> oil and have long beards. The women, also of a good height, have fine large
> eyes, pretty teeth, European traits, a soft skin. Nature was pleased to grant them
> perfect bodies.[32]

As Tcherkézoff has remarked, Europeans had long associated light skins
with 'noble' and dark skins with 'ignoble' savages, in the Pacific as elsewhere; and the French were predisposed to find these people attractive.[33]
By the same token, in the Society Islands chiefly people and 'arioi wore
sunshades, oiled their bodies with mono'i (scented oil) and tried to stay out
of the sun, making their skin white and their bodies sleek and appealing;
and light skins were considered a mark of high status and beauty.[34] When
Bougainville and his officers went ashore, Ahutoru led the way, dressed
in European costume. He was welcomed by about three hundred people
who carried him on their shoulders and then sat down around him, listening raptly to his tales about what he had seen on board this strange vessel.
An inquisitive crowd, none of them armed, surrounded the Frenchmen,
touching them and pushing aside their clothes to examine their bodies.
The local chief, Reti (also known by his title, Teri'i-tua), a tall, intelligent man about forty-five years old with a deep scar on his forehead,
greeted the strangers courteously, leading them to a long house where
five or six women welcomed them, putting their hands on their breasts
and exclaiming 'Taio!' ('Bond friend!'). Reti's father, a wrinkled, white-
bearded man, was present, but this old chief seemed cautious and uneasy.
As Bougainville remarked: 'His thoughtful and suspicious air seemed to
shew that he feared the arrival of a new race of men would trouble those
happy days which he had spent in peace'[35] – an uncanny echo of Vaita's
prophecy. This house (probably Pereue, the 'arioi house at Hitia'a) was

eighty feet long and twenty feet wide. Inside, a wickerwork cylinder about three feet long and covered with black feathers hung from the rafters (a *to'o* or image to contain an ancestor god), and a male and a female *ti'i* (ancestor figures, guardians of fertility) stood on tall pedestals carved with open-work, one upright and the other leaning against the wall.

After this welcome, Reti seated his guests outside on fine mats, where his servants served them with fruit, dried fish and water. Bougainville was enchanted by this repast, later remarking that 'we had a golden age meal with people who are still living in that happy time'.[36] Following the meal, Reti dressed his guests in bark cloth and presented Bougainville and a junior officer, the Chevalier d'Oraison, with *taumi*, chiefly breastplates in the shape of a crescent, decorated with shark's teeth and black feathers, putting these around their necks. In order to impress their hosts, one of the officers fired his pistol at a bird on a tree, terrifying them. Shortly afterwards when the Prince of Nassau, realising that one of his pocket pistols was missing, complained to Reti, the chief flew into a rage, striking some of the men in the house and stripping several others. When he could not find the pistol he presented the Prince with a fine mat as an apology.

Bougainville and his companions now walked back to the boats where two *'arioi* musicians invited them to sit on a grassy bank and entertained them, one singing a gentle, plaintive song while the other played on a three-tone nose flute – as Bougainville remarked, 'a charming scene, worthy of Boucher's brush'[37] (a French artist of the period who produced many Arcadian scenes, including images of flute players and studies of Venus, Cupid and the Graces). He invited the chief and three of his companions to dinner on board the frigate, where they were entertained with flute, cello and violin music, and a fireworks display that surprised and frightened them. That night Bougainville noticed that fires had been lit on the islets on the reef at Hitia'a, guiding the canoes in safely through the coral outcrops.

When Reti came out to the ship the next morning, he brought a pig and some chickens along with the stolen pistol; and Bougainville sent all of the scurvy sufferers ashore with a guard of thirty soldiers and some sailors to fill the water casks and set up the shore camp. The Prince of Nassau, the Chevalier d'Oraison and Fesche, one of the volunteers, went with them. On the beach they were greeted by a large crowd whose leaders presented the Prince with a pretty young woman, urging him to sleep with her on the spot, but he made his excuses, offering her gifts instead. At Reti's house they were given a meal, and afterwards the Prince was offered a very young girl about twelve or thirteen years old and urged to have sex with her on a fine mat in front of all these people. Fesche, who was present, gave a salacious account of what happened, replete with references to Helen of Troy and Eve before the Fall:

> [He] makes her the gift of an artificial pearl that he attaches to her ear, and ventures a kiss, which was well returned. A bold hand led by love slips down to two new-born apples rivals of each other and worthy like those of Helen to serve as models for cups that would be incomparable for their beauty and attraction of their shape.
>
> The hand soon slipped and by a fortunate effect of chance, fell on charms still hidden by one of their cloths, it was promptly removed by the girl herself whom we then saw dressed as Eve was before her sin. She did more, she stretched out on the mat, struck the chest of the aggressor, making him understand that she was giving herself to him and drew aside those two obstacles that defend the entrance to that temple where so many men make a daily sacrifice.[38]

As the Prince caressed the girl, however, an *'arioi* musician began to play on his flute and the spectators, each carrying a plantain branch, sat around them in a circle. Embarrassed by the presence of so many witnesses, the Prince could not play his part, although 'an Indian used very singular means to further excite my desires'.[39] As we have seen, in Tahiti young girls might be offered to visiting high chiefs, and sex was performed in public by young *'arioi* on ceremonial occasions to excite and arouse the gods. The Prince of Nassau was being honoured by being asked to take part in this kind of ritual. Charmed by the innocence of these gestures, he exclaimed in his journal: 'Happy nation that does not yet know the odious names of shame and scandal!'[40]

When Bougainville came ashore that afternoon, Reti was talking with his father and several elders, who were unhappy that the shore camp was being erected. Picking up several of the soldiers' kitbags, Reti put these in a boat and told Bougainville that he and his men must sleep on board their vessels at night. Bougainville replied firmly that his men would remain on shore for eighteen days to collect fresh food and water, putting eighteen stones down on the ground; and when a solemn old man tried to take away nine of these pebbles, the commander would not allow it. Finally, Reti and his companions reluctantly gave their consent for Bougainville and his men to stay ashore for fifteen days, offering them a large canoe shelter with matting walls under which they could pitch their tents. To thank them he invited them to supper in his tent, and the Tahitians ate heartily, although one of them managed to filch Bougainville's opera glasses from his pocket. After supper Bougainville ordered the sailors to fire twelve rockets for his guests, a display that terrified them. That night Reti posted his own men as sentries and Bougainville, the Prince of Nassau, some of the soldiers and thirty-four men who were suffering from scurvy went to sleep in the tents under the canoe shelter. Reti, who slept nearby, had nightmares about the fireworks all night; and every time he awoke with a start, he sent placatory gifts to his visitors. When one of his wives arrived at daybreak he offered her as a bedmate to the Prince of Nassau, intending this as a compliment to his *taio*. When the Prince demurred, considering the woman to be old and ugly, this insult strained their new friendship to its limits.

Now that the shore camp had been established, the islanders helped the sailors to fill the water casks, cut wood for firewood and collect antiscorbutic plants, and provided them with fruit, fish, shellfish and delicious large crabs and crayfish. Fortunately, April was a time of plenty in Tahiti, when a new crop of breadfruit was harvested.[41] Although Bougainville had brought more than twice as many men to the island as the *Dolphin*, there was enough food to feed them all for a brief period. During their stay the French thanked the islanders for their labour with gifts of nails, but nevertheless the Tahitians constantly pilfered from the camp, hiding in a nearby swamp and using long hooked sticks to filch things from the tents. As Bougainville remarked, despite the fact that their houses had no walls the islanders rarely seemed to steal from each other, and he mused that perhaps they had no idea of personal property. In Tahiti, though, the god Hiro (in some genealogies, the ancestor of Tamatoa I, the high chief of Ra'iatea)[42] was the patron of thieves, and a daring theft was regarded with admiration. Before attempting such a feat, a man or his wife would go to Hiro's *marae*, where they implored the god to help him by making him invisible. If the theft failed, however, the culprit could be killed, and thieves might be taken out to sea in a canoe and dropped overboard, lashed to a large stone. For this reason theft was infrequent on the island, but the treasures brought by the Europeans were irresistible; and in any case, the strangers were taking local resources without payment, or accepting gifts from the islanders without making return presents.

During this visit the islanders frequently offered the French young girls to sleep with, no doubt seeking to acquire the *mana* and *ora* (life force) of these sacred strangers, enhancing the fertility and power of their lineages.[43] According to Fesche, however, such a girl often found sex with one of the strangers an ordeal, weeping when it was over, 'but would easily recover her composure and make a thousand caresses to her new spouse as well as to all those who had been witnesses'.[44] On one occasion, a distinguished elder brought three lovely young women into

Bougainville's cabin and urged him to have sex with them. The commander refused, but was so distracted by these seductive visitors that one of them managed to purloin an achromatic glass from his cabin, and he had to send some sailors to chase their canoe in order to retrieve it. As Bougainville remarked, this was a sailor's Paradise; and as he and his companions discussed these amorous delights during their meals, a shipboard narrative emerged depicting Tahiti as an island Eden whose people made love in public without shame or false modesty.[45] Bougainville quoted Virgil, invoking Venus, Dido and Cythera, the island of Aphrodite, to express his admiration:

> As they went into houses, they were presented with young girls, greenery was placed on the ground, and with a large number of Indians, men and women, making a circle round them, hospitality was celebrated, while one of the assistants was singing a hymn to happiness accompanied by the sounds of a flute. "O Venus, for they say it is you who grant rights to those who seek hospitality, may it be your pleasure to make this a happy day for those who set out from Troy and one our descendants will remember." [Virgil, *Aeneid*, I: 731–33.] Dido then offers the delights of her home in the style of this island.
>
> Married women are faithful to their husbands, they would pay with their lives any unfaithfulness, but we are offered all the young girls. Our white skin delights them, they express their admiration in this regard in the most expressive manner . . . These people breathe only rest and sensual pleasures. Venus is the goddess they worship. The mildness of the climate, the beauty of the scenery, the fertility of the soil everywhere watered by rivers and cascades, everything inspires sensual pleasure. And so I have named it New Cythera (the island of Aphrodite).[46]

The ship's surgeon Vivez went so far as to suggest that the Tahitian men were ill favoured by Priapus, the Greek phallic god, and that their women 'took the French for envoys from Vulcan and Venus without realising that they themselves were granting a similar benefit'.[47] The Prince of Nassau, whom the islanders quickly recognised as the most aristocratic among the strangers, was particularly favoured by the young women. As he wrote, describing one of these encounters:

> I was strolling in a charming place, carpets of greenery, pleasant groves, the gentle murmur of streams inspired love in this delicious spot. I was caught there by the rain. I sheltered in a small house where I found six of the prettiest girls in the locality. They welcomed me with all the gentleness this charming sex can display. Each one removed her clothing, an adornment which is bothersome for

pleasure and, spreading all these charms, showed me in detail the gracefulness and contours of the most perfect bodies.

They also removed my clothing. The whiteness of a European body delighted them. They hastened to see whether I was made like the locals and pleasure quickened this research. Many were the kisses, many the tender kisses I received! Throughout this scene, an Indian was playing a tender tune on his flute. A crowd of others had lined up around the house, solely preoccupied with the spectacle . . . I lived on good terms with the Indians whom I liked greatly. Appreciative of the small gifts I made them, they displayed a real affection towards me.[48]

The Tahitians were fascinated by the white skin of the strangers, because as mentioned earlier, a pale complexion was a sign of high status in the islands, associated with daylight and the sun. They could not believe, however, that the French had brought no women with them, and one day Ahutoru (who was living on board the *Étoile*) expressed doubts about the sex of Jean Baret, Commerson's valet, exclaiming '*Vahine!*' ('Woman!') and making unequivocal proposals to her while the naturalist sat beside his servant, looking annoyed and disconcerted. Vivez, who disliked the naturalist, described the sequel with some relish. The next morning when Commerson and Baret went ashore to collect plants, she was seized by hundreds of island men who yelled out '*Vahine!*', and a man was carrying her off in his arms when an officer drew his sword and stopped him. The following day Baret and her master went ashore again, and while Commerson was looking at some shells, several Tahitians seized her and stripped her naked, assuring themselves that Baret was indeed a woman. In this way her imposture was revealed, to the mingled amusement and annoyance of her shipmates.

After this ordeal Baret stayed on board the *Étoile*, but Ahutoru, who had become fascinated by her, paid her ardent attentions, asking if she was married. It was not until Commerson told him that his valet was a '*maou*', without knowing exactly what this meant (a *mahu* was a man who dressed and lived as a woman, an accepted role in Tahitian society), that he lost interest, although he still enjoyed it when she combed and powdered his hair. As Vivez remarked, now that her gender had been disclosed Baret became more relaxed with her shipmates, no longer stuffing her breeches with cloth, and 'finished the voyage very pleasantly, having suitors on all sides who did not lessen her fidelity to her master'.[49]

During these first days at Hitia'a the French sailors wandered about freely on shore, greeted on all sides with warmth and friendship. As Bougainville exulted:

I thought I was transported into the garden of Eden; we crossed a turf, covered with fine fruit-trees, and intersected by little rivulets, which keep up a pleasant coolness in the air . . . A numerous people there enjoy the blessings which nature showers liberally down upon them. We found companies of men and women sitting under the shade of their fruit-trees: they all greeted us with signs of friendship: those who met us upon the road stood aside to let us pass by; everywhere we found hospitality, ease, innocent joy, and every appearance of happiness amongst them.[50]

Inevitably, however, there were misunderstandings and clashes with the local people. On the evening of 9 April a group of warriors hid in the grass around the shore camp, trying to take things from the tents, although the patrols prevented them from coming too close to the encampment. Finally, in frustration, they pelted the sentries with stones, and when one of the soldiers chased the leading culprit, slashing at him with his sword, he hit a banana tree instead, deflecting the weapon. Alarmed by this violence, some of the women and children fled from the village.

Early the next morning, a very imposing chief, burly and more than six feet tall, arrived at Hitia'a. This was Tutaha, an ally of Reti's and an enemy of Purea and Amo.[51] Tutaha was a leading 'arioi and warrior from the Pare-'Arue district and the regent for his great-nephew Tu, a young aristocrat who apart from Teri'irere was the highest-ranking chief on the island. Although Tutaha was eager to have his great-nephew recognised as the paramount chief of Tahiti, this ambition was at imminent risk, because at this time Purea and Amo were building the great new marae at Mahaiatea for Teri'irere's installation. After befriending Captain Wallis, Purea and her high priest Tupaia had stitched the red pennant from the Dolphin to Te Ra'i-puatata, the maro 'ura or red feather girdle that Tupaia had brought from Taputapuatea. Eager to recruit European allies of his own, Tutaha hastened to Hitia'a to meet the French, bringing gifts of pigs, chickens, fruit and bark cloth which he presented to Bougainville; and in return the commander presented him with silks, tools, nails and beads, although he startled the great warrior by firing a pistol ball through a plank of wood to demonstrate the power of his weapons.

After this display, Tutaha invited Bougainville to the house where he was staying, offering him one of his young wives as a bedmate. He had taken Bougainville as his taio or ritual friend, and it was proper for a taio to sleep with his friend's wife, providing that she was willing. This idyll was soon shattered, however, along with Tutaha's chances of forging a close alliance with the French. During an argument, a soldier shot one of the Hitia'a men at point-blank range. When the islanders came to

Bougainville in great distress to complain about the killing, he sent the ship's surgeons to examine the body while a woman sat beside it, crying bitterly and anointing the corpse with coconut oil. When none of his men would confess to the murder, more people fled from Hitia'a, taking their belongings with them, and Ahutoru left the *Étoile* to join his compatriots. It was quiet that night at the shore camp, although one man approached, carrying a pig and crying out '*Taio! Taio!*' ('Friend! Friend!').

That night Duclos-Guyot warned Bougainville that their anchorage was unsafe, with jagged coral outcrops on the sea floor. Worried about the risk to his ships and that their relationships with the islanders were unravelling, Bougainville decided to cut short his visit to the island; and on 11 April he went on board the *Étoile* to tell them that he intended to sail in two days' time. Véron's notebooks, which contained the astronomical observations that he had made in Tahiti, had been stolen (no doubt because this seemed to be a ritual object), so Bougainville sent him ashore to repeat these observations and check the longitude of Tahiti. Commerson had already sketched a small Tahitian canoe and some tools and weapons in his notebook; and he and Bougainville, the surgeon Vivez, and Saint-Germain, the clerk on board the *Boudeuse*, now bartered for 'curiosities' (artefacts), including specimens of bark cloth and several adzes which were brought back to Paris.[52] When Tutaha came out to the ship with a gift of pigs that afternoon, Bougainville gave him an axe, a mirror and a small bell as return gifts; and this was the last time that he saw the great warrior.

Early on 12 April 1768, the wind turned to the south. The month of Au Unuunu had arrived, notorious for its stormy weather. As the wind gusted violently, two of the frigate's anchor cables rubbed against the coral and parted. Swinging in the wind, the *Boudeuse* collided with the storeship; and as the sailors worked frantically to separate the two vessels, the frigate's men hauled in the ship's remaining anchor ropes, fixing a spare anchor to the *Boudeuse*'s south-east cable and dropping it to the bottom. This steadied the frigate, but two of their irreplaceable anchors had been lost. In the midst of the chaos, Bougainville was told that his soldiers had killed or wounded three men at the shore camp, and that the rest of the islanders were fleeing from Hitia'a. He hastened ashore where he learned that some soldiers who had left the camp without permission had beaten an islander who refused to give them his pig, although they had offered two nails for it. When several of his friends came to rescue the man, the soldiers had fixed their bayonets and wounded or killed three of them. When the Prince of Nassau arrived in the village the people had surrounded him, weeping, kissing his hands, clutching his knees and begging for his help. The Prince drew his sword, and beating four of the soldiers with the flat edge of the blade drove them back to the camp, where they were put into irons.

Apoplectic with rage, Bougainville questioned these men in front of the Tahitians and threatened to summarily execute them, making their comrades draw lots to hang them and sending for the chaplain to give them the last rites. Fortunately for these soldiers, however, there was no firm evidence against them. That evening when Reti came to the camp, he carried a plantain branch which he offered to the Prince of Nassau, kissing his chest, weeping and crying '*Taio, taio, mate*', which Fesche translated: 'You are our [ceremonial] friends, and yet you kill us.'[53]

Bougainville was furious with his men. As the Prince of Nassau exclaimed in his journal that night: 'We saw our two ships on the verge of perishing on the coast. What would have become of us 6000 leagues from our fatherland in an island unknown in Europe, among people who were angry against us! What a situation!'[54] Fearful that they were about to be attacked, Bougainville doubled the guard around the shore camp. At 7 p.m. that evening a man dressed in bark cloth and foliage leaped into the camp, crying out '*Taio, mate!*' ('Friends, you kill us!'), jumping around and 'screaming like a devil'.[55] Later that night two muskets, some swords and a cauldron were stolen from the guard tent. A sailor who had grabbed a lantern to look for the thieves noticed several men crouching in the grass and fired at them, and six or seven other shots were fired.

Things were going from bad to worse. That night a severe storm struck Hitia'a, and at 2 a.m. an easterly squall drove the *Boudeuse* towards the rocks. Bougainville was woken and rushed on board his ship, but fortunately a land breeze sprang up at the last minute that saved her from disaster. At daybreak, however, two more of the *Boudeuse*'s anchor cables parted, and the ship was left swinging close to the beach on a single rope. During the night some warriors had sneaked out to the buoys and cut the cables. The captain of the *Étoile* sent his men across with a large anchor which they fixed to a new cable and quickly lowered, but at 10 a.m. this cable also parted. Just as shipwreck seemed imminent a south-westerly breeze blew up and saved them. Another anchor was sent over from the *Étoile* and when the wind shifted back to the east this was lowered. The storeship was anchored in sandy ground, and by his quick thinking the *Étoile*'s captain La Giraudais had saved the frigate.

After daybreak on 14 April the Prince of Nassau went ashore with Fesche, his irascible clerk Saint-Germain and two others to find Reti and attempt a reconciliation. Reti had left his house and the village was deserted, but some people escorted them to the place where the chief was now staying, carrying them on their backs across the river. Women came up to them, kissing their hands and weeping, 'their faces wet with tears'. Almost two hundred people followed them, and when they came to Reti's house the chief came out holding up a plantain branch which he gave to the Prince, putting his arms around him and his companions, weeping bitterly. As Reti drove away the bystanders, Fesche wrote later, he and his companions felt stricken with guilt and remorse: 'These various spectacles brought tears to our eyes. Were these Savages? Certainly not, on the contrary we were the ones who had behaved like barbarians and they acted like gentle, humane and well-regulated people. We murdered them and they only did good to us.'[56]

After greeting the Prince of Nassau, Reti led him and his companions to a hut where he gave them a meal before escorting them back to the shore camp, followed by a procession of islanders carrying pigs, chickens and fruit. Bougainville, seeing this from the ship, came ashore with gifts of silk cloth, tools and nails which he presented to the chief, assuring him that he would find out who was responsible for the killings and punish them. Reti responded by embracing him, and soon the camp was full of islanders who brought more refreshments. When Bougainville saw two soldiers chasing some of these people away, one of them brandishing a stick, he grabbed the stick and punched the culprits, although the chiefs quickly ran up to save them from further punishment.

That night the wind died down and the sea was calm. The boats that had been sent to take soundings found a pass through the reef, and the next morning Bougainville instructed La Giraudais to take the *Étoile* through this pass and cruise off the coast. The last of the water barrels were filled, and while the shore camp was being packed up some islanders brought a pig (no doubt a sacred *'arioi* pig) and asked Bougainville to demonstrate the power of firearms by asking one of his men to shoot it. The commander agreed, but when the pig dropped dead these people were frightened; and when a soldier shot two parrots flying on the wing shortly afterwards, they fled in terror. Bougainville sent some of his men to sow some seeds in a garden that he had made for Reti – maize, wheat, beans, peas, lentils and various vegetables – and presented the chief with a couple of turkeys and a goose and a gander. That afternoon he formally took possession of the island for France, setting up an oak plank in the canoe shed carved with a long inscription describing an Act of Possession and burying a bottle beneath it sealed with wax, containing a paper inscribed with the names of the ships and their officers. Although Wallis had claimed the island for Britain nine months earlier, the Hitia'a people told Bougainville nothing about the British visit. Now that they were about to sail from Tahiti the local people seemed disconsolate, the women weeping and the men urging them to return soon to Hitia'a.

At 6 a.m. the next morning Reti arrived on board with a gift of bananas, a pig and other items including some bark cloth and a beautiful large woven sail,[57] weeping and embracing the Frenchmen. Ahutoru was with him, and when he begged Bougainville to take this young man with him to France, Bougainville agreed, promising to ensure that Ahutoru was brought back to Tahiti. Reti presented the young man to each of the ship's officers, saying that this was his *taio* and the son of an *ari'i* (high chief) from another district, and asking them to treat him as a bond friend. After this ceremony Ahutoru farewelled a lovely young girl in a canoe alongside the ship, giving her three pearls from his ears and embracing her fondly. Fesche was sceptical about this arrangement, remarking acidly: 'I am firmly of the belief that this poor wretch will long regret his foolish action, as I consider his return to his home to be impossible . . . The main motive that makes him act in this way is his desire to be married for a while with some white woman.'[58] Bougainville named his passenger 'Louis de Cythère' but Ahutoru, who regarded the commander as his ritual friend, exchanged names with him and called himself 'Poutaveri', the Tahitian equivalent of 'Bougainville'. After ordering the men to set sail, Bougainville realised that they were struggling to raise the anchors with the capstan and signalled to three canoe-loads of women alongside the *Boudeuse*, throwing them some pearls and asking them to strip themselves. At this alluring sight the sailors heaved with a will, hauling in the cables with alacrity.

As soon as Reti left the ship, Bougainville ordered the sails to be set and the four anchor cables were dropped, leaving the anchors on buoys. A land breeze carried the *Boudeuse* towards the eastern passage, but as they passed the reef the wind died, and the tide began to drive the frigate towards the coral. The longboats and barges, which had been lowered to retrieve the anchors, arrived just in time to tow the frigate away from the rocks. The sailors managed to retrieve two anchors, but they were so exhausted that they could not weigh the others. That night a strong gale blew up and Bougainville was forced to hoist in the boats, abandoning two more of his precious anchors. According to island histories, the shark god of Hitia'a, who lived in the harbour, had been so offended by the unauthorised presence of the 'canoes without an outrigger' that he bit their anchor cables in two, forcing these strange vessels to leave the island.[59]

After his ten-day visit, Bougainville had no idea that he might have affronted the local gods; nor was he aware that his men had infected local women with syphilis.[60] As the Tahitians later attested, the hair and nails of those who had been afflicted with this dreadful disease fell out, the flesh rotted from their bones and they died in miserable isolation. Furthermore, he had been told nothing about the recent fighting on the island. Rather, he thought that life on Tahiti was idyllic. On 16 April 1768 he wrote in his journal: 'Farewell happy and wise people, may you always remain what you are. I shall never recall without a sense of delight the brief time I spent among you and, as long as I live, I shall celebrate the happy island of Cythera. It is the true Utopia.'[61]

Ahutoru at the Opéra

As they sailed away from Tahiti in a fresh breeze, heading north-north-west, the French ships passed a small green atoll where Ahutoru told Bougainville that they could obtain fresh provisions, and he had many mistresses. He called this island 'Oumaitia' (Me'eti'a, an island to the east of Hitia'a, which was regularly visited by Tahitians), although in fact this was Teti'aroa, an island north-north-west of Hitia'a under the control of the Pare-'Arue chiefs, who periodically visited these islets. The *'arioi* also frequented Teti'aroa, entertaining themselves with song, dance and feasting, fishing for dolphin and tuna, and making themselves beautiful by fattening their bodies and lying in the shade to whiten their skins, a custom known as *ha'apori'a*.[1] A plump, pale *'arioi* or chief was a living embodiment of *ora* – well-being and prosperity – and this custom was particularly favoured by those men who were fond of *'ava*, because drinking too much *'ava* gave them scaly skins, red, inflamed eyes and a haggard, skinny look – a disconcerting sign of scarcity and famine.[2] After a stint at the islets, however, they were transformed, once more looking sleek, pale, plump and healthy.

As a ceremonial friend of Reti, the chief of Hitia'a, Ahutoru was a man of *mana*. His father was a chief from Tahiti and his mother a 'captive' from Ra'iatea,[3] no doubt another chiefly woman who had been exiled during the attacks by the Borabora warriors. There are no surviving paintings or drawings of Ahutoru, but according to the French he was about thirty-five years old, five foot two inches tall and not handsome, at least by European standards. However, he was an adventurous soul, and as soon as the French ships arrived off the coast Ahutoru had boarded the *Étoile*, determined to join them. The local people were enthusiastic about his plan to travel with the strangers to their homeland, and Bougainville was also keen to support him, for as he wrote later:

It was to be supposed that he spoke the same language as his neighbours, that his manners were the same, and that his credit with them would be decisive in our favour, when he should inform them of our proceedings with his countrymen, and our behaviour to him.[4]

The languages and customs of Polynesia were far more diverse than Bougainville realised, however, and his priorities for the expedition and Ahutoru's were different. Several days later while he was watching the night sky, the young islander named a dozen stars, pointing out those that marked the bearing of Tahiti, and told Bougainville that if they sailed north-north-west for two more days on the bearing of a particular star, they would arrive at an island inhabited by his allies where they would be given fresh food and women. It is likely that Ahutoru was referring to Ra'iatea, although they had already sailed past this island. Using explicit gestures, Ahutoru indicated either that he had a child ashore or had been born there; and when the ship kept sailing west he grabbed the wheel and frantically tried to turn it in that direction. As a sailor pulled him away from the wheel Ahutoru seemed distraught, and at dawn the next day he climbed to the top of the mast and stayed there all morning, gazing sadly in that direction.

Over the next few days Bougainville was ill with a high fever; and Ahutoru was disconsolate. He told the commander that if there were no women where they were going, they could cut off his head. On 3 May 1768 they sighted an island where canoes came out to examine their vessels. This was one of the Manu'a group in Samoa, but Ahutoru, who knew nothing about Samoa, asked whether this was France. Eight or ten canoes came alongside, with people who looked different from the Tahitians, with darker skins, and although Ahutoru stripped off his European clothes and spoke with them, they did not understand him (which is not surprising given that Samoan is a West Polynesian language, not mutually intelligible with Tahitian). These islanders would not come on board, and unlike the Tahitians they were not interested in iron. According to Vivez, these people swam like fish, ignoring the sharks that swarmed around them, or catching them by hitting the water with an oar, holding out bait on a stick placed inside a large noose of rope and snaring the shark when it bit on the bait. Ahutoru quickly lost his enthusiasm for landing at these islands – as Bougainville remarked: 'Our Indian seemed to hold the[se people] in contempt and showed clearly that he had no wish to go with them'[5] – and he urged Bougainville to kill them.[6]

As the ships sailed through the Samoan archipelago, passing Ta'u, Ofu, Tutuila and Upolu, the French were so impressed by the speed and manoeuvrability of the local canoes, which sailed twice as fast as their vessels, zipping across their wakes, that they called these the 'Navigator Islands'. A week later when the ships arrived at Futuna and Uvea, Ahutoru was desperate to go ashore to 'make a sacrifice to Venus'.[7] Bougainville, who sympathised with his passenger, described him as an intelligent, shrewd man who had already mastered the workings of the ship and the roles of each crew member, although he had not yet learned a single word of French and found it difficult to pronounce the language. Despite these challenges, Ahutoru was able to convince his companions that he knew all the phases of the moon, and he accurately predicted the weather from signs in the sky. He indicated that in Tahiti the people believed that the sun and moon were inhabited, provoking Bougainville to exclaim, 'What Fontenelle taught them about the plurality of worlds?'[8] – a reference to Fontenelle's speculations about whether or not the other planets in the solar system were inhabited.[9]

During these conversations, which depended upon a combination of sign language and a smattering of Tahitian acquired by the French, Ahutoru was able to give his shipmates the first insights gained by any Europeans into Polynesian astronomy and navigation:

> The better instructed people of this nation . . . have a name for every remarkable constellation; they know their diurnal motion, and direct their course at sea by them, from isle to isle. In these navigations, which sometimes extend three hundred leagues, they lose all sight of land. Their compass is the sun's course in daytime, and the position of the stars during the nights; which are almost always fair between the tropics.[10]

Ahutoru also told Bougainville and others about life in his homeland, describing the customs of human sacrifice and infanticide, and the wars that convulsed the islands at frequent intervals. Bougainville's first impression that Tahiti was the true Utopia was quickly tempered by these conversations, and accordingly his account of life on the island in the published account of the voyage is much less rhapsodic than the descriptions written at the time of his visit.

By 19 May, about a month after leaving Tahiti, the sailors began to exhibit symptoms of venereal disease 'of all the types known in Europe'.[11] When the surgeon examined Ahutoru he found him riddled with these infections, although Ahutoru indicated that he and his compatriots were not greatly troubled by them. Bougainville was still glad that he had not allowed any of the sailors suffering from these disorders to go ashore in Tahiti; but as noted earlier, eighteenth-century medical knowledge of venereal disease was imperfect and it was not known that syphilis, for example, can be infectious but asymptomatic for long periods.[12] Like the British, the French introduced venereal diseases to Tahiti, although the main source of infection was clearly Wallis's men, who had transmitted these maladies to many of the women with whom they slept. Also as mentioned earlier, unmarried 'arioi girls made love freely during their festivals, although 'arioi wives were faithful to their husbands; and it was the young girls (often virgins, or those who had not yet given birth) in particular who were presented to the Europeans. The sexual practices associated with the cult of 'Oro and taio bond friendships ensured that venereal infections spread quickly around the island, and just nine months after Wallis's visit the people at Hitia'a were already stricken with these diseases.

When the ships arrived at Vanuatu (which Bougainville named the Great Cyclades after a group of Greek islands) on 22 May, Ahutoru went ashore at Aoba Island with Bougainville, the Prince of Nassau and an armed guard, watched by a suspicious group of black-skinned warriors armed with bows and arrows. When the warriors threw stones and shot a few arrows at the French, the soldiers fired their muskets, killing or wounding some of these men. At Aoba the sailors collected firewood and a few bananas and coconuts, and Bougainville and his officers took possession of Vanuatu for France. Once again Ahutoru (whom Bougainville called 'Louis') spoke of these people with contempt and understood nothing that they said. They seemed even more alien to him than the Samoans.

As they sailed from Aoba, Bougainville, who had heard the shipboard gossip about Commerson's valet, finally went across to the Étoile to confront Jean Baret. Weeping, she confessed that the rumours were true and she was indeed a woman. After being orphaned and losing a lawsuit for her inheritance, she had been left in penury; and in desperation she had dressed as a male and hired herself to her master as his valet. Bougainville accepted this story, which conveniently absolved Commerson from blame, writing about Baret with genuine admiration:

> She will be the only one of her sex [to have circumnavigated the world] and I admire her determination all the more because she has always behaved with the most scrupulous correctness. I have taken steps to ensure that she suffers no unpleasantness. The Court will, I think, forgive her for this infraction of the ordinances. Her example will hardly be contagious. She is neither ugly nor pretty and is not yet 25.[13]

Supplies on board the ships were again running low, and the sailors were subsisting on horse-beans, bacon and rotting salt beef. In their desperation they supplemented their diet with rats, and ate the ship's goat and a dog, which tasted quite good. Not surprisingly, Bougainville was becoming desperate to find fresh food and water. When the ships reached the Great Barrier Reef off Australia on 6 June, however, he decided not to land on this great continent, saying that the English explorer Dampier had described it as a 'barren land' and adding, 'judging from its approaches it offers no promise of any facilities for the settlement of a colony that would be useful to its mother country'.[14]

Having thus dismissed Australia, Bougainville headed north to the south-east coast of New Guinea and past the Louisiade archipelago. During this passage the weather was stormy and wild, and again he was forced to cut the crew's daily rations. In order to keep up their spirits he adopted a cheerful demeanour, trying to hide his concerns and quoting from *The Aeneid* in his journal: 'He feigns hope with his face, suppresses the deep grief in his heart' (*The Aeneid*, I: 209).[15] Ahutoru also remained cheerful, although he was bored and frustrated by their failure to land at any of these places. Bougainville praised the islander's wit and good humour, his gift for mimicry and his habit of composing chants to commemorate their experiences, adding that 'he forgets neither kindness nor harm done to him, but he is grateful and has no vindictiveness'.[16]

On 2 July as the ships sailed through the strait between Choiseul and Bougainville Island (named after the French explorer), the boats were sent into Choiseul Bay where they fired on a group of warriors in canoes who resisted their landing and captured two of their craft, one of which carried a partly cooked human jawbone. Concluding that these people were cannibals, Bougainville echoed Ahutoru's racial attitudes, commenting: 'We note that the blacks are much nastier than the Indians whose colour is closer to white.'[17] The ships carried on to New Ireland where they anchored on 6 July in an uninhabited harbour,[18] visited by Philip Carteret (the commander of the *Swallow*, the *Dolphin*'s consort ship) just eleven months earlier. Carteret had nailed a lead plaque to a tree recording the details of his visit which one of Bougainville's men found damaged on the beach, bringing it to his commander. The French expedition set up a shore camp in this 'wet, unpleasant hole', where they replenished their supplies of wood and water, staying there for almost three weeks while Véron took the astronomical observations that enabled him to accurately establish the width of the Pacific. When a sailor who had been bitten by a sea snake was treated by the ship's surgeons and recovered, Ahutoru exclaimed ruefully, 'Alas, poor Tahiti' (*Aue aue Tahiti*), remarking that when people on his island were bitten by sea snakes, they always died. Despite such remarks, he was an ardent patriot who never accepted the superiority of Europeans over his own people. As Bougainville remarked: 'It is incredible how far his haughtiness went. We have observed that he was as supple as he was proud; and this character at once shews that he lives in a country where there is an inequality of ranks, and points out what rank he holds there.'[19]

As the ships sailed along the coast of New Ireland, canoes approached on several occasions, pelting them with stones. The bread and salt meat on board were almost inedible and the men were dropping with scurvy; and by 25 August there were forty-five sick men on board the *Boudeuse*. As they sailed past New Guinea and through a labyrinth of islands towards the Dutch East Indies, conditions on board became dire. As Bougainville exclaimed in despair: 'There have been many arguments about where Hell is situated, truly we have found it!'[20] Finally, on 2 September 1768 they dropped anchor at Kayeli Bay in Buru, a Dutch outpost (now part of Indonesia), overjoyed to have reached a European settlement. The Dutch resident treated the officers to a superb supper which they ate with intense appreciation – as Bougainville remarked, 'this . . . was one of the most delicious moments of my life'.[21] He purchased fresh provisions for his crew and sent the sick men ashore to recuperate.

The countryside around Kayeli Bay was charming, with green hills, plains and forests, although there were enormous crocodiles in the nearby rivers; and the Dutch Resident entertained them in his Chinese-style house, manned by 100 slaves from Macassar and Seram. Ahutoru was deeply impressed by Kayeli, the first European outpost that he had visited:

> This European establishment [made a great impression] on our Cytheran. One realises that his surprise must have been great when he saw men of our own colour, and houses, gardens and domesticated animals in large numbers and in such a range, and at the hospitality that was shown in so open and knowledge-able a manner.
>
> He began by making them understand that he was a chief in his own country and that he was travelling with his friends for his own pleasure. He endeavoured to imitate us exactly during our visits, when out walking, or at table . . . He often asked us whether Paris was as attractive as this factory.[22]

Ahutoru, who had already realised that life on board the ships was governed by a strict chain of command, saw that status also dominated life in European settlements, and responded by insisting upon his own aristocratic background. It is probable that at Buru he was also alerted to the differences between European nations, because Bougainville often talked with the Dutch resident about British ambitions to take over the spice trade. It may have been there that Ahutoru told Bougainville about Wallis's visit to Tahiti, which the French commander had not heard about during his sojourn at Hitia'a.

After five days at Kayeli the ships sailed to Butung, where they anchored briefly, and one of the sailors acquired a monkey (which according to the French, Ahutoru thought was a man – a misunderstanding, as in Tahitian a monkey was described as an *'uri ta'ata* or human animal);[23] then on to Sulawesi and along the north coast of Java, anchoring at Batavia on 28 September 1768. They stayed here for two weeks, the officers living in a fine furnished hotel owned by the Dutch East India Company. Delighted by this elegant city with its hospitable inhabitants who invited them to feasts and concerts, they watched Dutch plays and Chinese comedies and pantomimes, and walked about the city admiring its grand houses, gardens and wide streets with their canals and avenues of trees. The canals also acted as sewers and breeding places for mosquitoes, however, and many visitors to Batavia were stricken with dysentery or malaria. Despite the delights of the city, almost every officer and man in the expedition contracted some disease, and when Ahutoru fell ill with dysentery he dubbed Batavia *'fenua mate'* – the land of death.

So many of the French sailors were still suffering from these diseases when the expedition headed west for Mauritius (or Île de France as it was then known, a French possession off the east coast of Africa) that they could barely work the ship, and they had a miserable passage. Upon their arrival at Mauritius, seventy men from the *Boudeuse* were transferred to the local hospital, although most were discharged back to the ships during their month-long stay on the island. The vessels were repaired and provisioned, and Bougainville gave Commerson, Jean Baret and Véron the astronomer leave to stay at Mauritius – Véron to observe the 1769 Transit of Venus at Pondicherry in India; and Commerson and his mistress to study the botany of Mauritius and Madagascar (and rescue the expedition from scandal). Although during the voyage Ahutoru had told his shipmates about the wars between islands and districts in the Society Islands, the hierarchical distinctions between different ranks, and the customs of human sacrifice and infanticide, Commerson had sailed on the storeship, not the frigate, and he was largely unaware of the less idyllic aspects of life on the island. While his boxes of notebooks from the voyage remained an unsorted jumble, the naturalist drafted a rhapsodic account about life in Tahiti which he despatched from Mauritius to France, where it was published in the newspaper *Mercure* in December 1769.[24]

In his *Post-scriptum on the Island of New Cythera or Tahiti*, Commerson drew upon Thomas More's *Utopia* (1516) which described a perfect society in a hidden South Sea Island; and the writings of Jean-Jacques Rousseau with his ideas about 'noble savages' who lived in a state of nature, without property, without inequality and without dissension, in absolute freedom including freedom in love.[25] From the time of the ancient Greeks, the South Sea (like outer space in the twentieth century) had provided Europeans with a blank slate for thought experiments about social life, including differing approaches to sexuality. This literary tradition included Plato's account of Atlantis (400 BC), a society ruled by philosopher-kings and located on an antipodean continent; *L'isle des Hermaphrodites* by Arthus, describing a voyage to an island inhabited by hermaphrodites who worshipped Cupid, Bacchus and Venus; Francis Bacon's *New Atlantis*, where explorers from Peru discovered a society dedicated to scientific enquiry whose laws of marriage were handed down from Solomon; and *La Terre Australe Connue* by Gabriel de Foigny, a lapsed Franciscan monk, recounting a shipwreck on another hermaphrodite island in the South Sea whose inhabitants procreated in a mysterious fashion.[26] Like Bougainville as he left Tahiti, Commerson described the island as a true 'Utopia' where people worshipped the gods of Love:

> Born under the most beautiful of skies, fed on the fruits of a land that is fertile and requires no cultivation, ruled by the fathers of families rather than by kings, they know no other Gods than Love. Every day is dedicated to it, the entire island is its temple, every woman is its altar, every man its priest. And what sort of women? you will ask.
>
> The rivals of Georgian women in beauty, and the sisters of the unclothed Graces. There, neither shame nor modesty enforces their tyranny: the action of creating one's fellow creature is a religious act . . . Strangers are all welcome to share in those happy mysteries, it is even a rule of hospitality to invite them: so that the fortunate Utopian continually enjoys both his own feelings of pleasure and the spectacle of those of others . . .[27]
>
> As regards the simplicity of their manners, especially their honest treatment of their women, who are in no way subjugated among them as they are among the Savages, their fraternity, their horror for spilling human blood, and their hospitality to foreigners, our admiration and gratitude require us to leave to the newspapers the task of writing more fully on each of these articles.[28]

Commerson's lyrical, glowing vision of Tahitian society evoked a Utopia that should exist somewhere on earth, if not in Tahiti, where people live in peace and freedom and make love in all innocence; and the *Post-scriptum* made a vivid and lasting appeal to European imaginations. According to Commerson, even in Mauritius Ahutoru continued to illustrate his contention that these islanders worshipped only the goddess of love, recording in one of his notebooks the refrain of a wistful song that the young Tahitian sang about Mauritius which Commerson primly translated into Latin – a 'Land which is miserly with pussy'.[29]

After leaving Mauritius on 10 December 1768 the ships sailed to the Cape of Good Hope where Bougainville enjoyed the excellent local wines, and the Dutch governor was hospitable; and then to Ascension Island. At Ascension they again crossed the track of Carteret in the *Swallow*, finding a bottle in a cave with the details of his visit just three days earlier. On 25 February 1769 they finally caught up to the *Swallow* at sea, and Carteret presented Bougainville with an arrow that he had collected during his voyage. As they left the *Swallow* behind, Bougainville noted that Carteret's ship seemed very small and slow, appearing to stand still even when it was under sail, and remarked how much the British captain must have suffered in so poor a vessel during his long journey. Indeed, he showed more sympathy for Carteret than Wallis, or the British Admiralty that had despatched his little, cranky sloop on a voyage around the world. After passing the Azores, as the *Boudeuse* anchored in St Malo on 16 March 1769 Bougainville exclaimed triumphantly: 'I entered [the port] having lost only seven men, during two years and four months, which were expired since we had left Nantes.'[30]

As the first Tahitian to sail on board a European vessel, Ahutoru had made an extraordinary voyage. During his visits to Samoa, Vanuatu, the Great Barrier Reef, Choiseul, Buru, Butung, Batavia and Mauritius, he had encountered a remarkable diversity of places and peoples. Although in his home islands the cosmos was structured as a concentric array of domed skies curving down to the sea, embracing the different island groups, during this odyssey Ahutoru sailed through all of these horizons.[31] Like many of his shipmates, when he arrived in France he was still weak from the illness he had contracted in Batavia and took some months to recover. According to de la Condamine, a famous mathematician and explorer, at the time of his first meeting with Ahutoru the young islander was suffering from a cold and a fever. He described him as intelligent and lively, with a remarkable sense of smell which he used to tell the difference between a man and a woman. When the scientist, who was rather deaf, put his hearing trumpet against Ahutoru's ear he quickly realised its purpose, exclaiming in Tahitian, 'dead ears!' (Bougainville, who had brought back a glossary of 300 to 400 words in Tahitian, must have provided this translation).

Noticing a painting of a scantily clad Venus that hung in Condamine's study, Ahutoru pretended to lift the cloth that preserved the goddess's modesty, and made explicit gestures that the scientist considered too gross to describe in writing. According to Condamine, Ahutoru was unable to pronounce more than half of the consonants in French, and none of the nasal vowels (because Tahitian has no nasal vowels, and fewer consonants than French).[32] He and Bougainville decided to ask Pereire, a linguist and fellow member of the Royal Society of London who specialised in teaching deaf-mutes to speak, to teach French to Ahutoru; but Pereire evidently focused upon learning Tahitian himself instead, because when Ahutoru left France his French was still almost non-existent, whereas Pereire published an abridged Tahitian vocabulary as an appendix to the second edition of Bougainville's *Voyage*.[33]

However, while the *philosophes* were fascinated by Ahutoru, he preferred high society in Paris. According to Denis Diderot, Bougainville must have been an entertaining guide:

> [He] has a taste for the amusements of society: he loves women, plays and good food; he accepts the whirl of fashion with as good grace as he did the inconstancy of the element on which he has been tossed. He is amiable and gay: a true well-balanced Frenchman.[34]

Ahutoru also met the Duke of Orleans, the Prince of Conti and the young Duke of Chartres, and at a dinner party given by a leading light in the Académie des Sciences he was introduced to Charles de Brosses, the President of the Académie, who had written about voyages of discovery to Terra Australis. According to Condamine, Bougainville was very fond of Ahutoru, never allowing anyone to call him a 'savage', and bought him a coat with gold frogs, a cloth jacket and an ostrich feather for these occasions. Once Ahutoru had recovered from his illness Bougainville took him to walk on the ramparts and to see the tightrope dancers in the Tuileries (probably Les Grands Danseurs, a troupe of acrobats and actors who performed stunts that included walking the tightrope with a child in a wheelbarrow, and a monkey that danced on the tightrope).[35] Although he could not speak French, Ahutoru often roamed around Paris on his own, purchasing things in the shops and never paying too much for them. Bougainville took him to meet the King and Queen at Versailles, and they dined together in many aristocratic houses in Paris where Bougainville titillated his contemporaries by recounting the shipboard fable of the Island of Love, free of sexual inhibitions. As Louis de Bachaumont reported after his visit with Ahutoru to the French court:

[The savage] has adapted very well to this country; he affects to find nothing surprising about it, and he showed no emotion at all when he saw the beauties of the chateau of Versailles. He likes our cooking very much, eats and drinks with presence of mind; he is easily intoxicated, but his great passion is for women, and he shows no discernment in his choice.

M. de Bougainville claims that in the country where he took this savage, who is one of the supreme chiefs of the land, men and women indulge in the sins of the flesh in an utterly immodest manner, they copulate on the first mat they find, in full view of heaven and earth. Hence the idea of calling the place the *Island of Cythera*, a name that it also deserves for the great quality of its climate, soil, situation, environment and produce.[36]

Fascinated by Bougainville's stories, the Duchess of Choiseul (the wife of Bougainville's patron) took a particular interest in Ahutoru, spending a large sum of money to provide him with tools, seeds and cattle when he left Paris, and accompanying him to the Opéra, which became his favourite entertainment. Ahutoru used to watch the performances from the galleries behind the boxes, revelling in the dancing and music.[37] From Isherwood's study of popular entertainment in eighteenth-century Paris, it seems that the Opéra had much in common with *heiva* (*'arioi* performances) in Tahiti. Like *'arioi* performances on ritual occasions, the stately productions at the Opéra (also known as the Académie Royale de Musique), sponsored by the Crown, featured mythical themes, drama, singing and dancing accompanied by instruments; while in the performances at the Opéra Comique and the fairs, actors staged Rabelaisian farces about the loss of virginity or cuckoldry with the liberal use of explicit sexual and excremental humour, which must have reminded Ahutoru of the satirical skits performed by the *'arioi* players as they travelled around the islands.[38]

Some of the bawdiest farces in Paris were shown in the private theatres of the nobility, followed afterwards by sex with mistresses or prostitutes; and no doubt Ahutoru attended some of these entertainments. As an exotic attraction in his own right, Ahutoru got to know many of the actresses and dancers in Paris, including a German dancer, Mademoiselle Heinsel, to whom he gave an *'arioi* tattoo. The sexually graphic nature of popular entertainment in eighteenth-century France no doubt explains why Bougainville and his companions were charmed rather than shocked by their encounters with the *'arioi*, and by the sexual hospitality they were offered on the island. Whereas in Paris such explicit sexual displays were regarded as libertine and obscene, in Tahiti the erotic performances of the *'arioi* were joyous, celebrating the fertility of the gods, and to the Frenchmen these seemed innocent and idyllic by comparison.

At the Opéra Comique, too, some of the dramatic fables performed by the actors were set in fictional Utopias, drawing contrasts between the social behaviour of their inhabitants and current mores in Paris. There is thus a close link between French popular drama in the eighteenth century and the works of the *philosophes*, who wrote more serious reflections on similar themes, using the fictional musings of visiting Brazilians or Tahitians to critique their own society. As a living 'Utopian', Ahutoru, along with Commerson's idyllic portrait of life in Tahiti and Bougainville's published account of his voyage, inspired a number of works in this genre including Nicolas de la Dixmérie's *Le Sauvage de Taiti aux Français* (1770), which includes a long letter supposedly written by Ahutoru to the French people as he left France;[39] and the more famous *Supplément au Voyage de Bougainville* by Denis Diderot (written in 1773). The *Supplément* begins with a dialogue about Bougainville's voyage which includes the following exchange:

A: Have you seen the Tahitian whom Bougainville took on board and brought to this country?

B: I've seen him; he is named Aotourou. The first land he saw he took for the native land of the explorers. Either they had deceived him about the length of the voyage, or, naturally misled by the apparent short distance from the shore of the sea where he lived to where the sky seemed to limit it at the horizon, he was ignorant of the real extent of the earth. The idea of the communal enjoyment of women was so well established in his mind that he threw himself upon the first European woman that he met and prepared very seriously to treat her with true Tahitian courtesy.

He was bored among us. He never ceased to sigh for his own country, and I am not surprised. Bougainville's *Voyage* is the only one which has given me a taste for any other country than my own.[40]

This dialogue is followed by a passionate lament from a Tahitian elder Orou (loosely based on Reti's father), who decried the evil consequences of Bougainville's visit including the introduction of venereal diseases and sexual perversions. In his lament Orou exclaims: 'We follow the pure instinct of Nature. You have attempted to erase its character from our souls!'

Although he was feted in France, by the end of his stay Ahutoru had spent two years away from Tahiti, and he was homesick. According to the Abbé Delille's romantic musings, when he visited the Jardin du Roi and came across a tree that also grew in Tahiti, Ahutoru threw his arms around it, weeping bitterly: 'A thousand charming things rose up before his eyes – the beautiful fields and blue skies which had seen him happy, the river he had swum with powerful strokes, his father's house and the woods all round, woods that echoed with his sweet love songs – he thought he saw them again and his tender soul at least for a moment was in his homeland once more.'[41] At last, in March 1770, Ahutoru had his wish: he was embarked on the *Brisson* at La Rochelle which took him to Mauritius, escorted by a merchant who was a passenger on the same vessel.

Eager to have Ahutoru as an ally and advocate in his home island, the Ministry of the Marine sent orders to the governor and superintendent of Mauritius to hire a ship to take him back to Tahiti, and Bougainville donated 36,000 francs (a third of his fortune) to equip this vessel. Several trunks were filled with the clothing, jewellery and other objects given to Ahutoru at Versailles and in Paris; and the King gave 1200 piastres for the purchase of goods at Mauritius to send with him to Tahiti. High diplomacy was also involved, because the French Government asked the King of Spain whether Ahutoru's ship might stop at the Philippines en route to his home island; and he gave his permission.[42] During his earlier visit to Mauritius, Ahutoru had stayed with Poivre, the governor of the island, and during the voyage on the *Brisson* he constantly talked about his friend 'Polary' and how greatly he looked forward to seeing him again.

When the ship arrived at Mauritius on 23 October, Ahutoru ran immediately to Poivre's house where he greeted the intendant with caresses. He sat beside the governor at the dinner table, treating him like a father. Poivre sent Ahutoru to the local Lazarist priests to learn some French, although they compiled a Tahitian vocabulary instead; and the intendant soon began to organise an expedition to return Ahutoru to Tahiti and to search for the Southern Continent, where it was hoped new sources of spices would be discovered. Soon Marion du Fresne, a longtime officer of the French India Company who had set himself up as a merchant in Mauritius when the company had collapsed, was commissioned to lead the expedition. Marion took advice from Commerson, and for a time Commerson and l'Abbé Rochon (a member of the Académie des Sciences and a skilled astronomer) planned to sail with Ahutoru to Tahiti. The King paid for one of the ships, the *Mascarin*, which was fitted out at his expense, and advanced the costs of the wages, supplies and trade goods for both ships, while Marion mortgaged his property in Mauritius to purchase the second ship, the *Marquis de Castries*. Crews and officers were recruited for the voyage, including the nephew of the Governor of Mauritius. Poivre purchased lavish gifts for Ahutoru and the chiefs in Tahiti, including tools, iron, utensils, seeds, rice, ox, cows, goats, and 'indeed everything which I think should be useful to the good Tahitians'.[43]

Just as the ships were about to sail in early October 1771, however, a smallpox epidemic broke out on the island. Shortly after the ships left Mauritius, smallpox boils erupted on Ahutoru's body and he came down with a very high fever. Marion headed straight for Madagascar, but only two days later Ahutoru died from this terrible disease.[44] This first of the Polynesian travellers to Europe never returned home to Tahiti to regale his friends and family with tales of his extraordinary adventures.

A Polynesian Venus

At the time of Bougainville's voyage, the forthcoming Transit of Venus in 1769 was creating great excitement among the scientific community in Europe. A generation earlier Edmund Halley, a member of the Royal Society in Britain, had predicted the timing of this rare astronomical event; and it was thought that if the Transit could be accurately observed during its next two occurrences in 1761 and 1769, a number of cosmological dimensions (including the size of the solar system) could be calculated. Unfortunately, however, the 1761 observations had failed because of bad weather and a lack of scientific co-ordination; and like the Académie des Sciences in Paris, the Royal Society in London resolved to do everything possible to ensure that the 1769 observations were successful. In November 1767 (when Bougainville set sail for the Strait of Magellan) the Royal Society set up a committee to organise the British observations of the Transit which decided to send observers to various locations around the world, including two to the South Sea, nominating Alexander Dalrymple, a distinguished hydrographer with long experience in the north-west Pacific (whose burning ambition it was to discover Terra Australis) as one of the Pacific observers. In the course of their planning, Thomas Hornsby, the Professor of Astronomy at Oxford, pointed out that although the Transit would be widely visible in the northern hemisphere, it could only be viewed from a small area of the Pacific Ocean. The latitudes and longitudes for the islands that he listed in this region were old and inaccurate, however, and it quickly became clear that the expedition would have to 're-discover' whichever island was selected as the site of the Pacific observations.

In February 1767 the Council of the Royal Society petitioned King George III for money to fund a British expedition to observe the Transit in the Pacific; and after that, decisions followed in quick succession. In March of that year the King agreed to support the voyage; and the Navy Board purchased a Whitby collier, which it renamed the *Endeavour*. When

Dalrymple insisted that he would sail on the ship only if he could command it, in early April the first Lord of the Admiralty informed the Earl of Morton, the President of the Royal Society, that such an arrangement would be 'entirely repugnant to the regulations of the Navy'.[1] Dalrymple resigned, and in mid-April James Cook, a master in the Navy and a skilled surveyor and cartographer who had trained in Whitby colliers and observed an eclipse of the sun, was appointed to command the *Endeavour*. In early May the Royal Society appointed Charles Green (an astronomer who had sailed with Nevil Maskelyne to test Harrison's chronometer) as the main Pacific observer for the Transit, with Cook as the second observer. In mid-May when Captain Wallis arrived back in England in the *Dolphin* and reported the discovery of Tahiti to the Admiralty, along with a top-secret estimate of its position, there was great excitement, as this seemed a likely site for observing the Transit. On 25 May James Cook was made a first lieutenant; and soon afterwards the Earl of Morton asked the Admiralty to allow Joseph Banks, a wealthy young fellow of the Society 'well versed in natural history', and his suite of seven people to join the voyage.[2] At this time, too, at the Royal Society's suggestion, Tahiti was officially selected as the expedition's destination. The island was located in the right part of the Pacific Ocean for the observations; it was claimed by Britain and not Spain; it was beautiful and fertile, and inhabited by people who were friendly at the time that the British had left the island. When Wallis reported that his men had sighted land to the south of the island that might be Terra Australis, the prospect of a voyage to Tahiti seemed irresistible.[3]

Joseph Banks, the twenty-five-year-old botanist who represented the Royal Society on this expedition, was a well-connected young gentleman educated at Eton, Harrow and the University of Oxford. As one of his teachers had lamented: 'There is a great Inattention in Him, and an immoderate Love of play . . . tho' in other respects we agree extremely well together; as I really think Him a very good-tempered and well disposed Boy.'[4] Since that time, however, Banks had discovered a passion for botany. When his father died in 1761, his mother shifted from Revesby Abbey, their country seat in Lincolnshire, to a house near the Chelsea Physic Garden in London, where Banks got to know Philip Miller, the chief gardener and a Fellow of the Royal Society. Three years later when he turned twenty-one, Banks inherited a fortune of £6000 a year and promptly brought Israel Lyons from Cambridge to teach a summer course in botany at Oxford, which he attended. Lord Sandwich (the First Lord of the Admiralty from 1748–1751) lived nearby in Chelsea, and they soon became friends. Sandwich was witty, clever and good company, a member of the notorious Hellfire Club who kept a mistress and conducted

Joseph Banks wearing a Māori cloak

flagrant affairs, and soon initiated the young Banks into the delights of a libertine lifestyle. Sandwich was also a Fellow of the Royal Society and a founder of the Society of Dilettanti, which promoted artistic taste and the study of classical antiquity, and Banks became a member of the Dilettanti and a reader at the British Museum. There he met Dr Daniel Solander, a favourite student of the great Swedish naturalist Carl Linnaeus who was cataloguing the museum's natural history collections, Thomas Pennant, and Gilbert White of Selbourne, all ardent naturalists.

Eager to make discoveries of his own, in 1766 Banks accompanied a naval friend on an expedition to Newfoundland where he collected plants, animals and geological specimens, described the local Indians and some of their customs, and got to know William Broughton Monkhouse, the *Niger*'s surgeon who would sail on the *Endeavour*. It is possible that he also met James Cook, who was surveying the coasts of Newfoundland and Labrador at this time and stopped at St John's during Banks's visit. Upon returning to England, where he found that he had been elected a member of the Royal Society, Banks hired a young Quaker draughtsman, Sydney

Parkinson, to draw the birds, fishes and insects that he had collected in Newfoundland. Dr Solander helped Banks to catalogue his collection of plants, inspiring him with an ambition to go to Sweden to study under Linnaeus himself, although at this time the Linnaean system had a dubious reputation. In his more lyrical writings Linnaeus often referred to plant fertilisation as 'marriage' and the male and female organs in plants as 'husbands' and 'wives', likening the calyx to a marriage bed, the filaments to spermatic vessels, the anterae to testicles, the dust to sperm, and the style to the vagina – similes that linked the scientific collection of plants with sex. Affronted by these connotations, the first edition of the *Encyclopaedia Britannica* in 1768 blasted the 'alluring seductions' of Linnaean taxonomy, declaring: 'Obscenity is the very basis of the Linnaean system.'[5]

Although Banks was attracted rather than repelled by botany's risqué reputation, the science was even more alluring. During this period, Linnaeus's binomial system for classifying plants and animals was becoming the basis for a global taxonomic project, with new species and genera being collected and classified around the world. A scientist who discovered and described a new species had the right to name it, gaining immortality in the process; and in 1767 when the Royal Society expedition to the Pacific was being planned, Banks became entranced by the prospects of the voyage. After studying Rousseau and de Brosses' work about voyages of discovery to Terra Australis, and their advice about how any expedition to the great unknown continent should be organised, Banks remarked to one friend: 'The South Sea at least has never been visited by any man of science'; while to another he declared: 'My Grand Tour shall be one round the whole globe!'[6] Supported by Lord Sandwich, he decided to join the expedition; and in July 1767 the Admiralty gave its formal approval. Banks gathered a magnificent array of scientific equipment, rumoured to have cost him at least £10,000 – including a bell tent for expeditions ashore and a dinghy for collecting at sea; medicines and chemicals, razors and knives; machines, nets, trawls and hooks; glass jars, paper presses, telescopes and microscopes; an armoury of pistols and guns; and a fine library of books on exploration and natural history.

At a dinner one night, Banks spoke about the voyage with such infectious zest that his friend Dr Daniel Solander, that charming 'philosophical gossip', leapt to his feet and vowed to accompany him. True to his promise, Solander joined the expedition as its chief naturalist,[7] along with Herman Spöring, his clerk at the British Museum, a Swede who had studied surgery, instrument-making and natural history. Banks also hired Sydney Parkinson, his Quaker draughtsman, and Alexander Buchan, a landscape painter, as the expedition's artists; and added two of his servants from

Revesby, two negro servants, a boy called Nicholas Young and two dogs to his entourage.

While these arrangements were being made, the Earl of Morton, the President of the Royal Society, drafted a set of 'Hints' on what information Banks and Cook should gather about any places they might discover, particularly the Southern Continent; and how they should treat its inhabitants. It is likely that the Earl, who had been briefed about Wallis's visit to Tahiti, was shocked by the violence of the *Dolphin*'s clashes with the Tahitians. Morton's 'Hints', which are remarkable for their tolerance and restraint, made a powerful impression on Cook and his *Endeavour* companions, influencing their conduct during this and subsequent Pacific voyages. The Earl urged Cook and Banks:

> To exercise the utmost patience and forbearance with respect to the Natives of the several Lands where the Ship may touch.

> To check the petulance of the Sailors, and restrain the wanton use of Fire Arms.

> To have it still in view that sheding the blood of those people is a crime of the highest nature:— They are human creatures, the work of the same omnipotent Author, equally under his care with the most polished European; perhaps being less offensive, more entitled to his favour.

> They are the natural, and in the strictest sense of the word, the legal possessors of the several Regions they inhabit.

> No European Nation has a right to occupy any part of their country, or settle among them without their voluntary consent.

> Conquest over such people can give no just title; because they could never be the Agressors.

> They may naturally and justly attempt to repell intruders, whom they may apprehend are come to disturb them in the quiet possession of their country, whether that apprehension be well or ill founded.

> Therefore should they in a hostile manner oppose a landing, and kill some men in the attempt, even this would hardly justify firing among them, 'till every other gentle method had been tried.[8]

At about the same time, the First Lord of the Admiralty was drafting Secret Instructions for the voyage that ordered Cook to search for the Southern Continent. According to these Instructions, after observing the Transit of Venus at Tahiti, Cook should sail south to 40 degrees in search of Terra Australis. If the continent did not appear, he should sail west to 35 degrees until he reached its coastline or the east coast of New Zealand charted by the Dutch explorer Abel Tasman. If he discovered Terra Australis, he should cultivate an alliance with its inhabitants, trading with them but always being on his guard against surprises. With their consent, Cook should take possession of various places on the continent in the name of the King of Great Britain. The Instructions show an insouciant assurance – after purchasing a collier and appointing a master to command her, the Admiralty had promoted him to lieutenant and ordered him to sail around the world to observe the Transit of Venus, and while he was about it, to discover the last great unknown land-mass on the planet.

The ship selected by the Admiralty, the *Endeavour*, a cat-built barque from Whitby, was small, sturdy and sea-kindly, her hull sheathed with iron nails. The barque's official complement was seventy men, although at the last minute this was raised to eighty-five including twelve marines. When Banks and his scientific party were added, there were ninety-four men on board the *Endeavour*. Compared with Wallis's frigate the *Dolphin* with her crew of 150, or Bougainville's two ships which brought 340 men to Tahiti, this was a small party, but then the *Endeavour* was only 106 feet long. The ship was altered to accommodate the extra men, jamming them in with their provisions and equipment; and the officers were shifted to grim little cabins on the lower deck, while Cook had to share the Great Cabin with Banks and his scientists and artists. Having just achieved his ambition to become a commissioned officer, however, Cook was in no mind to quibble about these arrangements.

James Cook had every right to take pride in his appointment, for in many ways he was an unlikely choice to command this expedition. A farm labourer's son from Yorkshire, Cook had joined his first ship when he was seventeen years old (at a time when most boys went to sea at twelve or thirteen); and when he was given the command of the *Endeavour* he was forty years old and still a ship's master. In an era when promotion in the Royal Navy depended largely on patronage, Cook had few strings to pull, and he had won this command by sheer capability. As he later wryly acknowledged:

[I am a] man who has not the advantage of Education; . . . but has been constantly at sea from his youth, and who, with the Assistance of a few good friends gone through all the Stations of a Seaman, from a prentice boy in the Coal Trade to a Commander in the Navy.[9]

James Cook

James Cook's seafaring career began when he was apprenticed to
Captain John Walker, a Quaker merchant and shipowner at Whitby. He
had a great regard for his master, living with the Walker family ashore and
experiencing the Quaker lifestyle of simplicity, moderation, honesty and
self-discipline. The merchant fleet in Whitby was a fine school for seamen,
with high standards of cleanliness, well-maintained ships and fresh provisions, and while serving on Walker's colliers Cook also taught himself
mathematics and navigation. He showed great promise, and after promot-
ing him to mate in 1755, Captain Walker offered him the post of master.
Cook was restless and ambitious, however, and decided to join the Navy
instead where he hoped to win a commission. He joined the Navy as an
able-bodied seaman and over the next three years was quickly promoted to
master's mate, boatswain and then master in the Channel Service. In 1758
his ship crossed the Atlantic to Canada, where he took part in the siege of
Louisbourg and helped to chart the St Lawrence River for the attack on
Quebec. Samuel Wallis commanded one of the ships in the British force
on that occasion, while Louis-Antoine de Bougainville was in charge of
a group of French soldiers. When Quebec fell, Cook was transferred to

Nova Scotia and Newfoundland where he produced a magnificent set of charts of those islands. In 1764 he was given his first command, the schooner *Grenville*; and two years later accurately observed an eclipse of the sun, publishing the results in the *Philosophical Transactions* of the Royal Society.

Although James Cook was a brilliant seaman, he was modest and unassuming; and he got on well with Joseph Banks, perhaps associating him with his father's employer in Yorkshire, a kindly gentleman who had sponsored Cook's early education. Cook was allowed to bring five men with him from the *Grenville* to the *Endeavour*, including his wife's cousin Isaac Smith (whom the Tahitians spoke of as his 'son'), an able surveyor and cartographer; while the Navy transferred six experienced Pacific hands from the *Dolphin* – the third lieutenant John Gore, a fine seaman and passionate sportsman who had sailed around the world with both Byron and Wallis; Robert Molyneux, the *Endeavour*'s capable, hard-drinking master, who had been a master's mate under Wallis in the *Dolphin*; Charles Clerke, the high-spirited, engaging master's mate who had sailed as a midshipman under Byron, and whose account of meeting 'giants' at Patagonia had been published in the *Philosophical Transactions*;[10] Richard Pickersgill, a master's mate with Wallis and a skilled surveyor; Francis Wilkinson, a sailor with Wallis who was promoted to master's mate on the *Endeavour*; and Francis Haite, a forty-two-year-old seaman with Byron who became a carpenter's yeoman. Cook's second lieutenant, Zachary Hickes, a steady and experienced seaman, was already suffering from the consumption that killed him during the voyage; while William Monkhouse, the hard-drinking surgeon who had sailed to Newfoundland with Banks, was appointed as the *Endeavour*'s surgeon, along with his brother Jonathan who joined as a midshipman.

Cook's experience as a master proved invaluable in preparing the *Endeavour* for a voyage around the world. After months of hard work the barque sailed down the Thames, anchoring in the Downs on 3 August 1768. Ten days later Cook sent a message to London telling Banks and Solander that the ship was ready to set sail and that their servants and luggage were already on board. When Banks received this message he was at the opera with a young woman to whom he was rumoured to be engaged, Harriet Blosset, the ward of the nurseryman James Lee; and that night he drank heavily to disguise his emotions. The next day he and Solander hurried in tearing high spirits to join the *Endeavour*, but the weather turned foul and the ship stayed at anchor. It was not until 25 August 1768 that James Cook wrote in his journal:

At 2 p.m. got under sail and put to sea having on board 94 persons including Officers Seamen Gentlemen and their servants, near 18 months provisions, 10 Carriage guns 12 Swivels with good store of Ammunition and stores of all kinds.[11]

As they headed away from the coast of England, Banks was seasick, but he and Solander were soon revelling in the voyage. Hard-working, affable and uncomplaining, Banks and Solander were ideal travelling companions. They quickly developed a daily routine, working from 8 a.m. to 2 p.m., describing their collections and reading books from the ship's library in the Great Cabin, and again from four o'clock until it got dark; and Cook often shared in their debates and discussions. During the voyage the *Endeavour*'s Great Cabin became a travelling learned society, and they learned a great deal from each other during these sessions. Perhaps sparing a thought for Miss Blosset, when they reached the latitude of Africa on 10 September, Banks wrote in his journal:

> Today . . . we took our leave of Europe for heaven alone knows how long, perhaps for Ever; that thought demands a sigh as a tribute due to the memory of freinds left behind and they have it; but two cannot be spard, twold give more pain to the sigher, than pleasure to those sighd for.[12]

When the *Endeavour* arrived at Madeira soon afterwards, Cook punished two of the sailors for refusing to eat fresh beef and issued onions as an anti-scorbutic; and Banks and Solander stayed with the English consul, who provided the 'gentlemen' with horses so that they could collect plants and shells.[13] On 18 September the *Endeavour* set sail again, and in early November when they arrived off the Brazilian coast, the Portuguese authorities, finding it difficult to believe that this small collier was a King's ship on a scientific mission, placed a guard around the vessel and refused the scientists permission to go ashore. As Solander wrote to a friend back in England:

> How mortifying that must be to me and Mr Banks you best can feel, especially if you suppose yourself within a quarter of a mile of a shore, covered with palms of several sorts, fine large trees and shrubs, whose very blossoms have had such an influence upon us, that we have ventured to bribe people to collect them, and send them on board as greens . . . for our table. We have, nevertheless, by fair means and foul, got about 300 species of plants, among them several new, and an infinite number of new fish.[14]

After this frustrating visit the *Endeavour* sailed from Rio, thousands of butterflies fluttering around her mastheads; and on 25 December the crew celebrated Christmas by getting 'abominably drunk', although fortunately the winds were moderate while the sailors were incapacitated.[15] On 11 January 1769 they sighted the coast of Tierra del Fuego where the Royal Society scientists went ashore, putting the ship at some risk as it tacked on and off the coast. Afterwards, as Cook remarked in exasperation, they 'return'd on board bringing with them several Plants Flowers &c most of them unknown in Europe and in that alone consisted their whole Value'.[16]

At the Bay of Good Success the next day, Cook and his companions met a forlorn group of Ona 'Indians' whom he described as 'perhaps as miserable a set of People as are this day upon Earth'.[17] Eager to add new specimens to their botanical collections, on 16 January Banks and Solander, with Monkhouse, Green and Buchan the landscape artist, accompanied by Banks's four servants and two sailors to carry their baggage, travelled into the interior, climbing up wooded hills to a boggy plain. During this expedition Buchan had an epileptic fit, and when it began to snow, Solander lay down and went to sleep, as did Richmond, one of the black servants. When Banks sent the others ahead to make a fire and urged Solander towards it, Richmond would not stir and the other black servant was left to keep him company. Unfortunately, these two men had filched a bottle of rum, and that night they froze to death in a drunken stupor. When the rest of the party returned to the ship, the irrepressible Banks took out one of the ship's boats and went fishing, looking for more new species.

On 21 January Cook headed for Cape Horn in fair and moderate winds, rounding the Horn thirty-three days later. This was a fine passage compared with that of Bougainville, who had taken two months to sail around the Horn, and Wallis, who took three months to pass through the Strait of Magellan. As they sailed westward across the Pacific, the sailors began to fall ill with scurvy; and Banks, who had swollen gums, pimples and a sore throat, drank lemon juice to cure himself. Cook began to question the existence of the Southern Continent; and even Joseph Banks, a firm believer in Terra Australis, had his doubts, writing in his journal:

> When I look on the charts of these Seas and see our course, which has been Near a streight one at NW since we left Cape Horne, I cannot help wondering that we have not yet seen land. It is however some pleasure to be able to disprove that which does not exist but in the opinions of Theoretical writers, of which sort most are who have wrote any thing about these seas without having themselves been in them.

They have generaly supposd that every foot of sea which they beleivd no ship had passd over to be land, tho they had little or nothing to support that opinion.[18]

At last, on 3 April, they sighted land – Vahitahi atoll in the Tuamotu Islands, where naked warriors marched along the shore brandishing long clubs. The *Endeavour* sailed past Akiaki and Hao (which Bougainville had also seen); Marokau and Ravahere, where armed warriors boarded two canoes and came after them; and Reitoru, Ana'a and Me'eti'a to the east of Tahiti, which Wallis had briefly visited. On 10 April the sailors caught a blue shark (an *ata* or incarnation of Ta'aroa) while birds wheeled around the vessel. That evening some people claimed that they had sighted land to the west, but it was cloudy and no one could be certain.

On 11 April 1769, to Captain Cook's great relief, the mountains of Tahiti appeared on the horizon. On shore in Matavai Bay, however, the people were terrified. Since Bougainville's departure, despite the idyllic reputation that Tahiti had acquired in Europe, another war had broken out on the island, and Purea and Amo's people had been defeated. Matavai Bay was now occupied by the conquerors and their allies, led by Tutaha, the great warrior leader of Pare-'Arue. As soon as they saw the British flag fluttering in the breeze they remembered the bond friendship that Purea had forged with Captain Wallis, and supposed that he had come back to avenge his friends and allies. Memories of the *Dolphin*'s attack on the fleets in Matavai Bay were still vivid, when muskets and cannons had been used to devastating effect, and Tutaha's people were expecting ruthless reprisals.

Like all disputes in the Society Islands, the recent war in Tahiti revolved around a contest over *mana*; in this case tracing back to a struggle between two brothers in Papara a generation earlier – Aro-mai-i-te-ra'i and Tuitera'i,[19] the younger brothers of Te'e'eva, the first-born in the senior line of the Tevas. As mentioned earlier, after a battle in Papara, this aristocratic woman had fled to Ra'iatea where she married Ari'ima'o (or Shark Chief), a son of Tamatoa I, and bore Mau'a, the heir to the Tamatoa title. In her absence, her two young brothers struggled over the succession to the Papara titles, the elder brother Aro-mai-i-te-ra'i arguing that now their older sister had gone to Ra'iatea, he was the rightful person to succeed his father, while his younger brother Tuitera'i disputed this, saying that only the first-born child had the automatic right of succession.

The Teva clans had supported Tuitera'i, the younger brother; and Aro-mai-i-te-ra'i was banished from Papara, nursing his grievances.

In the next generation, when Tuitera'i's son Amo succeeded his father and became chief of the Tevas, he married Purea, the first-born child of the chief of Fa'a'a district on the north-west coast of the island. When they planned to invest their young son Teri'irere as the *ari'i rahi* or paramount chief of the island, however, Aro-mai-i-te-ra'i's descendants bitterly opposed this ambition. At this time in Tahiti, women who were the first-born in aristocratic families had a powerful influence in deciding the succession to sacred titles;[20] and as the first-born in the senior lineage of the Tevas, Te'e'eva (like Purea) was one of these 'Great Women'. When she decided to support Teri'irere as the paramount chief of Tahiti, Te'e'eva sent her nephew Fa'anounou accompanied by the high priest Tupaia to Papara with the *maro 'ura* (red feather girdle) known as Te Ra'i-puatata and an image of 'Oro, carrying these sacred objects to Teri'irere and his family.

Although as the first-born child of Amo and Purea, Teri'irere had a strong claim to succeed his father as the bearer of the *maro tea* or yellow feather girdle of the Tevas, this was contested by Aro-mai-i-te-ra'i's descendants. The *maro tea* was associated with rain and fertility; only the most senior among the Tevas could wear this sacred insignia; and Tuitera'i (Amo's father and Teri'irere's grandfather) had been a younger brother. During Wallis's visit, furthermore, in order to strengthen her son's claims, Purea had forged a ceremonial friendship with the British commander, and after his departure, as mentioned earlier, her high priest Tupaia had commemorated this alliance by stitching the red pennant from the *Dolphin* to Te Ra'i-puatata, the *maro 'ura* he had brought for the young chief from Taputapuatea. If Teri'irere was installed with both the red and yellow feather girdles at Mahaiatea, the great new *marae* that was being built in Papara, the *mana* of 'Oro, the *mana* of the Tevas and the *mana* of the British would come together, giving Teri'irere unprecedented powers.

In Tahiti, however, only one high chief could wear the *maro 'ura* at one time, thus being recognised as the *ari'i maro 'ura* or paramount chief of the island. To further complicate matters, during this period the Papara *maro 'ura* was not the only red feather girdle in Tahiti. The young high chief of the northern district of Pare-'Arue, Tu (or Tu-nui-e-a'a-i-te-Atua, as he was formally known) also had claims to a *maro 'ura* through his mother Tetupaia-i-Hauviri, another Great Woman and the eldest child of Tamatoa III from Ra'iatea,[21] and his claims were strongly supported by his great-uncle Tutaha. When Tetupaia married Teu, the chief of Pare-'Arue, linking the Pare-'Arue lineage with the Tamatoa clan of Ra'iatea and the Mato clan in Huahine,[22] she brought a red feather girdle from her family in 'Opoa which was lodged at Taraho'i *marae* in Pare. Her father was Ari'ima'o's younger brother; wheareas Teri'irere's claim to the *maro 'ura* from Ra'iatea came through Te'e'eva, Ari'ima'o's high-ranking widow.[23] Through his ancestor who had married the daughter of an earlier Vehiatua, Tu also had kin ties to that high-ranking dynasty in southern Tahiti. Despite Teri'irere's various claims to *mana*, therefore, Tutaha, the leading *'arioi* and Tu's regent, considered that his great-nephew had the stronger claim; and he was adamantly opposed to Teri'irere's installation.

Tutaha, a tall, imposing *'arioi* about sixty years old, had befriended Bougainville during the French commander's visit. He was a wily politician, and while the great *marae* at Mahaiatea was being built he set about gathering allies to oppose Teri'irere. In order to do this, he played upon these old enmities. Aro-mai-i-te-ra'i's granddaughter Purahi, the first-born in her family, considered herself senior to Amo (as her grandfather was Tuitera'i's older brother, and her mother was his eldest sister). She bitterly resented the elevation of Teri'irere over her eldest son, Vehiatua II, who, given his descent from Aro-mai-i-te-ra'i, also had a strong claim to the *maro tea*. Her husband Vehiatua, the high chief of southern Tahiti, had his own reasons for hating the Papara lineage, whose ancestors had killed his grandfather;[24] and with Purahi's blessing he joined Tutaha in the alliance against Teri'irere. In addition, Tutaha recruited allies from the heart of Purea's family – including Vave'a, the sister of the high chief of Mo'orea, who had married Purea's youngest brother, and was infuriated that Purea was trying to elevate Teri'irere over her son Teri'i-vaetua.

Despite the growing opposition to Teri'irere's installation, Purea and Amo were unmoved. After Bougainville's departure the *marae* at Mahaiatea had been completed; and as the eleven stone steps of its *ahu* or altar rose into the sky, higher than any other *marae* in the Society Islands, a chant was composed in its honour:

> Look at Mahaiatea!
> Papara now has two mountains
> One is Mount Tamaiti
> The other is Mahaiatea![25]

In order to collect the huge quantities of food and gifts required for Teri'irere's installation, Purea declared a *rahui* over the main resources on the island – choice foods, bark cloth, canoes and fine mats. Only a leading chief was entitled to impose such a ritual restriction, however;[26] and outraged by Purea's presumption, Vave'a and her daughter Itia decided to break the *rahui*.

Mahaiata marae *at Papara*

In those days, if a *rahui* was in force and a guest of equal standing came
to visit, all of the food that had been collected under the restriction had to
be offered to the visitors and the *rahui* was broken. Invoking this custom,
Vaveʻa boarded her clan's double canoe with its shelter in the prow, a privilege reserved for high chiefly families, and had herself paddled to the gap
in the reef opposite Mahaiatea. According to the oral histories, when she
saw the great canoe approaching, Purea stood on the beach and hailed it,
calling, 'Who dares to venture through the sacred pass? Do you not know
that the Tevas are under a *rahui* for Teriʻirere-i-toʻoaraʻi? Not even the
cocks are permitted to crow, or the ocean to storm at this time!' Vaveʻa
replied haughtily in the name of her son: 'It is Teriʻi-vaetua, the *ariʻi* of
Ahurai!' Undaunted, Purea answered, 'How many paramount chiefs can
there be at one time? I know only of one, Teriʻirere-i-toʻoaraʻi. Down
with your shelter!' Shamed by this response, which denied her son's status,
Vaveʻa wept and slashed her head with a shark's tooth, but Purea was adamant and her sister-in-law was forced to return to Faʻaʻa.

Next, ʻItia (formally known as Tetuanui-reia-i-te-Raʻiatea), Vaveʻa's
eldest child and Purea's niece, took their lineage's sacred canoe and set
off for the pass through the reef at Mahaiatea. Again Purea stood on the
beach and refused to welcome ʻItia ashore, denying the chiefly status of
her brother and telling her to pull down her shelter. ʻItia was a bolder

woman than her mother, however, and despite Purea's fury she came ashore and sat on the beach at Mahaiatea, where she slashed her head with a shark's tooth, dug a hole in the beach and let her blood flow into it. This was a call for revenge, as her blood in the soil of Mahaiatea demanded blood in restitution.

Shaken by Purea's disregard for her kinsfolk, Amo's younger brother Manea, the high priest of the Tevas, stood on the beach and rebuked her, reminding her that as paramount chief, Teri'irere's position would depend upon the support of all of his family and their allies. Quoting a clan proverb, he declared, 'The drums of Mata'irea are calling for a *maro 'ura* for Teri'irere. Where will you wear the *maro 'ura*? In Nu'urua and Ahura'i. One end of the *maro* holds the Porionu'u, the other end the Tevas; the whole holds the Oropa'a.' With this proverb, Manea was reminding Purea that Te Ra'i-puatata represented all of Teri'irere's kinsfolk. One end of this red feather girdle was decorated with two tongues, each symbolising a district of the Porionu'u people, while the other end was decorated with eight black feather tongues, each representing one of the clans of the Teva. The girdle as a whole symbolised the Oropa'a (or Pa'ea) people; and without their support he would be nothing. Purea was unrelenting, however, retorting, 'I recognise only Teri'irere.' Affronted by her stubbornness, Manea dried the blood from 'Itia's face with bark cloth, wiping away the feud as far as he and his family were concerned.[27]

Although Teri'irere had powerful support, it was being weakened by these machinations. Concerned about Tutaha's role in orchestrating the opposition to Teri'irere, Tupaia urged Purea to have the great warrior killed, but she refused to entertain his suggestion. Instead, Amo sent a herald around the island carrying a *vane* or banner made of red baize from the *Dolphin* and fringed with red feathers, summoning the chiefs of the surrounding districts and islands to Teri'irere's installation, which they had timed to coincide with the Matahiti (First Fruits) celebration in December, when the first breadfruit crop would ripen. The chiefs invited to the ceremony included Tepau of Ahurai, Purea's eldest brother; Tu of Pare-'Arue, Teri'irere's main rival; Pohuetea of Puna'aui'a, a great fighting chief; Puni the elderly war leader from Borabora who had conquered Ra'iatea, Taha'a and Huahine; and Vehiatua I, the old fighting chief of Tai'arapu. Some of these leaders accepted the invitation, but when the red banner arrived at Tai'arapu, Vehiatua struck it down contemptuously, exclaiming, 'Why would we let this flag pass through our district?', tearing the banner into pieces and sending the scraps back to Amo. An experienced campaigner, the old chief quickly mustered his forces before Amo could summon his allies; and he and his warriors descended on Papara.

Before Teri'irere's investiture could take place, in December 1768 Vehiatua and his allies attacked Papara. When the canoes of the opposing forces fought inside the reef off Mahaiatea, the bodies of those who fell floated to the coral bottom where the cuttlefish lodged in their skulls, so that the battle was named *Mata toroa* after this circumstance. In the bloody land battle that followed, Tutaha's army from Pare-'Arue and the Puna'aui'a warriors led by Pohuetea fought alongside Vehiatua's army and hundreds of Amo's men were killed, leaving the beach at Mahaiatea strewn with their bones. In conflicts of this kind on the island, the punishment for defeat was terrible. Children were speared through the head and strung on cords, women were spread-eagled and disembowelled, while leading warriors were beaten flat with clubs, or their heads and genitals were tightly bound with sacred sennit. Houses were burnt, pigs were captured, gardens destroyed, breadfruit trees cut down and left to rot and coconut trees were decapitated.[28]

After the battle as the victorious warriors rampaged across Papara, the *rauti* or war orators urged Tutaha's army to annihilate their enemies:

> Be like the blasting north wind
> Weed out the water mint (refugees)
> Look for the red *taro* (able-bodied survivors)
> Leave no one alive
> Disembowel the hen (the enemy clan)
> Do not leave a red root behind
> Be deaf to their entreaties
> Be like the roaring ocean
> Put the sky (the chief) beneath your feet
> Let us have the anger
> Of Ta'aroa, whose curse is death![29]

When they came to Mahaiatea, the warriors seized the gifts that Purea had received from Captain Wallis, including a goose and a turkey, threw down the stones of the great *marae* and destroyed its sacred idols. They did not capture Amo, however, who escaped to the mountains with Tupaia, Purea and Teri'irere. His enemies caught and killed his younger brother Ma'i instead, and as an ultimate insult Vehiatua had Ma'i's body cooked in an oven. At the height of the battle, Pohuetea, the formidable *ari'i* of Puna'aui'a, and his ally To'ofa of Paea seized the red feather girdle Te Ra'i-puatata and the image of 'Oro from Taputapuatea, carrying these sacred objects to 'Utu-'ai-mahurau *marae* on the west coast without Vehiatua's knowledge.[30] When the battle was over, Vehiatua took the bodies of many of the dead to his home district in Tahiti-iti where he built a *marae* at Tai'arapu decorated with their skulls (which held their spirits and *mana*), naming this grisly monument Te-ahu-upo'o (the wall of skulls).[31]

Although he had joined with Vehiatua's forces, Tutaha did not support Vehiatua's ambitions for his son. He was determined that, instead, his great-nephew Tu would become the paramount chief of Tahiti. In order to achieve this he made peace with Purea and Amo, allowing them to retain their chiefly status while taking control of their district;[32] while Teri'irere retained the *maro tea* of his Teva ancestors and continued to play a vital role in the fertility rituals. During the peace-making ceremonies Teri'irere and Tu, and their fathers Amo and Teu, became *taio* or bond friends, securing both the truce and Tu's position; while Teri'irere was married to Tu's eldest sister, binding him into Tu's kin group. Later, the Teva clans blamed Purahi, Vehiatua's wife, for the disaster that she had brought upon her people, singing a song of bitter recrimination:

> Papara is prostrate
> The mountain [the *ari'i* Teri'irere] is laid low
> By the great army of Hui and Tai'arapu
> Only one now stands on the shore, the *Marae*,
> You are the cause of our downfall
> You have sinned, Purahi
> Against the *reva 'ura* [installation ceremony] of your *ari'i*
> That was broken up by Tai'arapu
> And brought about our ruin.[33]

Captain Cook in Arcadia

On 12 April 1769 when the *Endeavour*, her sails billowing in the breeze, headed in to Matavai Bay, Tu's people gazed at the ship in consternation. Matavai Bay had been Captain Wallis's headquarters, and Wallis had promised his *taio* Purea that he would return. If this was his vessel, he was bound to avenge her defeat; and after sending the young chief into hiding, Tutaha despatched canoes out to the ship, their crews taking offerings of bananas, coconuts, breadfruit, small fish and *vi* or Tahitian apples and crying out '*Taio! Taio!*'

The former *Dolphin*s under Wallis – John Gore, the third lieutenant; Robert Molyneux the master; Richard Pickersgill, a master's mate; and Francis Wilkinson – gazed eagerly into the canoes, looking in vain for their old friends and lovers. Since their crushing defeat, however, Purea and her people no longer visited Matavai Bay, and this had become enemy territory. The only person that they recognised was Fa'a, the white-bearded old man who had handled the trade during the *Dolphin*'s visit, whom Cook invited on board and showered with presents. When he began to give himself airs, Banks dubbed the elder 'Nestor' after the garrulous, boastful old statesman from Homer's *Iliad*. Cook sent the pinnace ahead of the ship to anchor off Hiro's Rock, marking the shoal where the *Dolphin* had grounded; and the next day when the *Endeavour*'s anchors rattled down into the bay, Sydney Parkinson sketched the spectacular volcanic skyline from the deck of the ship. As he noted in his journal that night, 'the land appeared as uneven as a piece of crumpled paper, being divided irregularly into hills and valleys; but a beautiful verdure covered both, even to the tops of the highest peaks'.[1]

During the long voyage from England, the *Dolphin*s had often boasted about their affairs with beautiful island women, and the delights to be obtained in Tahiti for a spike nail or a hatchet. Determined to avoid the uncontrolled barter of iron for sex that had developed during the

A View of Matavai Bay

Dolphin's visit, however, Cook announced a set of rules to regulate the exchanges between his men and the local people. Partly inspired by the Earl of Morton's 'Hints', these rules began by admonishing the sailors to 'endeavour by every fair means to cultivate a friendship with the Natives and to treat them with all imaginable humanity'.[2] Only those individuals authorised to trade could exchange goods with the islanders; and if any man lost his tools or arms, the value of these would be charged against his pay, and the same rule applied to any supplies taken from the ship without permission. When one of the sailors, Samuel Jones (a twenty-two-year-old Londoner) breached the new rules, Cook had him tied to the rigging and he was given a dozen lashes, watched by his crestfallen shipmates.

After the flogging, Cook took the longboat ashore, accompanied by Fa'a, Joseph Banks and Dr Solander, the astronomer Charles Green, a party of marines in their scarlet coats and John Gore, the *Endeavour*'s third lieutenant, who had a smattering of Tahitian from his visit on the *Dolphin*. Fa'a guided them towards the *Dolphin*'s old watering place where he suggested that the British might set up their shore camp; and the marines went through their drill, watched by a terrified crowd of islanders. Memories of the *Dolphin*'s cannons were still vivid, and after a pause their leader approached the strangers, prostrating himself, creeping on his hands and knees and offering Cook a green plantain branch as a sign of friendship. When Cook accepted the bough, Tu's people seemed astonished and extremely relieved. Each of Cook's companions was also given a branch, and the islanders led them in procession to a place where they scraped the ground bare of plants and laid down their plantains, followed by the marines and the rest of Cook's party. After this ceremony of peacemaking, Gore led the party along the coast to show them Purea's 'palace', followed by an inquisitive crowd. As they walked through the woods, Banks thought that he was in heaven:

> We walk'd for 4 or 5 miles under groves of Cocoa nut and bread fruit trees loaded with a profusion of fruit and giving the most gratefull shade I have ever experienced, under these were the habitations of the people most of them without walls: in short the scene we saw was the truest picture of an arcadia of which we were going to be kings that the imagination can form.[3]

Gore, on the other hand, was disconcerted, because since his visit during the *Dolphin*'s voyage everything had changed. Where large houses, canoe sheds, double canoes and stone *marae* had once stood, there were now only a few temporary houses inhabited by servants. When they reached the site of Purea's great *'arioi* house, they found it occupied by a garden of barkcloth plants, although a few of the pillars were still standing in the grass. While this was the height of the Season of Plenty in Tahiti and the autumn harvest festival was approaching, they saw only two pigs and no chickens, whereas formerly these animals had been abundant. Many of the people were suffering from some kind of itch (probably a symptom of venereal infection) and few of them were willing to approach the Europeans. None of the high-ranking people who had previously befriended them appeared, and the district seemed largely deserted. Instead of the warm greetings he and the other *Dolphins* had expected, they were treated with reserve and suspicion. Despite Gore's chagrin, however, Banks and his companions were in raptures. After months at sea, it was wonderful to be back on land, and the shady woods, scented flowers, sandy beaches and sparkling rivers were delectable.

Early the next morning, 14 April, several double canoes came alongside the *Endeavour*, bringing out two stately envoys. As soon as these men entered the Great Cabin they took off their bark-cloth robes, dressing Cook and Banks in these garments. In exchange, Cook gave each of them beads and a hatchet, while the crews of their canoes boarded the ship, swarming up the rigging and grabbing at everything they saw. Because

Cook had shown no sign that he wished to avenge Purea, Captain Wallis's bond friend, the warriors took this as a sign of weakness. They had brought out several pigs but would only exchange them for hatchets, a sign that the price of pork had shot up since the *Dolphin*'s visit; breadfruit, however, were still plentiful, as they usually were in April on the island. Apologising for their companions' unruly behaviour, the envoys invited Cook to accompany them to a point south-west of Matavai Bay, in the Pare-'Arue district. To their evident relief, Cook accepted the invitation, and with Joseph Banks, Dr Solander, Dr Monkhouse and the marines, they set off together in the boats, heading for Pare.

When they landed on the beach at Point 'Utuha'iha'i – where the tomb of the Pomare family now stands – the envoys led them to a large *'arioi* house where Tutaha (whom Banks immediately dubbed 'Hercules' because of his magnificent physique) welcomed his guests to Tahiti. An imposing stature was the mark of a high chief in the Society Islands, and at over six feet tall, Tutaha was an impressive figure. Cook and Banks were also tall, however, each about six feet tall – unlike Tutaha's former *taio* Bougainville, who had been quite short, and Captain Wallis, who was so ill during his visit that he could barely stand upright.[4] Tutaha presented each of his guests with a cock, a hen and a long piece of perfumed bark cloth, and in return Banks took off his silk neckcloth, ceremoniously presenting this with his linen handkerchief to Tutaha, delighting the great war leader. During the *Dolphin*'s visit, Tutaha had stayed away from Matavai Bay and now he was apprehensive, supposing that given their bond friendship with Purea, the British would feel obliged to avenge the 'Queen' and her people. Cook knew nothing about the recent battles, however, and oblivious to these political complexities, he greeted the Pare-'Arue war leader in an affable manner.

After these exchanges, Cook and his companions walked about the houses, where women pointed at mats and lay down seductively, offering them sex. During the voyage to Tahiti, Joseph Banks had revelled in the shipboard gossip about the delights to be enjoyed with island women, but on this occasion, as he noted ruefully, 'there were no places of retirement, the houses being intirely without walls, [and] we had not an opportunity of putting their politeness to every test that maybe some of us would not have faild to have done had circumstances been more favourable'.[5] After walking along the beach for about a mile, Banks and Cook were greeted by another crowd of people, led by a dignified, bearded, middle-aged man with frizzled black hair. This was Tepau (more formally known as Tepau-i-ahura'i), the chief of Fa'a'a, a district on the north-west end of the island, who like Tutaha was a senior *'arioi*. Although Tepau was

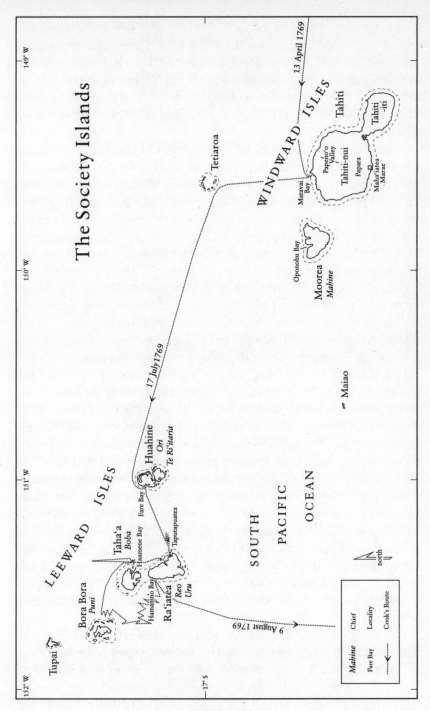

The Society Islands

Purea's eldest brother and the *ari'i* of her lineage, during the recent war he had sided with Tutaha and his wife's sister Vave'a against his sister Purea and her husband's people. Like Tutaha, Tepau had good reason to be worried about the *Endeavour*'s arrival; and he presented Banks, Cook and each of their companions with a green bough and seemed overjoyed when they put their hands on their chests and said '*Taio*,' accepting his offer of friendship.

After these exchanges, Tepau led his guests to a place where a feast of raw fish and breadfruit had been prepared, and his wife Tomio sat beside Banks, feeding him with fish and coconut milk. Disappointed by his companion, whom he considered old and ugly, Banks beckoned to 'a very pretty girl with a fire in her eyes that I had not before seen in the countrey',[6] inviting her to sit beside him. Ignoring Tepau's wife, he showered the girl with beads and other gifts, deeply offending the older woman. While he was thus diverted, Dr Solander and Dr Monkhouse had their pockets picked, Solander losing an opera glass and Monkhouse a snuffbox. As soon as Banks realised what had happened, he stood up and struck the butt of his gun on the ground, making a loud rattling noise. As the onlookers fled in alarm, Tepau picked up objects and hurled these in a fury at his people as they fled, scattering 'like sheep' in all directions.

Disconcerted by this theft, Tepau tried to console Solander and Monkhouse with gifts of rolls of bark cloth, but when Banks insisted that they wanted the stolen objects returned, he went off to find them. Half an hour later he came back, beaming and bearing the snuffbox and the opera glass case, but when the case was opened it proved to be empty. Determined to recover their stolen property, Tepau took Banks by the hand and they walked rapidly for about a mile until they reached a house where a high-born woman was sitting. Tepau gave this woman some cloth, Banks presented her with beads at Tepau's instruction and she went off, returning about half an hour later with the opera glass and the beads in her hands, which she handed over to Tepau. Delighted to have retrieved the stolen objects, Tepau brought these back to their companions. When he insisted that Dr Solander should still accept the bark cloth as compensation for the theft, Banks dubbed him 'Lycurgus' as a token of his sense of justice.

Like Bougainville and Commerson, as he walked about this island with its mountains, grassy plains, tall, stately men draped in flowing bark cloth and glorious, bare-breasted women, Banks was irresistibly reminded of images from Greek and Roman antiquity. In eighteenth-century Europe, every educated person was drilled in the classics (although Banks had been a reluctant classical scholar); and European art and literature were riddled with references to Greek and Roman mythology. Almost as soon as he stepped ashore, Banks labelled Tahiti 'Arcadia' after the mountainous home of the Greek god Pan, and he named various Tahitian chiefs 'Nestor' (after the wise but boastful old Greek warrior); 'Hercules' (the greatest of heroes, renowned for his strength and courage); 'Lycurgus' (a statesman and orator); 'Epicurus' (the famous devotee of pleasure); 'Mentor' (Odysseus's friend and wise advisor to his son); 'Solon' (the Athenian poet and statesman); and 'Ajax' (another famous warrior). It was as though he had stepped back into a mythical time where love was free and he walked like a king – a vision so alluring that it was largely undisturbed by subsequent experience. Cook, on the other hand, the matter-of-fact, self-educated Yorkshireman, was largely unmoved by such fantasies; and he was determined to maintain discipline and keep his men under control during this visit to the island.

Early the next morning, 15 April, Captain Cook went ashore with Banks, Solander and Parkinson, escorted by armed sailors and marines, at the eastern end of Matavai Bay, where he planned to set up a fort to protect the observatory. A crowd of unarmed spectators began to gather; and in order to keep these people back, Banks drew a line in the black sand with the butt of his musket, ordering the islanders not to cross it. After walking along the beach, they fixed on Te Auroa, which they named 'Point Venus' in honour of the Transit of Venus, as the best site for a fortified camp. Today at Point Venus, a tall, white, brick-edged lighthouse towers over the peninsula, and groves of coconuts and casuarina trees shade the mouth of the Tuauru River, where no traces survive of Cook's visit. When a local chief arrived, escorted by Fa'a, Cook tried to tell them about his plans to build a fort on the point and they seemed contented with his explanation. The sailors pitched Banks's tent while Hicks and Green joined Cook and Banks, walking into the woods with the rest of the Royal Society party to look for pigs and leaving Jonathan Monkhouse (a midshipman and the surgeon's brother) in charge of the little encampment. When they reached the banks of the Tuauru River, Banks killed three ducks with one shot, terrifying his Tahitian companions so much that they all fell flat on their faces.

Soon afterwards, Cook heard a rattle of musket shots from Point Venus. Gathering his party in alarm, he rushed back to the tent, where Monkhouse reported that after performing some comic tricks to distract the sentry, an islander had shoved the man and stolen his musket. When the midshipman ordered the marines to fire, they shot into the crowd, wounding two people before chasing the thief and shooting him dead, although they could not find the musket that he had taken. As Parkinson remarked, the marines had obeyed the order to fire 'with the greatest glee imaginable, as if they had been shooting at wild ducks'. Upon hearing this report, Banks exclaimed in horror: 'If we quarrelled with those Indians, we should not agree with angels!'[7] He immediately crossed the river with Fa'a to talk with the Tahitians, and managed to persuade about twenty of these people to return with him.

Before they would cross the river, however, the islanders picked up plantain branches and put their hands on their chests, calling out '*Taio*'. When they reached Point Venus they sat down with Cook and his companions, and finding them friendly, sent for coconuts and drank coconut milk with them, laughing and joking. The theft of the sentry's musket was a marvellous coup – for Tu's people, supposing that the British were their enemies, regarded them as fair game. According to Tahitian custom, however, it was proper to kill a thief who had been caught in the act, and these men were matter-of-fact about the shootings. The Earl of Morton had urged Cook to avoid such incidents, instructing him 'To check the petulance of the Sailors, and restrain the wanton use of Fire Arms'; and Banks, who thought that the young officer had been overzealous, was amazed to find the islanders so unconcerned by the death of their companion. Cook ordered the sentry to be clapped in irons for neglect of duty, and when the tents were struck they returned to the ship. Alarmed about this breach of discipline, early the next morning Cook read out the Articles of War to the crew, with its sonorous roll call of punishments, and a sailor was given twelve lashes for disobeying orders. Afterwards the ship was warped into a new position so that its guns faced Port Venus. The Tahitians evidently understood this as the sign of an imminent attack, because Fa'a did not visit them that day and only a few islanders appeared on the beach, although they seemed quite friendly, supplying the sailors with fruit and coconuts.

Buchan, the young landscape artist, had been ill for several weeks, and during the previous day he had suffered another epileptic fit and now lay in his hammock in a coma. That night he died. Upset by his loss, Banks exclaimed in his journal:

> I sincerely regret him as an ingenious and good young man, but his Loss to me is irretrevable, my airy dreams of entertaining my freinds in England with the scenes that I am to see are vanishd. No account of the figures and dresses of men can be satisfactory unless illustrated with figures: had providence spar'd him a month longer what an advantage it would have been to my undertaking but I must submit.[8]

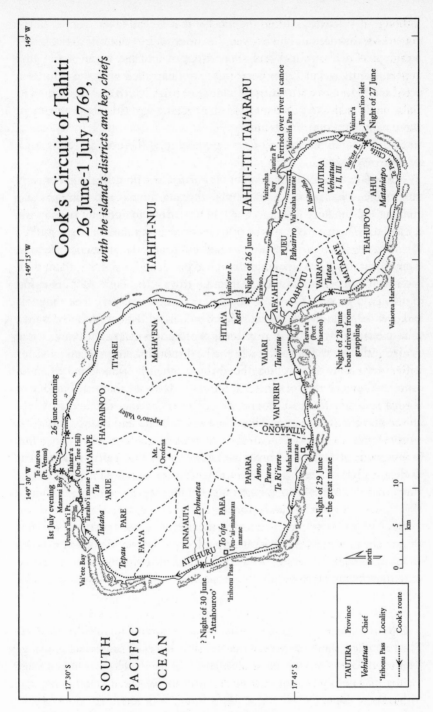

Cook's Circuit of Tahiti

Wary of offending the islanders, Banks advised Cook against burying Buchan ashore, and his corpse was taken out to sea where the burial
service was read, and his body was dropped into the ocean. Later that
morning, Tutaha and Tepau came out to the ship, each bringing a plantain
branch, a pig, roasted breadfruit, yams and fruit, which they presented to
Cook and Banks as a peace offering. During the day, the observatory tent
was pitched on Point Venus and equipped with astronomical instruments,
and Cook and Green stayed on shore that night to observe an eclipse of a
satellite of Jupiter.

The following day, fresh breezes blew across the point as the sailors and
the marines laboured on 'Fort Venus', digging ditches and ramparts and
erecting the timber palisades. The site was protected on one side by the
sea and the Tuauru River on the other, with an islet standing in the middle
of the river. The local people worked alongside the strangers, helping
them to cut down the trees and dig the ground, and supplying them with
breadfruit, coconuts and fruit. Although it was the height of the Season
of Plenty, pigs were scarce, probably because so many of these animals
had been killed in the recent fighting. Cook asked Banks and Dr Solander
to take charge of the trade with local people, and that night Banks came
ashore and slept in the fort. Early the next morning when Tepau and his
wife Tomio came to visit him, they brought their household goods and a
canoe shelter as a temporary house. As soon as he realised that Banks was
the highest-ranking man among the strangers, Tepau decided to adopt
him as his *taio*; and dressing Banks in a fine mat and a red bark-cloth robe
– the costume of a black leg *'arioi* – he gave him a meal of pork and *poipoi*
(a dish made of fermented breadfruit mixed with coconut milk) and went
to sleep in Banks's tent. Later that day, Tepau's son, a handsome young
man of about twenty-two, joined them for supper.

That evening Green and Monkhouse, the surgeon, walked into the
woods where they found the body of the man whom the marines had shot
several days earlier lying on a raised platform. The bier was sheltered by a
thatched roof, and weapons, a hatchet, some hair and a coconut with some
water had been placed beside the corpse. Fortunately they were repelled
by the stench and did not approach the body, which was virulently *ra'a*
or sacred.

Over the next few days, a small village sprang up inside the fort.
This included Banks's three tents housing himself, Solander, Spöring,
Parkinson, Green and his two servants; a tent for the officers and another
for the marines and sailors on shore duty; the observatory; a cook tent
with a large copper oven and a ship's forge; with a tent for the coopers
and sail makers outside the fortifications. Tepau and the other Tahitians

A Burial Platform

who visited the fort were fascinated by this encampment. Tepau began to imitate the strangers, learning to eat with a knife and fork, and gazing in admiration at Sydney Parkinson's pencil sketches of his fellow Tahitians (although none of the finished portraits appears to have survived), naming each person as he looked at their image. At the same time, Banks and his entourage were investigating Tahitian life, collecting words for a Tahitian vocabulary and a variety of artefacts, while Parkinson drew many of these objects in his sketchbooks – breastplates or *taumi* decorated with pearl shell and dog's hair, weapons, paddles, slings, tattooing instruments, bark-cloth beaters, tools, fish-hooks, baskets, stools, musical instruments, the fly whisks with carved handles that the Tahitians used to keep away the island's swarming flies.[9] When a young girl showed Parkinson how to dye red bark cloth, the artist sketched the neat baskets in which she kept the leaves and other ingredients she used to make different colours.

On 21 April, Cook went to inspect the funeral bier (or *fare tupapa'u*) that Green and Monkhouse had discovered, approaching the corpse so closely that his Tahitian companions shrank back in horror. Concluding that the islanders must believe in an afterlife given they provided the dead man with food, drink and tools, Cook added wryly, 'if it is a Religious ceremoney we may not be able to understand it, for the Misteries of most Religions are very dark and not easily understud even by those who profess them'.[10] At the same time, the Tahitians must have been wondering about the British, and whether they were gods or people. After killing this man in a mysterious fashion, the strangers kept returning to his corpse, where the spirit of the dead man still lingered. At a funeral bier, the realm of the gods entered the world of everyday life, and the site was so *ra'a* or sacred that any islander who had approached it without following the proper rituals would have dropped dead or been stricken with some foul disease; yet the British seemed to go there with impunity. It was at once ghoulish, and puzzling.

Early the next morning Tutaha arrived at the fort with a gift of two pigs, accompanied by a party of eight *'arioi* who played flutes and sang to entertain the strangers. Tepau soon followed, bringing two large fish as a gift for his *taio*. As Sydney Parkinson sat sketching trees, people and fish, the flies swarmed onto the paper and ate the paint, wrecking his drawings, until a mosquito net was hung over the table where he was sitting. Even then, they had to put a fly trap beneath the mosquito net to kill the flies that managed to get under the netting. Tutaha had brought an axe which he asked the blacksmith to repair, and when Banks, Solander and the officers examined it, they discovered that it was of French manufacture. Although Banks insisted that the axe must be from the *Dolphin*, whose trade goods had been purchased from old iron shops in London where the stock was sourced from all over Europe, the others argued that a French ship must have visited the island since the *Dolphin*'s departure. They were right, because Tutaha must have obtained this axe from Bougainville when they became *taio* at Hitia'a. Later that day, six swivel guns were mounted at the fort, and the family of fishermen who lived on the point abandoned their houses. Soon afterwards the old man Fa'a (who must have been a priest) arrived at Point Venus and prophesied that in four days' time the *Endeavour* would fire its guns upon his people.

Despite these tensions, Cook thought it safe for his men to go ashore, and on 23 April he gave them liberty under certain conditions. While they were at Tahiti they would not be provided with shipboard provisions, but must eat local foodstuffs. They were forbidden to go beyond One Tree Hill or commit any violent act, and any man who breached these instructions would be confined to the ship for the rest of their visit. As soon as the sailors were out of sight, however, they began to live out their shipboard fantasies. As Wilkinson (a master's mate and a former *Dolphin*) noted with pleasure: 'We find the woman of this Island to be very Kind in all Respects as Usal when we were here on the *Dolphin*';[11] and Molyneux (a mate and another *Dolphin*) added laconically: 'Every man has his Tayo (or Freind) ... but the women begin to have a share in our Freindship which is by no means Platonick.'[12] Iron and other European goods must have featured in these exchanges, and unable to prevent them, Cook and his officers turned a blind eye. During his visit ashore, Molyneux looked for 'the Queen' and his other former friends, but found only three people whom he remembered, an old man and his son and a young woman – who could tell him nothing about Purea.

Over the next few days, Joseph Banks and other members of the Royal Society party began to explore the area beyond Point Venus. With the astronomer Charles Green, Banks was the first to leave the fort, climbing about three miles into the hills, accompanied by Tepau, who complained bitterly that the steep ascent would kill him. On their way back to the fort, Banks examined the funeral bier of the man who had been shot, lifting up the bark cloth wrapped around the corpse – a breach of the death *tapu* (sacred restriction) that terrified his companions. The following day Banks and Dr Solander walked eastward across a fertile plain to a steep hill by the ocean. Clambering around its slopes, they came to another plain with large houses and wealthy-looking people where the Papeno'o River ran out of a deep, beautiful valley. When they returned to Matavai Bay that night, Tepau was so relieved that Banks had returned safely from this perilous expedition that he and his family wept as they greeted him.

Yet, despite Tepau's kindness, Banks did not trust his *taio*. On 25 April Solander lent his knife to one of Tepau's kinswomen, who forgot to return it, and the next morning when Banks found that his knife was also missing, he flew into a rage and accused Tepau of the theft, although the chief was adamant that he knew nothing about it. When an islander produced a rag in which three knives were wrapped, one of which proved to be Solander's, Tepau seized it and stalked off to the doctor's tent before restoring the other two knives to their owners. In a fury the chief began to search everywhere for Banks's knife, until one of the young botanist's servants, who had tidied it away the previous day, realised what he was doing and handed the knife to his master. Gazing at Banks reproachfully Tepau burst into tears, indicating by signs that if he ever stole from his *taio*, Banks could cut his throat, who hastened to present him with gifts as reparation. He had insulted the chief without just cause, as no *taio* would steal from his friend, and that night he wrote in his journal: 'His behavior has . . . given me an opinion of him much superior to any of his countreymen.'[13]

Two days later Tepau dined with Banks, bringing with him a companion whom Banks named 'Epicurus' in honour of the enormous meal that he ate on this occasion. Although Banks entertained himself by giving such nicknames to the islanders (which apart from the classical names included such delightful epithets as 'Sniggle-mouthed Jack', 'Square Kate', 'Mrs

Yellow Face' and 'Fine Wild woman'),[14] he was beginning to learn their proper names, despite the linguistic difficulties on both sides. Banks wrote Tepau's full name as 'Tubourai tamaide' (Tupuro'a-i-Tamaiti?), for instance, while the Tahitians called him 'Topane' (Tepane); Dr Solander was called 'Tolano' and Jonathan Monkhouse 'Mate' (death), because he was in command when an islander had been shot; while Captain Cook was known as 'Tute'. Although these names were not very accurate, at least they were getting to know each other as individuals. Banks also learned that the island was called 'Otaheite' (Tahiti), and from that time on, he and Cook referred to it by its proper name. After dinner that evening, Tepau farewelled his friend, but soon returned in a fury. Taking Banks by the arm, he led him to a place where Henry Jeffs, the ship's butcher, was standing, indicating by signs that this man had gone into his house where he took a fancy to a stone axe, offered his wife Tomio a nail and demanded that she hand it over. When she refused, Jeffs had seized the axe and, throwing down the nail, brandished a reap hook and threatened to cut her throat if she protested. Jeffs had little to say in defence of his actions, and Banks promised Tepau that the butcher would be punished the next day on board the *Endeavour*.

Very early the next morning, 28 April, another of Tepau's wives (for in Tahiti most chiefs had several wives) stood outside the gate of the fort, weeping bitterly and slashing her head with a shark's tooth. As the blood poured over her face, this woman spoke in a loud, melancholy tone, mopping up the blood with a piece of bark cloth before throwing it into the sea, a gesture demanding vengeance for the insult to Tomio and her family. Shocked to see her so upset, Banks took her in his arms and tried to comfort her while the other Tahitians in the tent ignored them, chatting and laughing. Among them was a 'fat, bouncing, good-looking dame'[15] who had just arrived with several companions and a large quantity of bark cloth. As soon as Robert Molyneux, the ship's master and a former *Dolphin*, entered the tent, he recognised this woman, telling his companions with great excitement that this was the *Dolphin*'s 'Queen Oberea', while Purea also recognised Molyneux, greeting him with joy. Gazing at this famous personage, about whom he had heard so much in Europe, Banks described her as about forty years old, 'tall and very lusty, her skin white and her eyes full of meaning, she might have been hansome when young but now few or no traces of it were left'.[16] It was no wonder that Purea was unmoved about the insult to Tepau and his family, however, because her elder brother had sided against her in the recent war, and they were at loggerheads.

On this occasion Purea was accompanied by Tupaia, and when

Molyneux took them out to the *Endeavour*, Lieutenant Gore immediately recognised the high priest-navigator. Captain Cook welcomed them both to the Great Cabin, where he gave Purea a number of presents, including a doll that he whimsically told her was an image of his wife in England. Purea stayed on board the *Endeavour* for several hours, exploring the ship and confiding to Molyneux that after the *Dolphin*'s visit she and her husband Amo had been attacked and dispossessed of all their lands. When Purea came ashore again, Tutaha had just arrived at Matavai Bay, and as she passed him Purea triumphantly brandished the doll in her enemy's direction. After the defeat of her people and the devastation of their district, Purea must have been elated at that moment. Uneasy to see her and Cook on terms of warm friendship, Tutaha became agitated, calming down only when Cook also took him on board and gave him gifts including a doll of his own, which he probably took to be some kind of *ti'i* or ancestor figure from England. Shortly afterwards Purea and her entourage left Matavai Bay and returned to the east coast of the island, where she was staying.

Distracted by Purea's visit, Banks forgot to ask Captain Cook to punish Jeffs for his conduct towards Tepau's wife, although Tomio reminded him of his promise on several occasions. Early the next morning, he escorted Tepau and his wife out to the ship and told Cook about what had happened. Determined to uphold his rules for dealing with the islanders, Cook ordered Jeffs to be punished, explaining his crime to the crew 'in the most lively manner, and ma[king] a very Pathetick speech to the Ship's Company'.[17] While the ship's butcher was being stripped and tied to the rigging, Tepau and his family watched quietly, but as soon as the flogging began, Tomio began to weep and cry out, and pleaded with Cook to stop this brutal punishment. Although in wartime in Tahiti, and when thieves were caught in the act, people were harshly treated, there was no precedent for flogging. Cook did not relent, however, and Jeffs received his full sentence of twelve lashes with the cat-o'-nine-tails.

Later that morning a fleet of about thirty double canoes sailed into Matavai Bay, where they landed several hundred people. Uncertain about their intentions, Cook ordered two more guns mounted on the deck of the *Endeavour*, and another two at Fort Venus. When he made enquiries, Banks was informed that these canoes had brought Purea back to Matavai Bay, and that the 'Queen' was still asleep in her canoe shelter. To his surprise, when Banks went to visit her, he found Purea lying naked in the arms of Pati, a young man about twenty-five years old. Unabashed, she put on her loincloth, and dressing Banks in fine bark-cloth garments escorted him to the fort, accompanied by her favourite attendant, Teatea, a beautiful young *'arioi* who was a niece of Amo's. It is likely that about this time, Banks began his affair with Teatea (whom he described as 'a fine Grecian girl' and 'my flame').[18] These signs of renewed friendship with the British delighted Purea, but deeply concerned her enemies Tutaha and Tepau; and that evening when Banks went to visit Tepau, he found him and his family in a melancholy mood. Banks was mystified until one of the officers reminded him that, four days earlier, Fa'a had prophesied that in four days' time the *Endeavour* would fire on the islanders. That night Cook ordered the watch to be doubled on board the *Endeavour* and the men slept with their weapons beside them.

Early the next morning, 30 April, Purea came out to the ship with a pig which she exchanged for a hatchet. When Banks went ashore, Tomio came running into the tent to tell him that Tepau was dying. Seizing him by the hand and insisting that her husband had been poisoned by some food that a sailor had given him, she led him to their house where Tepau was lying against a post, vomiting violently. After examining a remaining scrap of this 'food' that had been wrapped in a leaf, Banks realised that the chief had swallowed a wad of chewing tobacco and told Tomio to give him coconut milk to drink, which quickly cured him. Reassured by this act of kindness, Tutaha visited the ship the next morning, entering the Great Cabin where he poked into every chest and drawer. Cook humoured the great chief, and when Tutaha noticed an iron replica of a Tahitian adze made in England and begged for it, he readily handed it over. During this visit, Tutaha was accompanied by a man who was so sacred that he had to be fed by hand. He was either a priest, or a chief who was under a temporary restriction because a relative had died, or the *tapu* of birth had not yet been lifted from his eldest child by the *amo'a* rituals; but on this occasion there was no woman to feed him. At dinner this man sat stolidly at the table, not touching his food, until one of Banks's servants took pity on him and fed him by hand.

That afternoon the observatory tent was erected inside Fort Venus and the astronomical quadrant and other instruments were taken ashore for the first time. There were now forty-five armed Europeans living in the fort, including the officers and gentlemen; and with its sentries, ramparts, palisades and guns, Cook considered Fort Venus impregnable. Early the next morning, however, when he and Charles Green came ashore to set up the astronomical quadrant, they were horrified to find that it was missing. This vital piece of equipment had been landed in a small packing case and stored in Cook's empty tent overnight, with an armed sentry on guard. While the Tahitians regarded the theft of this sacred object from

Fort Venus

the British as a brilliant coup, Cook was aghast, because he and Green had sailed around the world to observe the Transit of Venus, and without the quadrant their mission would be futile. After offering a large reward for its return he had the fort searched; but there was still no sign of the missing instrument.

While the fort was being searched, Banks ran off in pursuit of the thief, crossing the Tuauru River. On the opposite bank he met Tepau who made a sign using three straws in his hand, indicating that his countrymen had opened the box and examined the quadrant. Telling Banks that the instrument had been carried off to the east, Tepau joined him, Green and a midshipman as they chased after the thief. At every house that they passed, Tepau asked for news and received encouraging replies. It was extremely hot, however, and after they had run and walked for about four miles, Tepau pointed to a promontory another three miles off, saying that the quadrant had been taken to that place. Taking stock of their situation, Banks realised that they were on their own and unarmed except for his pair of pocket pistols, but after sending the midshipman back to fetch Cook and some armed men, he and Green proceeded in pursuit of the precious instrument.

When they arrived at the point, they found one of Tepau's people holding up a part of the quadrant. A crowd of islanders gathered round, and as they began to jostle 'rather rudely', Banks drew a circle in the sand and, brandishing his pistols, indicated that they must not cross this line. Impressed by his aplomb, the islanders drew back and before long the quadrant case was produced, along with a horse pistol and some reading glasses which were handed over to Banks, together with several other pieces of the quadrant. When Green examined these items he found that some small pieces of the instrument were still missing, and Tepau sent people off to find them. When all of the parts of the quadrant had been recovered, except for its stand which Tepau promised to retrieve, Banks and his companions packed up the stolen items in the case and began to walk back towards Fort Venus.

By this time the midshipman had arrived back at the fort and reported that Banks's party had become isolated. Cook ordered his officers to detain the chiefs and the double canoes if they tried to leave the bay, and after mustering the marines, chased after Banks and his companions. At sunset about four miles from the fort, the two parties finally met each other and hastened back to Point Venus.

At 8 p.m. when they reached the encampment, they found that Tutaha had been captured and was being held inside the fort, which was surrounded by a large, agitated crowd. That afternoon when Tutaha and the other chiefs noticed Cook and his marines running into the woods, they had panicked and tried to flee the bay in their canoes. Obedient to Cook's orders, Gore, the third lieutenant who was left in charge of the *Endeavour*, despatched a boat to chase the canoes. Some of these craft escaped, but when the boat intercepted a double canoe carrying Tutaha and his party, they jumped overboard and began to swim ashore. Determined not to let the chief escape, the boatswain leaned over and grabbed Tutaha by the hair, hauling him into the boat. A chief's hair and head were imbued with the *mana* or sacred power of his ancestors, however, and this was a terrible insult. Tutaha had been taken to the fort, weeping with terror and convinced that he was about to be killed, where Second Lieutenant Hicks detained him. When Cook and Banks arrived at Fort Venus, Tepau and all their people wept over Tutaha, aghast at the insult to this great leader. Tutaha sent for two pigs as a peace offering which he presented to Cook, but it was not until he had left the fort and was surrounded by his people that he stopped crying.

Tutaha was from the Pare-'Arue district, however, not Ha'apape, the district around Matavai Bay (which his warriors had devastated); and the local people were not sorry to see him humiliated. When Parkinson went ashore that afternoon he walked through the woods, stunned by the noise that the cicadas were making. Arriving at a clearing, he saw people bringing large baskets of breadfruit to a long house, piling them up and redistributing the fruit to a crowd that had assembled. At the height of the Season of Plenty, an entire district sometimes gathered to bake their breadfruit in one huge communal oven; and this must have been one of those occasions.[19] Although pigs and chickens were scarce, the 'arioi usually gathered at this time for the autumn harvest festival, when the celebrations were particularly brilliant, with feasts, foot and canoe races, and contests with spear and javelin.[20] Unmoved by Tutaha's plight, the Matavai people were carrying on with their preparations.

Back on board that night, Cook, Banks and the officers tried to work out how the Tahitian had managed to steal the quadrant. During the previous evening at sunset they had seen a man crawling along the river-bank behind Fort Venus, who ran away as soon as he was challenged. Immediately afterwards Cook had walked around the fort, ordering the drummer to beat the tattoo three times to summon the sailors and marines, but as soon as Cook's back was turned the man must have crawled into the tent and taken the packing case. Although he was astonished at the thief's audacity, Cook was overjoyed to have recovered this vital piece of equipment. Fortunately, Banks had brought a set of watchmaker's instruments with him on board the *Endeavour*, and Solander's clerk Hermann Spöring, who had trained as a watchmaker, spent the evening working on the astronomical quadrant, restoring it to good working order.

Tutaha, who had not been involved in the theft of the instrument, was enraged by the way that he had been treated. Early the next morning he sent a messenger demanding an axe and a shirt in return for the two pigs he had given to Cook, and the release of his double canoe, which the British had impounded. This messenger told Cook that Tutaha was determined to stay away from him and his people for at least ten more days; and no provisions were traded that day and very few Tahitians appeared in Matavai Bay, although one woman came out to the ship with her child whom she said had been fathered by one of the men from the *Dolphin*. Cook's men had also seized Purea's double canoe, but she and her allies must have been thrilled by the ignominious way in which Tutaha had been handled; and when Tupaia (whom Banks described as at least forty-five years old and 'Oberea's right hand man who was with her in the *Dolphin's* time')[21] came to collect Purea's canoe that afternoon, he stayed with the British until dusk, spending the night in the canoe with Pupu, his 'dolly' (as Banks called her).

The following day, 4 May, a number of people from Mo'orea arrived at Fort Venus, who dictated the names of twenty-two islands lying in the seas around Tahiti to Captain Cook. Later that day, Cook and Green set up the two astronomical clocks, one in Cook's tent under a double guard and the other in the observatory. No breadfruit or other provisions were brought out to the ship or the fort that day, as Tepau and his people continued to reproach the British for the way that Tutaha had been treated. Nevertheless, Banks managed to persuade Tepau to give him five long baskets of breadfruit from the recent distribution, each holding more than twenty breadfruit. Worried about the way that the supplies of fresh food were drying up, Cook instructed Tutaha's messenger, who arrived again to demand the axe and the shirt, to tell the chief that he and Banks would visit him the next day, bringing these items.

Early the next morning, Tutaha sent more envoys out to the ship, who seemed extremely uneasy until Cook, Banks and Solander boarded the pinnace. When Cook and his companions arrived at Point 'Utuha'iha'i they found the harvest festivities in full swing.[22] As they were greeted by a huge crowd who crowded around them, a tall, fine-looking man in a white bark-cloth turban struck these people with a long white stick and threw stones to clear a pathway so that Cook and his party could come ashore. As this man led them to meet Tutaha, the crowd chanted *'Tutaha taio!'* ('Tutaha is your friend!'). They found Tutaha sitting under a large tree, surrounded by a group of elders who gazed at them gravely. When Tutaha invited Cook and his companions to sit beside him, asking for the axe and the shirt, Cook presented him with the shirt and a broadcloth poncho, made in Tahitian style and trimmed with tape, which Tutaha immediately donned, giving the shirt to one of his companions.

Soon afterwards, however, Purea and several of her women companions came to sit beside Cook and Banks, and Banks accompanied her to a nearby house to get out of the sun. This infuriated Tutaha, who stalked off in a rage, sending a messenger to tell Cook and Banks to join him at the pinnace. They found Tutaha sitting under an awning and joined him there for a while, tasting the breadfruit and coconuts that he had brought before accompanying him to a courtyard beside the *'arioi* house, fenced with low bamboo rails, where a wrestling match was under way. When Tutaha went to sit at one end of the arena, which was filled with at least 500 spectators, he invited Cook, Banks and their party to join him.

Although the spectators at this match were almost all men, Purea soon made her appearance in the arena. Cook and his companions decided not to sit with Tutaha but walked about with Purea instead, watching in fascination as groups of wrestlers entered the arena, stooping with their bodies curved and their left arms close to their sides, and striking their left chests and forearms hard with their right hands, making loud, explosive noises. When a man challenged an opponent, he linked the fingers of his two hands in front of his chest and moved his elbows up and down, flapping them like wings (evoking the feathered god Ta'aroa and his power), until his opponent returned the signal. The protagonists tried to grab each other by the thighs, loincloth or hair until one of them was thrown on his back, while the old men in the 'arioi house chanted and performed a dance for the victor. Tutaha had ordered a feast of two roasted pigs, some breadfruit and coconuts for his guests, but because Purea was still in close attendance upon Cook and his companions he ordered his people to carry one of the roasted pigs to the boat and escorted his guests to the beach, leaving Purea behind. Cook and Banks were famished by this time, and as they rowed out to the ship the delicious aroma of roasted pork tantalised them throughout their four-mile journey. On board the *Endeavour* they dined heartily, and Cook gave Tutaha more presents.

Now that Tutaha and the British had made an uneasy peace, the Pare-'Arue people once again brought abundant breadfruit and coconuts out to the *Endeavour*. The following day, 6 May, Tutaha visited Fort Venus with a gift of five long baskets of breadfruit and some coconuts; and the next day he arrived with four roasted pigs, sending one on board as a gift with some breadfruit and bartering another for a broadaxe, before leaving for the east side of the island. After his departure, however, it was once again very difficult to get fresh food, the local people insisting that all of the food supplies in the district and to the east belonged to Tutaha, and could be bartered only with his permission. In the Society Islands it was customary for visiting parties to bring provisions with them, and although they were lavishly feasted on the first few days of their visit, they ate their own food thereafter. Contrary to this custom, this party of strangers seemed determined to rely upon local supplies, which were being rapidly depleted; and their insulting behaviour towards Tutaha still rankled. To make matters worse, the Season of Scarcity (which formally began on 20 May, when the Matari'i or Pleiades sank below the horizon) was only a few weeks away, and would be marked with more rituals and feasting. Determined not to run out of food at this crucial time, it seems that Tutaha had imposed a *rahui* (or ritual restriction) on the district.

The Transit of Venus

In the Royal Navy, it was notorious that commanders found it much easier to keep their men under control when a ship was at sea and the sailors were working. When they went ashore, the sailors invariably got into trouble – they drank, brawled, broke the law and slept with local women. Aware of these dangers, Cook was determined to maintain discipline during his visit to Tahiti; and in particular, he wanted to prevent his men from infecting the islanders with venereal diseases (also known as 'Cupid's itch' or 'the curse of Venus' during the eighteenth century).[1] These disorders included gonorrhea and the pox (or syphilis), a hideous disease that progressed to skin eruptions and, in the later stages, agonising pains and rotting skin, muscle, lips, noses and inner organs. Before they landed at Tahiti, Cook had ordered William Monkhouse to examine the sailors for these diseases; and after the surgeon assured him that only one of the crew was infected, this man was kept out of contact with the island women. According to the *Endeavour*'s muster roll, however, at least seven of the sailors were treated for venereal diseases during the month before they reached the island; and in fact, any man who had contracted syphilis and many of those who had caught gonorrhea during their visits to Rio de Janeiro and Tierra del Fuego must still have been infectious, despite being asymptomatic by the time of Monkhouse's examination.[2]

In early May when some of the sailors began to show the symptoms of venereal diseases, Cook was bitterly disappointed. He tried to contain the outbreak by forbidding the infected men to sleep with Tahitian women. The crew were stubbornly uncooperative, however, as were the officers and members of the Royal Society party, most of whom had lovers on shore (listed in Solander's notebook as Aururu or 'Mrs Toaro' (Gore); Tiare or 'Mrs Boba' (Molyneux); Teatea Hautia, 'Mrs Tate' (Clerke); and Tuarua, 'Mrs Eteree' (Green)). Joseph Banks had his beautiful 'flame'

Teatea; and even the prim young Quaker artist Sydney Parkinson had a girlfriend, Piari'i or 'Mrs Patini'.[3] As Cook noted in frustration:

> I have reason (notwithstanding the improbability of the thing) to think that we had brought [venereal disease] along with us which gave me no small uneasiness and did all in my power to prevent its progress, but all I could do was to little purpose for I may safely say that I was not assisted by any one person in ye Ship, and was oblige'd to have the most part of the Ships Compney a Shore every day to work upon the Fort and a Strong guard every night and the Women were so very liberal with their favours, or else Nails, Shirts &c were temptations that they could not withstand, that this distemper very soon spread it self over the greater part of the Ships Compney.[4]

The Tahitians found Captain Cook's attempts to urge chastity upon his companions incomprehensible, however. They saw no link between sexual intercourse and the new diseases, which they believed were caused by the anger of the gods, particularly the gods of the British. Far from

The Quaker artist Sydney Parkinson

avoiding Cook's shipmates, it made sense for them to ally themselves with these powerful strangers, and to do this they forged *taio* relationships with the British, creating bonds between their lineages and families and those of their visitors. These relationships invariably included sexual exchanges; for instance, the *taio* friendship between Tepau and his wife Tomio and Joseph Banks included Tomio's sisters, two of whom became 'Mrs Green' and 'Mrs Parkinson'.[5] As Dr Solander reported with ribald glee, on one occasion when Banks entered his tent with Tomio, 'the first thing he saw was Shyboots Parkinson in bed with the girl's sister'.[6]

Cook was thus greatly relieved when Tepau assured him that his men had not been responsible for introducing these diseases to the island. According to the chief, these disorders were brought by two 'Spanish' ships which had visited Tahiti some ten months earlier. These ships, commanded by 'Toottera' (Duclos, the captain of the *Boudeuse*), had anchored in a bay on the east coast called 'Ohidea' (O Hitia'a) whose chief was 'Orette' (Reti).[7] During their visit, the crews had purchased quantities of pigs and chickens, and had been kind to the islanders, killing only one man who had stolen from them. There was a woman on board one of these ships, the first European woman that the islanders had seen; and when the strangers sailed to the westward, promising to return nine months later,[8] one of the islanders volunteered to go with them.[9] They had left these diseases (or '*mate*') behind them, and among those who were first infected, hair and nails dropped out, flesh rotted from their bones (symptoms of syphilis), and they died in miserable isolation. Later, however, the priests had discovered a cure, or at least a treatment that left those infected with only mild symptoms.[10] When Banks showed the Tahitians the flags of various European nations and asked them to indicate the flag flown by these vessels, Tepau (who is unlikely to have visited Hitia'a at that time) pointed at the Spanish colours. He was mistaken, of course, because these stories referred to Bougainville's visit to Hitia'a, almost exactly a year earlier. It was polite of Tepau not to blame the British for bringing venereal diseases to the island, because as we have seen, the *Dolphin*'s crew were the first to infect local women (although from his account, it seems that the French introduced syphilis to the island).

If Cook's attempts to prevent the spread of venereal infections baffled the islanders, they also put him at odds with his men, who already resented his order forbidding the sentries to shoot islanders who were caught stealing. The shortage of pork was another cause of disaffection, because Cook, who was acting as the ship's purser, refused to make this up from the ship's supplies. On 5 May, Robert Molyneux, the *Endeavour*'s master, noted that 'this scarcity of Pork causes great murmurings which begun in a Quarter least expected & serves to shew that People may be Guilty of the Highest Ingratitude'.[11] Two days later he informed Cook that some of the sailors had been talking in a mutinous manner:

> I accquainted the Captain with some Mutinous words spoke by some of the People the Fact being prov'd the Captain was going to Proceed to Punish the delinquents, I interpos'd & a Pardon was granted on Promise of Better Behaviour for the future. I had many reasons for doing this as I well knew the Spring that cause'd these commotions.[12]

Mutiny was every captain's worst nightmare, and this was bad news for Cook. Molyneux made this report on a Sunday, when the *Endeavour*'s crew were off duty and idle. Tahiti was a seductive place, with its sandy beaches and coral reefs, plentiful fish and vegetable foods (at least at this time of year), and alluring, golden-skinned young women; and it is not surprising that the sailors were tempted to think of escaping the long voyage home and a life of poverty under the grey skies of England. When it became clear that his attempts to control sexual exchanges between his men and the Tahitians were futile, Captain Cook decided to ignore the matter. Obtaining a promise of good behaviour, he gave the offenders a chance to redeem themselves.

About this time, a new craze swept among the sailors, who began to trade for shells, fish-hooks and any other item of local manufacture, hoping to make a fortune by selling these 'curiosities' upon their return to England. Since Tutaha's arrest it had been difficult to purchase food on the island, and when Purea and Tupaia arrived back at Matavai Bay on 9 May, bringing large quantities of coconuts and breadfruit to barter, this was greatly appreciated. Purea brought a broken axe and several pieces of old iron from the *Dolphin*, which she asked the blacksmith to mend; and Tupaia told Banks that although the *Dolphin* had been the first ship to anchor at Tahiti, the local people had known about iron since a European ship had been stranded on a reef off a nearby island many years ago. Its crew had defended themselves bravely before being overwhelmed and slaughtered; and when a canoe from this island had arrived at Tahiti, bringing two dead bodies and some iron bolts from the ship, the crew were so warmly welcomed that they were still living on the island. Like the story of Bougainville's visit, this tale was a little garbled, combining as it did events from the wreck of the Dutch navigator Roggeveen's ship on Takapoto in the Tuamotu in 1722 with his fatal brush with the people of Makatea a month later. All the same, it is clear that by now some Tahitians were managing to convey quite complex information to the British, and individuals on both sides were beginning to learn each other's languages.

Over the next few days Cook ordered the sailors to make a small garden and plant some seeds that he had brought in sealed bottles from Mile End in London, while the carpenters caulked the *Endeavour*'s quarterdeck and the sailors mended the rigging. People from other districts were eager to see the strangers; and on 12 May a double canoe arrived at Point Venus with a man and two young women sitting under its awning. These were probably 'arioi arriving for the ceremonies that marked the sinking of the Pleiades (Matari'i) below the horizon on 20 May, when the Season of Scarcity (or Matari'i-i-raro) formally began. Banks went to meet these people on the beach, accompanied by Tupaia, who was acting as his ceremonial advisor. As the visitors landed, the islanders formed a lane, and the leading man from the canoe, who must have been a priest, laid down a dozen young plantain trees and other plants at its far end. Picking up each of the plantains in turn, he walked towards Banks and, handing a plantain to Tupaia, pronounced a short sentence and gave Banks a small bunch of parrot's feathers (or 'ura, used in Tahiti to summon the gods) – the *maro tai* offerings, made upon arriving at another island. After this man had laid down three lengths of bark cloth, one of the young women (whose name Banks later gave as 'Ourattoa' ('Ura-atua?')), wearing a large quantity of bark cloth wrapped around her, stepped on the bark-cloth runner.[13] According to the missionary Orsmond, a woman wrapped in this way (known as *tihi tomo*) could hardly move, and sometimes almost suffocated; and during such presentations women often fainted.[14] On this occasion, however, the young woman walked a short distance towards Banks, turning around twice and, slowly unwinding the cloth, let it fall gracefully to the ground. The man laid three more lengths of bark cloth upon the first and she repeated the performance, stepping on the bark cloth, turning herself around and unwinding more of the cloth from her body. Finally, when three more lengths of bark cloth were laid down, she stepped onto these and turned herself around, unwinding more bark cloth and letting it drop until she was nude, exposing 'her naked beauties'.[15]

After this presentation Tupaia rolled up all the bark cloth and gave it to Banks, whom the young woman embraced. Tantalised by the display, Banks took this girl by the hand and led her to the tent, followed by her female companion, trying to persuade them to stay with him. Although Banks could be forgiven for thinking that both the girl and the bark cloth were gifts,[16] in Tahiti wrapping a person or thing in bark cloth or fine mats was a way of at once acknowledging and containing their *mana* (ancestral power) – images of the gods were wrapped in layers of bark cloth, and on ceremonial occasions chiefly people were also wrapped in many layers of bark cloth or finely woven garments. On the other hand, unwrapping bark cloth from a person or thing released their *mana*, and when a woman was unwrapped in this way, this was a ceremonial act rather than a gesture of sexual enticement.[17] On this occasion the young woman would not yield to Banks's entreaties, and soon afterwards returned to her canoe. Fortunately for the young botanist, his ardour was not utterly frustrated, because Purea arrived soon afterwards with his sweetheart Teatea.

Early the next morning Banks went shooting in the woods, and afterwards went to visit Tepau. When they had been talking for a while, the chief grabbed the gun from Banks's hand, cocked it, and holding it up in the air, pulled the trigger, although fortunately it misfired. Banks, who had often warned Tepau not to touch his firearms, was furious, scolding the chief and threatening to shoot him. Tepau stood patiently under the onslaught, but as soon as Banks had crossed the river, the chief and his family abandoned the house they had built near the fort and moved back to Pare. When Banks was told about this, he and Molyneux hurried to Pare where they found Tepau and his people sitting in a melancholy huddle. Some of them were crying, and as the Europeans approached, an old woman slashed her head with a shark's tooth until the blood ran down over her face, in a gesture of mourning. When Banks assured Tepau that he was no longer angry, the chief agreed to return to Point Venus; and a double canoe was launched which took them back to the fort, where Tepau and Tomio spent that night in Banks's tent as a sign of reconciliation.

On 14 May, a Sunday, Cook decided that divine service should be celebrated. He rarely conducted prayers himself, probably because in his youth he had lived with Captain Walker, who like other Quakers did not hold with priests or religious rituals. A ship's tent was set up in Fort Venus as a temporary church, and Tutaha, Tepau and Tomio, and Purea, Pati and Teatea all attended the service, which was conducted by the ship's surgeon William Monkhouse.[18] During the ceremony, Banks sat between Tepau and Tomio who carefully imitated his movements, standing, sitting or kneeling to pray; and telling the other islanders in the fort to keep quiet. The Tahitians must have thought that this was a ritual in preparation for the setting of the Pleiades, and that Monkhouse was some kind of priest (for in Tahiti priests were often also healers), because later that day there was a curious sequel. A young man more than six feet tall lay at the gate of the fort where he made love to a girl about ten or twelve years old, urged on by Purea and several other women. Although the girl seemed reluctant and frightened, the women instructed her how to play her part, which as Cook observed, 'appear'd to be done more from Custom than Lewdness'.[19] As mentioned above, during the great seasonal festivals public sex by young *'arioi* was peformed to arouse the desire of the gods; and it seems that Purea (a leading *'arioi*) had staged this performance to entice the gods of the British. That night an islander stole an iron-bound cask full of water from outside the fort, right under the sentry's nose, showing that Hiro had made him invisible. Hiro was said to be a son of 'Oro, and spectacular thefts of this kind were associated with the *'arioi* cult. Some years later, the missionary Ellis quoted a chief as saying, 'We thought, when we were pagans, that it was right to steal when we could do it without being found out. Hiro, the god of thieves, used to assist us.'[20]

The next morning, 15 May, Tepau warned Banks that another cask was about to be stolen, and at sunset he and Tomio lay down beside the casks, but a sentry had been posted and Banks managed to persuade them to sleep in his tent. At midnight when the thief came back, the sentry fired his musket and he ran off into the darkness. The following day it pelted with rain, and a double rainbow rose over Fort Venus. According to the *'arioi* traditions, when 'Oro first came to earth he had arrived on a rainbow; and a double rainbow was a spectacular sign of the god's presence and power. That evening, Tepau accompanied by his wife Tomio and Purea with her attendants Pati and Teatea set aside their disagreements, sleeping together in Banks's tent; and when the thief returned once again to the fort, the sentry fired his musket, but the powder was damp and the gun misfired. The beginning of the Season of Scarcity (Matari'i-i-raro or Pleiades-below) was imminent, and on 18 May all of the chiefs except Tepau and Tomio left the bay in a flotilla of canoes for the ceremonies that marked this occasion. Later, other canoes arrived bringing large quantities of *vi* to barter, which the ship's cook made into apple pies for the sailors. The next day a canoe identical to the double canoes that Wallis's men had seen at Nukutaveke in the Tuamotu Islands landed in Matavai Bay with two large pigs, but its crew refused to trade these animals, saying that they were intended for Tutaha.[21]

During the visit of the Nukutaveke canoe, Tepau went into a tent in Fort Venus where he took seven large nails from a basket. When Banks's servant told him that Tepau was hiding a large nail under his clothing, Banks went to the chief's house and demanded an explanation. Tepau confessed and handed over the nail, although at first he told Banks that he had sent it to Pare. Banks was inclined to forgive his friend on this occasion, telling Tepau that if he returned the other nails the incident would be forgotten. In Tahiti, however, a *taio* had a right to his friend's property, and hoarding was regarded as greedy and selfish. Tepau had showered gifts on his friend and was entitled to share his property in return, but Banks did not understand this and regarded Tepau's action as stealing.

Baffled and insulted, that night Tepau and his family emptied their house and once again moved back to Pare.

The next day, 20 May, the Pleiades sank below the horizon, marking the formal beginning of the Season of Scarcity. The day after was a Sunday, and when Purea, Pati and Teatea arrived back at Fort Venus, William Monkhouse again conducted divine service. After dinner, Purea's lover Pati went for a walk, but when he returned and asked to be readmitted to the fort, Purea told the sentries to refuse him. When they ignored her and let him in, after looking at him disdainfully, Purea made advances to Banks instead, who remarked sardonically: 'Oborea . . . seems to act in the character of a Ninon d'Enclos [the dazzling mistress of an eighteenth-century Parisian salon] who satiated with her lover resolves to change him at all Events, the more so as I am offerd if I please to supply his place, but I am at present otherwise engag'd; indeed was I free as air her majesties person is not the most desireable.'[22] After his return to England, however, Banks told a different story about this encounter, reporting that after he and Purea had slept together, 'she dismissed him with evident Contempt, informing him that he was not to be compared with her own Men and requesting that for the future he would devote his attention to the Girls of his suite'.[23]

On 22 May there was a violent storm, with torrents of rain, thunder and lightning – another sign of 'Oro's power. The tents were soaked, and Cook was worried that the *Endeavour* would be wrecked on the reef. Over the past few days Tutaha had sent several messengers to ask Cook to visit him at Pare, promising that he would give him some pigs; and that afternoon, Cook despatched Lieutenant Hicks as his emissary. When Hicks arrived at Pare, however, he found that Tutaha had shifted to Fa'a'a, Tepau's district, and when he followed him there, Tutaha greeted him and gave him a pig, promising that if he stayed overnight more pigs would be brought. The pigs did not materialise, and Lieutenant Hicks returned to the ship without them.

On 25 May, Tepau and Tomio returned to Point Venus, looking apprehensive. Banks gave them the cold shoulder, unwilling to renew their friendship until Tepau returned the nails he had taken. William Monkhouse had also befriended Tepau, and much to Banks's annoyance the surgeon went to Tepau's house and invited him and Tomio into the fort. The chief made numerous excuses, however, saying that he was hungry, had a headache and must sleep, and he did not take up Monkhouse's invitation; and soon afterwards he and Tomio returned to Fa'a'a. Although Banks and Solander were able to obtain enough fish to feed the officers and the sick, pork was now extremely scarce, and the sailors were shooting duck,

Tahitian snipe and rats to augment their diet. As Molyneux observed: 'It is Easy to Kill 1000 [rats] in a day as the ground swarms & the Inhabitants never disturb them. I have laid in the woods several nights & among other particulars I observ'd the rats play'd about me as indifferent as about a Tree: in eating rats we quite outdid the Indians who Obhor them as Food.'[24]

The next day Monkhouse accompanied Tepau and Tomio to Pare. Because he had been conducting divine service, the Tahitians had decided that he was a priestly expert, naming him 'Matamata'u' or 'awesome person'.[25] Tepau took him to some 'arioi rituals, which were so sacred that intruders were struck down and killed;[26] and it was probably at this time that Monkhouse watched the erotic dancing that he later described to Cook, who wrote in his journal:

> [The] Arreoys have meetings among themselves where the men amuse them-selves with wristling &c and the women in dancing the indecent dance before mentioned, in the Course of which they give full liberty to their desires but I believe keep up the appearance of decency.
>
> I never saw one of those meetings. Dr. Munkhouse saw part of one enough to make him give credit to what we had been told.[27]

Although in everyday life the Tahitians were very modest, carefully concealing their genitals when washing and bathing, during their meetings young 'arioi danced naked, celebrating the potency of the ancestors. The islanders' everyday speech was also sexually graphic, and in his vocab-ulary Dr Solander collected many terms describing sexual exchanges.[28] After their competitive games, too, young girls exposed themselves in their victory dances, as Sydney Parkinson reported:

> We saw a favourite game, which the young girls divert themselves with in an evening; dividing themselves into two parties, one standing opposite to the other; one party throws apples, which the other endeavours to catch . . . Now-and-then one of the parties advanced, stamping with their feet, making wry mouths [grimaces which he sketched in his notebook], straddling with their legs, lifting up their cloaths, and exposing their nakedness; at the same time repeating some words in a disagreeable tone.[29]

The young Quaker was shocked by these antics (even though his girl-friend 'Mrs Patini' (Parkinson) was probably among the performers), remarking that 'thus they are bred up to lewdness from childhood, many of them not being above eight or nine years of age'.[30] As the Bounty mutineer Morrison later noted, however, these gestures were performed as a way of mocking their adversaries, and the girls who exposed themselves were extremely modest and timid in private, allowing no liberties from the Europeans who mistook these displays for sexual provocation.[31]

Two days later, on 28 May, Cook decided to visit Tutaha, who was still sending him messages of invitation. Accompanied by Banks, Solander, Tepau and Tomio, Cook went in the pinnace to Fa'a'a on the west coast of the island. When they arrived, they found that Tutaha had moved further south to a *marae* in Atehuru (no doubt 'Utu-'ai-mahurau *marae* in the Pa'ea district on Point Teone-ahu),[32] where after the attack on Mahaiatea, Pohuetea's warriors had taken the red feather girdle Te Ra'i-puatata and the image of 'Oro from Taputapuatea. Ever since that time, Tutaha's people had been forced to go to Atehuru whenever the great rituals featuring these sacred objects were performed, rather than carrying them out on their own *marae*, Taraho'i.

The Pleiades or Matari'i had already sunk beneath the horizon, and the ceremonies that marked this occasion were over. The rituals that formally opened the Season of Scarcity were still under way, however, and when they landed on the coast, Cook and his companions walked for some time until they came to a bay where Tutaha was sitting under a tree, surrounded by a large crowd of people, including Purea, Tupaia and many of their friends. Cook and Banks presented the great warrior with a yellow petticoat and other gifts, and he gave them a pig in return, promising that more pigs would be brought in the morning, but did not offer them lodgings. Lines of canoes were drawn up on the beach, bringing visitors to this occasion. Cook and his party had left their boat behind and had no food or shelter, and Cook and the midshipmen were invited to one house and Dr Solander to another, while Purea gave Banks a bed under the awning in her canoe, next to Tutaha's.

That night Banks and Purea went to sleep early, as was the custom on the island. Because the night was hot, Banks stripped off the fine clothes that he was wearing – a white jacket and waistcoat with silver frogs, with two pistols and a small powderhorn in the pockets. He handed these garments to Purea, who promised to look after them; but when he woke up at about 11 p.m. and felt for his clothes, he realised that they were missing. He woke Purea to complain of his loss; candlenuts were lit; and Tutaha and Purea rushed off in search of the thief, returning empty-handed half an hour later. Banks still had his musket, which he had neglected to load the previous evening. In the commotion he felt vulnerable, not knowing where Cook and his other companions were staying. Tupaia stood beside

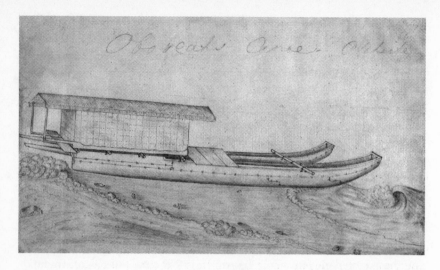

Purea's Canoe

him, however, and eventually Banks gave the high priest his musket and went back to sleep, telling the other people in the canoe that he was sure that Purea and Tutaha were doing everything they could to recover his possessions. Soon afterwards he was awakened by the sound of music, and walking to a place where a *heiva* (*'arioi* performance) was under way, he found Captain Cook, looking disconsolate, who reported that he had lost his stockings, which he had placed under his head as he slept, while each of the midshipmen had lost a jacket. Shortly after they discovered their losses, Tutaha had arrived with some *'arioi* musicians, four flautists and three drummers with some singers, who entertained them for about an hour to console them. Cook was not amused, however, grumbling that 'the Musick and singing was so much of a peice that I was very glad when it was over'.[33]

Deciding that nothing more could be done that night, Cook and Banks went back to bed. When Banks awoke early the next morning, he found Tupaia sitting beside him with his musket and the rest of his clothes which he had guarded all night, and Purea gave Banks a bark-cloth poncho which he donned instead of his lost jacket. When Tutaha appeared soon afterwards and he and Cook asked him to retrieve their stolen garments, however, neither the great warrior nor Purea seemed interested in doing anything about it. By now, Banks and Cook were convinced that Purea and Tutaha had conspired to rob them. A chief's clothing was imbued with his *mana*, and these garments had probably been taken for the rituals at 'Utu-'ai-mahurau *marae*, along with Te Ra'i-puatata, the famous *maro 'ura* held at this *marae* into which the red bunting pennant from the

Dolphin had been sewn, to implore the gods to return with an abundant harvest during the next Season of Plenty. At 8 a.m. when Dr Solander arrived from the house where he had slept, they discovered that he had been luckier, as he had lost nothing. For the rest of the morning they tried to persuade Tutaha to return their clothing or to give them the extra pigs he had promised, but when he ignored them, they walked back to the boat, seething with frustration.

Back at the pinnace, which was anchored opposite 'Irihonu Pass, they found ten or twelve Tahitians swimming in a raging surf, which Banks thought would have killed most Europeans. They pushed the stern of an old canoe out to the breakers, diving under the waves, and when they caught a wave, one or two of them climbed into the stern and rode it swiftly almost to the beach, watched by the fascinated strangers.[34]

The Transit of Venus would occur on 3 June 1769, and this day was rapidly approaching. Following the Earl of Morton's 'Hints', Cook decided to have observations made simultaneously in several different locations: Fort Venus; the east coast; and Mo'orea, the island just north-west of Matavai Bay. The carpenters worked furiously to repair the longboat, and Cook put Lieutenant Gore in charge of the Mo'orea expedition, which included Joseph Banks, Dr Monkhouse, Herman Spöring, Jonathan Monkhouse, Tepau and Tomio. Lieutenant Hicks led the expedition to the east coast of Tahiti, accompanied by Charles Clerke and Richard Pickersgill, both of the mates and Saunders, a midshipman; while Captain Cook and Charles Green were in charge of the Fort Venus observations, along with the master Robert Molyneux, Dr Solander and the ship's carpenter, William Satterly.

On 1 June, Gore and his party took the longboat to Mo'orea, landing on Irioa islet just inside the reef, guided by a local canoe; while the pinnace headed for Ta'aupiri islet off the north-east end of the Hitia'a district, not far from Bougainville's anchorage. After the observatory tents were pitched, the instruments were set up and tested. At sunrise on 3 June the weather was fine, without a cloud in the sky. Banks waited until the first contact between the planet and the sun had been observed, and then went ashore at Mo'orea to trade for provisions, where Ta'aroa, the high chief of the island (Ta'aroa-ari'i, a title attached to the high chiefly line in Mo'orea) and his sister Nuna came to greet him. As they approached, Banks unwrapped a bark-cloth turban from his head and laid it down, and they sat upon this together while Ta'aroa presented him with a pig as a gift to his god, a dog as a *taura* (rope) to bind them as *taio*, and a quantity of coconuts, breadfruit and dried fish.[35] Afterwards Banks sent a canoe to the observatory to fetch gifts for his visitors, and when the canoe returned it brought Tepau and Tomio to join them. Banks presented an adze, a shirt, some beads and nails, looking glasses and scissors as his *maro tai* or gift to the local gods, and Tomio, who was related to Ta'aroa, gave him a shirt and a long nail.

After these exchanges, Banks took his chiefly companions to the islet, where he let them gaze through the telescope at the sight of Venus crossing the sun, explaining that he and his comrades had come to observe this celestial event. Apart from the sun and moon, the planet Venus (Aphrodite to the Greeks, another link with the goddess of love) was the brightest object in the southern sky, and in Tahiti this planet was known as Ta'urua-nui, the beautiful eldest daughter of Atea (the mother of the stars), placed in the sky by the creator god Ta'aroa as a sign of peace and prosperity. During the time of creation, Ta'urua-nui had sailed her star canoe across the sky, begetting numerous stars and constellations; before guiding the trickster god Hiro on his voyages of exploration.[36] During his visit to the Underworld Ta'urua-nui had slept with Tafa'i, another famed explorer, helping him to rescue his father; and a beautiful woman by this name had also been the cause of the wars between Papara and southern Tahiti several generations earlier. The Tahitian chiefs must have understood the observations of the Transit as some kind of ceremony dedicated to Ta'urua-nui, the goddess worshipped by island navigators. That afternoon Banks returned to Mo'orea to explore and collect plants, and when he returned to his tent on the islet at sunset, three beautiful girls followed him in their canoe and spent the night with him. The next morning he returned to Matavai Bay, although these young women pleaded with him to stay with them on Mo'orea.

After this expedition Banks was elated, but Cook was disappointed by the observations that had been made. Although the day had been fine, a dusky shade around the body of the planet made it impossible to ensure consistency in the measurements taken by different observers. In addition, Cook was dismayed to find that while the observations were under way some of his men had broken into one of the storerooms and stolen a hundredweight of spike nails. When one of the culprits, Archibald Wolf, was found with seven nails in his possession, he was given two dozen lashes but refused to betray his accomplices. On 5 June Cook decided to honour the King's birthday, which had been delayed by the Transit; and one of the ship's tents in Fort Venus was prepared for the feast, which Tepau, Tomio and Tupaia attended along with the ship's officers and gentlemen. During the toasts when they tried to teach the islanders to pronounce King George's name, the closest they got was 'Kihiargo';

while as Banks observed with amusement, 'Tupia to shew his Loyalty got most enormously drunk'.[37]

From this time onwards, Tupaia attached himself to the British. This high priest, navigator, politician, warrior and scholar from Ra'iatea, who according to the missionary Richard Thomson was 'reputed by the people themselves . . . to have been one of the cleverest men of the islands',[38] had been trained in the school of learning (or *fare-'ai-ra'a-'upu*, houses for 'eating' sacred prayers, where high-born students were taught chants and incantations about the creation of the cosmos, genealogies, navigation, astronomy, the calendar and kin group proverbs and histories) attached to Taputapuatea *marae*.[39] As a navigator and high priest of 'Oro, Tupaia was intrigued by the eclipse of the sun that he had observed with the British during the *Dolphin*'s visit, and now by their observations of the star Ta'urua-nui. He was also fascinated by the Royal Society party, who were studying Tahitian, collecting vocabularies and lists of personal names, and trying to understand local customs. Joseph Banks, the elegant, wealthy young gentleman, was the highest-born man on board the *Endeavour*, and he enjoyed Tahitian company, particularly that of the women. Even Banks's flashes of arrogance and anger seemed proof of his *mana*, and Tupaia gravitated towards him. Along with Purea, the high priest had forged a ritual friendship with Captain Wallis, and now he transferred this loyalty to 'Tepane'. After their recent defeat at the hands of Tutaha and his allies, it was comforting to be in the company of these powerful strangers, whom he hoped might help him to free his home island from the Borabora invaders.

Like many *'arioi*, Tupaia was also an artist, and over the followir.g weeks he spent a great deal of time with Sydney Parkinson and Herman Spöring, Banks's two draughtsmen. Until recently, a series of ten watercolour drawings that survive from the voyage were thought to have been made by Banks himself, but in 1997 a letter from Banks came to light that describes one of these sketches (which depicts a European exchanging a piece of white cloth for a large crayfish with a Māori warrior), attributing it to Tupaia:

> Tupia the Indian who came with me from Otaheite Learned to draw in a way not Quite unintelligble. The genius for Caricature which all wild people Possess Led him to Caricature me & he drew me with a nail in my hand delivering it to an Indian who sold me a Lobster.[40]

The eyes on human figures in these drawings are identical to motifs in Lapita pottery, dating back to the earliest colonisation of Polynesia;

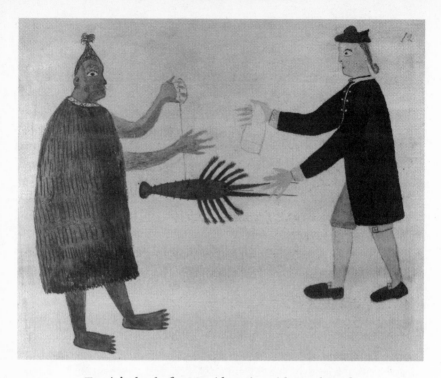

Tupaia's sketch of a Māori bartering with Joseph Banks

while the dominant colours of black, ochre and red brown are the main colours in bark-cloth painting (in fact, it is possible that Tupaia's drawings are coloured with Tahitian dyes). These sketches have other distinctive features, including a two-dimensional rendering of three-dimensional structures such as *marae* and, as Jenny Newell has pointed out, lovingly detailed images of plants showing their roots in the soil in x-ray style.[41] Some *'arioi* were skilled at painting and dying bark cloth, and Sydney Parkinson made a detailed study of these techniques, perhaps instructed by Tupaia.[42] From the surviving sketches, which include studies of *'arioi* musicians, and canoes lined up outside an *'arioi* house with warriors posed on their fighting platforms, it is plain that in his artworks, Tupaia focused upon the *'arioi* cult and ritual life in the Society Islands. He often worked alongside both Parkinson and Spöring, studying their artistic techniques; and on many occasions they sketched the same subjects.

It seems likely that Tupaia was also an expert in tattoo, an artistic tradition that originated with the gods in the Society Islands. Tahitian tattoo featured naturalistic images of 'coconut and bread-fruit trees, with convolvulus wreaths hanging round them, boys gathering the fruit, men engaged in battle, or . . . carrying a human sacrifice to the temple, . . . every kind of animal, . . . and weapons of war',[43] which may have inspired the style of his sketches; and Banks, Parkinson and others from the Royal Society party all took tattoos in Tahiti,[44] memorialising the *taio* relationships that bound them into Tahitian families, giving them local names, ancestors, enemies and allies.

During Banks's absence at Moʻorea, a high-born old lady (one of Tomio's relatives) had died. A canoe awning was raised on posts and railed around with bamboo, shading the body that was covered in fine bark cloth, with fish and meat beside it. Below the awning lay crumpled piles of bark-cloth rags, smeared with blood where the mourners had slashed themselves with shark's teeth. In a nearby house, visiting mourners were resting and sleeping, and the Chief Mourner's costume was stored in another building. When Banks visited the bier, Tepau told him that unless foodstuffs were provided for the dead person the gods would eat their body instead,

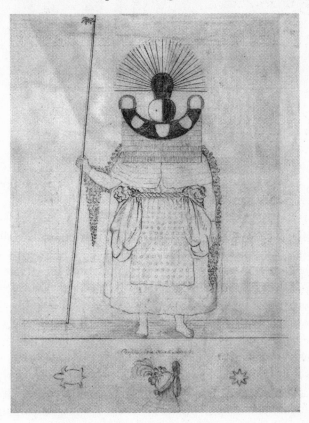

Spöring's sketch of the Chief Mourner

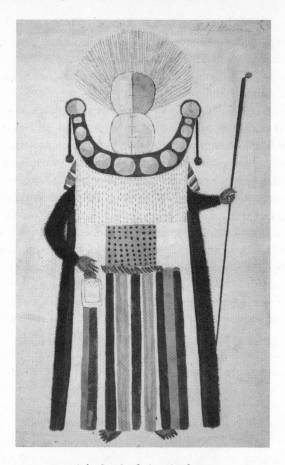

Tupaia's sketch of the Chief Mourner

condemning the spirit to languish in the dark underworld, as opposed to living a life of pleasure in Rohutu-no'ano'a, the perfumed paradise where there was no old age or sickness, and the spirits of chiefs and 'arioi lived a life of pleasure.[45]

On 9 June, Tepau, who was acting as the Chief Mourner, donned his fantastic costume. Both Spöring and Tupaia sketched this regalia, which was extremely sacred and highly prized. Over his face Tepau wore an iridescent mask, the *parae* after which the costume was named, made of four polished discs of pearl shell stitched together. One of the discs was black and the other was white, with a small hole for his right eye to look through. The black disc evoked the Po, the dark world of the spirits, while the white disc with the small hole was the Ao, the bright world of people from which the dead woman was departing. The two upper discs were both black, summoning up the Po, and surmounted by a crown of red-tipped tropic bird tail feathers – the rainbow (a harbinger of 'Oro). As Babadzan has pointed out, this mask almost blinded the wearer, a reminder of Uhi, the blind old female guardian of the Po, the dark land of the dead; and Hema, Tafa'i's father who had been blinded before his son rescued him from the underworld.

Below the mask Tepau wore a curved wooden board or *pautu*, decorated with five polished pearl shells in memory of Hina, the moon goddess, which covered his mouth and shoulders. From this wooden crescent hung the *'ahu-parau*, a shimmering array of little rectangles of iridescent pearl shell stitched together in rows in tribute to the Pleiades, the eyes of dead chiefs turned into stars. Over his body the chief wore a ceremonial poncho or *tiputa* decorated with an 'apron' or *'ahu-'aipu* decorated with rows of discs of polished coconut shell; around his neck, a tangled mass of sennit cord.[46] The coconut shell discs evoked the coconuts with which Tafa'i restored Uhi's and then Hema's sight, allowing his father to escape from the Po; while the braided, coloured sennit around his neck was the 'skin' of Tane, the god of peace and beauty. In this costume, Tepau had the power to galvanise the gods, so that his wife's kinswoman could make her way safely to Rohutu-no'ano'a, the *'arioi*'s perfumed paradise. As the Chief Mourner, he was bound to kill or wound anyone who breached the *tapu* of mourning, brandishing a clapper made of pearl shells to warn of his approach and wielding a lethal long club (or *paeho*) edged with shark's teeth, with which he could strike down anyone foolish enough to stray across his path, although he would not touch a fellow *'arioi*.[47]

Impressed by this costume, Banks was so intrigued that he asked his *taio* if he could accompany him the next time he performed the ritual. Tepau agreed, and the following day Tepau, dressed in the Chief Mourner's costume and accompanied by his wife Tomio, a boy and several other women led Banks to the funeral bier where he stripped off his European clothes, tying a strip of bark cloth around his waist while the women daubed his face and head with a mixture of candlenut soot and water, like an *'arioi* initiate. The young boy in their party had already been blackened from head to foot, and when they were prepared, Tepau prayed beside the body and near his own house, and they ran into the fort, 'to the surprize of our friends and affright of the Indians who were there, for they every where fly before the *Heiva* like sheep before a wolf'.[48] After emptying the fort, they proceeded to a place where about one hundred people were gathered, who fled in all directions when they saw them and hid from the *heiva*. When all of these people had vanished, Tepau led the *nevaneva* or 'crazy people' (a term used to describe the mourners, and *'arioi* possessed by 'Oro) back to his house where he took off his costume, and they washed themselves in the river.

Tupaia's sketch of 'arioi *musicians*

Archery was a sacred pursuit in Tahiti, practised by chiefs, and the next day, Lieutenant Gore, who was a keen sportsman, challenged Tepau to an archery competition.[49] However, while in European archery the aim is to shoot accurately at a target, in Tahiti the goal was to shoot the arrow as far as possible. Although neither man was skilled at the other's technique, when Tepau demonstrated the Tahitian style of archery the arrow travelled 274 yards. After two sailors spoiled the fun by seizing several bows and arrows from the islanders, Cook had them punished with two dozen lashes.

These light-hearted exchanges continued on 12 June when a group of travelling 'arioi musicians invited Banks to join them at their evening performance. In times of peace the younger 'arioi led a life of pleasure, roving in groups from one island to another, sleeping with the most beautiful girls and being showered with food and gifts by the chiefs in the districts where they staged their dramatic performances (or 'upa 'upa).[50] On this occasion a large crowd had gathered to listen to the 'arioi musicians, two flautists and three drummers, who sang songs in praise of their European visitors while Tupaia made a sketch of their performance. As Banks remarked, once again evoking the classics: 'These gentlemen like Homer of old must be poets as well as musicians.'[51] Seeing that their guests were enjoying the performance, the 'arioi asked Banks and his companions to sing them an English song, which they did to the applause of the assembled crowd; and according to Banks, one of the 'arioi liked their music so much that he told them he wanted to go to England to learn how to sing.

The next day, however, the mood turned sour. During a walk in the woods, William Monkhouse picked a flower that grew on a tree at a *marae*, a terrible desecration. Angered by the surgeon's impiety, a man came up behind him and struck him; and when Monkhouse grabbed this man and tried to punch him, two more men came up and, seizing the surgeon by the hair, freed their compatriot and ran off. That night an islander, no doubt seeking retribution for Monkhouse's *hara* or wrongdoing, sneaked into the fort and, using a forked stick, hooked an iron oven rake over the palisade. Although this was 'contrary to the opinion of everybody',[52] Cook had forbidden the sentries to fire at the Tahitians, even when they were stealing; but now his patience ran out and he decided to put an end to this 'insolence'. During the day a fleet of twenty-five double canoes had arrived from a fishing expedition to Teti'aroa, loaded with their catches, and early the next morning Cook took an armed party and seized the vessels, hauling them into the river behind the fort. When the chiefs protested, Cook told them that unless they returned everything that they had stolen from the British, he would burn their canoes.

At noon the oven rake was returned to the fort, but none of the other objects that Cook had listed, including the musket stolen from the sentry, Banks's pocket pistols, a sword belonging to a petty officer and the water cask taken from the fort. Tutaha's friends blamed Purea for these thefts, while her friends blamed Tutaha; and Tutaha was so angry with Cook that he forbade his people to bring any more fruit to the fort or the *Endeavour*. When Banks returned to Fort Venus that night from a shooting expedition in the woods, he thought that Cook had acted unwisely in confiscating the canoes:

> The Canoes pretty certainly did not belong to the people who had stolen the things. I confess had I taken a step so violent I would have seizd either the persons of the people who had stolen from us, most of whoom we either knew or shrewdly suspected, or their goods at least instead of those of people who are intirely unconcerned in the affair.[53]

This was self-righteous of Banks, however, because Cook was simply following the Earl of Morton's instructions and trying to avoid further violent confrontations.

No food was brought for barter the next morning, and the fish in the canoes began to rot and stink. When some individuals who were not the proper owners began to take provisions from the canoes, Cook could not stop them, as he did not know the rightful owners of these vessels. Although Tepau and Tomio remained at Point Venus, Tutaha stayed away; and on 17 June when Banks and Gore went to Pare to shoot ducks, Tutaha and his family packed up their household and left the district. The winter solstice (which would occur on 21 June) was imminent, when the gods and the 'arioi would depart from the island, and it is likely that Tutaha was taking his great-nephew Tu to the rituals at 'Utu-'ai-mahurau *marae* on this occasion. The following day, after a boat was sent to collect new ballast for the *Endeavour*, tensions ran even higher. Finding no suitable rocks and ignoring the violent protests of the local people, the officer had begun to pull down stones from the local *marae*, angering the gods (who might refuse to return to the island the following summer). The islanders hastily sent a messenger to Fort Venus to tell the British what the officer was doing, and Banks set off at once with Lieutenant Gore to settle the dispute, which they did by sending the men to the river where there were plenty of suitable stones.

On 19 June, while Tutaha and his entourage were absent, Purea, Teatea and Tupaia took the opportunity to return to Fort Venus, for the first time since the theft of Banks's jacket. They arrived in a double canoe loaded with plantains, breadfruit, a pig and a dog (which Spöring sketched during this visit). Although Purea blamed Pati, her lover, for stealing their clothes, Cook and Banks rebuffed her, sending her away and refusing to accept her presents. She wept bitterly, going off to sleep in her canoe; and the next morning when Cook relented and finally accepted her gifts, Banks allowed Purea and her women to lie in the marquee. Banks took Teatea to his own tent while Dr Monkhouse and one of the lieutenants paired off with two of Purea's other female companions. At nightfall when Monkhouse and the lieutenant decided to move into Banks's tent, the surgeon, wanting some privacy, pushed out one of Purea's women and tried to force Teatea to leave the tent, although she wept loudly in protest. Already at odds with Monkhouse and infuriated by the liberties he was taking, Banks shouted at him angrily and they quarrelled at the tops of their voices, while Purea and her women retreated to their canoe. Fearing that this might end in a duel, the other members of the Royal Society party intervened, and Banks left his tent instead and joined Teatea in Purea's canoe.

Early the next morning when tempers had cooled, Purea arrived at the fort with a gift of provisions, including a very fat dog. In Tahiti, dogs were kept as pets, given their own names and fed on coconut, breadfruit, yam and other vegetables; and their flesh was prized as chiefly feast food. During the presentation, Banks was given a basket of provisions which included a cooked dog's thigh, and when he and his companions tasted this meat they found it delicious. They decided to have Purea's dog for dinner, and Tupaia offered to cook it for them. The priest suffocated the dog by holding his hands over its mouth, which took about a quarter of an hour, then singed its body over hot stones, scraping off the hair with a shell. Using the shell, he cut open the dog's belly and removed its entrails, washing these carefully in the sea, and put the blood into coconut shells. Breadfruit leaves were laid on stones that had been heated in a shallow pit (about a foot deep), and the dog's carcass along with its liver, heart and lungs was doused with the blood, wrapped in leaves and laid on the stones, and more hot stones were piled on top of the bundle. The pit was filled with earth, well patted down, and the oven was left to cook for about four hours. When the dog meat was served, Cook, Banks and Solander ate it with gusto, although the others refused to touch it. As Cook exclaimed in his journal: 'It was the opinion of every one who taisted of it that they Never eat sweeter meat, we therefore resolved for the future not to despise Dogs flesh.'[54] After this tasty meal, Cook resolved to return the canoes to their owners when they asked for them.

Despite the shattering defeat of her people, Purea still hoped that, with British assistance, her son Teri'irere might be installed as *ari'i maro 'ura* or paramount chief of the island. As Cook and Banks had evidently forgiven her for the theft of their clothing, and had quarrelled with Tutaha, the prospects of a renewed alliance seemed brighter. She sent a messenger to Papara, and early the next morning, 21 June – the day of the winter solstice and the farewell to the gods – her husband Amo arrived at Fort Venus with a boy about eight years old, riding on a man's back, and a young woman about twenty years old. As they approached the fort, all the islanders including Purea dropped their garments to their waists as a sign of respect and veneration.[55] This was her son Teri'irere, whose investiture at Mahaiatea *marae* had provoked the recent war. This *tama-aitu* or 'god-child' was so sacred that he had to 'fly' to Fort Venus so that his feet did not touch the ground; and the 'fine, wild woman' with him was To'imata[56] (or Te-ari'i-na-vaho-roa), the sister of Tu, his greatest rival.

When Tu and Teri'irere's people had made peace after the recent fighting, the two young *ari'i* became bond friends; and despite the difference in their ages, Teri'irere was betrothed to Tu's sister. Although the young chieftainess was eager to look around the fort on this occasion, Amo would not permit her or Teri'irere to enter the British compound. They were accompanied by a woman named Titi, who ceremoniously presented Cook with a bright yellow garment bordered with red and decorated with crosses, copied from their 'Spanish' visitors. This was Amo's first direct contact with Europeans, and they found him shrewd and intelligent, asking many thoughtful questions about England and British customs.

Noting the respect paid to Teri'irere, Cook asked about the boy; and Purea and Amo assured him that he was 'the Heir apparent to the

Pohuetea

Sovereignty of the Island, and as such the respect was paid to [him], which was due to no one else except the *Areedehi* [*ari'i rahi*], which was not Tootaha, but some other person who we had not seen, or like to do, for they say he is no friend of ours and therefore will not come near us'.[57] This was a mischievous reference to Tu, the young high chief of Pare-'Arue, who after the battle of Mahaiatea had been installed with the red feather girdle brought by his mother Tetupaia from Ra'iatea. Throughout this visit, Tu kept away from Captain Cook and his men, because Tutaha did not trust them. Although Teri'irere and Tu were now *taio* or ritual friends, Purea and Amo were intent upon driving a wedge between Tutaha and the British; and their efforts were largely success-ful. After this visit by Teri'irere, Tutaha became even more angry and disaffected.

On 23 June, two days after the winter solstice, Cook discovered that a Portuguese sailor was missing from the ship. Shortly afterwards one of Tutaha's servants told him that the deserter was at Pare with his master, and when Cook offered him a hatchet to fetch the sailor back, the man went off to Pare. That evening the sailor was brought back to the fort and reported that as he headed towards the boat the previous day, three Tahitians had approached him in a friendly fashion, crying out 'Taio, taio'. After walking some distance with him, however, they had seized him and dragged him to the west end of the bay, where they stripped him and put him in a boat. They then took him to Pare, where Tutaha gave him some clothing and asked him to stay with him. After making some enquiries, Cook found that this story was true and excused the sailor from punishment.

Over the next few days, Tutaha ensured that no more provisions were brought to the fort; but despite this, on 24 June, Tepau and Tomio came to visit Banks, bringing him gifts including a large piece of fine bark cloth which they asked him to give to his sister 'Opia' (Sophia).

On the next day, a Sunday, Pohuetea (also known as Potatau, or more formally Tetuanui-e-marua-i-te-ra'i), the warrior *ari'i* of Puna'aui'a who had fought against Amo and Purea in the recent war, arrived at Fort Venus. A majestic figure, Pohuetea was accompanied by his wife Purutihara, a woman as strapping and tall as her husband. As even his close friends and chiefs from other districts sought to ally themselves with the British, Tutaha was being increasingly isolated.

Circling the Land

Just as the gods and the *'arioi* were departing for the Season of Scarcity, Captain Cook decided to leave Matavai Bay for a time. He was tired of the difficulties that attended a long stay on shore – libidinous, grumbling sailors, quarrelsome chiefs and light-fingered islanders. The Admiralty had ordered him to produce detailed charts of each place that he visited, along with descriptions of their natural resources and people; and Joseph Banks was eager to collect more plants and make further observations of the islanders. Cook and the young botanist decided to take an excursion together along the east coast of Tahiti, and at 3 a.m. on 26 June they boarded the pinnace and set off, rowed by two sailors and guided by a man named Tuahu.[1]

The day was calm and pleasant, and as the sun came up, the sea sparkled, coconut palms waved on the beaches and brilliantly coloured fish darted below them in the lagoon. After five hours of rowing along the coast they landed at Ha'apaiano'o (named 'Whapaiano' on Cook's chart) at the mouth of the Papeno'o Valley, which Banks had formerly visited on foot with Dr Solander. The local chief, 'Ahio', greeted them, along with two people whom they had met at Matavai Bay: a man called Teaitupoaro and a young woman, both of whom had accompanied Banks when he ran with the Chief Mourner. They took him to their house where they showed him the body of the old lady whom they had mourned on that occasion, the young woman explaining that when she inherited the old lady's land she had shifted to this district, bringing the corpse of her kinswoman with her.

After a brief stay at Ha'apaiano'o, Cook and Banks decided to walk to Hitia'a, Reti's district, guided by Teaitupoaro. As they walked, the boat followed them along the coast, taking soundings. Despite the long months at sea they were both very fit, walking many kilometres during this part of their journey. Cook was curious to see the bay where the 'Spanish' ships had anchored, and when Reti, the chief of Hitia'a whose *taio* Ahutoru had sailed with Bougainville, met them on the banks of the Mahatearo River, he freely answered Cook's questions, showing them the place where the ships had anchored inside the islets Puaru and Ta'aupiri (where Lieutenant Hicks and his party had observed the Transit of Venus). He also took them to the watering place and the site where his visitors had erected their tents, showing them the holes in the ground made by the tent poles. Banks found a shard of pottery nearby, and convinced by this evidence that the chief was telling the truth, gave Reti a cross which the chief erected on the campsite.

Eager to carry on with his survey, Cook returned to the pinnace and asked Teaitupoaro if he would accompany them as their guide. Upon setting out from Matavai Bay, Cook had not intended to travel around the island, but Banks was an ebullient, high-spirited companion, and it was intoxicating to be away from Matavai Bay, the local chiefs and his crew, exploring this beautiful island. Throwing caution to the winds he decided to carry on with their journey, despite the risks: they were a very small party with only one musket and several pistols between them, little ammunition, no food and just a few trade goods to barter. Teaitupoaro was hesitant, however, protesting that after leaving Hitia'a they would enter enemy territory outside the sphere of Tutaha's influence, where the people would surely kill them; and it was not until he saw them loading ball into their musket and pistols that he agreed to go with them. His caution was understandable, because they were heading straight towards Tahiti-iti (little Tahiti), the southern part of the island ruled by the great warrior chief Vehiatua, who had recently attacked Purea and Amo at Mahaiatea.

Rowing until nightfall, they reached the Taravao isthmus in the middle of the island, which according to Teaitupoaro was still in allied territory. They saw few houses ashore, but several double canoes were drawn up on the beach whose occupants made them very welcome. Among them was 'Ura-atua (literally, red feathers of the gods), the young woman who had ritually presented bark cloth to Banks at Matavai Bay, and she gave him a meal and invited him to sleep in her canoe. Early the next morning Cook and Banks went for a walk to examine this low, marshy isthmus, which almost cut the island in two. Teaitupoaro explained that Taravao was the boundary between Tahiti-nui (large or northern Tahiti), where Tutaha was the most powerful leader, and Tahiti-iti (small or southern Tahiti) or Tai'arapu, which was governed by Vehiatua; and that the islanders often portaged their canoes across this isthmus from one side of the island to the other.

After this hike, Cook, Banks and Teaitupoaro boarded the pinnace and headed south-east to Anuhi (now Pueu) in Tahiti-iti. When they arrived, the chief Maraeta'ata (whose name Banks translated as 'the burying place of men') and his father Pahiriro (taker of boats) came to greet them. As Banks commented, 'despite their terrible titles' these men were very friendly;[2] and when Cook and Banks came ashore, all of the crowd except for Maraeta'ata stripped their garments down to the waist, honouring them as high chiefs. Following this ceremony Teaitupoaro became quite cheerful, saying that these people would not now kill them, but warning his companions that they had little meat to offer. Indeed, Banks noted that they had been given no pork or breadfruit thus far in their journey. After some hesitation, Maraeta'ata presented his guests with a very large pig, receiving a hatchet in return; and when they looked around at the crowd, they recognised only two people. None of these people was wearing any beads or ornaments from the *Endeavour*, although several wore some ornaments from the 'Spanish' ships, and Maraeta'ata showed Banks and Cook two twelve-pound shot, one marked with an English broad arrow, which he said that 'Tutero' (Duclos), the commander of those ships, had given them (although in fact these shot came from the *Dolphin*).

From Anuhi (now Pueu), Cook and Banks proceeded on foot, sending the pinnace ahead to Tautira towards the southern end of the island. After walking about seven kilometres across a wide, fertile plain they came to the Vaitepiha River, in the heart of Vehiatua's territory. As they crossed the river by canoe, the crowd of Tahitians who accompanied them swam across like 'a pack of hounds taking the water'.[3] In this spectacular valley,

Vaitepiha Bay

sheltered by ranges of high jagged mountains rising up out of a deep gorge, where the Vaitepiha River flows out towards the flats, winding into the lagoon, the chief orator of southern Tahiti used to chant in the main 'arioi house, Pararo:

> The mountain above is Tahua-reva
> The assembly ground is Ti'ara'a-o-Pere
> The river is Vaitepiha
> The marae are Pure-ora [dedicated to Ta'aroa] and Taputapuatea [dedicated to 'Oro]
> The harbours are Vaiuru'a, Vai-o-nifa and Te-'afa [in Tautira Bay]
> The high chief is Te-ari'i-na-vaho-roa or Vehiatua-i-te-mata'i
> The 'arioi house is Pa-raro
> The chief 'arioi is Te ra'a-roa.[4]

After hearing so much about the 'ari'i rahi' or 'King' of southern Tahiti, Cook was eager to meet this venerable warrior. Passing the ruins of some very large houses, they arrived at Tautira Point where they found Vehiatua I (formally known as Vehiatua-i-te-mata'i),[5] a very old, thin man with a white beard and hair, sitting near some canoe awnings with a beautiful young woman about twenty-five years old. Their meeting was brief, even perfunctory, with no presentation of gifts or ritual greetings, no doubt because Vehiatua was very suspicious about their intentions. Later, their guides told them that the young woman at his side (who may have been his eldest daughter) had as much influence in Tahiti-iti as Purea had once had in Tahiti-nui. Teari'i ('the high chief'), Vehiatua's eldest son, was also present, and after exchanging a pig for gifts he agreed to guide Cook and Banks on the next stage of their journey.

After leaving Tautira, Teari'i led his companions across a cultivated plain where the streams ran in stone-edged channels and the coast was protected by a stone sea wall. The houses were neither big nor numerous, but they saw many large canoes pulled up on the beaches, longer than those at Matavai Bay. These canoes had high prows and sterns with forked poles on which Banks guessed that large images were hung, like those that he had seen hanging up in their houses (although fishing lines for dolphin and tuna were in fact slung from these forked poles). On almost every point there was a stone marae and several inland, more highly ornamented with carving than those in Tahiti-nui. These marae had ti'i with ancestors standing on top of each other's heads (which Teari'i explained was the mark of a burying ground), and unu boards set upright on the marae, carved with latticework topped by figures of birds and men, one featuring a cock painted red and yellow. Although the region seemed very fertile, they were not given a single breadfruit during this part of their journey. All the breadfruit trees in the district had been stripped bare and the people were living on Tahitian chestnuts (or *mape*), fermented breadfruit paste (*mahi*) and wild mountain plantain (or *fe'i*). In this part of the island, the breadfruit season was over, and the Season of Scarcity had already begun.[6]

By now Cook and Banks were exhausted, and when they went to meet the pinnace they found that the two guides who had accompanied them from Tahiti-nui had stayed with Vehiatua, thinking that their companions would return that night to Tautira. Teari'i and another local man agreed to accompany them in the boat and they rowed south along the coast until they came to a small island called Tiareiti, where Teari'i guided them into a snug cove on its south-east coast, where a deserted long house stood beside a small creek. They had brought very little food with them, just a bit of salted beef and no bread, because as Banks explained, 'for that we depended on the natives who had on all former occasions been able to supply us with any quantity of Breadfruit'.[7] According to Banks, a chief sitting down to a meal would often eat three breadfruit, three fish, fifteen large plantain and a quart of *mahi* or fermented breadfruit at one sitting,[8] and during the Season of Plenty he had become accustomed to this kind of repast. Driven by hunger, he walked into the woods to look for more provisions but found only one house where the people gave him a firebrand, one-and-a-half breadfruit and some Tahitian chestnuts, which he and his companions baked and shared for supper with a couple of roasted ducks and curlews. Still hungry, Banks bedded down that night under an awning from a canoe that had followed them from Tautira, while Cook and the others slept in the long house; and during the night their guide Tuahu came to join them, lying down beside the captain.

Early the next morning Banks and Cook went ashore again, hoping to find some houses and more food for breakfast. As they walked along the coast they passed several *marae* by the Vai'ote River where skulls and vertebrae lay carelessly strewn on the stone pavements, no doubt belonging to enemy warriors killed during the recent fighting. They saw no houses, but came across several large canoes drawn up on a beach near a group of people who included some of their acquaintances from Tahiti-nui. Delighted, they greeted these people eagerly; but when they asked them for food their acquaintances put them off, saying that they could have some later. When Banks, who was famished, demanded that they fetch him some coconuts from the palms on the beach, which were richly laden with nuts, they agreed to his request but did nothing about it, not even when he threatened to cut down one of these palms with a hatchet. These people did not own the trees and could not pick the coconuts, but fortunately the owners of some of the trees soon arrived, having almost stripped them bare when Banks approached and bartered for all of the nuts they had gathered. These were loaded into the pinnace, and farewelling their friends and Vehiatua's son, Cook and Banks carried on down the coast, guided by Tuahu.

Along this stretch of coast the reef was irregular, with high cliffs (Te Pari) plunging straight into the ocean. On these precipitous cliffs they saw just a few houses perched on ledges, one or two breadfruit trees and many mountain plantains. Following a canoe through Tutataroa Pass into the lagoon, they rowed along a coastal plain that Tuahu told them was very fertile. This was Ahui (now Vaipoiri), part of the Teahupo'o district, where a chief named Matahiapo came out to greet them. His people produced numerous coconuts and about twenty breadfruit, which they bartered for a very high price, while the chief traded a pig for a glass bottle. In this bay Banks noticed an English goose and a turkey cock, both immensely fat and very tame, which the people treated as pets, saying that these animals had been left by the *Dolphin*. In a nearby *'arioi* house they saw fifteen freshly cut underjaws fastened to a semicircular board which hung at one end of the house; and when Banks asked the local people about these grisly objects, they refused to answer. Jawbones were war trophies, and almost certainly these came from warriors killed in the attack on Papara or a more recent skirmish. When they returned to the pinnace, Matahiapo accompanied them as their guide, although he wanted them to greet the people at every *fenua* or estate along the coastline, stopping the pinnace on a number of occasions.

Later that afternoon when they reached a large bay in the Vaiuru (now Vaira'o) district, Matahiapo pointed out a long house in which he said they could spend the night with his friend, a chief named Tuivirau. When they landed, Tuivirau greeted them warmly, and ordered his people to cook for them. By now they had plenty of provisions that the different chiefs had given them – about 30 breadfruit and some plantains and fish, enough for the next two days. Banks stayed close to the women, hoping that one of them would offer him a bed, but although five or six of these women flirted with him, seeming to promise more than a night's lodgings, eventually they all wandered off and left him. Deflated, Banks went to the *'arioi* house where supper was being served, which he ate with Cook, Tuivirau and Matahiapo and their companions. Matahiapo was evidently an important chief, because when Tuivirau prepared a supper of *popoi* (a paste of breadfruit, plantains and coconut milk mixed in a coconut shell), he fed him with his own hands. After the meal, Tuivirau showed Cook and Banks where they could sleep, and they sent for their cloaks from the boat, stripping themselves and sending their clothes into the pinnace for safekeeping, intending to spend the night dressed only in bark cloth. Later that evening when Matahiapo complained of the cold, Cook had a cloak fetched for him, trusting this affable, helpful chief, and they lay down to sleep beside him.

Almost as soon as he had dozed off, however, Cook was shaken awake and told that Matahiapo had vanished with the cloak; and Tuahu confirmed this story. Jumping up in a fury and brandishing one of his pocket pistols, Banks yelled that the thief must be captured. As their companions began to sidle out of the house, Banks grabbed Tuivirau's brother, a fine-looking man, declaring that unless he helped him to catch Matahiapo, he would shoot him. This man guided them along the coast for about ten minutes, running in the dark, when they met an islander coming back with the cloak. The chief had fled, 'by that means escap[ing] a severe thrashing which we had decreed to be a proper reward for his breach of trust'.[9] When they returned to the long house, finding it deserted, Banks went off to find Tuivirau and his companions. Assuring them that he and Cook were only angry with Matahiapo, he managed to persuade them to return to the long house where they all went off to sleep again. At 5 a.m., however, they were woken by the sentry who reported that the pinnace was missing. In a panic they rushed to the beach with the two sailors, but although the night was clear and the sea shone in the starlight, the boat had vanished. Thinking that the pinnace had been stolen and that they were about to be attacked, they prepared to defend themselves, although they were only four men armed with one musket, two pocket pistols, and no spare ammunition. Fortunately, fifteen minutes later the boat drifted back into sight, riding on its grapnel with the returning tide, and greatly relieved, they returned to the long house for breakfast.

After breakfast Cook and Banks set out again, rowing west until they reached Afa'ahiti, the last district in Tai'arapu, governed by a chief called Moe. Moe was busy building a house and was eager to obtain an axe, but unfortunately they had none left to give him. When they returned to the pinnace, Moe and his wife followed them for several miles in their canoe before inviting them to land. His people had a large pig, but Moe wanted an axe for it; so Cook promised that if he brought this pig to Matavai Bay, they would give him a large axe and a nail. After consulting his wife, Moe agreed, giving them a roll of bark cloth in token of this promise.

Back in the pinnace, they were rowed up the coast to Vaiari where they encountered several of their old friends, including Tupaia. The high priest took them straight to the local *marae*, a very neat stone pavement on which a pyramid of palm nuts about five feet high had been erected, decorated by three human skulls in a row, white and perfect, near a small carved stone image about forty-five centimetres high (a stone *ti'i* or resting place for a spirit) under a thatched shelter. Lying beneath a nearby *fata* (sacrificial platform) were the skulls of twenty-six pigs and six dogs. No doubt because Tupaia was with them, when they returned to the beach a remarkable large figure made of basketwork, seven feet six inches high and very bulky, was shown to them. It was covered with white feathers to represent its skin, and black for its hair and tattoos; wore a loincloth to cover its genitals; and on its head had four knobs, three in front and one behind, which they were told were *ta'ata iti*, or little people (perhaps descendants of this ancestor). According to the local elders, this image was called 'Maui' after the *atua* (ancestor god) who had slowed the sun in his tracks and pulled up islands from the ocean; but although these people tried to explain its meaning to the British, they found their account unintelligible. From the little that they could understand, this image was used as a 'puppet' in some of their *heiva* or *'arioi* gatherings.

From Vaiari, Cook, Banks and Tupaia took the pinnace up the coast towards Papara, hoping to spend the night with Purea and Amo. When they landed, however, they found that their friends had already gone to Matavai Bay to meet them. At Purea's house, a small, neat building with slatted bamboo walls, her father made them welcome. Afterwards, Tupaia led them to a point by the ocean where they had noticed a grove of *toa* or casuarina trees, and as they approached they were amazed to find a stone pyramid with eleven steps, 'a most enormous pile, certainly the masterpiece of Indian architecture in this Island so all the inhabitants allowed',[10] hidden among the trees. This was Mahaiatea, the great *marae* that Tupaia, Purea and Amo had built for Teri'irere's installation. When they measured its *ahu* or stone pyramid, they found that it was 267 feet long and 87 feet wide at the base, with eleven steps each four feet high edged with a course of white, square coral blocks, some large and all neatly polished, laid on top of courses of uniform, round pebbles. The foundations of the *ahu* were faced with squared reddish rocks, some almost five feet high, while on its summit stood the figure of a bird carved in wood, with the broken stone image of a fish lying beside it.[11] It seems that the steps of the *ahu* in this and similar *marae* represented the tiered heavens,[12] while the stone image must have been the *puna* (or sacred emblem) of Ruahatu, the sea god who created the pass through the reef opposite Mahaiatea, and controlled the fertility of the local fisheries.[13] In front of the *ahu* lay a large, square pavement surrounded by

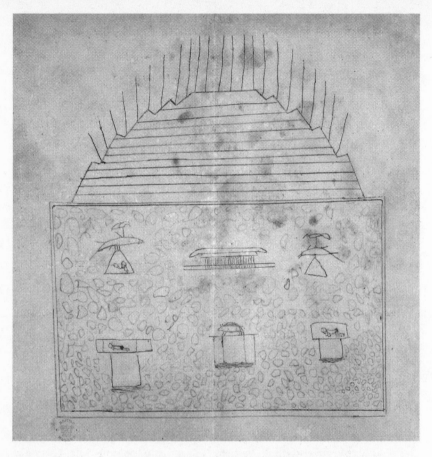

Tupaia's sketch of Mahaiatea marae

stone walls, 360 feet long by 354 feet wide, with *toa* and plantain trees growing upon it.

While trying to explain the different parts of this *marae* to Cook and Banks, Tupaia completed two remarkable sketches of Mahaiatea, each showing its high, stepped *ahu*; the sacred trees that shaded the *marae*; the *fata* or sacrificial platforms that carried pigs as offerings for 'Oro; and the paved plaza and the *fare atua* or god-house (shown in one of the sketches apparently hanging off a vertical stone wall, although in fact this was the paved plaza drawn without using European conventions for perspective). Cook and Banks were deeply impressed by the workmanship in this edifice, which was constructed of solid stone without any mortar, although some of the steps of the *ahu* sagged in the middle and it seemed to be in ruins. A hundred yards or so to the west they saw another pavement with several *fata* about seven feet high, carrying the skulls of around fifty pigs

Another sketch by Tupaia of Mahaiatea marae

and many dogs. This was the ancient *marae* of Teto'orara'i, which also belonged to Amo and Teri'irere. According to Cook, these *marae* stood on a low point about a hundred yards from the ocean.

Once the most impressive *marae* in Tahiti, Mahaiatea now lies hidden at the end of an obscure dirt pathway winding down to the beach between houses and gardens. Since Cook's time the coast has been eaten away, and the sea almost laps at the foot of the *ahu*, which has been reduced to a high, tumbled heap of rubble, covered with casuarina and other trees. According to Teuira Henry, in 1865 at the insistence of the French governor the stone steps of Mahaiatea were demolished to make a bridge over a nearby river, which was soon swept away in a flood.[14] At the time of Cook and Banks's visit, however, the great battle of Mahaiatea had been fought only six months earlier, and as they walked back to Purea's house along the beach, bones crunched under their feet. When they examined these remains, they found that they were mainly human ribs and verte-brae. Shocked by this grisly sight, they asked Tupaia about these bones, who told them that in December 1768 the Tai'arapu people had attacked this *marae*, killing many of the local people and forcing Purea and Amo to fly to the mountains. The victorious warriors burned all the houses and took away the pigs and other animals, including the turkey and the goose they had seen with Matahiapo; and the jawbones they had seen hung up in his house were trophies from this battle. That evening there was rain and lightning, a sign of 'Oro's presence.

After passing the night in Purea's house, early the next morning they rowed further up the west coast, dodging amongst reef and shoals until they came to Atehuru, near 'Utu-'ai-mahurau *marae*. There they were welcomed by 'their intimate friends' – probably Purea and Amo – who gave them a good supper, although they explained that the next breadfruit crop would not ripen for at least another three months. The following morning, 1 July, was wet and windy, the first bad weather they had expe-rienced since setting out on their circuit of the island. Cook and Banks had been fortunate, given they had taken no dry clothing with them in the pinnace. After paying a brief visit to Tutaha, they returned to Matavai Bay, bringing two large pigs and the chart that Cook had made during his circuit of the island. Afterwards Tupaia and Banks worked together, recording many of the coastal place names on this chart, which in its final draft includes the names of districts and settlements around the island.[15]

Although Cook and Banks did not know this, their circling of the island echoed an ancient ritual practice. According to the missionary John Orsmond, when food and other gifts were distributed at a major cere-mony, the leading *'arioi* announced the gifts, 'in imagination [circling] all round Tahiti and Moorea making mention of the mountain – Assembling ground – River – Point of land – Harbour at the place, and the Chief's name [of each district]. Every priest on officiating before the Marae had to do the same. They never erred.'[16] In the same way, when a chief returned home after a visit to another place, he made a circuit of the island, visiting one district after another; and when a party of *'arioi* visited another island they made offerings at the main *marae* and then progressed around the coastline, giving performances in each district in succession. And when a new high chief was installed, his supporters sent his *vane* or banner in a

circuit around the coastline to each main *marae*, where the *vane* was ritually welcomed, or struck down if the succession was contested. Thus
when Cook and Banks travelled around the coast of Tahiti, visiting the
different districts, this was a powerful statement of *mana* – explaining
why Vehiatua and his people in southern Tahiti (traditional enemies of
the visitors' northern friends) had been so reluctant to receive them; and
why Tupaia was delighted to see them safely back in northern Tahiti. And
when Banks sat down with Tupaia to write down place names around the
coast on a chart of the island, recording them in this new form of *tatau* (or
tattoo – as the islanders called writing when they first saw it), this seemed
yet another new way of asserting *mana* or control over the island.

Upon his return to Matavai Bay, Captain Cook found that the ship's provisions had been surveyed and the water barrels were full. Now that the
breadfruit season was over, food was increasingly scarce, and the gods
had departed the island. Cook also decided to leave the island as soon as
possible. Eager to heal the breach with Tutaha and the other chiefs, he
thought it best to return the canoes that he had confiscated. Consequently,
when Pohuetea, the stately chief of Atehuru, came to visit him and asked
the captain for a particular canoe, Cook readily agreed; although when a
number of the islanders vehemently protested, he realised to his chagrin
that Pohuetea was not the rightful owner. Despite Pohuetea's protests that
he had exchanged this canoe with Cook for a pig, it was taken away from
him. The great warrior was so humiliated and angry that for the rest of
the day he and his wife would not speak to the British or even look at any
of them.
    Now that their departure was imminent, on 3 July Banks and Dr
Monkhouse went on an excursion up the Tuauru Valley. After climbing
for about two miles, they met several people coming down from the valley
with loads of breadfruit on their backs. Banks had noticed that although
the trees around the bay were bare, a few breadfruit were still being delivered to the coast, and these people explained that because the breadfruit
trees up the valley cropped later than those on the coast, they provided
some supplies when the other trees failed. According to the missionary
William Ellis, the Tahitians had at least fifty named types of breadfruit
that ripened at different times of the year.[17] Reflecting upon the plentiful
supplies that the *Dolphin*'s crew had received at about this time of year,
Banks realised how terrified the islanders must have been during that visit.
The islanders often told him about 'the terrour which the Dolphin's guns
put them into and when we ask how many people were killd they number
names upon their fingers, some ten some twenty some thirty, and then say

"*worrow worow*" [*ua rau, ua rau*, hundreds and hundreds], the same word as is usd for a flock of birds or a shoal of fish'.[18] The *Dolphin* had only spent a month at Tahiti, however; whereas the *Endeavour* stayed in Matavai Bay for almost three months, arriving after a destructive war on the island; and it is not surprising that by this time local supplies had been depleted.

About four miles up the valley, Banks and Monkhouse found a cluster of houses on both sides of the river, and eventually they came to the last house in the valley, where the owner gave them drinking coconuts as a refreshment. After climbing about six more miles up a rough, steep track, they arrived at a beautiful waterfall that tumbled down sheer cliffs a hundred feet high. At this place a rope of plaited hibiscus bark had been lowered over a cliff thirty feet tall, so that people could climb up to gather wild plantains on the upper plateau. Banks looked for gold and other minerals in the valley, but could see only volcanic rock in all directions, which made him think that the high islands he had seen must be the remnants of a great continent drowned by sea after a violent volcanic convulsion, speculating that perhaps this had been the fate of the Great Southern Continent.

Over the next few days, Cook worked hard to get the *Endeavour* ready for sea while Banks planted a large number of different kinds of seeds that he had brought from Rio de Janeiro (including watermelons, oranges, limes and lemons), making gardens in a range of soils and locations. Unfortunately, none of the seeds (except for the mustard seed) that Cook had brought from London had germinated, probably because of the way in which they had been stored. During one of these excursions, Banks watched curiously as a girl about twelve years old was tattooed on the buttocks with a large multi-toothed chisel that was struck rapidly, penetrating her skin. She bore this quietly for a time, but when the pain became too intense she began to weep piteously, held down by two women who sometimes scolded and hit her, and at other times urged her to be patient.

On 6 July the guns were carried on board the *Endeavour*, and Purea and Amo sent for Teri'irere who arrived with his betrothed wife, although again Amo prevented her from entering Fort Venus. During that day, Banks was warned that the man who had stolen the quadrant had returned to the bay, intending to rob them once more before they left the island, and many people offered to sleep in the fort that night to protect their property. Nothing was taken, but during the following day when the carpenters began to dismantle the fort, breaking down the gates and palisades for firewood, the thief stole the staple and hook from the great gate, accomplishing his ambition. As soon as Banks was told about the theft, he and his companions set off 'in full cry much like a pack of fox hounds',[19] running and walking for six miles, although unluckily they ran right past the thief, who had hidden himself in a brook among some rushes. When they returned to the fort, Tepau gave Banks the staple and hook, which he had managed to retrieve. Food was running short in the bay, and the following morning Purea arrived with four small pigs as a tribute to their friendship.

Two nights later two marines escaped from the fort, which by this time had almost been dismantled. Clement Webb, steward of the gun-room, had fallen in love with a local girl; while Samuel Gibson, his sworn brother (or *taio?*) and reputedly a wild young man, also had a Tahitian lover. Tutaha had promised them land and servants if they joined him, and when they left the fort they fled to the west side of the island (no doubt to Pare). Cook decided not to act at once, but to wait in case they voluntarily returned to the *Endeavour*. By now, time was running out for any islander who wanted to procure iron tools or weapons, and that night when two foreign sailors went for a walk, a man struck one of them on the forehead with a large stone and stole his knife, while his companion was also slightly wounded.

By dawn the next morning the marines had still not returned to the ship. Determined not to tolerate any desertions, Cook decided to take a number of chiefs hostage until the deserters were brought back to the *Endeavour*. He sent Hicks to visit Tutaha, with orders to lure the chief into the pin-nace and bring him back to Matavai Bay, convinced that if he had Tutaha in his power, the people would do anything he wanted. Purea and Teatea, Banks's 'flame', Tepau and Tomio, Pohuetea and his wife Purutihara, and Nuna, the chieftainess of Mo'orea, were all gathered in Banks's tent, and after the pinnace departed they were told that they would not be allowed to leave. At first they could not believe what they were hearing, but when they realised that the British were in earnest, they offered their assistance to capture the deserters.

Cook agreed, and Tepau and Pohuetea sent some of their people with the midshipman Jonathan Monkhouse, and the corporal of marines, a man named John Truslove, to track down the missing men. At dusk when Hicks arrived back at the ship with Tutaha, Cook ordered that the other chiefs should also be brought out, and Tepau and Tomio, Purea, Pohuetea and Purutihara were taken out to the *Endeavour*, weeping inconsolably and trembling with fear. At 9 p.m. some islanders arrived with one of the desert-ers, Clement Webb, and took him out to the ship, where Webb told Cook that the midshipman and the corporal had been captured and disarmed and were being held at Pare by Tutaha's people, who also had Gibson with them. He had been sent to tell Cook that they were determined to keep his men captive until their chief was released. Unwilling to bargain in this way, Cook immediately despatched a large party of armed men under Hicks in the longboat to free his men, accompanied by Tupaia as a 'voluntary prisoner' – a remarkable gesture of confidence in the British. Tupaia guided the longboat to the Pare where the captured men were held, and the armed party landed just before dawn and freed their comrades, taking Gibson a prisoner.

Although the chiefs had been terrified when they were first taken on board the *Endeavour*, they relaxed a little when Cook assured them that he would not hurt them. At about 8 a.m. the next morning when the armed party returned with Jonathan Monkhouse, Truslove and Gibson, Monkhouse told Cook that the guides sent by the chiefs had been very troublesome, refusing to tell them where they were going, and leading them into an ambush where a number of armed warriors had seized them. Afterwards, when Webb was sent back to the ship to tell Cook what had happened, the islanders had quarrelled amongst themselves, coming to blows, some arguing that their captives should be freed immediately while others insisted that they should be kept until Tutaha was liberated. Cook now told his captives that they would be released as soon as his men's weapons were returned, and when the guns were brought back to the ship shortly afterwards, Cook sent the chiefs on board the boat, giving each of them a gift as they left the *Endeavour*.

Banks had spent the night in his tent at Fort Venus. That evening when a large crowd surrounded it, many of them armed, he walked amongst them, displaying considerable courage. As the chiefs were rowed ashore the next morning, the people were overjoyed, but when the hostages saw Banks they glared at him in fury: 'No sign of forgiveness could I see in their faces, they lookd sulky and affronted.'[20] Ignoring their anger, he walked along the beach to Purea, and four pigs were soon brought to him: two from Purea and two from Tutaha. Both Tahitians were still extremely angry, however; and as Cook remarked: 'Thus we are likely to leave these people in disgust with our behaviour towards them, owing wholly to the folly of two of our own people.'[21] That afternoon the remaining tents were struck and taken on board; the small bower anchor, whose stock had been found riddled with sea worm, was repaired; and that night all the sailors and the Royal Society party slept safely on board the *Endeavour*.

After the defeat at Mahaiatea, Tupaia's position on the island had become tenuous. When the *Endeavour* had arrived at Matavai Bay and he, Purea, Amo and Teri'irere renewed their alliance with the British, they put their lives at risk; and Tupaia's decision to guide the British longboat to Pare was the last straw for Tutaha. Now that his British friends and protectors were about to leave Tahiti, Tupaia was in imminent peril, and he decided to go with them. When he told 'Tepane' that he had decided to join the expedition, Banks was overjoyed, offering to support him during the voyage:

> Tupia . . . is certainly a most proper man, well born, cheif *Tahowa* [*tahu'a*] or preist of this Island, consequently more skilld in the mysteries of their religion; but what makes him more than any thing else desireable is his experience in the navigation of these people and knowledge of the Islands in these seas; he has told us the names of above 70, the most of which he has been at.
>
> The Captn. refuses to take him on his own account, in my opinion sensibly enough, the government will never in all human probability take any notice of him; I therefore have resolvd to take him. Thank heaven I have a sufficiency and I do not know why I may not keep him as a curiosity, as well as some of my neighbours do lions and tygers at a large expence than he will probably ever put me to; the amusement I shall have in his future conversation and the benefit he will be of to this ship, as well as what he may be if another should be sent into these seas, will I think fully repay me.[22]

Here one can see Banks, the future President of the Royal Society and doyen of Pacific exploration, already anticipating future voyages; but at the same time demonstrating a sense of superiority over the islanders, speaking of Tupaia as a 'curiosity' and a 'wild man' like those exhibited in fairs and sideshows in Britain, even while acknowledging his intelligence and knowledge.

Taking a miniature of Banks and several small farewell presents, Tupaia went ashore to visit his friends while Banks and Herman Spöring went to Point 'Utuha'iha'i to visit Tutaha's *marae*, Taraho'i, which Spöring sketched on this occasion. Several of their friends (perhaps Pohuetea and his wife Purutihara, who later called herself Captain Cook's 'sister') greeted them, willing to overlook their recent imprisonment; and they accompanied Banks to Tutaha's house to see Purea, where they made peace with each other. Many of the other people from the *Endeavour* also went ashore, farewelling their *taio* and lovers and giving them presents and receiving gifts in return. That night Tupaia went with Banks out to the ship, sleeping on board for the first time.

On 13 July at dawn, the sailors raised the *Endeavour*'s stream anchor. A little later, Purea and Teatea from Papara, Nuna from Ra'iatea, and Pohuetea and Purutihara from Puna'aui'a (but not Tutaha, Tepau or Tomio) came out to the ship, weeping softly as they farewelled their friends, while the commoners in the canoes lamented at the tops of their voices, crying out *'Aue! Aue!'* and making a deafening racket. By 11 a.m. when all the ship's boats had been secured, Tupaia stood on the deck with his attendant, a young *'arioi* musician boy named Taiato, weeping a little as he sent down a shirt for Tutaha's favourite wife. As the ship set sail, he and Banks climbed to the topmast where they stood waving at the canoes, and when they came back down to the deck the high priest looked exhilarated. Cook remarked that although a number of the islanders had offered to sail with them, they chose Tupaia because he seemed to know more about 'the Geography of the Islands situated in these seas, their produce and the religion laws and customs of the inhabitants than any one we had met with and was the likeliest person to answer our purpose'.[23] As Molyneux added, Tupaia was 'infinitely superiour in every Respect to any other Indian we have met with, he has conceiv'd so strong a friendship for Mr. Banks that he is Determined to Visit Britannia'.[24] The Ra'iatean navigator was off on his greatest voyage.

Tupaia's Ship

As the *Endeavour* sailed from Tahiti, according to Richard Pickersgill, 'by Tobias Directions we stood to the Wt in Quest of some Islds which he said lay that way not far distant'.[1] Tupaia was a star navigator trained at Taputapuatea, one of the most famous voyaging centres in Polynesia, and during the weeks before they sailed, the high priest had passed on some of his knowledge to Cook and Molyneux, the ship's master. His *taio* friendship with Joseph Banks made it possible for him to share this sacred information with his friend and his people, and once he decided to sail with Banks to 'Britannia', Tupaia had his own ideas about where the *Endeavour* should be heading. In particular, he wanted to visit Huahine, where he had estates and titles and the high chief Ori was an ally and friend of Ari'ima'o, the former high chief of Ra'iatea. Above all, he wanted to take this powerful ship to his homeland, and with the help of Cook and his men, free Ra'iatea from the Borabora invaders.

Cook had his own reasons for allowing Tupaia to pilot the *Endeavour*. During his meetings with the high priest at Matavai Bay, he had come to respect Tupaia's knowledge of the seas around Tahiti, and now that he was once again sailing into uncharted waters, he was eager to learn everything he could from the island navigator. In addition, Tupaia had convinced him that it would be possible to obtain plentiful supplies of fresh food in the Leeward Society Islands; and Cook wanted to give his men time to recover from the venereal infections that they had contracted in Tahiti before heading south in search of Terra Australis. When he told Cook and Molyneux about the surrounding archipelagos, Tupaia had passed on some of the basic information taught to star navigators – island lists, recited in the schools of learning. These lists included a brief description of each island – its name; size; whether it was low or high; whether or not it had a reef; the location of good harbours; the main foodstuffs produced there; whether or not it was inhabited; whether or not the people were friendly; and the name of its *ari'i* or high chief. In more advanced sessions, the novices were also taught the bearing of each island; the 'star path' or succession of stars to follow during the night on a voyage between each particular island and another;[2] the sailing time for the voyage from a known point of departure; and the chants recording particular sequences of islands.[3] Sometimes the navigators also sketched the sailing courses between islands in the sand on a beach, along with the coastlines, reefs, passages and harbours of these places.[4]

Star navigators were expected to memorise all of this information, but Cook and Molyneux wrote it down. During their sessions with Tupaia, Cook recorded a list of seventy-two[5] and Molyneux a list of fifty-five islands,[6] with the approximate bearings of each island from Tahiti. No information about the star paths was written down, presumably because it was too difficult for Tupaia to share this information with the British when the names of the stars and the configurations of the constellations were all different. Cook's island list and Molyneux's have only thirty-nine islands in common, indicating that during his conversations with these two men, the high priest-navigator shared different fragments of his navigational knowledge. More than half of the island names on these lists can be readily linked with islands on contemporary charts (fifty-five from a combined list of eighty-nine island names), although the lists also include islands that have no cartographic equivalent – for instance Tumu-papa, a name that refers to the creator Tumu (Ta'aroa's phallus) and Papa, the Earth; and those names beginning with Hiti-, evidently drawn from the story of the ancestral voyager Rata (Hiti-teare, Hiti-tautaureva, Hiti-tautaumai, Hiti-poto, Hiti-te-tamaruire etc.).[7] The identifiable islands are spread across a vast oceanic expanse around the Society Islands, from the Marquesas and Tuamotu Islands in the east, the Austral and Cook Islands in the south, and the islands of Samoa, Tonga, Tokelau and Fiji in the west – an east-to-west sweep of more than 5000 kilometres; although Tupaia made it clear that he had visited just twelve of these places himself: eight in the Society Islands, two in the Australs and two in the Tongan archipelago.

Cook found the information given in these lists too 'vague and uncertain' for practical use, however (as indeed it was without the star paths), and before they sailed from Tahiti, he and Banks also began to work with Tupaia on a chart of the Leeward Society Islands, trying to translate his knowledge into cartographic space.

Quickly grasping the idea of mapping, Tupaia produced a remarkable chart of Ra'iatea (his home island), Taha'a, Borabora and Maurua, showing their coastlines, passages and reefs, and images of mountains drawn

Tupaia's chart of Ra'iatea

without perspective (like his sketches of *marae*); with many place names
of islets, passages and settlements written around the coasts in Banks's
handwriting.[8] From this chart and Tupaia's descriptions, Cook learned
about the Leeward Society Islands to the north and west of Tahiti, many
of which had not been previously visited by Europeans (at least as far
as Cook knew); and he was keen to explore the archipelago and add
more islands to his charts of the Pacific, while Tupaia was eager to visit
his homeland. On 13 July 1769 when they sailed west from Matavai Bay,
therefore, Cook already had some idea of where they were heading. He
was confident about Tupaia's geographical knowledge and glad to have
him as his pilot.

When the atolls of Teti'aroa came into sight, Tupaia told Cook and
Molyneux that these islets were governed by the 'King of Otahite' (i.e.
Tu) and used for fishing expeditions.[9] Early the next morning while
Mo'orea and Tahiti were still visible to the south, 'Saunders Island' (now
Maiao) came into sight, which Tupaia called 'Tapuaemanu'. Later that
day, Clement Webb and Samuel Gibson, the two marines who had tried
to desert at Tahiti, were released from confinement, and each was given
a flogging of twenty-four lashes; and at sunset Huahine and Ra'iatea
loomed over the horizon just as Tupaia had predicted. Unfortunately,
Pickersgill did not describe how the high priest gave his directions to the
steersman – perhaps by pointing, or sign language, or instructions in a
mixture of Tahitian and English (because by that time Tupaia had learned
some English, while some of the Europeans had learned some Tahitian).

The next morning, 15 July, was misty, with light, uncertain breezes;
and when the wind died later, Tupaia stood in the stern windows of the

ship, chanting to Tane for a breeze and scolding the god when it did not blow up immediately:

> Toobaiah praying in the afternoon, in the stern-windows, called out, with much fervour, O Tane, *ara mai, matai, ora mai matai* [*ara mai matai, ara mai matai*]; which is to say, Tane (the god of his Morai) send to me, or come to me with a fair wind; but his prayer proving ineffectual, he said, *Wooreede waow* [*ua riri au*], I am angry.[10]

Tupaia was summoning Te moana-roa-no-Tane, a wind sent by Tane that was accompanied by clear blue skies, telling his shipmates that this wind would begin to blow when the sun was at the meridian and take them straight to Huahine.[11] The missionary Orsmond recorded one of the chants used by island navigators on such occasions:

> Oh Tane, god of beauty, Lord of the fleets, of the deep ocean
> Take care of your people
> Carry us in the hand of your *mana*, right to our destination
> Give us a wind astern, a wind from the east
> Let us sail as fast as a child's canoe with a coconut leaf for a sail
> Let us sail as smoothly as on a sea of oil, or a bed
> Let the crests of the waves be low
> Carry us to Apotara (a landing place on the west side of Huahine harbour).[12]

Joseph Banks mocked Tupaia's efforts, however, remarking that although the high priest 'often boasted to me of the success of his prayers, . . . I plainly saw he never began till he saw a breeze so near the ship that it generaly reachd her before his prayer was finished'.[13] Despite Banks's scepticism, a fine breeze blew up at the time that Tupaia had predicted, carrying them straight to Huahine.

Early the next morning as they approached the north-west coast of the island, several canoes came out whose crews seemed very frightened. Tupaia talked with these people, who had never seen Europeans before, reassuring them that the strangers were friendly. Eventually a leading chief of Huahine, Ori (also known as Mato), a fine-looking man six feet four inches tall with a great mop of hair, came on board with his wife.[14] When Tupaia introduced Ori to Cook, the chief exchanged names with the captain, taking him as his *taio*. As the *Endeavour* approached the pass leading into Fare Harbour, Tupaia sent an islander to dive down and measure the depth of its keel, impressing Cook with his caution; and guided the ship safely into the harbour.

Fare Harbour, Huahine

Upon landing at Fare the high priest stripped his garments down to his waist, a sign of respect to the local gods, and asked William Monkhouse (whom he recognised as the *Endeavour*'s *tahu'a* or priest) to do the same. Gesturing that Cook, Banks, Solander and Monkhouse should stand behind him, Tupaia sat opposite a group of chiefs who had gathered in a long house, the main *'arioi* house on the island. He chanted for almost fifteen minutes while Ori gave the responses, and afterwards he presented Ori with two handkerchiefs, a black silk neckcloth, some beads and two small bunches of feathers as a *maro tai* offering to the local gods; while the chief handed Tupaia a return gift of plantains and other sacred plants. Two other chiefs spoke for the Huahine people, presenting Tupaia with plantain plants and two small bunches of feathers, and at the end of this ceremony Ori gave coconuts and a pig to the British for their own gods. As Cook remarked with a rare, wry flash of humour, 'thus they have certainly drawn us in to commit sacrilege, for the Hog hath already received sentence of death and is to be dissected tomorrow'.[15] Immediately after this ritual, Tupaia took Monkhouse to the local *marae* to pay his respects to Tane, presenting two handkerchiefs to the god as an offering; and afterwards he presented Monkhouse with a pig.

From these rituals, it is clear that Tupaia was taking Cook, Banks, Solander and their shipmates on an *'arioi* voyage. The ceremonies he had just enacted were those performed when a party of *'arioi* visited another island, although the gifts that Tupaia presented on this occasion were relatively modest. According to Orsmond, when visiting *arioi* arrived at an island they were invited to the local *'arioi* house and made welcome, and the black leg *'arioi* from the visiting party presented their *maro tai* (sea voyage offering) to the local gods, chanting:

> There is your sea voyage offering, o god!
> A fine mat, *'ura* feathers, *'arioi* cloth
> A pig, half a breadfruit, and a bunch of braided coconut leaves
> They are for our safe arrival at this island.
>
> Let your shadow be one of *aroha* [love, compassion], o god!
> Let no harm befall us while we are at this island
> Until we sail away
> Listen to our request, o god![16]

After these exchanges the head priest of the visiting *'arioi* went to the local *marae*, as Tupaia had just done, taking red feather amulets and a piece of coral rock from his home island as an offering to the gods of the island. Polynesian navigators still follow this ritual; for instance at Taputapuatea in Ra'iatea, where sailors who have arrived on voyaging canoes often leave pieces of stone or shell necklaces from their home islands in front of the small shrine where 'Oro's *fare atua* (or god-house) once stood – a poignant tribute to their ancestors.

Tupaia was a familiar figure on Huahine, with estates at Ta'areu, Maeva, Fai'e and Farerea, and seats on two local *marae*, Manunu and Mata'irea;[17] but his arrival on this occasion was unprecedented. His appearance on board this weird craft, the first European ship they had ever seen, was disconcerting, but also a sign of hope; because according to James Magra (one of the sailors who had a good grasp of Tahitian), the Borabora warriors under Puni who had conquered Ra'iatea were also in the process of trying to subjugate Huahine.[18] Like Tupaia, at this time Ori was hostile to Puni and his warriors, complaining that they came every month or six weeks to raid his island, killing everyone who opposed them, and he begged Cook to destroy them. It is probable that Tupaia had brought the *Endeavour* to Huahine because he hoped to persuade Cook to join Ori and his warriors in an attack on Borabora; but Cook was unwilling to get involved in inter-island warfare. Contrary to island custom, he resolutely refused his friends' pleas to attack and kill Puni's marauding warriors.

The following day, Banks, Parkinson and Spöring went ashore at Fare Harbour, where they examined some large boat-houses, their pillars carved with the heads of men, dogs and other patterns; and visited a god-house at a local *marae*, escorted by Taiato, Tupaia's young *'arioi* attendant. Banks was aggrieved by the high priest's absence, grumbling that he was 'too much engagd with his freinds to have time to accompany us'.[19] He and his companions carefully examined the *fare atua* or god-house at this *marae*, which Parkinson and Spöring both sketched; Banks describing it as a wooden chest with a lid tightly sewn on, supported on two poles by a row of little carved arches (the ribs of Ta'aroa, whose body had been transformed into the first god-house). A round hole at the end of the *fare atua* was stopped up with bark cloth, which Banks did not touch because he did not want to offend the local people; although when he looked at the god-house the next day the cloth was gone and it was empty, no doubt to protect its contents from such impious scrutiny. After Cook's refusal to attack Borabora, ignoring Ori's urgent entreaties, the high chief spent most of his time with Tupaia, although when the *Endeavour* was about to sail he came to farewell Cook and his companions. Cook gave Ori some medallions and a small metal plate stamped with an inscription, *His Brittanick Maj. Ship Endeavour, Lieutt Cook Commander, 16 July 1769, Huaheine*, asking him to present these to any other visiting commander. The high chief must have considered this a gift of some significance, because he promised to keep it always in his possession.

At daylight on 20 July as they sailed from Fare Harbour, Tupaia told the helmsman to steer the ship west, heading directly for 'Opoa on the south-east coast of Ra'iatea. When they arrived at Oatara islet off the coast of 'Opoa, Tupaia went in the pinnace with Molyneux to take soundings, guiding the ship through the sacred pass, Te Ava-mo'a. As the ship entered the lagoon, two canoes came out, each bringing a chiefly woman who carried an *'arioi* pig as an offering in recognition of this extraordinary arrival. When these two women boarded the *Endeavour* and presented their pigs, they were each given a spike nail and some beads, which delighted them. After talking with these women, Tupaia, who always spoke of the Borabora warriors with dread, told Cook that his enemies were planning to attack the *Endeavour* the next day. In order to avoid a confrontation, Cook hurried ashore with Joseph Banks, Dr Solander and Tupaia, who guided them to Taputapuatea, the headquarters of the *'arioi* cult where he had been trained. With his companions standing behind him on the beach, Tupaia repeated the ritual he had performed at Huahine, chanting to the gods and presenting his *maro tai* or sea voyage offering to 'Oro.

When the ceremony was over, Cook ordered the English Jack (a white flag with the red cross of St George) to be hoisted on a pole. As the marines lined up in their scarlet coats, standing at attention, Cook read a proclamation formally taking possession of Ra'iatea, Taha'a, Huahine and Borabora in the name of King George III of Great Britain. For the Tahitian onlookers, this was an astonishing sight. Years earlier when the Borabora warriors had attacked Taputapuatea, Vaita, the priest of 'Oro, had prophesied that a canoe without an outrigger was coming, bringing a new kind of people who would take over the islands. In the company of these powerful strangers and in defiance of the Borabora conquerors, Tupaia had accomplished this prediction, bringing the 'canoe without an outrigger' to Taputapuatea and guiding the 'glorious children of Tetumu' ashore. Escorted by their red-coated warriors (the marines), the strangers had just proclaimed the *mana* of their gods over Taputapuatea, the most sacred site in the Society Islands.

Tupaia now led his companions to the great *marae*. Banks described Taputapuatea's main *ahu* as a stone platform about eight feet high, faced with immense coral slabs and with many carved planks or *unu* on its summit. A large roasted pig lay on the sacrificial platform (*fata*) next to the *ahu*, which Sydney Parkinson drew in his sketchbook; and in a large house nearby, the sacred *marae* drums were stored. Here they were greeted by priests called *heiva*, who wore high wickerwork headdresses (or *fau*) decorated with feathers, feather garments adorned with round pieces of mother-of-pearl, and *taumi* or breastplates fringed with white dog hair and decorated with plaited twine woven into intricate patterns,

Taputapuatea marae, Ra'iatea

over which rows of green pigeon feathers alternated with semicircular rows of shark's teeth; and Parkinson also sketched one of these men. The priests were attended by small boys, smutted with charcoal, who helped to place the sacrifices for the gods on the *fata*. Near the main stone platform, four or five god-houses (*fare atua*) known as 'Oro stood on posts, each with its long canoe-shaped chest supported on a row of little carved arches, where poles were inserted so that the priests could carry the gods in procession.

Driven by curiosity, Joseph Banks put his hand inside one of these god-houses and grabbed a parcel wrapped in mats, about five feet long by one foot thick, tearing the matting apart with his fingers. This must have been the *to'o* (god-image) of 'Oro himself,[20] and after ripping the matting, Banks tugged at the sennit binding around the image. This was the *'aha-mata-iti a Tane*, the multi-coloured sennit associated with Tane, the god of beauty, ritually wrapped around 'Oro as his 'skin' in a ritual that 'gave the beauty of Tane to 'Oro and the power of 'Oro to Tane'.[21] Horrified by this sacrilege, the priests 'behaved so coolly that the captain did not know what to make of them. Toobaiah, who was with him, seemed to be quite displeased. We did not know the occasion of their reservedness.'[22] This was obtuse, because the god-houses were intensely *ra'a* or sacred. The *to'o* or image of 'Oro was the god himself, and when Tane's sennit was wrapped around the *to'o*, the ritual was so sacred that a human sacrifice was always offered.

Although Tupaia was also aghast at Banks's temerity, he was still hoping to persuade the British to attack the Borabora warriors. Leading them to a nearby *'arioi* long house, he showed them rolls of bark cloth, and a model canoe about three feet long hung up in the house upon which eight lower jawbones were suspended, explaining that these were the jaw-bones of Raiatean men, hung there as trophies by the Borabora invaders. Banks and Solander walked further along the coast, where they came to another god-house whose base was also decorated with the jawbones of defeated warriors. As mentioned earlier, *marae* in Tahiti were described as mouths that consumed everything that came within their reach, and jaw-bones (taken from the bodies of ordinary warriors, and fastened together into *'titi taa'* or 'strings of jaws')[23] were a fitting tribute to 'Oro. Banks and Solander saw only a few people in this district and they seemed demoralised and impoverished, no doubt because of the devastation caused by the raids of the Borabora warriors.

Wandering around the coast the next morning, Banks saw many large arched canoe-houses. Ra'iatea was famous for its canoes, and the men in these houses were making or repairing *pahi*, the double sailing canoes

Canoe house in Ra'iatea

that were used on their voyages to other islands, dexterously dubbing out the hulls with their stone adzes. These *pahi* were large, some as much as seventy feet long, with planks sewn onto a solid keel, and Spöring and Parkinson both completed detailed drawings of these craft with their high curved prows and crab-claw sails; while Banks described how they were built, adding that 'we saw several of them at Otahite which had come from Ulhietea [Urietea or Ra'iatea] and Tupia has told us they go voyages of twenty days'.[24] During his discussions with the navigators at Ra'iatea, Banks learned that they preferred to use the middle-sized *pahi* for their longer voyages, sometimes staying at sea for several months (although they had to land on an island every fortnight or twenty days to get fresh food and water, which they carried on board in large bamboos), and that they steered their canoes by the sun and the stars:

> In their longer Voyages they steer in the day by the Sun and in the night by the Stars. Of these they know a very large part by their names and the clever ones among them will tell in what part of the heavens they are to be seen in any month when they are above their horizon; they know also the time of their annual appearing and disapearing to a great nicety, far greater than would be easily beleivd by an European astronomer.[25]

During this brief stay at 'Opoa, Banks and Solander explored various *marae* and canoe-houses and searched inland for new plants, without much success; while Cook and Molyneux surveyed the north and south coasts of the island. Dr Monkhouse was put in charge of the trade with local people – much to the indignation of the sailors, who were forbidden to barter for curiosities or have sex with the local women. Tupaia sometimes accompanied Banks and Solander on their botanising expeditions, but the high priest spent most of his time with his 'arioi friends and the priests at Taputapuatea, no doubt exchanging news, recounting his adventures with the British, and discussing ways of getting rid of the Borabora invaders. When Cook sailed from 'Opoa Harbour he ignored Tupaia's advice, heading for the noa (common, non-sacred), northern Iriru pass rather than for Te Ava-mo'a, the ra'a (sacred) pass to the south, almost wrecking the Endeavour on the coral in the process. He had to wait at anchor until 25 July when a north-west breeze came up which carried the ship through the northern pass and out into the open ocean.

As they sailed along the east coast of Ra'iatea and Taha'a, the adjoining island, Tupaia pointed out the Toahotu pass into Ha'amene Bay, telling Cook that this led to a very good harbour; and when they came to the wide channel between Taha'a and Borabora, Cook intended to head east between the islands, but the winds were contrary so he carried on north, sighting Tupai, a low atoll that according to Tupaia was inhabited by three families, and produced only coconuts and fish. The next day they turned south again, frustrated by the wind, reaching Toahotu Pass on the eastern side of Taha'a where Molyneux went ashore with Banks and Solander to barter for provisions. The people of Taha'a greeted the strangers with awe, dropping their garments to the waist, and the travellers obtained three pigs, twenty chickens and innumerable plantains at this island, which were boiled and eaten on board the Endeavour instead of breadfruit or bread, because the ship's bread was so full of weevils that it tasted like mustard.

On 29 July when the wind changed, Cook steered towards the high craggy peaks of Borabora. The island looked barren, and they could see a large salt lagoon between the beach and the mountain. According to Tupaia, these people had plenty of pigs, fruit and chickens; and although there was no passage through the reef on the east side of Borabora, a good pass through its western reef led into a fine harbour. Cook was keen to visit this island but Tupaia dissuaded him, saying that its inhabitants were bold warriors who would certainly attack him and his people. He told Cook that when a European ship had been wrecked at Borabora some years earlier, the inhabitants had killed all of the crew and taken the iron from the vessel (although probably Cook did not understand him properly, and he was in fact referring to the wreck of Roggeveen's ship in the Tuamotu

Islands). In the event, Cook did not land on Borabora, but headed instead down the west coast of Taha'a. When Maurua (now known as Maupiti) came into sight, Tupaia reported that this island was very fertile, although there was no pass through its reef big enough for the *Endeavour*. Pointing to the Paipai pass opposite Hurepiti Bay on the west coast of the island, he said that there was a good anchorage behind it. His expert knowledge of the islands was obvious, and Banks remarked, 'we now had a very good opinion of Tupias pilotage, especialy since we observd him at Huahine send a man to dive down to the heel of the ship's rudder; this the man did several times and reported to him the depth of water the ship drew; after which he has never sufferd her to go in less than 5 fathom water without being much alarmd'.[26]

After noting a leak in the *Endeavour*'s powder room, Cook decided to careen the ship for repairs at one of the bays on Ra'iatea. At Tupaia's suggestion they headed for Rautoanui Pass on the west side of the island opposite Ha'amanino Bay, the high priest's home district. As they approached the pass, the tide flowed out so strongly that the ship lay to that night, visited by large numbers of canoes. On 1 August 1769 the boats were lowered, warping the *Endeavour* through the pass and into Ha'amanino Bay, a snug little cove where a freshwater river still winds out to the bay through groves of coconut trees. Tupaia told Banks and Solander that he owned estates around this harbour, as well as in other districts of Ra'iatea (at Tevaitoa, Punaroa, Tetoaroa Bay, Ha'ava Valley, Utautua, Urupai, Uturoa, Tepua Valley, Hamoa Valley, Fa'aroa Valley and Farepa), but that all of his lands had been seized by the Borabora invaders. He identified his *marae* on Ra'iatea as Tainu'u in the Tevaitoa district, the largest *marae* on the island and traditionally associated with the royal family from Rarotonga,[27] and Taputapuatea at 'Opoa.[28]

Ha'amanino was an *'arioi* headquarters, and when Banks, Solander and Parkinson went ashore, escorted by armed sailors, the inhabitants crowded around them, competing to carry the British on their backs over streams and muddy patches. At a long *'arioi* house when the crowd parted to let them through, they found a mat about thirty feet long laid on the ground with several pretty little girls sitting at one end, accompanied by a young woman. As Banks remarked, 'without stirring [they] expected us to come up to them and make them presents, which we did with no small pleasure for prettier children or better dressd we had no where seen'.[29] One of these little girls was dressed in red bark cloth, with a large quantity of plaited hair around her head, a chiefly ornament, and as Banks and Solander approached her:

She stretchd out her hand to receive the beads we were to give, but had she been a princess royal of England giving her hand to be kissd no instruction could have taught her to have done it with a better grace. So much is untaught nature superior to art that I have seen no sight of the kind that has struck me half so much.[30]

In another of these houses an *'arioi* performed a comic dance, donning a wickerwork helmet or *fau* about four feet high (which Parkinson also sketched), an *'arioi* warrior's headdress decorated with feathers edged with shark's teeth and tropic bird feathers).[31] This man danced gracefully, sometimes slowly and at other times turning his head rapidly so that his headdress whirled, almost touching the faces of people in the crowd and

Tupaia's sketch of an 'arioi dancer in Ra'iatea

'arioi *dancing in Ra'iatea*

making them laugh heartily, especially when he did this to the British. Afterwards they were shown the inside of a *fare atua* or god-house, decorated on the outside with jawbones and full of bundles wrapped in bark cloth; and when Banks managed to persuade a priest to unwrap one of these bundles, they found that it contained a skull complete with its jawbone. Although Banks speculated that these bundles contained the skulls of those on the victors' side who had died in battle, while the jawbones hung on the outside of the house belonged to those who had been defeated, the priests resolutely refused to answer any questions about these relics.

The following day, 3 August, Cook, Banks and Solander took the pinnace up the north-west coast of Ra'iatea to survey the coastline and barter for fresh food, while the officers supervised the loading of ballast and the carpenters repaired the leaks in the powder room. They went ashore at a bay called Tapioi, where a *heiva* (or *'arioi* troupe) with three drummers, two female and six male dancers entertained them for several hours. Tupaia, who accompanied them, explained that the performers in this troupe were all high-born people. The female dancers had *tamau* or headdresses made from cords of plaited human hair (which Banks measured after the performance, estimating that the cord in each headdress was more than a mile long) wound around their heads, interspersed with scented white flowers. They wore black bodices with bunches of black feathers on each shoulder, and short, thickly ruffled red and white skirts over white bark-cloth petticoats; and one of these women had three large pearls suspended from her ears.[32] The women stood on a large mat, and as they danced they advanced sideways along it, rapidly rotating their hips to make their ruffled skirts and long petticoats shimmer, sometimes standing, and at others sitting or resting on their knees and elbows, moving their arms, hands and fingers with incredible rapidity. Although Banks and his companions found the dancers' hip movements erotic, these had no particular meaning, for their hands and arms told the story.[33]

From time to time the dancers twisted their mouths in grimaces that their visitors found grotesque. This was the *hura*, a stately dance performed by high chiefly women. An old man, their teacher, called out between each dance, announcing the next item. The dances were greeted with enthusiastic applause; and during the interludes, the male performers (known as *fa'ata*) acted out a kind of farce in both dance and speech, representing a battle between the Borabora warriors and those of Ra'iatea in which the

'Arioi *dancer grimacing during the* hura

latter were defeated.[34] According to Parkinson, the actions mimed by the men during this last scene were extremely 'lascivious'.

The following day Banks and Solander went ashore again at Ha'amanino Bay, where the local people confirmed everything that Tupaia had told them about his lands around the harbour, pointing out some of his estates or *fenua*. They told Banks that most of the people now occupying Ha'amanino Bay were originally from Borabora, and that Puni, the high chief of that island, would soon be arriving. For Tupaia, this return to his conquered birthplace was sad and humiliating, and he gave one of the sailors, James Magra, a long account of the invasion of Ra'iatea and his own subsequent history which is almost indistinguishable from the oral narratives about this period collected by the early missionaries on the island. According to Tupaia's own account, Borabora had been a place of exile to which the high chiefs of Tahiti and other islands had despatched thieves and other malefactors. The outcasts soon became pirates, however, and began to attack those who had banished them. When Puni (who was now almost ninety years old) became the leader of the Borabora warriors, they attacked and conquered Taha'a, before attacking Ra'iatea, where Tupaia had been a subordinate chief. The Ra'iatea people had fought bravely, resisting the invaders over a three-year period until Puni killed their high chief. Afterwards his young son was immediately declared his successor, and invested with the *maro 'ura* at Taputapuatea. After a final attack during which Tupaia was wounded, the young chief was forced to flee to Tahiti, followed by Tupaia who soon became Purea's lover and the high priest of Papara. When Tutaha, the uncle of Tu, began to scheme against Purea, according to Tupaia he advised her to have him killed but she refused; and when the people of Tahiti-iti invaded Papara soon afterwards, Tutaha became the regent for the new high chief of the island. After conquering Purea's people, Tutaha and his allies allowed her, her son Teri'irere and Tupaia to retain their ritual privileges.[35]

Puni must have been worried about visiting the British, given that they had arrived in the company of Tupaia, his inveterate enemy. The next day, instead of coming himself, he sent three very pretty young girls with gifts of pigs and chickens to welcome them to the island. Cook and Banks were eager to meet this famous warrior, and the following evening when they went to visit him at the bay where he was staying, Puni greeted them without ceremony. Banks was deflated by his first sight of this great conqueror:

The King of the *Tata toas* [ta 'ata toa, warriors] or Club men who have conquerd this [island] and are the terror of all other Islands we expected to see young,

lively, hansome &c &c but how were we disapointed when we were led to an old
decrepid half blind man who seemd to have scarce reason enough to send hogs,
much less galantry enough to send ladies.[36]

Cook was also unimpressed by Puni, but when the high chief invited
him to visit his headquarters at Putuputu (now Hurepiti) Harbour on the
west coast of Taha'a, he thought it politic to accept. Very early the next
morning he and Dr Solander went in the pinnace and longboat, escorted
by Puni and a number of canoes, and proceeded to Hurepiti, which had
many large houses and fine canoes. When they landed, Cook presented
Puni with an axe in the hope that the chief would encourage the local
people to be generous, but Puni was still fearful and soon departed. They
obtained few provisions during their visit to this deep inlet, although
Cook completed a chart of the harbour.

During that day, Banks stayed behind with Tupaia at Ha'amanino Bay,
bartering for 'curiosities', and neither of them met Puni. No doubt Tupaia
was avoiding an encounter with his enemy. Instead he and Banks accompanied Parkinson to the *heiva*, where the male *'arioi* divided into two
groups, one group dressed in white and the other in brown bark cloth, and
performed a sequence of five or six skits; the chief of the 'brown' group
giving his servant a basket of meat to look after, while the 'white' group,
who were evidently thieves under the protection of Hiro, attempted
to steal it. Their efforts were in vain until at last the servant fell asleep,
and they gently lifted away the basket in triumph. Tupaia and Parkinson
sketched the three female dancers at this *heiva*, and Tupaia told his companions that the troupe would move slowly around the island over the
coming weeks, entertaining the people. When Solander and Banks visited
the troupe the next day, recording their names, they were given a quantity
of bark cloth and a 'very good dinner'. The ship was now plentifully supplied with pigs, chickens, plantains and yams, and at noon on 9 August
when the *Endeavour*'s anchors were raised, as Banks noted laconically, 'we
again Launchd out into the Ocean in search of what chance and Tupia
might direct us to'.[37]

In fact, as the *Endeavour* sailed away from the Society Islands, Tupaia lost
control of the voyage. Although he urged Cook to head west where he
said there were plenty of islands, some of which he had previously visited
in a voyage that 'took 10 to 12 days going thither, and 30 or more coming
back'[38] (two of which Cook identified as Tafahi and Niuatoputapu in the
Tongan archipelago, both of which are included in Tupaia's island lists),[39]
Cook turned south instead, following his instructions to search for Terra

Australis. He was curious about Tupaia's story, however, asking him how he and his companions had managed to sail home again from the western islands against the prevailing winds. In response, the high priest told him about westerly wind shifts in November to January which his people used to sail to these islands, returning home when the winds changed back to an easterly direction. When Cook asked Tupaia whether there were any islands to the south, and whether he had heard of any large land-masses on that bearing, Tupaia replied that the most southerly island that he had ever visited was Moutou (the old name for Tupua'i in the Austral Islands), south-east of Tahiti; and although his father had told him about islands further south, none of these was very large as far as he knew. If Cook continued to sail south, however, he would find an island called Manu'a a little to the east of their current course (according to the island lists collected a little later by the Spanish, Manu'a, a large, uninhabited island with a lagoon, was the homeland of the first inhabitants of Huahine). Although 'Manu'a' has often been identified with a group of islands by this name in the Samoan archipelago, these lay west, not south; and yet, as Johann Forster later noted, Tupaia had an accurate sense of his bearings throughout this voyage, identifying these with the directions of particular winds (the Tahitian equivalent of cardinal points on a compass).[40]

On this occasion the winds were unfavourable for a visit to Manu'a, however; and on 12 August when they passed this island without sighting it. Tupaia said that it was now 'e topa [it falls]', a term also used for the setting of the sun. On their current bearing, he said, they would soon arrive at another island called 'Hiti-roa', which he had visited twenty-three years earlier; although these people had had no further contact with the northern islands. At noon the next day when 'Hiti-roa' (Rurutu, one of the Austral Islands) loomed over the horizon, Tupaia recited the names of a number of other islands to the south and the south-west, most of which also began with Hiti- (the islands to the south being Tupua'i and Raivavae in the Austral Islands, and those to the south-west being associated with the story of the ancestor Rata's great voyage). That night the high priest fished for tuna from the deck of the *Endeavour*, using his own rod and a mother-of-pearl lure, although his rod broke when the first big fish struck the lure.

When they approached Rurutu the next morning, Banks, Solander and Tupaia went ashore in a ship's boat commanded by Lieutenant Gore, where they were challenged by about sixty warriors who stood on the beach brandishing long lances. As the boat rowed along the beach, two men dived into the sea and tried to swim out to them. They were soon left behind, however, and when two others swam out, they also failed

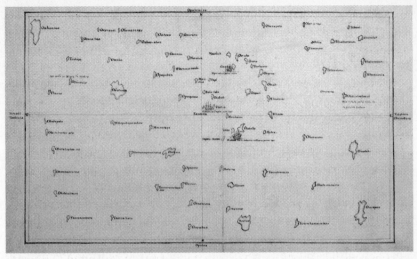

Tupaia's chart (with Cook) of the islands around Tahiti

to reach the strangers. When one warrior finally reached the boat, Gore refused to allow him on board. Tupaia told Banks that the people on this island had only one canoe (explaining why they no longer had contact with the northerly islands); and when this small, narrow, highly carved craft pushed off from Avera Bay and approached the boat, its crew (who seemed friendly at first) soon jumped on board and tried to capture this strange vessel. Two muskets were fired overhead and they quickly jumped into the sea, but one of the sailors fired again, wounding one of these men with a musket ball that grazed his forehead.

As the boat rowed in towards the beach, a single warrior armed with a long spear challenged them. The challenger was soon joined by another warrior wearing a tall cap decorated with tropic bird tail feathers, and garments striped in red, yellow and brown. When an older man joined them, evidently a priest, he asked where the strangers had come from. As soon as Tupaia replied that they came from Tahiti, the elder began to chant at the top of his voice. Tupaia gave the responses, but at the same time warned Gore and Banks that these people were hostile. Although some of the local people laid down their weapons and approached the boat, bartering some cloth and a few weapons, Gore decided not to attempt a landing, because his men had only muskets without bayonets, and if these weapons got wet in the surf they would be useless.

After this futile expedition the boat returned to the ship, and the next day they sailed south from Rurutu. On the following day everybody on board was deceived by a cloud on the horizon which they mistook for an island or the Unknown Southern Continent. Tupaia, who had offered a name for this 'island', was deeply chagrined when he discovered that it was a mirage. Now that he had reached the limits of his voyaging experience, he began to pass on more of his geographical knowledge to Cook and Banks, describing a total of about 130 islands (including some further south) and sketching a chart of the islands around Tahiti.[41] When Cook drafted the final version of this chart,[42] he misunderstood the Tahitian words for north and south (which identify north as the direction towards which the south wind blows and vice versa), thus reversing the positions of a number of islands;[43] and translated the distances travelled between islands, described in 'nights' by Tupaia, into estimates of cartographic distance, resulting in further distortions. In addition, Cook used his own charts to locate the islands that he had thus far visited, so that the positions of the Society Islands and some of the Tuamotu in this version of Tupaia's chart are quite 'accurate' according to cartographic convention. There are also islands on the chart that don't exist in cartographic space, which is not surprising given island navigators dwelt in a world in which ancestor gods were real and islands could swim like fish, behaving in ways that were fundamentally different from the world described by Western science.

There has been much debate about this chart, with some scholars trying to 'correct' it in various ways; while others have regarded it largely as a mythological projection.[44] Both kinds of explanation, however, try to grasp Tupaia's depiction in purely European terms – the first tries to translate it into cartographic space while the second characterises his chart as fantastic, dismissing the kind of world in which Tupaia navigated. A fascinating new study that comes closer to a Tahitian cosmos demonstrates that Tupaia's map has little to do with cartographic space, but rather draws upon the ways in which navigators in the Society Islands conceived of the oceanic environment. Their knowledge of the surrounding seas was organised into lists of islands with sets of bearings (elaborated as 'star paths', or successions of stars that rose and set on the bearing of a destination island) radiating out from each island. This study argues that Tupaia's chart is a combination of such 'plotting diagrams', each with a different orientation, only one of which corresponds to the cardinal points added by Cook; an approach that allows at least forty islands on Tupaia's chart to be reliably identified.[45]

While working on this chart with Tupaia, Banks and Cook also drew upon the high priest's knowledge to produce 'Descriptions' of life in Tahiti and the Society Islands – Cook liberally copying from Banks's version. These accounts briefly describe the islands themselves, and their inhabitants, with descriptions of their physique, tattoos, clothing and ornaments, personal hygiene and ideas of modesty; houses, sleeping arrangements, cultivations and eating habits; music, dancing and other entertainments (including the *heiva*). They also give accounts of the *'arioi* society and its customs; leadership, including the roles of chiefs and priests; fishing gear, canoes, navigation, and the divisions of time; their language, with vocabularies; ways of handling marriage, illness and death; religion and *marae*; and Tahitian ideas about property. The 'Descriptions' are taxonomic in nature, based on a standardised list of topics, and are based both upon what Tupaia told them and the things that Cook and his companions had seen in the islands (or often a combination of both), frequently generalising from particular observations and incidents described in their journals.

A number of the observations included in these 'Descriptions' do not also appear in the journals. Cook noted, for instance, that when Tupaia attempted to calculate the population of Tahiti, he counted the number of fighting men mustered by each district (which added up to a total of 6780 warriors).[46] Cook added that most of the inhabitants lived on the coastal plain in scattered houses (which are marked on his charts), surrounded by fruit trees and plantations of bark-cloth trees, rather than in villages. In his generalised account of Tahitian navigation, Cook also argued that the Pacific must have been settled from west to east, a judgement vindicated by contemporary scholarship:

> In these Pahee's as they call them . . . these people sail in those seas from Island to Island for several hundred Leagues, the Sun serving them for a compass by day and the Moon and Stars by night. When this comes to be prov'd we Shall no longer be at a loss to know how the Islands lying in those Seas came to be people'd, for if the inhabitants of Uleitea have been at Islands laying 2 or 300 Leagues to the westward of them it cannot be doubted but that the inhabitants of those western Islands may have been at others as far to westward of them and so we may trace them from Island to Island quite to the East Indias.[47]

In his more expansive 'Description', Joseph Banks gave an excellent account of the ritual separation of the sexes in Tahiti, particularly the prohibition on men and women eating together, or touching food prepared by members of the other gender. He confessed that on one occasion 'I myself spoild a large heap of [*mahi* – fermented breadfruit] only by inadvertently touching some leaves that lay upon it as I walkd by the outside of the house where it was. The old directress of it told me that from that circumstance it would certainly fail and immediately pulld it down before my face.'[48] Banks also claimed that while no woman would dare to approach the main *marae* of their district, they had their own *marae* 'where they worship and sacrifice to their Godesses'.[49] It appears that although men in Tahiti were relatively *ra'a* or sacred compared with women, who were relatively *noa* or profane, some women were of such high descent that they were more *ra'a* than men; and these 'Great Women' transcended the prohibition on eating with men or food prepared by men, and had *marae* and *'arioi* lodges of their own.

Although some later accounts of Tahitian society describe men and women (perhaps unmarried?) as sleeping in different houses, according to Banks a man and his wife slept in the middle of their dwelling, near the other married people of the household. Next to them lay the unmarried women, with the unmarried men at a little distance, while the *teuteu* or servants slept outside. He commented that because these houses had no walls, there was no privacy, 'even [for] those actions which the decency of Europeans keep most secret',[50] speculating that perhaps it was for this reason that local conversation was often ribald, which the Tahitians greatly enjoyed but the British considered indecent. Premarital sex was not frowned upon, and when the young girls danced and sang, their words and actions were sometimes highly erotic, although they were expected to give up this kind of dancing once they were in a stable relationship.[51] Many high-born people, however, practised 'free liberty in love', having serial affairs but destroying any children that were born from these unions. These people, known as *'arioi*, had meetings where the young women danced the 'indecent dances, . . . [giving] full liberty to their desires'; while the men wrestled and had other entertainments.

Banks added that the Tahitians were very skilled in predicting the weather, which they did by examining the arch of the Milky Way, saying that if this curved in one particular direction all night, the wind would come from that quarter the next day. He reported that although Tupaia was eager to teach him and his companions about the gods in Tahiti, this proved almost impossible, because the priests in the islands discussed such matters in a specialised language. Indeed, Banks's account of Tahitian religion was garbled, although he did grasp that Tumu and Papa were two of the original beings in the cosmos.[52] Because of his *taio* friendship with Banks, Tupaia was keen to instruct him in these esoteric matters, because it was impossible to understand life in Tahiti without a knowledge of the gods; but Banks was a devout empiricist, and his cosmological assumptions about the world did not sufficiently coincide with Tupaia's to allow such a conversation. In addition, the vocabularies collected by Banks, Molyneux and Parkinson are relatively brief and schematic, relying heavily on gesture as the primary means of communication. Although they managed to communicate sufficiently well with Tupaia for many practical purposes, when it came to more complex topics, they could never be certain that they truly understood what he was saying.

It is easy, however, to imagine the conversations between Tupaia, Cook and the Royal Society scientists and artists as they sat in the *Endeavour*'s Great Cabin, surrounded by a clutter of charts, books, sketches, specimens of animals in bottles and plants pressed in paper, with bundles of seaweed dangling from the ceiling. This endless journey south must have been a revelation for the high priest, because as he explained to his friends, voyages in the islands usually lasted a maximum of twenty days. As the voyage went on and the weather became colder, the yams on board began to rot and the pigs and chickens died; and by 28 August Tupaia was complaining of pains in his stomach. Two days later when a very large, faint comet appeared in the sky, he declared that this was a sign that the Borabora warriors were about to attack Ra'iatea. As the weeks went by, Dr Solander also began to suffer from scurvy. Banks opened one of the bottles of essence of lemon juice, and the ship's cook made them a delicious pie with preserved North American apples. By 1 October flocks of small birds flew about the ship and pieces of seaweed floated on the surface of the sea, which they took to be signs of land – perhaps Terra Australis.

On 6 October 1769 in light breezes and fine weather, Joseph Banks observed:

> At half past one a small boy who was at the mast head Calld out Land. I was luckyly upon deck and well was I entertaind, within a few minutes the cry circulated and up came all hands, this land could not then be seen even from the tops yet few were there who did not plainly see it from the deck till it appeard that they had lookd at least 5 points wrong.[53]

On this occasion Tupaia had no identification to offer, because this large land-mass was beyond the limits of his known world. As Banks reported in excitement, there was 'much difference of opinion and many conjectures about Islands, rivers, inlets &c, but all hands seem to agree that this is certainly the Continent we are in search of'.[54] The winds were light and variable, and it was not until two days later that the *Endeavour* sailed into Tūranga-nui or 'Poverty Bay', as Cook named it, a wide bay on the east coast of the North Island of New Zealand. When he saw a palisade on an offshore island, Tupaia guessed that this must be a *marae*, while his British companions thought that it might be an enclosure for deer or cattle (although in fact it was a fortified village).

As the *Endeavour* sailed in to the bay several canoes crossed its wake but quickly returned to shore, seeming to take little notice of this strange apparition. According to the tribal histories, however, there was wild speculation on shore. Some local people guessed that this must be a floating island, heading into their harbour, while others thought that it was the great ancestral bird that had flown to the homeland, Hawaiki, to fetch the *kūmara* or sweet potato. When they saw 'a smaller bird, unfledged (without sails), descending into the water, and a number of parti-coloured beings, but apparently in the human shape, also descending, the bird was regarded as a houseful of divinities. Nothing could exceed the astonishment of the people.'[55] Still others recalled a prophecy by Toiroa, a priest from a school of learning at Mahia to the south, when he fell into a trance and spoke with his gods. His back arched and the fingers of his raised hands splayed out, as he darted about like a lizard, chanting:

Tiwhatiwha te pō	Dark, dark is Te Pō [the realm of ancestors]
Ko te Pakerewhā	It is the red and white strangers
Ko Arikirangi tēnei rā e haere nei.	It is the high chief from the sky that is coming.[56]

It seemed likely that these were the red and white strangers, but no one was certain whether these beings were ancestors, gods or people.

That afternoon when Cook, Banks and Solander went ashore on the west bank of the Tūranga-nui River, they left four of the ship's boys guarding the yawl. As the officers explored a small fishing camp on the west bank, the boys wandered down onto the beach, where they were challenged by four warriors who came down from a nearby hill, gesticulating with their spears to challenge the strangers. When the boys yelled for help and tried frantically to row down the river, one of the warriors pulled back his spear to throw it at the yawl (a challenge demanding that they declare their identity); and the coxswain, alerted by their cries, shot him dead with his musket. This was Te Maro from Te Aitanga-a-Hauiti, the kin group that occupied the lands east of the river.

The next day when Cook, Banks, Solander and Green returned ashore with Tupaia, escorted by a party of marines wearing their scarlet jackets, a war party quickly gathered on the opposite side of the river where they performed an impassioned *haka* (war dance) in protest against the shooting. As he listened, Tupaia realised that he could understand what these people were saying. Ra'iatea and Tahiti were among the homelands of Māori, and Tupaia, a gifted linguist who had visited different Polynesian archipelagos, could decipher the sound shifts between their languages.

Calling out to the warriors, he assured them that his companions only wanted fresh food and water; but at the same time he warned the British that these people could not be trusted. When Tupaia finally managed to persuade one of the warriors to swim across the river, this man landed on a rock at the edge of the tide –Te Toka-a-Taiau, a famous landmark and a boundary marker between tribes where a *mauri*, a sacred stone from the homeland, had been buried. When the warrior refused to come any closer, Captain Cook put down his musket and approached him, and they pressed noses in greeting. Some of his companions now ventured across the river, and when one of these men seized Green's sword, Banks and his comrades fired simultaneously, killing one of these men – Te Rākau from Rongowhakaata, a chief from the west side of the river. Tupaia, whose gun was loaded with small shot, fired last, hitting two warriors in the legs and crippling them – in this dangerous situation, he had no hesitation about using European weapons.

Later that day three young boys were captured from a fishing canoe and brought on board the *Endeavour*, where Cook hoped to befriend them. Tupaia talked with these boys, asking them about their gods, their chief, local place names and customs; although when they told him that they ate their enemies, he reacted with horror. That night he stayed with the boys, comforting them when they woke up in terror. The next day when Tupaia went ashore he approached the dead bodies of the two men who had been shot, watched by a party of local warriors. He gave the boys a scarlet coat to lay on the corpse of their dead kinsman, and spoke to these people. Tupaia was a high priest of 'Oro from Havai'i (the old name of Ra'iatea), the homeland of Māori, and in these situations he could say what he liked, as the British could not speak Māori. Very likely these people identified Tupaia with 'Ariki-rangi', the high chief from the sky whose arrival Toiroa had predicted. He could speak their language, and had arrived in a strange *waka* (canoe) with these bizarre, powerful companions. As in Tahiti, red was the colour of the gods, and afterwards the descendants of these people cherished this coat for its extraordinary associations, naming it 'Te Mākura' and using its scarlet glow to predict the outcome of battles.[57]

After leaving Tūranga-nui, the *Endeavour* sailed south, and when the wind died and the ship was becalmed off Ongaonga, the man who had pressed noses with Cook on Te Toka-a-Taiau caught up with them in his canoe, and told Tupaia that the young fishermen had told their families that the strangers had treated them kindly. News of Tupaia's presence was spreading along the coast, and a number of chiefs came alongside the ship in their canoes, their faces painted red with ochre, the sacred colour. At the north end of the Māhia peninsula, an *ariki* (or high chief) boarded the *Endeavour*, gazing about in amazement. Off Waikawa, an island off the peninsula where an ancestral canoe had left another *mauri* stone from the homeland, Hawaiki, a party of warriors paddled out, faces daubed with red ochre, ready to challenge this extraordinary vessel. As they hurled their spears against the *Endeavour*'s hull, Cook ordered a great gun loaded with musket balls to be fired into the water, and the gun boomed and flashed – a spectacular demonstration of ancestral power.

Off the Ngaruroro River several days later, a man wearing a red cloak and covered in *kokowai* or red paint, the sacred colour, came out and talked with Tupaia, who asked him for the names of the local chiefs and places around this great bay (which Cook now named 'Hawke's Bay'), presenting him with gifts of iron and bark cloth. The following day when a canoe from another part of the bay came alongside, it brought out another leading chief and an old priest (perhaps Toiroa himself?) who chanted and performed rituals as they paddled towards this weird vessel. At first their exchanges were amicable, but when Tupaia's young companion Taiato went down the ship's ladder to barter with these people, the warriors pulled him down into their canoe. According to the oral histories, Tupaia shouted '*Mai, mate koe!*' ('You will be killed!'), but their ancestors replied defiantly, '*Kahore he rākau o te hunga o Hawaiiki; he pū kakaho, he korari!*' ('The people from Hawaiki have no weapons, only reeds and flax stalks!').[58] At Cook's order, the marines lined up and fired, killing several of these warriors, and when his captor fell wounded, Taiato jumped into the ocean and was hauled back on board the *Endeavour*. Later he brought Tupaia a fish as an offering for his god, and the high priest told him to throw it back into the ocean.

At Cape Turnagain, Cook tacked to the north, sailing back up the east coast of the North Island. After sailing past Poverty Bay the *Endeavour* anchored in a small bay called Anaura, where they were greeted by two heavily tattooed chiefs, one of whom wore a red feather cloak, no doubt the *ariki* (high chief) of this district, while the other wore a fine cloak decorated with transverse stripes of white dogskin. Perhaps the *ariki* and Tupaia became bond friends, because the encounters in this part of the country were peaceful. When they went ashore at Anaura, a man presented Dr Monkhouse with the body of a mummified child, a tribute to these supernatural strangers.

At Uawa or Tolaga Bay, just south of Anaura Bay, where a famous school of learning (known as Te Rāwheoro) that specialised in tribal lore and carving was sited, Tupaia was welcomed ashore, and had long conversations with the high priest of this *whare wānanga*. These must have been

*The poupou collected by Captain Cook or Tupaia at Uawa, New Zealand, as
recently restored in Dresden*

extraordinary exchanges, as the local *tohunga* (priest) asked Tupaia for news of the island homelands, known to Māori as 'Rangiatea' (Ra'iatea), 'Hawaiki' (Havai'i, the ancient name for Ra'iatea), and 'Tawhiti' (Tahiti). No doubt they talked about Tupaia's remarkable experiences on board the *Endeavour*, and the high priest told them about 'Oro. According to Banks, 'they seemed to agree very well in their notions of religion only Tupia was much more learned than the other and all his discourse was heard with much attention'.[59] Among other things, Tupaia asked this priest about the practice of *kai tangata* or cannibalism, sharply criticising this custom. Given the practice of human sacrifice in Tahiti, this might appear hypocritical; but in the Society Islands it was the gods rather than people who consumed the spirits of enemies, and it is likely that Tupaia considered cannibalism to be blasphemous.

During his stay at Uawa, Tupaia sketched a ship and some boats on the wall of the rock shelter in Opoutama ('Cook's Cove') where he slept. More than sixty years later, the local people showed this drawing to Joel Polack, a British trader, saying that it was sketched by Tupaia. Some fragments of rock drawings still survive in this shallow cave, high on the northern cliffs in this small, sheltered haven. According to Polack, local Māori called the shelter 'Tupaia's cave', and they showed him the well dug in the cove by Cook's men.[60] During this visit the high priest also painted a striking watercolour of Joseph Banks exchanging white cloth for a large crayfish. Banks, Parkinson, Spöring and Tupaia were taken out to Pourewa Island, where their guides showed them a carved canoe and an unfinished carved meeting house with carved *poupou* (ancestral wall panels) stacked against the walls.

One of these *poupou*, an ancestral portrait daubed in red ochre, may have been presented to Tupaia on this occasion, because a wall panel finely carved in the local style was brought back to England, where it was sketched and later vanished, recently reappearing in Tübingen in Germany.[61] The high priest made a remarkable impression on the local people, and it is likely that they wanted to honour him with the gift of an ancestral image. Children born during his visit were named after him, and although there are still people in the district who are reputed to be his descendants, it is likely that their family name arose from this circumstance.[62]

Tupaia's presence on board the *Endeavour* made the ship's passage around the coastline of New Zealand unlike any other during the early contact period. It was as though a great voyaging canoe had arrived from Hawaiki (the island homeland) with a high priest on board; and Māori were at once fascinated and frightened by this weird craft and its occupants. As they sailed northward to Whakatane in the 'Bay of Plenty', as

Cook named it, Tupaia talked with the crew of a fast-sailing double canoe, and afterwards they performed songs and dances for him, made speeches and chased the *Endeavour*, pelting the ship with stones and smashing some of her stern windows. At the tip of the Coromandel peninsula, another sacred site where an ancestral canoe had deposited a *mauri* stone from the homeland, two carved canoes came alongside the *Endeavour* where their crews performed an impassioned war dance, once again defending a sacred site from the strangers. Tupaia called out to their crews, telling them to go ashore or his companions would kill them, and admonishing them by saying that the sea was a place free for all travellers.

During this circumnavigation of New Zealand, double canoes often sailed ahead of the ship, taking news about Tupaia and the extraordinary vessel that was coming. At the Bay of Islands, when the high priest told the local people to give up cannibalism, they passionately defended the custom. While the ship lay becalmed off the Karikari peninsula further north, six canoes came alongside where Tupaia talked with the people about their land and their ancestors' voyages:

> They told him that a distance of three days rowing in their canoes, at a place called *Moorewhennua* [Muriwhenua], the land would take a short turn to the southward and from thence extend no more to the West. This place we concluded must be Cape Maria Van Diemen, and finding these people so intelligent desird him to enquire if they knew of any Countries besides this or ever went to any.
>
> They said no but that their ancestors had told them to the NW by N or NNW was a large countrey to which some people had saild in a very large canoe, which passage took them up to a month: from this expedition a part only returnd who told their countreymen that they had seen a countrey where the people eat hogs, for which animal they usd the same name (*Booah*) as is used in the Islands. And have you no hoggs among you? said Tupia. – No. – And did your ancestors bring none back with them? – No. – You must be a parcel of Liars then, said he, and your story a great lye for your ancestors would never have been such fools as to come back without them.[63]

By the time that they reached Totara-nui (Queen Charlotte Sound) in Cook Strait between the North and South Islands, news of this extraordinary vessel had sped before them. As they sailed into the sound, a *tohunga* (priest) stood on a small island in the entrance, dressed in a strange costume, and performed rituals with a cloak and feathers. Afterwards, canoes flocked alongside the ship whose crews talked eagerly with Tupaia 'about their antiquity and Legends of their ancestors'.

Soon after their arrival in Queen Charlotte Sound, Cook, Banks and Tupaia went exploring in a nearby cove, where they saw the body of a dead woman floating on the water. When they landed and found human bones in some food baskets, Tupaia interrogated the people, asking, 'What bones are these?' They answered, 'The bones of a man.' 'And have you eat the flesh?' 'Yes.' 'Have you none of it left?' 'No.' 'Why did you not eat the woman who we saw today in the water?' 'She was our relation.' 'Who then is it that you do eat?' 'Those who are killed in war.' 'And who was the man whose bones these are?' '5 days ago a boat of our enemies came into this bay and of them we killed 7, of whom the owner of these bones was one.'[64] At Totara-nui, Tupaia also acquired further geographical information for Cook, reporting that: 'They knew but of 3 lands one of which lay to the N which they would be 3 months in going round [which Cook identified as 'Aeheino mouwe' – *Ahi no Maui* – Maui's fire, the North Island]; another which we was upon they could go round in 4 days and a Third lyeing SWtd of which they had but a very Imperfect knolledge and called it Towie poe namou [*Te Wai Pounamu* – Greenstone Waters, the South Island].'[65] From Cook's comments, it is obvious that he already had a shrewd idea that New Zealand was not part of the Southern Continent, but was made up of islands, and that the old chief's information reinforced his opinion.

After leaving Queen Charlotte Sound, the *Endeavour* sailed south down the east coast of the South Island. Although Banks was still convinced that they had found Terra Australis, Cook was almost certain by now that New Zealand was a group of islands. On 28 February 1770 Tupaia told his shipmates that it was New Year's Day in Tahiti, when the Matahiti or First Fruits ceremony would be held, and they celebrated the festival with him. On 9 March they rounded the south cape of the South Island of New Zealand, 'to the total demolition of our aerial fabrick called continent', as Banks ruefully confessed. Sailing up the west coast, far out at sea to avoid a lee shore, they reached the west side of Cook Strait where Tupaia and Taiato went angling and caught a boatload of fish for their shipmates. During their six-month circumnavigation of New Zealand, as Cook noted with satisfaction, Tupaia had been an invaluable guide and companion:

> Should it be thought proper to send a ship out upon this service while Tupia lieves and he to come out in her, in that case she would have a prodigious advantage over every ship that have been upon discoveries in those seas before; for by means of Tupia, supposeing he did not accompany you himself, you would always get people to direct you from Island to Island and would be sure of meeting with a friendly resception and refreshments at every Island you came to.[66]

Sadly, however, Tupaia's time of usefulness to Cook and the voyage was almost over. The *Endeavour* headed east across the Tasman Sea towards the eastern coast of Australia, where in late April 1770 Cook went ashore with Tupaia at Botany Bay. When the high priest tried to talk with some of the local Aborigines, however, they looked at him in utter incomprehension, shaking their spears in defiance. He did not understand a word that they said; and although he sketched several of the local fishermen in their tiny canoes, these people found him as terrifying as the British, and ran away whenever he approached them. At Bustard Bay to the north, where they found little fresh food, Tupaia dismissed the local Aborigines as *Taata Eno* (*ta'ata 'ino* – bad people). At the same time, he was finding the shipboard provisions of salt meat and ship's biscuit inedible, and as the supplies of fresh food ran out he began to suffer from scurvy. The *Endeavour* was almost shipwrecked on the Great Barrier Reef, and when it was careened at Endeavour River for repairs, Tupaia went off hunting and shooting and soon cured himself by eating shellfish, wild bananas and taro. Increasingly, however, his shipmates were no longer prepared to tolerate his proud demeanour, and he became lonely and morose, no doubt wishing that he had never set off on this miserable voyage.

When the *Endeavour* left the east coast of Australia, heading for the East Indies, Tupaia almost vanishes from the shipboard records. By the time that they arrived at Java Head south of Batavia in the Dutch East Indies, the high priest was very ill with scurvy, craving fruit and root vegetables but refusing to take any European medicines. As soon as they arrived at Batavia, where fresh food and vegetables were abundant, he began to recover. Walking around the streets of Batavia with his young servant Taiato, Tupaia was astonished by the canals and the houses of this bustling city, although he was disgusted to find that some of these dwellings had indoor toilets, which he considered a filthy custom. Taiato was enthralled, 'almost mad with the numberless novelties which diverted his attention from one to the other, he danc'd about the streets examining every thing to the best of his abilities'.[67] When Tupaia realised that the different groups of people in the city each wore their own costumes, he donned his own bark-cloth garments again; and one day while he and Banks were out walking, a man approached them and asked if Tupaia had ever previously visited Batavia. In this way they learned about Ahutoru's visit to Batavia with Bougainville, and Banks realised that the 'Spanish' ships about which they had heard so much in Tahiti were in fact French. They were also regaled with stories about Jean Baret, Commerson's female assistant, whose presence on board had created a delectable scandal.

Māori crying out for Tupaia

After several weeks in this unhealthy city, however, Tupaia fell ill again, this time with malaria or dysentery, both of which were rife in Batavia; and Taiato caught a chest infection that quickly turned into pneumonia. Banks, Dr Solander and their servants were also suffering from an intermittent fever, and Tupaia was soon so unwell that Banks began to despair of his life. When the high priest asked to leave the ship to escape into the fresh air (blaming his illness on the houses that crowded around the harbour, blocking the free circulation of the air), Banks took him to a wooded islet in the harbour and had a tent pitched for him where the winds blew more freely.

Soon after this move, Banks's illness also came to a crisis, with fits that made him faint, and the ship's surgeon William Monkhouse fell ill and died shortly afterwards. The day after Monkhouse's funeral, Banks, who was confined to his bed, was told that Taiato had died, and that Tupaia was heartbroken at the loss of his young companion, 'whoom I well knew he sincerely lovd, tho he usd to find much fault with him during his lifetime'.[68] According to Parkinson, the high priest lay in his tent on the island, weeping and calling out, 'Taiato! Taiato!' On 20 December 1770 Banks was told that Tupaia had also died. With the death of Taiato the high priest's last link with his homeland had been lost, and life no longer seemed worth living. With no one to perform the proper rituals, it is unlikely that Tupaia's spirit made its way to Rohutu-no'ano'a, the '*arioi*'s perfumed paradise. Instead, Tupaia and Taiato were buried side by side on Eadam Island, a convict hell-hole in Batavia Harbour.

After Tupaia's death, Captain Cook remarked that: 'He was a Shrewd Sensible, Ingenious Man, but proud and obstinate which often made his situation on board both disagreable to himself and those about him, and tended much to promote the deceases which put a period to his life.'[69] Cook had also fallen ill at Batavia, which may explain these churlish comments, but Tupaia deserved a more generous epitaph. He had guided the *Endeavour* safely through the Leeward Society Islands, freely sharing his navigational and ritual knowledge with Cook and his companions. After failing to persuade Cook to help him to free his homeland from the Borabora invaders, he had continued to act as a diplomat and interpreter in all subsequent contacts between the British and Polynesian peoples.

Tupaia had also learned to execute watercolours in the European style, and to sketch charts, and everyone on board the ship acknowledged his formidable intellect. During the *Endeavour*'s voyage around New Zealand, Māori thought that this was Tupaia's ship, and when Captain Cook returned during his later voyages they came out, calling for Tupaia, singing songs about him, and weeping when they heard that he had died at Batavia. At Uawa (Tolaga Bay), where he had spent so much time with the local priests and was revered as a great *tohunga* (knowledgeable expert), when they were told of his death they chanted:

'A koe mate aue Tupaia [*Kua mate koe, aue Tupaia*]' – 'You have died – alas, Tupaia!'

The Viceroy of Peru

During the voyages of Wallis, Bougainville and Cook, the Spanish had anxiously watched these British and French incursions into the Pacific. After Francis Drake's 1569 expedition through the Strait of Magellan and up the coasts of Chile and Peru, where he had seized a treasure-trove of bullion, British buccaneers periodically raided the Spanish colonies in South America, causing mayhem; and although France fought alongside Spain against Britain during the Seven Years' War (1756–63), the Spanish were almost as uneasy about her intentions. After vehement protests by the Spanish government, Bougainville had been forced to give up his settlement in the Falkland Islands, although he was compensated for his losses; and as soon as the Spanish discovered the small British outpost at Port Egmont, they sent a force of five frigates from Buenos Aires to the island and forced them to surrender, almost provoking a renewal of war between Britain and Spain, although the crisis ended in a diplomatic stand-off. In June 1766, when the Spanish ambassador in London, the Prince of Masserano, complained to General Conway about the British voyages into the South Sea, the General remarked blandly 'that since the French go there the English may go too'.[1] Soon afterwards, Julian de Arriaga, the Spanish Secretary of State for the Indies, fearing that the British had established a colony on the coast of Patagonia or perhaps on Davis's Land (a high island off the west coast of South America reported to have been discovered by Captain Davis, a British buccaneer), sent orders to the Viceroy of Peru to have these places searched for a British outpost.

The Viceroy of Peru, Manuel de Amat y Junient, was a formidable, aristocratic Catalan who had won a reputation for military prowess in Africa before taking up his appointment as Governor of Chile. He had reorganised the Chilean Army, built towns and fortifications, and subdued the Indian population, gaining a reputation as a capable and enterprising, if autocratic, leader. In 1761 when Amat was appointed the Viceroy of

Manuel de Amat, Viceroy of Peru

Peru, he was given almost regal powers over a vast province that stretched from the Pacific to the Cordillera of the Andes, and from the second to the thirty-second parallel south. As Viceroy, he presided over the courts of justice, the councils of finance and war, and served as the captain-general of the armies on both land and sea. The only restraint on his powers was the Royal Audience, a council empowered to watch over the 'education and good treatment in spiritual and temporal matters' of the Indians; and although this council reported directly to King Carlos III, Amat was also its president.

When the British captured Havana in 1762 and a British squadron cruised close to Callao, the main port of Peru, Amat strengthened the Peruvian Army and Navy and personally supervised the construction of new coastal works and fortifications. He also commissioned a number of major civil structures in Lima – an elegant promenade; the Plaza de Toros, a bullfighting ring; a cockfighting arena; and hospitals and churches. Amat was a hot-tempered, passionate man, and he could be arrogant and haughty. His critics accused him of corruption, saying that he made huge profits from the sale of licences and royal offices, and delighted in the scandal provoked by his flamboyant affair with a young *creole* opera singer, Micaela de Villegas or 'La Perricholi'.[2]

Convinced that the British and the French were trying to establish outposts in the South Sea, Amat was suspicious of any British or French vessels that approached his territories. When a ship from French India, the *St Jean Baptiste*, arrived off the coast of Peru during 1770, he had the vessel impounded on the grounds that Surville must have been looking for Davis's Land. Soon afterwards he despatched two ships commanded by Don Félipe González to search the Patagonian seaboard for a French settlement, and to look for Davis's Land, whose precise location was unknown. The expedition found Easter Island instead, previously visited by the Dutch navigator Roggeveen in 1722, reporting that 'San Carlos' (as they named it) was a likely place for a foreign colony.[3] Shortly thereafter, Amat received a despatch from Arriaga ordering him to establish a settlement on Easter Island; followed by a brief account of Captain Cook's visit to 'King George's Island' or 'Otaheite' to observe the Transit of Venus, with royal orders to explore that island.[4]

After receiving these instructions, Amat began to organise another expedition to examine Easter Island as a potential Spanish colony, and to find and explore Tahiti. The *Santa Maria Magdalena*, or the *Águila* as she was commonly known, the best vessel for the purpose in the Peruvian fleet, had been damaged at sea and required extensive repairs, delaying the voyage. This frigate with its 22 eight-pounder guns and crew of 231 men was commanded by Don Domingo Boenechea, a good-humoured, skilled navigator who had served in the Atlantic, the Mediterranean and North and South American waters, fighting the British. His senior lieutenant, Don Tomás Gayangos, a high-born young man, had risen through the ranks and later became a rear-admiral; while Don Juan Ruiz de Apodaca, one of the ship's sub-lieutenants, was a Basque from a noble family, only twenty years old when he joined the *Águila*. He collected a Tahitian vocabulary during the voyage, drafted charts of the island and, like Gayangos, later had a stellar career, becoming Commander-in-Chief of the Spanish Navy. Another of the sub-lieutenants on board the *Águila*, Don Raymundo Bonacorsi, wrote a vivid journal of the voyage to Tahiti; while Juan de Hervé, the master, who had visited Easter Island with González, sailed as the expedition's pilot.

Although the officers were generally well-born and Spanish, the *Águila*'s crew was diverse, because Peru's population included Indians from different language and kin groups, *chapetón* (whites born in Spain), *creole* (whites of Spanish descent born in South America), blacks, and those born of mixed marriages in different combinations. Several Peruvian Indians were recruited for this voyage in the hope that they might be able to understand the languages of Tahiti and Easter Island, although this proved to be an illusion. There were also marines on board, including an intelligent young marine with a gift for languages named Máximo Rodríguez, who had previously sailed to Easter Island. Most of the sailors were recruited from the poorer sections of Peruvian society, and none was a foreigner, as at this time foreign sailors were not permitted to sail in the South Sea on board Spanish vessels.[5]

Before she sailed, the *Águila* was loaded with provisions for the sailors, and a supply of trade goods for the islanders – hundreds of flannel shirts in different colours for the men and white cotton shirts for the women; assorted garden tools, knives, thread and sail needles; fishing line and fish-hooks; many different types of seeds and potatoes; brass hoops, hawk's bells, innumerable beads in many colours; combs, earrings and even rosaries. Amat also gave Boenechea a detailed set of orders, instructing him to investigate Easter Island more closely; and to find Tahiti and circumnavigate and chart the island, and discover whether or not it was inhabited. He and his officers were permitted to choose whether to head first for Tahiti or Easter Island. When they arrived at those islands, however, they must treat the 'natives' with the utmost gentleness and humanity.

> You will acquaint yourselves with their customs, rites and mode of government, both in time of Peace and in time of War . . . You will furthermore bring them to understand the protective influence and incontestable rights of our Catholic King over all the Islands adjacent to the vast dominions he owns, and spare no effort for inducing them by gentle means to come to a fair and reasonable compact with us.[6]

Having learned about Tupaia's role during Cook's Pacific voyage, Amat also suggested that some 'priests or wizards' from the island might likewise be persuaded by gentle means to come to Lima; or maybe four or five smart young lads could be brought to Peru for instruction in Spanish and the Christian religion. He ordered Boenechea to select a crew member who should devote himself to compiling a dictionary of the island languages, and seeking information about their customs. If Tahiti had been already settled by foreigners, the captain and his officers should weigh up whether or not to risk an attack on their vessel.

In the case of Easter Island, King Carlos III had vowed that the inhabitants should be rescued from their 'miserable Idolatory', and instructed Boenechea to seek the islanders' permission for a small missionary settlement to be established. He should locate a site for a small fort where a chapel might later be built; and ensure that the entire island was carefully examined. Amat also arranged for two Franciscan friars, Father José Amich and Father Juan Bonamó, to accompany the expedition. Amich, a mathematician and former master of King's ships from Barcelona, had joined the missionary college of Ocopa in the upper Amazon, where friars from Europe were trained to take the gospel to the heathen. They took the vow of chastity and poverty and were devoted to the Virgin Mary.[7] In South America, however, Mary had become associated with the Earth Mother, mountains, birds and flowers[8] – Indian elements that aroused anxiety in the Vatican, prompting an 'Extirpation of Idolatry' in which investigators from the Inquisition were sent into local communities, seeking to abolish indigenous beliefs and ritual practices. Along with the practice of forcing the Indians to labour in the silver mines, escalating taxes and other injustices, this campaign led to violent clashes with Andean communities. In 1766, just a year after Amich joined the college at Ocopa, nine of its missionaries were killed by a local chief; while in 1767 all but one of the sixteen remaining missionaries were killed by the Piro Indians. During that same year the Jesuits were expelled from Peru; and in 1768 when two large groups of Franciscans arrived at Ocopa from Spain by order of King Carlos,[9] it is likely that Amich's companion on the voyage, Father Juan Bonamó (an Italian), was among them.

Differing ideas about sex also helped to provoke these conflicts. Within the Catholic Church, chastity was a virtue, monogamy was the rule, and premarital sex a sin; whereas for the Indians, polygamy was a traditional practice, and trial marriage was regarded as a sensible step before entering a permanent relationship. Priests tried to use the confessional to force their congregations to adopt Catholic mores (for example, an early confessional manual in Peru included several hundred questions on sexual behaviour); and polygamy was harshly punished. Yet at the same time, indigenous approaches to sexuality infiltrated many aspects of Peruvian life, to the despair of the Church hierarchy.[10] By the eighteenth century in the grand convents in Lima, nuns dressed in silk and jewels received male visitors; while in the city concubinage was so common that 'it is considered a shame to live without a concubine'.[11] Indeed, Viceroy Amat himself (then in his sixties) was involved in a passionate affair with La Perricholi, a twenty-year-old opera singer, scandalising the Church and Lima society.[12]

The *Águila* was taking the Catholic faith to new South Sea Islands, however, and the conduct of its crew was intended to be exemplary. Boenechea was ordered to ensure that his sailors did not commit any 'rudeness nor least sign of impropriety' against island women, bring women on board or ramble unsupervised on shore; while the friars were to study the island languages and watch over the sailors to ensure that there was no 'harshness and rough treatment' towards the natives.[13] Determined to keep this voyage a secret, Amat also ordered Boenechea not to open his sealed orders until he was ten leagues off the coastline of Peru.

On 26 September 1772 the *Águila* sailed from El Callao in a fresh

PLATE 1: *A Polynesian Venus*

PLATE 2: The Birth of Aphrodite *by Botticelli*

PLATE 3: *A Tahitian war canoe*

PLATE 4: *The Great Sea Battle in Matavai Bay*

PLATE 5: *French wallpaper, 1804, A Scene in Tahiti*

PLATE 6: Resolution *and* Adventure *in Matavai Bay*

PLATE 7: *Ha'amanino Bay*

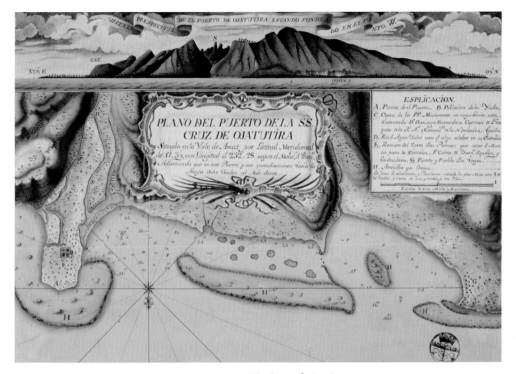

PLATE 8: *Spanish chart of Tautira*

PLATE 9: *Captain Cook witnesses a human sacrifice at ʻUtu-ʻai-mahurau* marae

PLATE 10: *Papetoʻai Bay in Moʻorea*

PLATE 11: *The Death of Captain Cook in Kealakekua Bay*

southerly breeze, and that evening Boenechea summoned his officers, opening the sealed packet of orders in their presence. When the officers' council met early the next morning and read the instructions, they decided to sail first to Tahiti, and then to Valparaiso to load fresh provisions, and afterwards to Easter Island. Although the bearings of Tahiti had been suppressed by the British, the Spanish authorities had somehow managed to procure this information; and the *Águila* headed west-south-west towards the latitude of the island. After a month at sea they sighted Tauere, an atoll in the Tuamotu and a new discovery, where Lieutenant Gayangos took a boat to the reef but found no safe landing place. The following day they sighted Haraiki, another new discovery; and on 3 October Ana'a came into sight, where about a hundred men, women and children waved green branches in an exuberant welcome. Although some of the heavily tattooed inhabitants carried pointed lances, they seemed very good-humoured. Lieutenant Bonacorsi took the boat close in to the reef, but again no safe landing place was found and they returned to the *Águila*.

On 6 November a small high island, Me'eti'a, appeared on the horizon, where two canoes came out to the ship, each bringing two tattooed men who asked for nails. The master's mate, Don Angel Cuidad, took a boat around the island, discovering a place that allowed some of his men to scramble ashore, finding the local people very friendly. The next morning canoes flocked around the ship, bringing out fish, plantains, coconuts and fruit to barter. This time Lieutenant Gayangos took the boat ashore, and when he returned to the ship he reported that he and his men had been warmly welcomed by about a hundred people who guided them along a steep path to two small clusters of houses. There they found a human jawbone hanging in a hut, some small carved wooden stools, a black-and-tan puppy with pointed ears, large pigs in a pen, and nearby a stone temple with a stepped platform and posts carved with the images of dogs. An old man presented them with a pig; and after some good-humoured exchanges they returned to the boat, accompanied by three of the islanders who came with them as far as the *Águila*. Two of these men then climbed into a canoe, while the other, a cheerful individual who had taken a liking to the carpenter's mate, decided to accompany the strangers to Tahiti. Pronouncing the name 'Tahiti', he pointed to the west, indicating the direction of their destination. At this time Me'eti'a was under the control of the chiefs of southern Tahiti, and canoes regularly sailed between the two islands. The *Águila* set sail, and at eight o'clock the next morning when a high peak came into sight their guide shouted 'Tahiti! Tahiti!', naming each bay and headland as it came into sight. At one o'clock that afternoon a large fire flared up on the southern coast of the island.

On shore in southern Tahiti the inhabitants must have been wondering whether this was Captain Wallis or Captain Cook, or perhaps the French commander Bougainville returning to the island. Shortly after the *Endeavour* sailed away in August 1769, war had once again broken out on the island. Emboldened by the gifts that he had received from the British, the great fighting chief Tutaha decided to install his great-nephew Tu as the *ari'i maro 'ura* or paramount chief of Tahiti, and once again he had mustered his allies. On this occasion Reti, the chief of Hitia'a and Bougainville's *taio*, joined Tutaha's army, and an inconclusive battle was fought in his district between Tutaha's forces and those led by Vehiatua I, the old warrior chief of southern Tahiti. Shortly afterwards there was another clash at Hitia'a, and this time Tutaha's forces gained the advantage. The warriors of both sides rested for some months, but during 1770 hostilities broke out again and a sea battle was fought off Hitia'a. As the two fleets paddled towards each other and the slingsmen from the Tai'arapu war canoes unleashed a barrage of stones at their enemies, Tutaha's warriors flinched, and afterwards the battle was derisively named 'Taora ofa'i (shower of stones)'.[14] Once again the outcome was inconclusive, and their leaders decided that the next time they met, only one side could claim the victory. They agreed to take their fleets far out to sea where the canoes of each would be bound together when they clashed, so that none could flee from the conflict. The encounter on this occasion was bloody, and the warriors fought each other to a standstill. During this battle both sides lost so many men that when the fleets finally broke apart neither could chase the other, so they limped back to their own districts, leaving many dead and wounded warriors in the water.

Disappointed by the outcome of these battles and fearing that 'Oro had deserted him, Vehiatua set sail for Ra'iatea to seek the support of the war god. In his absence the warriors on both sides rested for several months, building new canoes, letting their wounds and injuries heal and recruiting new allies. In 1771 some of the Papara people, who had not forgiven Tutaha for his part in the attack on Mahaiatea *marae*, decided to make peace with Vehiatua and joined the Tahiti-iti army, while many of the Pa'ea people decided to fight with the Pare-'Arue force led by Tutaha and his east coast allies. As they prepared for the battle, the *rauti* or war orators on both sides sent messages taunting each other for their cowardice in the previous clash, and challenging their enemies. According to the early missionaries, these *rauti* spoke so eloquently that people would walk right across the island to hear them; and when Tutaha's fleet, numbering about three hundred canoes, paddled out to the deep ocean from Te Auroa (Point Venus) and formed into divisions, lashing their canoes together, Paeti'a, a *rauti* from Point Venus, mounted the fighting platform of his canoe and addressed his comrades, inspiring them by recounting the heroic deeds of their ancestors, reciting all the battles that they had fought and won, and praising those chiefs who had performed the most spectacular deeds of bravery.

On this occasion Tutaha had mustered the largest fleet in living memory, and when they clashed with the enemy fleet off Teto'a-o-Hiro (Hiro's Rock, named Dolphin Rock by Captain Wallis) at Matavai Bay, the canoes of the opposing fleets were lashed together. The canoe carrying Teu and his young son, the sacred chief Tu, was placed at the rear of their fleet, but at the height of the battle its crew cut the ropes, raised the sails and fled to Teti'aroa. When they saw their high chief deserting them, Tutaha's warriors began to waver. That evening when Vehiatua's canoe was seen returning from Ra'iatea, the Tahiti-iti forces were elated while Tutaha's men were disheartened. Before Vehiatua could join the battle, however, darkness fell. The fleets separated and that night the warriors slept in their canoes on the ocean, eating a little and resting for the battle in the morning.

By dawn the canoes had drifted into Matavai Bay, and Tutaha's warriors, seeing that they were close to their own territory, fought with renewed ferocity. At the same time, encouraged by Vehiatua's return and believing that the power of 'Oro was now on their side, the fleet from Tahiti-iti also fought fiercely, attacking their enemies at close quarters. So many warriors were killed in this clash that sharks flocked into the harbour, and when a canoe drifted away from the battle, the sharks attacked the wounded men who hung from its sides, ripping them to pieces. The sea was reddened with their blood, and this battle was named 'Te-tamai-i-te-tai-'ute 'ute' (the battle of the red sea). Finally a sea breeze blew up which drove the canoes ashore, but the tide of the battle had turned against Tutaha's men, and many of his warriors, finding themselves in home territory, scrambled ashore and fled into the mountains. Dead combatants were strewn along the beaches, and Vehiatua's men collected the bodies of their enemies, piling them up in a towering pyramid at Taunoa as an offering to 'Oro. When the bodies in this great pyramid began to rot they were attacked by rats, so that this *ahu* (altar) of corpses was called Te-fare-'iore (the house of rats'). In their triumph Vehiatua and his allies rampaged along the coast, destroying canoes, houses, trees and gardens, and killing men, women and children, before returning to their own districts laden with plunder. Several days later Tu and Teu, who had retreated to Mo'orea after their flight, returned to Pare and made a temporary peace with Vehiatua.

Despite the devastation that Vehiatua had inflicted upon his army,

Tutaha was not cowed but bided his time to seek revenge. Although Tu's father Teu was unwilling to renew the struggle, Tutaha was determined to avenge his defeat. He summoned Tu, his great-nephew, and marching with him at his side mustered another great army of warriors. This time Amo and Purea's brother Tepau (the *taio* of Joseph Banks) fought with Tutaha, engaging Vehiatua's warriors at Afaina near Papara, but once again the outcome was disastrous for the Pare-'Arue army and its allies. During the fighting both Tutaha and Tepau were killed, and the Tai'arapu warriors carried their bodies to Tutaha's own *marae*, 'Utu-'ai-mahurau at Atehuru, where they were disembowelled as a gesture of contempt. Their bowels were hung up in a breadfruit tree for the birds to peck at, while parts of their remains were taken back to Tai'arapu and buried at the *marae* at Tautira;[15] and Vehiatua exiled many of the surviving warriors to the Tuamotu Islands.[16]

During this fatal battle Tu escaped, fleeing to the mountains where he joined his father Teu. When Vehiatua's army sought to complete their victory by seizing the *maro 'ura* for Vehiatua's young son and heir, however, Tu's warriors joined those of his *taio* Teri'irere and Pohuetea, the *ari'i* of Puna'aui'a, and repulsed the southern Tahiti warriors with great slaughter.[17] When peace was made on this occasion, Tu and Vehiatua's young son (Tu's second cousin by a marriage in a previous generation)[18] became *taio* or bond friends. Vehiatua I was an old man, and shortly after the peace-making he died and was succeeded by his son Paitu, this young man inheriting his title Vehiatua Teari'i-ta'ata-'ura'ura (high chief of great sacredness),[19] although he had no *maro 'ura* of his own. He was installed as Vehiatua II, and Tu became his *taio*. With Vehiatua II's support, Tu was now invested at 'Utu'ai-mahurau *marae* in Atehuru with the famous red feather girdle Te Ra'i-puatata which Tupaia had brought from Ra'iatea, and recognised as the *ari'i maro 'ura* or paramount chief of the island. Amo and Purea had now retired from active politics, although Teri'irere remained a significant figure as the wearer of the *maro tea* (yellow feather girdle) of the Tevas, and the ritual guardian of rain on the island. As for Vehiatua II's mother, Purahi, after losing her husband she married Ti'itorea, a black leg *'arioi* who was now her son's regent. The arrival of a new European ship off Tahiti-iti aroused anxiety among the victors and hope among the defeated. Both sides planned to forge *taio* relationships with the new arrivals and recruit them as allies.

On 7 November 1772 when the *Águila* approached the south coast of Tahiti, the wind died and the frigate was becalmed. Squalls blew off the land, making a landing impossible. Two days later the first canoe came out to the ship, bringing a man who offered the Spaniards plantains and coconuts, exchanging these for small knives. Soon afterwards another canoe came alongside, and two men boarded the *Águila* who had an animated conversation with the man from Me'eti'a. After this discussion their passenger told Boenechea that there was a good harbour ashore; and finally, on 12 November 1772, Lieutenant Bonacorsi took a boat, an armed crew and some marines to look for wood, fresh water and ballast south of Tautira. About forty canoes came out, flocking around the boat as it rowed through the Vaionifa passage. There were many houses along the shore and about 500 people stood unarmed on the beach, 'the whole of them in a very merry mood, and making a great hullabaloo'.[20] When their passenger from Me'eti'a, who now told them that he had been born in Tahiti-iti (southern Tahiti), pleaded to go ashore, pointing out his mother and father in the crowd, they landed him among his people. The locals indicated a spot in Vaiuru'a Bay (which the Spaniards now named 'Puerto Santa Maria Magdalena') where the frigate could anchor, which suggested to Bonacorsi that other European ships had previously visited this harbour. In fact, this was wrong. Captain Wallis had sailed past Tautira, while Captain Cook and Joseph Banks visited southern Tahiti by boat, but the two British captains had anchored their vessels at Matavai Bay; and Bougainville's two ships anchored off Hitia'a on the north-east coast of the island.

The following morning the officers' council on board the *Águila* resolved to send the launch inside the reef to take soundings and examine the eastern coastline. The next day the boat, under the command of Lieutenant Francisco Berdesoto, rowed up the coast towards Hitia'a. As they sounded along the shoreline, canoes surrounded the launch, one carrying the local *ari'i* (Reti, Bougainville's bond friend), while about two hundred people stood on the beach, waving out to them in welcome. The *ari'i* cried '*Taio! Taio!*', and stepping into the boat presented Berdesoto with some fish and showed him places where he could find fresh water. When Berdesoto returned to the ship, he reported that Hitia'a was an unsafe anchorage (a fair assessment, since Bougainville's vessels had narrowly escaped shipwreck in this bay). After dinner the *Águila* headed northwards again, but at three o'clock the frigate struck on a rocky shelf just north of Hitia'a. As soon as he was warned that the water was becoming shallow Boenechea luffed the *Águila* out to sea, but as the ship spun around, the rudder jammed on the rocks. The commander sent all the sailors forward but still the ship did not budge until the topsails were hoisted, driving the *Águila* off the reef and tearing off three stern planks and the tiller, although fortunately the inner skin of the hull was undamaged.

After the carpenter had fitted a spare tiller, Boenechea headed the *Águila* back out to sea, tacking off the south end of Tahiti.

Over the next few days the weather was squally with contrary winds, and it was not until 18 November that the *Águila* headed back towards the island. When Hervé took the boat in through Vairu'a Pass, examining the anchorage that the islanders had indicated during their first visit, the rising of the Pleiades or Matari'i was only two days away, marking the formal beginning of the Season of Plenty (or Matari'i-i-ni'a). That evening when he returned to the ship, Hervé was accompanied by Ti'itorea, the strapping black leg *'arioi* who was now Vehiatua II's stepfather and regent, and the political leader of southern Tahiti. During this visit, Ti'itorea handled all of the exchanges with the Spanish, keeping the young *ari'i* well away from the strangers. Ti'itorea seemed relaxed and cheerful, bringing a pilot out to the ship who offered to guide the *Águila* in to Vairu'a Bay. The next morning the boat was sent ahead to mark the passage and the frigate sailed in to the harbour where it moored the following day. When Boenechea ordered the diver to examine the ship's hull, the man reported that although part of the rudder was missing and the false keel and part of the cutwater had splintered when the *Águila* struck the coral shelf, the keel itself was undamaged. The officers held a council meeting and decided to carry on with the expedition, sending some sailors ashore to fill the water casks and collect ballast. They also decided that the launch should go around the island to chart the coastline; and carpenters were despatched inland to find suitable timber to repair the vessel.

Soon afterwards Ti'itorea brought an English axe out to the ship and asked to have it repaired, although it was not his own property; and during this visit he forged a *taio* relationship with Boenechea, the Spanish commander. As Bonacorsi remarked: 'Each of the [*ari'i*] took one of us for his particular *tayo* to such good effect that we could never separate ourselves from such a one for one instant.'[21] When two more chiefs boarded the ship they were shown the Spanish and French colours, which they ignored, but when Boenechea showed them an English flag they told him that a ship flying these colours had spent five months in Tahiti, sailing around the island before departing ten months earlier. They added that its captain had a big nose, and ate with a two-pronged fork.[22] This account referred to Captain Cook's three-month visit to Tahiti, during which he and Joseph Banks took a boat right around the island, although the *Endeavour* had departed more than three years earlier. Another man who came out to the ship told the Spaniards about twenty other islands in the seas around Tahiti, which Boenechea listed in his journal; pointing towards the bearing of each island, naming it, counting on his fingers the number of days it took to sail there, and using gestures to indicate its size, height and out-line.[23] These visitors explained that the people of the Tai'arapu district were presently at war with Mo'orea, whose chief had sheltered Tu during the recent battles. To make matters worse, the high chief of Mo'orea now claimed to be Tu's successor, while according to these people this status belonged to Ti'itorea's 'younger son' (Vehiatua II's younger brother). The islanders were eager to barter, and as Bonacorsi remarked:

> They are exceedingly shrewd and quick-witted in their dealing; but they are at the same time very straightforward and by no means given to cheating, so that whenever one of our people was not satisfied with what he had bought they would at once give back what they had accepted for it.[24]

On 5 December, Boenechea sent Lieutenant Gayangos, Father Amich, the second master Rosales, four marines and an armed crew off on the launch, ordering them to sail around the island, charting the coastline and finding out as much as they could about local conditions. Gayangos began his journey by heading the launch up the east coast, thus circling Tahiti in the opposite direction to Captain Cook and Joseph Banks during their boat trip around the island. After rowing out to sea through the Vaionifa passage, Gayangos came to 'a fairly deep bay' which he charted and named 'La Santissima Cruz de Ohatutira' – Vaitepiha Bay, Vehiatua's headquarters at Fatutira (now known as Tautira). Heading north, the launch soon arrived at Anuhi in the Pueu district, which he named 'Puerto La Virgén', where the son of the local *ari'i* and his wife came out in a large canoe to greet them. The young chief stepped into the launch and guided Gayangos and Amich to his house where his father, the *ari'i* Pahairiro, embraced them with pleasure and presented them with coconuts, plan-tains and breadfruit. In return the Spaniards gave Pahairiro a machete, two small knives, a mirror and some toy bells, and the *ari'i* led them to the nearby women's house, where he asked the marines to fire off their muskets. When they did so, the women fled in terror, bumping into each other, tripping and falling over one another in panic.

After this visit the Spaniards rowed out to sea again through Ti'itau Pass, followed by a fleet of canoes, and passed the small islet of Motu Nono. When the launch anchored at Vaito'are near the southern bound-ary of Hitia'a, north of the Taravao isthmus, canoes flocked out bringing plantains, coconuts and other fruits for the strangers. Gayangos and his companions slept on board that night, although early the next morn-ing they were woken by ear-splitting claps of thunder, a downpour of rain, and a strong wind that cracked the mast (a sign of 'Oro's power).

After making some repairs they rowed back to Vaito'are, where a local man escorted three of the crew up a nearby hill for a view of the isthmus. When they came down the steep track, this man went ahead to prevent them from falling.

Tainui, the son of Reti (the high chief of Hitia'a and Bougainville's *taio*), who was about eighteen or twenty years old, now invited the Spaniards to his house where he presented them with coconuts and plantains. When he offered to guide them on their circuit of the island, they gladly agreed, and Tainui slept ashore that night, joining them in the morning with a lavish supply of fish and fruit. As they sailed up the east coast, the launch was surrounded by a fleet of fishing canoes. From mid-November to mid-December, the Season of Plenty opened with a period known as Teta'i (the Season of the Sea) when the people went fishing for tuna and other species. The first day of the tuna season was extremely sacred, and only one canoe went out to sea to catch the first fish, which was offered to the gods, while the rest of the people ashore stayed in their houses, fasted, and observed a strict silence.[25] By December, however, the fishing season was in full swing, and on this occasion the high chief Reti soon joined them, presenting Gayangos with a boatload of fish and receiving a machete and a small knife in return. When Reti offered to escort the launch on its tour around the island, along with his son and his wife's brother Taruri, Gayangos hesitated, pleading a shortage of provisions; and the chief went off and returned with piles of food. His people filled four beakers of water for the journey, and as the launch was about to leave, his wife, his sister and his son's wife arrived by canoe, shouting at them from a great distance. Reti sent them the knife and machete that Gayangos had given him, and the lieutenant added two mirrors, some strings of beads and toy bells as gifts to console the women, before ordering the launch's sail to be hoisted, setting off for the north-east point of the island.

At 1 p.m. the boat crossed Matavai Bay, heading for Pare-'Arue, the home of Tu, who according to Reti now held dominion over the other chiefs in the island. Although Tu's army had been defeated in the recent war, he had been invested with the red feather girdle that his mother Tetupaia had brought from Ra'iatea (which he wore only at Taraho'i, his own *marae* in Pare); and after peace was made, he had also been invested with Te Ra'i-puatata at 'Utu-'ai-mahurau *marae*. His status as *ari'i maro 'ura* or paramount chief of the island was now generally recognised – in part because his mother was now the senior 'Great Woman' on Tahiti, and such women held powerful sway over the chiefly titles. Although Tu's great-great-grandfather had come from the Paumotu Islands, arriving through the Taunoa passage at Pare-'Arue where the local chief took him as his *taio*, and eventually succeeding to his *taio*'s titles, Tu's mother Tetupaia, the daughter of Tamatoa III, had such high status that it made up for this doubtful pedigree.[26] In the *'arioi* gatherings, the chief *'arioi* of Pare-'Arue used to chant:

> The mountain above is Mahue
> The assembly ground below is Vai-rota
> The water inland is Pu-'o'Oro
> The point outside is Ahu-roa
> The *marae* are Tara-ho'i and Rai-a-mau,
> The harbour outside is Ua,
> The high chief is Tu-nui-a'a-i-te-atua
> The under chiefs are Ari'i-peu and Ari'i-Pa'ea
> The chief messenger is Turuhe-mana
> The *'arioi* house is Na-nu'u
> The schools of learning are Va-uri, Utu-mea and Fare-fatu
> The principal teacher is Matau.[27]

His great-uncle Tutaha had kept Tu away from previous European visitors, but now the young *ari'i* felt strong enough to handle such encounters. As the launch entered the lagoon at Pare, the Spaniards saw a crowd of people standing on the stone *ahu* (which had seven or eight steps) of Taraho'i *marae*, yelling and waving. Eager to meet the paramount chief, Gayangos raised the Spanish ensign; and as a fleet of canoes surrounded the launch, about five hundred people led by eight heralds carrying long white rods emerged from a grove of trees, escorting Tu along the beach opposite their anchorage. Gayangos gave Reti a roasted chicken and some fresh bread, and sent him in a canoe to give these to the *ari'i maro 'ura* (high chief of the red feather girdle). When Reti returned he made a long speech, inviting Gayangos to come ashore in a double canoe. Escorted by the sergeant and a marine, Gayangos was paddled to the beach where he was carried ashore on the shoulders of one of the paddlers. The crowd pressed about them so closely that they could not move until two men with white rods cleared a way through the throng, escorting them to Tu's dwelling.

Tu (or more formally Tu-nui-a'a-i-te-atua) was a very tall, well-built young man about twenty years old and six feet three inches tall, with black eyes and an aquiline nose. He sat on a mat in an oval house with three women beside him, guarded by four men holding white rods and surrounded by about five hundred of his people. When Tu greeted Gayangos, calling him his *taio*, and Gayangos replied in kind, the young

Tu, paramount chief of Tahiti

ari'i embraced the lieutenant in delight, kissing him on the forehead. Taking off his own bark-cloth robe he wrapped it around the lieutenant's shoulders; and his three female companions, whom Tu introduced as his mother and two sisters, went through the same ceremony. When Gayangos presented the women with the gifts that he had brought for this purpose, they seemed thrilled, especially with the mirrors. A fourth woman joined them, another of Tu's sisters, who also took off her garment, draping it around Gayangos's shoulders. As he had given away all of his other gifts, he presented her with his handkerchief.

According to Gayangos, Tu trembled constantly during this meeting with the first Europeans he had seen, never taking his eyes off the carbine that the lieutenant wore slung over his shoulder. In an effort to reassure him, Gayangos unslung his weapon and handed it to the sergeant, addressing Tu as his *taio*. Using sign language, he tried to explain that he and his people had come from a large country, sailing for two months to reach his island. Drawing a large circle in the sand to represent Peru, Gayangos put a tiny dot beside it to represent Tahiti. Although Tu and his family seemed mystified by this performance, they were overjoyed when the lieutenant indicated that after returning to his own country he would come back with axes, knives and other presents. A very old lady (perhaps eighty years old) now arrived and greeted Gayangos warmly, presenting him with more bark cloth. Glancing at the sergeant and the marine, who were both armed, she exclaimed '*Pupuhi!*' ('Shoot!'), shut her eyes and pretended to fall to the ground; but despite this ominous pantomime she invited Gayangos to stay for a meal, saying that she would feed him with her own hands. Gayangos refused politely and returned to the beach, where one of the islanders asked him to fire his carbine. He obliged, firing it in the air, to the great 'astonishment and admiration' of the people; and after this demonstration a canoe took him back out to the launch and they carried on with their journey.

When they reached Vai'ete Bay (now Pape'ete), more canoes came out to greet the Spaniards, bringing two men who told them that the *ari'i* of this district was a man named Tomaheni. This *ari'i* and his wife soon came out to the launch, accompanied by a chief from Mo'orea named 'Ami'. At this time Vehiatua II's people were at war with Mo'orea, having become entangled in a dispute over the high chieftainship of that island, and although Reti greeted these men politely he soon turned his back and clapped his hand over his mouth, urging discretion upon his companions. When the Mo'orea chief began to malign Ti'itorea (Vehiatua's regent), saying that he and his people were thieves and robbers, Tomaheni joined in this indignant tirade. Gayangos asked them whether any European ship had visited Mo'orea, and Ami replied that they had seen a ship off the southern coast of the island but it had soon sailed away (presumably the *Dolphin*, which had sailed past Mo'orea). This man was so suspicious of the Spaniards that he and his companions slept that night on board double canoes at a safe distance from the launch, keeping three lights burning all night on board their vessel.

At dawn the next morning Gayangos and his company were woken by a raucous chorus of cocks on the shore. As they headed along the coast to Pa'ea, a fleet of canoes came out to meet them, one of which brought the tall, stately *ari'i* of Puna'aui'a, Pohuetea (or Potatau, as he was now known), accompanied by three of his kinswomen. They boarded the launch, presenting bark cloth to the strangers along with coconuts, roast breadfruit and some very yellow sweet potatoes. Pohuetea had befriended both Cook and Banks but he was also affable to the Spaniards, ordering his people to fill their water containers. After making a long speech of welcome he went off fishing, leaving two of his kinswomen, Purutifara and Taina, with Gayangos and his companions. When he returned several hours later with an eleven-kilo tuna, Pohuetea lamented that another of these fish had run away with his tackle, and asked Gayangos for some hooks, showing him one that he had made himself out of iron. When the lieutenant gave him four large nails he was delighted, and explained that the iron for his hook had been given to him by some strangers who had visited the island (Captain Cook and Joseph Banks), travelling around it in their boat; and Gayangos gave him a machete, three small knives, three mirrors, toy bells and some beads to seal their friendship. At dusk that evening Pohuetea offered one of his kinswomen to Gayangos as a bed-mate, suggesting that the lieutenant could make love with her in his canoe while he stayed on the launch; and he seemed astonished when Gayangos refused, not realising that the Spaniards had been forbidden to sleep with local women.

Early the next morning as they rowed down the west coast of Tahiti to a large bay called Papara, Pohuetea explained that this district was ruled by a chief named Amo (Purea's ex-husband and Teri'irere's father). Entering the lagoon they rowed to Pururu islet, anchoring in its lee as large canoes flocked around the launch, bringing out plantains and coconuts. One of these canoes carried two large kites used for divination, which were cov-ered with bark cloth stretched on cane frames and had a long tail made of feathers. When Reti and the other islanders went ashore that night, they indicated that they would return again the next morning. They seemed reluctant to visit southern Tahiti, however, which was enemy territory; and at daylight when Gayangos headed for the bay on the west side of the Taravao peninsula, followed by a number of canoes, Reti, his brother-in-law and his son were not among them. Passing Hava'e Bay (which they named 'San Dámaso') they ran along the southern coast until they arrived back in Vaiuru'a Bay. During their six-day circuit of Tahiti, Gayangos, Amich and their companions had met most of the main chiefs on the island, and found no evidence of European settlements. They also com-pleted a vocabulary and drafted some excellent charts of Matavai, Tautira and the entire island, which they named 'Amat's' after the viceroy who had sponsored the voyage.

During this early contact period, each of the European commanders who visited Tahiti gave it a different name. Captain Wallis called it 'King George's Island' after his monarch; Bougainville named it 'Nouvelle Cythère' (New Cythera) after the birthplace of Aphrodite, the goddess of love; Cook used the local name, 'Otaheite' (Tahiti); and Boenechea named it 'Amat's' after the Viceroy of Peru – an illuminating choice in each instance. By some strange quirk of history, Britain, France and Spain had managed to divide the island among them, associating themselves with different districts and lineages. Wallis had anchored in Matavai Bay, but allied himself with Purea and Amo of Papara and their Teva-i-uta people from the west coast; while Bougainville anchored off Hitia'a on the east coast, allying himself with Reti, the high chief of that eastern district. Like Wallis, Cook had anchored in Matavai Bay, where he forged an uneasy alliance with Tutaha, Tu's regent and the leader of the Pare-'Arue district, although he and Banks also maintained friendly relationships with Purea and Amo of Papara. Now Boenechea had arrived off the southern coast of the island, associating himself with Vehiatua II, the high chief of Tahiti-iti, and the Teva-i-tai people, although Gayangos also forged a *taio* relationship with Tu. As each commander took particular leading chiefs as their *taio*, names, gods, genealogies, enemies and allies were exchanged, shifting Tahitian history in new directions.

When Gayangos returned to the *Águila*, he found that during his absence some of the Tai'arapu people had been stricken by an influenza-like illness, and several of those afflicted had died. In Tahiti, *tahu'a* or priests had the power of life or death, calling on their gods to heal people or to harm them; and local people were well aware that there were priests on board the *Águila*. No doubt they concluded that the Spanish gods and their priests were inflicting these sicknesses upon them. Ti'itorea was among the sufferers, and when he and Purahi said goodbye to Boenechea, they accused him of bringing this malady to the island. The Spaniards had arrived at the time of the rising of the Pleiades, when the Season of Plenty began, a time of rejoicing that marked the beginning of the fishing season and the approach of a new breadfruit harvest. These illnesses were ominous, however, suggesting that the gods, priests and chiefs of the island were under attack by the gods of the strangers. The islanders now began to ask the Spaniards when they planned to leave the district, and many of them deserted Vaiuru'a Bay, although canoes from other districts were still arriving at the frigate.

During the launch's absence, Boenechea had distributed a pair of nanny goats and a kid, a cock and a hen, two pairs of pigeons, some guinea pigs, and assorted vegetables from Peru (potatoes, sweet potatoes, garlic, onions, maize, wheat, beans, chickpeas, squashes, melons and watermelons) among the local people; and the sailors sowed seeds and roots ashore. Some of these plants were already sprouting when the frigate left the island. During their stay in Vaiuru'a Bay the officers had befriended some local men, and four of them decided to accompany the Spaniards to Lima – Pautu, a skilled diver about thirty years old; Tipitipia, a young man of about twenty-six; Heiao, a 'lump of a lad' about eighteen; and Tetuanui, a young boy about thirteen years old who travelled with his father's permission. When the launch arrived back in Vaiuru'a Bay, the district was almost deserted; and when Boenechea set sail from Tahiti-iti on 20 December 1772, warping the ship through the pass and leaving the launch to recover the kedge anchor, almost no one stood on the beach to farewell them.

After leaving Vaiuru'a the *Águila* headed for Mo'orea to examine that island for signs of European settlement. The officers' council had resolved to reconnoitre the island by boat, but when contrary winds made this impossible they agreed to return to Valparaiso before visiting Easter Island. During the journey back to Peru the officers and the friars often talked with the four Tahitians, and as they began to understand them better, they learned a good deal about life on the island. The 'Descriptions' that Boenechea, Bonacorsi and Amich wrote during this passage were based upon these conversations, as well as their observations during their visit to the island. Among other things, they remarked that most of the *ari'i* whom they had met in Tahiti were very corpulent, some so obese that they could hardly stand upright. Fatness and height were signs of prosperity and power in Tahiti, and the *ari'i* embodied these values. The Spaniards thought that there were eight high chiefs on Tahiti, each ruling his own district; and although all of these *ari'i* acknowledged Tu as the paramount chief, Bonacorsi remarked: 'I do not think they render him much obedience, as each one rules his respective district.'[28] The Spaniards estimated the population of Tahiti at a minimum of 10,000 people, with the districts of Papara on the west coast, Tai'arapu in southern Tahiti, and Pare-'Arue being the most densely populated. According to Boenechea, the people in southern Tahiti had at least 1500 to 2000 large canoes (suggesting a much larger population). Amich, the Franciscan friar, remarked of the Tahiti-iti people that 'their besetting vice is lasciviousness; . . . and it would seem that they are not jealous, for they make offer of their women to strangers';[29] and Boenechea added:

> The women carry the upper hand in everything, and whatever articles were obtained from us on board this Frigate were got for them: the others begged with exceeding importunity in the names of the women for whatever we had, so much so that they became a great nuisance to us. They tendered their women to use quite freely, and showed much surprise at our non-acceptance of such offers. The latter were also wont to make advances themselves, but with some show of coyness.[30]

The Spaniards had learned almost nothing about Tahitian religion, however, although during the passage to Peru, Pautu, Tipitipia, Heiao and Tetuanui periodically gazed up into the sky and offered sacrifices to their *atua* (god), and told the Spaniards that during these rituals at home, their god came among them in the form of a whirlwind. As Amich commented:

> We could not be sure whether they have any religion; they certainly had no house of worship, though they appear to observe some sort of idolatry, for they carry certain rudely carved wooden figures on their canoes, which represent human forms; but they in no wise worship they, nor do they resent their being scoffed at by strangers. Their cemeteries [in fact *marae*] are . . . small rectangular platforms faced all round with two or three high steps built in with stone. They are ornamented with a number of large wooden effigies – for the most part figures of an obscene character.[31]

The *Águila* made a rapid passage back to Peru, and on 21 February 1773, just two months after leaving Tahiti, they anchored in Valparaiso Bay to take on fresh water and provisions. Two days later a ship's boy and a marine who had been suffering from scurvy died, and Tipitipia became ill with 'indigestion . . . [and a] malignant calenture [fever]'.[32] He was baptised and named 'Joseph', and soon afterwards died. The officers decided to carry on with their expedition to Easter Island, accompanied by the three surviving Tahitians; but close to their destination the *Águila* sprang a leak near the stern, and they decided to return to Valparaiso, arriving back in the harbour on 31 May. The master Juan de Hervé immediately sent a report to the Viceroy, passing on some additional information that had been acquired from the islanders during their passage.[33]

According to Hervé, during this journey Pautu reported that many months earlier an English ship commanded by 'Tepane' (Banks) had visited Tahiti. These people had killed four islanders in order to take away their women; and when one of the sailors deserted, an armed party was sent in search of him. When they could not find him they had captured Tu's 'father' (Tutaha) and locked him in the bread room (a reference to the desertion by the marines, Webb and Clements, from the *Endeavour*, and Cook's decision to hold Tutaha and other chiefs hostage on board the ship). If Tutaha had indeed been locked in the bread room – a detail not mentioned in the *Endeavour* journals – this would have been a devastating insult, because cooked food was inimical to *ra'a* or ancestral power. After Tepane's ship had sailed away, two other ships commanded by 'Tootera' (Duclos) had visited Hitia'a with a 'very pretty woman' on board, who never went on shore; and the islanders captured one of these men and stripped him naked, taking his musket. At night these people had brought large, thick rods on shore which they mounted on forked sticks, putting something white beneath their lower ends, and watched the stars and the moon (a reference to Bougainville's visit with Commerson's female 'valet', Jean Baret; combined with Cook's observations of the Transit of Venus). When these ships had sailed from Hitia'a, they had been forced to abandon a large anchor. Given the rudimentary knowledge that Pautu and the Spanish had of each other's languages, it is not surprising that the Spanish understanding of these events was somewhat garbled.

The islanders also told the Spaniards that in Tahiti trifling thefts were punished by tying the thief's hands and setting fire to his beard; but that if a thief stole a cloak, a canoe or some other treasure, he was bound hand and foot, a large stone was tied around his neck and another to his thighs, and he was taken out to sea in a canoe and thrown overboard. If a thief was not caught in the act, however, he was not punished, because he must be under Hiro's protection. When a high chief like Vehiatua I died and his widow remarried, her new husband took over the rule of the district; but as soon as she died, the power would pass to her son, Vehiatua II. Hervé described this young man, whom Cook had known as Teari'i (the high chief), as 'a great friend of mine and a young fellow of fine presence, some seventeen or eighteen years old', adding that he already controlled part of the Tai'arapu district.[34]

According to Pautu, when a pig was offered to the gods, the head went to the priest while the loins were given to the chief or *ari'i*, so that the owner received hardly any of the animal's carcass. Each high chief had a large *pahi* or double voyaging canoe that carried fifty men, although the largest of these were in Ra'iatea. If women came on board, a small deck-house was erected on the canoe; and when they went ashore, they used the deckhouse as a shelter. When the Spaniards remarked that they had seen no such vessels during their visit to Tahiti, Pautu assured them that the local *pahi* were all away on a visit to Ra'iatea. At certain times of the year, he explained, canoes from Tahiti travelled to Ra'iatea, and at other times when the weather was favourable, canoes from Ra'iatea came to Tahiti (a reference to the ritual exchanges between these two islands that were all that remained of the great inter-island alliance for the worship of 'Oro). When they arrived at the port of El Callao in June 1773, Pautu and his two young companions were given a warm welcome; and shortly after-wards they were taken to Lima, where they were lodged in the Viceroy's palace.

Tute's Return

Back in England, when the *Endeavour* anchored in the Downs on 12 July 1771 after her voyage around the world, they received a rapturous welcome. Cook was only a lieutenant, however; and most of the glory of the voyage went to Joseph Banks and Dr Solander, who had brought back a treasure-trove of new species of plants and animals, along with many artefacts and drawings. Although Terra Australis Incognita had remained elusive, the Swedish botanist Linnaeus wrote to Banks in great excitement about his discoveries, ending his letter with a Latin salutation: '*Vale vir sine pare*, Farewell O unequalled man!'[1] This was heady stuff for a twenty-seven-year-old, and intoxicated by his new fame Banks almost forgot who had commanded the *Endeavour*. While Cook was writing his reports to the Astronomer Royal about the South Sea tides and the Transit of Venus, and completing a series of meticulous charts of the places that they had visited, Banks frequented the Royal Palace at Richmond; talked with King George III about his gardens at Kew; received an honorary degree from Oxford; and began to plan a second Pacific expedition, this time with two vessels, to make another search for the Unknown Southern Continent.

After jilting Harriet Blosset, Banks also boasted about his sexual exploits with the women he had met during his journey, provoking a satirical riposte in the *Town and Country Magazine*:

That curiosity which leads a voyager to such remote parts of the globe as Mr B- has visited, will stimulate him when at home to penetrate into the most secret recesses of nature. As nature has been his constant study, it cannot be supposed that the most engaging part of it, the fair sex, have escaped his notice; and if we may be suffered to conclude from his amorous descriptions, the females of most countries that he has visited, have undergone every critical inspection by him. The queens, and women of the first class, we find constantly soliciting his company, or rather forcing their's upon him: at other times we find him visiting them in their bed-chambers, nay in their beds.[2]

This was followed by a flurry of salacious poems by anonymous authors, including a mock letter from Purea (or Oberea), the Queen of Tahiti, to her faithless lover Opano (Banks):

> Read, or oh! say does more amorous fair
> Prevent *Opano*, or engage his care?
> I, *Oberea*, from the Southern Main,
> Of slighted vows, of injur'd faith complain.
> Though now some European maid you woo,
> Of waiste more taper, and of lighter hue;
> Yet oft with me you deign'd the night to pass,
> Beneath yon breadfruit tree on the bending grass.
> Oft in the rocking boat we lay,
> Nor fear'd the drizly wind, or briny spray.
> Who led thee through the woods impervious shade,
> Pierc'd the thick covert, and explor'd the glade.[3]

Although Banks took it for granted that he would lead the next Pacific expedition, the Admiralty promoted Captain Cook instead, and the Naval Board invited him to select the vessels for the voyage. Now a master and commander, Cook chose two sloops from a Whitby shipyard, valuing their seaworthiness, their capacity to hold cargo, and their ability to be careened for repairs; but when Banks saw the *Resolution* he was outraged, thinking it far too small a vessel for such a voyage. He planned to take a large party of artists and scientists (and even two horn players) on this new expedition, and demanded that an extra upper deck and a raised poop be added to the *Resolution*. Lord Sandwich supported his friend and the work was carried out, but when the sloop went on a trial run from the Downs, she almost capsized. As Charles Clerke, who had sailed with him on the *Endeavour*, wrote wryly to Banks: 'By God, I'll go to sea in a grog-tub, if required, or in the *Resolution* as soon as you please, but must say I think her the most unsafe ship I ever saw or heard of.'[4]

After this debacle the Naval Board took charge, sending an army of shipwrights to undo the alterations. When Banks saw the *Resolution* again, stripped of her additions, he threw a tantrum and ordered all of his things to be taken out of the ship. Unimpressed by these antics, Sir Hugh Palliser, Cook's long-standing patron and now Comptroller of the Navy Board, refused to make any further changes to the sloop; and in a fit of pique Banks withdrew from the voyage. Cook had recruited twenty of the *Endeavour*'s crew for this expedition, however, including Charles Clerke as his second lieutenant – Banks's high-spirited, good-humoured correspondent who had sailed with Byron and Wallis on the *Dolphin*; Richard Pickersgill as third lieutenant, the capable, hard-drinking Yorkshireman who had also sailed on the *Dolphin* with Wallis; and John Edgcumbe as lieutenant of marines. Samuel Gibson, the hot-headed young marine who had tried to desert at Tahiti, was promoted to corporal; while Robert Palliser Cooper, a relative of Sir Hugh's, became the *Resolution*'s first lieutenant. Tobias Furneaux, a gentle, humane officer who had sailed on the *Dolphin* with Samuel Wallis (to whom he was related by marriage), had the command of the *Adventure*, the consort ship; and he was joined by his second lieutenant James Burney, the novelist Fanny Burney's sailor brother who had voyaged with Byron on board the *Dolphin*, and Jack Rowe, an unruly young sailor whose family in Devonshire was closely related to Furneaux's.[5] Although Banks had been popular during the *Endeavour* voyage, the sailors had little sympathy for his predicament, one of the midshipmen, John Elliott, remarking acerbically:

> It has always been thought that it was a most fortunate circumstance for the purpose of the Voyage that Mr Banks did not go with us; for a more proud, haughty man could not well be, and all his plans seemed directed to shew his own greatness, which would have accorded very ill with the discipline of a Man of War.[6]

After the contretemps with Banks, the scientific party was reduced to two astronomers, one for each ship; plus a botanist with his assistant and an artist who were recruited at short notice. The astronomers were William Wales, who had observed the Transit of Venus at Hudson Bay in 1769, and William Bayly, who observed the Transit at the North Cape. During this voyage, their task would be to test the accuracy of several different types of chronometer and fix the location of the places that were visited. Johann Forster, a distinguished German naturalist and Lutheran pastor who had translated Bougainville's *Voyage* into English, replaced Dr Solander as the expedition's botanist, although he proved to be cantankerous and self-important; while his son George, who sailed as his assistant, was as clever but much better-tempered. Like George, the artist William Hodges, a gifted landscape painter, was well liked by the sailors. This was a much bigger expedition than Cook's previous voyage, with 112 sailors and marines and eight civilians on board the *Resolution*, and 81 sailors and marines and two civilians on the *Adventure* (203 men in total, compared with 94 men on board the *Endeavour* – but still far fewer than the 340 men on board Bougainville's two vessels). Despite Banks's

Johann and George Forster

defection, an impressive array of scientific equipment was sent on board the *Resolution*. When Lord Sandwich and Sir Hugh Palliser visited the two ships at Plymouth and announced that their crews would be paid their back wages, giving the petty officers and the sailors a two-month advance, the men celebrated by getting riotously drunk. The *Resolution*'s buoy came adrift and the ship was almost wrecked on the rocks at the entrance to Plymouth Harbour, before the voyage had even started.

While preparing for this expedition, Cook had charted the tracks of all known voyages in the Pacific (although he knew nothing about the Spanish expeditions from Peru to Easter Island and Tahiti). He concluded that if there was a Southern Continent it must lie in the high southern latitudes of the Indian or Pacific Oceans, or around longitude 140 degrees west, which ran through the Marquesas and the Tuamotu Islands. He decided to use Queen Charlotte Sound in New Zealand as his base for exploring the far southern reaches of the Pacific, and Tahiti for exploring the seas around 140 degrees west. On 13 July 1772, having restored order on board, Cook gave the command to set sail.

After making brief visits to Madeira and St Jago, the ships arrived at the Cape of Good Hope where Cook learned more about Marion du Fresne's visit to Madagascar and Ahutoru's death from smallpox; and a young Swedish naturalist, Anders Sparrman, joined the Forsters. When the astronomers checked the chronometers, they were delighted to find that K1, Kendall's famous copy of a watch by John Harrison, had only gained about a second a day during their passage, although the other chronometers proved unreliable. After a month at the Cape, Cook headed south again; and as the ships entered the high latitudes, drenched by towering waves and freezing winds, and the rigging froze solid and snow drifted in the sails, Johann Forster turned to Virgil's *Aeneid* for consolation. Crossing the Antarctic Circle, whales sounded around the ships and penguins paraded on the icebergs, but no land was discovered. In these miserable conditions the sailors were stoical, but when the surviving sheep and cattle were put in a compartment next to Johann Forster's cabin, he lamented:

> I was now beset with cattle & stench on both Sides, having no other but a thin deal partition full of chinks between me & them. The room offered me by Capt. Cook, & which the Masters obstinacy deprived me of, was now given to very peaceably bleating creatures, who on a stage raised up as high as my bed, shit & pissed on one side, whilst 5 Goats did the same afore on the other side.[7]

During February 1773 in thick fog, the two ships were separated. After sailing the *Resolution* south for another fortnight, still looking for Terra Australis, Cook finally turned north towards New Zealand.

Before heading for Queen Charlotte Sound – the agreed rendezvous on the northern end of the South Island – Cook took the *Resolution* into Dusky Cove on the west coast, which Joseph Banks had been eager to explore during the *Endeavour*'s voyage. In this pristine green fiord Cook and his men spent six weeks fishing, shooting birds and seals, brewing spruce beer, collecting wood and fresh water, making charts and occasionally meeting nomadic families of Ngāti Mamoe hunters and gatherers. Heading north again, on 17 May the *Resolution* entered Cook Strait, where six large waterspouts danced dangerously around the vessel. In Queen Charlotte Sound they found the *Adventure* at anchor in Ship Cove, battened down for the winter. Furneaux, an easy-going commander, had failed to persuade his men to follow Cook's strict regime of cleanliness and eating greenstuffs, and they were suffering from scurvy. Many of them had also caught gonorrhea during an unrestrained orgy with local women, infected during the *Endeavour*'s visit three years earlier. According to Furneaux, when the first canoe approached the *Adventure* in the sound, their leader had held up a green bough and cried out 'Tupaia! Tupaia!'; and when they heard that the high priest had died in Batavia these people were dismayed, asking whether the British had killed him.

When Furneaux came on board the *Resolution*, Cook ordered him to make his men eat wild celery and scurvy grass, and prepare the *Adventure* for the voyage to Tahiti. Over the next few days as canoes kept arriving at Ship Cove, their crews asked for nails, hatchets and glass bottles and called out for Tupaia, lamenting bitterly when they heard that he had died in Batavia. They offered their womenfolk for barter, and Cook's crew joined the *Adventure*'s men in a riot of debauchery. Unable to control his men, Cook remarked despondently:

> Such are the consequences of a commerce with Europeans and still more to our Shame civilized Christians, we debauch their Morals already too prone to vice and we interduce among them wants and perhaps which they never before knew and which serves only to disturb that happy tranquillity they and their fore Fathers had injoy'd. If any one denies the truth of this assertion let him tell me what the Natives of the whole extent of America have gained by the commerce they have had with Europeans.[8]

Over the next few weeks as canoes from other districts began to arrive in the sound, their leaders stood up in their carved vessels, making speeches, chanting, and asking for Tupaia. As Cook remarked, the high priest had made a remarkable impact upon Māori:

> It may be ask'd, that if these people had never seen the *Endeavour* or any of her crew, how they became acquainted with the Name of Tupia or to have in their possession such articles as they could only have got from that ship, to this it may be answered that the Name of Tupia was at that time so popular among them that it would be no wonder if at this time it is known over the great part of *New Zealand*.[9]

A cargo cult had developed around the high priest, based upon his reputation as a priest and navigator who had arrived from the homeland on a strange craft packed with wondrous objects. Among Māori, Tupaia's name was now surrounded with an extraordinary mystique. As George Forster mused:

> So much had [Tupaia's] superior knowledge, and his ability to converse in their language rendered him valuable, and beloved even among a nation in a state of barbarism. Perhaps with the capacity which Providence had allotted to him, and

which had been cultivated no farther than the simplicity of his education would permit, he was more adapted to raise the New Zeelanders to a state of civilization similar to that of his own islands, than ourselves, to whom the want of the intermediate links, which connect their narrow views to our extended sphere of knowledge, must prove an obstacle in such an undertaking.[10]

After three weeks in the sound, Cook staged a display of fireworks, and on 7 June 1773 the ships sailed out of Cook Strait, heading south-east in search of Terra Australis. Despite Furneaux's best efforts, the crew of the *Adventure* had refused to eat their anti-scorbutics and were now riddled with scurvy as well as gonorrhea, making it difficult to work the ship; and to his annoyance, Cook was forced to send some of his own crew to man the *Adventure*.

After a long, frozen passage during which no land was sighted, Cook turned north for Tahiti. Threading his way through the Tuamotu archipelago, he complained bitterly about Bougainville's failure to publish the positions of the atolls he had visited, because it was almost impossible to see these low islands. When they passed Me'eti'a on 15 August, Captain Furneaux came on board; and afterwards Cook set a course for Vaitepiha Bay on the south-east end of Tahiti and retired to his cabin. He awoke next morning to find that the ships were heading straight for the reefs and hastily ordered the steersman to haul off to the north, narrowly escaping shipwreck on the coral.

As they edged up the south coast of Tahiti, the wind died, becalming the ships; and Cook ordered the boats lowered to tow them away from the coral. During these manoeuvres a canoe came out to the ships carrying two men wearing narrow belts and bark-cloth turbans who cried out '*Taio! Taio!*' These men handed up a green plantain branch as a sign of peace, and when this bough was placed in the *Resolution*'s main shrouds, more than two hundred canoes flocked out to the vessels, where their crews eagerly exchanged coconuts, plantains, breadfruit, fish, birds and artefacts (including flutes, drums and cloth beaters) for beads and small nails. A tall, stately chief named Tai came on board with his wife and two sisters, and Clerke gave this chief a black silk cravat, which he immediately wrapped around his neck. When they asked about Tutaha, Tai told them that the great warrior had been killed by the fighting-men of southern Tahiti; and that the *ari'i* of southern Tahiti, the elderly warrior Vehiatua I, had since died and been succeeded by his son, Vehiatua II.

After this discussion, Tai and his family went below decks, where his sister Marora'i took a fancy to a pair of sheets on an officer's bed. This man offered them to her in exchange for sex, and although she hesitated, after a time she agreed. They were soon interrupted, however. According to Anders Sparrman, 'Our people, enchanted by the hundreds of docile and agreeable young females, naked to the waist, who surrounded our ship, felt the Paradise of Venus herself was within their grasp';[11] and as the sailors gaped at this entrancing spectacle, an inflowing current swept the *Resolution* towards the reef, and the ship struck on the coral with a resounding crash. As the amorous officer rushed from his cabin, Cook stamped furiously on the deck, shouting orders and swearing 'Goddamn! Goddamn!' as the ship repeatedly struck on the rocks. A bower anchor was put in the boat, and the sailors, assisted by the islanders, lowered it and managed to haul the sloop off. Soon afterwards a breeze blew up from the land, saving the *Resolution* from almost certain destruction. When the unlucky officer returned to his cabin, he found that his mistress had vanished, along with his bed linen. The *Adventure* was also swept towards the reef, but was saved at the last moment when several anchors were dropped, which later had to be cut loose, along with the *Resolution*'s bower anchor. That night as the ships tacked off the coast, Captain Cook retired to his cabin in a sweat and with terrible pains in his stomach – the first sign of the intestinal disorder that was to plague him during the rest of this voyage.

Early on the morning of 17 August 1773 the ships sailed in to Vaitepiha Bay, Vehiatua II's headquarters. This young high chief had guided Captain Cook during his 1769 trip around Tahiti-iti; and he was soon told that 'Tute' was back, this time with two ships, although 'Tepane' (Banks) and 'Tolano' (Solander) were not with him. Since Cook's last visit, however, Vehiatua's people had killed Tutaha and Tepau (Banks's *taio*, who had since been succeeded by his son), and he must have expected merciless reprisals. During their brief visit to southern Tahiti eight months earlier, furthermore, the Spaniards had said many harsh things about the British, and his stepfather Ti'itorea had forged a *taio* relationship with Boenechea, the Spanish commander.

As the ships anchored in Vaitepiha Bay, a number of canoes came out to exchange goods with the British sailors; and when several men took coconuts that had already been purchased, throwing them overboard so that they could be sold again, a sailor struck them with a whip, which 'they bore patiently'.[12] Two men who claimed to be *ari'i* came on board, where Cook gave them shirts and axes in exchange for promises of pigs (which were never delivered). Women swam naked in the lagoon and some came on board, including several girls only about nine or ten years old who were presented to the sailors. As George Forster remarked, 'our sailors were perfectly captivated, and carelessly disposed of their shirts and cloaths to gratify their mistresses . . . The view of several of the nymphs swimming nimbly all round the sloop, such as nature had formed them, subvert[ed] the little reason which a mariner might have left to govern his passions.'[13]

When Cook and Furneaux went ashore at Tautira, a cheerful crowd of islanders led them along the east coast, some carrying their guests on their shoulders across the Vaitepiha River, telling them to hold on by crossing their ankles. When they were told that these ships came from Britain, these people cried out for Tupaia, Banks and Solander, and several of them recognised Cook and Furneaux from their previous visits. On a wild, bushy point, Cook and his companions were shown a terraced stone pyramid, overgrown with shrubs, which they were told was the burial place of Vehiatua I, the venerable warrior whom Cook had met in 1769. There were about fifteen carved wooden figures (or *ti'i*) standing on this *marae*, each about eighteen feet high and facing out to sea, some carved with six or eight human figures standing upon each other's heads, the male and female figures alternating but always with a male figure at the apex. Nearby, a platform stood laden with bananas and coconuts as offerings for the god of the *marae*.

Although these people were affable, as soon as Cook and Furneaux began to barter for food they ran into difficulties. It was August, in the midst of the Season of Scarcity, and the plains around Tautira were brown and parched. To make matters worse, Vehiatua II had placed a *rahui* on the pigs and chickens in his district and his people refused to barter any of these animals, saying that it was strictly forbidden. Furthermore, none of the Tahiti-iti people forged *taio* relationships with Cook and his people during this visit, presumably on Vehiatua's orders. The next morning when Captain Cook sent the boats along the south coast to try to recover the lost anchors, the sailors raised the *Resolution*'s bower anchor but were unable to retrieve the anchors from the *Adventure*. Later that day, George Forster went ashore in this glorious bay, which he described as an Elysium:

> The plain at the foot of the hills was very narrow, but always conveyed the pleasing ideas of fertility, plenty and happiness . . . The slopes of the hills, covered with woods, crossed each other on both sides, variously tinted; and beyond them, we saw the interior mountains shattered into various peaks and spires . . . We entered a grove of breadfruit trees, on most of which we saw no fruit at this season of winter . . . Tall coco-palms nodded to each other; the bananas displayed their beautiful large leaves. A sort of shady trees . . . bore golden apples . . . Indeed a variety of wild species sprung up amidst the plantations, in that beautiful disorder of nature, which infinitely surpasses the trimness of regular gardens.[14]

When Cook went ashore he was met by a large crowd led by three men dressed in red and yellow bark-cloth garments and turbans, each carrying a long wand and one accompanied by his wife. According to these men, they were the *'opu nui* ('big bellies' or *marae* attendants) or *ta 'ata no te atua* (the people of the god) at the local *marae* – presumably Vai'otaha, the main *marae* of this district. When Cook returned to the *Resolution* for dinner he was escorted by the two young sons of a chief named Puhi, whom he invited to share his meal. One of these young men took the opportunity to steal a knife and a pewter spoon from Cook's cabin, however, jumping overboard and fleeing in his canoe. As he sat at a distance, laughing, Cook fired three musket balls over his head and sent a boat to capture him. The young chief swam ashore; and when the boat pursued him to the beach, a crowd of angry islanders pelted the sailors with stones. Cook sent another boat to protect his men, ordered a four-pounder to be fired which cleared the beach, and took a third boat himself and captured two large canoes. Bayly the astronomer, who was on shore at the time, witnessed the terrified islanders fleeing to the mountains, hiding in the reeds when they saw any of the British and then hastily fleeing again. Later that afternoon when the bay was deserted, one of the ship's boats was sent out to sea to bury the body of a marine, Isaac Taylor, who had died that morning from consumption and asthma.

Early the next morning when some islanders came out to the *Resolution* to ask for their canoes to be returned, Cook decided to give them back their craft because the supply of food to his ships had dried up. In any case, as one of the sailors, James Magra, remarked, there were good reasons why the islanders took things from the British: 'Is it not very natural, when a people see a company of strangers come among them, and without ceremony cut down their trees, gather their fruits and seize their animals, that such a people should use as little ceremony with the strangers, as the strangers do with them; if so, against whom is the criminality to be charged, the christian or the savage?'[15] In fact, however, the Tahiti-iti people had allied themselves with the Spaniards and considered the British to be their enemies, and fair game. Later that day, after watching women beating bark cloth with grooved wooden mallets, the Forsters walked up a little valley where a man welcomed them, spreading plantain leaves on the stone pavement in front of his house. He produced a wooden stool for Johann and fed them with baked breadfruit and a basket of *vi* or Tahitian apples. After shooting a pigeon, which frightened his host, Johann swam in the river and then returned to the ship with his son, where they arranged their specimens and completed some drawings.

The following day when the Forsters returned ashore, they saw a quantity of bark cloth that had been washed in the river hung up to dry; and groups of men and women eating separately from each other. Near a house they noticed a semicircular *taumi* or breastplate airing in the sunshine, decorated with feathers and shark's teeth, but the owner would not part with it for anything that they could offer. Wandering past houses scattered among fruit trees, shrubs covered with scented flowers, and well-tended gardens of bark-cloth plants, taro, yams and sugar cane, they arrived at the house of Tai, the chief who had visited the *Resolution* with his two sisters. Although the officer who had slept with one of these girls, Marora'i, showered her with presents, she would not sleep with him again, ignoring his entreaties. As George Forster observed, during this visit to Tahiti the chiefly women rarely demeaned themselves by making love with the strangers; and the married women declined all offers, simply saying with a smile, 'No', or remarking, 'I am married'.[16] As Teuira Henry later noted (on the authority of her missionary grandfather, John Orsmond): 'Young girls, some of whom were the cherished daughters of the highest people of the land, were carefully guarded and chaperoned by the chief arioi woman, and their persons, being regarded as sacred, were respected by all members of the society.'[17]

During the successive visits of Wallis, Bougainville, Cook and Boenechea, these women had discovered that these strangers were not gods, but human; and that sex with them was often followed by new and disgusting diseases. According to William Wales, the astronomer, by this time the role of sleeping with European visitors had been relegated to a relatively small number of commoners and war captives:

> I have great reason to believe that much the great part of these [women] admit of no such familiarities, or at least are very carefull to whom they grant them. That there are Prostitutes here as well as in London is true, perhaps more in proportion, and such no doubt were those who came on board the ship to our People. These seem not less skilfull in their profession than Ladies of the same stamp in England, nor does a person run less risk of injuring his health and Constitution in their Embraces.
>
> On the whole I am firmly of opinion that a stranger who visits England might with equal justice draw the Characters of the Ladies there, from those which he might meet with on board the Ships in Plymouth Sound, at Spithead, or in the Thames; on the Point at Portsmouth, or in the Purlieus of Wapping.[18]

During their visits ashore at Vaitepiha, the islanders were almost invariably good-humoured towards the British. They wheedled for presents, saying '*Taio, poe!*' or 'Friend, a bead!'; and when George Forster teased them by mimicking their requests, they burst out laughing. During these exchanges the islanders named Johann Forster 'Matara', his son George 'Teuri', Hodges 'Reo', and Sparrman 'Pamani'. Although George was enchanted with Tautira, admiring its lovely waterfalls, flowering plants and bright birds, Johann complained that he had found few new species in the bay, and the ship was so crowded with visitors that he could not dry his specimens on deck but had to use the ship's oven instead. Nevertheless, he and his companions were beginning to learn more about life on the island, visiting one *marae* with a tiered *ahu* and a funeral bier nearby upon which a woman's corpse lay draped in white bark cloth. Beside this a female mourner sat disconsolately in a hut, and a dead bird wrapped in a mat lay outside on a sacrificial platform. Although they offered beads and a nail to this woman, she would not touch their gifts or even look at them, strictly observing the *tapu* of mourning.

Johann Forster also noticed that all the *ari'i* whom they met in Tautira had very long fingernails, presumably to show that they did no manual labour. On another of their excursions they came across a very fat man, the chief of the district, who lay lolling with his head on a wooden pillow while two servants prepared his dessert, fresh and fermented breadfruit and bananas mashed together with a black basalt pounder – the practice of *ha'a-pori'a*, during which a chief was fed to make him plump and sleek, as a sign of the power and prosperity of his lineage.[19] While the servants were preparing his pudding, a woman fed this 'Tahitian drone' with a large fish and several breadfruit, cramming big pieces into his mouth. Even here, they realised, there was inequality and excess, and George (who had radical leanings) was dismayed by this spectacle:

> We saw a luxurious individual spending his life in the most sluggish inactivity, without one benefit to society, like the privileged parasites of more civilized climates, fattening on the superfluous produce of the soil, of which he robbed the labouring multitude.[20]

During these excursions, the *'arioi* often entertained the Europeans with flute music, dancing, singing and wrestling. They found Hodges's drawings entrancing and asked the Forsters endless questions about their country, the name of their captain, how long they would stay and whether they had any wives on board. Nevertheless, they always hid their pigs and chickens, such was the force of the *rahui* or ritual prohibition; and whenever the strangers asked them about Vehiatua, they said that he was away from the district, although the young *ari'i* kept sending messengers to Cook promising to visit him.

On 21 August, Tuahu, the man who had guided Cook and Banks during their 1769 boat trip around the island, boarded the *Resolution* where he asked after Tepane (Banks), Tolano (Solander) and Tupaia. When he heard that Banks and Solander were both well, and that Tupaia had died from sicknesss, not violence, he seemed relieved. Tuahu gave Cook a long account of the recent wars; and when Cook showed him the chart of Tahiti that he had drafted during their journey, he was enthralled, pointing out each district in turn and reciting its name. He also gave Cook his first information about Boenechea's visit to Tahiti-iti, calling his ship '*Pahi no Pepe*'; adding that it had lain at Vaiuru'a Harbour for five days where one of the crew (whom the islanders called 'Pahutu') had run ashore; and claiming that it was this man who had told the *ari'i* not to barter any pigs to the Spaniards. As George Forster observed ruefully: 'It is a melancholy truth, that the dictates of philanthropy do not harmonise with the political systems of Europe!'[21] In fact, however, they had misunderstood Tuahu, who was trying to tell them that Pautu, a thirty-year-old islander, along with three others, had sailed away to Lima with Boenechea. He also told Cook about the *apa no Pepe* or 'Pepe's illness', an acute viral infection that the Spaniards left behind them which affected the head, throat and stomach and often proved to be fatal.[22] Sometime during that day, Cook heard that the young *ari'i* Vehiatua II had arrived at Tautira.

Early the next morning, Cook, Furneaux, several of the officers, the Forsters and Sparrman went ashore to meet the young *ari'i rahi*. They found him sitting on a four-legged wooden stool surrounded by his people, while some of his attendants prepared the chiefly beverage '*ava*. Cook was escorted by a man named Pao who had been living on board the *Resolution*; and as they approached, the crowd lowered their upper garments as a sign of homage to their high chief. Vehiatua II made room for Captain Cook to sit beside him on his stool, while Furneaux and the others sat down on large stones. George Forster described the *ari'i* as a dignified, fair-skinned young man about eighteen years old, five feet six inches tall, with sandy hair reddened at the tips, and a mild, anxious expression. He was accompanied by his stepfather Ti'itorea, a corpulent, robust man tattooed with solid black blotches in various shapes on his arms, legs and hips (an emblem of his black leg '*arioi* status), consulting him constantly during this meeting. Cook gave the young *ari'i rahi* a length of red baize, a bed sheet, a broadaxe, a knife, nails, looking glasses and beads, with which he was delighted; but when Johann Forster presented Vehiatua with a tuft of feathers fastened to a wire and dyed bright crimson, the people cried out '*Aue!*' in loud admiration. In exchange for these gifts, the young high chief presented his visitors with a pig. He remembered

Captain Cook from their excursion together during Cook's *Endeavour* voyage (when Cook had known him as 'Teari'i' (the high chief)), and enquired after Joseph Banks. He also asked how long they intended to stay in his district, remarking that he hoped that they would spend at least five months with his people. When Cook answered that he intended to leave southern Tahiti the next day, Vehiatua was dismayed, promising him more pigs if he would stay longer. During this meeting the crowd of about five hundred people became rowdy, although the *ari'i rahi*'s attendants occasionally called out for silence, hitting anyone who did not listen with their bamboo staves.

When he realised that Cook would not change his mind, Vehiatua II walked arm in arm with him along the banks of the Vaitepiha River. He asked the names of the sailors, enquired whether their wives were on board, and when he heard that they had no women with them, jovially urged them to seek wives among his people. The sun was very hot, and they soon retired under a long shelter (the local *'arioi* house). The young *ari'i rahi* talked with Cook and his companions about the Spanish ship, saying that it had visited Tahiti-iti five months earlier and stayed there for ten days (although in fact, Boenechea had visited Vaiuru'a Bay eight months earlier and stayed there for a month). As far as the British visitors could make out, the Spanish captain had hanged four of his own people, while a fifth had escaped the same fate by running away, although this man, Pahutu, had later died – another misunderstanding, as Vehiatua was trying to tell them about Pautu and his three companions who had sailed away to Lima. During this discussion, Ti'itorea, who had taken the Spanish commander Boenechea as his *taio*, asked whether the British had a god in their country, and if they prayed to him. When Johann Forster, the Lutheran pastor, assured him that they had a god who had created the world, to whom they often prayed, Ti'itorea seemed delighted, repeating these comments to his companions.

As dinner time approached, Captain Cook took out his watch. Vehiatua was fascinated, examining the watch eagerly and gazing at its whirring wheels. After listening to its ticking, he exclaimed that it 'talked'; and when Cook tried to explain that it measured the hours in the day, the young *ari'i rahi* remarked that it was like a little sun, moving through the sky. After farewelling Vehiatua and Ti'itorea with a hearty '*Taio!*', Cook and his party returned to the ships for dinner. Later that afternoon, when Cook visited Vehiatua, remarking that he was going to Matavai Bay because his people had no pigs to give him, the *ari'i rahi* sent for two pigs which he presented to Cook and Furneaux. In a gesture of appreciation, Cook instructed a Scottish marine to play the bagpipes, a performance which sent Vehiatua, Ti'itorea and the other islanders into raptures. By this time the young high chief had visibly relaxed and was enjoying their company, chopping up little sticks and felling banana trees with one of their hatchets, and asking them innumerable questions.

That evening Cook and his companions returned to their ships, and early the next morning, 24 August, the two vessels were towed out of the harbour and sailed up the east coast, leaving Richard Pickersgill, the *Resolution*'s third lieutenant (who was now enjoying his third visit to Tahiti) at Tautira with a party of armed men and the cutter to collect the pigs that Vehiatua had promised. As they sailed along the east coast in a light land breeze, Johann Forster forgot his woes, quoting Virgil's description of the Elysian fields:

> 'They reached the places of joy and the grassy groves of the Happy Ones, and the homes of the Blessed. Here a more wholesome air clothes the plains in a brilliant light, and they have their very own sun and stars to enjoy. Some were exercising themselves in the grassy fields of sport, playing games and wrestling on the yellow sand; some beat out rhythms with their feet and sang songs . . . He [Aeneas] saw others to left and right feasting on the grass, and singing a joyful hymn in chorus, amid a scented grove of laurel, whence the mighty stream of Erydanus rolls through the woodland to the upper world.' [*The Aeneid* VI, 638–56.][23]

The next morning when Vehiatua and his retinue arrived on the beach at Tautira, they seemed surprised to see that Pickersgill had been left behind with so many armed men. When the young high chief asked the third lieutenant to fire a musket at a target, Pickersgill obliged and the crowd tumbled backwards in fear. The shot made only a small hole, however, so Pickersgill loaded his gun with small shot and blew the target to pieces. Amazed by the power of his weapons, Vehiatua begged him and his party to stay on in Tahiti-iti, sending women to try to persuade them; and that afternoon the *ari'i* bartered eight pigs for axes, judiciously choosing small axes for the little pigs and big ones for the larger hogs that his people had brought to Tautira.

Pickersgill had no intention of staying in Tahiti-iti, however; and that afternoon he set off in the cutter in pursuit of the *Resolution* and the *Adventure*. A squall blew up off Hitia'a, where a fleet of canoes came out to invite them ashore. One man offered them food and clothing; and when another man, Reti's 'brother' Taiuri, assured Pickersgill that if he spent that night at his house, he could sleep with his daughter, as Pickersgill remarked, 'this was an offer not to be rejected'. This man boarded the cutter, stripping off Pickersgill's wet clothes and dressing him in dry bark cloth before taking him ashore. On the beach, they were greeted by a crowd of at least 5000 people who picked up their guests, jubilantly carrying them on their shoulders to Reti, Bougainville's *taio*. According to Pickersgill:

> I was led round a numerous Family of reverent old men and Presented to Each of them by the King, they all expressing their utmost Pleasure and Satisfaction at my paying them a Visit, a House was Prepair'd Victuals drest the Cocoa Nut trees robbed of their fruit, and all was joy and mirth; we supped together; nor were the men neglected they haveing an other House and every attention shewn them.[24]

Although Reti and his people were delighted to meet the British, they did not ask about Ahutoru and barely reacted when they heard that he had died. After supper, Pickersgill sent an armed party to take the boat out into deep water, assuring his hosts that this was simply a precaution against thieves. Afterwards, as he remarked in his journal: 'The Hymneal Songs being allready perform'd we retired to rest untill the Blushing Morn told us it was time to depart.'[25]

The following morning, 25 August, Pickersgill took the cutter up the coast east of Matavai Bay, where he found the *Resolution* and the *Adventure*. As he boarded the *Resolution*, two canoes came out from the bay, flying feather streamers and bringing Fa'a, the old priest who had attached himself to the *Dolphin* during Wallis's visit and to Captain Cook during his visit on the *Endeavour*. Fa'a exchanged gifts with Johann Forster, taking him as his *taio*, and seemed overjoyed to see Cook and Pickersgill, solemnly listing the three occasions upon which 'Tute' (Cook) and 'Petero' (Pickersgill's Tahitian name) had now visited the island. When the ships hauled around Point Venus, huge crowds stood on the beaches; although at 4 p.m. as the anchors rattled down into the bay, most of these onlookers ran away 'like startled deer',[26] running past One Tree Hill and heading for Pare. Almost all of these people had bared their torsos, except for one tall man with a bush of frizzy hair whom Fa'a identified as the paramount chief Tu, running nimbly among his people. Soon afterwards a chief named Maraeta'ata boarded the ship with his wife, a fine-looking woman; and they and their companions took *taio* among the officers and gentlemen, exchanging gifts and names with them. (*See Plate 6*.)

As George Forster noted, the people at Vaitepiha Bay had been 'infinitely more reserved, and in some degree diffident of our intentions',[27] and did not take *taio* among Cook's people. This was presumably because although Joseph Banks had been a bond friend of Tutaha, Vehiatua I's enemy, Boenechea was a *taio* of Ti'itorea, Vehiatua II's regent. Realising that Spain and Britain were often at war, the people of Tahiti-iti had adopted Boenechea's enemies as their own. According to James Magra, moreover, the islanders showed a remarkable fidelity to their bond friends: 'To such there is no service that they will not readily submit, nor any good office that they will not readily perform; they will range the island through to procure them what they want, and when encouraged by kindness and some small presents and tokens of esteem, no promises or rewards will influence them to break their attachments.'[28] Like his *taio* Vehiatua II, the paramount chief Tu was now in a difficult position, because he had taken Lieutenant Gayangos as a *taio* during the Spaniard's brief visit to Pare; and at first he also took it for granted that the British would treat him as an enemy. The Matavai people were very friendly to the sailors, however. That night, as the moon shone down on a calm, silvery sea, the Tahitians talked with their new *taio* on board the *Resolution*, and told them about the recent wars, while Samuel Gibson, the marine who had attempted to desert from the *Endeavour*, acted as their interpreter. They assured the British that Tu was now the paramount chief of Tahiti, and that even Vehiatua had to lower his garments to the waist in his presence; and when they talked about Tu's hasty flight from the British, they laughed, saying '*mata'u*' ('afraid'). George Forster marvelled that these people seemed to hold no grudges about Wallis's attack on Matavai Bay:

> We now saw the character of the natives in a more favourable light than ever, and were convinced that the remembrance of injuries, and the spirit of revenge, did not enter into the composition of the good and simple Taheitians. It must surely be a comfortable reflection to every sensible mind, that philanthropy seems to be natural to mankind, and that the savage ideas of distrust, malevolence, and revenge, are only the consequences of a gradual depravation of manners.[29]

Now that Tu was widely (if not universally) acknowledged as the *ari'i maro 'ura* or paramount chief of Tahiti, Captain Cook was eager to forge an alliance with him. Early the next morning tents were erected on Point Venus for the sick men and the coopers, and afterwards Cook went in his boat with Captain Furneaux, Sparrman and the Forsters, escorted by Maraeta'ata and his wife, to visit Tu at his home in Pare. As they passed Taraho'i *marae*, Maraeta'ata and his wife lowered their upper garments; and when Cook remarked that this was Tutaha's *marae*, Maraeta'ata corrected him, saying now that Tutaha was dead, this *marae* belonged to Tu. By this time, Tu had been invested at Taraho'i *marae* with the red feather girdle that his mother Tetupaia had brought from Ra'iatea; and with Te Ra'i-puatata, the red feather girdle that Tupaia had brought from Taputapuatea, now held at 'Utu-'ai-mahurau *marae* in Atehuru. When they arrived at Pare where a crowd of about 1000 people greeted them with shouts of acclamation, and they found the young paramount chief sitting in a reed-fenced enclosure about twenty yards square, surrounded by a circle of high-ranking men and women who had stripped off their upper garments. Some sailors were sent ahead with gifts which they ceremoniously put down in front of the young *ari'i*, and after this presentation Cook and his party were invited to sit in front of Tu and his retinue. To clear a way for them, the heralds (known as Tu's *hoa* or companions) struck at the crowd with their long bamboo rods, hitting these people until they shifted.

During Cook's previous visit to Matavai Bay, Tu had been kept away from the British. Cook was delighted to meet the young paramount chief at last, whom he described as a strongly built, robust young man about twenty-five years old, six feet three inches tall, with a prodigious mop of frizzy hair and a majestic, intelligent demeanour. During their visit the *ari'i maro 'ura* sat cross-legged on the ground with his mother, his aunts, his sisters and two younger brothers around him, all stripped to the waist; and when his father Teu (or Hapai), a tall, thin, grey-bearded man, arrived soon afterwards, he also stripped his garments to the waist in homage to his son, a gesture that disconcerted George Forster. Although Tu presented his guests with red, perfumed bark cloth, Cook refused this gift, saying his presents were for friendship's sake and required no return; and he ordered the bagpiper to play for Tu and his people, who seemed enchanted by this performance. When Tu asked after Tupaia, he seemed unconcerned to hear about his death; and he enquired after Banks, Solander and others in the Royal Society party from Cook's previous voyage, although he had met none of these people. He promised to give Cook plenty of pigs, confessing that he was afraid of his guns; and as Cook remarked, 'indeed all his actions shew'd him to be a timerous Prince'.[30] Tu was often accused of cowardice, although as Ari'i-marau later noted, a young *ari'i rahi* was taught to be gentle and thoughtful:

> The people are like a crying child, easily coaxed with gentle words, easily enraged by ill treatment. The heart of the Arii must be as great as his power; he must be ever ready to do good, never weary of listening to the cry of his people, with ears and eyes open to the law.
>
> Break the sudden rage that shakes your body, that clouds your brow. Reflection is a good master. Wisdom and a gentle heart are the best spear that an

Arii can have. The head of government must not be seen with grinding teeth, with lifted voice, with frowning brows, with passion-shaken body, with angrily beating heart like that of the plebian, for whom alone such things can be fit.

Meditate before speaking. Your words are flashes of lightning, as mighty as the clap of thunder, they cannot be recalled. Watch your people. Arouse not that which will pain you – you may not be able to find the cure.[31]

When they returned to Point Venus for dinner at noon, Cook found that Bayly and Wales had erected their observatory tents on the same spot as where the tents had been pitched for the 1769 observations of the Transit of Venus.

Early the next morning Tu paid a return visit to Cook, sending a gift of a pig, two large fish, baskets of fruit and rolls of bark cloth out to the *Resolution*. When Cook invited him on board, Tu would not stir from his canoe until the captain had been swaddled in bark cloth as a mark of peace and friendship. His younger brother boarded the ship first, and when he assured Tu it was safe, the young paramount chief followed with his sister and many other high-ranking people. Cook gave them gifts, and each of Tu's companions adopted *taio* among the officers and gentlemen, and shared their breakfast. These Tahitian aristocrats were amazed to see the British drinking hot tea, and although Tu ate nothing (as he was too *ra'a* or sacred), his attendants feasted heartily. As soon as Tu saw Johann Forster's spaniel, a fine dog although filthy with tar and grease, he asked for it; and when the dog was given to him, he handed it to one of his *hoa* or heralds, who carried it everywhere with him. When Furneaux came on board he had a breeding pair of goats with him which he presented to Tu, who sent these animals ashore in his canoe.

Later that morning when Tu and his retinue landed with Captain Cook at Pare, the people shouted out in joy. Tutaha's elderly mother, who was waiting on the beach, greeted Cook with floods of tears, holding his hands tightly and crying out, 'Tutaha the *taio* of Tute is dead!' Moved by her grief, Cook had tears in his eyes, although Tu soon pushed the old lady aside. He seemed jealous of her relationship with Cook and quickly dismissed her; although Cook managed to meet her that afternoon and gave her some presents. That night a number of young women danced on the decks of the ships and ate with their lovers (contrary to Tahitian custom). As George Forster remarked:

This evening was as completely dedicated to mirth and pleasure, as if we had lain at Spithead instead of O-Taheitee. The women assembled on the forecastle, and one of them blowing a flute with their nostrils, all the rest danced a variety of dances usual in their country, amongst which there were some that did not exactly correspond with our ideas of decency. As soon as it was dark they retired below decks, and if their lovers were of such a quality to afford them fresh pork, they supped without reserve, though they had before refused to eat in the presence of their own countrymen, agreeably to that incomprehensible custom which separates the sexes at their meals.[32]

Although Cook had tried to restrain his men, knowing that they would be passing on more venereal infections, this proved impossible; and the island women were baffled that Cook refused to sleep with any of them. Misunderstanding his scruples for impotence, they dismissed him as '*Old, and good for nothing*'.[33]

Like those at Tautira, the pigs at Matavai Bay had been placed under a *rahui* or ritual prohibition. Eager to procure fresh meat for his men, on 28 August Cook sent Pickersgill with the cutter to Atehuru to see whether, despite the Season of Scarcity, the chiefs of that district still had some pigs to barter. Followed by a fleet of about a hundred canoes, Pickersgill set off along the west coast; and when he landed that afternoon at a sandy bay in Puna'aui'a, he was greeted by Pohuetea, the *ari'i* of the district – the tall, powerful *ari'i* whom Gayangos had recently met during the Spaniard's trip around Tahiti. During Captain Cook's first visit to the island, Pohuetea had been taken hostage on board the *Endeavour*, and although they had been reconciled before Cook had sailed, he was still wary of the British. When Pickersgill presented him with a large axe and gave each of his womenfolk a mirror, asking him to bring pigs to the ships, Pohuetea replied that he was too frightened to go to Matavai Bay, but if the lieutenant would wait, he would obtain some pigs for him. Pickersgill had to return to the ships that afternoon, however, and decided to leave it for another day. Just as they were about to depart, one of Pickersgill's men realised that his powderhorn had been stolen; and when Pickersgill told Pohuetea about it he sent his men off in pursuit of the thief, who soon returned with the stolen item.

During Pickersgill's absence, when Tu boarded the *Resolution* he presented Cook with a second pig, a large fish and more fruit and bark cloth, and went to the *Adventure* to make a similar gift to Captain Furneaux. As soon as Tu returned to the *Resolution*, Reti and his companions, who were already on board, hastily dropped their garments to their waists – a compliment they also paid to Tu's sister and younger brother as close kin of the *ari'i maro 'ura*. When Cook escorted Tu to Pare, the bagpiper played and some of the sailors danced the hornpipe to entertain him; and afterwards when the young paramount chief asked his people to dance in reply, they danced in their own style and then performed a hilarious parody of the hornpipe. The next day, Cook, accompanied by Furneaux, visited Tu, and presenting him with a broadsword, buckled this weapon around his waist, although the young *ari'i* seemed extremely uneasy and soon asked whether he could remove the sword. On this occasion Tu escorted his guests to an *'arioi* theatre where they were entertained by three drummers and Tu's sister danced to the drums, wearing a particularly elegant costume decorated with long tassels of feathers that hung down from her waist.[34] Afterwards four *'arioi* men performed skits in which Cook's Tahitian name, 'Tute,' was often mentioned. During these burlesques, as the Forsters remarked, the comics were always male, with men also playing the female parts. When Cook and Furneaux returned to their ships, their hosts loaded the boats with cooked fish and fresh fruit and vegetables.

Cook had still obtained very few pigs, however, and on 30 August he sent Pickersgill again to see whether Pohuetea had collected the pigs that he had promised. When Pickersgill arrived at Puna'aui'a, he found the *ari'i* sitting in his house among a huge crowd of his people. He gave his visitors a lavish meal, and they slept there that night. Pohuetea had not gathered the pigs, though, because he did not know that they were coming; so Pickersgill decided to go to Papara to visit 'old Queen Oberea' to see whether she had any pigs for him. When Pickersgill tried to land at Papara, however, a herald ordered him not to step ashore. Determined to see Purea, Pickersgill ordered his men to aim their muskets at this man; and holding up a plantain branch as a sign of submission, the herald led them to a house where they rested while a messenger was sent to Purea, who lived about two miles away. When she arrived, she assured Pickersgill that she was now very poor and had no pigs to give him. Although she asked fondly after her friends from the *Dolphin* and the *Endeavour*, Purea barely mentioned Tupaia, her former high priest and lover. The next morning when Pickersgill and his party walked back to Pohuetea's house, the *ari'i* offered to accompany them back to the ships if the third lieutenant would promise on a small bunch of red feathers that the British would not shoot him. After he did this, holding on to the red feathers, Pohuetea and his former wife (who regarded herself as Cook's 'sister') boarded the pinnace with four pigs as gifts for Cook – two sent by Amo and two from himself – although many of his people tried to dissuade him from accompanying the British, weeping bitterly.

During Pickersgill's absence from Matavai Bay, several marines and a sailor from the *Adventure* had gone ashore where, according to later reports, they raped several women. There was a fight and loud yelling on the beach, and when Cook sent an armed boat to find out what was going on, they returned bringing these men in irons. Although Tu had promised to visit Cook that morning, he decided to stay away, sending his counsellor Ti'i instead with a pig, some fruit, and a message that he was too *mata'u* (afraid) to visit the *Resolution*. In front of Tu's envoy, Cook ordered his men to bring the culprits to the gangway, where each of the three marines was given eighteen lashes and the sailor twelve; and he instructed Furneaux to punish any others in his crew who had been involved in the riot. After loading three sheep from the Cape of Good Hope into his boat, Cook set off to Pare with Ti'i, Furneaux and Johann Forster to find Tu. At Pare, they were told that Tu had fled to a place further south; and when they arrived there, Tu had already departed. Later that afternoon when Tu arrived with his mother to see Cook, his mother wept bitterly, although Cook tried to reassure them, presenting the young *ari'i* with the sheep and ordering the bagpiper to play for him. Finally, Tu sent for a pig which he presented to Cook, and another which he gave to Furneaux, as a sign of reconciliation. When a little pig was brought for Johann Forster, however, one of Tu's relatives stood and made an angry speech, and a large pig was produced instead and given to the naturalist. Cook and his companions also produced their iron goods and other trinkets, distributing these freely, and in return the Europeans were all bundled up in bark cloth as a gesture of reconciliation.

While Cook, Furneaux and Johann Forster were away on this expedition, George Forster and Sparrman also went ashore. Still furious about the events of the previous night, the old man Fa'a met them on the beach, although he seemed much happier when they told him that the culprits had been severely punished. The two young botanists took a guide and climbed up one of the valleys behind Pare, high into the mountains, to look for new species of plants. As they passed a large *hutu* (Barringtonia) tree they saw a group of people gathering the nuts, who explained that they crushed these and mixed them with a particular kind of shellfish to stun fish in the lagoons. When the young botanists turned back again, stumbling and sliding down the steep slopes, they handed their muskets to their guide who led them down safely, taking them to one of the valleys behind Matavai Bay where a man and his daughter invited them to dinner. A fine mat was spread on the ground, and the two young naturalists sat down while the women massaged their arms and legs, which were tired and aching. They were given an excellent meal and showered this family with nails, knives and beads, thanking them profusely for their kindness. As they walked back down the valley, they met a man who was preparing red dye for bark cloth, and some women who showed them how to use this dye for decorating bark cloth with patterns.

Cook was now eager to leave Matavai Bay, and on 1 September 1773 the observatory and its instruments were loaded on board the *Resolution*. Although the spring equinox on 21 September was approaching, when the *'arioi* would return from their homes, Captain Cook was about to leave the island. At 3 p.m. that afternoon when Lieutenant Pickersgill arrived back in the bay, accompanied by Pohuetea, his wife and one of their friends, the chiefs presented Cook with the four pigs that they had brought, bearing themselves with great dignity. Soon afterwards a young man named Porea came to Cook, begging to sail with him to 'Peretani' or Britain; and Cook agreed, thinking he might be useful during the voyage. When Porea asked for a hatchet and nail for his father, Cook handed these items over; but at sunset, after the ships had set sail, a canoe came out and demanded in Tu's name that the young man go back with them. Convinced that he had been tricked, Cook told these men that he would release the youth as soon as they returned the hatchet and the nail that he had sent to his father; but assuring him that this was impossible, they paddled back to shore. As the *Resolution* sailed away from Tahiti, Porea stood at the stern of the ship, weeping bitterly, until Johann Forster and Cook took pity on him, assuring him that from now on they would be his *metua* or parents. In gratitude, the young man hugged them and soon regained his composure.

During this visit to Tahiti, Cook and his companions learned more about the chiefly system on the island. The red feather girdle could be worn by only one high chief at a time, who was recognised as the *ari'i maro 'ura* or paramount chief, although this was not always the eldest son of the deceased paramount chief. The *ari'i rahi* (or leading high chiefs), who were titleholders who held ceremonial sway over a number of districts and whose powers including the right to place *rahui* or sacred restrictions over the resources in their districts, often contested the succession. They in turn were distinguished from the *ari'i* (high chiefs of particular districts); the *ra'atira* (lesser chiefs or landowners); the *manahune* (commoners), who comprised the vast mass of the population; and the *teuteu* (or hereditary servants). In comparing this arrangement with the feudal system in Europe, George Forster remarked that there was no poverty in Tahiti and the people seemed genuinely fond of their chiefs, treating them in many ways as equals. Although some kinds of food (for instance, turtle, a sacred creature associated with 'Oro) were reserved for the *ari'i*,[35] the high chiefs paddled their own canoes and worked alongside the ordinary people; although some *ari'i* were more indolent than others. Further, although corpulence was a sign of chiefly status, Tu, the most sacred chief on Tahiti at this time, was lean and well-muscled. The prestige claimed by certain lineages in various districts seemed to rise and fall according to the strength of character and intelligence of particular chiefs and their supporters, the marriages and alliances that were forged, and their success or failure in the wars that periodically flared up between the different lineages, districts or islands.

As for the sailors, they adored their visit to Tahiti. As they sailed away, one of the crew, John Elliott, summed up their impressions of the island:

> This Island appeared to us to be the Paradice of those Seas, the Men being all fine, tall, well-made, with humane open countenances; the Women beautiful, compaired with all those that we had seen, of the Middle Size, zingy suple figures, fine teeth and Eyes, and the finest formed Hands, fingers and Arms that I ever saw, with lively dispositions. And tho the Men were inclined to steal little things from us, yet the Women seemed free from this propensity. In fact, when we were on shore here we felt ourselves in perfect ease and safety.[36]

Hitihiti's Odyssey

After leaving Matavai Bay, Cook headed west for Huahine, following the track of his voyage with Tupaia through the Society Islands. As they entered Fare Harbour on 3 September 1773 through a narrow gap in the reef, the *Adventure* failed to tack successfully and grounded on the coral; and had to be hauled off with boats and anchors. Eager to ensure that his trade goods kept their value, Cook forbade his men to engage in barter; and given the scarcity of food in Tahiti he was delighted to see the canoes flocking out from Huahine laden with fruit, pigs and chicken. When they landed at Fare, Porea proudly escorted them ashore, wearing a linen frock coat and trousers and carrying Captain Cook's powderhorn and shot pouch. He pleaded with his companions to pretend that he was a British sailor, and when they addressed him as 'Tom' he answered 'Sir', pronouncing this 'Soro'. Porea refused to speak any Tahitian during his visit to Huahine, instead using a kind of gibberish that he insisted was English. At Fare, the local people told Cook that Ori (or Mato), who had changed names with him in 1769, was still alive and eager to see him; and that his son Teri'itaria was now the *ari'i rahi* of the island, the previous high chief having died since Cook's last visit.

The next morning when Cook went ashore to meet Ori, accompanied by Captain Furneaux and Johann Forster, a priest who had appointed himself as their guide gave them three plantain branches, telling them to decorate these with large nails, looking glasses, medals and red feathers, and instructing Johann Forster on how to manage their side of the ritual and make the *utu* – the gifts announcing their arrival. As the decorated boughs were handed to Ori one by one, the priest told Forster to call out that the first branch was for the *ari'i* or high chief of the island; the second for the *atua* or god; and the third from Cook for his *taio* Ori. After a pause, five plantain stalks were ceremoniously delivered to the boat in reply, another priest announcing that the first, with a pig, was for the visiting *ari'i* 'Ori' (or Cook, as they had exchanged names) from the *ari'i rahi* òf Huahine (Ori's son Teri'itaria, a boy about seven years old); the second, with a pig, from the god of Huahine for his god; the third, also with a pig, for Tetumu (the *ata* or incarnation of Ta'aroa's phallus); the fourth, with a dog, as a *taura* or bond to tie Cook's and Ori's people together; and the last, with another pig, from 'Tute' (or Ori) for his *taio* 'Ori' (or Cook). Finally, Ori sent Cook the small piece of pewter inscribed with the details of the *Endeavour*'s visit to Huahine that his friend had given him in 1769. When he received this memento Cook stepped ashore, holding up his plantain branch, and embraced his *taio*. Ori, a thin, old man about fifty years old with rheumy eyes, greeted him with tears trickling down his cheeks, and presented Cook with another pig and some bales of bark cloth. He asked after Tupaia, and when he was told how he had died, seemed to accept his fate with equanimity.

While these exchanges were under way, George Forster and Anders Sparrman, who also landed at Fare that morning, walked to Ori's house through orchards of fruit trees, groves of perfumed shrubs and flourishing gardens. When they shot a white-bellied kingfisher and a grey heron as specimens, some of the local people protested vehemently, saying that these were sacred birds or *atua*. In the Society Islands such birds were *ata* (or incarnations) of the gods, carrying their spirits to the *marae* so that they could enter the *to'o* or god-images.[1] The next morning when Ori paid a visit to Cook on board the *Resolution* with his sons, they received Cook's gifts with indifference but seemed delighted when the bagpiper played for them. The next morning, George Forster and Sparrman went ashore again, visiting a large double war canoe under construction. They described the two hulls of this craft as eighty-seven feet long, joined by eighteen squared beams twenty-four feet long which projected beyond the hulls on both sides, and strengthened by three longitudinal spars, so that 144 paddlers could sit on the beams. This canoe had a fighting stage twenty-four feet long and ten feet wide, supported by four carved pillars, and the prow and stern were both decorated with large carved human figures. The canoe builders explained that when Huahine had been attacked by the Borabora warriors ten months earlier, their *ari'i rahi* was killed and had been succeeded by Teri'itaria, and that afterwards Ori had made peace with Puni, the paramount chief of that island, becoming his *taio* or bond friend in order to maintain Huahine's independence from Borabora.

At the watering place that morning, a tall man named Tupai, dressed in red bark cloth and with bundles of feathers hanging at his girdle (the costume of a leading *'arioi*), tried to stop the people from bartering their animals and breadfruit to the British. This was understandable, because during this brief visit to Huahine Cook's men obtained three hundred pigs, thirty dogs and fifty hens, almost exhausting the local resources, which were still scant on the island. The Season of Scarcity was just ending, and the new breadfruit crop had not yet ripened. When Tupai threatened one of the officers and seized a bag of nails from the captain's clerk, Captain Cook ordered him to give these back; and when he refused, Cook grabbed the two large clubs that Tupai was carrying, brandished his sword when Tupai resisted and gave the clubs to a sailor, ordering him to smash these weapons and throw them into the sea. Infuriated by this insult, Tupai stormed off in a rage. Later that afternoon when Sparrman went off botanising on his own, two men approached him, calling themselves his *taio*. Evidently Tupai was one of these men, and after guiding the young botanist far inland, he grabbed Sparrman's hunting knife from its scabbard and hit him on the head with its hilt, stunning him; and when the young man stumbled and almost fell, they tore his jacket from his back, grabbed his belt and black satin waistcoat, and took his silk handkerchief, a knife and a small microscope. When Sparrman tried to run away the two men attacked him again, hitting him on the head and shoulders, stripping off his shirt and trying to take off his trousers. Fortunately, when some other islanders came on the scene the assailants ran away; and the rescuers took off their own bark-cloth garments, wrapping them around Sparrman who stood there dazed, half naked and bleeding, and took him to Ori's house, where they told the chief what had happened.

Ori was distraught when he heard about the attack, weeping out loud and promising to recover every item that had been stolen. He escorted Sparrman back to Fare, although as soon as Ori boarded the pinnace with Cook, his people began to weep loudly, his wife and daughter slashing their heads and shoulders with sharp stones and begging the *ariʻi* not to accompany the British. Ori was resolute, however, saying to his people, 'Ori [Cook] and I are friends, I have done nothing to forfeit his friendship, why should I not go with him?'[2] As Cook remarked: 'Friendship is Sacred with these people. Oree [Ori] and I were profess'd friends in all the forms customary among them, and he had no idea that this could be broke by the act of any other person.'[3] After dinner, some of Ori's people brought back Sparrman's knife, scabbard and a part of his waistcoat, but his other stolen possessions had vanished. Because Ori had been so helpful, Cook resolved to take no further action to punish the theft, a decision that angered Johann Forster, who protested vehemently that his failure to punish violent robberies would endanger every European who subsequently visited the island.

The following morning, Cook decided to leave Huahine. Accompanied by Johann Forster and Furneaux, he went to Ori's house to farewell his friend, presenting him with gifts including a copper plate engraved with the details of his latest visit in the *Resolution*. Embracing Cook with tears in his eyes, Ori asked if some of his people who were on board the *Adventure* could be sent ashore; but when Cook sent a boat to fetch them it returned with only one person on board, a tall, slim, dark-skinned young Ra'iatean named Ma'i who had joined the *Adventure* when it arrived at Huahine and was eager to travel to England. Because Ori had already left the ship, Cook decided to let the young man sail on the *Adventure*, although he was surprised that Furneaux wanted to take him to England.

Although Cook described Ma'i as 'dark, ugly and a downright black-guard' (in eighteenth-century parlance, a low-born person),[4] according to Ma'i's own account he was a *hoa* or chiefly attendant, the second son of a landowner in Ra'iatea who had been killed by Puni's warriors in about 1762. After his father's death Ma'i had fled to Tahiti, and during the great naval battle between the *Dolphin* and the Tahitian fleet in Matavai Bay he was wounded in the side with a musket shot. Afterwards he had apprenticed himself to a priest, travelling with him throughout the Society Islands, the Tuamotu and the Cook Islands. Ma'i may also have visited the Marquesas, because he spoke of sailing to an island seven days to the east, where the people spoke a different language and had tattoo patterns different to those in the Society Islands. Eventually he returned to Ra'iatea, where he was captured in a battle by some of Puni's warriors and taken with other captives to Borabora. They had escaped death only when a woman from Ra'iatea, a *taio* of one of these warriors, begged for their lives; and afterwards they managed to steal a canoe and fled to Huahine.

Ma'i was well liked by his shipmates. As George Forster remarked: 'He was not an extraordinary genius like Tupia, but he was warm in his affections, grateful and humane; . . . polite, intelligent, lively and volatile.'[5] When the ships set sail from Huahine on 7 September, heading for Ra'iatea, he cried out for his friends, weeping bitterly. Like Tupaia, Ma'i was determined to free his homeland from the Borabora invaders, and told his shipmates that if Captain Cook did not help him, he would tell his fellow islanders not to give the British any provisions.

The next morning when the ships arrived off Ha'amanino Harbour, Tupaia's birthplace in Ra'iatea, the wind was blowing straight out of the bay; and while the vessels were being warped through the pass, Rufera, a burly, athletic, black leg *'arioi* from Borabora, came out to the *Resolution*

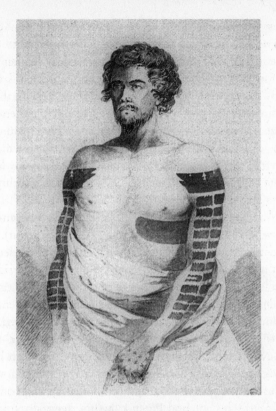

A Knight of Borabora

carrying a small pig and a plantain branch; and when everyone else ignored him, presented his pig to Johann Forster. This man was impressive
and statuesque, his arms tattooed in large black squares, his breast, belly
and back in thick black bands, and his thighs, buttocks and hands a solid
black. That afternoon another Borabora *'arioi*, Herea, a very stout, heavily tattooed man, fifty-four inches around the waist and with long wavy
black hair down his back, came on board and exchanged names with
Johann Forster – perhaps because the islanders regarded the elder Forster,
a Lutheran pastor, as the high priest of this expedition.

The sailors were so impressed by these black leg *'arioi*, whom they
dubbed the 'Knights of Bolabola', that they decided to set up a society of
their own, tattooing a black star on the left side of their chests and calling
themselves the 'Knights of Otaheite'. To celebrate their new brotherhood
they cooked and ate dogs, just like the Society Islanders; and sensing their
danger, the dogs that they had obtained at Huahine skulked around the
ship, refusing to eat and drink and hiding in corners. Both Rufera and
Herea asked Captain Cook about Tupaia, but as Borabora men they were

his bitter enemies and expressed no sorrow when they were told that he had died at Batavia. After the conquest of Ra'iatea, Puni, the paramount chief of Borabora (who wore a *maro tea* or yellow feather girdle, the insignia of the most aristocratic line in Borabora), had allowed 'U'uru (more formally known as Vetea-ra'i-'u'uru, the son of Tamatoa II by his third wife, and half-brother to Tu's mother Tetupaia) to remain as the *ari'i maro 'ura* or red feather girdle high chief at 'Opoa; although at the same time he appointed 'Boba' (Tapoa), his close relative and anointed successor, to rule over the adjoining island of Taha'a.⁶ According to Ma'i, Puni was now very old and almost blind, but still cheerful and merry, and much loved by his people. He sponsored *'arioi* games and festivities with enthusiasm, and had invented many new entertainments himself. During the *Endeavour* expedition Cook had visited Puni, but on this occasion the great warrior retreated to Maupiti Island as soon as he heard of their arrival, fearing that the British had come to free Huahine and Ra'iatea from his dominion.

On 9 September Cook went ashore to visit 'U'uru's brother Reo, whom he had met during his 1769 visit to the island. Reo, a robust, medium-sized man with a wispy, reddish-brown beard and an intelligent, cheerful face, welcomed him warmly and asked to exchange names with him. When Captain Cook agreed, Reo asked after Tupaia and listened with intense interest to the story of his voyage and death in Batavia. He was accompanied by his wife, his son and Poiatua, his fourteen-year-old daughter, a charming, beautiful girl with a lovely voice. After this meeting the Forsters went off looking for specimens, and when they shot several kingfishers and two herons (although they knew from their time in Huahine that these were sacred birds, the *ata* or incarnations of gods), Poiatua burst into tears, while her mother and the other women were also very upset. When Reo saw the Forsters, he gravely asked them not to kill any more of these birds on the island.

As Cook had discovered during his visit there with Tupaia, Ha'amanino Harbour was an *'arioi* headquarters, and once again he and his companions were treated to a series of *'arioi* performances. On 10 September, for instance, when Cook visited Reo, he was entertained with a *heiva* performed by three drummers, one female (Reo's niece) and seven male actors, who enacted a farce depicting a thief who was caught in the act, but managed to escape with his prize. The next day, Reo's daughter Poiatua and another high-born young woman danced the *hura* (a chiefly dance) on fine mats laid out in an enclosure between two houses, one of which sheltered the audience and the other the musicians. These girls wore bodices made of brown *'arioi* bark cloth with red and white bark-cloth ruffles

Poiatua, a Polynesian Aphrodite

around their waists, layered white bark-cloth petticoats, and high turbans on their heads made from plaited hair decorated with white flowers. As they danced to the drums they rotated their hips, standing, sitting and lying down, twisting their mouths awry and making graceful, elegant gestures with their arms and hands as an old *'arioi* man danced with them, calling out the actions. Afterwards five male *'arioi* actors performed a skit ridiculing Reo and the other chiefs who were present; danced an 'indecent' dance, mimicking the sexual act; and took turns to belabour each other, evidently depicting the Borabora conquest of the island. One of these men was so skilful that Lieutenant Burney dubbed him 'Garrick' after the famous actor in London. Although Cook and his companions attended many *'arioi* performances during this visit to the Society Islands, however, none of them was invited to the most private *'arioi* gatherings (unlike the first voyage, when the surgeon Monkhouse had enjoyed this privilege). As Johann Forster noted:

> There are other dances usual in their nocturnal festivals with the Arreeoys, which, none of our ships company had an opportunity of seeing, and according to the accounts of the natives extremely indecent and lascivious; these are called t'eai-morodee and the women exhibiting them too-aha [tu'a'a – lewd, shameless, indecent].[7]

After this performance of the *hura*, 'U'uru, the *ari'i maro 'ura* at 'Opoa, paid a stately visit to Captain Cook, presenting him with a pig and receiving lavish gifts in return. During this meeting the chiefs recited the names of a number of islands, including Rimatara and Tupua'i in the Australs; Hao in the Tuamotu; Maupiha'a and Fenua'ura in the Society Islands; Vava'u and 'Uiha in the Tongan islands; Upolu in the Samoan archipelago; Rarotonga in the Cook Islands; and Aurea and Tautipa, islands that appear on Tupaia's island list but cannot now be identified. Other people told the Forsters about an island called 'Hiva', which was inhabited by a race of giants. All of these islands were included on Tupaia's chart, although his knowledge of the far-flung islands had been far more extensive.[8]

On another excursion to the north of Ra'iatea, George Forster became tired and bargained for a ride in a canoe; but when the owner demanded an exorbitant price the young naturalist angrily refused, calling this man a scoundrel. Johann Forster was watching, and when the owner of the canoe tried to grab his son and seize his musket, he aimed his gun, shooting the man in the back with small shot as he ran off. Back at the ship, when Johann told Cook what he had done, Cook laughed at first, but at supper that evening he rebuked him for shooting the islander. Johann, who had long resented Cook's refusal to punish the islanders for theft, reacted violently, retorting that he was not answerable to Cook, and threatening to tell King George about Cook's failure to exercise proper control over the islanders. Hot words were exchanged, and when Johann challenged the captain to a duel, Cook had him thrown out of the Great Cabin. If Forster had been a sailor, this would have been mutiny, an offence punishable by death; but he was a civilian and Cook was left fuming with frustration.

The next morning when Cook sent Lieutenant Pickersgill with Jack Rowe (the *Adventure*'s mate) to fetch bananas from the adjoining island of Taha'a, Johann Forster and Sparrman asked whether they could accompany them. Glad to see the back of the elder Forster, Cook gave them permission. When they landed at Ha'amene Harbour, they were invited to a *heiva* where the local *ari'i*, a thin, elderly man named Ta, asked Johann

Forster to sit beside him. At this *heiva* a group of young people (novice *'arioi*) wearing red sashes, their bodies glistening with scented coconut oil and their heads decorated with tufts of human hair, paraded two by two and laid down bundles of bark cloth in front of the *ari'i* in a *huapipi* ceremony, a ritual celebration of prosperity and fertility that initiated them into the *'arioi* society, watched by a woman dressed in a Chief Mourner's costume whose face and body were blacked with charcoal.[9] When a bystander scuffled with one of the drummers they were both thrown out of the arena; and afterwards three young girls aged between five and ten years old danced, followed by three male *'arioi* who acted out a skit depicting a successful theft from some sleeping people.

That night when Pickersgill, Rowe, Forster and Sparrman went to sleep in the local *'arioi* house, Ta kept them company. During the night, however, the sentry heard someone moving around the house, grabbed the 'thief' by the hair and beat him with the butt end of his musket. When a candle was lit and they found that the 'thief' was none other than Ta, they laughed heartily at his misfortune. Brooding over this insult, the next morning Ta escorted his guests to a feast at the village of Tapoa (Puni's nominated successor), although the *ari'i* was absent; and during this meal their mat-bag full of items for barter was taken. Johann Forster was still furious over Cook's failure to punish the attack on his son; and Jack Rowe was notorious for his high-handed approach to the islanders. (As Lieutenant Burney later remarked, 'some of our young folks behav[e] in a very foolish, arrogant manner, drawing their Swords to fright them & pretending to be in a passion at trifles'.)[10] Lieutenant Pickersgill obviously agreed that the islanders should be taught a lesson, and they went on a rampage, taking Ta hostage at gunpoint, firing their muskets and seizing mats, pigs, pearl shells, breastplates, drums and costumes from the houses in Tapoa's village. Ta was so terrified that he fouled himself; and when they seized the *heiva* costumes, the elderly male and female guardians crept towards them, half-crouching and half-kneeling and each with a dog in their arms in a gesture of submission. Pickersgill refused to release Ta until the mat-bag had been returned with all its contents, however; although when this was done they let him go and took the boat back to Ra'iatea.

During their absence Reo had given Cook a feast, serving him and his companions two roasted pigs, piping hot breadfruit, plantains and drinking coconuts. The men ate before the women, and when Cook offered Reo a glass of Madeira he drank it down with relish, unlike most of the islanders who disliked the taste of alcohol. Afterwards Porea prepared *'ava* and drank about a pint of this beverage, which left him red-faced and so drunk that he had to lie down on the floor of the cabin. The next day one of the *Adventure*'s sailors had a scuffle with a local man, although when he and his friend were confronted by three burly warriors armed with clubs, they took to their heels. When stories arrived at Ra'iatea about the rampage in Tapoa's village on Taha'a, with reports that some of the people there had been shot, Reo stayed away from the ship, and Porea handed Cook's powderhorn to one of the sailors and disappeared. He had met a girl in Ra'iatea, and Cook thought that he had abandoned the expedition for this reason.

Later that day Hitihiti, a very handsome, well-dressed young *'arioi* about seventeen years old and a close relative of Puni, came to tell George Forster that he wanted to sail with them to England. It seems likely that this young man was the nephew of Tetupaia (the mother of Tu), because this is the name of her sister's son on some genealogies; and according to those accounts one of his uncles had married Puni, a woman from the chiefly lineage of Borabora. In this case Hitihiti was a very aristocratic young man, a member of the same aristocratic family as Tupaia, and no doubt hoped to follow in the great priest's footsteps. Although George assured him that the voyage would be dangerous and uncomfortable, Hitihiti was determined to go and his friends eagerly supported him; and when George presented this young *'arioi* to Cook, he agreed that Hitihiti could take Porea's place on board the *Resolution*.

Concerned that tensions on the island were spiralling out of control, Cook now decided to leave Ra'iatea. When he went to invite his *taio* Reo to a farewell dinner, he was not at home; and when he finally found his friend, Reo's mother threw herself into his arms, weeping bitterly. After assuring Reo of his friendship, Cook returned to the ship and summoned Johann Forster to the Great Cabin, where they shook hands and agreed to set aside their differences. Ma'i, who was now on board the *Adventure* (listed in the muster roll as 'Tetuby Homy' (Te Tupai Ma'i)), was delighted and relieved to hear that they were about to leave the island. A few days earlier several Borabora warriors, having heard him boast that he would fetch guns from England to drive them off Ra'iatea, had been about to ambush Ma'i when he was warned of the attack, escaping at the last moment by abandoning his clothes on the beach and frantically swimming back to the *Adventure*. That afternoon when Hitihiti's friends came out to the *Resolution* to farewell him, they brought bales of bark cloth and balls of *mahi* or fermented breadfruit, as well as an attendant to care for him during his journey. There was plenty of fresh meat on board, because Cook and his men had obtained at least five hundred pigs during their visit to Ra'iatea. Early the next morning when Reo arrived with more presents for Cook, he was accompanied by his daughter Poiatua who asked for the green awning from the captain's boat for her canoe, although Cook did not give it to her. As the sails filled in the breeze, Reo wept bitterly, urging his *taio* to return to Ra'iatea with his sons. As George Forster wrote in his journal that night: 'The simple child of nature, who inhabits these islands, gives free course to all his feelings, and glories in his affection[s]', quoting the classics: 'When Nature gave tears to man, she proclaimed that he was tender-hearted, and tenderness is the best quality of man' (Juvenal, *Satires*, 15).[11] Cook, the unsentimental Yorkshireman, simply remarked: 'In short, the more one is acquainted with these people the better one likes them, to give them their due I must say they are the most obligeing and benevolent people I ever met with.'[12]

On 17 September 1773 as he sailed away from Ra'iatea, Cook set a course to the west in a fresh gale, heading for the islands that Tupaia had been so keen to visit three years earlier. Hitihiti (or Mahine as he was also known, a name that he had acquired by exchanging names with Mahine, the paramount chief of Mo'orea) was seasick, although he felt better after eating pieces of raw dolphin and shark dipped into salt water and several balls of fermented breadfruit. As he ate, Hitihiti repeated a prayer, setting aside a small portion of the food for his *atua* or god. Several days later on a Sunday, when the *Adventure*'s crew gathered on deck for divine service, Ma'i (or 'Jack', as the sailors called him) was terrified, fearing that he was about to be offered as a human sacrifice, although Lieutenant Burney managed to reassure him.

On 2 October the ships anchored off the small Tongan island of 'Eua, where a chief named Taione came out to the *Resolution* and exchanged gifts with Cook, placing each of the small presents he was given on his head and saying *fakafeta'i* or 'thank you'. He escorted Cook, Furneaux, the Forsters, Sparrman, Hitihiti and Ma'i ashore, leading them to a delightful house surrounded by a lawn and flowering trees where they were welcomed by a huge crowd, none of whom was armed, who greeted them with shouts of pleasure. When Taione seated his guests on fine mats Cook ordered the bagpiper to play, although as Sparrman remarked ruefully: 'Our Scots virtuoso, who had been accustomed to arouse general delight in Otaheite with his wailing bagpipes, seemed here to be denied all approbation.'[13] Nevertheless, three young Tongan women responded courteously by singing in harmony, snapping their fingers in time; and the Europeans sang (especially Sparrman, who loved singing comic Swedish songs on such occasions), accompanied by a violin and zither. Soon afterwards Cook and his companions were taken to another house where a fine feast was spread and they ate heartily, particularly Ma'i and Hitihiti. Although these two young Society Islanders tried to communicate with the 'Eua people, they could understand only a few of the words that they said, which is not surprising, given Tongan is a West Polynesian language, quite different from Tahitian. There was no good watering place on 'Eua, however, and Cook decided to leave the island the following morning.

During this brief stay at 'Eua, as Ma'i and Hitihiti began to work with the Forsters on a vocabulary of Tahitian and a description of life in the Society Islands, it soon became obvious that they stood on opposite sides of the struggles that divided their home islands. Hitihiti was a close relative of Puni, the conqueror of Ra'iatea who had sent both Ma'i and Tupaia into exile; while Ma'i hated Puni with all his heart for conquering his homeland. When he heard Hitihiti delivering a speech to a blue king-fisher that the Forsters had shot, addressing it as 'Puni's *atua* [god]', Ma'i exclaimed sardonically that the Europeans had killed Puni's god; and as far as possible, he stayed away from the young *'arioi* from Borabora.

On 6 October as the ships sailed up the west coast of Tongatapu (the island of the sacred chiefs of Tonga, previously visited by Abel Tasman in 1643), the local inhabitants waved little white flags in greeting. When they arrived at the district of Hihifo a minor chief named Ataongo came on board who exchanged names with Cook and escorted them ashore. This island seemed very fertile, with fenced gardens, flowering shrubs, plantations and neat paths between the houses. When the local inhabitants brought their goods to barter, Hitihiti and Ma'i discovered to their delight that these included dancing aprons and headdresses decorated with bright red feathers, bargaining eagerly for these treasures. Hitihiti urged Cook to buy as many of these feathers as he could, as they would command a very high price in Tahiti; saying that a piece ornamented with red feathers only two fingers wide would buy a large pig in the Society Islands. After talking with the Tongans for a time, Ma'i and Hitihiti began to manage the sound shifts and understand them a little, 'convers[ing] with the natives much better than we could have done after a long intercourse with them'.[14] That night a number of naked, unmarried girls swam out to the ships and came on board, and as George Forster confessed, 'our seamen took advantage of their disposition, and once more offered to our eyes a scene worthy of the Cyprian temples'.[15]

Furious at this debauch, the following day the Tongan men began to steal from the British. One man dived under the pinnace to try to take its grappling iron, while another attempted to wrestle its oars from the sailors. A sailor's jacket was stolen, and the thief was shot with small shot; and when George Forster and Sparrman went botanising and became separated in the woods, a warrior grabbed at George's musket. Another crawled through the scuttle into the master's cabin, seizing a ruler, his log-books, the *Daily Assistant* and the *Nautical Almanac*, a sword and a copy of Pope's *Homer*. When the sailors in the pinnace saw this man drop these prizes into his canoe they chased him, firing a musket ball into its stern; and when he threw these things into the water and dived overboard, they rowed after him, finally hauling him into the pinnace with a boathook.

Cook had made a serious error in exchanging names with Ataongo, a lesser chief; and the next day when he was presented to a much higher-ranking chief named Latunipulu (Tuʻilakepa Latunipulu, the sister's son of the sacred chief Tuʻi Tonga), the chief sat there sullenly in silence. To make matters worse, when one of the local men took a nail from Johann Forster without giving anything in return, the irascible botanist thumped him with a heavy wooden dart; and seeing that the islander was about to retaliate, drew his sword and slashed him across the back. Cook was incensed and decided to leave the island at once, ordering his men back to the ships while the Tongans watched impassively. As the ships set sail, a canoe came alongside the *Resolution*, a man furiously beating on his drum as the paddlers drove their canoe in time through the water; and Cook set his course south, heading down to New Zealand. In his journal, Johann Forster quoted *The Aeneid*:

> 'All together they veered out the sheet, and . . . let the sails out now to port then to starboard: together they turned and turned the yards high above: The winds they wanted carried the fleet along.' [*The Aeneid*, V: 830.][16]

On 8 October as the sloops sailed south past the small island of ʻAta, heading for New Zealand, the mood on board was merry. Ten days later they sighted Table Cape on the east coast of the North Island of New Zealand, where people sat on the point and gazed at the ships, although no canoes came out to greet them. Cook wanted to spend some time at Queen Charlotte Sound before sailing south again to search for Terra Australis; and as they sailed south past Cape Kidnappers several canoes approached the ships, bringing out two dignified chiefs who boarded the *Resolution*. Hitihiti offered these men gifts of young coconut trees and yams and urged them to plant them ashore, but they could not understand what he said and largely ignored him. These chiefs, who had heard about the *Endeavour*'s visit to New Zealand, must have been hoping to meet the famous high priest, Tupaia. Although Hitihiti was probably a relative of Tupaia, he had none of his charisma; and after performing a *haka* or war dance the chiefs returned to their canoes. That night the wind blew up, and several days later the ships were caught in a terrible storm. Tossed by howling gales and drenched and battered by high waves, the *Resolution* and *Adventure* were blown out to sea and lost sight of each other.

When the winds died down again, Cook tacked the *Resolution* in to Queen Charlotte Sound, the agreed rendezvous, noting with dismay: 'We did not find the *Adventure* as we expected.'[17] On 3 November 1773 when the anchors splashed into the green, still waters of Ship Cove, several canoes came out, bringing people whom Cook recognised from his 1770 visit to the sound. When they went ashore, Hitihiti took a musket, and with his first shot killed a shining cuckoo feeding on seedheads in a garden that Cook's men had planted. As Johann Foster remarked, the Society Islanders had very acute eyesight, often spotting birds or animals long before the Europeans could see them. Despite his best efforts, however, and unlike Tupaia, Hitihiti could not understand or speak Māori. As an experienced navigator, the high priest had visited many Polynesian islands and mastered the sound shifts between different Polynesian languages; but this was the first time that Hitihiti had left the Society Islands. Although the young 'arioi may have lacked Tupaia's sacred knowledge, however, he shared his chauvinistic habit of mind, urging Māori to grow coconuts and yams and pointing out faults in their way of life. Although the local elders had tolerated such comments from Tupaia, they found them highly inappropriate when delivered by a callow youth who could barely speak their language; and Hitihiti was not popular among them.

The sailors went fishing and began to repair their battered vessel; and soon afterwards an elder named Te Wahanga and his family, who had met Cook during his previous visit, returned to the sound in a canoe loaded with greenstone chisels, adzes and women. There was an orgy on board the *Resolution*, and Hitihiti joined in with enthusiasm. Disgusted by the nightly revels taking place on his ship, Cook decided to leave the sound as soon as possible. When the local people heard that the ship was about to sail, however, a flotilla of canoes set out for Admiralty Bay where they raided their enemies for more cloaks, weapons and greenstone. On 22 November when Pickersgill and some other officers went ashore at Indian Cove, they found a group of women weeping and slashing themselves with obsidian in mourning for their menfolk who had died during this battle, while a group of warriors cut up the body of one of their enemies. The heart of this young man was impaled on a forked stick on the prow of their canoe, while his other body parts lay on the ground; and when one of the warriors jauntily speared the discarded lungs of this man and offered them to Lieutenant Pickersgill, he refused, but bartered for the head, carrying his trophy back to the *Resolution*. Shortly afterwards,

Charles Clerke, the ship's practical joker, staged a macabre barbecue on board, grilling a piece of the cheek from the severed head on a gridiron and offering the sizzling meat to a local warrior who ate it with relish. Cook and Hitihiti were away on a visit to Motuaro Island, looking at the gardens that the sailors had planted, and when they returned to the ship Cook asked Clerke to repeat the demonstration, no doubt because his earlier reports about Māori cannibalism had been greeted with scepticism back home in England. When Clerke obliged, Hitihiti stood transfixed with horror, weeping and vehemently declaring to Clerke and the warriors who savoured the meat that they were vile and no longer his friends; and when they laughed, he ran away. Like Tupaia, Hitihiti was horrified by the practice of *kai tangata* (literally, 'eating people'), although human sacrifice was commonly practised in the Society Islands. Shortly after this gruesome demonstration Cook decided to leave Queen Charlotte Sound. Instead of searching for the *Adventure*, however, on 25 November 1773 he headed south once more, looking for the Unknown Southern Continent.

On 12 December at 62 degrees south, Hitihiti saw his first iceberg. During his visit to New Zealand he had gathered a bundle of little sticks, one for each island they had visited since leaving Ra'iatea, no doubt intending to add their names to the lists of islands memorised by island navigators; and now he added another stick for this *fenua teatea* or 'bright land', which he described as 'white, evil, useless'.[18] As the *Resolution* headed further south and the sails froze solid and icicles hung in the rigging, Cook ordered a fire to be lit in the Great Cabin, where Hitihiti worked with the Forsters on their vocabularies and accounts of island customs or quietly unpicked the red feathers from the objects that he had bought in Tongatapu. The fresh food had run out and the sailors were now living on reduced rations – mouldy bread, hard dried meat, stinking water, and soup crawling with maggots. When they realised they would not be returning to England that year, a mood of sullen depression spread among the crew. There were fights; and when Cook punished a midshipman by giving him a flogging and sending him before the mast, the sailors began to mutter, because this was contrary to naval tradition.

After he crossed the Antarctic Circle for a second time, Cook's stomach pains returned. On 30 January 1774 at an unprecedented 71 degrees south, the *Resolution*'s path was blocked by a vast, glittering icefield, and Cook confessed in his journal: 'I whose ambition leads me not only farther than any other man has been before me, but as far as I think it possible for man to go, was not sorry at meeting with this interruption, as it in some measure relieved us from the dangers and hardships, inseparable from the navigation of the South Polar regions.'[19] As soon as the *Resolution* turned

north, Cook's illness got worse, and after taking a purge to relieve his
constipation he was stricken with violent vomiting – a classic symptom
of intestinal obstruction. When the ship's surgeon gave him a mixture
of castor oil, camomile tea and ipecacuanha to ease the nausea, he had
an attack of hiccups that lasted for twenty-four hours. It was not until
26 February that Cook could sit up in bed, and Johann Forster sacrificed
his favourite dog to make a meat broth to feed his captain. Although Cook
drank it down ravenously, he was still emaciated, and did not regain his
strength for the rest of the voyage. Scurvy was rife on board, and along
with the sailors, George Forster was also suffering from its symptoms –
swollen, bowed legs, rotting gums, excruciating pains, and livid, purple
blotches on his body. In order to obtain fresh supplies, Cook decided to
set a course for Easter Island, visited by the Dutch explorer Roggeveen in
1722 and by the Spanish ships sent by the Viceroy of Peru in 1770.

On 11 March 1774 when Easter Island loomed above the horizon, the
sailors (including Hitihiti) hung over the railings. After 103 days at sea,
they were yearning for greenery, fresh food and water, but as they approached the coastline they could see that this island was barren and parched,
with no spreading trees, waterfalls or fresh pools of water. Although the
ranks of tall, brooding stone statues along the coast were impressive,
few gardens or animals were visible. These people had only a few small
canoes made of short lengths of wood sewn together, and there were no
high timber trees on the island. As the *Resolution*'s anchors splashed into
Hangaroa Bay, a bold, energetic man named Maruahai with leg tattoos
and earlobes stretching almost to his shoulders came on board and talked
with Hitihiti, who was delighted to discover that their languages were
closely related. The next morning when Cook and his companions went
ashore, they found that the local people had only a few chickens and sugar
cane, bananas, sweet potatoes, yams and plantains to barter. They grew
their food plants in deep holes dug in the ground, mulched to preserve the
moisture, and lived in long, thatched houses with stone foundations and
roofs like the upturned hulls of large boats. The islanders were unarmed
and terrified of firearms, because during Roggeveen's 1722 visit the Dutch
sailors had shot many of their ancestors. Most of the islanders were thin
and tattooed, with elongated earlobes and faces painted with red-brown
ochre and daubed with white or yellow streaks; and many went almost
naked, as bark cloth was scarce on the island, although one man proudly
sported a jacket of blue woollen cloth while another had a red and white
chequered handkerchief acquired during the Spanish visit to the island
three years earlier.

Using Hitihiti as an interpreter, the islanders explained that the great carved stone statues with their red topknots (the sacred colour) commemorated former *ari'i* or high chiefs, reciting the names of the various ranks of images – Hangaroa, Hangatupou, Hangahivi and Hangamahanga, and so on – and the names of the individual statues, which Johann Forster carefully recorded. They treated these monuments with veneration, although many had been toppled from their stone platforms. One day while Hitihiti was ashore with William Hodges, who sat sketching one of these statues, a man snatched his black hat from the young *'arioi*'s head and ran off with it, leaving Hitihiti standing there speechless. Shortly afterwards another man seized Hodges's hat; no doubt because hats and headdresses were sacred in Polynesia, imbued with the *mana* of those who wore them. The islanders bartered their own feather headdresses, necklaces, ear ornaments and some fine wood carvings representing both men and women for coconut shells, cloth and nails; including one elegant carving in yellowish wood of a woman's hand with her fingers curved upwards as though she was dancing. Hitihiti bargained eagerly for the headdresses, especially those decorated with man-o'-war bird feathers, and some of the carvings; and later he gave the carved hand to Johann Forster, who upon his return to England presented it to the British Museum. A few of the local women acquired goods from the sailors by sleeping with them, several of them boarding the *Resolution* and sleeping with one man after another – as George Forster commented caustically, 'emulating the famous exploits of Messalina' (the sexually voracious wife of the Emperor Claudius).[20] In fact, however, they saw only thirty women among about seven hundred men during their visit to the island, so it is likely that most of the women had been hidden.

Although Cook was still very weak, he could not resist exploring this island with its enigmatic statues, and after one of these excursions he was once again stricken with acute stomach pains. Many of his men were still suffering from scurvy, however, and they had obtained little fresh meat, fruit, vegetables, wood and water. Cook decided to leave Easter Island and set a course for the Marquesas, which Mendaña had visited in 1595, and as they sailed away from Hangaroa, Hitihiti added a stick to his bundle, summing up his impressions of this island by remarking succinctly: '*Ta'ata maitai, fenua 'ino* (good people, bad land).'[21]

On 6 April 1774 they sailed past Fatu Hiva, Motane and Hiva Oa in the Marquesas, looking for a good harbour; and when Tahuata came into sight Cook headed for this green island, narrowly escaping shipwreck when a sudden squall drove the *Resolution* towards the rocks off Vaitahu Bay. About fifteen canoes came out, their crews offering *kava* plants as a sign of peace, although they had slings tied around their foreheads and piles of stones in their narrow canoes. These warriors were fine-looking men, tattooed from head to foot with bars, scrolls, chequers and spirals, and although Hitihiti called out to them, they would not come on board the *Resolution*. Early the next morning they brought out quantities of bread-fruit to barter; but when Captain Cook, the Forsters and Hitihiti stepped into the boat to go ashore, a warrior grabbed an iron stanchion to which the boarding ropes were tied, jumped overboard with it and swam to his canoe. A warning shot was fired overhead but he took no notice, even when a second shot was fired; and when one of the officers came up on deck and saw this, he aimed his musket, fired and shot the man through the head. He fell back dead in his canoe, and as it began to fill with blood one of his companions tried to bail it out, laughing hysterically; while another man sat there looking distraught. According to George Forster, Hitihiti 'burst into tears when he saw one man killing another on so trifling an occasion. Let his feelings put those civilized Europeans to the blush, who have humanity so often on their lips, and so seldom in their hearts!'[22]

Despite this violent beginning, Cook was determined to land at Tahuata to fetch fresh water and food for the sailors. Drums boomed in the hills as crowds of armed warriors gathered on the beach, and a canoe came out bringing a man who carried a pig over his shoulder. Cook presented this envoy with a hatchet, and when he, Hitihiti, the Forsters and Sparrman landed with a party of armed marines, they were confronted by about a hundred armed warriors, their leaders wearing woven coconut headbands decorated with round pieces of pearl shell with tortoiseshell filigree, and black cock plumes or man-o'-war bird feathers. Making friendly gestures, Hitihiti asked these men to sit down, explaining as well as he could that the man who had been shot was a thief, and that he and his companions only wanted to barter for fresh food, wood and water. Marquesan and Tahitian are closely related dialects, and these warriors seemed to understand him, leading the strangers to a stream where the sailors began to fill the water casks, guarded by a line of armed marines, while the officers exchanged breadfruit, bananas and plantain for small pieces of iron.

Early the next morning as canoes from the nearby islands gathered around the ships, Cook and Hitihiti went ashore where they were greeted by Honu, the local *hakaiki* or high chief,[23] accompanied by a very beauti-ful woman and her daughter, the only women present on this occasion. An intelligent and good-humoured man, Honu conversed readily with Hitihiti, telling him the names of the surrounding islands. Hitihiti was delighted with the Marquesans, bargaining for a drum and some orna-ments, and demonstrating the art of making fire by rubbing dry hibiscus sticks together, which astonished these people. The red feathers that he and his companions had acquired at Tongatapu were highly prized in these islands, and the Marquesans eagerly bartered their headdresses, breast-plates, earrings and other objects for these treasures. When the shore party returned to the ships for dinner, the waves were so high that the boat was almost swamped, and Hitihiti decided to swim out to the *Resolution* rather than run the risk of being capsized on the reef.

The following morning when Cook went ashore, he discovered that the midshipmen had been bartering red feathers and other goods without permission, spoiling the rates of exchange. Cook was still unwell; and he decided to return to Tahiti as soon as possible to fetch more fresh provisions. While he was bartering for a few last pigs, some men brought women down to the beach and offered them to the sailors. Cook hated this kind of sexual barter, and when he struck a sailor for 'neglect of duty' the islanders exclaimed in surprise, 'He beats his brother!' The Forsters were very impressed by the Marquesan chiefs, with their robust build, energetic manner and lack of ostentation, unlike the languid, obese *ari'i* whom they had met in the Society Islands; and George Forster compared them with Nireus, the most handsome of the Greek warriors at Troy.[24]

After leaving the Marquesas the *Resolution* sailed into the Tuamotu archipelago; and on 17 April sighted Takaroa, where Cook sent an armed boat ashore and Hitihiti eagerly bartered for long-haired white dogs, saying that their hair was highly valued for making breastplates in the Society Islands. When warriors began to gather on the beach, the young *'arioi* warned his companions that these men were about to attack; and the sailors quickly returned to the boats. As they rowed away from the island, the warriors hurled stones at the strangers and then sat down on the beach, talking at the tops of their voices.

As they sailed past three more small atolls in the Tuamotu, Hitihiti counted up his bundle of sticks, with one stick for each of the islands upon which they had landed during this remarkable journey – 'Eua and Tongatapu in the Tongan archipelago; Te Wai Pounamu, the South Island, and Fenuateatea, the name given by Hitihiti to the North Island of New Zealand; Teapai, as he called Easter Island (although this seems to have been the name of a district); Tahuata in the Marquesas and Takaroa in the Tuamotu. He must have later passed on this information to the *'arioi* navigators, because from 1775 onwards some of these names (which were not included in the lists dictated by Tupaia in 1769) appear in the island lists collected by the Spanish – Vaitahu (the bay where the *Resolution* anchored in Tahuata in the Marquesa Islands), which was said to be high, populous and productive and inhabited by people very like the

Tahitians; Pounamu, described as barren, with very high mountains, few fruits but many fish, and inhabited by cannibals (the South Island of New Zealand); and Fenuateatea, said to be large and fertile, inhabited by white people who dressed and spoke like Tahitians (the North Island of New Zealand).[25] The young *'arioi* had also acquired a store of fabulous gifts for his friends and relatives – red feathers from Tongatapu; carvings and man-o'-war bird feather hats from Easter Island; long-haired white dogs from Takaroa and the presents that his shipmates had given him; along with endless yarns about his extraordinary adventures and the amazing places that he had visited.

The Red Feathers of 'Oro

Since 1768, eight Society Islanders had sailed away on European ships; and of these explorers, Hitihiti was the first to return to the islands. When the *Resolution* anchored in Matavai Bay on 22 April 1774, two high-born young *'arioi* came on board and greeted Hitihiti with delight. They removed his European clothing, took off the fine bark-cloth garments they were wearing and wrapped them around him, adopting him as their *taio*. When Hitihiti showed them some of the objects that he had collected, especially the bright red feathers that he had acquired at Tongatapu, they were ecstatic; and when he gave them a few of these treasures, they were speechless with joy. As George Forster noted, Hitihiti was thrilled to leave the ship and go ashore: 'It is no wonder that a native of the Society Isles should prefer the happy life, the wholesome diet, and the simple dress of his countrymen, to the constant agitation, the nauseous food, and the coarse awkward garments of a set of seafaring Europeans.'[1] Canoes flocked out to the ship bringing live mullet in troughs fixed between the hulls of double canoes, and quantities of breadfruit and fruit; and although George Forster and Captain Cook were still suffering from the 'dry gripes', as they ate their fill of *vi* or Tahitian apples their symptoms began to ease. That evening several women came on board, and as George Forster remarked, 'the excesses of the night were incredible'.[2]

Eager to check the chronometers on board against the well-attested longitude of Matavai Bay, William Wales went ashore the next morning to set up the astronomical tent with its instruments. When they landed, Cook and the Forsters were greeted by Tu's father Hapai (a thin, grey-bearded man also known as Teu) and Tutaha's elderly mother; and a man escorted them to his house where he fed them a delicious baked pudding made of scraped coconut meat and taro and presented them with fine garments perfumed with scented oil. When the Tahitians saw the red feathers from Tongatapu, they were wild to procure them; quantities of pigs, chickens and other provisions began to arrive at the trading place, and women offered themselves to the sailors. After the poverty that they had witnessed during their previous visit, Matavai was now thriving and prosperous, with many new canoes and houses under construction, gardens everywhere, and plenty of pigs and chickens around the houses. Even the goats that Captain Furneaux had given Tu had had a pair of kids. It was the height of the Season of Plenty; the people were using the iron tools acquired during previous European visits to rebuild their houses and canoes, and there were no signs of food shortages. Cook's trade goods were almost exhausted, but as Hitihiti had promised, one tiny patch of red feathers (or 'ura) glued to bark cloth or wickerwork, or one man-o'-war bird plume, was enough to buy a large pig, such was the value of these sacred objects. That night as the sailors celebrated the festival of St George, the patron saint of England, groups of women danced on the main deck, the quarterdeck and the forecastle; and afterwards, 'the pleasures of Venus were joined to the usual orgies of the festival'.[3]

Two days later during a violent thunderstorm, the *Resolution* was struck by lightning. As a blue flame flashed along a copper chain running from the masthead into the sea, a violent clap of thunder shook the ship, reminding the islanders of the bond between the Europeans and 'Oro. When Tu came out to greet Captain Cook, he was amazed and delighted to see the store of red feathers that Cook had acquired in Tongatapu; and when Cook presented some to him, he was overjoyed. Pohuetea, the tall, imposing *ari'i* of Puna'aui'a, his new wife and his former wife Purutihara (a towering, powerful woman who had met Cook during the *Endeavour* voyage and called herself his 'sister') also came out to the ship, bringing three large pigs to barter for red feathers. After feasting on fresh pork, chicken, breadfruit, plantains, taro and *vi*, Cook, George Forster and the sailors began to recover from their illnesses; and Cook acquired a taste for the delicious baked puddings that he was offered.

Since the defeat of Tutaha and his allies by Vehiatua I and the deaths of Tutaha and Tepau in battle, the Tahiti-iti warriors had turned their attention to Mo'orea. As Gayangos had been told during his visit to the island, the young chief Vehiatua II had clashed with Mahine, the *ari'i rahi* of Mo'orea, over the succession to the paramount chieftainship of that island. Mo'orea lay off the west coast of Tahiti, and its chiefly family was closely intermarried with the Tahitian chiefly lineages. Although the paramount chief Mahine, a black leg 'arioi, was married to the sister of Amo, the *ari'i* of Papara, they had no living children; but his sister Vave'a was married to Teihotu, a younger brother of Tepau, and she wanted her son Mahau (also known as Metua'aro, or more formally as Teri'i-tapunui) to

Hitihiti

succeed her brother as the high chief of Mo'orea. This young man was very well connected, and his sister Pateamai had married Vehiatua II's younger brother. At first Vehiatua's youngest brother had been sent to Mo'orea to claim the succession; but when Mahine had the boy killed, war broke out with the people of southern Tahiti. Afterwards Mahine decided to adopt his wife's nephew as his son and heir, infuriating Vave'a and her daughters, who considered Mahau more worthy to succeed his uncle as the paramount chief of Mo'orea; and when they sent Mahau with his sister Itia to Mo'orea to claim the succession, Mahine forced them to fly to Pare, where they were now living under Tu's protection.

On 26 April when Cook, the Forsters and several officers went to Pare to pay Tu a formal visit, they found themselves in the midst of this controversy. A spectacular fleet was drawn up on the beach – 160 double canoes with high carved, red-painted sterns, decorated with striped and chequered banners (identifying the gods of each division), black feather bundles and feather streamers. The hulls of these canoes were loaded with stones, clubs and spears, and their fighting platforms each carried between eight and twenty warriors wearing layered garments in white, red and brown with ornate breastplates, while a few of these men were distinguished by towering wickerwork helmets (or *fau*) decorated with feathers. The largest of these canoes was 110 feet long and 14 feet wide and carried 50 paddlers; and the war fleet was attended by about 70 smaller craft, some with thatched shelters for the chiefs while others (which they called *marae*) were lined with palm leaves to carry corpses after the forthcoming battle. Fearing that this fleet had gathered to attack the *Resolution*, Cook was uneasy, although when he landed on the beach the warriors greeted him with competing shouts of '*Taio no Tu!*' ('Tu's friend') or '*Taio no To'ofa!*' ('The friend of To'ofa!'). As he stepped ashore, To'ofa, the 'Admiral' of the fleet and a leading chief of Pa'ea, greeted Cook with great courtesy, taking his right hand to lead him to his canoe; while Ti'i, one of Tu's uncles and counsellors, grabbed him by the left hand to take him to his *taio* Tu – 'so that between one party and the other I was like to have been torn to pieces'.[4] When the armed sailors landed on the beach, Captain Cook pulled himself free; and when he turned to Ti'i and asked about Tu, To'ofa, a very tall, vigorous and noble-looking old man, stalked off and vanished.

Pohuetea, the *ari'i* of Puna'aui'a, was also present on this occasion, and when Cook asked him why this fleet had gathered, he replied that Amo had allied himself with Vehiatua II and they were going to attack him, despite Tu's reservations; while others reported that they were going

'Arioi *war canoes*

to fight against Mahine. As Cook freely admitted, however, his grasp of Tahitian was still very imperfect, and these people were trying to explain a complicated situation. It seems that To'ofa, as 'Admiral' of the fleet and the Pa'ea war leader, disputed Mahine's right to anoint any successor as high chief of Mo'orea other than Mahau, Vave'a's son and a member of the *ari'i* lineage in his own district; while Vehiatua II was angry with Mahine for killing his youngest brother. Cook estimated that the Atehuru alliance (which included the districts of Fa'a'a, Puna'aui'a and Pa'ea) had mustered 8000 warriors for this naval review, their leaders distinguished by long round 'tails' of green and yellow feathers that hung down their backs; and given the number of districts on the island, he guessed that Tahiti must have a population of around 240,000 people.[5] After returning to the ship for dinner, Cook and the Forsters went to Pare where they found Tu, who was avoiding them because, during Cook's absence, some of his clothes had been stolen. When he realised that his *taio* did not intend to avenge the theft, however, Tu escorted Cook and his companions past groves of fruit trees, scented shrubs and clear pools to a cluster of fine houses where they chatted until sunset, the women joking and punning in high good humour.

The next morning To'ofa sent two large pigs out to the *Resolution*. When he joined Cook and Tu for dinner, the 'Admiral' inspected every part of the ship with meticulous attention, particularly the masts, ropes and tackle, and asked Cook to give him cables and anchors. This silvery-haired chief, with his rotund paunch and cheerful, open face, was sensible and intelligent; and Cook was annoyed with himself for having turned down his invitation to inspect the war fleet. Tu showed To'ofa how to use a knife and fork, and how to drink grog, calling this strange beverage *vai no Peretani* (water from Britain). During their conversation, when Cook jokingly offered to join in the attack on Mo'orea, Tu and To'ofa hesitated at first, then smiled and refused his assistance, saying that this would give too much *mana* to the Mo'orea people. The next day Vehiatua II sent a pig to Cook, asking for red feathers in return; and when Pohuetea visited Cook, he was so avid for red feathers that he offered his wife to him, and when Cook declined this honour, offered his towering war helmet instead,[6] demonstrating the extraordinary value placed upon these sacred items. During these visits the chiefs listened raptly to Hitihiti's stories about his adventures, although they scoffed at his tales about white rocks that turned into water, rain that turned into white stones, and days when the sun did not set, while his accounts of the cannibals in New Zealand filled them with horror. As William Wales remarked:

I have always thought the situation of a Traveller singularly hard: If he tells nothing which is uncommon, he must be a stupid fellow to have gone so far, and brought home so little; and if he does, why – it is a hum, – aye – a toss up of the Chin; and, – 'He's a Traveller!'[7]

When the chiefs asked Hitihiti for gifts – the Marquesan and Easter Island headdresses, the baskets, clubs, bark cloth, fine mats and red feathers from Tonga that he had acquired during his travels, all of which were highly prized in Tahiti – he dared not refuse them; but when he showed them the preserved head of the Māori boy collected in Queen Charlotte Sound, they gazed at it in dismay, naming it the 'man-eater', and remarked that, according to the oral histories, long ago there had also been cannibals in Tahiti.

On 29 April an islander who had stolen a water cask was sent ashore and tied to a post by the tents. Although Tu begged for his freedom, Cook had the man responsible flogged with two dozen lashes; and afterwards To'ofa made an eloquent speech castigating his people for the way that they treated the British:

> How can you act in so shamefull a Manner as to steal from your friends, who bring you every thing that is good & usefull? do not they bring you Axes, Knives, Nails, Red Feathers, Beads, &c and give them to you for Hogs, Breadfruit Cocoa-Nuts, &c. things that you can spare; and could they not, if they were not your friends, easily kill you, and take them for nothing? but they do not do so. – They are your friends! Why then do you rob them? If you will steal, Steal from the Tiarabo [Tai'arapu] men, and the Men of Eimeo [Mo'orea], who are your Enemies, & fight with you; but steal not from them![8]

When To'ofa had finished his speech, Cook ordered the great guns to be fired and the marines went through their drill, marching, wheeling and firing their muskets in volleys; and after this display To'ofa and his elderly wife accompanied the Forsters to Pare. When he talked with the Forsters, To'ofa was astonished to learn that Captain Cook was not the High Admiral of Britain, and that Banks was not King George's brother; and when he heard that there were no coconuts and breadfruit in England, he lost interest in that far country. The next morning when Cook went ashore at Matavai Bay, the crews of ten war canoes demonstrated their fighting tactics, paddling the canoes ashore and dragging them quickly up the beach where the warriors leaped out, fully armed, and engaged in a sham fight with some men who were hiding in the bushes. Several young men stood high on the curved sterns of the canoes holding white rods, acting as lookouts. During that day while the canoes lay on the beach, Hodges made sketches for his painting of the war fleet at Pare, while Johann Forster likened these great canoes to the ships of Greek antiquity, with their star navigators and warrior heroes.

The following day, Reti, Bougainville's *taio*, arrived at the *Resolution* to ask Cook and Johann Forster whether they would see his friend 'Poutaviri' (Bougainville) when they returned to Europe. When Johann Forster remarked that this was not impossible, the vigorous, grey-haired *ari'i* urged him eagerly, 'Tell him I am his friend, and long to see him again at O-Taheitee.'[9] According to Reti, when Tutaha had been killed during the battle with Vehiatua's army, he had been fighting at his side. Later that day Cook was told that Hitihiti had married the daughter of a Matavai chief and intended to stay in Tahiti. According to a midshipman who attended the ceremony, Hitihiti and his bride had been seated side by side, holding hands and surrounded by ten or twelve people, mainly women, who chanted while Hitihiti and his bride gave short responses. They were presented with food, some of which Hitihiti gave to his wife, and afterwards they bathed in the river. Soon afterwards Hitihiti came on board with his bride, a very short, plain young girl who asked his shipmates for presents. Hitihiti was very popular on board the *Resolution*, and while some of the sailors urged him to sail with them to England, George Forster tried to dissuade him, pointing out the dangers of the journey. Another young man, Nuna, was eager to sail as Johann Forster's servant, although when the elder Forster suggested this to Cook, the captain turned him down flat, to Forster's intense annoyance.

Perhaps because on this occasion the British had brought a treasure-trove of red feathers with them, the atmosphere was peaceful and relaxed; and as the Forsters and Sparrman roamed around the hills looking for new species of plants, they were welcomed everywhere and sometimes slept ashore. According to Johann Forster, most of the inhabitants of Tahiti lived in dwellings scattered along the lower reaches of the valleys or around the rim of flat land that surrounded the island, and the interior was wild and uninhabited, with only a few scattered dwellings. The houses had open sides and were beautifully sited, shaded by groves of trees, surrounded by scented shrubs and scattered among coconut and breadfruit trees, banana and plantain plantations. The taro gardens were irrigated by stone weirs in the rivers, while the *aute* or bark-cloth trees were grown in meticulously cultivated plots with manured soil sprinkled with shells. Johann Forster thought that Tahiti was far more productive than most parts of England or France, because with thirty-five breadfruit trees an acre, each acre could feed twelve people over eight months of the year; and he estimated that there were at least forty square miles of bread-fruit plantations on the island. With fermented breadfruit paste, yams, taro, plantains and bananas to feed them during the other four months of the year, he calculated that the island could support a population of at least 200,000 people (close to Cook's estimate); and it did not surprise him that despite the devastation caused during the recent wars, the islanders had quickly recovered their prosperity.[10] The islands around Tahiti also provided specialist products that they obtained on their canoe-borne expeditions – perfumed oil in bamboo containers from Borabora and Taha'a; hair from the white long-haired dogs of the Tuamotu Islands to decorate the warriors' breastplates; and bright red feathers from the parrakeets on the uninhabited island of Fenua'ura (Manua'e in the Scilly Islands), about ten days' sail west of Tahiti. While the 'arioi voyages were chiefly dedic-ated to the worship of 'Oro, they also fostered a desire to excel in dancing, sports and dramatic performances and a love of adventure, providing many opportunities for gift exchanges. The Europeans fitted neatly into this gift economy, with their own specialist goods (iron, red cloth, glass and now red feathers) and entertainments to offer.

Everyone was eager to obtain a supply of these treasures before the *Resolution* left the island; and on 7 May when Tu's father Hapai came out to the ship, knowing how highly the Europeans prized this regalia, he presented Captain Cook with a *parae* or Chief Mourner's costume. According to Hitihiti, when a man died, a woman donned this costume and acted as the Chief Mourner, terrorising the people with her shark's-teeth-edged weapon; and when a woman died, a man wore the costume and led the mourning rituals. This was a generous gift, and as George Forster remarked, Tu's family 'appeared to be very much beloved among the nation, who in general are extremely fond of their chiefs. In return, their behaviour to every body was so affable and kind, that it commanded a general goodwill.'[11] Teri'irere, the high-born son of Purea and Amo, also came out to the ship with his *taio* Tu and Tu's younger brother Ari'ipaea, who stayed on board for supper, regaling his hosts with a long history of the wars in Tahiti.

The end of the Season of Plenty was now approaching, and on 20 May when the Pleiades set below the horizon, the Season of Scarcity would begin. Once again, however, Captain Cook was leaving the island. While the *Resolution* was being prepared for sea the next day, an islander grab-bed a musket from a sentry who was asleep at his post and ran away with his prize. As soon as Tu heard about the theft, he fled with his younger brother, fearing that Cook would take them hostage. Ti'i, Tu's uncle

and counsellor, stayed with Cook, promising that the musket would be
returned; but when six large canoes loaded with baggage from the houses
sailed around Point Venus, Cook boarded the pinnace and intercepted
these vessels. Scenting danger, their crews assured him that Tu was at the
shore camp while they were on their way to the *Resolution*, and he let
them pass; but as soon as they reached the ship they paddled off at high
speed. Furious at being hoodwinked, Cook chased them in the pinnace,
his crew firing their muskets, and captured five of these canoes, bringing their passengers on board the *Resolution*. According to these people,
the *ari'i* Maraeta'ata, whom Cook had met during his previous visit to
Tahiti, had been responsible for the theft of the musket; although he and
his family had escaped by diving from their canoe and swimming ashore.
When Hitihiti and Ti'i came out to the ship, however, they assured Cook
that, on the contrary, Maraeta'ata had had nothing to do with the theft of
the musket, which had been stolen by one of Vehiatua's people. Taking
them at their word, Cook released the hostages, although at the same time
he threatened that unless the musket was returned he would burn every
boat on the island. Later that afternoon when some islanders arrived at the
shore camp with the musket, along with other items – a two-hour glass
and some cloth that had been stolen from a marine – they told Cook that
one of Maraeta'ata's men had indeed been responsible for the theft. As
he wrote dolefully in his journal that evening: 'In this particular I believe

War Canoe, Tahiti

both Tee [Ti'i] and Odiddy [Hitihiti] willfully deceived me.'[12]

No women slept on board the *Resolution* that night and no provisions arrived at the ship, and when Cook went to visit Tu at Pare the next morning he rebuked him for running away, assuring the young *ari'i maro 'ura* that, as his friend, he was angry only with Maraeta'ata and his people. Two days later, encouraged by news of this dispute with Tu's people, Purea and Amo separately visited the *Resolution*. Purea presented Cook with two pigs, receiving several red feathers in return, but Amo was almost ignored during his brief visit. That night, at Tu's request, Cook fired the ship's cannons, ordered the marines to perform their drill and mounted a display of fireworks that terrified and enchanted the Tahitians. As sky rockets, air balloons and serpents streaked across the sky a thunderstorm broke over Matavai Bay, with loud claps of thunder and flashes of lightning; and the islanders trembled, fearing that 'Oro was angry with the Europeans for usurping his powers.

On 14 May 1774 when To'ofa came out to the ship, bringing *taumi* or warriors' breastplates for Cook and the Forsters as farewell gifts, his legs were so swollen (with gout, according to Johann Forster, although probably he was afflicted with elephantiasis) that he could not climb up the side of the *Resolution*. A chair was slung for him and he was hoisted up on deck, where Cook gave him an English pennant and showed him how to fly it. When Hitihiti, who had accompanied the 'Admiral', told his friends that he had decided to stay in Tahiti, Johann Forster urged him to reconsider, saying that unless he returned to Ra'iatea, his family would think that the British had killed him. During this conversation Hitihiti proudly confessed that he had slept with Purea the previous night, which he regarded as 'a great honour and mark of eminence'.[13] Hapai and all of his family except Tu also came out to the ship, where they presented Johann Forster with two fine 'tails' of green and coloured feathers and a Chief Mourner's costume. When a fleet of forty canoes appeared around the point at Pare during these farewells, Cook and his officers went off in the boat to inspect them. These canoes, lashed together in divisions of three or four, belonged to the smallest district on the north-west coast of Tahiti. In each canoe a man stood in the stern, marking time with a green branch and indicating whether the right or left rank of paddlers should drive their paddles through the water. Watching their manoeuvres, Johann Forster compared these canoes with the triremes of Greece and Rome, which also had stages for their rowers. When these craft landed on the beach, their high, round sterns kept the decks dry, and the warriors jumped ashore in divisions and engaged in a sham fight, wielding clubs and ducking and jumping to avoid their opponents' weapons. When they fought with spears, the defenders put the points of their weapons on the ground and used them to parry the flying spears, which they did with great dexterity.

On the beach, Cook met Tu, standing beside his large new double canoe which was about to be launched. Tu had planned to name this canoe 'Tahiti' but Cook persuaded him to name it 'Peretani' (Britain) instead, presenting his *taio* with a grappling rope and an English Jack and receiving a pig and a large turtle in return. When Tu took his new canoe out to the *Resolution*, flying the English Jack, the sailors saluted him with a hearty three cheers. That day Tu dined on board for the last time and urged the Forsters to stay with him, saying that, if they agreed, he would make them *ari'i* in Matavai and Pare. When he talked with Cook, Tu confessed that despite their apparent amity, neither To'ofa nor Pohuetea were his friends. The great battle between their fleets and Mo'orea's would be fought at sea five days after the *Resolution*'s departure, when Vehiatua II's fleet would join them. Although To'ofa and his allies had been urging Tu to take part in this battle, he was reluctant to do so. Often described as timid and cowardly, both by some of his compatriots and by various European visitors, Tu did not like fighting; and on this occasion, even though the interests of his future wife Itia and her brother Mahau were at stake, he hesitated to attack Mahine. Cook and Tu were now on excellent terms, which Cook attributed to his policy of restraint in dealing with the islanders (although it also had a good deal to do with the red feathers that he had brought to the island):

> Three things made them our fast friends, Their own good Natured and benevolent disposition, gentle treatment on our part, and the dread of our fire Arms; by our ceaseing to observe the Second the first would have wore off, and the too frequent use of the latter would have excited a spirit of revenge and perhaps taught them that fire Arms were no such terrible things as they had imagined, they are very sencible of the superiority they have over us in numbers, and no one knows what an enraged multitude might do.[14]

After dinner when Tu left the ship, Cook saluted the *Peretani* with three guns; and during the salute an Irish gunner's mate slipped overboard and began to swim ashore. Like the Forsters, this man had been offered land, a house and a beautiful wife if he stayed on the island, but one of the officers spotted him and Cook sent a boat to pick him up, punishing the defector by putting him in irons for a fortnight. Hitihiti had finally decided to sail with them to Ra'iatea, and he came on board accompanied by four young men from Borabora (one of whom was Hitihiti's brother, and another his servant) and a beautiful young girl from Ra'iatea who was eager to visit her parents. When they farewelled their friends, an officer gave this girl some clothes to wear and she dined with them in their mess, breaking the prohibition on eating with men and 'laugh[ing] at the prejudices of her country-men with all the good sense of a citizen of the world'.[15] As the ship sailed away from Matavai Bay, heading for Huahine, the people in the canoes wept bitterly, as if they were parting with members of their own families.

On 15 May 1774 when the *Resolution* arrived at Fare Harbour, Cook's *taio* Ori (also known as Mato) came out with the medal and copper engraving that Cook had given him during his previous visits, along with a pig and some *'ava* roots to welcome his *taio*, but no rituals of welcome were performed on this occasion. Ori seemed unwell, with red, inflamed eyes and a parched, scaly skin, a sign that he was drinking too much *'ava*. During Cook's previous visit he had humiliated a senior *'arioi* named Tupai, and since his departure Tupai and his people had risen up and were in open rebellion. To make matters worse, the beginning of the Season of Scarcity was only a few days away, with the setting of the Pleiades on 20 May. That night as the islanders sat chatting in their houses, lit by glowing candlenuts stuck on sticks, Porea (the young Tahitian who had joined the ship during their previous visit to that island, but had vanished at Ra'iatea) came out to the *Resolution*, to tell Cook and the Forsters that he had not left the expedition of his own accord. Eight months earlier when the ship had been preparing to sail from Ra'iatea, and he went ashore to say goodbye to his young mistress, her father had attacked him, stripping him of his European clothes, beating him and tying him up until after the *Resolution* left the island; although eventually he had escaped to Huahine, where he had been kindly treated.

Tupai and his friends were still bitterly hostile to the British, and when the Forsters went ashore at Fare to collect specimens the next morning, their servant, who had lagged behind, was attacked and knocked over by five or six warriors. Although Johann Forster fired at these men, his musket flashed in the pan, but they still ran away. When Cook stormed ashore to complain of this outrage, Ori and his elders, assuring him that they had no control over these people, urged Cook to shoot them. That evening at an *'arioi* performance, the beautiful young girl from Ra'iatea who had accompanied the Europeans to Huahine was mercilessly satirised. The *'arioi* actors (including the 'Garrick' who had entertained them during their earlier visit to Ra'iatea) lampooned her liaisons with the Europeans, enacting the hostile reception that she would receive back home in Tahiti so vividly that she burst into tears and fled from the arena, comforted by her British friends while others in the audience wept in sympathy. That night, however, several local women who had promised to go out to the ship did not make their appearance. Tupai was a senior *'arioi*, and this skit was another way of seeking his revenge, humiliating all those who befriended the British.

The following day this girl was accosted in a house and stripped of her European clothing. She fled back to the *Resolution* and refused to go ashore for the rest of their visit. Soon afterwards when a man tried to steal the second lieutenant's powderhorn, the officer struck him so hard with his musket that he bent the barrel; although another man who snatched a small box holding red feathers from a sailor managed to escape with his prize. At about the same time, several of the petty officers (the surgeon's mate Anderson, Colnet and Vancouver) went off to shoot birds, and while they were recharging their muskets, another man stole a bag containing two hatchets and some nails. Johann Forster railed against Cook's leniency: 'None is punished for his Audaciousness & Robbing; & they grow bolder every day for this reason: in case one were shot dead, the rest would be so alarmed, that no thefts would more be committed, & it would cause more honesty among them & greater Security for Europeans.'[16] The next day a man confronted Charles Clerke, the ship's second lieutenant, holding up a stone and defying Clerke to shoot him, saying, 'This stone is for you!' Rumours ran around the crew that the islanders were about to attack the *Resolution*; and although Cook was sceptical, he ordered twenty stands of muskets to be kept ready in case of an ambush.

On 20 May (the day when the Matari'i or Pleiades sank below the horizon and the Season of Scarcity formally began) the first lieutenant Palliser Cooper, Clerke and Burr, one of the master's mates, went shooting ducks in a lagoon. Cooper hit two ducks with one shot, which splashed down into the lagoon; and when he ordered an islander to fetch them and the man refused 'to be [his] Water-Spaniel', Cooper punched him and shot at him with his musket, which flashed in the pan. While the gun was still misfiring, a group of warriors attacked Cooper and his companions, giving them a thrashing; and although Burr managed to shoot several of these people, he was also overpowered, stripped and beaten. A friendly chief who arrived on the scene drove off the assailants and sent his people to recover the items that had been taken. As soon as Cook heard about this affray he hurried ashore, took possession of a large house and held two chiefs as hostages. When the officers arrived, bruised and battered and their garments in tatters, Clerke (who was devoted to Cook) confessed that they were largely to blame for what had happened.

The next morning Hitihiti came out to the ship carrying twenty-two leaves from a tree, with a message from Ori imploring Cook to bring twenty-two armed men to arrest the assailants. When Cook went ashore with Hitihiti to discuss the matter with Ori, his *taio* told him that the men who had attacked the officers were his enemies who had rebelled against him. Cook decided to teach these people a lesson, and mustering an armed party of forty-eight men including eighteen marines, the Forsters and Sparrman, he went inland led by Ori, who marched ahead of them brandishing a long spear pointed with a barbed stingray tail. As they crossed a marsh and marched towards a deep ravine, the crowd around them grew bigger and Hitihiti became nervous, warning Cook that some of these people were rebels who planned to ambush them. Cook ordered his men to fire their guns by platoons, demonstrating that they could keep up a continuous fire; and when some islanders approached and presented him with plantain branches, two dogs and two pigs as a sign of submission, he decided to abandon this expedition and returned to his vessel. As Wales noted sardonically: 'At 4 p.m. the Armed Party returned; having, according to the strict, literal meaning of some Poet or other, who, I have utterly forgot: "March'd up the Hill, and then – March'd down again."'[17]

Exasperated with Huahine, 'this island of rogues' as Sparrman called it,[18] Cook decided to leave for Ra'iatea. Although they had obtained few pigs on this island, where red feathers were not highly valued (the Huahine people were followers of Tane, not 'Oro, and red feathers were not used in Tane's worship), the ship was loaded with breadfruit and coconuts. That afternoon when the Forsters noticed an unfamiliar type of canoe crewed by men with tattooed faces, they were told that these people had been blown to Huahine from Mataiva atoll in the Tuamotu archipelago. Although Hitihiti's brother and his two friends had decided to stay behind at Huahine, an emissary from Ori to Puni accompanied them when they sailed from Fare, heading for Ra'iatea.

On 24 May 1774 when the *Resolution* anchored at Ha'amanino Harbour, Tupaia's birthplace, Cook's *taio* Reo came out to the ship. (*See Plate 7.*) Delighted to see Hitihiti and Hurihuri (Ori's emissary) on board, Reo invited them and Cook ashore for a feast and a *heiva* the next morning. When they arrived at his house, they were greeted by five old women who wept bitterly, slashing their heads with shark's teeth. A fleet of *'arioi* canoes was drawn up on the beach, seventy of which had sailed from Huahine several days earlier to the east side of Ra'iatea (presumably on a visit to Taputapuatea for the rituals to mark the setting of the Pleiades), carrying about seven hundred people. Women were cooking 'large and luxurious dinners' while '*ava* was being prepared and consumed; and according to Hitihiti, who revered the '*arioi* society, many of its leading members were present on this occasion.

George Forster had a good deal to say about the '*arioi* during this visit to Ra'iatea, presumably on Hitihiti's authority, given he was a junior member of the society. He noted, for instance, that

> the arreoys enjoy several privileges, and are greatly respected throughout the Society Islands. They feast on the choicest vegetables, and on plenty of pork, dog's flesh, fish and poultry, which is liberally furnished by the lower class, and for their entertainment, make to one another presents of *ahous* [cloaks] & other things . . . They are amused with music and dances, which are said to be particularly lascivious at night, when no other spectators but themselves are admitted.[19]

According to Johann Forster, these private performances, which were part of the fertility rituals dedicated to 'Oro, were called *te 'ai moro iti*.[20] He added: 'They keep great meetings at certain Seasons, where they eat & drink the inebriating Pepper-Drink & lay with women & have Dances & Comedies exhibited to them. They are of both Sexes, but less Women than Men, & the latter are all warriors.'[21] Although some '*arioi* were married, others had temporary mistresses; and when they heard that the '*arioi* killed any children that were born to them, the Forsters tried to persuade Hitihiti to leave the society.

Because Ra'iatea was the headquarters for the worship of 'Oro, the ship's stock of red feathers had an extraordinarily high value, and many of the sailors found women to sleep with during this visit. On 27 May, Reo and Tapoa, a tall, handsome young '*arioi* from Borabora who was betrothed to Puni's twelve-year-old daughter, came out to the *Resolution*. Although Johann Forster, Sparrman, Rowe and Pickersgill had recently ransacked his village on Taha'a, Tapoa seemed ready to overlook the matter. His mistress Teina was pregnant, although when Johann Forster asked her about the child, she said that she would kill it as soon as it was born. When he protested, she assured him that while the god of England might be offended by this custom, her god approved of it; although if they promised to take her child to England and gave her a hatchet, a shirt and red feathers, she might decide to keep the baby. Teina laughed uproariously as she said this, and stopped teasing only when Hitihiti scolded her, assuring her that the British considered infanticide to be very wicked. That afternoon the chiefs took Cook and his companions to an '*arioi* performance which began with a dance by Poiatua, Reo's beautiful daughter, who moved gracefully, twisting her lips in wry grimaces (called *utu roa* or 'big lips') to tremendous applause. Her display was followed by a skit that must have been inspired by the conversation between Johann Forster and Teina. A large, brawny *'arioi* with a bushy black beard impersonated a woman in labour, sitting on the ground between the legs of another man who held him tightly to his chest. A large white cloth was spread over their legs, and as the bearded man groaned and wriggled, crying out '*Aue! Aue!*' ('Alas! Alas!'), there was a violent convulsion and a third clown emerged from under the bark cloth, trailing a long cord behind him. As the mother chased her 'baby', squeezing her 'breasts' and sometimes stroking them up his backside, and pressing his nose to flatten it (which was done to babies in the islands to improve their looks), the men in the audience laughed uproariously while the women looked on with demure smiles.

At breakfast the next morning when Poiatua and her companions came out to the *Resolution*, the young woman who had sailed with the British from Tahiti welcomed them warmly. Later that morning the Forsters were taken to a large stone temple sixty feet long, described as the *marae no Parua* (or Tupaia's *marae*, because Parua was Tupaia's birth name). Their hosts were adamant that Tupaia was an *ari'i* or high chief, although during their previous stay at Ra'iatea his Borabora enemies had as insistently denied this. No doubt they denied the high priest's aristocratic status because they had conquered his people. When Reo joined Cook for dinner that day, he drank about twelve glasses of wine and a stiff tumbler of grog without becoming intoxicated; afterwards escorting Cook, Wales and their companions to a *heiva* where his daughter Poiatua danced again, followed by a skit featuring five *'arioi* actors who held up pieces of bark cloth, threw these down or hid them under a mat, chanting and dancing with ludicrous gestures. This skit ended with a sham fight, the winner of which was crowned with green boughs while the others danced around him. The next day at another *heiva* two little girls danced, followed by Poiatua who on this occasion danced in a costume decorated with European beads, and was presented with many gifts at the end of her performance.

During this visit, as they watched the *'arioi* eating lavish meals, perfuming their hair, singing, dancing, drumming or playing the flute in their long houses at night, lit by candlenut tapers, the British marvelled at the ease of their lives. The *'arioi* were meticulously groomed, bathing twice a day in a beautiful pool that had been enlarged and lined with rocks, anointed themselves with *mono'i* (perfumed oil), and frequently changed their bark-cloth costumes.[22] While most of the sailors envied the *'arioi*, Johann Forster saw in this society the seeds of corruption, comparing their existence with the opulent debauchery of the aristocracy back in Europe.[23] Like European grandees, he said, they seduced young women, although he qualified this by saying that only some girls slept with the *arioi* warriors during their festivals, 'officiat[ing] on these occasions like the priestesses and nymphs of the Paphian and Amathusian Goddess'.[24] Only Hitihiti seemed unhappy, because his relatives were plaguing him for gifts but otherwise ignored him, and now he had only a few red feathers left which he intended as a gift for Puni. He would gladly have sailed with them to England, but when Cook told him that this was impossible because he would not visit the Society Islands again, he decided that after the *Resolution* had sailed he would return to Tahiti. During that day the iron rudders and tillers from the pinnace and the cutter were stolen, along with the boat's grapnels, although when Cook informed Reo of the thefts, the rudders and the grapnels (but not the tillers) were quickly returned, along with a huge offering of breadfruit.

On 30 May Hitihiti invited Cook, the Forsters, Reo and his family, and some leading *arioi* to a feast at his family estate on the northern end of Ra'iatea. This estate was now in the possession of his brother, who presented their guests with some small hogs and *'ava*, and baked a large hog in an earth oven. Cook had brought several bottles of brandy, and after mixing the brandy with water, he offered the grog to the *arioi* who drank freely and soon went to sleep. Hitihiti drank so much *'ava* and grog that he had to be carried back to the ship, dead drunk. Two days later a rumour ran around the island that two ships had arrived in Huahine, bringing Mr Banks and Captain Furneaux back to the islands. They described the ships, Banks and Furneaux in such detail that at first Cook was convinced that the stories were true, until a *taio* of Johann Forster's assured him it was a hoax. Cook was now planning to leave Ra'iatea, and that night he invited the chiefs to a fireworks display, although many of the fireworks fizzled, disappointing the spectators.

Early the next morning the Forsters went to visit a *ta'ata-'orero* (or learned man) called Tutavai, who told them about the gods of the Society Islands. According to this expert, 'Oro was chiefly worshipped at Tahiti, Mo'orea, Ra'iatea and Taha'a; Tane at Huahine; the god Tu at Maurua; and the creator god Ta'aroa at Tapuaemanu (or Mai'ao); while the god Maui was responsible for earthquakes. When a priest looked up to the sky, the *atua* or god, who was invisible to others, came down to talk with him. Although the major gods were honoured with offerings of pigs, chickens and other food, the lesser gods were only saluted with a hissing sound. After death, the spirit of a person often lodged in a *ti'i* or wooden image which was placed near their *marae*; other spirits inhabited an island named

Manu'a, in the shape of strong tall men with fiery eyes who ate unwary travellers. Priests inherited their roles, serving the gods all of their lives; and the high priest of an island was always an *ari'i*. Alongside the priests there were also teachers who instructed their students about geography, astronomy and other matters; and to end his lesson, this learned man dictated to the Forsters the names of the compass points, and the names of the lunar months in the Society Islands calendar.

After dawn on 4 June 1774, Reo with his family, 'U'uru the *ari'i* of 'Opoa and his family, and Tapoa the *ari'i* of Taha'a came out to the *Resolution* to farewell Cook and his companions. They wept bitterly, urging them to return again to the island, and Reo asked Cook the name of his marae. When Cook replied 'Stepney', the name of his parish in London, they all repeated loudly, '*Tepene marae no Tute!*' ('Stepney, Cook's *marae!*') Soon afterwards Hitihiti came on board, where he asked Captain Cook to *tatau* (tattoo) some writing for him to show other Europeans who might land on the island; and Cook wrote him a 'Certificate of Good Behaviour'. It was King George's birthday, and as a special mark of his favour Cook let Hitihiti fire a cannon as part of the ship's salute to the monarch. When Hitihiti farewelled his British friends, he was heartbroken. According to George Forster,

> poor [Hitihiti]'s heart seemed torn to pieces by the violence of his grief. He ran from cabin to cabin, and embraced every one of us, without being able to speak a single word. His tears, his sighs, his looks were eloquent beyond description. At last the ship set sail; he got into his canoe, and continued standing upright, whilst all his countrymen were seated. He looked at us, then hung down his head, and hid it in his garments.[25]

As they sailed away from Ra'iatea, they could see Hitihiti standing in his canoe, still waving to his friends on board the *Resolution*.

Three Tahitians in Lima

In June 1773, while Captain Cook was still sailing among the icebergs, Pautu, Heiao and Tetuanui arrived in El Callao in Peru on board the *Águila*. This was not the first time that Polynesian explorers had reached South America. According to archaeological evidence, the South American sweet potato and bottle gourd had arrived in Polynesia between AD 1000 and 1100,[1] and chicken bones with DNA descended from Polynesian ancestors were recently found in a site in Chile and dated to AD 1400 – suggesting that, by then, Polynesian navigators had reached the coast of South America.[2] The numbers of these first explorers were not great, however, and their voyages left few visible traces. A little over a hundred years later, when the Spanish arrived in Peru in AD 1531, they conquered the Incas and the Empire of the Sun and changed its inhabitants' lives forever. These three Tahitians were the guests of the Viceroy of Peru; and as they travelled on the dusty road six miles along the coast to Lima, they crossed a colonial landscape of farmhouses, vineyards, fields of sugar cane, groves of banana palms and citrus orchards.

The city of Lima was set upon a hill, its adobe houses painted in warm, light colours, their ironwork balconies bright with flowers. From a distance, the city was dominated by the steeples and domes of its churches; the black, rocky heights of the Cordillera of the Andes looming above the spires. The Viceroy's palace was impressive, with a series of stately reception rooms where Amat held audience with his subjects. In one salon, decorated with portraits of former viceroys, Amat met the Indians and *mestizo*s (half-breeds); in a second, he met the *chapetón* (Spaniards from Spain) and *creole*s (Spaniards born in South America); and in a third, where portraits of the King and Queen of Spain were hung, he met women who wanted to speak with him in private. The rooms were lit with candelabra and furnished with carved Spanish chests, tables and chairs. Don Manuel de Amat y Junient Plannella Aumerich y Santa Pau, second son of the first marquis of Castellbell, represented the Spanish King in Peru, and he lived in regal style.[3]

Eighteenth-century Lima was a lively city with a diverse population. The *chapetón*, or Spaniards from Spain, dominated high society and held the most prestigious positions; followed by the *creoles*, Spaniards born in Peru and descended from the *conquistadores*. There were also blacks living in Lima, often freed slaves, because slavery was gradually being abandoned during this period; along with Indians from many different groups who had escaped from the pueblos to the city. The kings of Spain had instructed successive viceroys to ensure that the Indians did not 'suffer any damage to their persons or their property; on the contrary they shall see to it that these peoples are treated with justice and kindness';[4] but according to Amat, corruption was rife and the Indians were forced to work in the gold, silver and mercury mines under inhumane conditions. Factory owners, cane and cotton growers, landowners, and even the priests and magistrates who were supposed to protect the Indians exploited them mercilessly instead, getting them into debt and treating them as slaves. Amat told the King that unless these abuses were curbed, 'it will not be long before the realm comes to total desolation, the Indians will be gone, the villages extinguished as the people seek refuge and asylum in the cities'.[5] In earlier times the Inquisition had conducted tribunals to try to wipe out traditional beliefs in Indian parishes, using torture and humiliations that provoked bitter resentment, although by this time it was relatively inactive. Uprisings among the Indians were still harshly suppressed, however – for instance in 1743 when Atahualpa II ('the last Inca') and his followers were captured, hung, drawn and quartered; and after rebellions in the provinces in 1771 and 1773. Although Amat was sympathetic towards the Indians, he considered that 'too much indulgence was harmful to the state' and that exemplary punishment was essential on such occasions.

Despite the sufferings of the Indians and the blacks, public life in Lima was gay and brilliant. At births and marriages, and when viceroys were installed, there were festive celebrations, and during the Carnival in February, people soaked each other with water, drank *chicha* (maize beer), and became drunk and amorous. Rough humour and sexual licence were commonplace on such occasions. During religious processions, bells were rung and fireworks were lit, while people dressed as devils with tattooed faces and bodies painted red and blue banged stones together and blacks carried cardboard effigies of giants. There were also masked balls; and in the theatres, comedies, burlesques, vaudeville and sketches were performed and blindfolded acrobats danced on tightropes. There was a university in Lima, and some of the aristocrats had vast libraries and studied Voltaire, Diderot and Rousseau, books banned by the Inquisition. As for the women, according to Max Radiguet: 'The woman of Lima has at one and the same time something of the wasp and the humming bird. She has, like the former, a fine corsage and a sting, which is the epigram; she has the dazzling colour and capricious, uneven flight of the latter, and from both an immoderate love of flowers and perfumes.'⁶ These women loved gossip, and were fond of satire and banter. Music was popular in Lima, and people played the harp and the guitar, and sang with pleasure. They were also passionately fond of cockfighting and bullfighting, and during his term as Viceroy, Manuel de Amat built a new bullfighting ring and a cockfighting arena in the city.

Love-making and affairs were also popular pastimes. According to Frezier:

> Even if the Spaniards [in Peru] are sober when it comes to wine, they show little restraint as regards continence in the matter of love, they yield to no nation, they freely sacrifice their property to this passion. They rarely marry within the Church, but are all engaged in open concubinage, which has nothing scandalous about it, in their eyes; far from it, it is a disgrace not to be attached to a mistress, whom they keep on condition that she is for them alone.⁷

The Viceroy was a case in point, because soon after his arrival in Peru, the sixty-year-old Amat had become infatuated with Micaela de Villegas, a charming, buxom teenager feted for her talents as an actress and singer. Micaela's mother traced her descent from a line of viceroys, but when she fell in love and married a poet who was rumoured to have Indian blood, she was disowned by her family. After Micaela's father died, the family had been left impoverished and the young girl went onto the stage, having several liaisons with older men before she met the Viceroy.⁸

La Perricholi, as she would become known, was a fiery, flamboyant young woman. She loved the limelight, and had a hot temper. She is said to have quarrelled furiously with the Viceroy when, by royal fiat, he expelled the Jesuits from Peru and confiscated their property. When they were reconciled, Amat built her a house with ponds, lakes, a formal garden and a small theatre in the French style, decorated with gold and roses. In 1771 she became pregnant and bore Amat a son, 'Manuelito', whom he adored; and when Pautu, Heiao and Tetuanui were installed in the Viceroy's palace, they must have met Micaela and her little boy. The Tahitians had learned some Spanish on board the *Águila*, while Máximo Rodríguez, the young marine who sailed with them, was studying their language. He lived with them in the Viceroy's palace, working on a Tahitian vocabulary, learning Tahitian and teaching them Spanish. Amat took a personal interest in the islanders, inquiring into their way of life, providing them with elegant clothing, and ensuring that they enjoyed their time in Lima. Cockfighting, for instance, was also a Tahitian passion, and Pautu and his companions would have been taken to the cockfighting arena that Amat had built; and the theatre where Micaela sang and acted.

In August 1773, however, after only two months in Lima, Heiao contracted smallpox. On his deathbed, he was baptised 'Francisco José Amat', taking the Viceroy's surname. As Amat remarked, his death 'upset me since my intention and desire was always to return them so that their Indian compatriots could hear of the kindness with which they had been treated and the advantages they experienced in this country'.[9] During October of that year, after receiving religious instruction, Pautu and Tetuanui were baptised in Lima Cathedral, with the rector of the parish and the lieutenant colonel of the fort at Callao (the Viceroy's nephew) standing as their sponsors – Pautu taking the name 'Tomás' while Tetuanui was baptised 'Manuel' after the Viceroy.[10] The following month there was an uproar in the palace when Amat broke off his relationship with Micaela. She had quarrelled with the director of her play on stage, striking him across the face with a riding whip. According to contemporary accounts, when the crowd screamed out for her to be jailed, Amat ordered her to apologise for her behaviour; and when she refused, he threw her out and banned her from the stage for a two-year period.

After the *Águila*'s arrival from Tahiti, Amat had sent a report of the voyage to the Navy Department in Spain, and the royal officials decided that a Catholic mission should be established on the island. The Tahitians who had sailed on the *Águila* to Lima were to be sent home, accompanied by a party of armed men and several missionaries, to introduce 'the true religion' to the islanders.[11] In late 1773 when Amat received these orders, he began to organise a second expedition to Tahiti, recruiting two more Franciscan friars from the mission college at Ocopa – Father Gerónimo Clota, a Catalan, and Father Narciso Gónzales, a native of Extremadura in Spain. A portable house was ordered to shelter them during their time on the island, along with cassocks, vestments (including a crimson set, the sacred colour in Tahiti) and other ecclesiastical items – a portable oratory with a picture of Our Lady of Monserrate, a crucifix, a missal, candlesticks, a chalice, wafers, a bell, an altar cloth in crimson and yellow (the colours of 'Oro), and rosaries, medallions and crosses to distribute to the islanders. Máximo Rodríguez, the young marine who was becoming quite fluent in Tahitian, was appointed as the expedition's interpreter, and a schedule of 100 questions was drafted for him to answer during his stay in Tahiti, including items such as the following:

7. Is it true that when they conquer any district they set up a statue or Eti [*ti'i*] in sign of possession?

. . .

10. Make sure as to the truth or otherwise of the alleged apparition of the Devil in the form of a shark in the sea; and whether he helps them, as is said, to regain the shore when their canoes founder.

. . .

19. Which are the islands holding most commerce with that of Amat?

. . .

43. Do they adopt evil courses at a very early age?

. . .

51. Are there any giants or pigmies, and how tall are they?

. . .

78. Learn how many Islanders the English killed, and whether they bore the latter any ill-will for it, and the same as regards the French.

. . .

93. Are they much given to the vice of women?

. . .

100. Might it be easy to concentrate them in a town?[12]

These questions, which evince a degree of familiarity with life on the island, were probably drafted by Amat himself with Rodríguez's help, after talking with the Tahitians. Such 'interrogatories' or long questionnaires were also used by the Inquisition, however, and it is possible that this list was compiled by one of the Viceroy's clerical advisors.

Once again, Don Domingo Boenechea was appointed to command the *Águila*, with Don Tomás Gayangos as his senior lieutenant and Juan de Hervé as his pilot; in addition, Juan Pantoja y Arriaga (a young man in his early twenties) was appointed as the second pilot on this voyage. In order to establish the mission, it was decided that on this occasion the *Águila* would be accompanied by a storeship, the *Júpiter*, commanded by Don José de Andía y Varela, a Chilean. As their departure approached, the *Júpiter* was loaded with clerical equipment, the portable house, trade goods, medicines, bandages, tools, candles, cooking utensils, oil, honey, brandy and wine; six months' provisions for the sailors; and rice, biscuit and other dried goods for four men during a one-year stay on the island. Cattle and other livestock were also brought on board, although it was clearly expected that the Tahitians would largely feed the friars.

Finally, Pautu and Tetuanui were sent on board; and on 20 September 1774 the *Águila* and the *Júpiter* sailed in company from El Callao in a fresh breeze, heading for Tahiti.[13] Four days later Tetuanui ('Manuel') fell ill with smallpox, a tumour erupting on his left shoulder that had to be cut open. The storeship was slow and ponderous, and on 5 October when the two ships lost sight of each other during a storm, the *Águila* left the *Júpiter* behind. Two days later a *mestizo* cabin boy was flogged on board the frigate with 100 strokes and forced to wear a double iron collar for soliciting a pageboy to commit sodomy. On 29 October they sighted Tatakoto atoll, one of the islands in the Tuamotu and a new discovery for the Europeans, where seven or eight corpulent warriors armed with spears walked along the beach, following the ship's passage. Over the next few days they sighted other islands in rapid succession – Tauere, Tekokoto, Hikueru and Haraiki.

On 6 November when the *Águila* approached Ana'a, a large fire flared up on shore. Boenechea ordered the sails to be struck and Gayangos, Pautu, the second pilot, a sergeant and four soldiers were sent ashore in an armed boat. As the boat rowed towards the north-west end of the island, 150 chanting warriors stood on the beach, armed with clubs, spears and slingshots. They beckoned to the strangers, but the surf was too high for a landing, so Gayangos ordered Pautu to swim ashore to talk with them. When Pautu hesitated, saying that he was too afraid, two of the sailors swam the mooring rope to the rocks, and he followed them by diving into the ocean. At that instant, however, several warriors hauled on the mooring rope while others attacked with a barrage of stones flung by slingshots, and the soldiers fired their muskets in the air to frighten them. Pautu and the sailors scrambled back on board; and as they rowed along the coast, they saw a wooden cross leaning on a beach which seemed to be very old. Although Quirós had erected a wooden cross when he visited Ana'a in 1606, it is unlikely that this was the original cross, and it may have been a replica made by the local inhabitants. Giving a sailor two knives, Gayangos instructed him to place the knives on the beach as a peace offering; but as soon as this man reached the shore, several warriors jumped out of the bushes and he beat a hasty retreat to the boat. When the warriors saw the knives lying on the beach, however, they exclaimed in delight, making signs of peace; and they were given more knives and biscuits in exchange for coconuts, a pearl-shell necklace, a bow and a woven loincloth. Several of these men now jumped into the water and waded out to the boat to talk to Pautu, recognising him as a Tahitian by his tattoos, although they could barely understand each other.

Boenechea, who had agreed to meet the *Júpiter* off Ana'a, tacked the *Águila* around the island for several days, waiting for the storeship. On 9 November, however, after a violent thunderstorm, Boenechea decided to leave his station and head for Tahiti. Sailing past Tahanea, another new discovery, and Motutu'a, on 13 November they sighted Me'eti'a, an island that as Pautu told them was ruled by a chief subordinate to Vehiatua, the *ari'i* of southern Tahiti. As the ship approached Me'eti'a, two canoes came out, their crews greeting the Spaniards as *taio* or bond friends. As soon as they recognised Pautu some of these men boarded the *Águila*, including one old man who greeted him with joy, pressing noses with him. When they asked Pautu about the other Tahitians who had accompanied him to Lima, they were shocked to hear that Tipitipia and Heiao had died in that far country. As for the young boy Tetuanui ('Manuel'), he was still lying ill below decks, and they sent him a gift of a fresh fish.

Later that afternoon when the chief of Me'eti'a came out in a small outrigger canoe bringing a load of grass for the livestock, he and his people were given blue beads, knives, fish-hooks and coins from the Royal Treasury. When Boenechea showed him the head of King Carlos on one of these coins, saying that this was his *ari'i*, a great leader who ruled many lands, this man laughed heartily; and he asked the commander how long it would take to reach the King's country. Shortly afterwards, more canoes arrived alongside bringing a group of Tahitians who were living on Me'eti'a, including a man named Hipatea who brought out a small pig for Pautu; and the brother of Manuel's mother who brought two piglets for the boy and two small cloaks. About five or six of these Tahitians were eager to return home, and at Pautu's urging, Boenechea agreed to give them a passage back to their homeland.

On 14 November 1774 the skyline of southern Tahiti came into sight. Early the next morning Boenechea addressed the crew, ordering them to deal fairly with the local inhabitants and forbidding them to have any relations with Tahitian women. He warned that any violation would be punished by a flogging over the cannon; and had his orders nailed to the masthead. At about 8 a.m. when sails were sighted off the coast, they thought that this might be a British ship. As the strange vessel approached, however, the *Águila* lowered a Maltese pennant with a blue flag and fired a cannon, the signal of recognition, and as the ship responded in kind they realised that this was the *Júpiter*, which had arrived off southern Tahiti eight days earlier.

During Captain Cook's brief visit to southern Tahiti six months earlier, Vehiatua II and his people had remained loyal to the Spanish, refusing to establish *taio* relationships with the British. On 6 November 1774 when the *Júpiter* arrived off the coast, the black leg *'arioi* Ti'itorea and another chief named Utai, who recognised the Spanish flag, joyously welcomed Andía y Varela and his men, inviting the ship's commander, his quartermaster and armed sailors to accompany them to Tautira. Despite the illnesses that had followed the Spaniards' last visit, the leaders of Tahiti-iti acknowledged their *mana*. Utai was terrified of muskets, though, and when a spark flew from a sailor's flint and steel, he tried to throw himself into the ocean. Upon their arrival at Tautira, where a thousand people waited on the beach, the storeship's crew had been given drinking coconuts and plantains, while Andía and the quartermaster were presented with bark-cloth garments. They returned to the storeship, delighted with their reception; and since that time the *Júpiter* had been cruising off the coast, waiting for the *Águila*.

As the two ships sailed in company towards the southern coast of Tahiti, Boenechea despatched the launch with an armed party commanded by Don Raymundo Bonacorsi (a sub-lieutenant who had sailed on the 1772 voyage to Tahiti), with orders to explore the coast from Papara to Hitia'a, and locate the best harbour for the ships to anchor. Accompanied by Pautu, Máximo Rodríguez and Don Diego Machao, a sub-lieutenant of marines, Bonacorsi took the launch along the east coast towards the district of Tai'arapu, entering Vaiuru'a Bay through a pass in the reef where innumerable canoes flocked around them. Once again, the Spaniards had arrived at the beginning of the Season of Plenty, a favourable time to visit the island; and this time they had brought back a Tahitian who could tell his fellow islanders about his adventures in the strangers' homeland. One of Pautu's brothers-in-law, a man named Temaeva, stood up in his canoe and stepped into the boat to greet Pautu as they came through the pass, kissing him on the cheeks and temples; followed by Pautu's uncle, who came out in his canoe, weeping and inviting them ashore. When they landed in front of his house, Pautu's relatives crowded around them, wailing when they heard that Tipitipia and Heiao had died in Peru, kissing Pautu and hugging his legs, staring at his Spanish costume and listening raptly to tales of his amazing experiences. Inside the house, Pautu's mother and two sisters sat crying, although they paused to embrace Bonacorsi and Máximo, thanking them for their kindness to Pautu and presenting them with fruit and fish. Afterwards, Bonacorsi and Máximo walked through pouring rain to the house of Tipitipia's father, where a group of old men had assembled. Tipitipia's father had already heard about his son's death in Lima, and he wept as he greeted Bonacorsi and his companions. Soon Máximo was seated among the old men, talking to them, who seemed delighted when he told them that he intended to remain with them on the island.

Soon afterwards, when Manuel's parents arrived at the house, weeping and asking after their son, Máximo reassured them, saying that Manuel was still on board the ship because he had a sore on one shoulder, but that they would see him very soon. Bonacorsi decided to carry on to Vaitepiha Bay, and as they rowed towards this spectacular harbour Pautu told the Spaniards that Tu, the ari'i of Pare-'Arue, who was now recognised as the ari'i maro 'ura or paramount chief of Tahiti, was currently visiting Tautira. During the peace-making rituals that ended the recent wars between the people of Pare-'Arue and southern Tahiti, Tu and Vehiatua II had become taio or bond friends; and ceremonies hosted by Ti'itorea, Vehiatua's step-father and regent were being held to ratify their friendship. Off Tatatua Point, Ti'itorea and his wife Purahi came out in a double-hulled canoe to greet them, informing the Spaniards that English ships commanded by one 'Tute' (Captain Cook) had recently visited this harbour (referring to Cook's August 1773 visit with the *Resolution* and *Adventure*).

Another canoe soon came racing out towards the launch, bringing Vehiatua II, a light-skinned, corpulent young man about twenty-two years old, with lank, sandy brown hair. Pautu greeted his ari'i with rever-ence, taking off his hat and trying to remove his Spanish clothing so that he could give it to him. Although Máximo managed to stop Pautu from taking off most of his clothing, he insisted upon giving his belt and a netted sash to Vehiatua, while all the other islanders lowered their gar-ments to their waists in a gesture of homage to the high chief. According to Máximo, Vehiatua seemed less healthy than he had been during their 1772 visit. His skin had become scaly (a symptom of drinking too much 'ava) and he seemed dull and befuddled. Shortly afterwards another canoe arrived bringing the paramount chief Tu with his parents, sisters, and his younger half-brother Hinoiatua, a tall, good-looking young man who was now the chief of Ti'arei on the north-east coast of Tahiti-iti. This was Tu's younger brother, also known as Ari'ipaea (or more formally as Teari'i-fa'atau), who was sixteen at this time; and to avoid confusion, he will be referred to as 'Ari'ipaea' from this time forward.[14]

Unlike Vehiatua, it seems that Tu had no compunction about forging taio relationships with his friends' enemies; and as Máximo took the lead in many of these encounters, it seems that Tu mistook his status. Although he had recently adopted Captain Cook as his *taio*, the paramount chief greeted the young marine warmly and exchanged names with him. Tu confirmed the stories about Cook's two recent visits, identifying the British flag and showing them a plaited bag decorated with black and white beads which he said came from these ships, which were commanded by 'Tute' (Cook) and 'Pono' (Furneaux). During this conversation the launch rowed to Farea'ari in the district of Pueu, where the sailors sounded the bay; and when Bonacorsi went ashore with the two *ari'i* to fetch water, wood and fire, the islanders crowded around so closely that Vehiatua had to order the heralds to hit them with their batons to keep them back. Later that afternoon, Tu and Vehiatua came out again to the launch with gifts of fish, bananas, coconuts and a sucking pig and were given fish-hooks and knives in return, and stayed there chatting with Pautu and Máximo until nightfall.

At dawn on 16 November, Tu and Vehiatua escorted the launch to Anuhi in the Pueu district, where Pahairiro was the *ari'i*. As they rowed along, Tu asked Máximo to open his shirt, curiously examining the rosary that he was wearing around his neck and asking him about the cross. Máximo told him that this image kept away the *tupapa'u* or spirits of the dead (meaning the 'Devil'), while Pautu tried to explain the ritual of baptism; and when Tu asked whether he might also be baptised and have a cross like the one that Máximo was wearing, the young marine assured him that, in time, he would receive religious instruction from the friars. Upon their arrival at Anuhi (which they named 'Puerto la Virgén') they were greeted by another tumultuous crowd led by Pahairiro, Vehiatua's father's brother, a strong, corpulent, grey-haired man about seventy years old whom Gayangos had met during his 1772 visit. The old chief greeted Bonacorsi and Máximo with obvious pleasure, presenting them with bark cloth, and he seemed overjoyed to see Pautu alive and well. Bonacorsi gave Pahairiro an axe and two small knives, and in return the old chief gave him a pig; but because there was no room in the boat, the sub-lieutenant could not accept this offering.

As the launch sailed up the east coast to Hitia'a, the district governed by Reti, Bougainville's *taio* (who had farewelled Captain Cook just six months earlier), Tu and Vehiatua explained that they had recently quarrelled with Reti. They said nothing, however, about the naval attack on Mo'orea that had been imminent when Cook left the island, although they had both been intimately involved in that expedition. According to the missionary Richard Thomson's account, after Cook's departure Tu's and Vehiatua's fleets had sailed to attack Mahine in support of Mahau's claim to rule Mo'orea; but once again, seeing the strength of their combined

forces, Mahine had decided not to fight. Instead he sent his herald to pro-
pose peace, saying that he would allow Mahau to resume his role as *ari'i
rahi* of the island. The fleets had landed peacefully, and their crews were
royally feasted. When all the local food was consumed they returned to
Tahiti, and this futile expedition was remembered as 'Afaiutua' (carrying
baggage).[15]

Outside the reef at Hitia'a, Tu and Vehiatua farewelled their Spanish
companions and headed back to Tautira. Teta'i, the fishing season, had
begun, and soon afterwards fishing canoes came out bringing Reti, a tall,
strong, cheerful man about fifty years old with a deep scar on his forehead,
who stepped into the launch and invited them ashore. He was accompanied
by his daughters, and when Bonacorsi presented them with gifts, saying
that he had come to sound their harbour, Reti showed him where the sea
floor was rocky or sandy, and pointed out the spot where Bougainville had
lost his anchors. After a brief visit ashore to collect water, wood and fire,
Bonacorsi and his men returned to the boat to cook their meal. The canoes
crowded around, their crews yelling so loudly that the Spaniards were at
their wits' end until Máximo thought of a diversion, announcing that his
companions were eager to barter for *'iore* (Polynesian rats). All of the
canoes immediately rushed ashore, but before long the locals were back
again, flocking around the launch, some in canoes and others swimming,
holding up rats by their tails, some dead and some alive. Fortunately, when
Máximo confessed that this was a trick and told them to throw the rodents
away, they thought that it was hilarious.

The launch headed south again, and when they arrived at Anuhi,
Máximo was sent ashore in a canoe to ask for water, food and fire. When
he told the local *ari'i* Pahairiro that he intended to stay on the island with
the two missionary friars, the old chief seemed delighted; and as the launch
left the next morning, he came out with his wife with gifts of coconut and
bark cloth. At Tautira, where one of Tu's sisters came out in her canoe
with its awning and invited Máximo, her adoptive 'brother', to join her,
they escorted the launch back to Vaiuru'a Bay where Tu was staying with
his *taio* Vehiatua II. During their journey she gave the young marine bark-
cloth garments and a woven mat as a gesture of friendship, and would not
accept an axe in return, although these were highly prized on the island.
When they arrived at Tai'arapu, Pautu landed at his family's house, where
his sisters wept loudly as soon as they saw him. The sailors filled the barrels at a beautiful spring, and rowed to Vaiuru'a Bay where a large crowd
was waiting, Tu and Vehiatua among them.

After Máximo told the *ari'i* that he and his companions were going to
visit the Vaiaotea harbour in the Teahupo'o district, Tu returned to the

beach but Vehiatua and one of his leading men, Taruri, decided to accompany the young marine. Taking Vehiatua's canoe in tow, they sailed up the west coast towards Vaiaotea, where Machao the sub-lieutenant, Máximo and Pautu went ashore with Vehiatua and his henchman. As they walked along the beach, they came to a very large canoe shed in which two big canoes were stored, each with a cabin on their decks (probably the district's ceremonial canoes, belonging to the high chief and his family), and some war canoes each with a *pa'epa'e* or platform upon which the warriors stood in battle. The local men demonstrated their fighting techniques, telling Máximo that they were at war with Mo'orea. In another shed there were several of the canoes known as *pahi*, used to travel to other islands. The fact that the voyaging canoes were stored separately from war canoes and ceremonial canoes is intriguing, suggesting that long-distance voyaging was considered to be distinct from other types of seafaring activity.

After Pautu disappeared into the crowd, an islander sidled up to them and offered to show them 'Taitoa's' burial platform. According to Máximo, Taitoa had been Vehiatua II's 'stepfather', a grey-bearded, tall, good-looking old warrior famed for his battles against Tu's father whom the Spaniards had met during their previous visit to the island. His bones now lay on a thatched platform in this weedy, tumbledown enclosure. The identity of this 'Taitoa' is puzzling, however. As a high-born woman, Purahi no doubt had a number of liaisons, and perhaps Taitoa was her second husband (and Ti'itorea her third). As Máximo and his companions approached this sacred spot, a man carrying a small pig and a plantain branch laid them down as an offering to avert the anger of the gods. It was dangerous to approach such a place, because the spirit of the dead person still lingered around their corpse. According to Teuira Henry, if such a *hara* (or offence against the power of the gods) was committed, 'sure judgement upon the guilty priest, people, and the land was supposed to follow, and if concession and judgement were not quickly made, the priest, it is said, would die in great agony by a curse from the gods'.[16]

The islanders were horrified by the Spaniards' temerity, and Máximo and his companions moved away from Taitoa's funeral bier towards two other enclosures where the corpses were still quite fresh. Although Vehiatua's companions tried to stop them, saying that no one should approach these places for fear of being attacked by the *tupapa'u* or spirit of the dead person, who would tear out their eyes, Máximo retorted that these fears were groundless, and persisted in going towards the bier. Back at the launch, they found Pautu surrounded by his family, his sisters still weeping, cutting their heads with sharp stones and shark's teeth and smearing their bodies with blood in mourning for those who had died during his absence. Although Máximo told Pautu that he was wrong to consent to such a ceremony, Pautu simply changed the subject. From the beginning, Máximo adopted an attitude of superiority towards many Tahitian customs, urging the islanders to drop them, and he deliberately breached many sacred restrictions. Back at the boat, Vehiatua sent the Spaniards gifts of a baked pig and baskets of plantains and breadfruit; and that night they slept on board the launch.

At dawn on 18 November Bonacorsi took the launch south towards Vairaaʻo, where Pautu and Máximo went ashore to visit the parents of Heiao, the young Tahitian traveller who had died in Valparaiso. As they walked along the beach towards the house of the local chief Tuivirau, however, their path was blocked by a tumultuous crowd who refused to make way even when the heralds beat them with rods; and they were forced to return to the boat. When Captain Cook and Joseph Banks had visited Tuivirau during their 1769 circuit of the island, there had been a confrontation in his district after a boat-cloak was stolen; and no doubt the ariʻi wanted to avoid any more clashes with Europeans. Turning south again, the Spaniards returned to Vaiuruʻa Bay where Máximo and Pautu went ashore to check on a garden that Boenechea's men had planted during their previous visit. It was overgrown with weeds, and all of the plants had died. Soon afterwards Máximo heard that Tu's parents had arrived at Vaiuruʻa to offer prayers to Punuamoevai (Punua-sleeping-in-the-water), a god of the Teva-i-tai lineages associated with rain, fisheries, fertility and the land breeze known as Paetahi.[17] This was presumably one of the ceremonies associated with Tetaʻi, the Season of the Sea, when the ʻarioi returned to the seashore and the first fish were offered to the gods. Máximo joined his adoptive 'parents' at their marae before returning to the boat, where the Spaniards slept that night, drenched by showers of heavy rain, a sign of the god's presence and power.

Early the next morning, 19 November, Tu, his brother Ariʻipaea and their younger brother Vaetua, along with Vehiatua, his stepfather Tiʻitorea and his mother Purahi, boarded the launch to visit the frigate. As soon as they headed out to sea, however, the weather changed abruptly. Strong, gusty winds began to rock the boat, and as black clouds billowed up on the horizon, they headed back into Vaiuruʻa Bay where Tu sent one of his servants to climb a coconut palm and look out for the frigate. As other attendants prepared a meal, the lookout sighted the Águila, and packing up their supplies (which included quantities of dry coconuts, bananas mashed with yams and breadfruit, and baskets of tiny fish wrapped in banana leaves and roasted), all of the Tahitians except Purahi and Tu's young brother Vaetua boarded the launch and set off once more for the frigate, arriving safely on board two hours later. On deck, Tu presented Boenechea with his own cloak and waist-mat, saluting him as an *ari'i* and calling him his *taio*; and Boenechea responded by presenting Tu, Vehiatua and Ti'itorea each with an axe in the name of King Carlos III. As the weather worsened, Boenechea ordered the steersman to head the frigate out to sea to avoid the risk of shipwreck.

Over the next three days the *Águila* was battered by a violent storm, tacking about in the open ocean out of sight of the coast of southern Tahiti. The chiefs dined with Boenechea in his cabin, although they would only eat bread, pork and chicken; and Pautu fed Tu by hand, because Tu was so intensely sacred that he could not touch cooked food. Every time the ship tacked, a cannon shot was fired as a signal for the sailors, sending Tu into a frenzy of fear, which Ari'ipaea explained by telling the Spaniards that many of his people had been killed by the British – no doubt a reference to Wallis's attack on Matavai Bay, when so many Pare-'Arue people had been killed by musket- and cannon-fire. If Tu had been present on that occasion, he would have been about fifteen years old, and it must have been a traumatic experience.

Ari'ipaea, a strongly built, serious young man with one mole on his lip and another on his right cheek, also told Boenechea and his companions about Cook's first visit to Tahiti, saying that the British had gazed at the stars. When he described Cook's 1773 visit to Tautira and Matavai Bay, he told them that his sailors had forcibly taken some local women. According to Ari'ipaea, when the warriors gathered to attack them in reprisal, many of the islanders were shot. (This must refer to the incident reported in the British journals during Cook and Furneaux's 1773 visit, after three marines and a sailor from the *Adventure* tried to have 'unwanted intimacies' with some Tahitian women. They got into a fight with their menfolk and were later flogged as a punishment – although the shootings were not mentioned in the British journals.) Fearful that his men were about to be attacked, Captain Cook had sailed away to Ra'iatea, spending fifteen days at Ha'amanino Bay, and then carried on to Huahine, accompanied by a young man named Hitihiti. According to Ari'ipaea, whose account of these events was largely accurate, although the sequence was muddled, after visiting Vaitahu (Tahuata, in the Marquesas), the strangers had returned to Ha'amanino Bay where they left Hitihiti with a shotgun, a barrel of powder, a sword and an axe; before sailing to Matavai Bay where they bartered their Tongan red feathers to great advantage.

On 23 November Purahi arrived alongside the *Águila* in a double canoe, tossed by waves so high that her craft almost capsized. When he saw his wife weeping in the canoe, Ti'itorea also burst into tears, and after

Double canoe, Society Islands

they had talked for a while he told Boenechea that he and the other chiefs were anxious to go ashore. Apparently Tu's people were distraught about his absence, fearing that the Spaniards had taken him to Lima. In response Boenechea pointed out the danger of trying to go ashore in these stormy conditions, and Tu agreed to wait until the next day, thanking the commander for his concern and addressing him as his *taio*. Purahi's canoe was hauled aboard and she slept on the *Águila* that night, refusing to give up her sheets and pillow the next morning (because they had become *tapu* or imbued with ancestral power from her body). The weather was now more settled and as the frigate headed back towards the southern coast of Tahiti, Purahi's canoe was lowered and one of her servants took it ashore while the chiefs boarded the launch, accompanied by Arriaga, Don Juan de Manterola, the lieutenant of infantry, Rodríguez and a sergeant and two soldiers. Mist hung low over the land, and when it cleared they went through the Vaionifa pass, surrounded by a milling crowd of canoes, landing at Vaiuru'a Harbour.

Tu's parents and many of his kinsfolk were waiting on the beach, and when the *ari'i maro 'ura* landed, about three hundred of these people formed a large circle around him, weeping loudly, the women lowering their clothes to the waist, covering them with mats, slashing their heads and upper bodies and smearing themselves with blood in thanksgiving for his safe return. During his absence the Pleiades had risen above the horizon (on 20 November), formally announcing the beginning of the Season of Plenty. Because he wore the *maro 'ura*, Tu was imbued with ancestral power, and his presence at the rituals heralding the Season of Plenty was necessary to summon the gods who would bring *mana* and *ora* (well-being) to his people; while his loss would have been a disaster. The priest or *tahu 'a* made a speech, holding up a number of plantain branches and every now and then throwing one of these at Tu's feet to punctuate his oration. When Tu responded with a speech of his own, heralds with long poles kept the crowd back. Finally, the priest laid a small dog at Tu's feet and the ceremony came to an end. The women went to wash themselves in the ocean while the chiefs regaled the crowd with stories about their adventures on board the *Águila*. Later, Vehiatua asked Arriaga to have a musket fired at a canoe, and when the ball passed through both sides of the hull the islanders were astonished. Vehiatua begged to try this for himself and they let him shoot the musket, although one of the Spaniards also held the weapon to ensure that there were no accidents. After dusk, all of the Spaniards except Máximo were ferried out to the boat, and one of the officers almost drowned when he was tipped out into the rolling surf. That night they slept on board the launch, drenched by showers of driving rain.

Boenechea's Burial

Very early the next morning while it was still dark, the Spaniards were awoken by a chorus of cocks crowing on the land. It was calm and cloudy, and at 6 a.m. Ti'itorea's canoe arrived alongside the launch, laden with gifts for Boenechea. When the sailors went ashore to collect fresh water and grass for the livestock, Máximo returned with them, and Arriaga decided to row to Tautira to look for the frigate, accompanied by Vehiatua and his people. At Tautira, Vehiatua and Máximo went ashore, where they asked one of the local men to climb a coconut palm and look out for the ships, but he could see no sign of their sails. That night there was a wild storm, with thunder and lightning. When the *Júpiter* finally came into sight the next morning, they headed out and boarded her. Apart from Máximo, the Spaniards were afraid of sleeping ashore among the Tahitians, and were overjoyed to be back on board one of their own vessels.

During his time out at sea, Boenechea had decided that of all the harbours they had inspected, Vaitepiha Bay was the best place to establish a mission. (*See Plate 8.*) There was a good anchorage, and an area of flat, fertile land beside the Vaitepiha River where the mission house could be erected. In fact the village of Tautira was intensely sacred. Sited on the 'head of the fish' (a reference to the island as a great fish that had swum away from Ra'iatea), this was the first place in Tahiti where a *marae* had been dedicated to 'Oro. As the chief *'arioi* of Tautira used to chant:

> The mountain above is Tahua-reva
> The assembly ground is Ti'ara'a-o-Pere
> The point outside is Tautira
> The river is Vai-te-piha
> The *marae* are Pure-ora [under Ta'aroa's sway] and Taputapuatea [Sacrifices from Abroad]
> The high chief is Vehiatua-i-te-mata'i

The *'arioi* house is Pa-raro
The chief *'arioi* is Te ra'a-roa![1]

At 2 p.m. on 27 November 1774 the *Águila* and the *Júpiter* anchored in Vaitepiha Bay; and soon afterwards Tu and Vehiatua came out to the *Águila*. When they came on board they brought gifts of bark cloth, fine mats, breastplates, pigs and fruit for Boenechea, receiving axes, knives, shirts and other prized objects in return. Canoes crowded around the ships, bartering plantains, coconuts and breadfruit for European items; and the commander escorted the two *ari'i* to his cabin, accompanied by eight or ten of the leading chiefs. When they were seated, Boenechea told Tu and Vehiatua that he had decided to erect a house at Tautira for Máximo and the two missionary friars, asking if they would be willing to give land for this purpose, and whether they would take care of his people. Both chiefs agreed with delight. Assuring Boenechea that he would provide men to help with the construction of the house, Vehiatua offered to go ashore the next day with Gayangos and Father Narciso to select the site; and the chiefs retired to the quarterdeck, talking to each other with obvious pleasure. Until now, access to the European ships with their iron goods, clothing and powerful weapons had been almost exclusively controlled by the people of the northern coast, at Matavai Bay and Pare-'Arue; and the people of southern Tahiti had missed out on this traffic. Now that Tu and Vehiatua were *taio* or bond brothers, both would benefit from having the Spaniards located in Tautira (rather than at Hitia'a or Papara, for instance). At 6 p.m. the *Águila*'s sails were furled, the sailors cheered 'God save the King!', and the two chiefs and their companions boarded their canoes and returned ashore to share this momentous news with their people.

At daybreak the next morning when Vehiatua came out to the ship, he invited Gayangos and the two friars to go ashore and choose the site for the mission. They were accompanied by Pautu, Máximo and two marines, and when they landed at Tautira, Vehiatua led them to a large house where the local elders had assembled. Vehiatua sat at the head of the house while a chief sat in each corner, and they debated the matter for two hours until an agreement was reached about how a site should be selected. Walking around the bay, Gayangos found an area of good soil on the outskirts of the village; and when he asked Vehiatua for permission to erect the mission house on this spot, the chief said that he would have to ask his mother Purahi, as she owned the land, but he was sure that she would agree. Purahi gave her consent, but insisted that the mission house should be sited as far as possible from Vai'otaha *marae*, which stood nearby. Her hesitation was understandable, because Vai'otaha was one of the most significant *marae* on the island – the first in Tahiti to have been dedicated to 'Oro's worship. The site selected for the mission was about 150 yards from the Vaitepiha River and quite close to the sea. The river was brackish at this point, and although there were irrigated taro gardens and several houses on the site, Vehiatua agreed that these could be shifted. People arrived that afternoon to dig up the crops and remove their houses; and when they began to clear the site the following morning, Tu's younger brother Ari'ipaea worked among them.

Over the next few days, an armed guard was sent ashore each morning to protect the sailors who worked as axemen and labourers, and to prevent them from mingling with the Tahitians or sleeping with their women. They did not succeed, however, because as Arriaga later noted, some of the local women had already contracted venereal diseases and many of the Spanish sailors became infected during this visit.[2] When the sailors went to bathe, the island women sometimes danced naked on the beach before joining them in the water. As they watched these men felling trees, the Tahitians were amazed by the ease with which their iron axes cut through the wood; although as many breadfruit trees and coconut palms, so crucial to the local way of life, came crashing down, they began to express their disquiet. People from other districts were arriving in Tautira, eager to barter with the Spaniards, sometimes tricking them by giving them old bark cloth or mats in which the rents and holes were cunningly disguised. On 28 November when Manuel's father arrived at the frigate to see his son, he embraced the boy closely, gazing at him and 'marvelling at the stories he related about his time in Lima'.[3]

Now that the sailors were spending more time ashore, there were more disputes with the local people. On 30 November a ship's boy from the *Júpiter*, Pedro Carvajal, was thrown into irons for quarrelling with some islanders and threatening to have them shot. The punishment flag was flown on board the storeship; but before the boy could be flogged, Vehiatua and Ari'ipaea arrived on board, pleading with y Varela to free him. Y Varela finally relented, and when he invited Vehiatua to join him for dinner in his cabin, the chief ate with a knife, fork and spoon, copying the Spanish officers and asking for wine at the proper intervals, praising it with genuine delight. The following morning, however, when one of the sailors in the shore party washed his shirt and spread it on a bush to dry, the garment vanished. The sailor flew into a rage, brandishing a knife at some of the local people and threatening to cut their throats or shoot them unless his shirt was returned immediately; and Máximo hurried out in a canoe to the *Águila* to report this dispute to his superiors. When Gayangos and the pilot Juan de Hervé rushed ashore to reassure the chiefs, they found Tu — who seemed terrified — at his parents' house; but after Gayangos embraced the paramount chief and sat down with his mother Tetupaia, with whom he had a *taio* relationship, Tu calmed down a little.

Máximo and Hervé then went to see Vehiatua, who was also very apprehensive, assuring him that the sailor would be punished for threatening his people. The launch crew was mustered and made to stand in a line so that the chiefs could identify the culprit; and when they pointed him out, his hands were tied and he was placed under arrest and taken to the launch. Although Tu and Vehiatua begged Gayangos to free this man and insisted on accompanying them out to the *Águila*, Boenechea ordered the punishment flag to be flown and had the sailor trussed over a gun for a flogging. The chiefs begged so insistently for the man to be freed, however, that the commander finally relented, and had the man clapped in irons and forbade him to go ashore again. Afterwards Tu and Vehiatua thanked Boenechea warmly and dined with him, staying on board until after the Angelus had been recited.

On 2 December, Reti, the *ari'i* of Hitia'a, arrived at Tautira with his family. Greeting Gayangos by his forename and surname, he embraced him affectionately, presenting him with bark cloth, mats, fruit and a large pig, and receiving two axes, six knives and other objects in return. Reti complained to Gayangos that although he and his son had accompanied the lieutenant around the island during his previous visit, the Spaniards had decided to establish their mission in Tautira instead of Hitia'a; and although Gayangos assured him that this was only because the anchorage at Hitia'a was unsafe, and that they were still *taio* or bond friends, the *ari'i* was not consoled. That afternoon the carpenters went up the Ataroa Valley to look for trees, accompanied by Máximo and some of Vehiatua's people, where they blazed about ninety breadfruit trees. The next morning when the trees began to be chopped down, the people protested angrily. Vehiatua asked Máximo to stop the felling, saying that his people had complained that they would die of hunger. Vehiatua demanded an axe for every two or three trees, saying that Tute's (Cook's) people had paid as much; but Máximo retorted that in that case a ship full of axes would have to be sent from Lima, and they would have to leave the island. Relenting, Vehiatua appointed one of his chiefs, a man named Taitoa (who, if he carried his father's title, may have been Vehiatua's half-brother), to ensure that the axemen felled only those trees that did not fruit properly, or were remote from any settlement. He sent about two hundred of his men up the valley, who hauled the logs to the river for the Spaniards, and floated them down to Tautira.

On 4 December, a Sunday and a day of rest, when Vehiatua came out to the *Águila*, asking Boenechea to lend him the boat so that he could go to Vaiuru'a, the commander refused. After mass, a fleet of about two hundred canoes laden with provisions and led by two large *pahi* sailed into Vaitepiha Bay, the islanders explaining that these canoes had come from Pare for the festivities celebrating Tu's bond friendship with Vehiatua. Boenechea was not convinced; and apprehensive that his ships were about to be attacked, he ordered the cannons to be loaded with round and grape shot and the small arms primed. As they approached the frigate, however, the fleet wheeled about and headed for Tautira, dashing towards the beach in tight formation. About two hours later, there was a scuffle on shore. Men armed with long weapons began to attack the visiting canoes, seizing the provisions on board and cudgelling their crews, who retaliated with enthusiasm. Fearing that his men might be harmed, Boenechea ordered the yawl to be lowered and piped away with an armed crew; but as soon as they saw this the Tahitians laughed uproariously, saying that this was only a *rave* or sham fight between the people of Pare and southern Tahiti, who were celebrating Tu's visit to their district.

The arrival of this fleet and the scramble for its cargo announced the raising of the *rahui* on the resources that had been reserved for the opening of the Season of Plenty. On this occasion, the Tahiti-iti people were also celebrating the bond friendship between Tu and Vehiatua II. Such ceremonies always began with a *pa'iatua* ritual to renew the images of the gods and recharge them with ancestral power. Afterwards, when the first breadfruit and bananas were carried to the district's main *marae* (Vai'otaha, in this case), they were offered to the gods to ensure the ongoing fertility of these crops. Each district sent several new canoes to the ceremony laden with sacred objects, accompanied by a fleet of other canoes loaded with supplies of pigs, dogs, fruit, bamboos of *mono'i* or scented oil, offerings of bark cloth and other treasured items. After landing on the beach, the crews were welcomed by the priests and walked in a procession to the *marae* with their offerings, the chiefs dressed in fine mats and accompanied by warriors blowing conch-shell trumpets. At the *marae*, the priests chanted their prayers; and the high priest put a selection of the sacred offerings on a platform for the gods. This was the signal for the people standing around the *marae* to demand their share of the provisions; and when the host chief announced that everything not reserved for the gods was now available, the spectators would run to the place where the provisions had been piled. Fighting, snatching and scrambling, they grabbed their share, sometimes hurting each other in the scuffle; and this was followed by a great feast, with *'arioi* performances, dancing, singing, boxing matches and wrestling. The patron god of this festival was Ro'o-ma-Tane, a god of the *'arioi*, whose festivities dominated this celebration.[4]

Now that the celebrations heralding the Season of Plenty were under way in Tautira, this was a bad time for breadfruit trees to be felled or for a mission to be built in the district. That afternoon, the festivities were interrupted when some islanders complained to Máximo that a sailor from the *Júpiter* had given a woman a handkerchief for sex, lay with her and then took back his gift. They wanted to kill him for this insult, but when Andía y Varela heard the story he had the culprit put in irons and sent on board the storeship. The next morning on board the *Júpiter*, the punishment flag was raised, a cannon was fired, and the sailor was given fifty lashes. On this occasion the *ari'i* did not protest, remarking that this was very different from the way that the British had dealt with similar incidents. Andía assured them that this was because the Spaniards and the British had different religions; and that, unlike the British, his people respected women. The next day when some coconut palms were felled, one of these trees crashed onto a sailor and broke his spine, killing him outright. Convinced that the ancestors had struck down the sailor for cutting down these trees, and fearful that the Spanish would punish them, Tu and his people fled into the mountains. Boenechea hurried ashore and assured Vehiatua that he did not blame them for the accident, asking him to tell Tu to come back down. A funeral mass was held the following morning, and the sailor was buried close to the mission shelter with a small cross set upon his grave. The islanders, who watched the ritual intently, were appalled to see earth being shovelled and stamped down over the corpse, which they regarded as an act of disrespect to the dead man and his spirit.

On 8 December the Spaniards held their own celebrations in honour of 'The Most Pure and Immaculate Conception of Our Lady the Virgin Mary'. The frigate was decorated with garlands and bunting, and at sunset the sailors gave three cheers for King Carlos III, although they did not fire the cannons for fear that this would terrify the local people. The following day the *Águila* was decorated for the Princess's birthday, and the Tahitians, seeing the Spaniards in a festive mood, resumed their celebrations. That afternoon an *'arioi* festival or *heiva* was held at Tautira, which Máximo described in an account of Tahitian customs he was writing for the Viceroy – an irreplaceable document that unfortunately was later lost in the Lima archives. Luckily, Andía y Varela also wrote an account of this *heiva*, which was attended by the entire population, including the *ari'i maro 'ura* Tu and his family. According to y Varela, some of the dances were performed by two young boys dressed as women who wore barkcloth wings at their waists, carrying a small wand decorated with feathers and following the cues of their 'dancing master' (the leader of the 'arioi troupe). The dances at this *heiva* were 'extremely immodest'; and when several young girls performed a respectable dance (the *hura*), they screwed their mouths awry in a gesture so hideous that, according to y Varela, it must be inspired by the Devil. The musicians played nose flutes with three holes, a range of sharkskin drums, and two slit gongs, one longer and thicker than the other, which were struck with two small sticks to make a harmonious sound.[5] Y Varela added that although most of the Tahitian women were tall, beautiful and charming, 'there are some dissolute hussies amongst them, as in every place, [but] those who do not belong to that class evince modesty in their clothing, their mien and their behaviour'.[6]

Although this was a time of celebration, all was not well in Tautira. On 10 December, Vehiatua sent the people of the inland valley into exile for refusing to bring their tribute to the ceremonies, and for plotting to kill him and replace him with another *ari'i*. The valley's inhabitants must have been outraged that so many of their breadfruit trees had been felled for the mission, while most of the trees in Tautira had been spared. At dawn the next morning when Ari'ipaea came out to the *Águila*, dressed in an old uniform jacket with epaulettes given to him by one of the officers, he informed Boenechea that these people had taken up arms against Vehiatua, and that Vehiatua and Tu were on their way to quell the rebellion. Boenechea immediately sent an armed party ashore under the ensign Don Nicolas de Toledo to protect the mission house and the working party, and as they rowed ashore these men could see the warriors setting off up the valley, straggling in loose order, armed with spears, slings and clubs; many of the leading warriors wearing *taumi* or breastplates decorated with dog's hair, pearl shell and shark's teeth. Ti'itorea wore a 'crown' on his head, neatly woven of coconut husk fibres; while some of the leading warriors had towering wickerwork helmets (*fau*) with a kind of screen over their faces, the ordinary fighting men protecting their heads with thick white bark-cloth turbans.[7] Many of these men also proudly displayed shreds of European clothing – the arm of a jacket, the leg of some trousers or a dirty, torn shirt; while a few warriors wore grotesque masks and made 'all kinds of feints and gesticulations' – probably the *rauti* or war orators.[8]

Tu had about four hundred men and Vehiatua had two hundred warriors; and when their armies met at the mouth of the gorge they fought a brief skirmish with the rebels, who were greatly outnumbered, killing two of their chiefs and chasing the rest into the mountains. When the victorious forces arrived at the enemy village they burned down the houses, felling fruit trees and destroying the gardens. As they wandered back to the beach the warriors were laden with bark cloth, mats, pigs and fruit, and eighty of them triumphantly carried the thatched roof of one large house on their shoulders (presumably the *'arioi* house of the enemy district). As each of the captains arrived, he presented a plantain branch to Vehiatua, and one of these men also handed over one of the enemy chiefs, whom he had captured. Although they threatened to kill him, this man was eventually pardoned; and when Tu joined them, Vehiatua handed one of his plantain branches to the paramount chief in recognition of his senior status. They were delighted to see the armed party of marines by the mission, thinking that Boenechea had sent these men to help in their battle, and went out to the frigate to thank him, recounting the story of their victory with deep satisfaction.

The next morning the first section of framing for the mission shelter was erected, more breadfruit trees were felled, and the single donkey that they had brought from Lima died, and was cooked and eaten by the Tahitians. That afternoon Máximo was summoned to visit Tu's sick aunt (a woman named Tutara'a), in the hope that he might cure her. He found a *tahu'a* (priest) chanting over the invalid, holding up a plantain branch and some leaves while her relatives wept in despair, declaring that it was impossible that she should recover. When Máximo took the sick woman's pulse, he found that it was racing; and when he asked her how she felt, she replied that she ached all over. Although this woman was probably suffering from influenza, Máximo diagnosed a 'suppression of the menses' and suggested that she should be bled, which was done the next day. The following morning when he gave her medicine from the ship and urged her to have her other arm bled by the 'plebotomist' from the storeship, she hesitated; but after Máximo told her that unless her relatives and the priest withdrew, he would stop his treatment, she agreed. The next day the invalid was feeling much better, and another woman came to Máximo, asking him to treat an abscess on her cheek, which he did with ointment.

Although Máximo had no medical training, the Tahitians were clearly hoping that as the *taio* of their *ari'i rahi*, he would be close to his own gods and know how to cure these new afflictions; and the young marine did not disabuse them. On 17 December, Vehiatua came to complain that two of the sailors had cut grass and picked fruit from the sacred trees on Vai'otaha *marae*, a terrible *hara* or offence against 'Oro, who was punishing his people with these illnesses. Although Boenechea gave strict orders that actions of this kind must be avoided in future, another influenza epidemic had broken out on the island; and that afternoon Ti'itorea and Purahi left for Papara, where several of the leading chiefs had already died of a severe chill and fever. Although the Spaniards attributed these illnesses to the Tahitians' daily habit of bathing in the sea at sundown, the Tahitians blamed them on the arrival of the Spaniards and their incessant *hara* or breaches of *tapu* restrictions.

On 20 December when the portable mission house was brought ashore, guarded by an armed party, Vehiatua asked his leading counsellor Taitoa to take care of the ironwork and tools because a thief had announced that he was going to steal them. The house was quickly erected under the thatched shelter, and Vehiatua suggested he should sleep in the house that night with Máximo. When he saw how their beds were placed, however, he asked for these to be turned around, so that their heads (the most *tapu* parts of their bodies) rather than their feet faced Vai'otaha *marae*. The following day, 21 December, was the summer solstice, celebrated by a *para 'a Matahiti* or 'ripening of the year' ritual during which the first fruits of the breadfruit harvest were offered to the gods, and those who had died during the past year were ritually recognised as *'oromatua* or ancestral spirits. Once again, however, the Spaniards had brought illness in their wake, and there is no indication that the ritual was performed at Vai'otaha on this occasion. Instead, the festival must have been shifted to another district. When the Spanish friars visited 'Oro's *marae* on that sacred day, they saw a priest's house to one side of the stone temple, and a platform on a pole where the priests laid offerings of plantains, cooked food and branches, set into a stone pavement between the priest's house and the 'altar' (or *ahu*). There were also small standing stones set into the pavement where the priests and *ari'i* leaned during the ceremonies, although some of these were left vacant for deceased ancestors.[9] On the other side of the *marae* stood three high *ti'i* (carved poles), one wider than the others and carved with five nude women with their genitals prominently displayed; and the other two carved with male figures. There were two other *marae* close to the mission, each with a priest's house and platforms for offerings.

The mission house had been erected in a *ra'a* or sacred part of the bay, where the various *marae* were concentrated. The friars' visit to Vai'otaha *marae* had been inauspicious, however; and later that morning they heard that Pahairiro, the strapping old high chief of Anuhi whom the Spaniards had visited earlier, had died of a chill and fever. No doubt the *tahu'a* or local priests saw this as the consequence of the friars' visit to the sacred *marae*, which had affronted the gods of the island. When he heard the news of Pahairiro's death, Vehiatua wept, 'but not very much' according to Máximo;[10] and all the chiefs set off for Anuhi for the mourning rituals. Tu's mother 'Faiere' (as Máximo always called her, although she is known as 'Tetupaia' in the genealogies), a stately, large, good-hearted woman, told Máximo that he must go with them, because through his bond friend-ship with her son, he was a relative of Pahairiro.

When they arrived at Anuhi, their canoes were hauled ashore. Taking off their good clothing, two of the women in their party wrapped little mats around their waists to stop their bark-cloth robes from being spoiled when they slashed their heads and upper bodies. The mourners walked towards Pahairiro's house, the men in front and the women behind; each of the chiefs pulled up a young plantain shoot; and the commoners began 'to howl just as if they were dogs' to announce that the mourners were coming. Outside the house, Tu gathered his people in a circle and threw down his plantain branch, and the two women approached the funeral bier with offerings of bark cloth, where they stood and slashed themselves. After this ritual of mourning they threw down the bloodied bark cloth and sat beside the bier, weeping, while Vehiatua sat with the dead man's family. Pahairiro's corpse lay wrapped in bark cloth, his hands resting on his chest with a little bunch of red feathers clasped in his fingers and another in the fold of his loincloth, as a link with the ancestor gods. The bark-cloth offerings were piled up in a heap, and when the wailing was over, these were carried to a cleared place nearby, where the chief would later be buried.

When this ceremony was over, Tu asked Máximo to sit beside him and tell his people about Spain and its territories, how the Spanish fought their battles, and about the damage caused by cannon-fire. As soon as Máximo assured them that warriors dressed in armour could not be shot, Tu urgently requested the Spaniards to bring him a helmet and a coat of mail. When they began to speak about religion, Tu told Máximo that the Tahitian gods were so powerful that if any of their *tahu'a* or priests became angry with the young marine, they could simply take some of his spittle, put it in a piece of coconut and bury it; and that after two days Máximo's testicles would be so swollen that they would reach the ground (a symptom of ele-phantiasis or *fe'efe'e*, which was endemic in the Society Islands). Máximo reacted scornfully, demanding that a priest should immediately put this to the test, Tu ordered one of his men to begin the incantation, as no *tahu'a* were present; but when Máximo burst out laughing, mocking this man's performance; and Tu and his people were flummoxed. After the chiefs had retired to their canoe awnings to sleep, Máximo approached Pahairiro's body – which was being fanned by four men, each holding a stalk of the ginger plant with which they wiped away the blood and swished away the flies – breaching the death *tapu*. That night the young marine was forced to sleep on a pile of plantain leaves and no one offered him shelter, even when it was pouring with rain.

On 26 December, Vehiatua went out to the *Águila* to farewell Boenechea, saying that he and his people were going to Vaiaotea in the Teahupoʻo district to entertain a party that had arrived from Raʻiatea (no doubt an *'arioi* troupe that had come for the Matahiti celebrations). While he was on board, however, the *ariʻi* went below decks with his 'servant', who must have been a *mahu* (a man who lived as a woman, an accepted role on the island), where one of the sailors followed them. When he entered the sergeants' mess, he found the servant performing oral sex on the *ariʻi*. Horrified, the sailor punched Vehiatua and thrashed his companion with a stick; and without a word, the two Tahitians boarded their canoe and went ashore, although none of the officers knew why they had departed so abruptly. In Tahiti, the *ariʻi* were often attended by *mahu*, and although the chiefs had sexual relationships with women, the custom of also having sex with these *mahu* was taken for granted.

Later that afternoon there was an uproar in Tautira, and afterwards all of the canoes put off in confusion, heading for the east point of the bay. Other people were seen running into the hills, led by Tu and his retinue; and when the yawl, commanded by Don Juan de Manterola with a sergeant and four armed men, landed on the beach, they found one of the *Júpiter*'s men, Franscisco Navarro, being carried away unconscious, with blood running from his head. After washing his clothes this man had spread three of his shirts and two pairs of trousers on some bushes to dry, and when they vanished, Navarro had grabbed one man and punched another who happened to be standing nearby. As soon as he let this second man go, however, his victim grabbed a large stone and hit the sailor three or four times on the head, leaving him for dead. When he heard about the attack, de Manterola sent for Gayangos, asking him to come ashore and talk with Vehiatua, who was sitting inside the mission house with Máximo, weeping bitterly. When Gayangos arrived, he assured the young *ariʻi* that they were not angry with him; but asked him to have the assailant brought so that they could find out whether or not he was guilty. After the way that he had been treated on board the *Águila*, however, Vehiatua was unwilling to help the Spaniards, although he sent out a search party. His men returned about an hour later, bringing a man from the inland valley whom they insisted was the offender, although the man protested vehemently, saying that he had been away collecting firewood at the time of the quarrel. Gayangos mustered Navarro's shipmates, and when he asked them if they could identify this individual, they all insisted that this was not the culprit. Vehiatua was furious, loudly reproaching his men for misleading him. Another chief arrived shortly afterwards who told Gayangos that in fact the man who had attacked Navarro had acted in self-defence, because the sailor had punched him once without good reason; and when he tried to hit him again, the man had picked up the stone to defend himself.

It is probable that one of Vehiatua's men had taken the shirts and trousers as a reprisal for the assault on his *ari'i* on board the *Águila*; and that the prisoner who was delivered to the Spaniards was one of the inhabitants from the inland valley who had rebelled against the high chief. When Boenechea heard what had happened, he summoned the officers' council who decided that the man had been falsely accused and should be released. An armed guard was sent ashore to collect all the tools and implements and shut up the mission house; and Boenechea sent a message to Vehiatua saying that 'in view of the ill return made for all the benefits he and his compatriots had received at our hands, it was no longer his wish that the Padres should remain on the island, and that on the morrow, we would take the house to pieces and have it conveyed on board again'.[11] As soon as he received this message, however, Vehiatua II swallowed his pride and begged the Spaniards not to leave, promising that he would hand over the assailant.

That night on board the *Águila*, the officers began to rail against the islanders. Nicolas de Toledo declared that they should have taken Vehiatua as a hostage until the delinquent was given up, just as Captain Cook had done in order to retrieve his deserters; but the friars disagreed, saying that the Tahitians would surely punish them for such an act as soon as the frigate sailed. Pautu was present, and when he tried to defend his compatriots, the officers shouted him down, saying that according to a man named 'Mavarua' (Mau'arua, the exiled paramount chief of Ra'iatea who was now living at Papara),[12] it was Pautu's fault that Vehiatua had not handed over the assailant, because he had warned the *ari'i* against the Spaniards. When they heard this, both Pautu and Manuel 'became very morose and said they would cast themselves ashore naked, that they wanted no clothes nor anything else from us, but only to stay in their own country; which made us wonder at their ingratitude'.[13] At 9 p.m. that evening Navarro regained consciousness in the infirmary, and was given extreme unction (the sacrament for anointing the sick) by the friars.

Early the next morning, Taitoa, Vehiatua's trusted counsellor, came on board to report that the sailor's assailant had been captured, and that Vehiatua was ready to hand him over. According to Taitoa, he had been unable to sleep the previous night because most of the chiefs did not want to give up this man and had argued bitterly about it. When Gayangos arrived ashore he found that Vehiatua had left for Vaiaotea, and he despatched Pautu and the interpreter to implore Vehiatua to return, assuring him of his safety. After what he had heard the previous night, however,

Pautu was determined to warn his *ari'i* to stay away from the Spaniards; and he went off on his own, leaving Máximo to make the journey with a guide. After they had walked for some distance, the guide, seeing that Máximo was very tired, offered to carry him on his back; and soon afterwards when they met two Tahitians in a canoe carrying a stolen sheep, which they were taking to Tu, these men offered to take Máximo with them.

Further along the southern coast they met Manuel's mother, who was going to fetch her son from the Spaniards. As they paddled past Pautu's house at Vaiuru'a, Máximo saw Pautu standing on the reef, wearing a loincloth. He had stripped off his Spanish clothing and yelled out to the two paddlers, telling them to capsize the canoe and drown 'Matimo' (as the islanders named the young marine). Although these men were afraid that Vehiatua and Tu would punish them for bringing Máximo, he reassured them, saying that Tu was his 'brother'. When they arrived at Vaiaotea, Vehiatua, who was surrounded by a large group of warriors armed with spears, greeted Máximo in tears. He ordered his men to lay their weapons aside and embraced the interpreter, who demanded that Pautu should be brought to him. When Pautu arrived, Máximo harangued him, describing the kind treatment that he and his companions received in Lima, where they had been housed in the Viceroy's palace and royally entertained, clothed and loaded with presents, accusing him of ingratitude. When Pautu made no answer, according to Máximo the elders abused him. That night the interpreter slept amongst Vehiatua's people, convinced that they would not harm him.

The next morning when Máximo returned to the *Águila*, he told Boenechea that Vehiatua would return to Tautira only if an unarmed officer went with him. Realising how reluctant the chiefs were to surrender this man, Boenechea sent Máximo ashore with a message to say that he had decided to absolve the assailant of blame, because Navarro had attacked him twice without justification. When he received this message, Vehiatua embraced Máximo gratefully, presenting him with a pig and a bunch of plantains as a mark of their friendship. He promised to return to Tautira the next morning, but said that Tu was now so terrified that he was unlikely to come with him. During the next afternoon, Vehiatua arrived at Tautira with Tu's brother Ari'ipaea and his mother Tetupaia to make peace with Gayangos and the other Spaniards. They said that they had been forced to slip away while Tu was asleep, or the paramount chief would never have allowed this meeting to occur.

On 30 December the shelter over the mission house was finished, and Vehiatua, Ari'ipaea, Tetupaia and a large retinue went to the *Águila* to visit Boenechea. When Vehiatua told him that, according to Pautu, the Spaniards planned to take him hostage, Boenechea retorted that the young man was a liar (although in fact Pautu was only reporting what he had heard on board the ship); and Vehiatua replied that he would tell his people to ignore him. At dawn the next day when Máximo reopened the mission house, he found it full of rats, and killed seventy-five of these creatures. The supplies, furniture and clerical equipment were landed and the Fathers were given fifteen packets of cotton and flannel shirts with which to reward the islanders who had worked on the mission shelter. That night they slept in the mission house for the first time, with Máximo, Manuel and his uncle beside them. At 9 a.m. the next morning, the troops and fifteen uniformed marines were landed and formed a guard of honour for the Holy Cross. Half an hour later the Cross was blessed and lowered into the boat, escorted by the officers and the ship's chaplains, and when they landed on the beach they were greeted by Fathers Narciso and Gerónimo. As the officers and chaplains formed a procession, carrying the Cross and singing the Te Deum, the guard of honour fired a round, terrifying the Tahitians who threw themselves flat on the ground. When the Cross was raised, a second round was fired; and after the friars celebrated mass, raising up the Host in the air, a third and final round was fired. At the same time, on board the *Águila* the sailors cheered 'God Save the King!' and the cannons fired a twenty-one-gun salute, again terrifying the Tahitians, although Máximo tried to reassure them by saying that this was just a *heiva* (entertainment) from Lima. Although Vehiatua and Tu were not present on this occasion, having returned to Vaiaotea to welcome the visitors from Ra'iatea, Ti'itorea had just returned from Papara with his wife Purahi, hoping that the Spaniards could cure him of a severe catarrh that all their family had contracted during their stay there – the second time that Ti'itorea had caught influenza during a visit by Boenechea and his companions.

Later that afternoon, the officers and the friars invited the chiefs to join them in the mission house. Boenechea was not present, but the paymaster de Andrade asked the chiefs (who included Purahi and Ti'itorea, but none of the other major leaders)[14] whether they agreed that the Fathers and Máximo should stay on the island. They all said that they were content and promised to protect them, but warned that if the people of Mo'orea attacked or a foreign ship arrived, they might not be able to honour that commitment. De Andrade impressed upon them the great power of the King of Spain, his dominion over all of the islands close to his territories, and his desire to instruct and befriend them; and assured them that as long as they kept their promise, Spanish ships would often visit them with tools and implements, and protect them from their enemies.

Early the next morning, the sentry on the *Águila* discovered two island-ers who had slipped on board to steal hoop iron. As soon as he saw them they dived overboard and swam beneath the frigate, but the boats were lowered and managed to capture them, although they kept on diving in an effort to elude their captors. These men were put in irons, and the next day each was given fifty lashes. Unsuccessful thieves received little sym-pathy in Tahiti, and after the flogging Purahi gave the miscreants a hearty kick and urged that the punishment should be continued, while Ti'itorea thrashed them with a paddle. Taitoa told the officers that they could drown the culprits if they liked, explaining the local custom by which thieves were taken out to sea in a canoe, their arms and legs trussed to a large stone, and thrown overboard. When Boenechea told them that he had decided to visit Ra'iatea before his ships returned to Lima, the chiefs had gifts of pigs and fruit sent out to the *Águila*. The commander despatched Máximo with a goat in a canoe with two paddlers, telling him to swap this animal for a nanny goat that was being held at Vaiaotea; and a number of cattle were sent ashore to the mission, which were given special names that were long remembered on the island – Riua, Piaoe, Mania, Mati, and so on.[15] When the marine arrived at Vaiaotea, the local headman welcomed him; and although he did not having a milking goat, he gave him a nanny in kid instead.

On 6 January 1775, Tu and Vehiatua returned to Tautira, accompa-nied by another fleet of 135 canoes laden with provisions, including 60 canoes with double sails from Teti'aroa, the atoll belonging to Tu's family where the chiefs and *'arioi* periodically went to rest and enjoy themselves. The Season of Plenty was now under way, and the gods and the *'arioi* were returning to Tahiti for the summer. When the canoes landed on the beach, there was another sham fight as the local people scrambled to grab the food; and Máximo went ashore and belaboured them with the flat of his sabre to stop them from seizing the provisions. That afternoon, at Ti'itorea's request, a portrait of King Carlos III was fixed to the wall of the mission; and later that day the frigate fired a signal gun to indicate that the ship would soon be sailing. On 7 January while the anchors were being weighed, the chiefs came out to farewell Boenechea, promising to take care of the missionaries during his absence. Many of the islanders begged for a passage to Ra'iatea; but Boenechea allowed only Mau'arua, the exiled high chief of that island (whom Gayangos described as Tu's uncle by blood),[16] and Puhoro, a navigator from Ma'atea, to accompany him as pilots for the *Águila*, although two servants of Tu and Vehiatua (sent by the chiefs to fetch *'ava* from the island) managed to stow away on board the frigate. On board the *Júpiter*, y Varela was accompanied by two Tahitians, one named 'Oromatua and the other Paparua. Later that morning the two ships sailed away to Ra'iatea, leaving Máximo, the friars and a party of sailors behind them.

Soon after the departure of the ships, a huge crowd of people from Ra'iatea and the other districts of Tahiti arrived at Tautira to resume the Matahiti festivities. At this time, the inter-island ritual exchanges for the worship of 'Oro were restricted to 'Opoa in Ra'iatea and Tautira in southern Tahiti; although the presence of the Spanish ships had disrupted this cycle. Each night these visitors crowded around the mission house, peering inside until the friars begged Ti'itorea and Purahi to have walls of wattle and daub built around the mission to give them some privacy. Ti'itorea agreed, and the work began right away. The following day, the garden was fenced to keep the spectators from trampling the plants, and the Fathers distributed six axes in the King's name to the chiefs to thank them for their assistance. More visitors kept arriving at Tautira; and on 10 January when Pautu arrived at the mission to see the friars, they were overjoyed, thinking at first that he had repented of his apostasy, but he had only come to fetch the gifts that he had received in Peru. When the friars opened the box in which these gifts were stored, they took out the swords and arms, and the rosaries and other religious tokens presented to him (given he was no longer Christian), handing the key of the box to Pautu, who gave it to Vehiatua and left the mission. The Fathers were devastated by Pautu's desertion, saying that 'the sorrow that we felt may be conceived, seeing that a soul so favoured of God and man was going to perdition, and that we should suffer the untold loss of all the host of heathen in these islands; inasmuch as henceforward we could but regard him as our enemy'.[17] No doubt Vehiatua wanted these treasures in order to redistribute to his guests at the Matahiti ceremonies. During the following day, four razors, a honing strap in its case, a handkerchief, a towel and a napkin were stolen from the mission; although Vehiatua retrieved most of these items and soon returned them to the friars.

On 12 January several women wrapped in long lengths of bark cloth made a ritual presentation to the visiting chiefs, twirling themselves and unwrapping the bark cloth from their bodies until they stood naked. According to Máximo, this ceremony (with which Joseph Banks had also been honoured) was known as a *ta'urua*; and it was followed by a *paraparau* or exchange of speeches during which the wars with Mo'orea were debated.[18] In the course of this discussion the chiefs asked Máximo whether, if the Mo'orea people attacked Tautira, he would fight with them; and they seemed astonished when he replied that he could only do this with orders from his superiors. Two days later another great fleet of

canoes arrived, and this time Vehiatua asked Máximo to go down to the
beach to prevent the sham fight over the provisions. Afterwards these
new visitors crowded around the mission, where the friars, who were
having dinner with Vehiatua, were driven almost to distraction by the
hubbub, which lasted until the *heiva* or *'arioi* entertainments began in the
late afternoon.

On 15 January the Fathers held a mass, and soon afterwards the chiefs
arrived with a retinue of about five hundred people who crowded inside
the mission house. When Purahi, who was accompanied by her youngest son, a 'very bright and prankish boy', demanded the gipsy costume
that Manuel was wearing for her son, the friars refused, saying that these
clothes had been a gift from the Viceroy. She began to strip the clothes
off the boy, retorting that her son was Manuel's chief, and this costume
belonged to him. Infuriated, one of the friars snatched the clothes from
her, except for a red silk sash that her son had already put on as a breech-
clout. During the tussle that ensued, Tu, Ari'ipaea and their father Teu
watched impassively, and afterwards they dined with the friars. Although
Teu's high-born wife Tetupaia accompanied them on this occasion, she did
not eat with the men; for as the friars noted, in Tahiti men and women ate
separately, and even slept separately unless they were married.[19] The fleet
of canoes departed that evening, and that night Tu and Vehiatua came to
warn Máximo that a ceremony would be held at Vai'otaha *marae* the next
morning where their god would appear in a white cloud, breathing fire.
They asked him to ensure that no fires were lit at the mission, and that he
and the friars stayed away from the *marae*. Instead, Máximo retorted that
he would certainly light a fire and visit the *marae* the next morning, leaving them nonplussed; although they told him that in that case he would
have to approach with a slow step without moving his arms, and wearing
only a loincloth.

On 16 January while Máximo and the friars were still asleep, the Matahiti
ceremony was held at Vai'otaha to celebrate the ripening of the year. As
soon as Máximo woke up that morning, however, he lit a fire and walked
to the *marae*, in defiance of the chiefs' earnest request that the Spaniards
should respect the customary prohibitions. The main ritual had already
ended, but he arrived in time to see the dance that the *'arioi* performed
for the *ari'i maro 'ura*. When one of the leading warriors told Máximo to
take off his upper clothing, he refused; and when Vehiatua asked him to
extinguish the fire at the mission, once again he refused to comply. The
chiefs were baffled. Such sacrilegious behaviour was almost unheard of,
as y Varela explained in his account of Tahitian customs:

They say that if they were to permit any one to enter or approach a *marae* the *Tupapau* [*tupapaʻu*: spirit of a dead person] would come by night and torment not only the defunct to whom the *marae* is dedicated, but the [priests] as well, and would do them no end of mischief. They regard this *Tupapau* as a sort of malignant spirit borne down through the air in the guise of a vapoury apparition or fiery serpent to wreak injury on their crops or trees or, it may be, to their health. They believe that it kills young children, and attribute both death and disease to its wiles.[20]

In spite of Máximo's *hara* (breach of *tapu*), the ceremonies continued the next day with an archery contest at the *marae*. Archery was a sacred pursuit in Tahiti, and while the competition was under way, the people were forbidden to light their fires. Only the *ariʻi* participated in this competition, and even they had to bare their chests in a gesture of respect to the gods. The *tahuʻa* (priest) opened the proceedings with a chant to ʻOro, asking that the contest should be successful, and the *ariʻi* stood on a stone platform. As the drums beat loudly, they shot off their arrows high into the air, greeted by shouts and exclamations from boys who were perched in trees to see whose arrow flew the greatest distance. At the end of the contest, the losing *ariʻi* had to provide a feast for the winner, with dancing and other entertainments.

On 18 January Máximo was called away to Irimiro, where a bull that the Spanish ships had brought was wreaking havoc. With the help of the local people, he managed to rope the bull around its legs, tying it up and lashing it to a pole. The following day he arrived back triumphantly at Tautira, leading the bull and welcomed by the foremost chiefs and their families. More visitors had arrived at Tautira, although Vehiatua had left the district, leaving the friars to fend for themselves. Tu stayed with the Fathers but did not try to check the visitors, who were now treating the friars with open contempt. They had disrupted the Matahiti celebrations by their untimely visit to Vaiʻotaha *marae*, and had tussled with Purahi, a 'Great Woman', in an unprecedented gesture of disrespect. Máximo himself had broken the *tapu* restrictions necessary for the success of the fertility rituals, and during his absence crowds of visiting *ʻarioi* had arrived at the mission after the *heiva* every afternoon to taunt the friars, yelling insults through the wicker screens, mimicking their 'speech and gesticulations', making obscene gestures and laughing uproariously at their discomfiture. As the Fathers lamented:

They called out to us through the screen round the house '*Guariro!*' which means 'thieves':- '*Neneva!*' which means 'fools':- '*Poreho!*' signifying shell-fish, but used among themselves to express the privy parts, making grossly obscene mockery of us the while; and others called us '*Harimiri*' which means 'old gaffers.' These terms we caught the meaning of ourselves; the rest, which were no doubt equally opprobrious, we did not understand. Meanwhile the women [looked on] with roars of laughter: the boys took their cue from the rest. We offered no retort. This lasted more than half an hour, and then they went home to their dwellings.[21]

During the fertility rituals on the island (and particularly during the Matahiti ceremonies), dances by the younger '*arioi* featured genital exposure and public sex. Not surprisingly, the Franciscan monks, who had taken vows of chastity, found these displays traumatic; and they must have protested in ways that affronted the '*arioi*. From this time onwards they were treated with dislike and derision, making their stay on Tahiti a miserable ordeal. When Máximo and Vehiatua arrived back at the mission, they found the house surrounded by an uproarious crowd of 2000 people. Ignoring the tumult, Vehiatua asked the friars for '*ava* from Lima (as they called alcohol), which they refused to give him, and some fish, and ate most of their food, sitting in the doorway of the house, eating plantains and drinking '*ava* until he became befuddled. Afterwards he lay down on Manuel's mattress to rest, with one of his servants fanning him with leaves. It must have been on this occasion that Vehiatua, annoyed by their refusal to give him alcohol and resenting the way that they had treated his mother, presented the Fathers with mountain taro or '*ape*, telling them that it was meant to be eaten raw. When they swallowed it, the '*ape* inflamed their mouths and throats, making them think that they had been poisoned. According to island histories, this trick was greatly relished by his people, who afterwards dubbed Vehiatua *Te-ari'i-no-te-maui* in honour of the trick he had played on the hapless friars.[22]

Later that afternoon the *Águila* arrived back in Vaitepiha Bay. The frigate had made a brief visit to Ra'iatea with Mau'arua, taking the exiled high chief back to his homeland, but they had been unable to anchor in any of the bays because of contrary winds. On 18 January Boenechea had fallen gravely ill and was given extreme unction, handing over the command of the expedition to his senior lieutenant, Gayangos, who decided to return to Tautira. When they arrived off Vaitepiha Bay on 20 January, Tu and Vehiatua came out with their retinues to greet the commander, despite the fact that his illness must have seemed a punishment for the innumerable *hara* or infractions of sacred restrictions by his people. Although the *ari'i* were disappointed that no '*ava* had been brought from Ra'iatea, they presented Gayangos with quantities of pigs and fruit. As Máximo reported to the acting commander, the friars were well but finding it very difficult to cope with the crowds that surrounded the mission each evening, holding a 'continuous orgie'.

On 21 January Gayangos took an armed boat under the command of Don Nicolas de Toledo to Matavai Bay, where the British had anchored; and Vehiatua, Tu and Ari'ipaea decided to accompany him on this excursion. They travelled to Matavai Bay, which Gayangos charted, returning via Hitia'a where their party was given a warm welcome. Reti's people presented Tu with three large roasted tuna, three live pigs, a large cooked pig, and coconuts, breadfruit and bananas. During their absence the chief Pohuetea had visited the ships, which were now being prepared for the voyage back to Peru. As soon as Tu and Vehiatua returned to Tautira, Gayangos summoned the chiefs on board and presented them with gifts from King Carlos III. When Ti'itorea received a gift that seemed less impressive than Vehiatua's, however, he was incensed, calling Gayangos 'bad' and 'miserly'; and Gayangos ordered him to be removed from the frigate. The next day Gayangos and Ti'itorea were reconciled, and when the acting commander asked the chiefs whether or not they agreed that King Carlos III of Spain should be the supreme chief over their island, they all assented except Tu, the paramount chief, who seemed 'somewhat distant' about this proposal.

On 25 January there was a display by *'arioi* dancers; and when it was over, Tu and Vehiatua left the bay with most of their followers for the Matahiti rituals in other districts. Boenechea was in his death throes, and again he was given extreme unction. He asked for the friars to be brought out to the *Águila*, although as soon as they arrived on board they complained to Gayangos that during the ship's absence they had been forced to cook for themselves, draw water and perform other menial tasks at the mission. To placate them, Gayangos ordered a sailor, Francisco Peréz, a man who knew about gardening, the care of livestock and other odd jobs, to look after them during their stay on the island. The friars sat with Boenechea until he died the following afternoon. As soon as the commander took his last breath, the ensign and jack on the *Águila*'s mast were lowered, the ship's bell tolled, and prayers were sung for his soul as his body was laid out in the cabin. At 8 a.m. the next morning the friars and the ship's chaplains held mass, attended by all of the officers; and Boenechea was taken ashore in the captain's boat, escorted by thirty marines with their lieutenant and ensign. As the boat was lowered, the *Águila* fired a salute of seven guns (acknowledging his rank). Chanting and carrying a cross, the Padres escorted Boenechea's body, dressed in his uniform with baton and sword, to the mission house, accompanied by the officers in a solemn procession, and he was buried in a coffin at the foot of the tall Holy Cross that had been erected to mark Spain's dominion over the island. The crowds of spectators were impressed by the wooden coffin and the stone paving that was placed over Boenechea's grave after the burial; although it seemed clear that the Spaniards' high chief had been killed by their gods as a punishment for the *hara* that his people had committed.

Early the next morning, two ship's boys were found to be missing. Tu and Vehiatua, who were on board the *Águila*, set off in hot pursuit of the deserters, assuring Gayangos that they would soon find them. The boys were discovered sleeping in a house at Anuhi, and were immediately taken back to the frigate. During their absence, three of the storeship's crew had threatened mutiny, and Gayangos sent three of his own men to replace them, clapping the offenders in irons. So many of the Tahitians wanted to accompany the ships to Lima that Gayangos was forced to have the frigate searched for stowaways. He decided to allow the navigator Puhoro (from Ma'atea) and the exiled high chief of Ra'iatea, Mau'arua, both of whom had sailed with him to Ra'iatea, to accompany him to Lima; while Andía y Varela chose two unnamed islanders, one from Ra'iatea and the other nominated by Tu, as his pilots. Vehiatua and Tu stayed on board the *Águila* until the last moment, their companions weeping bitterly as they farewelled the Spaniards, especially Taitoa and Tu's mother Tetupaia. As Vehiatua boarded his canoe, Gayangos told him that if any harm was done to the friars, he would return and execute him, set fire to the entire island and kill all of his people. Vehiatua responded mildly that Gayangos need not worry, because his people would look after them and give them fish and fruits; although if they were attacked by the people of Mo'orea, he could not guarantee their safety. At noon on 27 January 1775, the sailors singing their shanties, the ships set sail from Tautira in a fresh breeze, leaving Máximo Rodríguez, the two friars and the sailor Francisco Peréz behind on the beach – 'pretty woebegone', wrote Máximo in his journal, 'in our solitude, with no other refuge than God'.[23]

The voyage back to Lima was uneventful. On 30 January the two ship's boys who had deserted from the *Águila* were flogged over the cannon; and two days later Rurutu, one of the Austral Islands, appeared on the horizon. On 5 February they sighted Ra'ivavae, a new discovery for the Europeans, where Gayangos sent Mau'arua and Puhoro ashore in an armed boat. When he landed on the beach, Mau'arua was greeted by one old man, while other islanders tried to climb into the boat or flicked off the sailors' hats with their spears, laughing heartily. Several days after this visit, while Hervé was working on a large-scale chart of the islands that they had sighted, Puhoro asked him what he was doing and examined the chart intently. When he realised that it represented the islands east of Tahiti, he told Hervé that he had visited all of these places, naming each island and identifying it by the passages through its reef. He reported that there were many more islands in that direction, although he had visited only eighteen of them. When Hervé tried to explain about the four cardinal points, the navigator did not understand him, but told him which of these islands had pearls in their lagoons. He added that Me'eti'a, one of the islands they discussed, was only two days' sail south-east of Tahiti, and that periodically its inhabitants sailed to Tahiti to exchange their pearls for bark-cloth garments. According to Puhoro, Tapuhoe also had pearls in its large lagoon; and all of these islands were inhabited except for an island he called 'Tekokoto'.

When Gayangos, irked by the slow progress that the storeship was making, summoned y Varela on board the frigate, y Varela and his son, who had become quite fluent in Tahitian, talked with Puhoro about navigation in the islands. During these and other conversations, Puhoro dictated a list of fifteen islands to the east of Tahiti, including most of the north-west Tuamotu; and twenty-seven islands to the west, including many of the Society Islands, and Atiu and Rarotonga in the Cook Islands. As he listed each island, Puhoro described its topography and reefs, its main produce, whether or not the island was inhabited, the ferocity or otherwise of its inhabitants, sometimes the name of its ari'i, and how many days it took to sail there from other named islands. Significantly, this list, unlike those dictated by Tupaia to Cook and his companions, included several new islands – 'Pounamu', which was said to have very high mountains and a barren landscape, with plenty of fish, inhabited by cannibals (Te Wai Pounamu, the South Island of New Zealand); 'Fenua Teatea', inhabited by light-skinned people who could speak Tahitian, which was a larger and more fertile island (Aotearoa, the North Island of New Zealand); and 'Vaitahu', a high, very populous and productive island (in fact, a village on the island of Tahuata in the Marquesas)[24] – all of which Hitihiti had visited during Cook's second Pacific voyage.[25] Clearly, the island lists taught in the schools of navigation were constantly updated with information from subsequent voyages.

During this conversation, Andía y Varela also learned that in the islands navigators were known as fa'atere (literally, 'leader').[26] These men made long journeys, using a wind compass that divided the horizon into sixteen parts, with the cardinal points fixed by the rising and setting of the sun; and Andía recorded the name of each wind direction.[27] When setting out from port, the navigator tested the direction and strength of the wind, and assessed the direction of the swells. Using these signs and a feather and palmetto bark pennant on the mast to show any wind shifts, he set his course, using the stars at night and the sun during the daytime to fix his bearings. A *fa'atere* could distinguish the planets from the fixed stars, and they named the succession of stars used to voyage from one island to another after those islands. According to y Varela, they were brilliant navigators:

> Not only do they note by [the stars] the bearings on which the several islands with which they are in touch lie, but also the harbours in them, so that they make straight for the entrance by following the rhumb of the particular star that rises or sets over it; and they hit it off with as much precision as the most expert navigator of civilised nations could achieve.[28]

He also remarked on the uncanny accuracy with which Puhoro predicted the next day's weather each evening, 'a foreknowledge worthy to be envied, for, in spite of all that our navigators and cosmographers have observed and written about the subject, they have not mastered this accomplishment'.[29]

Finally, on 8 April 1775, when the two ships arrived back at El Callao on the Peruvian coast, their commanders hastened to report their findings to the Viceroy; and the four islanders – Puhoro and Mau'arua, the unnamed Raiatean and Tu's man who had sailed on the *Júpiter* – were taken to his palace. Amat was saddened to hear about Boenechea's demise, remarking: 'I felt his death very much due to his goodness and merit.'[30] Once again the Tahitians were housed in the palace, where they were treated with great kindness. During this time, Amat and La Perricholi remained estranged, and both were having other affairs; but the Viceroy was still visiting the theatre, the bullring and cockfights, and no doubt the islanders were taken to some of these entertainments. After only a month in Peru, however, Tu's man contracted smallpox, and like Heiao before him, died of this horrible disease and was buried in Lima.

Matimo and the Friars

Back in Tahiti, as soon as the *Águila* and the storeship *Júpiter* sailed from Tautira, Vehiatua and Tu departed, and Máximo followed them soon afterwards. The young marine was finding his life at the mission station almost intolerable. Fathers Clota and Gónzalez were cantankerous and impossible to please, and they often treated him as a servant. Although he disapproved of some Tahitian customs, Máximo was more at ease with his Tahitian friends than with the Franciscan monks. He was probably part-Indian; and Peruvian popular culture had much in common with life in Tahiti, with its love of festivals, dancing and music, and relaxed attitudes to sex. As a bond friend of both Vehiatua and the paramount chief Tu, Máximo was in a privileged position on the island; whereas in the mission station, the friars treated him harshly. After their disconcerting experiences with the 'arioi the Fathers now feared the islanders, approaching them with a mixture of arrogance and anxiety; and in turn, they were heartily disliked. As the friars quarrelled and complained, Máximo also came to regard them with a degree of contempt. After leaving the mission on 29 January 1775, he travelled with Taitoa as far as Afa'ahiti, walking across the Taravao peninsula (which his companions told him was haunted by *tupapa'u*, the spirits of dead people), to catch a ride by canoe to Vaiari (or Papeari) to meet Vehiatua and Tu, whom he found surrounded by their people.

After welcoming Máximo, Vehiatua quizzed him about Boenechea's funeral. Having heard his account, the *ari'i* told his followers that when someone died, it was better to bury the corpse in the ground according to the Spanish custom rather than to expose it on a platform in the Tahitian way, given the stench and the flies that buzzed around the body. Tu was also present, and he took Máximo to visit his great-uncle who was very ill, lying on the ground clothed only in a bark-cloth girdle. His attendants were fanning him with sprigs of ginger plants; and when Máximo told these people that they were making the sick man worse by giving him a chill, they answered that unless they kept fanning him, his god could not descend on a whirlwind and cure him. The young marine suggested that they should take this man to Tautira where the Fathers could treat him, and eventually they agreed. That night Vehiatua and his companions sat drinking 'ava, and although Máximo wrote in his journal that he was uncomfortable in their company, it is probable that he drank with them.

Early the next morning Máximo crossed the bay and headed south to Vaira'o, where the ari'i Tuivirau greeted him and presented him with gifts of bark cloth, pigs, plantains and coconuts. Afterwards he carried on to Mataoa'e, where the people stripped the clothing from their upper bodies in homage, laying a plantain shoot at his feet and greeting him as their ari'i. The high chief of this district, Tutea, an uncle of Vehiatua, ordered his people to entertain Máximo with a heiva, and nine women and two men danced for him, taking off their bark-cloth garments afterwards and piling them into a pyramid, which they presented to him before a crowd of 2000 people. When he refused to accept their gift, they marvelled at his generosity (according to his account); and when his paddlers arrived, he asked them for some 'ava to give to his hosts as Tutea had none in his district. The next morning Máximo walked to Vaira'o and from there travelled by canoe to Vaiari where he met Vehiatua and Tu, and they set off together with Ari'ipaea for the Taravao isthmus. As they journeyed, Vehiatua II showed Máximo a carved double canoe with an awning that sheltered a remarkable headrest carved in black stone, which he said came from Ra'iatea. When they crossed the isthmus, Tu's sick uncle stayed in his canoe as it was dragged along the track on rollers.

On 2 February they arrived back at Tautira, where Tu's father Teu was waiting for them on the beach, accompanied by a tahu'a (priest). As Tu sat down on the sand, a plantain branch, a bunch of yellow feathers fastened to a stick and a hog were placed before him. The priest delivered an oration, thanking the god of the sea for their safe arrival; and afterwards Tu and Ari'ipaea affectionately greeted their parents. Although as Tu's taio, Máximo was part of this family, he refused to participate in this ceremony, saying that this was not his custom and that he and his people acknowledged only one God, which according to him 'set them a-thinking'.[1]

When Máximo arrived back at the mission, hoping for a warm welcome from the Padres, they scolded him for staying away so long, saying that according to what they had heard, he had been drinking 'ava and sleeping with Tahitian women. Although Máximo indignantly denied these accusations, saying that he had spent all of his time with Tu and Vehiatua, and his friends supported his denials, he had spent a night on his own at

Mata'oae, where he had been welcomed as an *ari'i* and no doubt offered a girl to sleep with. Certainly the Tahitians later told Captain Cook that Máximo liked their women. When Tu's mother Tetupaia and her retinue arrived at the mission house soon afterwards, thinking that they had led him astray the friars turned this 'Great Woman' away. This was a grave insult, because according to island custom a chief never refused his hospitality; and the *taio* relationship between the young marine and Tu meant that the Fathers were bound to share their food with Tu's family.

During Máximo's absence some linen had been stolen from the mission, and Purahi and Ti'itorea accused Manuel's relatives of the theft. The following night when the friars caught a young boy hiding in the rafters of the mission shelter, they were enraged. The Fathers were also angry with the Tautira people for chasing their pigs, although these animals had been entering the villagers' houses and rooting around in their underground storage pits, devouring their *mahi* or fermented breadfruit. On 4 February when one of the Padres caught the villagers chasing one of his pigs, he lost his temper and pelted the people with stones, chasing them into their houses and forcing the occupants to flee in disarray, the women dropping their bark-cloth garments in panic. Later that morning, Máximo and the friars went to Vehiatua and told him that they had decided to move to another district where the people were more respectful. Soon afterwards, Vehiatua, Purahi and Ti'itorea arrived at the mission with some of the local chiefs, holding up plantain shoots as a sign of submission, weeping and saying that they were very hurt by these threats and would soon be leaving the district themselves; and begging the friars not to tell the Spaniards on the frigate that they had been unfriendly. The Fathers agreed, on the condition that the houses near the mission were abandoned so that they would no longer be troubled by their occupants, and Vehiatua agreed to this proposal.

At midday, however, the young *ari'i* suddenly fell ill. When his family sent for Máximo, he found Vehiatua lying in a faint on the ground with his head in his mother's lap. She and her female companions were distraught, while a priest with two plantain shoots stood beside them, praying to the gods for Vehiatua's recovery. Two attendants were fanning the *ari'i* with breadfruit leaves, and when Máximo told them to stop, they said that the breeze allowed the god to descend to relieve the sick man's suffering. Convinced that the *ari'i* had been stricken because he had offended the Spanish god, Vehiatua's family allowed Máximo to take charge of the invalid, even when he ordered a canoe awning to be brought and put Vehiatua inside it, covering him with bark-cloth wrappings and closing up the house with plaited palm-leaf screens. Telling his family to leave the young man in this stifling enclosure, he returned to the mission for supper. Later that evening when some of Vehiatua's relatives came to the mission to report that the young chief was feeling better, they remarked that their god was useless because he had been unable to help the *ari'i*, while the Spanish god was much more powerful. These people presented the friars with a quantity of fish to appease their wrath; and when Máximo and Father Gerónimo went for a stroll that evening they heard the priests in the *marae* beating the drums and calling for the *atua* (god) to come and cure the young chief; and the prayers and drumming carried on all that night.

Ever since the friars had accused Manuel's family of stealing linen from the mission, the boy had been desperate to leave them; and his *ari'i*'s illness was more than he could bear. On 5 February, saying that his mother was sick, Manuel went home to his family. During that day, Tu's family also came to the mission to farewell Máximo, saying that they had decided to return to Pare; no doubt because they were likewise terrified by Vehiatua's sudden illness. When Tu asked for a male and female Spanish piglet during this visit, the friars refused, upsetting the paramount chief, who remarked that they had given piglets to both Ti'itorea and Taitoa. Two days later, anxious to placate the Padres, Vehiatua ordered some of the rebels from the inland valley to work at the mission, erecting a bamboo fence around the kitchen garden and providing food for the Spaniards. Soon afterwards when the Fathers ordered Máximo and the sailor to share the work in the garden, the young marine protested, saying that although he was willing to pull his weight he needed time to write, because the Viceroy had asked him to collect a vocabulary and write a description of life on the island. Unmoved by his protests, the friars retorted that nothing of the sort was mentioned in their instructions, and that 'as to writing, they themselves were sufficient thereunto'[2] – a mistake, as Máximo's detailed journal of his time on Tahiti is infinitely richer than their intermittent jottings. If he was so well educated, they remarked sarcastically, it was remarkable that he had not been promoted by this time; and that as things stood, he must do as they told him. Although frugal living and hard work was part of the Franciscan ethic, most priests in Peru did little or no manual labour, requiring their parishioners to undertake this for them; and these monks were evidently no exception.

That evening when Máximo and Father Gerónimo went to see Vehiatua, they found that he was much worse. Although Máximo had ordered the young chief to stay wrapped up in the canoe awning, Vehiatua protested that it was stifling, and his head was hurting. As they talked, they could hear the local *tahu'a* yelling in the foothills, calling upon the gods to come and relieve the *ari'i*. When a high chief fell ill in Tahiti the priests went to summon the gods, and a herald went around the district dressed in green leaves, warning the people not to light their fires, cook food or go to sea in their canoes.[3] That night Vehiatua's relatives began to arrive from the surrounding districts, bringing bark cloth and other gifts as offerings for his recovery.[4]

Several days later, after dining with Máximo and the friars, Vehiatua had a fit of convulsions. Máximo and Father Gerónimo were summoned, and when they arrived found Vehiatua lying in one person's lap while others kneaded his legs or fanned him with breadfruit branches, and still others ran off to find pigs to offer at the *marae*. Father Gerónimo took his pulse, and finding that it was very weak, went to the mission to fetch oil of almonds. When he gave Vehiatua the oil in a draught of warm water, the *ari'i* coughed up a quantity of phlegm. They left him with his attendants, sweating and with a high fever, and returned to the mission to sleep. The next morning when Máximo went to see the *ari'i*, he found him lying out in the open air, without any shelter, and with offerings of hogs and plantain branches around his feet. He reproached Vehiatua, saying that if he did not follow their instructions they could no longer help him; although in fact the young high chief seemed much better.

Over the next few days the people of the inland valley brought food (including lobsters) for the friars and worked for them, building a fence around the kitchen garden and clearing the ground, where the Fathers planted broccoli, cabbages, endive, lettuces, watermelons, rice, tobacco, garlic and peaches. Despite the help that they were receiving, the Fathers were annoyed with Tu and Ari'ipaea, because when they came to visit Máximo they jumped over the fence into the mission enclosure without permission. Since Máximo had allowed this, they ordered the young marine to share the cooking with the sailor, despite his vehement protests. On 13 February, before Vehiatua and Tu set off for Vaiaotea, the two high chiefs came to farewell the friars. Manuel had not yet returned to the mission, and the Fathers asked Vehiatua to order the boy to come back because his period of leave had expired. The next day when Manuel arrived at the mission, however, the friars rebuked him so sharply for his absence that the boy was sure that he was about to be flogged, and promptly ran off again with his father.

A few days later when Purahi came to visit Máximo, she suggested that the ground in front of the mission house should be paved. To her horror, however, the Padres decided to use stones from Vai'otaha *marae* for this purpose; and although she tried to dissuade them, they would not listen and went with Máximo to take the stones from the *marae*. Aghast at this desecration, Purahi told them that the gods would surely punish her and she could no longer visit the mission, although she sent them a few fresh fish for their supper. At about this time, Father Narciso began to suffer from colic, vomiting and flatulence, which must have seemed a fitting punishment. Máximo's Tahitian was still imperfect, and this led to other misunderstandings. When some local people came to the mission several days later, they told him about Captain Cook, saying that he was the *ari'i* of Matavai Bay, who would return in seventeen months' time. As a patriotic Spaniard, Máximo was offended, replying that Cook would never dare to return to Tahiti while the Spaniards were on the island; but in fact he had misunderstood them. They were only trying to tell him that Cook had left the island seventeen months earlier.

On 19 February Purahi also fell ill. Fearing that the monks had caused her sickness, she asked Máximo to take her to Manuel, saying that the boy had lied to her about the Spaniards; but when Máximo asked the friars whether he could go with her, they refused, saying that he was on the island to act as their interpreter and must stay at the mission. As he remarked philosophically: 'I am beginning to see that they will pass the time in wrangling until there comes a change.'[5] Three days later, Purahi arrived at the mission to farewell Máximo and the Fathers. Her son was now very ill, and she had decided to accompany Tu's family to visit him at Vaiaotea. She wept as she said goodbye; and after they had left, Máximo got some of the local people to fetch several huts in which Tu had stayed during his time at Tautira and bring them to the mission. They hesitated, because Tu had slept in these shelters, making them *ra'a* or sacred; but the young marine insisted, using threats and ordering them to bring stones that had been trimmed for the *marae* to use as flooring and a hearthstone. By now Tautira was almost deserted, with only about eight people remaining in the village. The Tai'arapu people found themselves in a terrible dilemma, torn between their fear of reprisals if they did not do as the Spaniards demanded and their horror at the *hara* (breaches of *tapu*) that Máximo and the Padres were committing; and most of them abandoned the district.

On 25 February when Vehiatua's counsellor Taitoa arrived at the mission, he reported that Vehiatua was now so ill that he was paralysed, and that some of his people were coming to collect Pautu's chest so that it could be offered to the *atua*. After asking for a small live pig, some salt pork from Lima and biscuits and honey for the invalid, which the friars gave to him, Taitoa told them that Vehiatua had ordered the fisherman who looked after his net to keep them supplied with fish, while the 'rebels' in the inland valley had been commanded to supply them with plantains. When he asked Máximo and Father Gerónimo to visit Vehiatua, however, the Fathers refused on the grounds that the mission might be plundered in their absence; and again they asked for Manuel to be brought back to the mission. Later that day, Taitoa talked secretly with Máximo, saying that unless he went with him, the boy would never return; and they went together to Manuel's father's house, where the lad told his family that he was too afraid to go back to the mission because one of the friars and the sailor had threatened him, and 'they were all of them a rough lot'.[6] Even when Taitoa threatened the boy's family with exile if they did not return him to the mission, his weeping parents protested that the Padres would lock him up and carry him off to Lima, and that they could not agree. Some days later, Taitoa told Máximo that Manuel's family had another reason for avoiding the mission, claiming that they had stolen baize, bark cloth and axes from the friars.

Over the next few days, Máximo and the sailor took turns in the garden, transplanting tomatoes and sowing maize while Vehiatua's fisherman went out and fished for them, and the people of the inland gorge supplied them with fresh fish, plantains and bananas. On 5 March when Father Narciso fell ill again with flatulence and aching legs, Máximo gathered purslane ('pigweed') from Vai'otaha *marae* as a medicine to treat him – yet another *hara* or offence against the gods of the island.

Like Máximo, the sailor Francisco Peréz was finding life in the mission unbearable, and he became increasingly unstable. He threw stones at Vehiatua's billy goat, which had chased two of his nanny goats; and when a man at Taitoa's house asked him not to do this, he hurled a stone at him. On 10 March when Vehiatua, who was feeling a little better, arrived back at Tautira with Manuel and his family, he berated the boy's family for their offences against the Spaniards and they apologised profusely. Vehiatua took Manuel into the mission, where the friars welcomed and embraced him. Weeping loudly, however, the boy protested that he did not want to stay there; as the friars 'represented to him the ill he was doing, and that he ought to give heed to the great favour God had shown him in having brought about his baptism, etc., as well as the other kindness he had received from the Lord Viceroy, and other things that were told him for the good of his soul; but it was of no avail, and greatly to our grief, seeing that that soul was being lost'.[7]

The following day while Máximo was in Taitoa's house, talking with Vehiatua, Peréz burst in with a sword in his hand and stabbed one of the islanders who was quietly sitting there. Astonished by this unprovoked attack, Máximo took the injured man to the mission and bandaged his wounds. This man was one of Tu's family, and the Tautira people were terrified that they would be punished for this attack on the *ari'i maro 'ura*'s lineage. The offence committed by the sailor was compounded when Vehiatua asked the friars to give him a young boar so that he could breed it to a sow that he had in his possession. They refused; and when he asked to share their dinner, they likewise denied him. Instead, the monks ordered Máximo to prepare the meal; and as he did so, they complained that he was working too slowly. Infuriated by this treatment, Máximo said that he was not a menial and would not cook for them any more. Father Narciso flew into a rage, retorting that Máximo was not only a servant but mean and unworthy; while Father Gerónimo addressed him sarcastically as 'Señor Don Tal' – 'My Lord Sir So-and-so'. From that time onwards they refused to give Máximo paper and ink for his journal, and he had to write it in secret using a pencil or local dyes.

Later that day, Vehiatua announced that he intended to take the wounded man to Tu at Vaiaotea, and Máximo decided to follow him in order to retrieve a number of items that had been stolen from the mission. When they arrived at Manuel's father's house the next morning, Máximo accused the boy's family of stealing from the friars. One of the people in the house, weeping, handed over a large axe; and although at first Manuel's father protested that he had taken nothing, he eventually surrendered a bolt of cotton cloth. When Manuel arrived shortly afterwards and Máximo asked him to return various things that he had taken from the mission, the boy retorted, 'Not I! You son of a harlot!' In a fury, the young marine grabbed the lad and gave him a thrashing with a club; and when the father tried to stop him, the other people in the house stood there, too frightened to interfere.

As soon as Manuel's father let him go, Máximo went to see Vehiatua and told him what had happened. Upon hearing the story, the ari'i accompanied his taio back to Manuel's house, where he ordered the dwelling to be burned and its inhabitants sent into exile. Manuel's family came out of the house, weeping and begging for forgiveness; and when Máximo interceded on their behalf, Vehiatua told him that their fate was in his hands. After questioning Manuel, his father, and those who had accused them of stealing from the mission, Máximo realised that in fact they had taken much less than their accusers suggested. Although the boy and his father presented their ari'i with plantains and the last lengths of print that remained in their possession, Vehiatua still confiscated their lands and ordered his people to destroy their gardens, leaving only their houses standing.

After Vehiatua and his followers had left the settlement, Máximo followed in another canoe. As they paddled past Te Pari, the precipitous cliffs off the end of south-east Tahiti, a canoe beside them was swamped in the high seas. When Máximo arrived at Vaiaotea that evening, Tu's family greeted him with gifts, weeping; and Pautu appeared and threw himself on his knees before the young marine, crying bitterly. He told him that if the *Águila* came back to Tahiti, he would be happy to go on the ship to Lima, but that he could not live with them in the mission, because of the tales he had heard about the way that the Spaniards were behaving. When Pautu and Máximo began to regale Tu's family with stories about life in Peru and in Spain, they exclaimed in disbelief, saying that they must be insane. After farewelling these people, Máximo carried on to Mata'oae where the local people, who now regarded him as their *ari'i*, performed another *heiva* for him, dancing, singing, presenting him with bark cloth, mats and food, and introducing him to a dwarf who was scarcely three feet tall. After the *heiva*, Máximo returned to Vaiaotea where Vehiatua presented him with a double canoe for the Padres; and he delivered this to the friars, along with the items that he had recovered from Manuel's family.

On 18 March, a man who had been building a fence around the mission arrived, bleeding profusely and begging the Fathers to help him. Apparently this man had turned his wife out of their house, and since then she had been living with her father. That morning when he went to his father-in-law's house to have sex with his unwilling wife, his father-in-law and his wife had attacked him with a Flemish knife, wounding him badly. He dressed the slashes with plants but was eager for some ointment from Lima, saying that because the knife that had cut him was from Lima, he needed medicine from that place to cure him. When the friars refused, he left the mission in disgust, saying that he would not work for them any more. Although he had done his best they had treated him churlishly, and they could look for someone else to help them. The monks knew nothing of Tahitian ideas of reciprocity, according to which all gifts should be returned in generous measure, and the islanders found them stingy and graceless. That afternoon the headman of Tautira, a man named Tarioro, took a piglet from the mission, probably in retribution.

Several days later when Father Gerónimo and Máximo walked up the valley, the local people performed a *heiva* and delivered trimmed stones from various *marae* which the Spaniards used to pave the floor of the mission. The next day Father Narciso suffered another attack of flatulence, and when Máximo went to a *marae* to fetch purslane to treat the friar, a woman pleaded with him, weeping and begging him not to take it from that place, because her son was buried there. Ignoring her protests, he gathered some of the plant, and the next day more stones were brought from the *marae* to pave the mission. Soon afterwards Francisco Peréz also fell ill, and when Máximo went in search of more purslane, he had to go as far as Afa'ahiti where the *ari'i* Tavi presented him with bark cloth, coconuts, plantains, fish and a small quantity of the herb, saying that this was the last of these plants in the district. All the other purslane that grew on the local *marae* had been burnt, no doubt to stop the Spaniards from desecrating these sacred places. By this time the rebels from the valley had stopped supplying them with food and working on the fence; and the friars ordered Peréz to carry out these tasks instead. Several days later when the sailor presented the friars with a formal complaint about his working conditions (which Máximo had written for him), Father Narciso boxed his ears. As Máximo remarked despondently, 'there is no bond between us four, since each one considers himself alone, so that when some are quarrelling, the others are mere lookers-on'.[8]

Although the autumn harvest festival was usually held around this time, attended by crowds of *'arioi* and celebrated with feasting, dancing, skits, boxing, wrestling, shooting arrows and other diversions, on 5 April a messenger reported that Vehiatua was at Vaiari on his deathbed, surrounded by all of the other *ari'i*. Máximo was eager to visit the young high chief, and this time Father Gerónimo gave him permission. He travelled by canoe to Afa'ahiti, where the *ari'i* Tavi gave him a canoe awning as a shelter; and the next morning he accompanied Tavi and his people to Vaiari where they found Vehiatua lying on the laps of some female kin, with all of the objects that he had acquired from visiting ships scattered around him. Because he was suffering from a foreign disease, the priests must have thought the gods of the strangers would be placated by gifts from their native lands. Máximo embraced Vehiatua, who seemed glad to see him. Soon afterwards he noticed a man in the house thumping himself very hard and talking loudly, and when he enquired about this strange behaviour, Vehiatua's attendants explained that this man was possessed by the god, and that his ravings were the words of the *atua*. This individual was taking fine bark-cloth garments from various people in the house, and giving these to others. According to later accounts, men possessed by the gods in this way often wrapped their left arm in bark cloth and spoke in an imperious, vehement tone, trembling, with red, sparkling eyes; and on occasion they performed amazing feats – plunging their arm up to the elbow into a hard-packed pathway, scaling vertical cliffs, or spending hours underwater.[9]

Bewildered by the hubbub, Máximo left the house and went to see some other chiefs of his acquaintance. Later that evening Vehiatua was a little better, although when Máximo tried to persuade him to return to

Tautira, the *ari'i* said that he would not do this until the frigate arrived, because Máximo and his companions had desecrated the *marae* at Tautira and quarrelled with the local people. All the same, he ordered his people to present pigs and bark cloth to the young marine and to keep him entertained. When Vehiatua asked Máximo whether he needed anything else, hoping to secure the favour of the gods of the Spanish, the young marine mentioned a canoe and a net and the carved black stone footstool that he had seen earlier. Vehiatua instructed his people to find the best net that they had and gave him a fine canoe of his that had been named after the *Júpiter*, although he did nothing about the footstool. These gifts sealed a *taio* relationship between Vehiatua and Máximo, and afterwards Vehiatua's people always addressed the young marine as 'Vehiatua'.

Máximo had also heard that Pohuetea's sister-in-law Purutifara had some large pearls in her possession, and was curious to see them. He went to visit her, but when he mentioned the pearls she told him that an *ari'i* from Taha'a called Tepau had taken them and would not give them back to her. Vehiatua's former wife Tautiti also had some pearls; and when Máximo went to see them, he asked her why she and the young *ari'i* had parted. She told him that because they were first cousins, neither her parents nor Purahi had approved of the alliance. Later that afternoon during another visit to Vehiatua, Máximo examined some of the objects that had been placed at his *taio*'s feet, one of which was a book called *Mathematical Tables*, printed by Thomas Page in London; and when he asked for this book, Vehiatua gave it to him.

That evening as Máximo sat talking with Tu's family, they listened with rapt attention, although when he insisted that it was good for women and men to eat together, they protested that if they did this, they would be struck blind or crippled. The next morning, news came that the Papara people had rebelled against Vehiatua, although this district had been awarded to him in the recent peace settlement. When Vehiatua asked Máximo if he would help to suppress the uprising, the young marine replied that peaceful means must be tried first; and a messenger was sent in the name of the Spaniards to Teri'irere to warn him of the dire consequences of his actions. Soon afterwards Máximo returned to the mission in his new canoe, which had been hauled across the Taravao isthmus, bringing the new net with him. When he gave the net to Vehiatua's fisherman, however, asking him to catch fish for the mission, this man remarked that such a request was usually accompanied by gifts of pigs and bark cloth. When Máximo complied, the man added that he was unable to keep this net in his house, because it was *tapu* (having been transported in Vehiatua's canoe), while his house was *noa* (unrestricted or common).

On 13 April, news arrived in Tautira that Vehiatua had recovered from his illness, and was on his way to punish the Papara people for their rebellion. Two days later the Vaitepiha River flooded, sweeping the bodies out of several *marae* and swamping the mission garden and Vehiatua's *'ava* plantations – an ominous portent. That evening, Tavi, the *ari'i* of Afa'ahiti, arrived to report that the uprising in Papara had been suppressed, and that Vehiatua, who was feeling much better, planned to attend the victory celebrations. The next day, however, a messenger came to say that Vehiatua had suffered a relapse, and that two *tahu'a* or priests who were visiting Tautira were wanted to attend the *ari'i* at Vaiari. These were Temaeva, a high-ranking priest from Ra'iatea, and Manea, Amo's brother, the priest who had warned Purea about offending her kinsfolk before the fatal attack on Mahaiatea. After conducting prayers at Vai'otaha *marae*, the two priests set off with messages of sympathy from Máximo and the friars, who promised to visit the sick man soon. Shortly afterwards when Máximo went to Anuhi to borrow a canoe awning for Father Narciso to use during their visit to Vehiatua, Pahairiro's widow greeted him affectionately, but told him that because both her canoe awning and her daughter's were *noa*, they could not be used in Vehiatua's sacred canoe.

On 24 April Father Narciso and Máximo set off in their double canoe to visit the invalid. Stopping en route to rest the paddlers, they were told that the *ari'i* had gone ahead to Vai'uriri. When they arrived there at sunset, they found Vehiatua sitting up in his canoe awning, looking weak and unhappy. He greeted them affectionately and ordered a pig to be sent to their paddlers to reward them for their labours. At daybreak they were woken by the din of a crowd that had gathered outside their shelters, watching a strange flash streaking across the sky. When they cried out that this was their *atua*, Máximo tried to disabuse them; but as some stars appeared in the sky in the trail of the comet, they refused to take any notice. Afterwards when Máximo tried to visit his *taio* Tu, who was staying nearby, he could not make his way through the dense crowds, so he went with Father Narciso to farewell Vehiatua instead, who sent more pigs for their paddlers and asked them to fire off their muskets. They did so and said goodbye, leaving the *ari'i* in tears. When they reached the Taravao inlet, their canoe was hauled across the isthmus and the paddlers took them to Anuhi and then on to Tautira. There Máximo found that Peréz had been afflicted with an eye infection, and the sailor screamed all that night with the pain in his eyes, saying that it was driving him crazy.

On 7 May Máximo set off to visit Vehiatua again, taking some eggs that the sick *ari'i* had requested. He crossed the Taravao isthmus and went by canoe to Vaiari, where his *taio* was waiting. The *ari'i* was now so weak that he had to be supported when he sat up, and he wept as he welcomed Máximo. Unsympathetically remarking that his weakness was his own fault because he had ignored their advice, Máximo urged Vehiatua to return to Tautira for treatment. He also spoke with Purahi and the other chiefs, urging this course of action upon them; and when they eventually agreed, the invalid was put in a canoe with an awning and taken that evening to Toahotu. The next morning Máximo accompanied his *taio* to Vaira'o, where a number of boys who had been fattening themselves with breadfruit paste or *popoi* were presented to the *ari'i*, their bodies oiled, wearing scarlet loincloths, and their faces shaded by a plaited sunshade. This *huapipi* ritual (as Máximo called it), a celebration of fertility and prosperity, marked the progress of these boys through the grades of the *'arioi* society.[10] Reti, who attended this ceremony, explained to Máximo how his people had recovered one of Bougainville's lost anchors off Hitia'a by using large canoes and very thick ropes. It had taken them an entire day and night to raise it, and when they found that the iron was too hard to be fashioned into tools, they had given the anchor as a present to Puni, the *ari'i maro tea* of Borabora.

When they arrived at Vaiaotea three days later, his people wept to see Vehiatua so weak and wasted – an ominous sign for their collective well-being. The *tahu'a* went to the *marae* to pray for his recovery, and during these ceremonies no fires were allowed to be lit in the village. The next day Vehiatua's condition deteriorated, and his priests stood in the sea to pray for him and laid plantain branches around his house. Máximo visited the sick man and wrapped him up to induce a sweat, although his attendants tried to prevent this, saying that they had to keep on fanning to allow the god to descend into his body. Later, Máximo urged his *taio* to carry on to Tautira, but Vehiatua replied that his priests would not allow this because his god had not yet appeared at the *marae*, although the priests had gone out into other districts to summon him. The young marine carried on without his friend, and that night he slept at Ahui.

During that night, one of the paddlers, who was sleeping in the same shelter as Máximo, began to yell and walk backwards into the sea, gesturing wildly to indicate that he could see a *tupapa'u* (spirit of the dead). Máximo, who was alone with this man, tried to calm him; but when he saw that the paddler might drown himself, he summoned their companions. They arrived in great consternation, and placing a plantain shoot at the feet of this man, begged the *atua* not to harm him; and when the man cried out that one of his friends had just died, naming him, they went to check and found this man sleeping peacefully. The next morning Máximo carried on to Irimiro where Manuel approached him in tears, begging his pardon for deserting the mission. He had been to Teti'aroa, but returned home because he did not like it on the islets; adding that when the *Águila* returned, he would like to go with them to Lima. The boy was still unwilling to return to the mission, however, because of the outrages that the friars had committed; and later that afternoon Máximo returned on his own to Tautira.

On the evening of 17 May there was a violent thunderstorm. As lightning flashed and thunder boomed in the hills, the Vaitepiha River flooded again. Early the next morning the friars heard that Vehiatua was going to Fenua'ino islet off Vaiuru'a Harbour (where the worship of 'Oro had first been introduced to Tahiti) to offer sacrifices to his *atua*, presumably as part of the rituals to mark the setting of the Pleiades (Matari'i-i-raro) three days later, when the Season of Scarcity formally began.

Several days later when a leading man of Tautira fell ill, the sacred canoe was prepared for the invalid and the friars treated him with oil of almonds, improving his condition. The mission party were still quarrelling, however, and when Father Narciso rebuked Peréz for overworking some of his local helpers, the sailor went off in a huff to live with his friends at Tautira. On 31 May a messenger arrived with word that Vehiatua had arrived at Fenua'ino, where Máximo and Father Narciso decided to visit him, hoping to 'induce him to dismiss the tahua [*tahu'a* – priests] who were imposing upon him with their pretences and eating up his pigs without giving him any physic'.[11] The Tautira people warned Máximo that when the human sacrifice was offered at the *marae* on the islet the next day, no one would be allowed to light their fires, travel in their canoes or walk on the pathways, so they set off at once, announcing their arrival at Vaiuru'a by firing their muskets. Vehiatua sent a canoe to fetch them, and when they arrived at the islet they found the *ari'i* gravely ill, and offered him a meal of fried fish and biscuits.

That night Máximo and Father Narciso slept on the islet; and the next morning they presented Vehiatua with a mattress, baize sheets and a large blanket, receiving a baked sucking pig and a large pig for their paddlers in return. There were no women on this islet, because according to Máximo 'they have no place in these functions nor is their presence tolerated'.[12] While the young marine was talking with Vehiatua, urging him to stop the prayers of his priests as these were not making him any better, a man possessed by the *atua* rushed towards Father Narciso with a stone in his hand, ready to strike him down. Taitoa grabbed the man and sat him down by Vehiatua, in order that 'he might blurt out the tomfooleries that came into his head',[13] which were thought to be prophetic sayings. When Vehiatua remarked that if anyone interfered with this man they would die, Máximo immediately demanded his musket so that he could shoot him; although when the attendants begged him desperately to be still or he would make his *taio*'s illness worse, he relented. Before the human sacrifice was offered at the *marae*, Máximo and Father Narciso left the islet, 'not desiring to witness any more barbarisms'.[14]

On 5 June Máximo was invited to Tautira to take part in a *ta'urua* or distribution of pigs and bark cloth; and that night Vehiatua and his retinue arrived from Vaiaotea. The *ari'i* now had a severe cough, his arms and legs were paralysed, and he was running a high temperature; and the friars arranged for him to be shifted to a big house near the mission where they gave him oil of almonds in a draught of warm water, which relieved him. In the middle of that night when Máximo went to see his *taio*, he found him eating two coconut shells filled with fermented breadfruit. The young chief tried to hide the meal when he saw his friend, who reproved his attendants for giving Vehiatua this sort of food, pointing out that despite all the pigs that they were sacrificing to the gods, Vehiatua's health was not improving. The following day the *ari'i* felt a little better; and when the friars applied an ointment to his knees which relieved his pain, he was able to move around. Over the following days the Spaniards began to treat Vehiatua, feeding him Spanish dishes – egg flip flavoured with cinnamon (which he found too sweet), chicken stew, wood pigeon, maize porridge, rice and chocolate; and treating his knees with various ointments and a heated mixture of wine and anise. Father Narciso also shaved Taitoa in front of Vehiatua's people, to their amazement. When the *ari'i*'s fever dropped he was able to walk again, and soon afterwards a crowd of 3000 people gathered at Tautira to celebrate his recovery, entertained by the *'arioi* with dancing, skits and drumming.

On 14 June a group of boys who had spent a month ritually secluded in a canoe shed, wrapped only in thin bark cloth, eating and resting in order to make themselves pale and fat, were brought, glistening with coconut oil, for another *huapipi* ceremony. The leader presented each of these boys in turn to Vehiatua, announcing his name and district as the boy gave the *ari'i* a gift of bark cloth and was admitted to the *'arioi* society. Afterwards the people rushed among the boys to seize their multi-coloured loincloths, although on this occasion the boys wore two *maro* to make sure that when the outer one was removed they were not left naked. After the scramble, the drummers gave a performance, followed by an *'arioi* skit about a man with a jealous wife. The *'arioi* leader had the crowd in fits of laughter, and whenever the drums sounded, the *'arioi* chorus stood in a row, following his movements as they bent backwards and forwards, swaying in time to the music, gesticulating and moving their bodies very fast without shifting from their places.

The winter solstice on 21 June was fast approaching, when the gods would depart for the Po, the dark world of the spirits, and the *'arioi* would return to their homes. These rituals, which had also been performed during Wallis's visit to the island, ensured that the gods would return to Tahiti for another Season of Plenty. According to Moerenhout's later account, the ceremonies for this festival were particularly brilliant, with rituals at the *marae* followed by 'banquets, races, games, combats'.[15] On this occasion the *huapipi* ceremony at Tautira was followed by a *heiva* every afternoon over the next seven days, with drumming and dancing displays, wrestling matches, cockfighting and archery, watched by thousands of people who kept arriving from the various districts. Bark cloth and fine mats were presented to Vehiatua, while the friars continued to treat him with their concoctions – chicory syrup, syrup of violets, chocolate, and a dressing of 'frog plaster'. Despite this bizarre regime the young *ari'i*'s health improved markedly; and when one of the visitors stole a hen from the mission, Vehiatua threatened to have him killed, his eyes gouged out and his body offered as a sacrifice to the gods at Taputapuatea *marae* (presumably 'Utu-'ai-mahurau *marae*, the only *marae* on Tahiti at this time to hold an image of 'Oro). When another of Vehiatua's kinsmen from the district of Atehuru fell ill, he was also treated by the friars.

On 24 June, according to the Padres, 'a vast number of people arrived before the sun was up, and struck terror with their disorderly voices and yelling. They did their *Heyba*, which lasted an hour, without drums, and brought their performance to a close by all repeating one particular word (whose meaning we did not understand) over and over again together, with such force and loud yelling that it appalled one.'[16] This was almost certainly the *pa'iatua* ceremony, performed before each of the great seasonal festivals (including the farewell to the gods),[17] when a high chief was being installed, a new *marae* was founded, or in times of distress, when there was a drought or the high chief was thought to be dying,[18] to recharge the god-images at the *marae* with *mana* or ancestral power. Messengers were sent out to tell the people that the *marae* was about to be cleansed and the gods awoken and summoned:

> Awake and come tomorrow
> Bathe yourselves
> Feel your faces
> Draw on the white girdle
> And sit upon the lawn

To recite the *ahoa* (life-giving)
For weeding the *marae*
It is the awakening of the *ari'i*
The awakening of the people . . .
Sacredness tomorrow
Weeding of the *marae*
And in the early morning following
Awakening of the gods
The gods above, the gods below
The gods of the ocean, the gods of the land;
The gods within, the gods without,
They will all come to the ordinance
It is sacredness, holiness![19]

As the great *marae* drum sounded, people doused their fires and silenced their children. During the following day the *marae* was ritually weeded and cleansed by the chiefs, posts were erected as perches for the alighting gods, and that night the priests sent out spirit messengers to summon the *atua*. On the third and final morning the head priest would lead a procession to the *marae*, followed by four men carrying the image of the god of the *marae* in a portable god-house, while all the other priests carried the images of the gods of their districts in their arms, shouting '*Ho! Ho! Ho!*' to summon the *atua*. At the *marae*, the gods were unwrapped and oiled with scented oil, like the bodies of dead chiefs; and new red and yellow feathers were exchanged for old, sacred feathers being taken from the body of the main god of the *marae* and placed in the hollow images of the other gods to renew their power. After a sacred male pig was sacrificed, the gods were farewelled, and the participants were released from their sacred restrictions; followed by feasting and celebrations.

On this occasion, it must have been the loud '*Ho! Ho! Ho!*' to summon the gods that had terrified the friars. As mentioned earlier, many of the missionaries at Ocopa (the missionary establishment in the Amazon where Father Narciso and Father Gerónimo had been trained) had recently been killed by local Indians, and the friars there feared the Inca rituals, which they associated with human sacrifice. It is not surprising that during the farewell to the gods the Padres were intimidated by the huge crowds that had gathered at Tautira. Until this time there had been no *tahu'a* or priests at the festivities, because Vehiatua had banished them while he was being treated by the Spaniards; but they returned for this ceremony. The feasting and celebrations continued, and four days later there was an archery contest. The next day, the friars' pet monkey died, greatly mourned by the islanders; and on 2 July Máximo left Tautira to visit Tu, his other *taio*.

That afternoon Vehiatua fell ill again with a racking cough and high fever. Two days later there was loud drumming at Vai'otaha *marae* as a *tahu'a* made a long speech to a large, hushed crowd. During this oration the friars heard their own names mentioned, along with the names of Máximo, Francisco, Ti'itorea and Taitoa, although that was all that they understood. As Vehiatua's condition worsened, the *heiva* carried on for several days until 7 July, celebrating the smaller breadfruit harvest that occurred at about that time, when the *ari'i* finally took the *tahu'a*'s advice and left Tautira for his *marae* on Fenua'ino islet in Vaiuru'a Bay. Ten days later he returned to Tautira, still in a high fever, and asked the friars for a meal of sheep meat, biscuit and plantains. In the tussle over his treatment between the friars and the *tahu'a*, the young *ari'i* was vacillating between his own beliefs and those of the Spaniards. On 18 July Máximo arrived back at Tautira laden with bark cloth and mats, accompanied by four men struggling to carry a sacred stone bowl that he had been given during his two-week excursion around the island.

After leaving Tautira, Máximo had travelled up the east coast of the island. At Afa'ahiti, he had been entertained by Purahi, Vehiatua II's mother, and when he arrived at the large, well-populated district of Hitia'a the *ari'i* Reti had presented him with two roasted pigs and bales of bark cloth. At Maha'ena, the southern boundary of Tu's territories, the local *ari'i* showered him with gifts, which included an English cat left by Captain Cook and his people; and the young marine carried on to Ti'arei, where Tu's younger brother Ari'ipaea, another of his *taio*, was the high chief. Although Ari'ipaea (known as 'Hinoi' at this time) had been absent, his people greeted Máximo with a roasted pig and bark cloth, also addressing him as 'Hinoi'. The next morning Máximo set off for Onohea, a place belonging to Tu's mother Tetupaia; and later that day he arrived at Ha'apaino'o (or Papeno'o), a large and populous district where the *ari'i* was another brother of Tu (presumably his youngest brother Vaetua). On 5 July when Máximo was about to leave for Matavai Bay, this brother loaded two roasted pigs, two fishing nets and some bark cloth into his canoe. He arrived at Matavai Bay at sunset, where the local *ari'i* and his people greeted him warmly. As the crowds pressed around, this man took Máximo into one of the houses and posted a guard outside. Although a messenger was sent to invite Tu to Matavai Bay, Ari'ipaea arrived at midnight, addressing Máximo as 'Hinoi' (as he and Máximo had exchanged names), weeping and begging him to come with him to see Tu at Pare.

'Umete *from Taputapuatea, Tahiti*

The next morning the young marine was taken on a tour of Matavai Bay, a densely populated district, and Point Venus, where 'Tute' (Cook) and 'Pono' (Furneaux) had set up their fort. When they arrived at Pare later that day, Tu's huge retinue greeted him with joy, the chiefs honouring the paramount chief's *taio* by draping him with many lengths of bark cloth; and he slept in his canoe awning next to Tu's that night.

The following day, Tu's people showed Máximo some animals that Cook had given them – spaniels, goats, pigs, a goose, two sheep – and some ironware and British cloth, draped over the rafters of a great *'arioi* house. He gave them small knives and seeds, and on 8 July they presented him with gifts of fishing nets, canoes, food and bark-cloth clothing. The next day, Tu and his retinue escorted the young Peruvian to the boundary of this fertile, wealthy district, where his *taio* asked him if there was anything that he wanted. Máximo had heard about a large, black stone bowl that Tu had in his possession, and in reply he asked his *taio* for this sacred object. Although this *'umete* (bowl) was a prized relic, held at 'Utu-'ai-mahurau *marae* in the Atehuru district, along with the image of 'Oro and the *maro 'ura* brought from Ra'iatea to Papara, a chief could not refuse a *taio*'s request. Tu ordered the priests to bring the stone bowl to Máximo, and farewelled his friend in tears. When Máximo and Ari'ipaea arrived at Atehuru on 10 July, they were greeted at Pohuetea's house and presented with gifts of bark cloth, while another fiery trail (no doubt a meteor) streaked across the sky, watched by an uneasy crowd.

On 12 July Ari'ipaea and Máximo went via Puna'aui'a to Pa'ea, where Ari'ipaea, holding up a plantain branch, went with his *taio* to Taputapuatea *marae* to fetch the great stone bowl. He told Máximo that when the rituals to install a new *ari'i maro 'ura* of Tahiti were carried out at this *marae*, one part of the gathering cried out '*Ari'i!*' while the other part yelled '*Maeva!*' ('Welcome!'). As four men struggled to lift the sacred bowl into his double canoe, Máximo noticed a number of skulls lying on this *marae* (which his companions told him belonged to human sacrifices), along with three baked pigs on a sacrificial platform, and a small woven rush bower for the god. After handing over the stone bowl, Ari'ipaea returned to Pare. When he woke up early the next morning, however, Máximo found that the sacred *'umete* had vanished. Upon questioning the local people, he learned that one of Vehiatua's uncles had taken the stone bowl and buried it, but it was soon retrieved. Since Vehiatua had fallen ill, many of the islanders believed that the chief had been stricken by the Spanish god, and they were terrified of angering any of the mission party; and because Máximo was a *taio* of the leading chiefs on the island (Tu, Ari'ipaea and Vehiatua), they did not dare to disobey him.

On 14 July Máximo's party carried on to Papara, which he described as the largest district in the island, and densely populated. The young marine added that after the recent wars the district had been divided in half, one half being allocated to Purahi and Vehiatua, and the other to Amo – no doubt the reason for the recent uprising, when the Papara people refused to accept Vehiatua II as their *ari'i*. Amo greeted Máximo, giving him a pair of baked pigs and some bark cloth, and when he left the district on 16 July the young marine travelled by land, the stone bowl carried by his bearers, for fear that it would capsize their canoe off Mahaiatea *marae*. After he made brief visits to the districts of 'Atimaono, Vai'uriri and Vaiari, where he was showered with more gifts, his canoe was hauled across the Taravao isthmus. Máximo returned on foot to Tautira, where he heard that Vehiatua was once again very ill. As they approached the village, the drums were beating at Vai'otaha *marae* where prayers were being offered for Vehiatua's recovery.

When Máximo went to see Vehiatua the next morning, 19 July, his *taio* wept and complained that the friars had refused to treat him during his absence; and as Máximo remarked: 'I could not utter a word, for I knew he had right on his side.'[20] When Vehiatua asked for more of the ointment that had been applied to his legs, relieving the pain, Máximo, reluctant to tell him that the friars would not give it to him, assured him that it was all gone.

Over the next few days, there was a constant racket of chanting, flute music and loud drumming at Vai'otaha *marae*. The priests made speeches, praying, singing and chanting until past midnight each night; and on the evening of 22 July when prayers and a flute concert were performed in the invalid's house, one of the onlookers was possessed by the *atua*. The next morning they heard women crying loudly and people shouting out in Vehiatua's house; and when he went to investigate, Máximo found that his *taio* was on his deathbed. Purahi begged for his help, saying that if only the friars would treat her son, she would give them all of his possessions. The friars sent her a little medicine, and later they noticed a single line of men and boys carrying pigs and plantain branches to the *marae*, where they laid down their offerings and tried to summon the god.

On 24 July, Vehiatua was feeling a little better, and when he yawned the *tahu'a* declared that the god had entered his body, and that in ten days' time he would be cured. The next day a man possessed by the god arrived at Vehiatua's house, 'beating his chest with furious blows from both fists, rocking his head like a maniac, and making frightful grimaces with his eyes and mouth'.[21] This man declared that after some of Vehiatua's relatives had taken a sacred mat and two files belonging to the deceased chief Taitoa, his spirit had entered Vehiatua's body. If he was to be cured, these items must be returned immediately. After the objects were handed over, the *tahu'a* declared that Vehiatua would now recover, and they carried the sick man to the *marae* so that the god could restore his spirit to his body.

Three days later, Vehiatua took another turn for the worse, and on 27 July Purahi came to the friars in tears, again saying that her son was dying. When Máximo arrived and found his *taio* outside on a platform, he ordered the attendants to take him inside; although the news soon came that men had gone out to kill three human sacrifices to be offered at Vai'otaha *marae*. Purahi had begged the Padres to treat Vehiatua; although Father Narciso was willing, Father Gerónimo refused, saying that the *ari'i* would surely die and the people would blame them. That night a man from the inland gorge was killed as a sacrifice, and the Spaniards were told that four more human sacrifices were required. Fearing that they themselves might be offered up by these 'inhuman pagans', the friars barricaded themselves inside the mission station, lighting a lantern and intermittently firing their muskets to frighten the Tahitians;[22] although afterwards, when some of Vehiatua's family approached the mission, crying out '*Pare Gerónimo, mata'u, mata'u!*' – 'Father Gerónimo, we are terrified!' – Gerónimo told them that he had only been cleaning his *pupuhi* (gun).

The following day, a huge crowd arrived at Tautira to lament Vehiatua's illness. They formed into a procession, the women walking four by four, cutting themselves with shark's teeth, catching the blood on bits of white bark cloth, smearing it on their bodies until they were bloody all over and wailing '*Aue! Aue!*' As the friars reported: 'This immense throng came uttering loud lamentations with wailing and words which showed how great was the grief that was oppressing the hearts of these barbarians.'[23] The men came behind the women, laying down plantain branches for the god and small pigs for the *ari'i*, while the women presented him with large quantities of bark cloth. According to later accounts, when a high chief was on his deathbed, some of his people processed to the *marae* with ropes around their necks, offering themselves as sacrifices; and perhaps while the mission party were huddled in their station, this also happened.[24] Later that night there was loud yelling as the priests ran along the beach, summoning up the gods and begging them to return from the Po. Vehiatua suffered further convulsions, and the Spaniards were told that as soon as he died, the mission station would be plundered. Fearing for their lives, they kept guard until midnight. At midday the next day Vehiatua was carried in a litter to the mission, where the friars placed him on a couch. When the *ari'i*'s spokesman asked them, 'Are you angry?', they answered that they were not; and when he asked, 'Do you want to go away? Because if so we will be sorry,' Máximo replied that their only concern was that they would be plundered when Vehiatua died. The spokesman then assured them that the man who had made this threat had already been banished from Tautira. The friars castigated the sick man for allowing human sacrifices to be offered for his recovery, saying that such a thing would not be allowed in Lima; and shortly afterwards Vehiatua was carried away from the mission.

The following day Peréz quarrelled with another of the Tautira people, wounding him with his sword; and later that afternoon, hearing that a man and his son from Hitia'a had been killed and brought as human sacrifices to Vai'otaha *marae*, Máximo and Father Narciso went along a secret path and saw the bodies, plaited into palm-leaf bundles and hung on a pole between two trees. As soon as the *tahu'a* saw the two Spaniards, they ordered them to leave; although later the friars returned to their hiding place and saw another body being carried onto the *marae*. Fearful that the people might attack the mission, they kept watch again all that night. On 2 August they heard that the human sacrifices had now been taken to Taputapuatea (as 'Utu-'ai-mahurau *marae* was called at this time, because the image of 'Oro was kept there), and that one more sacrifice was still required. Although Ti'itorea and Purahi came to the mission in floods of tears, begging the friars to treat Vehiatua, again they refused to give him any medication.

On 6 August, hearing loud shouting and exclamations of grief, Máximo,

Peréz and the friars retreated into the mission house and barred the door. In the early morning a chief came to fetch Máximo, saying that Vehiatua wanted to speak to his *taio* one last time, and the young marine agreed to visit him. Máximo was afraid, because it was pitch black and people were milling around, yelling and screaming as drums beat frantically at the *marae*. As he was paddled across the Vaitepiha River, he saw pigs being taken as offerings to Vai'otaha *marae*. When he arrived at Vehiatua's house, his family embraced him, weeping loudly; and when he took his friend's pulse, he found that it was so weak it was almost imperceptible. Vehiatua was lying across the laps of his mother and his other female relatives, surrounded by all of his treasures; and just fifteen minutes after Máximo's arrival, he expired.

As Purahi abandoned herself to grief, groaning and weeping, Máximo gazed at the corpse – that of a fair-skinned, well-built youth about eighteen years old with tattoos on his lips, the palms of his hands and the soles of his feet. Vehiatua II had been an amiable and good-humoured friend, treating his *taio* (whom the islanders had named 'Oro-iti-maheahea – 'pale-faced, little 'Oro' – after the god) with tolerant affection. Máximo stayed with the mourners for a while before returning to the mission; and after mass when he returned with Father Gerónimo, they found Purahi clinging to her son's corpse – which lay stretched between two canoes under an awning, covered with striped, coloured bark cloth and adorned with a coronet of black feathers – slashing her upper body with a shark's-tooth instrument and covered with blood.[25] As soon as she caught sight of Father Gerónimo, Purahi burst into bitter reproaches, berating him for his refusal to treat Vehiatua, and he beat a hasty retreat; although she begged her 'son' Matimo to stay with her.

During that day no one went out fishing and no cooking fires were lit. Later that evening when a mourning party of Ahui people arrived at Tautira, armed with clubs, slings and weapons, Purahi sent them a messenger, begging them not to plunder the mission. In Tahiti, it was the custom when a high chief died for the inhabitants of the neighbouring districts to approach the enclosure where his body lay and ask to be admitted. When they were refused, this led to a fight in which the visiting mourners were always victorious.26 Concerned that these men might attack the mission, Purahi sent her younger son Tetuaounumaona (or Natapua),27 a good-looking boy about six years of age, to the mission to protect the friars, where they taught the child to make the sign of the cross and bless himself. Purahi also sent men to climb coconut trees so that they could give an advance warning of any party approaching the village. Fortunately, the Ahui chief was already at Tautira, and when the mourners from his district appeared he went to them with a plantain branch in his hand and told them not to harm the local people. The next morning when Vehiatua's body was taken to Vai'otaha *marae*, Purahi wept and slashed herself mercilessly, careless of her own suffering. She had eaten and drunk nothing since her son's death; although when Máximo tried to comfort his 'mother', she relented a little, and her family asked him to stay with Purahi to look after her. Over the next two days there were constant prayers and drumming at the *marae*, and the people stayed silent, lighting no cooking fires and fasting.

On 10 August a large crowd arrived from Vaiaotea, bringing gifts for Tetuaounumaona, Vehiatua's heir and successor. That night there was an eclipse of the moon – an evil omen indicating that a god was angry and devouring the planet.[28] Early the next morning messengers arrived with the news that Tu was now seriously ill; and that the Papara people were sending a human sacrifice for Vehiatua to Taputapuatea *marae*. Over the days that followed, crowds of people arrived from Mata'oae, Vaiari and Matavai with gifts of bark cloth and other treasures for the new *ari'i* and provisions for their own chiefs; and on 15 August a *pahi* landed from Ra'iatea, loaded with bark cloth, as a gift for Vehiatua III. Five days later Máximo and Father Narciso shot two sacred birds, but when they served one of these to the new *ari'i*, he refused to eat it, saying that it would make his eyes spin in their sockets. The next morning a party arrived from Atehuru headed by a man wearing a Chief Mourner's costume; and later more people arrived from Vaiaotea with gifts of bark cloth. Two weeks later, as the Vaiari people were leaving Tautira, Viriau, a very beautiful chieftainess from the village, collapsed with a pain in her chest; and when Máximo tried to bind a bandage around it, his friends told him to stop this or he would make her husband jealous. According to their account, she had been possessed by the spirit of Vehiatua II, her first cousin.

The mission party were now longing for the *Águila* to return. They set up a flagpole on the hill overlooking Tautira where they hoisted a home-made flag of bark cloth decorated with the Spanish arms. After the mourning rituals, Vehiatua's successor went to the islet in Vaiuru'a Bay to pray to his *atua* and eat turtle, a sacred food; and on 18 September he and his retinue returned to Tautira where a ceremony was conducted at Vai'otaha *marae*, and the chiefly women were admitted for a special ceremony. According to the islanders, this was a rare privilege, as women were not usually permitted to attend *marae* rituals. The spring equinox on 21 September was approaching, and most of their visitors were leaving the district for the celebrations. On 1 October when Máximo's clothes were stolen from his chest, he set off in hot pursuit of the thieves, chasing them as far as Vaiari;

and to Pare, where he asked Tu to retrieve his stolen property. That evening, Tu took his *taio* to an *'arioi* performance at a 'theatre' in Pare, where skits were performed to the amusement of the people. Máximo stayed that night with Teu and Tetupaia, talking with them about government on the island, music, and other customs for the account of Tahitian life that he was writing for the Viceroy.

The following day a high priest called Rae came to complain to Tu that Tu's own uncle had slept with his (Rae's) wife. After hearing his story, the paramount chief decided to exile his uncle for this offence, along with his family and even their dead relatives (whose bodies had been mummified and kept near their homesteads). Distraught, the uncle begged Máximo to intercede for them, and when Máximo spoke on their behalf, Tu relented. The next morning the offenders entered Tu's house with very slow steps, bared to the waist and looking downcast, carrying offerings of bark cloth, feather plumes and other treasures which they presented to the *ari'i* to requite their *hara* or wrongdoing. Soon afterwards Máximo decided to return to Tautira, accompanied by Ari'ipaea as far as Atehuru, where Pohuetea entertained them and delivered up the thief who had stolen his clothes. Although Pohuetea declared that this man should be tied up and thrown in the sea, Máximo decided that his punishment should be commuted to a sentence of banishment.

When Máximo returned to Tautira, Peréz and the friars were still squabbling. A fight broke out; and when he tried to separate them, Máximo got a thrashing. After the spring equinox, it was the custom for the *'arioi* to gather; and on 17 October people from all over Tahiti-iti began to arrive at Tautira with gifts of pigs and rolls of bark cloth for Vehiatua's younger brother, who was about to be installed as the *ari'i rahi* of southern Tahiti. There were speeches inside the chief's house, and during a great gathering at Vai'otaha *marae*, prayers were offered to the local deity Punua, along with other ceremonies (presumably the installation rituals) that the Spaniards did not witness. Afterwards there was a day of speech-making, dancing and other celebrations, followed by a great feast with twelve baked pigs, when the guests scrambled for their portions. Tired of the friars, Máximo had decided to set up his own household. On 30 October 1775 while he was working on his new house, helped by about five hundred people, messengers came to him to say that the *Águila* had been seen off the south coast of the island; and Máximo and Ti'itorea immediately boarded his double canoe and hastened out to the frigate.

Although the King had ordered the Viceroy of Peru to establish a permanent mission on Tahiti, the friars were now desperate to leave the island. When a large double canoe towed the *Águila* in to the bay, the Fathers sent

a letter to her new commander, Don Cayetano de Lángara, begging him
to take them back to Lima. After almost a year among 'a barbarous and
inhuman people', they said, their lives were at risk; and they implored
de Lángara to take them on board with their livestock and possessions.
Although some people might say that the Tahitians were 'gentle, affable,
well disposed and very friendly', the Padres insisted that this was only the
case when they were given frequent gifts; and on a number of occasions
– when a *tahu'a* or priest holding a stone had lunged at Father Narciso on
the islet off Vaiuru'a, for instance; or when people came to plunder the
mission after the death of Vehiatua, and had to be stopped from attacking
them – they had been in imminent danger. When de Lángara wrote back
to them, asking whether a mission could succeed on the island, the Fathers
answered in desperation, protesting that the Tahitians had 'a deeply rooted
belief in their sham god; in their errors they are blind to reason, in their
customs inhuman, and in their sacrifices execrable. They are people who
allow offenders to go unpunished; yet take the lives of innocent people.'[29]
They flatly refused to stay in Tautira unless an armed guard was left to
protect them; and de Lángara finally relented, allowing them to board the
ship with all their livestock except the chickens, which he said they should
give to Purahi, Vehiatua III and Ti'itorea, and any of the others who had
befriended them.

When the *Águila* had sailed from El Callao for this third voyage to
Tahiti, Mau'arua, the exiled high chief of Ra'iatea, had refused to leave
Lima, while the Raiatean who had sailed on the storeship was already
dead. Only the navigator Puhoro returned to Tahiti on this occasion,
receiving an ecstatic welcome from his family. After the frigate's arrival,
Máximo decided to return home to Lima; and when he went to say goodbye to his 'mother' Purahi, she wept bitterly, promising to look after the
mission house and all of its contents. As he said goodbye, he promised that
he would return to Tahiti. This time no islanders were allowed to sail on
the frigate – because, of the eight Tahitians who had visited Lima, four
had now died. The *Águila* sailed from Tautira on 12 November, towards
the end of the Season of Scarcity, heading back to Peru and arriving in El
Callao on 25 February 1776. When he received de Lángara's report, Amat
was furious that the mission had been abandoned, fulminating against
the friars for their 'lack of apostolic zeal'; although he was pleased with
Máximo's diary, his account of Tahitian customs, the great stone bowl
from Taputapuatea and other rare artefacts, thanking the young marine
by making him a halberdier in his company of archers.

The Viceroy was distracted at this time, however, and none of the items
that Máximo had brought was sent to Spain. In November 1775 Amat and

La Perricholi had been reconciled and no longer tried to hide their infatuation. When Micaela returned to the theatre she was greeted with a standing ovation, and Amat gave her a magnificent coach in which to ride through the streets of Lima. When news of this scandal reached the royal court, accompanied by rumours of corruption, Amat was recalled as Viceroy of Peru, and in May 1776 his successor arrived in Lima. Although Amat had a strong interest in Tahiti, the new Viceroy did not share his enthusiasm. The great stone bowl from Taputapuatea was given to his major-domo, who took it to his house where it was used for washing dishes in the kitchen – a terrible desecration, because cooked food is inimical to *tapu* or sacred power. As for Máximo Rodríguez's account of Tahitian customs, his vocabulary of Tahitian and various other precious artefacts that he had brought from the island, these were all lost. Fortunately, in 1788, after reading a Spanish version of Cook's journal of his third voyage, Máximo handed a copy of his diary to Amat's successor and reminded him of Tu's gift to the King. The stone bowl was retrieved and sent with Máximo's diary to the Secretary of State for the Indies; and Máximo was rewarded with a pension.

Over the years that followed, it is possible that Matimo and Mau'arua sometimes visited each other in Lima to discuss their extraordinary adventures. Amat's successors had other priorities, though, and this was the last Spanish expedition sent to the island. As for the stone bowl, it still survives and is now held in the National Museum of Anthropology in Madrid. This elegant object, carved out of black dolerite from Maupiti, perhaps with iron tools (given this stone is very hard), is a mystery, although there have been various conjectures as to its uses. Some say that it was used for sacred medicines, or for making *'ava* on high ceremonial occasions; while others have suggested that the viscera of human sacrifices were placed in this bowl so that the priests could read auguries from their twitchings. The paramount chief of Ra'iatea, Puni, had given this sacred bowl as a gift to Tu, who presented it to his *taio* Máximo, who delivered it to the Viceroy of Peru as a gift for the King of Spain. Indeed, at that time, the *'umete*, used in 'Oro's worship, was one of the most powerful objects in the Society Islands.[30]

Ma'i on Ice Skates

In October 1773 while Manuel de Amat was organising his second expedition to Tahiti, Captain Cook was preparing to take the *Resolution* and the *Adventure* back to England at the end of his second Pacific voyage. During a wild storm off the east coast of New Zealand, however, the two ships were separated for the second time during this expedition. As Captain Furneaux struggled to weather Cape Palliser in the *Adventure*, making so many unsuccessful attempts that the sailors named it 'Cape Turn and be damn'd', the seas were so mountainous that Ma'i, the young Raiatean commoner who had joined the ship at Huahine,[1] was terrified; although as the *Adventure* climbed up one huge wave after another, he 'cryed out with rapture . . . that it was a good Ship & the Sea could not sink her'.[2] At last when the winds almost drove the ship onto the Wairarapa coastline, Furneaux gave up and headed north to Uawa or Tolaga Bay, which Cook and Tupaia had visited in 1769.

When they anchored in Uawa on 5 November 1773, Ma'i, Furneaux and Lieutenant Burney went ashore, where the people asked them about the high priest, weeping bitterly when they heard that he had died and chanting, '*Aue, kua mate koe, e Tupaia!*' – 'Alas, Tupaia – you are dead!' The Aitanga-a-Hauiti people had been deeply impressed by this high priest-navigator from the homeland, Hawaiki, who had slept ashore in a cave in Cook's Cove, sketched a ship and canoes on its back wall, and conversed with the priests from the Te Rawheoro school of learning. The *Adventure*'s men eagerly bartered for crayfish, fish and *kūmara* (sweet potato), exchanging these for nails; filled the water barrels at Cook's Cove; and collected wood for the fire. During one of their expeditions ashore they found the mummified head of a woman adorned with feathers and other ornaments lying in a canoe, examining it curiously. This woman must have been a chief, because a painted canoe hull was an aristocratic memorial among Māori; and when they touched the preserved head the sailors breached the death *tapu*, gravely offending her relatives. Shortly afterwards a gallon of brandy for the shore party was stolen from the boat, probably in retribution; and although Jack Rowe (who along with Johann Forster, Anders Sparrman and Richard Pickersgill had rampaged across the island of Taha'a) urged Lieutenant Burney to take two of the local chiefs hostage, Burney refused, saying that it was too dangerous, and remarking unsympathetically: 'If Sailors won't take care of their Grogg, they deserve to lose it.'[3]

On 12 November the *Adventure* sailed from Uawa and headed south, hoping to find the *Resolution*, but was beaten back by contrary winds and had to return. When they set out again, the ship was hit by another ferocious storm off Cape Turnagain, and did not enter Queen Charlotte Sound until 30 November, when Captain Cook had already departed. After anchoring his battered vessel in Ship Cove, Furneaux took the boat ashore where he found a stump in the garden with an inscription carved on it, 'Look Underneath'. When the sailors dug beside the stump they found a bottle holding a roll of paper that read:

> As Captain Cook has not the least hopes of meeting with Captn Furneaux he will not take upon him to name any place for a Rendezvous. He however thinks of retiring to East Island about the latter end of next March – it is even probable that he may go to Otaheite or one of the Society isles; but this will depend so much on Circumstances, that nothing with any degree of certainty can be determined upon – James Cook.[4]

Although Furneaux was dismayed to find that Cook had not waited for him and his men, Ma'i was enthralled by this letter, and the fact that Cook had managed to convey this message to Furneaux in his absence. He made up his mind to learn to read and write; but over the next few days so many people on board the *Adventure* tried to help him, setting him tasks and giving him texts to copy, that according to Burney: 'The poor fellow's head was bothered – too many Cooks spoilt the Broth.'[5]

Over the next few days William Bayly set up the astronomer's tent in Ship Cove, and Furneaux sent Lieutenant Burney and Ma'i ashore with the surgeon's mate and three sick men to keep him company. The ship's bread was re-baked, and a deluge of rain almost washed away the water casks. They found none of the pigs that Cook had landed in the cove, although during one of his excursions Ma'i saw a hen and three chicks. Local Māori visited the ship every day, and on 12 December Burney made a cryptic entry in his diary: 'In Shag Cove – Kemp, Rowe, Omy & myself in the Great Cutter – Narrow Escape there.'[6] Clearly, they had had some dispute with the local people, but had managed to avoid the repercussions. Two nights later several men sneaked into the ship's tent, eluding the sentry, and took two muskets, a cutlass, several bags of linen and other goods. They had loaded most of this loot into their small canoe when the astronomer William Bayly saw them and fired, hitting one with small shot. Although they escaped into the woods, the next morning Burney found their canoe still loaded with these trophies, and a trail of bloodstains along the beach.

The following night, Burney ordered a fire to be lit in front of the tent. When the sentry put down his arms by the fire and went inside for tobacco, he looked back and saw a warrior, his body oiled and gleaming in the firelight. The sentry yelled out and the man disappeared; and when they searched the beach there was no sign of an intruder. Burney thought that the sentry must have been dreaming; but nevertheless he, Ma'i and the others lay down afterwards fully dressed, with their weapons beside them. An hour later the sentry roused them again, saying that three canoes were approaching the camp. On the beach, Lieutenant Burney ordered the sentry to fire a musket shot overhead; and after talking for a while, the crews of the canoes paddled away. The following night another small canoe with only three men on board made another attempt to sneak up on the shore camp, but once again they were detected. After the shooting, Ma'i and the British were no longer welcome in the Sound, and the next day Furneaux instructed Bayly to strike his tent and return on board the *Adventure*.

On 17 December Furneaux sent his kinsman Jack Rowe (whom he had promoted to master's mate) with the cutter to fetch greens from Grass Cove, with strict instructions to return by mid-afternoon, because he intended to set sail the following morning. Later that morning, the warriors who had stolen from the ship's tent on 14 December came and asked for their canoe; and although Burney was amazed at their 'impudence', it was so close to the time of their departure that he decided to hand it over. The ship's tent was struck and the launch hoisted on board, but by nightfall when the cutter still had not returned, Furneaux became anxious. Early the next morning he sent Lieutenant Burney and Ma'i in the launch with a well-armed party of sailors and marines to search for the cutter. Burney thought that Rowe had probably gone to explore East Bay; and that the cutter might have been damaged in an accident. As they sailed in to East Bay, Burney examined each cove in turn with his telescope and ordered his men to fire their muskets; and when he saw a man running along a beach towards the end of the bay, they searched two nearby villages but found nothing suspicious. At a small beach next to Whareunga Bay ('Grass Cove'), however, Burney saw a very large double canoe arriving with two men and a dog, who ran into the bushes as soon as they spotted the launch. By now Burney suspected that their shipmates were in trouble; but when he landed and searched the canoe, he was horrified to find a rowlock port from the cutter and a shoe belonging to one of the midshipmen. About twenty woven baskets were lying on the beach, and when the marines cut these open they found them full of roasted meat and fernroot, still warm from the oven. Nearby a hand lay on the ground which unmistakeably belonged to Thomas Hill, one of the sailors, who had had his hand tattooed in Tahiti with his initials –'T.H.' Aghast at the sight, and noticing a great billow of smoke rising from Grass Cove, Burney ordered his men to return to the launch and they sailed around the point, hoping to arrive in the bay before sunset.

At Grass Cove three double canoes and a single canoe were drawn up on the sand, and the beach was crowded with people. A fire blazed high up on the hills, whose slopes were 'throng'd like a Fair'. As soon as the launch appeared, the people on the beach retreated to a small hill; and as they approached the shore, Burney ordered his men to fire a musketoon into one of the double canoes, fearing that warriors might be concealed in its hulls. Afterwards they fired volley after volley into the crowd, until everybody ran away except for two very stout men (no doubt chiefs) who refused to retreat until one of them was wounded and had to crawl away on all fours. When they landed, the sailors found two bundles of wild celery that their shipmates had gathered, a broken oar, and at the back of the beach, a ghastly sight – dogs gnawing on the entrails of four or five men and the mangled, butchered remains of their comrades, including Jack Rowe's hand, with its scarred forefinger, various feet, and the head of Furneaux's black servant.

As they stood there, transfixed with horror, the master shouted that he could hear men gathering in the valley. Scooping the body parts of their shipmates into a hammock, they ran back to the beach where they demolished three of the canoes, made one last search for the cutter, boarded the launch and sailed away in the darkness, as a huge fire flared up on the mountainside. As James Magra wrote, 'the Lieutenant not thinking it safe to trust the crew in the dark, in an open boat, within reach of such cruel barbarians, ordered the canoes to be broken up and destroyed, and after carefully collecting the remains of our mangled companions, they made the best of their way from this polluted place'.[7]

Ma'i and the other men on the launch never forgot what they had seen at Grass Cove, and for the rest of his life Lieutenant Burney could speak of this horrific experience only in a whisper. Afterwards, he thought that the killings of his shipmates had not been premeditated, but provoked by a dispute with the local people and his men's own incautious conduct. He added that he had seen the people of Shag Cove – where he, Rowe, Ma'i and Kemp had had a 'narrow escape' six days earlier – at Grass Cove on this occasion. Whatever the cause, Furneaux had lost ten of his best men, including his kinsman Jack Rowe; and the next morning he ordered the anchors hoisted and hastened to the entrance of Queen Charlotte Sound, where they consigned the remains of their comrades to the ocean. The winds were contrary, however, and that night 'every Body on board [slept] under Arms expecting the Canibals to be down and board us'.[8] Early the next morning when the winds changed they escaped at last from that 'polluted place', fleeing south-east across the Pacific.

Knowing that he was unlikely to find Cook at Easter Island or Tahiti, Captain Furneaux decided to head south once more in search of Terra Australis, before returning quickly to England. After the killings in Grass Cove he was short-handed, and enlisted Ma'i as an ordinary seaman. It took them only a month to cross the Pacific to Cape Horn, rounding the Cape on a strong easterly current, and another month sailing east among the icebergs, searching for 'Cape Circumcision', an island reported by Bouvet, before heading north to the Cape of Good Hope, where they arrived on 19 March 1774. During his brief stay at the Cape of Good Hope, Furneaux wrote a report for the Admiralty about the killing and eating of his men in Queen Charlotte Sound, and a letter for Captain Cook describing the events in Grass Cove; dressed Ma'i in his own clothes, and took him to meet the Governor. Three weeks later the *Adventure* left for England, arriving back on 12 July 1774, exactly two years after they had set sail with Cook from Plymouth.

When the ship's anchors splashed down at Spithead, Captain Furneaux, James Burney and Ma'i travelled post-haste to London to report to Lord Sandwich. The First Lord of the Admiralty immediately summoned Banks, Solander and Dr Burney (James Burney's father) to this meeting; and Ma'i knew Banks as soon as he saw him, although he did not recognise Dr Solander, who had gained a lot of weight since his voyage on the *Endeavour*, until he heard him talking. When Ma'i saw Lord Sandwich's butler, he pointed at him, remarking in Tahitian, 'He is the King of the bottles'; and at Captain Furneaux, saying, 'He is the King of the ship'; and finally he declared to Lord Sandwich, 'You are the King of all ships.'[9] According to Fanny Burney, James's novelist sister:

> [Ma'i] was dressed according to the fashion of his Country, & is a very good looking man – my Father says he has quite an *interesting* Countenance. He

appeared to have uncommon spirits, & laughed very heartily many Times. He speaks a few English words – & Capt. Furneaux a few Otaheite words. – They had got Mr. Banks there, on purpose to speak with him – but Mr. Banks has almost forgot what he knew of the language. But you must know we are very proud to hear that our *Jem* speaks more Otaheite than any of the Ship's *Crew*. – this Capt. F. told my father, who was Introduced to this Stranger, as Jem's Father – he laughed, and shook Hands very cordially. [He] says that he is very fond of *Bunny* [Tepane], who spent a great part of his Time in studying the Language with him.[10]

Just a year before Ma'i's arrival in England, Hawkesworth's compilation of the voyages of the *Dolphin* and *Endeavour* had been published to popular acclaim, provoking intense curiosity about the Tahitians. Hawkesworth had extensively rewritten the journals of Byron, Wallis and Cook, however, introducing numerous errors in the process and embellishing them with titillating details. Some of these passages created a sensation – for instance, an episode in Tahiti when a tall young warrior and a very young girl had sex in public under Purea's instruction; or when Banks interrupted Purea making love in her canoe with her much younger lover; or the night that Banks spent with Purea, when his jacket with silver frogs was stolen. The book was extremely popular with the public, although the literary elite in London decried it. As Horace Walpole harrumphed: 'An old black gentlewoman of forty carries Captain Wallis across a river, when he was too weak to walk, and the man represents them as a new edition of Dido and Aeneas. Indeed, Dido the new does not even borrow the obscurity of a cave when she treats the travellers with the rites of love, as practised in Otaheite.'[11] The *Voyages* provoked a further flurry of anonymous poems; for instance, *An Epistle from Mr. Banks, Voyager, Monster-hunter, and Amoroso, to Oberea, Queen of Otaheite* which reproached Joseph Banks for abandoning his 'lover' Purea, the 'Queen of Tahiti', while deploring Hawkesworth's impact on English morality:[12]

> One page of *Hawkesworth*, in the cool retreat
> Fires the bright maid with more than mortal heat;
> She sinks at once into the lover's arms,
> Nor deems it vile to prostitute her charms;
> 'I'll do,' cries she, 'what Queens have done before;'
> And sinks, *from principle*, a common whore.[13]

Far from being chastened by these satires, however, Banks revelled in his notoriety; and in early 1773 when he and some friends travelled to the Netherlands to visit zoological collections and herbaria, he regaled his Dutch hosts with tales of his experiences on the island. When they asked him to pen an account to amuse the Princess of Orange, Banks wrote 'Thoughts on the manners of Otaheite', a sensuous snippet reminiscent of Commerson's descriptions of life on the island:

> In the Island of Otaheite where Love is the Chief Occupation, the favourite, nay almost the Sole Luxury of the inhabitants; both the bodies and souls of the women are modeld into the utmost perfection for that soft science. Idleness the father of Love reigns here in almost unmolested ease, while we Inhabitants of a changeable climate are Obligd to Plow, Sow, Harrow, reap, Thrash, Grind Knead and bake our daily bread . . .
>
> I have no where seen such Elegant women as those of Otaheite such [as] the Grecians were from whose model the Venus of Medicis was copied. The Luxury of their appearance is also not a little aided by a freedom which their differing from us in their opinion of what Constitutes modesty. [A] European thinks nothing of Laying bare her breast to a certain point but a hairs breadth Lower no mortal eye must Peirce. An Otaheitean on the other hand will by a motion of her dress in a moment lay open an arm and half her breast the next maybe the whole . . . and all this with as much innocence and genuine modesty as an English woman can shew her arm.[14]

By mid-1774, however, Banks's glamour was fading. Ma'i's arrival was a godsend, and Banks whisked the young islander off to his town house. He coached him carefully, and after only three days' instruction took him to meet the King and Queen at Kew. According to contemporary accounts, when King George greeted him, Ma'i replied politely, 'How d'ye do King Tosh!', asking him how many children he had, to the great amusement of the courtiers; and when the King presented Ma'i with a sword, he accepted it gracefully, buckling it to his belt. Like Ahutoru, a number of indigenous travellers brought to European centres had caught smallpox and died, and King George urged Banks to have Ma'i inoculated against this dangerous illness.

Less than a week later they dined with the Duke and Duchess of Gloucester, Ma'i dressed in his bark-cloth robes; and on 29 July a well-known physician gave the young Ra'iatean his smallpox inoculation. When he had recovered, Banks arranged for Ma'i to stay with Mr Andrews, the *Adventure*'s surgeon, who spoke good Tahitian; carrying him off to dinners with Lord Sandwich and the Fellows of the Royal Society. On 28 August Banks and Ma'i set off for a week at Hinchinbrook, Lord Sandwich's country estate, accompanied by Lord Sandwich and his mistress Miss Ray. There was a sailing

Ma'i meets King George and Queen Charlotte

party on Whittlesea Mere; and the following day Ma'i dug a deep hole in
the ground, lit a fire, heated some stones, placed mutton wrapped in leaves
on the steaming stones and covered it with earth. When it was cooked, his
companions pronounced the food delicious, asking him to cook again the
next day. Later that afternoon Ma'i was stung by a wasp, and came in with a
swollen hand, complaining that 'he had been wounded by a soldier bird'.[15]
A grand oratorio was performed at Hinchinbrook; and the next day at the
Duke of Manchester's estate, after one of the company gave Ma'i a shock
from an 'electrifying machine', he ran away and refused to return; while on
the Friday there was a fox hunt. Ma'i told his companions that he wanted to
return to Ra'iatea with men and guns in a ship, drive the Borabora invaders
off his estates and put his brothers on the land, and then return to England
and marry a young Englishwoman.[16] It was rumoured that during this visit
to Lord Sandwich, a notorious libertine and member of the Hellfire Club,
Ma'i had been introduced to ladies of leisure, his companions reporting that
he preferred slender Englishwomen with ruddy complexions.

After the house party broke up, Banks and Ma'i went off to Leicester
where they attended the races and a performance of Handel's *Jeptha*,
organised by Lord Sandwich, who performed on the kettledrums with
bravura. According to a spectator, throughout this concert Ma'i stood
in 'wild amazement'. At Leicester a 'sprightly agreeable lady' gave him
dancing lessons, and in the tearooms he gallantly handed cake and bread

Ma'i

and butter to the ladies. Banks had visiting cards engraved for Ma'i (one of which is now held in the British Museum),[17] which he politely left at people's houses; and when he paid his visits, wearing a velvet suit, he impressed those who met him as genteel and good-humoured. When he was introduced to the Duchess of Devonshire, who presented him with her pocket-handkerchief, embroidered with her crest, Ma'i kissed it and made an elegant bow. Banks also took him to the University of Cambridge, where he was greatly impressed by the professors. During a brief visit back to London, Ma'i talked with Sarah Banks, Joseph Banks's sister, who described him as 'a well behaved quiet sensible Man desirous strongly of associating with the best Company & behaving in a proper manner'.[18] When Sarah asked Ma'i whether he was eager to see Hitihiti again, he confessed that he was not, because Hitihiti was a 'Bolabola Man'. Afterwards Banks took him to the theatre, where Ma'i sat through the first two acts but was enchanted by the pantomime at the end, which must have reminded him of the *'arioi* skits in the Society Islands.

After visiting his Lincolnshire estate, Banks and Ma'i returned to London to attend the theatre and the opening of the House of Lords, where

King George deplored the 'daring spirit of resistance' in Massachusetts. Afterwards Ma'i went to dine with James Burney at his father's house, dressed in a court dress of Manchester velvet lined with white satin, lace ruffles, and the sword that the King had given him. Fanny Burney described Ma'i as tall, robust, very dark and not handsome, but with a pleasant face, and hands tattooed with dotted lines. He seemed polite, attentive and easy, and at the end of the meal when Mrs Burney proposed a toast to the King, he joined in heartily. When his carriage arrived, he told James Burney that he and Dr Solander were going to see twelve ladies; and when James translated, Ma'i understood, laughing and saying in English, counting on his fingers, '1. 2. 3. 4. 5. 6. 7. 8. 9. 10. – *twelve* – *Woman!*', and made an elegant bow as he farewelled each of the company.[19]

While Ma'i was being lionised in London society, Sir Joshua Reynolds painted his portrait. This painting, which has been regarded as one of the portraitist's masterpieces, depicted Ma'i as a 'noble savage', standing proudly in flowing white robes in front of a moonlit island. Reynolds, who painted this portrait for his own pleasure, exhibited it at the Royal Academy in 1776; and during his lifetime it was never offered for sale. When the noble family that had purchased the painting after the artist's death put it up for auction in 2001, there was a furore. Hailed as an 'eighteenth-century icon', Ma'i's portrait was sold to an anonymous foreign buyer; and when it seemed likely that it might leave Britain, the Department for Culture, Media and Sport barred it from export.[20] The Western dream of the 'noble savage', epitomised in this painting, was also reflected in *An Historic Epistle from Omiah to the Queen of Otaheite*, written at the same time, which portrayed the Ra'iatean as an innocent lost amidst the excesses of aristocratic life in Britain, longing for the simplicities of home:

> Can Europe boast, with all her pilfer'd wealth,
> A larger share of happiness, or health?
> What then avail her thousand arts to gain
> The stores of every land, and every main:
> Whilst we, whom love's more grateful joys enthral,
> Profess one art – to live without them all [. . .]
>
> [Europe's states] in cool blood premeditatedly go
> To murder wretches whom they cannot know.
> Urg'd by no injury, prompted by no ill,
> In forms they butcher, and by systems kill;
> Cross o'ver the seas, to ravage distant realms,
> And ruin thousands worthier than themselves.[21]

At about this time, however, Banks was becoming tired of Ma'i's company; and when Lord Sandwich invited him and the young islander to return to Hinchinbrook for Christmas, Banks declined. He had just been elected to the Council of the Royal Society, and was busily ordering his collections from his voyages. When Ma'i returned to London, he brought a letter from Sandwich expressing his dismay that Banks had not joined them at Hinchinbrook, and worrying about how Ma'i would manage living alone in London. As Sandwich reminded Banks: '[Ma'i']s safety must depend upon you & me; & I should think we were highly blameable if we did not make use of all the sagacity & knowledge of the world which our experience has given us, to do everything we can to prove ourselves his real friends.'[22] After this admonition from his friend, Banks put the young Raiatean back in the care of Mr Andrews, the *Adventure*'s surgeon, and they spent a quiet winter in London, where the young islander got to know the Chevalier d'Eon, the notorious diplomat, duellist and transvestite, who took him horse riding.[23] On one occasion they rode in great style along the Oxford Road until they reached the Pantheon, where Ma'i's horse stood stock-still and refused to budge, until finally he cantered back to his stable, Ma'i clinging on desperately, to the great amusement of the spectators.

In June 1775 when Ma'i accompanied Banks, Lord Sandwich and Miss Ray on an inspection of the Royal Fleet, boarding the *Victory* with its 100 guns, he was amazed to see this enormous vessel. During this tour they shot birds, visited the Observatory and attended plays; and at Plymouth Lord Sandwich received a letter that Captain Cook had sent from the Cape of Good Hope on his way back to England, describing the visits that he had made after leaving Tahiti to Tonga, Malakula, Erromango, New Caledonia, Norfolk Island and New Zealand. Soon afterwards a letter arrived from Dr Solander giving a breathless précis of the voyage, based on a report that he had received from Johann Forster: '260 new Plants, 200 new animals – 71° 10' farthest Sth – no continent – Many Islands, some 80 Leagues long – The Bola Bola savage an [in]corrigible Blockhead – Glorious Voyage – no man lost by sickness.'[24] In this letter Solander also inquired whether Ma'i would want to live with Hitihiti when the young 'arioi arrived back in England, but Ma'i was not keen on this prospect. Like the young islander, Banks was uneasy about the *Resolution*'s return. After his petulant withdrawal from the second voyage, Banks was not sure how Captain Cook might greet him; and he and Ma'i carried on with their tour of the shipyards with Lord Sandwich, rather than hastening back to London to await the *Resolution*'s arrival.

On 30 July 1774 when the *Resolution* anchored at Spithead, Cook wrote jubilantly in his journal: 'Hav[e] been absent from England Three Years and Eighteen Days, in which time I lost but four men and only one of them by sickness.'[25] Cook had every reason to rejoice, because during this voyage he had established that Terra Australis was a mirage, found many islands previously unknown to Europeans, survived a life-threatening illness, and brought his crew home safely to England. As John Elliott exclaimed, despite Cook's illness and the presence on board of the fractious botanist Johann Forster, along with a group of hard-drinking, quarrelsome midshipmen whom Cook referred to as his 'black sheep', the *Resolution* had been a happy ship: 'I will here do them the justice to say that No Men could behave better under worse circumstances than they did. The same must be said of the Officers, and I will add that I believe there never was a Ship where for so long a period, under such circumstances, more happiness, order, and obedience was enjoyed.'[26]

When Cook arrived in London on 6 August to report to Lord Sandwich, he looked tanned and fit; and he gave Dr Solander a friendly message for Banks, saying how much he had missed him during the voyage. Lord Sandwich was delighted with Cook, offering him a captain's place at Greenwich where he could enjoy a comfortable retirement, and promising Charles Clerke the command of a voyage to take Ma'i back to Tahiti, with Richard Pickersgill as his first lieutenant. On 9 August Cook was summoned to Richmond Palace, where he presented King George with charts from the voyage and was given his commission as post-captain. When Lord Sandwich, Miss Ray and Dr Solander visited the *Resolution* soon afterwards, they found a menagerie on board including three Tahitian dogs, a springbok, a suricate, and two eagles that Johann Forster intended to present to the Queen; and Pickersgill distinguished himself by producing the preserved head from New Zealand with two slices cut from its cheeks, making the ladies almost faint with horror. Afterwards Cook sent all of the 'curiosities' that he had acquired during the voyage to Dr Solander at the British Museum, including four casks with specimens of birds, fish and plants for Joseph Banks; and began to prepare papers for the Royal Society on fish-poisoning in the Pacific and the methods he had used to keep the *Resolution*'s sailors healthy during their voyage around the world.

When the newspapers announced that the *Resolution* was about to be refitted for another Pacific expedition, Cook wrote wistfully to John Walker, the Quaker shipowner in Whitby who was his former master:

> The *Resolution* . . . will soon be sent out again, but I shall not command her, my fate drives me from one extream to a nother a few Months ago the whole Southern

hemisphere was hardly big enough for me and now I am going to be confined within the limits of Greenwich Hospital, which are far too small for an active mind like mine, I must however confess it is a fine retreat and a pretty income, but whether I can bring my self to like ease and retirement, time will shew.[27]

Banks and Ma'i had not yet arrived in London, travelling instead to Yorkshire in Banks's huge coach with its cargo of books, maps, scientific equipment and trunks of specimens, where Ma'i befriended a young boy, a son of one of Banks's friends. The boy, George Colman, later recalled the day he went swimming with the Raiatean:

The coast of Scarborough having an easterly aspect, the early sunbeams shot their lustre upon the tawny Priest, and heighten'd the cutaneous gloss which he had already received from the water: – he looked like a specimen of pale moving mahogany, highly varnish'd; – not only varnish'd, indeed, but curiously veneer'd – for, from his hips, and the small of his back, downwards, he was tattow'd with striped arches, broad and black, by means of a sharp shell, or a fish's tooth, imbued with an indelible die, according to the fashion of his country.[28]

Eventually, however, Joseph Banks returned to London for a Royal Society dinner where he met Cook, and they made peace with each other. When Cook was made a Fellow of the Royal Society, Banks stood as his sponsor; and he took part in the Royal Society's decision to award Cook the Copley Medal for his contributions to the health of seamen. Captain Cook was the undoubted hero of the second voyage; and it was Banks who commissioned Nathaniel Dance to paint his portrait. Although Lord Sandwich had promised Charles Clerke (who had already circumnavigated the world four times – with Byron and Wallis, and with Cook on his two previous voyages) the command of the third Pacific voyage, Clerke had been thrown into the King's Bench prison after guaranteeing his brother's debts, where he contracted tuberculosis. The Admiralty consulted Cook on every detail in fitting out the *Resolution* and her new consort ship, *Discovery*, for the new Pacific expedition, which was to take Ma'i back home, and search for the fabled Northwest Passage through North America. In February 1776 at a dinner at Lord Sandwich's, when the glories of the voyage were being lauded, Captain Cook jumped to his feet and volunteered to lead the expedition.

The winter of 1776 was bitterly cold, with deep snows. The Thames froze over, and Ma'i learned to skate on the Serpentine River. According to Horace Walpole, Ma'i soon became a proficient skater, and he also mastered backgammon and chess, defeating several expert chess players. Among London philanthropists, however, there was concern that Ma'i was spending all of his time in disreputable company and learning nothing about Christianity or skills useful to his fellow islanders. Granville Sharp, a leading emancipist, gave the young islander lessons in English and the Ten Commandments, although their discussions tended to focus upon the Seventh Commandment, 'Thou shalt not commit adultery'. According to Sharp, when he explained the commandment to Ma'i:

'Oh!' says he, 'two wives – very good; three wives – very, very good.' 'No, Mr. Omai,' I said, 'not so; that would be contrary to the first principle of the law of nature.' – 'First principle of the law of nature,' said he; 'what that? What that?' – '*The first principle of the law of nature,*' I said, 'is, that *no man must do to another person any thing that he would not like done to himself.*' . . .'Well, Mr. Omai,' said I, 'suppose, then, that your wife loves you very much; she would not like that you should love another woman: for the women have the same passions, and feelings, and love towards the men, that we have towards the women.'

Ma'i sat and thought for a while, and then taking a pen from an inkstand, he laid it on the table and replied:

'There lies Lord S——' (a Nobleman with whom he was well acquainted, and in whose family he had spent some time); and then he took another pen, and laid it close by the side of the former pen, saying, 'and there lies Miss W——' (who was an accomplished young woman in many respects, but, unhappily for herself, she lived in a state of adultery with that nobleman); and he then took a third pen, and placing it on the table at a considerable distance from the other two pens, as far as his right arm could extend, and at the same time leaning his head upon his left hand, supported by his elbow on the table, in a pensive posture, he said, 'and there lie Lady S——, and cry!'[29]

The next time that Ma'i was taken again to Richmond Palace, King George told the young islander that he would soon be taken home to the Society Islands. When Ma'i visited the Burneys shortly afterwards, as Fanny Burney reported:

We asked if he had seen the King lately?
'Yes; King George *bid me*, – "Omy, you go home." Oh, very *dood* man, King George!'
He then, with our assisting him, made us to understand that he was extremely rejoiced at the thoughts of seeing again his native land; but at the same time that

he should much regret leaving his friends in England.

'Lord Sandwich,' he added, '*bid me*, "Mr Omy, you two ships, – you go home." – I say (making a fine bow) "Very much *oblige*, my Lord."'[30]

On 2 April when James Boswell, Samuel Johnson's biographer, met Cook at a dinner, he was greatly impressed by the famous navigator, remarking that 'he had a balance in his mind for truth as nice as scales weighing a guinea'; and reflecting how strange it was to see 'Cook, a grave steady man, and his wife, a decent plump Englishwoman, and think that he was preparing to sail around the world'.[31] Cook told Boswell that Ma'i wanted to take plenty of port wine and gunpowder back to Tahiti, but that he would not allow it. After this conversation Boswell became entranced with the idea of accompanying Cook on his next voyage; although when he confessed to Samuel Johnson that he was 'carried away with the general grand and indistinct notion of A VOYAGE ROUND THE WORLD', Johnson replied repressively: 'Why, Sir, a man *does* feel so, till he considers how very little he can learn from such voyages.'[32] At a dinner in Bath, when Boswell reiterated his desire to live for three years at Tahiti or New Zealand, to learn about people in a pure state of nature, Samuel Johnson was even more dismissive: 'What could you learn, Sir? What can savages tell, but what they themselves have seen? Of the past, or the invisible, they can tell nothing. The inhabitants of Otaheite and New Zealand are not in a state of pure nature; for it is plain they broke off from some other people. Had they grown out of the ground, you might have judged of a state of pure nature!'[33] And when Boswell defended the Tahitians, saying, 'I do not think the people of Otaheite can be reckoned savages', Johnson (who was allergic to Rousseau and all his works) exclaimed in exasperation:

Johnson: 'Don't cant in defence of savages!'

Boswell: 'They have the art of navigation.'

Johnson: 'A dog or cat can swim.'

Boswell: 'They carve very ingeniously.'

Johnson: 'A cat can scratch & a child with a nail can scratch.'[34]

Although Boswell visited Captain Cook at his home in Mile End to discuss the possibility of joining the expedition, after Banks's tantrums and Johann Forster's rages Cook was tired of sailing with civilian observers, and he was not encouraging (which was a pity, because Boswell would have written a magnificent account of the voyage). Cook had already recruited most of his officers, all younger than himself (he was now forty-seven, a grand old age in the eighteenth-century Navy), and there were many experienced Pacific hands among them. Despite his illness, Charles Clerke was given the command of the *Discovery*, supported by James Burney as his first lieutenant (who had sailed on the *Dolphin* under Byron and with Furneaux on the *Adventure*). John Gore, the mad-keen sportsman who had sailed with Byron, Wallis and on the *Endeavour*, became Cook's first lieutenant; although when Banks withdrew from the previous voyage, Gore had gone with him. There was also William Bayly, the *Discovery*'s astronomer, who had also sailed on Cook's previous voyage; William Anderson, an intelligent, capable Scottish surgeon; four petty officers; a carpenter, a cook and twelve able-bodied seamen, all of whom had sailed with Cook on previous voyages.

The new recruits included James King, the *Resolution*'s second lieutenant, a humane, kindly officer who had studied science in Paris and Oxford. Together with William Anderson, the surgeon, he replaced the civilian scientists who sailed on the previous two voyages. When King had asked Cook whether a scientific party would sail with them, to his consternation Cook exploded, shouting, 'Curse the scientists, and all science into the bargain!'[35] There was also John Williamson, the *Resolution*'s third lieutenant, who according to Trevenen, one of the midshipmen, was 'a wretch, feared and hated by his inferiors, detested by his equals & detested by his superiors; a very devil'.[36] As master of the *Resolution*, there was William Bligh, superbly capable as a surveyor and cartographer, but sharp-tongued and outspoken; and as her surgeon's mate, David Samwell, a Welsh extrovert and an ebullient lover of the 'Dear Girls'. This expedition had just one naturalist and one artist – respectively, David Nelson, a gardener from Kew who sailed on the *Discovery*; and John Webber, an accomplished landscape painter who was on board the *Resolution*.

In all, there were 114 men on board the *Resolution* and 73 on the *Discovery*. Cook was distracted, however, and the *Resolution*'s refit was shirked, so that the ship leaked like a sieve throughout the voyage. While the provisions were being loaded, Lord Sandwich sent a menagerie of domestic animals for Tahiti and New Zealand, including horses and cattle – in the hope that in New Zealand a better supply of meat might dissuade Māori from eating each other. In addition, there were laced hats and feathers, fine gowns and trousers, broadswords, cut glass, knives and forks, chessboards, spyglasses and assorted ornaments as presents for the islanders, portraits of the King and Queen and medicines for venereal diseases. Lord Sandwich presented Ma'i with his own suit of armour, especially made for him at the Tower of London; and in addition, an illustrated

Bible, suits, shoes, stockings, an assortment of tools, cutlery and crockery for his dwelling, along with furniture, drums and a wheelbarrow were brought on board for the young Ra'iatean. Some ingenious soul also sent toy models of horses, coaches, wagons and other objects so that Ma'i could convince his countrymen of the truth of his stories about England, along with fireworks, a jack-in-a-box, a puppet show, a German organ and an electrifying machine so that he could impress them with the wonders of Europe. On 11 June, Ma'i went to court to farewell the King, and several days later the *General Evening Post* reported that he had written a farewell note to his friends: 'Omiah to take leave of good friend. He never forget England. He go on Sunday. God bless King George. He tell his people how kind English to him.' Ma'i quickly made himself popular with his shipmates, with David Samwell reporting: 'Omiah is a droll Animal & causes a good deal of Merriment on Board.'[37] Finally, on 12 July 1776, after almost two years in England, Ma'i sailed on board the *Resolution*, heading home to the Society Islands.

Ma'i's departure inspired a flurry of anonymous poems, including a salacious squib, *Omiah's Farewell*, which described the islander's visit to England with coy references to Venus, Cupid and the Elysian fields, and recited his fond farewells to his lady admirers (particularly Lady Carew, who was rumoured to have succumbed to his exotic charms):

> This, on thy rosy pinions, Cupid, Bear
> To the soft hands of Lady C . . . fair
> To her white hands these plaintive strains I send,
> The beauteous Christian, and the Indian's friend:
> To her chaste bosom I confide my flame,
> And with an E. leave Omiah's fame
> Farewell, sweet Dame, with whom the roses blow,
> And lillies fairer than the fairest snow:
> Oft have I gazed with raptures on thy face,
> Admired thy majesty – ador'd thy grace.
> And from thy cherry lips instructions took,
> Beyond the learning of the wisest book.
>
> Untutor'd, wild, unletter'd I proclaim
> Myself an Indian – not the slave to Fame;
> The Slave of Love – no other God I own,
> No other God is to Omiah known.

Oft Lady C. hast thou promise made,
To sleep with me beneath the Breadfruit's shade,
For brighter suns, to leave this clouded sky,
And with Omiah share eternity.
For thee, her stores shall Otahietee pour,
And Venus guide each gay, delicious hour.[38]

Nor were these effusions the last British memorials to Ma'i. During a meeting with the young islander in London, the famous actor David Garrick had been inspired with the idea of a play featuring the Tahitian as a savage Harlequin; but when Ma'i featured on the English stage some years later, it was as the hero of a picturesque pantomime performed at the Theatre Royal, Covent Garden. Entitled *Omai: Or, a Trip Round the World*, this pantomime featured ingenious stage machinery, elaborate costumes, and backdrops based on the artworks brought back from Cook's Pacific voyages. In the plot, Ma'i is transformed into the son of Tu, the King of Otaheite, transported by Britannia to England where he woos the beautiful Londina and wins her from a Spanish rival, carrying her in triumph to his island home. In the grand finale, where Ma'i is crowned the King of Otaheite, the backdrop showed a royal palace with ships anchored before it and all the boats of different islands bringing ambassadors to salute their new ruler. After Ma'i's coronation, which was celebrated with dancing, wrestling and boxing matches, he and Londina were married, to the joyous acclaim of their people. The finale of the play featured a procession of islanders from different parts of the Pacific worshipping Captain Cook, as a giant portrait of Cook lying on a cloud, leaning against Britannia as an angel salutes him with her trumpet, descended against the backdrop into the eternal light of fame.

A Bare-chested Captain

On 12 July 1776 when Captain Cook set off on his third voyage of Pacific discovery, he had instructions to search for the southern islands recently found by Marion du Fresne and Kerguelen, before dropping off Ma'i at Tahiti, stopping at New Zealand en route if necessary. After that, he was to sail up the eastern coast of North America (into Spanish waters) to search for the Northwest Passage, which was rumoured to stretch across the frozen northern reaches of that continent. A rich reward had been offered for the discovery of the Northwest Passage, although the men did not know this until later in the voyage. After setting out from England, the *Resolution* made a brief visit to St Jago, and during this passage Ma'i showed his shipmates how to fish for dolphins with a rod and a white fly. While watching a meteor streaking across the sky, Ma'i declared that this was his *atua* (god), heading back to England. When they arrived at the Cape of Good Hope on 17 October, Samwell declared: 'The Governor & all at the Cape pay Captn Cook extraordinary Respect, he is as famous here & more noted perhaps than in England.'[1] Buoyed by this reception, Cook wrote ebulliently to Banks, assuring him that Ma'i had now recovered from the pox that he had caught in England, and passing on the young islander's greetings to his patron, Dr Solander, Lord Seaford and a good many others, including a number of ladies. When Charles Clerke finally joined them he took over the command of the *Discovery*; and Lieutenant Gore and Ma'i went off shooting, but potted only a few small birds. Cook had decided to buy more animals for the Pacific, and Ma'i gladly gave up his cabin to make space for four horses, bound for Tahiti. As Cook declared buoyantly in his letter to Lord Sandwich: 'Nothing is wanting but a few females of our own species to make the *Resolution* a complete ark.'[2]

During the passage from England, however, the *Resolution* leaked so badly that, in a letter to Banks, Lieutenant Gore declared roundly: 'If I

return in the *Resolution* the next Trip I may Safely Venture in a Ship Built
of Ginger Bread.'³ Cook had the ship recaulked, and on 22 November
1772 they sailed south-east to search for the islands found by the French.
At Kerguelen Island in late December they found the shore lined with
penguins that stood at attention to greet them; and when they arrived at
Tasmania, Ma'i showed himself to be an expert shot, killing a number of
geese. Ma'i had no great opinion of the Tasmanians, who went largely
naked, urinating where they stood, the men playing idly with their genitals. When he tried to talk with them, they did not understand a word that
he said, and he considered their women very ugly. When Cook urged one
of the Tasmanians to throw his spear at a target, he missed; and to convince him of the superiority of firearms, the young islander took aim with
his musket and blew the target to pieces, terrifying these people who fled
into the woods, to Cook's irritation.

Eager to obtain greenstuffs for the animals and fish, and scurvy grass
for his men, Cook decided to visit Queen Charlotte Sound in New Zealand
before heading to Tahiti. Lieutenant Burney had briefed him about the
killing and eating of his shipmates at Grass Cove; and four other sailors
(including Ma'i) from the *Adventure* had also enlisted for this expedition. Cook had often been frustrated by the lack of discipline on board
the *Adventure*, however, and he was inclined to blame Furneaux's men for
what had happened in Grass Cove. When the two ships sailed in to Queen
Charlotte Sound on 11 February 1777 the local people were extremely
apprehensive, although Ma'i waved his handkerchief to those on Motuara
Island, assuring them that 'we were their Friends'. They recognised Ma'i,
who talked with them about the Grass Cove killings; and when he told
them that Tute (Cook's Tahitian name) was on board, they came out to
the *Resolution* to greet him. During his brief visit to the Sound towards the
end of the second voyage, however, these people had managed to conceal
the killings from Captain Cook; and they remained very nervous, despite
the fact that, according to Cook, 'I did all in my power to assure them of
the continuence of my friendship, and that I should not disturb them on
that account'.⁴

When the *Resolution* and *Discovery* anchored in Ship Cove, the animals
were disembarked, as Samwell vividly recounted:

Today our Ship, which for variety of living Things she contained might be
called a second Noahs Ark, poured out the Horses, Cattle, Sheep, Goats &c.
with peacocks, Turkeys, Geese & Ducks, to the great Astonishment of the New
Zealanders, who had never seen horses or Horned Cattle before; these being all
feeding and diverting themselves about the Tents familiarised the Savage Scene

& made us almost forget that we were near the antipodes of old England among a rude & barbarous people.[5]

Māori gathered around the shore camp in some numbers, bringing weapons, tools and women to barter; although on this occasion many of the sailors refused to sleep with the women, whom they regarded as 'cannibals'. Although they were amazed by the animals he had brought, the local people were contemptuous that, for all his powerful weapons, Captain Cook showed no interest in avenging the death of his people. When Kahura, the chief who had led the attack on the *Adventure*'s men, made a provocative appearance alongside the ship, they begged Cook to kill him and seemed astounded when he refused. On 16 February when Cook, Ma'i and Captain Clerke went to visit Grass Cove where the *Adventure*'s men had been killed and eaten, they were formally challenged; and a local chief whom Cook had met during his previous visit told him about the affray. According to this man, one of the *Adventure*'s sailors had bartered for a stone adze, and when he took it without offering anything in return, its owner had snatched some bread and fish and was beaten by Furneaux's black servant. A fight broke out, Jack Rowe shot two of the local men, and when Kahura and his warriors came to their rescue, they had killed all of the British party as *utu* (revenge, equal return).

Like Māori, Ma'i was utterly baffled by Cook's refusal to avenge his *Adventure* shipmates. Lieutenant Burney also found it galling, writing in his journal: '[I]t seemed evident that many of them held us in great contempt and I believe chiefly on account of our not revenging the affair of Grass Cove, so contrary to the principles by which they would have been actuated in the like case. As an instance of how little they stood in fear of us, one man did not scruple to acknowledge his being present and assisting at the killing and eating the *Adventure*'s people.'[6] Many of the sailors were also bitter that Cook refused to avenge the fate of their comrades, particularly the former *Adventure*s; and soon after this visit to Grass Cove the *Resolution*'s quartermaster was flogged for 'insolence and contempt', an indication of this mood of disaffection.

Ma'i was anxious to recruit some attendants before returning home to the Society Islands, as a sign of his *mana*; and when a young man named Te Weherua, who had spent a good deal of time on board the *Resolution* during Cook's previous visits to the Sound, asked to accompany him to Tahiti, Ma'i asked Cook's permission, and Cook consented. Te Weherua was a high-born young man, and he was accompanied by a boy named Koa, who travelled with his father's approval. Cook was now ready to leave the Sound, and on 23 February when he ordered the shore camp packed up and the ships prepared for sailing, Te Weherua came on board with his attendant. Te Weherua's mother wept bitterly over her son, slashing her head with a shark's tooth, and Ma'i gave her two hatchets and several nails as farewell gifts. On 24 February the ships anchored off Motuara Island, where some people came out in canoes loaded with cloaks, greenstone ornaments, adzes and Polynesian dogs to barter to the British. Seeing Kahura in one of these canoes, Ma'i begged Cook to let him shoot this 'stout, active man', but once again Cook refused his permission.

The following morning when Kahura came out once again with his family and boarded the *Resolution*, Ma'i led him into the Great Cabin, crying out to Cook, 'There is Kahourah, kill him!' Shortly afterwards when Ma'i returned to the cabin and found Kahura unhurt, he flew into a fury, protesting, 'Why do you not kill him? You t[e]ll me that if a man kills an other in England he is hanged for it, this Man has killed ten and yet you will not kill him, tho a great many of his countrymen desire it and it would be very good.'[7] Captain Cook took no notice, however, even allowing Kahura to have his portrait painted by John Webber. Afterwards he mused: 'I must confess I admired his courage and was not a little pleased at the confidence he put in me.'[8] Cook's inaction was too much for Ma'i, and his shipmates. On board the *Discovery*, where Burney was the first lieutenant, the midshipmen and master's mates seized a Māori dog that one of their shipmates had purchased, and put it on trial for cannibalism. The dog was accused, tried and sentenced; and afterwards it was killed, skinned, cooked and eaten. In Polynesia, Cook's men had learned to eat dog, and they had also learned about *mana*, and the importance of avenging insults. In this mock trial – a popular form of 'rough humour' in England – his men were sending Captain Cook a powerful message about how cannibals ought to be treated.

Shortly after they sailed from Queen Charlotte Sound on 26 February 1777, Lieutenant King reported that there was 'a general disobedience among the people' and some meat was stolen. When Cook tried to force the crew to identify the offenders, they staunchly refused, and when Cook put them on a reduced allowance, they would not eat it, which King described as a 'very mutinous proceeding'.[9] On 29 March they arrived off Mangaia in the Cook Islands, where Ma'i called out to the crew of a canoe that had paddled out, saying that the ships had come in friendship. When these people asked where he and his companions came from and for the name of their leader, Ma'i asked them in his turn whether they ate people, which they indignantly denied. The chief boarded the *Resolution* and stumbled over a goat, asking the young Raiatean in alarm what kind of 'bird' this was. They found no safe passage through the reef at Mangaia, however, and carried on to Atiu, where people came out unarmed in their canoes to the *Discovery*, one man holding up a plantain branch and asking them, 'Are you the glorious sons of Tetumu?'[10] This was a reference to Vaita's prophecy about the 'glorious children of Tetumu', and there was a *marae* named Taputapuatea and an *'arioi* house on the north-west coast of the island.[11] Evidently the cult of 'Oro had already reached the Cook Islands. Many years later, in 1838, when the missionary John Williams sailed to Rarotonga with a Raiatean man on board, the Rarotongans asked this man why his people had killed the priests Pa'oa-tea and Pa'oa-uri at Taputapuatea, and what they had done with the sacred drum Ta'imoana.[12]

When Ma'i crossed to the *Discovery*, he and the Atiu man (who must have been a priest) went through a ritual, chanting in turns and pulling leaves from the frond of a coconut palm; and when they went to the *Resolution* the priest presented Captain Cook with a bunch of plantains, in turn receiving an axe and red cloth. The next morning when an envoy brought out more gifts for Cook and asked for a dog, which had evidently become extinct on this island, Ma'i gave him a pet dog of his own. Afterwards Dr Anderson and Lieutenant Burney went ashore, escorted by a group of armed warriors who led them inland to meet the high chiefs of Atiu, each of whom was decorated with fine red feather ornaments. As his boat landed on the beach, Ma'i was greeted by three Tahitians whose canoe had been blown to Atiu ten years earlier, and who talked with him eagerly, reporting that they had been kindly treated, and that the island was known as *Whenua no te Atua* because so many of its people were possessed by ancestral spirits. It may have been these Tahitians who had introduced the worship of 'Oro to the island. They led Ma'i and Lieutenant Gore to the meeting place where at least 2000 people had assembled, and Ma'i sent the high chief a bunch of red feathers and used a dagger to open a drinking coconut, which he presented with an elegant flourish to one of the women who danced for them.

After the dancing, the warriors refused to let Ma'i and his companions leave the meeting place; they were rudely jostled and many of their things were taken. When Ma'i saw an earth oven being lit, he asked in alarm whether the warriors were going to cook and eat them. Instead, the chiefs entertained their guests with wrestling matches and dances by men and then women; and Ma'i went through his weapon drill, performing a vigorous *heiva* as a finale. Laughing uproariously, the chiefs asked Ma'i about his companions; and he regaled them with fantastic tales about England, saying that in that country they had ships larger than their island, with guns that destroyed everything in their way. When the chiefs looked unconvinced, Ma'i took a musket cartridge, removed the ball and threw a coal onto it, making the cartridge explode. He warned the chiefs that unless they allowed him and his companions to return to their vessel by dusk, the ship's guns would blow their island to pieces. Impressed, the chiefs gave their visitors a lavish feast, with baked plantains and a roasted pig, offered Ma'i *kava* to drink, and sent a canoe to take Gore, Ma'i and the rest of their party back to the *Resolution*.

Cook now decided to carry on to Manua'e, an uninhabited island that he had sighted during his previous voyage, where he hoped to collect coconuts, greenery for the animals and scurvy grass for the sailors. On 6 April when they arrived at the island, however, they found to their surprise that it was now inhabited, and canoes came out, one carrying a chief wearing a red feather cap. According to Ma'i, these people paid tribute to the chief of Atiu; and they had seen two large vessels before, presumably the *Resolution* and *Adventure* during Cook's second voyage. Like the inhabitants of Atiu, the Manua'e people were light-fingered, grabbing a piece of salt meat that was being dragged behind the *Resolution* which they afterwards exchanged with Koa, Ma'i's younger attendant, for a piece of brown paper. They also tried to capture the *Discovery*'s cutter, hitting a sailor on the head with a paddle and grabbing Bayly's servant; although when two large armed boats were lowered they released their captive and fled. Again Te Weherua and Koa were astonished at Cook's restraint, remarking that 'of so many people within reach of our power, we have neither killed or made prisoners of any'.[13]

The ships were still short of water and fodder for the animals, and Cook decided to carry on to Palmerston Island, a large, uninhabited atoll. When they arrived on 13 April the boats went ashore where they found a carved piece of wood, set up on the beach and painted yellow, which Ma'i identified as a burial marker. Ma'i camped ashore on the island with Te Weherua and Koa, showing his shipmates how to find fresh water by digging in the sand, how to catch fish in the lagoon with a scoop net and capture the tame birds in the bush, and how to cook them in an earth oven. They were grateful, because they had plenty of delicious food to eat during the days that the ships anchored off the island; and Ma'i was delighted with this atoll, saying that he would like to return there with his family.

On 24 April the ships sailed past Niue, which Cook had visited during his previous voyage; and on 28 April during a thunderstorm they approached the high island of Nomuka in the Tongan archipelago, where Cook had landed three years earlier. An old man named Taipa came out to the *Resolution* and made a vigorous speech, pointing to the island (although Maʻi could not understand a word that he said); followed soon afterwards by a stout, robust chief named Tupoulagi, who brought Cook a large pig as a present. Tupoulagi offered his own house to Cook and Maʻi as a temporary abode, a pleasant dwelling set in an idyllic spot shaded by breadfruit and plantain trees and surrounded by gardens. Over the next few days Maʻi regaled Tupoulagi and the other leading Nomukans with tales about the power of King George and the great ships and cannons that he commanded, and his extraordinary adventures during his visit to England.

On 6 May a chief named Finau, a tall, regal man about thirty-five years old, arrived in a large sailing canoe from Tongatapu, accompanied by half a dozen beautiful young women. When Taipa introduced Finau to Captain Cook and Maʻi, he made a long speech explaining that Finau was the ruler of 150 islands, which he listed by name. In Tonga at this time, there were three senior chiefs – the Tuʻi Tonga, a sacred chief in the direct line of descent from the gods; the Tuʻi Haʻatakalaua, a secular chief appointed by the Tuʻi Tonga; and the Tuʻi Kanokupolu, appointed by the leaders of his own lineage, to whom much of this secular power had been delegated. Ancestral power passed through the female line in Tonga, and each of these chiefs was outranked by his father's sister – a little like the 'Great Women' of the Society Islands. At this time, it seems likely that Finau was acting as the Tuʻi Kanokupolu; and when he landed on the beach, Tupoulagi bowed his head to the soles of Finau's feet, followed by the other leaders of the island. When Finau went out to the *Resolution* an inferior chief ordered some men to leave Tupoulagi's house, beating them unmercifully with a club when they disobeyed and striking one man so hard that the blood gushed from his nostrils and mouth. After presenting Maʻi and Cook with gifts of red feathers, pigs and fruit, Finau invited them to visit Haʻapai, a northerly group of islands. The British were impressed by this man, finding him to be good-humoured, friendly and intelligent; and Maʻi, thinking that this was the highest chief in the Tongan archipelago, changed names with him, taking him as his *taio*.

During this visit Finau dined with Maʻi and Cook every day, and only Tupoulagi was permitted to join them. The chiefs were irrepressibly acquisitive, however; and when one of their high-born visitors was caught with a bolt from a winch hidden under his clothing, Cook had him flogged and tied up for several hours before he was released. On 14 May when they sailed for the Haʻapai Islands, Maʻi accompanied his *taio* Finau on board his canoe, which sailed much faster than the European vessels. During the day, Finau guided the ships, indicating the depth of the shoaling water by stretching his arms and pointing to the bearing of their destination island; and each night he and Ma'i slept ashore on a different island, bringing them gifts of fresh food every morning.

On 18 May when the ships arrived at Lifuka, a great ceremony of welcome was held. Ma'i and Finau escorted Captain Cook ashore, where the old man Taipa (who had also arrived by canoe from Nomuka) made a speech telling the people that Cook had come as a friend, and they must not molest him. By the following morning at least 3000 people had gathered; and 100 men arrived in procession bringing great loads of yams, plantains, coconuts, breadfruit, pigs and turtles, which they piled up in a large heap of food to Cook's left, and a smaller heap to Ma'i's right, because Finau was honouring him as a bond friend. There were displays of club fighting, wrestling and boxing, and when several sailors challenged the Tongans to wrestle and box, they were roundly defeated. After this entertainment Finau presented the heaps of food to Cook and Ma'i, and it took four boats to carry the provisions back to the ships. On board the *Discovery*, however, when Taipa's son was caught stealing a cat, Ma'i advised that he should be given 100 lashes on the grounds that the higher the rank the worse the crime. Although Clerke had him clapped into irons instead, this punishment enraged his father and the Nomuka people. The following day when Cook ordered the marines to perform their drill ashore, their performance was ragged and most of their shots missed the target. In response, Finau led about 200 warriors in a display of weapon handling that was performed with absolute precision. Seeing the Tongans beginning to mock his own people, Cook ordered the gunner to prepare a

Ma'i [extreme left] watches the night dances in Tonga

fireworks display. A water rocket was fired into the ocean, and as it burned underwater, rising and falling, and exploding like a clap of thunder, they were astonished, crying out *'Mate! Mate!'* ('We'll be killed!'); and when the sky rockets were fired, flying to an immense height before bursting into a cloud of smoke and falling sparkles, they yelled out in amazement. As Lieutenant King wrote:

> Such roaring, jumping, & shouting . . . made us perfectly satisfied that we had gaind a compleat victory in their own minds. Sky & water rockets were what affect'd them most, the water rocket exercis'd their inquisitive faculties, for they could not conceive how fire shoud burn under water. Omai who was always very ready to magnify our country, told them, they might now see how easy it was for us to destroy not only the earth, but the water & the Sky; & some of our sailors were seriously perswading their hearers, that by means of the sky rockets we had made stars.[14]

After this display, a troupe of beautiful women adorned with crimson hibiscus garlands danced in unison; and then a group of men; followed by some men who performed a skit (like an *'arioi* performance), making jokes about the fireworks, and more dancing. These dancers were sketched by John Webber, who showed Ma'i dressed in naval uniform, pointing towards the performers.

After watching these displays, David Samwell asked whether these were those 'fortunate Isles where all those Blessing are contained . . . that fancy fabled in her Age of Gold?', although he quickly qualified this by referring to the 'exorbitant Power of the Chiefs' and their 'barbarous Treatment of the common People' in Tonga.[15] When the dancing was over and an elderly chief sent the people away, Finau had the jungle searched for stragglers, having one man beaten so severely that he almost died. In fact, these alluring performances were a ploy. According to William Mariner, the first European to live in Tonga, the Nomuka chiefs were so angry about the affront to Taipa's son that during the night dances they had planned to ambush Captain Cook and his companions, kill them all and plunder their vessels. If Cook had not ordered the fireworks display that evening, it is almost certain that he and his men would have been caught unaware and slaughtered by the Tongan warriors.

Although Cook knew nothing about this plot, he must have sensed the hostile atmosphere, and he was eager to leave Lifuka. The next morning, however, Latunipulu, the sullen-looking high chief whom he had met during his previous visit to Tongatapu, arrived alongside in a large sailing canoe. As the sister's son of the current Tu'i Tonga, Latunipulu had very

high status, although Finau largely ignored him on this occasion. After the
failed ambush too, the Nomukans were still eager to avenge themselves on
the British, and they stole everything they could grab. There were more
floggings on board the ships, of both sailors and Tongans, and a thief
was wounded in the cheek with a boathook. On 23 May, Finau and Taipa
came alongside in a sailing canoe and told Cook that they were going to
Vava'u to fetch red-feathered caps as gifts for himself and Ma'i, urging
him to wait for them. On 26 May, however, Cook decided to shift the
ships to the southern end of the island, sending the *Resolution*'s master,
William Bligh, ahead to sound the bay. The next day a large sailing canoe
arrived alongside the ship bringing a straight-haired, extremely corpulent chief in his early fifties named Fatafehi Paulaho, who according to
his attendants was the 'King of all the Isles'. When he finally realised that
this sedate, sensible, good-natured chief was the Tu'i Tonga, the most
sacred chief in these islands, Ma'i was shattered to discover that his bond
brother Finau was not the highest-ranking chief in Tonga after all; and
when Cook accompanied the Tu'i Tonga ashore, Ma'i was so upset that he
refused to go with them.

The following morning when the Tu'i Tonga came out to the ship,
he brought out three caps covered with red feathers, one for Cook, one
for Clerke and one for Ma'i, mollifying the young Ra'iatean. Cook had
decided to leave Lifuka, however; and followed by three large sailing
canoes, one of which carried the Tu'i Tonga, on 29 May he set sail for
Nomuka. This was a difficult, dangerous passage, the ships threading their
way through a labyrinth of coral reefs and atolls, guided by William Bligh
in the cutter. Two days later, in squally, wet weather, they almost ran onto
a low sandy reef. They arrived safely, however, and the next morning
when Finau joined them he was forced to perform the obeisance, bowing
his head and touching the sole of the Tu'i Tonga's foot; and when the Tu'i
Tonga ate, Finau left the cabin because he could neither eat nor drink in
the Tu'i Tonga's presence. Ma'i was so disconcerted to see his *taio* Finau
abase himself before the Tu'i Tonga that he made a hash of interpreting
their exchanges. On 8 June they set off from Nomuka, the Tu'i Tonga and
Finau following the ships in different canoes.

The next morning as the ships approached Tongatapu, which Cook
had visited in 1773 with Ma'i and Hitihiti, the tide dragged the *Resolution*
onto a flat, shoaling reef where it hit a rock, and the *Discovery* struck a
coral outcrop, although fortunately neither of them grounded. As William
Bligh led the ships in to the harbour in the cutter, Finau and the Tu'i
Tonga sailed around them in their canoes, the royal canoe distinguished
by a bunch of red grass that hung from a pole on its stern, and sailing right

over several small canoes that got in their way, showing no concern when their crews were tossed in the ocean. On 10 June when the ships anchored off Tongatapu, Ataongo, the lesser chief with whom Cook had exchanged names in 1773, came on board and led Cook and Ma'i ashore to meet with the Tu'i Tonga. They were served food and *kava*, which only Ma'i drank, after Cook had watched young men and women preparing the drink by chewing the *kava* root and spitting it into a bowl, where it was mixed with water. Afterwards the Tu'i Tonga and Cook exchanged gifts, sealing their friendship. Cook put the two gunners, Anderson and Peckover, in charge of barter with the local people; and later the Tu'i Tonga escorted him, Ma'i and Clerke to Mu'a at the south-east end of the island, the sacred head-quarters of the high chiefs of Tonga, where he wanted to introduce them to a man whom he assured them was even more powerful than himself – a chief named Maealiuaki. This was the Tu'i Ha'atakalaua, a role lower in status than the Tu'i Tonga's but even more influential in the islands. When they arrived at this delightful spot, with its large houses and grassy fore-courts surrounded by gardens, and found that Maealiuaki was not there, Cook was angry at this apparent affront, before reflecting that probably Ma'i had misunderstood what the Tongans had told him.

The next morning Maealiuaki arrived at the landing place. This slen-der, dignified, grey-haired chief greeted Captain Cook in a kindly manner and invited him to sit beside him. Ma'i made a speech explaining why they were visiting the archipelago, with a Tongan interpreting (who presum-ably could speak Tahitian), and Cook presented the chief with a sword and some printed cloth. Despite this affable welcome, however, over the next few days the Tongans relentlessly stole iron and other goods from the British, and Captain Cook ordered punishments that escalated to new heights of severity. After seeing how harshly the chiefs treated their own people, he abandoned his usual restraint, flogging those who were caught stealing with two dozen, three dozen and four dozen lashes, ordering ears to be cropped off, and allowing his sailors to impale thieves with boat-hooks when they tried to swim away from the ships. At the same time, the floggings of his own men increased markedly, and at least eight were punished during this stay in Tongatapu.

Cook was obviously a powerful leader, and at this time the Tu'i Tonga and Maealiuaki were planning to install Fatafehi, the Tu'i Tonga's son, as his successor. They hoped to do this at the time of the *'inasi*, when the people gathered for the yam-planting rituals, and decided to recruit Cook's support for his installation. At the Tu'i Tonga's request, Fatafehi and Cook formally became friends during a ceremony performed under a bark-cloth canopy, with Ma'i sitting beside the young heir. When the ceremony was over, Maealiuaki presented Cook with a bark-cloth gar-ment decorated with patches of red feathers in honour of the occasion.

On 17 June thousands of people gathered in front of Maealiuaki's house, where Cook and his officers were seated. A procession of men brought small fish and small yams and laid these offerings down in two heaps, one for Captain Cook and the other for Captain Clerke; followed by displays of weapon handling and a series of formal dances accompanied by drum-mers, including one led by Finau, who was dressed in linen and wore pictures around his neck (perhaps the engravings from the second voyage that Cook had brought with him). Once again Cook responded by order-ing the marines to perform their drill, with a band playing drums, French horns and fifes in the intervals, but the music was so raucous and the drill so slovenly that the Tongans openly mocked their efforts. Te Weherua and Koa, Ma'i's young Māori attendants, performed a *haka* or war dance, which was greeted with great applause, and they were asked to give an encore; but afterwards when several of the sailors were challenged to wrestle and box and were soundly thrashed, Cook ordered the armourer to give another fireworks display, which made a better impression.

During this visit to Tongatapu, most of the sailors found women to sleep with (none of them high-ranking), and many of the men (including Te Weherua) contracted venereal diseases, introduced during Cook's previous visit to the island. Ma'i set up his own small house near the observatory where he slept with his Tongan girlfriends. Whereas during his previous visit to the island Ma'i had been overshadowed by Hitihiti, the high-born Borabora *'arioi*, the Tongans were now treating him with such respect that he became swollen-headed. He began drinking without restraint, and one day in a drunken fit got into an argument with the corporal of marines and struck the man, who punched him back. When Ma'i complained to Cook and Cook refused to punish the corporal, the young Ra'iatean stormed off with Te Weherua and Koa, saying that he would stay at Tongatapu; although when Cook sent him a kindly message, he quickly relented.

Up until this time relationships with the Tongan leaders had gener-ally been amiable, but on 20 June when a kid and two turkeys were stolen from the shore camp, Cook decided to take firm action. Suspecting that the chiefs were behind these thefts, he ordered the sailors to capture three canoes alongside the *Resolution*, and went ashore to the house set aside for the British where the Tu'i Tonga, Finau and other chiefs were talk-ing. Ordering the marines to put them under guard, he told the chiefs that they would have to stay there until everything that their people had stolen, including the missing animals, was returned to him. Hundreds of Tongans gathered outside the house, weeping and lamenting. When a large party of warriors assembled, Cook ordered the marines to surround the Tu'i Tonga with their bayonets pointed at his breast, and the warriors immediately withdrew. As soon as the turkeys, the kid and some iron tools were returned, Cook released the chiefs. The next day the Tu'i Tonga came to see Cook, his head covered with red pigment (the sacred colour), and took him ashore, where his people and Finau's, dressed in capes and aprons covered with red and yellow feathers, were piling up two huge piles of food between posts, each thirty feet tall, one of which was named 'Paulaho' after the Tu'i Tonga and the other 'Finau'. When they were finished, pigs, turtles and large fish were placed on top of these piles as a peace offering; and all these provisions were presented to Cook in a gesture of propitiation. That night there was more dancing and performances; and although the Tu'i Tonga danced, the atmosphere was sullen and sombre.

Despite the peace-making rituals, the Tongans were still bitterly angry about the way that their chiefs had been treated; and the following morning when William Bligh and John Williamson, the *Resolution*'s third lieutenant, went hunting in the interior, they were attacked by three men who stole their muskets. Later that afternoon, Samwell, who was trying to seduce a girl with some beads, was seized from behind and his pockets were picked. When Bligh and Williamson returned to the shore camp and told Ma'i what had happened, Ma'i immediately went to the Tu'i Tonga and Finau, demanding that the muskets be returned. Not surprisingly, the two chiefs fled at once, and Cook reprimanded Ma'i for interfering, although one of the muskets was brought back. By now the shore camp was almost deserted, and the Tu'i Tonga had his canoe ready to sail to Vava'u. Early the next morning an earthquake shook the shore camp, a sign that the gods were angry. Cook was now anxious to make peace with the Tu'i Tonga; and when a message came inviting him to accompany the high chief to the ritual centre at Mu'a, he accepted this invitation. The following morning the Tu'i Tonga escorted Cook to his family burial ground, where three mounds stood encircled by a stone wall, and held a *kava* ceremony as a gesture of reconciliation.

The Tongan warriors were not mollified, however, and at the shore camp they threw stones and pieces of wood at the sailors, teasing and taunting them. Infuriated by an insult, a marine loaded his musket with ball, and when a man snatched a tool from the carpenter, the marine shot him in the shoulder. Soon afterwards when some Tongans pelted a group of officers with coconuts, the officers chased and captured three of these men and brought them back to the shore camp. One of them was an attendant of the Tu'i Tonga, and although the high chief pleaded for his release, in a fit of rage Cook ordered the man to be tied to a tree, flogged with seventy-two lashes and his arms scored with a knife below the shoulders, while his relatives wailed, the women slashing their heads with shark's teeth. Observing this uncharacteristic conduct, the sailors wondered what was happening to Cook, who seemed to be losing his sense of humanity.

The Tongan chiefs were also given to harsh, arbitrary punishments, however, and the Tu'i Tonga seemed to accept Cook's behaviour. The 'inasi 'ufimui ceremony, which was marked by the rising of the Mataliki constellation, a sacred ritual to herald the planting season, was imminent. The Tu'i Tonga intended to install his son Fatafehi as his successor at this ceremony, and was anxious for Captain Cook to lend his *mana* to the occasion. On 7 July a flock of canoes set off for Mu'a, followed by Cook, Clerke and Ma'i in two boats. The 'inasi ceremony was about to begin, and when they met the Tu'i Tonga ashore, he begged them to take off their hats and let down their hair, because the gods were descending. A procession of about 250 men walked to the Tu'i Tonga's meeting house, each carrying small yams or bundles of plantains tied to a pole; and when Cook and his companions followed them to the ceremonial ground, they took off their hats, let down their hair as a sign of respect, and were invited to sit with the Tu'i Tonga and Fatafehi. As the ritual approached its climax, they were told that they would have to leave unless they also stripped to the waist. Although Ma'i readily complied, Cook refused; but when he tried to follow the Tu'i Tonga and Fatafehi to the burial ground, the warriors turned him back. Cook returned to the Tu'i Tonga's house where his companions were waiting, and by making a hole in a bamboo fence they spied on the ritual, during which thirty high-ranking women swaddled the boy in fine white bark cloth. When the ritual ended, they dined with the Tu'i Tonga and were entertained with boxing and wrestling matches; and that night Cook and Ma'i slept in the high chief's dwelling.

The next morning when the chiefs returned to the burial ground, Cook, who was still wearing his shirt and jacket, was again turned back by the warriors. Finally Cook acceded to their requests, and stripping off his shirt and jacket and letting down his hair, he joined in the ritual, running with a group of chiefs and sitting, eyes downcast, before the high chiefs in their shelter. As offerings were piled up before them, Cook and his group were sent to sit with their backs to the high chiefs; although when Cook sneaked a look, he saw a piece of roasted yam being broken and the pieces handed to the Tu'i Tonga and Fatafehi.

When some of the officers saw Cook taking part in this ritual, stripped to the waist and with his hair flying loose, they were astonished to witness so famous a Royal Naval commander abase himself before a 'savage'. As Lieutenant Williamson wrote:

> We . . . were not a little surprised at seeing Capt. Cook in ye procession of the Chiefs, with his hair hanging loose & his body naked down to ye waist; no person being admitted covered above ye waist, or with his hair tyed; I do not pretend to dispute the propriety of Capt. Cook's conduct, but I cannot help thinking he rather let himself down.[16]

Although during his previous two Pacific voyages Cook had upheld the dignity of his office, on this occasion he threw caution to the winds. Perhaps he was simply curious, because he wrote a marvellous account of this ceremony. Or perhaps after refusing to punish Kahura at Queen Charlotte Sound for the killing and eating of the *Adventure*'s men, and feeling the sting of his men's disapproval, his judgement had been disturbed. On that occasion Cook had held fast to the 'enlightened' values of the Royal Society, but in the process he alienated his men. As always, when things got too difficult on land, he decided to go back to sea. After giving farewell presents to the Tu'i Tonga, Fatafehi, Maealiuaki and Finau, Cook set sail on 10 July 1777, heading for the nearby island of 'Eua, which he had visited during his previous voyage.

It is interesting that although the Tongans told Cook about the nearby island groups of Fiji and Samoa, he showed no inclination to investigate these islands. The Tongans had described the Fijians as brave warriors and cannibals, and Cook had had enough of man-eaters. When he arrived at 'Eua on 12 July, he was warmly welcomed by Taione, a chief with whom he had exchanged names during his 1773 visit with Ma'i and Hitihiti to this island. Ma'i was also a great favourite at 'Eua; although when Taione offered to make the young Ra'iatean a chief if he stayed behind, Cook did not favour this proposal. They were welcomed with presentations of food, and wrestling and boxing matches; although on 1 July when two of the *Resolution*'s crew who had gone inland were stripped and returned to the landing place stark naked, Cook ordered the marines to go ashore and seize two canoes. Taione delivered up one of the thieves for punishment, who was carried out to the ship in irons, but Cook had lost his appetite for punishment and allowed the culprit to be ransomed the next morning in exchange for a large pig. It was time to take Ma'i home, and after one last *kava* ceremony and an exchange of gifts with Taione, on 17 July Cook set sail in a light breeze, heading for the Society Islands.

The passage was uneventful until, on 29 July 1777, a sudden, sharp gale split the *Resolution*'s sails and smashed the *Discovery*'s topmast. After a jury-mast had been rigged, they carried on past Tupua'i, one of the Australs, where two small canoes decorated with small pearl-shell circles came out to challenge the ships, the warriors brandishing their weapons and blowing on conch-shell trumpets. These men talked with Ma'i and beckoned for the British to come ashore, but Cook was not tempted, and carried on to the Society Islands.

Tute's Portrait

On 12 August 1777 as the ships approached the southern coast of Tahiti, Ma'i sat on the forecastle all day, weeping with joy as he gazed at the coastline. As for Te Weherua and Koa, they were beside themselves with excitement, scarcely able to believe that they would soon be arriving at this 'Promised Land', Tawhiti, the ancestral homeland of Māori. When some canoes came out from Tahiti-iti, manned by commoners who called out to Ma'i, however, he largely ignored them; and when another canoe came out bringing Ma'i's brother-in-law, who was visiting southern Tahiti, along with several other men who also knew Ma'i, including a chief called Utai, there were no tears or tender greetings. Rather, as Cook remarked in disappointment and surprise, 'there seemed to be a perfect indifference on both sides'.[1]

After a decade of European visits, it must have seemed to the islanders that almost as soon as a European ship sailed away from Tahiti, another appeared over the horizon. Wallis's 1767 visit had been followed by Bougainville the following year, and Bougainville's by Cook in the *Endeavour* in 1769. Three years after Cook had sailed away from Matavai Bay with Tupaia, the *Águila* arrived in southern Tahiti for a brief visit. When Cook and Furneaux visited Tahiti twice during his second Pacific voyage in 1773–74, Pautu, Heiao and Tetuanui were living in Lima; and when the *Águila* returned to southern Tahiti in late 1774, Cook was on his way back to England. By the time that Ma'i arrived in Britain, Máximo Rodríguez and the two Franciscan friars were living in Vaitepiha Bay. In 1775 while Ma'i was still in England, the navigator Puhoro returned home from his voyage to Lima, and 'Matimo' and the friars left the island on board the *Águila*. This small island had become a crossroads for British, French and Spanish ships, driven there by the winds of imperial ambition; and the Tahitians were becoming weary of the strangers, who so often left death and disputes in their wake. As for Ma'i, he was an exile from Ra'iatea

who had been living in Huahine; and compared with the high-born young
'*arioi* Hitihiti, he was a man of little consequence. By now three other
Society Islanders had returned from their travels to European settlements,
and the islanders were becoming blasé about these travellers, and the airs
and graces that they brought with them from those distant places.

When Ma'i took his brother-in-law down to his cabin and showed him
the red feathers that he had acquired in Tongatapu, however, giving him
a few of these treasures, the man was in raptures. As soon as he told his
companions on deck about this chiefly gift, all of them, including the chief
Utai, clamoured to take the young Ra'iatean as their *taio*. Although they
had snubbed him earlier, Ma'i readily agreed to these proposals, giving
each of them a few red feathers. As Cook remarked sadly: 'I expected that
with the property he [had been given] he would have prudence enough to
have made himself respected and even courted by the first people in the
island, but instead of that he rejected the advice of those who wished him
well and suffered himself to be duped by every designing knave.'[2] Cook
had other reasons to be chagrined, though, because when he showed Utai
and his companions the cattle he had transported with such infinite pains
around the world, they were indifferent, saying that during his absence
two ships much larger than his vessels had visited Vaitepiha Bay from
'Reema' (Lima), bringing fine pigs, dogs, goats and a bull which they had
left on the island.

During his second voyage, Cook had learned that after his *Endeavour*
visit to the island in 1769, a Spanish ship commanded by 'Pepe' had visited southern Tahiti. From the garbled understandings he had gained of
Boenechea's visit, Cook thought that a Spanish deserter had run ashore;
and he was alert to the possibility that other Spanish ships might have
visited the island. Through Ma'i, Utai now reported that since Captain
Cook's last arrival in 1774, the Spaniards had twice returned to Tautira.
During their first visit they had built a house and erected a tall cross in
the bay, beneath which their commodore had been buried after dying on
board his vessel. When the ships sailed away again, they had taken three
islanders with them to Lima, leaving behind two priests with a servant
and Matimo, a young Peruvian. As Samwell remarked, Matimo was popular among the Tahitians, 'conform[ing] to their customs & manners and
indulg[ing] himself with those pleasures which the island afforded, more
particularly among the Girls, which last Circumstance was so agreeable
to the Genius of these People that they looked upon him to be the best
Fellow among his Countrymen'.[3] Ten months later when the Spanish ship
had returned, it brought back only one of the Tahitians and took away
the priests and their companions. When he set sail again, their captain

had asked Vehiatua's mother to take care of the mission, assuring her that
he would return to the island. According to George Gilbert, one of the
midshipmen,

> the Spanish were very industrious in telling them that we were Pirates; that
> the English were a nation of very little consequence, and that they were much
> superior to us; which I suppose arises from their having larger ships, and their
> Officers being better dressed, which we took but little care about at those places.
> Notwithstanding these prejudices the Natives confessed that they liked us best;
> for the Spaniards would not permit them to come onboard their ships, but always
> keep them at a great distance whereas we were ever on friendly footing, and had
> the most intimate connexions with them.[4]

According to Cook, Matimo had also assured the Tahiti-iti people that
Britain had been destroyed as a nation; and that as for Cook, they had
met his ship at sea and sunk it with their cannons, sending his vessel and
her crew plunging down into the ocean. This was disconcerting news,
explaining the indifference with which they had at first been greeted.

During this conversation, Cook also learned that in his absence
Vehiatua II had died and been succeeded by his younger brother, Vehiatua
III. Purea, the 'Queen of Tahiti', had also died, although Tu and many of
his other friends were still living. The news of his cargo of red feathers
spread like wildfire, however, and although the Season of Scarcity was
approaching its height, early the next morning the ships were surrounded
by canoes packed with pigs and provisions whose crews shouted out for
'Tute!', clamouring for red plumes. As Cook commented: 'Not more
feathers than might be got from a Tom tit would purchase a Hog of 40 or
50 pound weight, but as every one in the Ships had some they fell in their
value above five hundred per cent before night.'[5] As Bayly remarked, even
the chiefly women succumbed to the craze: 'the women are thought to be
more friendly than on former voyages which are A tribute to the great
desire for red Feathers and numbers of fine women have come on board
the ship, & would cohabit for nothing but red feathers. As soon as they
had obtained a small Quantity by cohabiting once – have disappeared &
not been seen after by us either on board or on shore.'[6]

It was fortunate that Cook had procured so many red feathers in Tonga,
because axes and nails were no longer greatly valued, and without the
feathers it would have been impossible to provision his vessels. After the
ships anchored in Vaitepiha Bay, Ma'i's sister came out in a canoe loaded
with pigs and provisions to greet her brother, weeping and embracing
him tenderly, and Ma'i hurried her below so that his shipmates could not

see that he was also crying. Several chiefs came on board, and when Cook allowed them to put on the red feather bonnets that the Tu'i Tonga had given them, one of these men went to the galley window, preening himself and proudly showing off his headdress to the spectators alongside in the canoes, 'with great Complacency like some eastern Monarch adored by his subjects'.[7] According to Lieutenant King, when they went ashore at Tautira there were none of the tumultuous scenes of welcome that he had expected, and 'no remarkable bursts of surprise, applause or pleasure'.[8] The newcomers to the island were enchanted by Vaitepiha Bay, however, with its towering jagged mountains, its green valley and the 'fine stream of water' that wound down to the ocean, past picturesque houses and lush gardens. As soon as they landed, Ma'i took Captain Cook to meet an elderly man known as Etari, who sat under a canoe awning with plantain branches laid about his feet. Greeting this man with extreme deference, Ma'i addressed him as "Oro' and presented him with a tuft of red feathers on a stick, explaining to Cook that this was 'the God of Bolabola', a priest who was the *ata* or incarnation of the war god. Whenever this man left his shelter, the people carried him on a kind of handbarrow because his feet were so sacred that if they touched the ground it became forbidden to ordinary people.

Soon afterwards, Ma'i's mother's sister approached the young traveller, weeping at his feet; and as people gathered around and Ma'i began to regale them with tales of his adventures, Cook went off to look at the mission house that the Spaniards had erected. This prefabricated building was made of numbered oak boards, and had two rooms, with a table, bench, a bedstead and a large mahogany chest with a gilded hat and some old clothes inside. The building was protected by a large thatched shelter and stood on a stone pavement, surrounded by a palisade. A wooden cross about nine feet high stood outside, painted green and bearing the carved inscription '*Christus Vincit Carolus III imperat 1774*'. Angered by the effrontery of this inscription, which claimed the island for the King of Spain, Cook ordered his men to take the cross down and carry it back to the *Resolution*.

During this visit ashore, to his dismay Cook saw large Spanish pigs, two goats and three different breeds of European dogs in Tautira, along with some vines that the Spaniards had planted. The local people told him more about 'Matimo', whom they had liked and admired; although it was obvious that the Spanish friars had made no converts on the island. In their conversations with Cook, the Tahitians mercilessly satirised the monks, mimicking them counting their beads, blessing their food and performing other Roman Catholic rituals. As Samwell reported, although the islanders remarked that Matimo had slept with their women, 'they all unanimously condemn'd the flesh-subduing Dons, for that self denial which may be deemed meritorious in Cells & Cloisters, will be always looked upon with Contempt by the lovely & beautiful Nymphs of Otaheite'.[9]

Early the next morning when the horses were sent ashore, Ma'i and one of the officers (probably his friend Lieutenant Burney) mounted these animals and rode along the beach, Ma'i shooting his pistol over the heads

Ma'i goes riding on the beach at Vaitepiha Bay

of the crowd. At last Ma'i had managed to create a sensation, although when he was tossed off his mount the islanders laughed in derision. After dinner Cook summoned his men and told them about the search for the Northwest Passage and the £20,000 reward that had been offered for a successful discovery; and when he suggested that it might be better to save their grog now rather than to run out of spirits off the frozen coastline of Canada, the sailors unanimously agreed, saying that they were willing for their grog to be stopped except on Saturday nights, when they would mix it with coconut milk, toasting their wives and girlfriends back in England with this Polynesian cocktail. Now that they had arrived in Tahiti, that legendary paradise where their red feathers gave them the pick of the unmarried girls, the men were happy again; and Samwell reported that 'the Ships Company perfectly satisfied with these Reasons of Captain Cook & putting entire Confidence in him that he did every thing for the best, without the least hesitation unanimously agreed to the last Proposal . . ., which readiness to comply with his request afforded Capt. Cook much pleasure'.[10]

Over the next two days it poured with rain. On 15 August Vehiatua III sent his stepfather Ti'itorea with gift of two pigs and a message that he would visit Captain Cook the following morning. Dressing himself in a bizarre mix of English and Tahitian garments, Ma'i escorted Cook ashore to the place where Etari, the 'God of Bolabola', was waiting. During the voyage the young Raiatean had made a *maro 'ura* decorated with red and yellow feathers that he had collected in Tongatapu, intending this as a gift for Tu; and he took this precious object with him, showing it with great pride to the 'God of Bolabola'. Afterwards the priest was carried in his barrow to a house where they waited for Vehiatua III, a boy about twelve years old who arrived dressed in a scarlet-laced pair of Spanish breeches and a gold-laced Spanish hat, accompanied by his mother Purahi. When an orator spoke on behalf of the visitors, one of Vehiatua's people replied; then the priest spoke, followed by Ma'i, who were answered by the chief's orators. When Cook presented the young *ari'i* with a sword, a cotton gown and red feathers, he accepted these gifts with delight, exchanging names and taking Cook as his *taio*, and his mother Purahi took Captain Clerke as her bond friend. Afterwards Ma'i handed Vehiatua the red feather girdle that he had made, asking him to send it on to Tu so that it could be stitched to the royal *maro 'ura*; and at the sight of this prized object, Vehiatua and his family were overjoyed.

As mentioned earlier, Vehiatua had no red feather girdle of his own; whereas Tu now had two to wear on ritual occasions – the red feather girdle that his mother Tetupaia had brought from Ra'iatea, which he wore on Taraho'i, his family *marae*; and Te Ra'i-puatata, the famous red feather girdle that Tupaia had brought from Taputapuatea, which Tu wore for the ceremonies at 'Utu-'ai-mahurau *marae*. Vehiatua's family had been longing to have a red feather girdle of their own, and they could not resist the opportunity to keep Ma'i's gift for themselves, sending only a few of the red and yellow feathers to Tu. Although the Spaniards had assured the Tahiti-iti chiefs that the British were only *teuteu* or servants, these marvellous gifts gave the lie to that statement. Nevertheless, Vehiatua III and his family still spoke highly of Boenechea and his officers, saying that the Spanish sailors had been forbidden to sleep with their women, and made many gifts without expecting any return. These comments were no doubt politic, intended to inspire the British to a similar generosity; but when Vehiatua remarked that he had promised the Spanish commander that he would not allow the British to enter Vaitepiha Bay, Cook reacted angrily, retorting that they had no right to try to restrict his movements. In response, Vehiatua and his counsellors declared Cook 'the sole proprietor of the land, water & hogs, and in short conferr'd the sovereignty of the place upon him',[11] an honour sometimes paid to high-ranking visitors. Afterwards, the surgeon William Anderson mused:

> [The Spanish] took every possible means to avoid giving offence, were very severe in punishing their own people who offerd any injustice to the natives, even prohibiting too great a familiarity to prevent such accidents, distributed a great many things amongst them such as cloth, hatchets &c., and in short seem'd to have studied their good without expecting any thing in return. The consequence of this is that the natives have really acquired a kind of veneration for the people of that nation and seem to respect their moral character still more than admire their power, a proof that tender treatment may sometimes effect more than the force of arms.[12]

The next day Vehiatua III sent Cook a dozen pigs, fruit and bark cloth, and some of the officers visited Vehiatua II's funeral bier which stood by a creek near the Spanish mission. This was a large, thatched shelter hung with coloured cloth, mats, feather tassels and a length of scarlet Spanish broadcloth where Vehiatua II's body lay in state, guarded day and night by two men, with offerings of fruit lying nearby on a *fata* or altar for offerings. This place was so intensely *ra'a*, or sacred, that its guardians would not allow the British officers to venture beyond the outer palisade. That night Cook gave a fireworks display which astonished Vehiatua's people; and when he heard the islanders exclaim that 'the Lima ships had neither red feathers, nor fireworks!' he was delighted. The next morning, the navigator Puhoro, who had travelled to Lima and still remembered some Spanish ('*Si Senore!*', for instance), came out to the ship, where he spoke highly of the Spaniards. Ma'i, who was jealous to find another traveller like himself on the island, treated this man so roughly that they did not see him again. Later, Captain Clerke met Pautu, the diver who had also visited Lima, describing him as 'a low fellow and a little out of his sences'.[13]

During this visit, despite their assurances to Captain Cook, the Tahiti-iti people remained loyal to Boenechea and the Spaniards. Vehiatua's mother Purahi urged Cook to re-erect the cross outside the mission, and did not allow Ma'i to claim the Spanish mission house as a dwelling, although he offered her rich gifts for it. On 20 August Cook had the back of the cross inscribed with the legend '*Georgius tertius Rex Annis 1767, 69, 73, 74 & 77*', claiming the island for King George of Britain and listing the dates of the various British visits; and had it erected again in front of the Spanish mission to the pleasure of Vehiatua and his people. Tautira was a centre for 'Oro's worship; and that afternoon Lieutenant Williamson attended an *'arioi heiva* performed by two little girls, a young woman and two men, remarking that 'the whole concluded with a very obscene part perform'd by ye ladies, there are me customs in ye entertainments of the women, the relation of which tho' it might gratify curiosity, must offend modesty'.[14]

Not all of Cook's officers were enchanted with Vaitepiha Bay, however. Although the Tahiti-iti people entertained them every day with *heiva* or *'arioi* performances, Samwell thought Tahitian dancing much less graceful and entertaining than the night dances in Tonga; while Lieutenant King remarked that the paths in Tahiti-iti were muddy and slippery and the gardens chaotic, unlike the neat pathways and tidy fenced gardens in Tonga. He also thought that although the Tahitian women were beautiful, 'the men here fall far short in my Idea, in shape, air sweetness & manliness, of those in Tongatapu . . . If we want'd a model for an Apollo or Bachus we must look for it at Otaheite, & shall find it to perfection, but if for a Hercules or an Ajax at the friendly Isles [Tonga].'[15]

During Cook's visit to Tautira, his *taio* Tu sent him several plantain branches, urging him to return to Matavai Bay; and on 23 August while the ships were being unmoored, Cook and Ma'i went ashore to farewell Vehiatua III. As they talked with the young *ari'i rahi*, a man dressed in a girdle of plantain leaves joined them who spoke in a low, squeaking voice, warning Vehiatua not to sail with Cook to Matavai Bay and predicting that the ships would not reach their destination. Cook was annoyed, as he had suggested no such expedition. Although Vehiatua described this man as a *ta'ata 'ino* (bad person), his people took his prophecies seriously, believing that he was possessed by the god. While the oracle was speaking there was a downpour, and although everyone else ran for cover, he kept squeaking out his messages. According to Ma'i, when people were possessed in this way they did not know what they were doing; and sometimes a man in this state would give away all of his wealth to the 'arioi, and then come to his senses and realise that he had impoverished himself.

As soon as Cook boarded the *Resolution*, contrary to the oracle's prediction a light breeze sprang up from the east which carried the ship directly to Matavai Bay, where they anchored that evening; although the *Discovery* did not enter the bay until early the next morning. Twenty-four of the sailors on this expedition had previously visited the island; and hundreds of canoes loaded with young women, 'curiosities' and provisions surrounded the ships, their crews frantically crying out for 'Tute' (Cook), 'Pane' (Banks), 'Tate' (Clerke), Gore and their other friends on board the vessels. At last Cook was receiving the ecstatic welcome that he had expected, the people slashing themselves, weeping and embracing their *taio*. At 9 a.m. the next morning when Tu arrived at Matavai Bay with a fleet of canoes, he landed at Point Venus and sent a messenger to his *taio* Tute, welcoming him back to his district. Through his bond friendship with Tu, Captain Cook had already been made an *ari'i* of Matavai Bay, and Tu was overjoyed to see his friend again. When he disembarked, intending to outdo the Spanish, Cook sent the marines ahead dressed in their scarlet and white jackets to form a guard of honour on the beach. He and his officers wore their best uniforms, and Ma'i donned his most elegant suit. As the pinnace approached Point Venus, they found Tu sitting surrounded by a huge crowd, accompanied by his father Teu, his younger brother Ari'ipaea, a strongly built young man five feet ten inches tall, their younger brother (Vaetua) and three sisters (Ari'ipaea-vahine, Tetua-te-ahama'i and Auo). Cook approached and presented his *taio* with a suit of fine linen, a gold-laced hat, a silk dressing gown and slippers, some tools, a large piece of woven fabric covered with red feathers, and a red feather headdress from Tongatapu, which he put on Tu's head to shouts of acclamation. When Ma'i was brought to Tu, he greeted the paramount chief by kneeling and embracing his legs, and presented Tu with another piece of red-feathered cloth and a length of gold cloth from Britain.

Afterwards Tu and his family came out to the *Resolution*, followed by canoes laden with lavish gifts of food and bark cloth, where Cook gave them more gifts, showering Tu's sisters with looking glasses, beads and other trinkets; and the bagpiper played for them, to their intense delight. According to Samwell, when Tu offered his younger sister to Cook as a bedmate during his visit, Cook declined the honour as gracefully as possible. Soon afterwards Tu's mother Tetupaia arrived at the ship, a large, dignified, warm-hearted woman who wept at Cook's feet and gave him more rich gifts of food and bark cloth. Although at first Tu and his family ignored Ma'i, throughout these exchanges Cook treated the young Ra'iatean like a man of *mana*. He wanted Ma'i to stay in Tahiti with Tu and his family, because he could help Tu's people to look after the animals that he had brought for them from England. Although Cook hoped that 'the farther he was from his native island the more [Ma'i] would be respected',[16] instead the young Ra'iatean offended Tu and his family by lauding the power of the British King, implying that Tu's *mana* paled into insignificance by comparison:

> Omai began by magnifying the grandeur of the Great King; he compared the splendour of his court to the brilliancy of the stars in the firmament; the extent of his dominions by the vast expanse of heaven; the greatness of his power, by the thunder that shakes the earth. He said, the Great King of Pretanne had three hundred thousand warriors every day at his command, clothed like those who now attended the Earees [*ari'i*] of the ships, and more than double that number of sailors, who traverse the globe, from the rising of the sun to his setting . . .
>
> He said, the ships of war of Pretanne were furnished with poo-poos [guns] each of which would receive the largest poo-poo which his Majesty had yet seen within it; that some carried 100 or more of those poo-poos, with suitable accommodation for a thousand fighting men, and stowage for all kinds of cordage and war-like stores, besides provisions and water for the men and other animals for 100 or 200 days . . . That in one city only on the banks of a river far removed from the sea, there were more people than were contained in the whole group of islands with which his Majesty was acquainted.[17]

And when Tu realised that Ma'i had given a red feather *maro* intended for him to Vehiatua III, he was incensed with the young Raiatean, immediately despatching a messenger to Tautira to demand the *maro 'ura*; although Vehiatua sent back only a few red feathers and a human sacrifice for 'Oro by way of an apology.

After dinner Cook accompanied Tu and his family to Pare, where his men released a pair of peacocks, two geese, two turkeys and some ducks on the beach. Early the next morning the sailors delivered three cows and a young bull, two ewes and a ram and two female goats to Tu's family. The Spanish bull, a magnificent beast that had been claimed by Etari, the 'God of Bolabola', was already at Pare, along with some goats and the gander that Captain Wallis had given Purea during his visit to the island. That afternoon when Hitihiti came out to the *Resolution* he was given tools, clothing including a silk dressing gown, and other rich presents; but after hearing so much about the young 'arioi the officers were disappointed to meet him. According to Samwell, Hitihiti was 'one of the most stupid Fellows on the Island, with a clumsy awkward Person and a remarkably heavy look; he is married to a pretty woman who lives at Matavai; he frequently came on board to see us along with his Wife & was almost constantly drunk with Kava'.[18]

Over the next few days the sailors set to work erecting the observatory tents, recaulking the ships, overhauling the rigging and replacing the *Discovery*'s mainmast, which had been damaged in the recent storm. A garden was planted with potatoes, pineapples and melons, and some shaddock trees, and Ma'i planted cuttings he had taken from the vine that the Spaniards planted at Tautira, hoping that he could grow grapes and make wine on the island. After the departure of the friars the Tautira people had tasted the unripe grapes, and finding them bitter had trampled most of the plants into the ground. The sailors who had previously visited Tahiti were reunited with their *taio* and girlfriends, while girls from Vaitepiha Bay soon joined their sweethearts. With their red feathers to offer as gifts, the sailors had plenty of women to sleep with. As Rickman, one of these men, declared:

> We had not a vacant hour between business and pleasure, that was unemployed. We wanted no coffee-houses to kill time, nor Ranelaghs or Vauxhalls [the pleasure gardens in London] for our evening entertainments . . . In these Elysian fields, immortality alone is wanting to the enjoyment of all those pleasures which the poet's fancy has conferred on the shades of departed heroes, as the highest rewards of heroic virtue.[19]

On 27 August a messenger from Tautira reported that two large Spanish ships had anchored in Vaitepiha Bay, and that Matimo was on board. Producing some coarse blue Spanish cloth, this man described the ships so minutely that Cook was convinced that he was telling the truth. Although the *Discovery* had been careened for repairs and was lying on the beach without her mainmast, Cook had the *Resolution*'s guns hurriedly mounted and sent Lieutenant Williamson in the large cutter to spy on the Spaniards. Seeing these warlike preparations, the islanders deserted Matavai Bay, fearing that Cook was about to attack them. When the cutter arrived back the next day, Williamson reported that the story was a lie, but that their guide had jumped overboard, escaping punishment for his deception. That night, Tu and his family returned to Matavai Bay; and during a heavy overnight downpour a hammock and a barrel in the ship's tent were stolen. Later, William Bayly, disturbed by a thief who was trying to steal a small box containing red feathers from the observatory, seized the man by the hair. Although the thief escaped, Bayly was convinced by the frizzy mop of hair he had grabbed that the offender was Tu, because he had shown these feathers only to the paramount chief; but in any case, Tu and his brothers offered to guard the tents over the next few nights, and afterwards nothing significant was stolen.

On 30 August messengers from Mo'orea reported that there had been a rebellion on that island, and that Tu's friends had been forced to fly to the mountains. Cook had already been told that soon after his departure in 1774 the great fleet he had inspected had sailed to Mo'orea, led by the 'Admiral' To'ofa. As soon as the fleet appeared off the coast, however, Mahine's people had fled to the hills and avoided a battle. Now Mahine's people had risen up against Mahau, Tu's kinsman by marriage and the 'rightful' heir to the senior titles on the island; and when the messengers arrived at Tu's house in Matavai Bay, Cook listened to one of them giving a fiery speech, inciting Tu and his people to attack the rebels. There was a heated debate, with speakers arguing for and against such an action, while Tu sat silently, listening intently. Those chiefs who were eager to fight urged Cook to assist them; and because Ma'i was absent, Cook had to speak in his halting Tahitian, declaring that because the people of Mo'orea had done nothing against him and his men, he would not fight them. At the end of this meeting, Tu asked Cook to accompany him to Teu's house that afternoon, where the debate was resumed. During this discussion, Teu, who was very bitter against Mahine, told Captain Cook that some years earlier when Mahine had asked Vehiatua to send his young brother to Mo'orea as his successor, about a week after the boy's arrival Mahine had him killed. Afterwards he set himself up as the *ari'i* instead of Teri'i-tapunui (also known as Mahau),[20] the son of his sister Vave'a, bitterly offending the Tahiti-iti people and many others on the island.

That night a group of women performed a sultry dance on the banks of the Tuauru River, trying to awaken 'Oro-taua, the war god, in support of Mahau. According to the surgeon Dr Anderson, this performance

bespoke an excess of joy and licentiousness, though perhaps it might be their usual custom. Most of these were young women, who put themselves into seve-ral lascivious postures, clapp'd their hands and repeated a kind of Stanzas. At certain parts they put their garments aside and exposd with seemingly very little sense of shame those parts which most nations have thought it modest to conceal, & a woman more advanc'd in years stood in front, held her cloaths continually up with one hand and danced with uncommon vigour and effrontery, as if to raise in the spectators the most libidinous desires . . . The men flockd eagerly round them in great numbers to see their performance and express'd the most anxious curiosity to see that part just mentioned, at which they seem'd to feel a sort of rapture that could only be express'd by the extreme joy that appear'd in their countenances.[21]

Early the next morning To'ofa sent a message to Tu to say that a human sacrifice was about to be offered to 'Oro, seeking his support for the forthcoming attack; and as he was the paramount chief of the island, Tu's presence was required to summon the gods to the *marae*. Eager to witness this 'extraordinary and barbarous custom', Cook asked to accompany his *taio*; and when Tu agreed, they set off together in the launch with Pohuetea (the *ari'i* of this *marae*), Dr Anderson and the artist John Webber, Ma'i following behind in a canoe. At Motu Tahiri, a small island off the Fa'a'a district where they met To'ofa and his attendants, To'ofa asked Cook whether he would fight alongside them in the war against Mo'orea; and when Cook refused, To'ofa retorted angrily that it was strange that someone who always claimed to be their friend would not join them in fighting against their enemies. Before they sailed from the island, To'ofa gave Tu a tuft of two or three red feathers and a half-starved dog which was loaded into a canoe that followed them to 'Utu-'ai-mahurau *marae*.

As they came through the 'Irihonu (or To'ofaroa) pass at Pa'ea, they caught sight of this famous temple, built on a small point jutting out into the ocean which was also named 'Utu-'ai-mahurau.[22] When the black leg *'arioi* from Pa'ea spoke at their gatherings, he used to chant:

> The mountain above is Mahu-ta'a
> The assembly ground below is Taruru-'amo'a
> The points outside are Pa'ea and 'Utu-'ai-mahurau
> The rivers are Vai-atu and Vai-ra'a
> The *marae* is 'Utu-'ai-mahurau
> The passage for canoes is To'ofa-roa
> The high chief was Tevahi-tua-i-patea
> And the under chief was To'ofa
> The chief *'arioi* was Hita.[23]

Asking Cook to order the sailors to stay in the boat, Tu begged Cook, Anderson and Webber to take off their hats as they approached the sacred *marae*. They did so, and escorted by Tu and accompanied by a crowd of men and boys (with no women among them) they walked to the temple, where four priests and the *'opu nui* (literally, 'big belly') *marae* attendants were waiting. The human sacrifice, covered with palm leaves and trussed to a pole, was lying in a canoe in front of the *marae*, with water lapping against the hull. Two of the priests sat beside this canoe while the other two sat by the large stone *ahu* or platform. Cook stood at a distance from the *ahu* with Tu and several others, where one of the 'Big Bellies' brought a plantain branch and laid it in front of Tu, followed by another carrying a tuft of red feathers which he touched to one of Tu's feet, before retiring to a small *ahu* that stood on the beach. This was the 'bed of the gods' where the paramount chief stood during his installation, and the images of the gods rested during the ceremonies.[24] (*See Plate 9.*)

A priest now began a long prayer, periodically picking up a plantain branch and laying it down on the body of the human sacrifice, while a man stood nearby holding two bundles wrapped in bark cloth, one containing Te Ra'i-puatata, the famous *maro 'ura* from Ra'iatea, and the other containing the *to'o* (bound image) of 'Oro that Tupaia had brought with it from Taputapuatea. The man with the bundles containing these sacred objects joined the priests by the canoe, and after more prayers the plantain branches were taken off the corpse one by one and placed before the priests, and the body was lifted from the canoe and laid on the beach with its feet towards the sea while the priests stood around it, holding tufts of red feathers and praying to 'Oro. Finally, the body was laid down parallel to the sea, where a priest chanted for a long time before pulling some hair from its head and removing one of its eyes, which he placed in a green leaf and offered to Tu, who opened his mouth (allowing its spirit to enter his body) and presented the man with the tuft of red feathers that To'ofa had given him. This offering of the eye echoed Tafa'i's visit to the land of the dead, where he had gained power over its guardian (the old woman Uhi) by replacing her eyes, and rescued his father from the excremental underworld, where the gods had blinded him.[25] The man carried the eye, the red feathers and the tuft of hair back to the other priests, and when a kingfisher cried out, Tu exclaimed, 'That's the *Eatua* [god]!', explaining to Cook that this was a good omen.

The body was now carried from the beach to the inland side of the small *ahu*, where it was lain with its head towards the *ahu* and red feathers at its feet, below three carved *'unu* boards. As the bundles of bark cloth containing the *to'o* of 'Oro and the *maro 'ura* were laid on the 'bed of the gods', the great drums boomed, and the head priest implored 'Oro to help them defeat Mahine and their Mo'orea enemies, holding up To'ofa's tuft of red feathers as he did so. After a long chant in which Pohuetea took part, another tuft of hair was plucked from the head of the sacrifice and laid on the small *ahu*, while the red feathers were placed on the bundles of cloth, where they became imbued with their *mana*. The priests now carried the bundles, the red feathers and the sacrifice to a much larger *ahu*, situated further inland. This *ahu* stood about fourteen feet high and had a stone pavement in front dotted with a number of upright stones (the leaning places of the chiefs on the *marae*),[26] some of which were covered with bark cloth. The upright stones on the *marae* held the chiefly titles, and the titles held their genealogies, binding chief and land together.[27] The bundles of bark cloth containing the image of 'Oro and the red feather girdles, along with the red feathers, were leaned against the great *ahu* and the human sacrifice placed at its foot. As the priests prayed and the great drums beat loudly, a hole about two feet deep was dug in front of the stone platform where the *marae* attendants roughly buried the victim, covering it with dirt and stones.

As the body was placed in this grave a boy squeaked aloud, and Ma'i told Cook that this was the voice of the god speaking to them. The dog that To'ofa had given them was killed by having its neck twisted; and its fur was singed off, its guts thrown into a sacred fire and the organs laid on hot stones, where the blood was collected in a coconut shell and smeared all over the animal's body, making the sacrifice pleasing to 'Oro. As the great drums throbbed across the *marae*, a boy squeaked again loudly several times, calling upon the *atua* to eat these offerings. As soon as the priests had finished their prayers, the dog was placed with two others and three pigs on a large *fata* or sacrificial altar that stood near the small *ahu*, and the priests and the 'Big Bellies' (*marae* attendants) gave a kind of shout which ended that part of the ceremony. Afterwards, Tu, Ma'i and Cook went to Pohuetea's house where they spent the night, discussing the war and the omens that had occurred during the ceremony.

Early the next morning another pig was sacrificed, and Ma'i went off to see To'ofa, his new *taio*. By the time that Tu returned with Captain Cook to 'Utu-'ai-mahurau *marae*, the priests and a large number of men had gathered. Tu stood between the two great drums, close to the stone pyramid, inviting Cook to stand beside him. A plantain branch was laid at Tu's feet, and as the priests chanted, holding tufts of red feathers and an ostrich feather that Cook had given his *taio*, the red feathers were placed on the *fare atua* or god-house one by one, another pig was sacrificed, and the bark-cloth bundle containing the *maro 'ura* was opened and Te Ra'i-puatata was spread out on the stone pavement. Cook described this famous red feather girdle, the cause of so many wars, as a woven sash about five yards long and fifteen inches broad, with squares of bright yellow feathers and a few red and green ones pasted onto bark cloth, which was sewn to one end of the *Dolphin*'s red pennant. At one end of the girdle were eight horseshoe-shaped lappets fringed with black feathers, while the other end was forked. One part of the sash was incomplete, decorated only by the few feathers sent by Vehiatua from the girdle presented to him by Ma'i. There was also a sunshade, which seemed to be quite ancient, decorated with red tropic bird tail feathers. After the priests chanted the prayer of the *maro*, the sacred girdle and the red feather bonnet were wrapped again in bark cloth and laid on the great *ahu*. Afterwards the bundle containing the image of 'Oro was opened at one end; and when some red feathers were taken out, Cook could see the plaited sennit binding or 'skin' of the god, although he was not allowed to approach the sacred image. The entrails from the sacrificed pig were laid before the priests; and after watching their twitchings, one of the priests announced that the omens for the war against Mahine were encouraging.

After the entrails were thrown in the fire, the image of the god and the red feathers were replaced in the *fare atua* or god-house. Four large double canoes had been drawn up on the beach, each with a *marae* or sacred platform on board covered with palm leaves tied in intricate knots. These canoes held offerings of several small pigs, coconuts, plantains and breadfruit; and Tu told Cook that they belonged to 'Oro and would accompany the fleet when it sailed to fight Mahine. The human sacrifice or *ta'ata tapu* (sacred person) had been a middle-aged *teuteu* or servant; and on a ledge on the small *ahu* Cook saw forty-nine skulls belonging to previous sacrificial victims. Although the atmosphere was sombre, when Ma'i arrived in the middle of this ceremony the spectators gathered around him, asking him innumerable questions about his time in England, obviously feeling no need to keep quiet.[28]

According to Ma'i, this ritual was called the *pure ari'i*. When a human sacrifice was required for one of these ceremonies, the *ari'i maro 'ura*'s servants were sent to the *ari'i* of the various districts, each of whom nominated a victim. These men killed their victims by coming upon them unawares and hitting them on the back of the head with a club or a large stone; and when these human sacrifices were offered to 'Oro, the paramount chief had to be present. At this time, they were told, 'Utu-'ai-mahurau was the only *marae* in Tahiti where human sacrifices could be offered, because this was the place where the image of 'Oro and Te Ra'i-puatata were held. After a battle, the jawbones of enemies were also offered to 'Oro, and their bodies were brought to the *marae* where they were ritually buried. During the war against Vehiatua, for instance, the bodies of Tutaha and Tepau had been sent to this *marae*, their bowels cut out in front of the great stone temple and their corpses buried in different places on the *marae*, marked by upright stones – Tutaha, for instance, was buried near the small *ahu*, while the other dead warriors had been buried in a hole in front of the *ahu* as a thanks-offering for Vehiatua's victory. After peace had been made, Vehiatua's son and Tu had become *taio* or bond brothers; and later Tu was ceremonially invested with the *maro 'ura* Te Ra'i-puatata at this *marae* in the presence of the *ari'i* of the island, and recognised as the *ari'i maro 'ura* of Tahiti. Ma'i, who had been present when Tu was girdled with the red feather girdle, described this ceremony in some detail.

At the end of this ritual, Cook, Tu and Ma'i returned to Motu Tahiri, where To'ofa and his people were waiting. When the 'Admiral' asked Cook what he thought of the ceremony, and whether he and his men would join the attack on Mahine, Cook replied that the human sacrifice would not please the god, and that they would be defeated if they sailed against Mahine. These remarks infuriated To'ofa, and when Ma'i assured him that if he killed a man as a sacrifice in England, he would be hung by the neck, he was enraged, yelling out *'Ma 'ino! Ma 'ino!'* ('Bad! Bad!') and storming off, disgusted with the English and their perverse views. That night there was a *heiva ra'a* (sacred *heiva*) at Tu's house at Pare, during which his sisters danced, with comic interludes performed by male *'arioi* actors; while nearby two women and an old man beat gently on drums and sang softly, as about a hundred people listened silently to their music.

Over the next few days there were numerous feasts and entertainments. Ma'i gave a feast with fish, chickens, pigs and one of Cook's favourite puddings (made of breadfruit, ripe plantains, taro and palm nuts, individually scraped, rasped, mashed and baked, then mixed together with coconut milk and stirred over hot stones in a large wooden vessel). Several nights later, when Cook ordered a display of fireworks, many of the islanders were terrified when a table rocket accidentally flew into the crowd. Shortly afterwards there was a violent thunderstorm, convincing the people that 'Oro was angry with the British for trying to usurp his powers. Not to be outdone, Hitihiti also gave a feast, and afterwards Tu invited Cook to Teu's house where two women were being wrapped in vast quantities of bark cloth, with coloured cloth on top and two warrior's *taumi* breast-plates hung around their necks. When these girls were ready, Teu sent them on board the *Resolution* along with pigs and fruit as a gift to Cook, his son's *taio*, a ceremony that Ma'i attended dressed in his suit of armour. The next day Tu sent a gift of five pigs and a lavish supply of fruit out to the *Resolution* for Cook, while the islanders went fishing in the lagoon. As men and women stood in the water, beating it with sticks to drive the fish into a shoal, others walked with a seine net, encircling the seething mass of mackerel. When small nets were brought to collect the catch, there was chaos as the people ducked and dived to get their share. This was followed by another *heiva ra'a* at Tu's house in Pare, where his three sisters danced for Cook and his companions; and Cook visited the funerary bier of Ti'i, Tu's counsellor whom he had met during his last visit, whose embalmed body lay on the platform covered with bark cloth.

On 12 September, without telling Cook, Tu left Matavai Bay to assist at another *pure ari'i* ceremony at 'Utu-'ai-mahurau *marae*, featuring a human sacrifice sent there by Vehiatua. The next day at Pare, Tu ceremonially returned lands and pigs that had been confiscated from Tutaha's family to Tutaha's sons, one of whom had adopted Lieutenant King as his *taio*. Disappointed to have missed these ceremonies, Cook was upset that his *taio* had not invited him to join him on this occasion; and the next day he and Clerke went riding across the Matavai plains, followed by an astonished crowd of islanders. According to Lieutenant King: 'I believe they had never before seen any object which so highly rais'd their conceptions of our superiority over them: We want'd all these helps to give us a consequence in the Eyes of these people equal to the Spaniards.'[29] Although on several occasions Ma'i had tried to ride, dressed in his suit of armour and brandishing his sword, he had always fallen off his mount, ruining the spectacle. Cook was becoming increasingly frustrated with the young Ra'iatean, who was giving away his red feathers to 'refugees and strangers' (presumably other exiles from Ra'iatea) and strutted around Point Venus wearing carnival masks and other bizarre finery. Although Cook had hoped to marry him to Tu's youngest sister, Ma'i had an affair with a young commoner instead, who gave him a venereal infection and stripped him of his treasures. To make matters worse, he had forged a bond friendship with To'ofa, Tu's rival, offending the people at Matavai Bay and Pare. Nevertheless, Tu's people were fond of Te Weherua and Koa, Ma'i's Māori attendants; although Koa, who liked playing practical jokes, was sometimes worsted. One day when he was tormenting a young girl, for instance, she retaliated by calling him a cannibal and pretending to chew on her arm, reducing him to tears; although he got his revenge by mimicking her eating lice from her hair, a custom that she sometimes practised.

During Tu's absence, Reti, Bougainville's *taio*, arrived at Matavai Bay, and Tu's father Teu came to Point Venus, where he appointed guards to protect the British and their possessions. Each morning these guards claimed tribute from the girls who had spent the night on board the ships – a lucrative business. The islanders seemed less troubled than formerly by venereal diseases, and there were suggestions that the local priests had discovered a treatment that relieved or cured the symptoms. According to William Bayly, 'the natives pay no kind of Atention or fear of it – for when they were told & shewed that a man had the fowl disease they constantly say it would not hurt them'.[30] After their debauches, however, the sailors were becoming insubordinate, and some had to be severely punished for their 'licentious' behaviour towards the local women; while Lieutenant Williamson and the officer of marines Lieutenant Phillips (a close friend of Lieutenant King) quarrelled over a girl and fought a duel with pistols, each narrowly missing the other with his shot.[31]

On 14 September, messengers arrived from Pare to report that the fleet led by To'ofa and Pohuetea had sailed to Mo'orea to attack Mahine and his people. Apparently, when Mahine's fleet approached the canoes from Tahiti, however, the two sides found that they were so evenly matched that they did not engage with each other. Tu had refused to sail on this expedition, and the chiefs were blaming the ari'i maro 'ura for this inconclusive outcome, calling him 'a coward'.[32] Cook was ready to leave Tahiti; and he ordered the observatory tents to be struck and brought on board, and took the sheep to Pare and gave them to Tu. But to his annoyance, when Etari, the 'God of Bolabola', who had the Spanish bull in his possession, arrived at Pare, he refused to exchange this magnificent beast for one of Cook's young bulls and a cow, saying that it was destined for Borabora. Fearing that the priest would also claim the rest of his animals for 'Oro, Cook declared that if anyone took these creatures from Pare or killed them, he would return and destroy them. Afterwards, when Cook declared in frustration that 'instead of being a God [Etari] was the greatest Jackass he ever saw in his Life', Ma'i rebuked him – 'Ah Captain Cook! He is a very goog Gog! A very goog Gog Capt. Cook!'[33] – to the hilarity of the sailors.

On 21 September, the day of the spring equinox when the 'arioi assembled, Tu came to tell Cook that the Matavai fleet was about to sail for Pare; and Cook, who was eager to know more about Tahitian naval tactics, asked him if they would demonstrate their manoeuvres. There were about seventy large canoes in the fleet, decorated with banners and feather pennants and packed with spears and other weapons, carrying a thousand warriors, many wearing their taumi or crescent-shaped breastplates and some with black and red feather cloaks and headdresses. When Cook went ashore led by a party of marines playing the fifes and drums and carrying an English Jack, Tu escorted him and Lieutenant King to one of the great sailing canoes, while Ma'i boarded the canoe belonging to the chief of Matavai Bay. Outside the lagoon the two canoes paddled furiously towards each other, the warriors standing on the fighting stages, 'playing a hundred Antick tricks' and brandishing their weapons. Tu gave the orders to advance and retreat, manoeuvring his vessel; and finally the two canoes went head to head, Ma'i's warriors boarding Tu's canoe and Tu's crew jumping overboard to save themselves. According to Ma'i, in some battles the opposing canoes were lashed together to ensure that no retreat was possible, and the victors gave no quarter. After this mock fight, Ma'i put on his suit of armour, studded with brass, and mounted the fighting stage of a canoe which was paddled around the bay, although the islanders seemed unimpressed by this glittering spectacle; and during this excursion one of the knee joints in his armour broke, making the leggings useless.

While Captain Cook was involved in this review, Moana, the *ari'i* of Matavai Bay, invited some of the officers to his house, where they found a table prepared with benches around it – the first time that they had seen European furniture in an island dwelling. Moana gave them a lavish meal, afterwards providing them with young women as bedmates. When they farewelled him at dusk, they presented him with red feathers, and in return received gifts of bark cloth. Moana and his son Poeno were close allies of Tu; and at the *'arioi* gatherings, the black leg *'arioi* of their district (Ha'apape) used to chant:

> My mountain above is Orohena, the highest on Tahiti
> My courtyard below is Faaria
> My point outside is Fauroa [on the east side of Point Venus]
> My river is Faiai
> My *'arioi* house is Te Atita
> It is I, the chief *'arioi* Teaau,
> Confused by the cannon balls that whistle through our skies [a reference to
>   Wallis's attacks on Matavai Bay].[34]

The next morning a messenger arrived to report that after joining Pohuetea in an attack on Mo'orea, during which they had destroyed many houses and canoes, To'ofa's fleet had been worsted in a sea battle. Three of his men had been killed, and the 'Admiral' had quickly made peace with Mahine and returned to Atehuru. Upon his return, To'ofa was so angry with Tu for not joining his fleet that he was 'Irritated to a Degree of Madness, Abused of him Every where and was very glad to get any of us to Listen to him. He would Curse Ottou for an Hour together and Foam At the Mouth with rage.'[35] He threatened to attack Tu as soon as Cook's ships left the Society Islands, and when he heard this, Captain Cook, 'who had a mighty Friendship for Ottow [and] was a good deal Affected',[36] made an impassioned speech, declaring that he would return and destroy anyone who dared to attack his *taio*. Like Cook, Teu was angry with To'ofa, and accused him of making peace too hastily. When a messenger arrived to ask Tu to come to Atehuru, where another human sacrifice was about to be offered as part of the peace-making rituals, Cook, who was suffering from rheumatism and had an agonising pain down one side, sent Ma'i and Lieutenant King to accompany Tu to this ceremony instead. After his friends had departed, Tu's mother Tetupaia and a number of women came out to the *Resolution*, where they massaged Cook's body until the bones cracked, greatly relieving his suffering. They repeated this *romiromi* that night and the next morning, making 'my bones crack and a perfect Mummy of my flesh' until the pain disappeared.[37]

At Fa'a'a, when Tu, Ma'i and Lieutenant King arrived at To'ofa's canoe, his attendants awakened the great warrior. To'ofa was now completely lame, and when he sent a plantain branch and a dog which were laid at Tu's feet, he did not stir from his canoe. When King went to see him, the 'Admiral' asked whether Cook was angry with him, and King assured him that, on the contrary, Captain Cook was still his friend. Afterwards, To'ofa and Ma'i had a long conversation, Ma'i presenting To'ofa with red feathers, and To'ofa assuring the young Ra'iatean that he would give him a large sailing canoe and a crew of six *teuteu* or servants to sail it. Early the next morning when To'ofa's wife and daughter arrived at Fa'a'a to welcome him back from battle, they slashed their foreheads with shark's teeth, wiping the blood with white bark cloth which they threw into the ocean; and when Teri'irere, the son of Purea and Amo, arrived shortly afterwards, they repeated this performance. The men were served *'ava*, each drinking by himself and one of them getting so intoxicated that he suffered from convulsions. Afterwards, Tu, Teri'irere, Ma'i and Lieutenant King walked together to 'Utu-'ai-mahurau *marae*, where Mahine's brother laid a small pig and a plantain branch at Tu's feet, and they had a long talk together.

According to King, the ceremony at the *marae* began the next morning when eight large canoes led by To'ofa arrived and their leaders landed on the point, laying plantain branches at Tu's feet. After this presentation Tu and King walked to the main *ahu*, where the priests took up the bundles containing the *maro 'ura* and the image of 'Oro from the *fare atua* (god-house), carrying these ceremoniously to the 'gods' bed' where the human sacrifice had previously been lain. The priests chanted for a long time, lifting up and putting down plantain branches and sheaves of coconut flowers, until finally the head priest untied the bundle containing the red feather girdle, laid Te Ra'i-puatata at full length on the ground and wrapped it around Tu's waist as the *ari'i maro 'ura* held the red feather bonnet in his hand. After another long chant the head priest cried out

'*Heiva!*' and the people responded '*Ari'i!*'; repeating this three times and hailing Tu as the paramount chief of the island. Afterwards they proceeded to a low stone pavement on the opposite side of the small *ahu*, where Tu stood in front of the carved '*unu* boards while the same ritual was repeated. After three more shouts of '*Heiva!*' and '*Ari'i!*', Tu was divested of the *maro 'ura*, which was wrapped up again with a small tuft of red feathers that Tu had poked into its fabric, and replaced with the image of 'Oro in the *fare atua*.

When this ritual was over they went to Tu's house beside the *marae* where the chiefs sat around in a circle. A Tai'arapu (or southern Tahiti) chief opened the proceedings with a stiff, cold speech; followed by an animated, lively address by a chief from Atehuru. When Pohuetea made an eloquent speech rebuking Tu for not supporting them in the recent battle, he was answered by Tuti'i, Tu's orator, who gave an ironic response that provoked angry shouting. Mahine's brother delivered a spirited oration in reply, while an Atehuru man paraded about with a large stone on his shoulder and a sling tied to his waist. Afterwards an old man from Mo'orea spoke to a hushed crowd, and when the man who was carrying the large stone threw it down, the plantain branches at Tu's feet and the stone were taken to the *marae*, where the head priest chanted over them. This ended the ceremony, which ratified a six-month truce between To'ofa and Mahine.[38] Lieutenant King accompanied Tu back to Teu's house at Pare, where they found the old, grey-bearded chief raging against To'ofa for his folly in rushing to fight Mahine and making an imprudent peace settlement. Tu, who was very friendly with Lieutenant King, asked him to bring him plenty of red feathers and left-handed guns when he came back to Tahiti, assuring him that he would always be welcome and given plenty of pigs and other refreshments.

On 28 September 1777 the shore camp was packed up and the tents taken on board. Tu came out to the *Resolution* with a small, finely carved canoe as a gift for the *ari'i rahi no Peretani* – the King of Britain – asking that the King send him red feathers, axes, horses and half a dozen muskets in return. Webber had painted Tu's portrait during this visit, inspiring the paramount chief to ask for a portrait of his *taio*, Captain Cook. In return for the canoe, Cook now presented Tu with a large locked chest containing Webber's portrait of himself and gave Tu the key. At the same time, To'ofa fulfilled his promise to Ma'i, sending him a fine sailing canoe with a crew of six *teuteu* or servants to man it. When several of his sailors begged to be allowed to stay on at Tahiti, Cook refused; although when a number of the island women pleaded to accompany their British 'husbands' to

Ra'iatea, he allowed them to stay on board the *Resolution*. Their families loaded them with gifts of food; and according to Alexander Home: 'Almost Every man had a girl that Eat as much as himself and we lived in the Utmost Affluence.'[39] Early the next morning when a fresh easterly breeze blew up, the ships weighed anchor and set sail, and Cook fired a salute of seven guns for Tu, who left the *Resolution* soon afterwards with his mother Tetupaia, weeping as he farewelled his *taio*.

It was a low-key departure, however, for as Lieutenant King observed: 'The Men & women had so often taken leave of Europeans that they became more indifferent, & we had therefore few signs of regret.'[40] Ma'i had decked out his new canoe with a variety of feather streamers and flags – English, French, Spanish and Dutch; and as the two ships set sail, he followed them out of Vaitepiha Bay with Te Weherua and Koa on board. Sailing past Pare, Cook fired two guns as a final salute to his *taio*; and as Samwell remarked, 'no Man could be more esteemed & dreaded than Capt Cook was among them, who upon all Occasions preserved his Consequence with an admirable address, & the name of Toottee will be handed down to Posterity as the greatest Chief & a man of the greatest Power that ever visited their Island'.[41]

Ma'i guided the *Resolution* and *Discovery* to Papeto'ai Bay in Mo'orea, where they anchored the next morning. (*See Plate 10.*) A flock of canoes surrounded the ships, including several that had followed them from Tahiti, bringing other women who had been unwilling to farewell their British lovers. The bay was almost deserted, and the damage caused by To'ofa and his warriors during their recent attack was evident. The trees had been stripped of fruit and the houses were charred with fire or lay in ruins. As Alexander Home remarked, the people seemed poor and downcast, and everything bore 'the Meloncoly Marks of Depindoray [dependency] Slavery and Opression'.[42] The *Resolution* was full of rats, and Cook had the ship hauled close to the shore, laying out some spars as a gangplank for these animals, introducing European rats to the island. The following morning Cook and Ma'i went riding along the beach at Papeto'ai, astonishing the local people, although Ma'i forbade them to follow the horses. On 3 October, Mahine, who proved to be about forty-five years old, fat, scarred, bald and with only one eye, finally came out to the ship, accompanied by his wife, a 'sister' of Amo. As Home noted: 'We were much disappointed in Our Notions of this Champion of Liberty. We Expected to see A youthfull Sprightly Active fellow But Instead of that He Turned out An Infirm Old man more than half blind.'[43] He seemed very hesitant about meeting 'Tute', the bond friend of his enemy Tu, and only boarded the ship after much persuasion. Cook gave Mahine a cotton gown and some red feathers and exchanged names with him, which eased his fears; and he left the ship, returning soon afterwards with a large pig which he presented to his new *taio*.

On 6 October, however, when a kid that had been sent ashore with the other goats to graze was stolen, Captain Cook was furious; and when a man who boarded the *Resolution* confessed to the theft, saying that he had taken the animal as payment for breadfruit and plantains that the goats' keeper had taken, Cook had him thrown into irons. The next morning Cook sent a threatening message to Mahine, saying that unless the goat was returned to him at once, he would punish him and his people. The goats were sent ashore again, and that evening when the boat went to collect them they found that another of these precious animals, a nanny goat in kid, had been taken. When he heard about this second theft, Cook flew into a violent rage, stamping on the deck and threatening destruction to Mahine and all of his people. By this time the men were calling their captain 'Tute', his Tahitian name, and his temper had become legendary among them. As one of the midshipmen, James Trevenen, wrote in his journal:

> O day of hard labour! O Day of good living!
> When TOOTE was seized with the humour of giving –
> When he cloathd in good nature his looks of authority
> And shook from his eyebrows their stern superiority.[44]

And later:

> *Heiva:* the name of the dances of the southern islanders which bore so great a resemblance to the violent motions and stampings on the Deck of Captain Cook in the paroxysms of passion, into which he frequently threw himself upon the slightest occasion that they were universally known by the same name, and it was a common saying, both among officers and people, "the old boy has been tipping a *heiva* to such and such a one."[45]

Some local people offered to find the goat, but they gave misleading reports, which only worsened Cook's temper. He ordered all of the canoes in the bay put under guard; and in the morning when he was told that Mahine had fled to the other end of the island, he despatched two old chiefs with a midshipman and a master's mate to track down the goat, which the people said had been taken by a chief named Hamoa. Although the petty officers found Hamoa, his people gave them false assurances; and when his men returned empty-handed to the *Resolution*, Ma'i urged Cook to take a party of armed men, march across the island, and teach Mahine a lesson by shooting any of his people that they encountered. Early the next morning Cook set off with Ma'i to Hamoa's house, accompanied by one of the old chiefs and a party of thirty-five armed men; at the same time sending Lieutenant Williamson with three armed boats around the western end of the island. When they met a man en route and Ma'i begged to shoot him, however, Captain Cook refused his permission. At Hamoa's house, where the people denied any knowledge of the goat, some warriors ran into the bush and threw stones at Ma'i and the sailors. In a fury, Cook threatened that unless they delivered up the goat, he would burn their houses. When the people still professed ignorance, he ordered his men to set fire to eight houses and three large war canoes; and as they marched to meet the boats, Ma'i and his men burned six more large war canoes, plundered the houses, and took animals, tools and two canoes, ignoring the lamentations of the local inhabitants. As To'ofa's *taio*, Ma'i was eager to do as much damage as possible to his friend's enemies. They met the armed boats at Varari, on the north-west point of the island, the headquarters of Mahau, whom Cook considered the 'rightful heir' to the chieftainship of Mo'orea, and none of the houses and canoes in his district were damaged.

Not content with this rampage, the next day Cook sent another threatening message to Mahine, saying that unless the goat was returned, he would destroy every canoe on the island. After sending the carpenters ashore at 'Opunohu Bay to break up three or four more war canoes, Cook led an armed party to Paopao which demolished more houses, killed pigs and dogs, and smashed and burned more canoes; and they took away the planks of the houses to use for Ma'i's dwelling at Huahine. Finally, that evening the goat was returned to the *Resolution*. However, that night the young midshipman George Gilbert expressed the misgivings shared by many of his shipmates:

Where ever Capt Cook met with any Houses or Canoes, that belonged to the party (which he was informed) that had stolen the goat, he ordered them to be burnt and seemed to be very rigid in the performance of His orders, which every one executed with the greatest reluctance except Omai, who was very officious and wanted to fire upon the Natives . . . Several women and old men, still remained by the houses whose lamentations were very great, but all their entreaties could not move Capt Cook to desist in the smallest degree from those cruel ravages . . . and all about such a trifle as a small goat . . . I can't well account for Capt Cook's proceedings on this occasion as they were so very different from his conduct in like cases in his former voyages.[46]

Zimmerman, one of the sailors, echoed these sentiments, adding: '[W]e thought it rather extraordinary that O-mai himself and three of his boatmen, whom he had brought with him, executed the greater part of this destruction and behaved much worse than the Europeans.'[47] Even Lieutenant Williamson thought Cook too severe, remarking: 'I cannot help thinking the man totally destitute of humanity, and I must confess this once I obey'd my Orders with reluctance. I doubt not but Captn. Cook had good reasons for carrying His punishment of these people to so great a length, but what his reasons were are yet a secret.'[48]

There is no doubt that since the affair at Queen Charlotte Sound, Cook had become increasingly despotic, and was now behaving more like a Polynesian high chief than an enlightened Royal Navy captain. He had decided to teach Tu's enemy Mahine a lesson, no doubt intending to deter him from attacking his *taio* after his departure from the Society Islands. The next morning, 11 October, the ships sailed from Mo'orea with a number of the Tahitian girls still on board, following Ma'i's canoe to Fare Harbour in Huahine, where Ma'i had decided that he wanted to settle. In the dark early the next morning they heard a musket shot, the signal that land had been sighted, but in fact Ma'i had fired the shot because his canoe had almost capsized in a squall.

When they entered Fare Harbour and a Mo'orea man was caught with some stolen goods in his possession, Cook (who was not well) flew into another rage, ordering the ship's barber to shave this man's head and cut off his ears. The barber shaved the man's head and had begun to crop one ear when an officer, thinking that Cook could not be serious, stopped the punishment and ordered the man to swim ashore. As they landed at Fare, reports flew around the island about Cook's rampage across Mo'orea; and Cook was told that since his last visit to Huahine his *taio*, the old chief Ori, had been deposed in favour of his son, Teri'itaria. In fact, Ori had stepped down for his son before Cook's previous visit to the island; and his first wife Fa'atuara'i, a discreet, sensible older woman who had taken Joseph Banks as her *taio* in 1769, was now acting as her son's regent. Cook wanted Ma'i to settle down quietly at Huahine, and when Ma'i begged him to go with him to Ra'iatea and expel the Borabora men from his family estates, he would not hear of it.

The next morning Cook told Ma'i to dress himself in his best suit and they went to pay a formal visit to Teri'itaria. As Alexander Home commented, they found the young *ari'i rahi*, a boy about nine years old, riding on the back of one of his retainers:

This Boy is about 12 years Old and is attended by two Stout Lads whose Backs he Mounts when Ever he pleases So that they Stand in the Stead of a Horse or an Ass. This privalidge of riding upon people's backs seems to be Confin'd to the Royal Family. Though some times I have seen the young *Eris* [*ari'i*] Mount the Backs of the Vassels I should imagine that Omiahs Horses will be very Acceptable as it is plain that they have got a taste for riding.[49]

Ma'i began this meeting with a *maro tai* ceremony, thanking the gods for their safe landing and offering one tuft of red feathers to the god of the island; another for the *ari'i* to give to his god; and still others for King George, Lord Sandwich, Tute and Tate (Captain Clerke) and their ships, each with its own chant; placing each of these tufts at the feet of the high priest of Huahine. When the priest went away, taking these red feathers to the main *marae* of the island, Cook gave gifts to the young *ari'i*, in return receiving a presentation of pigs, fruit and bark cloth.

After this exchange of gifts, Cook spoke, saying that although he wanted to live with the Huahine people in friendship, he would not tolerate the kind of attacks that had happened during his previous visit to the island. He was followed by Ma'i, who told them fabulous stories about his adventures in Britain, lauding the power of King George and his army and navy. In Cook's name, he asked for a piece of land where he could build a house for himself and his servants; but added that if this was not possible, he would go to Ra'iatea and, with Cook's assistance, drive out the Borabora warriors. Hearing this, Cook assured the gathering that he would have nothing to do with such a venture, and that if Ma'i went to Ra'iatea, he must go as a friend and not an enemy to the Borabora people. A Borabora chief then stood up and declared that Huahine and everything in it was now Tute's, and that he could give whichever part of the island he liked to Ma'i for his dwelling.

At the end of these speeches, the chiefs agreed to grant Ma'i about an acre of land a little further along the beach, and Teri'itarea's mother promised that Ma'i and his possessions would be protected. The boundaries were pointed out, and Cook ordered the observatory tents to be erected on the site (which the people called 'Peretani' or Britain), and the carpenters set to work at once to build Ma'i a small dwelling. During the construction some iron tools were filched, for as Rickman remarked ruefully: 'The vigilance of Argos could not have secured the golden prize to them, from so many crafty Jasons.'[50] Over the next few days Te Weherua and Koa dug the ground; the sailors planted a garden with vines, shaddock trees, pineapples, melons and other crops; and the horse and the mare were brought ashore with a cow with a calf, goats, a pair of rabbits, sheep, cats, poultry and a monkey, which the Huahine people mistook for a person.

These animals were greeted with amazement, and every time that one of the officers went riding, according to Samwell, 'they were followed by Thousands of Indians running & shouting like mad People';[51] while the girls flocked to the ships, attracted by the sailors' red feathers.

This mood of peaceful goodwill was shattered when, on 22 October, a *heiva* was performed by candlelight by a party of *'arioi* from Ra'iatea. A girl 'as beautiful as Venus' danced for their guests; and while the officers watched enchanted, a man stole a sextant from William Bayly's observatory. When Cook was informed, he went ashore, stormed into the *heiva* house and brought the entertainment to an abrupt halt, berating the chiefs for the theft and demanding the surrender of the thief and the sextant. Seeing a Borabora man from Ra'iatea in the audience, Ma'i identified him as the thief, drew his sword and took him captive; and Cook ordered all of the large canoes in the harbour to be seized, to the amazement and anger of the Ra'iatean leaders. When the thief was taken on board the *Resolution* and clapped into irons, Ma'i made him confess where he had hidden the sextant, which was safely retrieved the next morning. Captain Cook, determined to make an example of this man who had displayed 'extraordinary impudence and audacity', ordered him to be flogged until his back was flayed, although he refused to cry out in pain.

Afterwards the man left the ship in a fury and went to Ma'i's garden where he tore up the grapevines that the sailors had planted, destroying many of the plants, breaking down the fences and releasing the two horses, four sheep and various poultry. When he was captured again and taken back to the ship, Cook ordered one of the sailors to shave this man's head and eyebrows and cut off both his ears, and he was thrown into irons on the quarterdeck, blood streaming down his body. Several days later the officers of the watch, pitying this man, let him go, to Cook's unrestrained fury. The mate was expelled from the *Resolution* into the *Discovery*, the midshipman was sent before the mast, and the two marine sentries were thrown into irons and given a dozen lashes each day over the next three days. The thief escaped, however, swearing that as soon as the ships had sailed, he would kill Ma'i and burn down his dwelling. Soon afterwards Cook was told that three large Spanish ships had arrived at Tahiti, but by now he was blasé about such reports, and took no notice.

By 26 October, Ma'i's house, which had a loft and a door with a lock, was finished, and his possessions were taken ashore. These included a bed, a table and chairs; and in addition to the portraits of the King and Queen, the electrifying machine and the jack-in-a box mentioned earlier, there was a hand organ, regiments of lead soldiers with coaches and horses, a compass, a globe of the world with charts and maps, cutlery, tin pots, kettles, drinking mugs, glasses and a Bible. As well, he had a saddle and bridle for his horse and mare, as he had now learned how to ride. Cook also left Ma'i a musket and bayonet, a brace of pistols, a fowling piece, gunpowder and pistol balls, swords and cutlasses – which were likely to be put into use, because Ma'i was determined to drive the Borabora invaders from his estates in Ra'iatea. His large sailing canoe was moored in front of the house, and his garden ran up into the foothills. Two days later Ma'i gave a feast for Cook, the officers and Ori's family at his new house. The ship's band performed a concert for the diners, with drums, trumpets, bagpipes, flutes and violins; Ma'i played the hand organ and demonstrated the electrifying machine; and Ori got drunk on wine, grog and other liquors. Afterwards there was a *heiva* followed by fireworks. Ma'i's brother and sister had now joined him, along with Te Weherua and Koa and the crew of the canoe that Ma'i had acquired in Tahiti. Despite his astonishing wealth, however, the Huahine people looked sideways at Ma'i, mocking him as an upstart, although they had a healthy respect for his weapons.

On 2 November Cook decided to leave Huahine, and when a breeze sprang up from the east, the anchors were raised and they sailed from the island, heading for Ra'iatea. As he farewelled Captain Cook, Ma'i burst into tears; and as he boarded the boat to go ashore, Cook asked him to send some white beads to the ship at Ra'iatea if he was being treated well, and black ones if he met with any misfortune. Now that Ma'i was being left behind, Cook had only good words to say about the young Ra'iatean:

> Whatever faults this Indian had they were more than over ballanced by his great good Nature and docile disposition, during the whole time he was with me I very seldom had reason to find fault with his conduct. His gratifull heart always retained the highest sence of the favours he received in England nor will he ever forget those who honoured him with their protection and friendship.[52]

Although he liked Ma'i, however, Cook was fond of Te Weherua and Koa and wished that he could take them to England. The sailors admired Te Weherua for his athletic strength, his good sense, and mild, noble disposition; while the boy Koa was full of fun, always entertaining his shipmates with his 'Monkey-tricks & the witty sayings of Wapping & St. Giles'.[53] As the boat carried them back to Huahine, Koa wept aloud and twice dived overboard; and it was only when he was forcibly restrained that he resigned himself to staying on the island.

On 3 November 1777 the ships arrived at Ha'amanino Harbour in Ra'iatea, Tupaia's birthplace, where Cook's *taio* Reo came out to the ship with his beautiful daughter Poiatua, whom Hodges sketched during this visit. Reo was also accompanied by his son and son-in-law, who brought out gifts for Cook; and he reproached his bond friend for not bringing Ma'i back to Ra'iatea, saying that he would have restored his estates to him (although Ma'i had been adamant that he could not live in peace with the Borabora invaders). Tapoa ('Boba'), the regent of Taha'a, also came out to the ships with his mistress Teina-mai, a good-humoured woman who by this time had borne him several children; and he had not married Puni's daughter, although they had been betrothed during Cook's previous visit. The titular chief of the island, 'U'uru, was still being permitted to play his ceremonial role and wear the *maro 'ura*, but the Borabora conquerors had left him with only a small piece of land and he was now very poor. Although 'U'uru hesitated to meet Cook because he had no gifts to give him, Cook met him anyway and gave him a number of presents. Several days later a canoe arrived from Huahine with four white beads, the signal that Ma'i was happy and well-treated, with a message that his goat had died and he would be glad of another and some axes. Cook sent these back to Ma'i on the canoe; and soon afterwards when the thief who had stolen the sextant and had his ears cropped arrived at Ha'amanino Bay and declared that he was now at peace with the British, Cook let the matter go.

On 12 November, John Harrison, one of the marines who had been flogged for releasing this man from his irons, deserted at midnight, taking his musket and uniform with him. Cook took two armed boats and pursued him, finding Harrison two days later, dressed in bark cloth and lying asleep between an older woman and a lovely girl who had decorated his head with red and white flowers. When the women burst into tears, Cook ignored them; and when the local chief came with a plantain branch and a small pig to make peace with Cook, he was abruptly sent away. Although about two hundred warriors had gathered, Harrison was already in the boat by the time they arrived, and they were too late to free him. Harrison's only excuse was that the older woman, who was from a chiefly family, had enticed him to live with her; and as a punishment Cook had him put into irons and given two dozen lashes. When the older woman came out to the ship afterwards bringing a large pig and gifts of food for Harrison, she was devastated when she heard about the flogging.

On 20 November the Pleiades rose above the horizon and Matari'i-i-ni'a or the Season of Plenty formally began; although none of the British mentioned any particular rituals on this occasion. Three nights later, no doubt encouraged by the relatively mild penalty meted out to Harrison, a gunner's mate, Thomas Shaw, and a midshipman from the *Discovery*, Alexander Mouat, who had fallen in love with a chiefly girl from Huahine, ran from the shore camp. A Tahitian friend of theirs named 'Pedro' carried them off in his canoe to the northern end of Ra'iatea; and when Clerke's armed boat arrived, they had already left the island. To ensure that the deserters were returned, Captain Clerke invited Poiatua, her brother Teura and her husband to join him on board the *Discovery*, offering them beads and knives; and when they came on board, he locked them in his cabin, where battens had been nailed across the windows. Poiatua wept inconsolably, and every morning during her imprisonment her female friends and relatives wept in canoes alongside the ship, swimming in the water, or on the beach opposite the anchorage, slashing their heads with shark's teeth and crying out *'Aue! Aue!'*, distraught at her captivity.

Convinced that Clerke must have acted without his *taio*'s knowledge, Reo pleaded with Captain Cook to free his children. Cook would not listen, however, replying that unless his men were brought back, he would carry the hostages away from the island. After hearing this, Reo plotted with the other chiefs on the island to seize 'Tute' and 'Tate' and keep them hostage until his children were released. Cook and Clerke usually bathed each evening in a freshwater pool upriver, but when Reo urged him to bathe that afternoon, Cook became suspicious and refused to leave the ship, telling Clerke to be careful. Clerke carried his pistol with him, deterring the would-be attackers; and when one of the Huahine girls – 'a Fat, Jolly girl [who] expressed great Horror at Fighting and Blood Shed'[54] – told her lover about the planned ambush, 100 armed men in two boats set off from the ships to protect Captain Clerke. As they landed, a group of warriors armed with clubs fled from the bush by the river into their canoes, and were fired at by the ships' boats. One of the *Discovery*'s sailors, who had just climbed into a canoe and was about to desert, panicked when he heard the firing and scrambled back on board again. Afterwards, the girl was given gifts of appreciation and sent back home by canoe to escape the enraged Raiateans. As Alexander Home reported:

> The Natives were Constantly Inviting us to Stay Amongst them. Their promise was a Large Estate and a Handsome Wife, and Every thing that was fine and Agreeable that their Country Afforded. It was not to be Wondered at that Such proposals were listened to by many and some of good Sense too, for it was by No Means Visionary Dreams of Happyness but absolutely real . . . It seemed Exactly the paradise of Mahomet in Every thing but Immortality.[55]

Sensing the mood of his men, Cook mustered the sailors and made an eloquent speech, saying that if they deserted, he would always get them back; and that no matter how much the islanders liked them, they were much fonder of their chiefs, whom he would take hostage until his men were returned – 'and dead or Alive, he'd have them!'[56] After sailing from Ra'iatea to Taha'a, the deserters had fled to Borabora; and Reo sent a message to Puni, begging him to return them, but there was no reply. Finally, on 29 November, Reo set off in his canoe to try to find them. Although the Season of Plenty had begun, during his absence his people refused to bring any provisions to the vessels; but eventually, on 4 December, a fleet of canoes returned to Ha'amanino Bay, one of them holding the two deserters, tied up and despondent. They had fled from Borabora to Tupua'i in the Australs, where they had finally been captured by Reo's men.

As soon as the deserters were on board, Cook had them clapped into irons and freed the three chiefly hostages. The gunner's mate was given two dozen lashes and released after a petition from the *Discovery*'s crew, and Mouat was sent before the mast. Captain Clerke, who was now very ill with the tuberculosis that he had contracted in the King's Bench jail, was much distressed by Mouat's defection, because his father, a brother officer, was a close friend who had commanded the *Tamar* during Byron's Pacific voyage; and mutiny was a terrible stain on any naval career. No doubt thinking of his own sons, Cook was inclined to be merciful to Mouat; as Lieutenant Williamson remarked: 'Captn. Cook had on this occasion all ye feelings of a parent, & often with great tenderness & concern us'd to say, how soon a young man, even without ye least propensity to Vice (& such was this young man) might by one boyish Action, make a worthy family miserable for ever.'[57]

After this quarrel Cook made peace with Reo and his family, giving them many gifts; and they were more or less reconciled. Three days later, the girls from Tahiti were told to leave the ships, because they were about to sail from the Society Islands. There were bitter lamentations, and the sailors were upset, although by this time more than thirty of the men were suffering from venereal infections. The winds were contrary, however, and it was not until 7 December 1777 that the ships finally set sail, heading for Borabora. Cook was eager to meet Puni again, and hoped to procure the large anchor from Bougainville's ship that had been salvaged by the Hitia'a people and sent to the old *ari'i rahi* as a present. Reo and eight other chiefs accompanied Cook on this passage. When they arrived at Borabora, Cook went ashore in the boat, accompanied by Reo and his companions. Cook was introduced to Puni, presenting the old warrior with a linen nightgown, a shirt, some handkerchiefs, a mirror, some beads and six large axes; and when he asked for the anchor, Puni immediately ordered three of his men to fetch it, and gave it to Cook before he would accept his presents. The winds were still contrary, however, and Cook and his companions did not stay long at Borabora. After farewelling Puni and Reo, they returned to their ships that afternoon and sailed away from the Society Islands, heading north towards the west coast of North America.

By this time a number of Cook's men had spent many months in the Society Islands. Charles Clerke, for instance, had sailed on the *Dolphin* with Wallis and on each of Cook's three voyages, spending almost a year in these islands over five different visits. Some of these men could speak quite good Tahitian, and their understanding of local customs was becoming increasingly sophisticated, as one can see from Cook's account of the *pure ari'i* ritual in Tahiti. They were now able to absorb quite complex information; and during this brief visit to Borabora, Lieutenant King was given a history of the wars between Borabora and the neighbouring islands that accords closely with the oral traditions. Since the Borabora conquest of Ra'iatea, Borabora had become the leading *'arioi* centre in the archipelago; and as they sailed away from the island, the *Discovery*'s surgeon's mate, William Ellis, gave a fine account of what they had learned about the *'arioi* during this visit to these islands:

> The society of the areeois is esteemed the most polite establishment in these islands; the members of which are always people of rank and fortune, and are distinguished by being tattooed in a peculiar manner, particularly those who are natives of Borabora . . . They generally go in companies of ten or twelve sail of canoes, and let them direct their course to whatever island they please, they are always certain of being well received; nay, if they have even been at war but a few days before the visit, all animosity is laid aside, and they are as perfect friends as if nothing had happened.
>
> One of their privileges is to keep two, three, or more women at once, who however must be members. They always wear the best cloth the islands produce, and eat many peculiar things, which others, even if arees, are not permitted to do. They are generally distinguished for their prowess, valour and activity in battle, and if any of them shew the least signs of cowardice, he is excluded from the society, and no one will associate with or speak to him.
>
> Their amusements during these meetings consist of boxing, wrestling, dancing, and making feasts and entertainments, at which crowds of female spectators attend, the fairest of whom are always made choice of by the conquerors. In general, they continue in this society to the age of thirty or thirty-five, when by suffering one of their children to survive, they debar themselves of the privileges of an arreoi. Many remain members all their lives, and die in a most emaciated state, occasioned by their very debauched way of living [or more likely, by the introduction of venereal diseases].[58]

As for Cook's sailors, they loved the Society Islands. Thomas Edgar, the *Discovery*'s master, called the Tahitian girls 'Angels', remarking that 'one of them, favord *me* with her Company & I can without vanity affirm it was the happiest 3 months I ever spent'.[59] George Gilbert, a sailor on board the *Resolution*, was sure that if Captain Cook had not been so determined to retrieve the deserters, most of the men would have run and stayed in the islands. According to Alexander Home, a midshipman on the *Discovery*, this was because the islands were irresistible:

> The Over flowing plenty, the Ease in which men live and the Softness and Delightfulness of the Clime, the women are Extremely Handsome and fond of the European, prodigiously insisting and Constantly Importuning them to stay, and their Insinuations are Backed by the Courtesy of the Chiefs and the admiration of the people in general. It is Infinately too much for sailors to withstand.[60]

As they sailed away from this 'paradise of Mahomet', heading for the icy waters off Canada to search for the Northwest Passage, it seemed to the sailors that the happiest part of their voyage was over. Indeed, a year later Captain Cook would be lying face down on the rocks on a beach in Hawai'i, bludgeoned to death by local warriors; and six months after that Captain Clerke perished from the tuberculosis that had plagued him throughout the voyage. When the ships returned to England, there was mourning and sorrow as well as celebration; and Captain James Cook was immortalised as a great European explorer, tragically killed by savage warriors, whose voyages had changed the face of the planet. (*See Plate 11.*)

Back in Europe, Tahiti had entered the realms of mythology. The neo-classical visions of Commerson, Banks and the Forsters were reflected in the idyllic paintings created by William Hodges and John Webber after Cook's second and third voyages. Their glimpses of an island Elysium inspired philosophical debates, novels and other artistic portrayals among European intellectuals; while the explorers' accounts of sexual life on the island gave these dreams an erotic glow. None of these visitors understood much about the 'Oro cult, or the 'arioi and their rituals for arousing the gods to ensure the fertility of the islands; and in Europe their descriptions of Tahitian customs such as public sex and genital exposure were viewed as titillating or disreputable, celebrated in salacious poetry or condemned as pornographic. In Britain, published accounts of Tahitian sexual life were thought likely to influence private behaviour, as one can see in reactions to Hawkesworth's account of a young Tahitian warrior making love with a little girl under Purea's supervision:

Our women may find in *Dr. Hawkesworths' Book* stronger Excitements to vicious Indulgences than the most intriguing French Novel could present to their Imaginations – our Libertines may throw aside *The Woman of Pleasure*, and gratify their impure Minds with the Perusal of infinitely more lascivious Recitals than are to be found in that scandalous Performance![61]

Likewise, the connection to private behaviour is found in a diary entry by Hester Thrale, the society hostess and friend of Samuel Johnson, about her relationship with Fanny Burney, James Burney's novelist sister:

> I have at length conquered all her Scruples, & won her Confidence & her Heart; 'tis the most valuable Conquest I ever did make, and dearly, very dearly, do I love my little *Tayo*, as the People at Otaheite call a *Bosom Friend*.

In France, by way of contrast, as Pamela Cheek argues in her book *Sexual Antipodes*, these dreamlike visions of Tahiti entered debates about public life, liberty and the State, particularly in the various accounts that were written about island Utopias where love is free and innocent, untrammelled by the conventions and corruptions of Europe – Sade's *Aline et Valcour*, for instance, or Diderot's *Supplément au Voyage de Bougainville*.

After his death in Kealakekua Bay, Captain Cook also achieved mythic status, idolised as the epitome of the enlightened European explorer, killed by savage warriors. In 1780, for instance, the poetess Anna Seward extolled him as an eighteenth-century Ulysses, mourning his death in a popular elegy that imagined the reception of the news in Tahiti. She described Tahiti as an Eden, an island of love; and Purea as a 'Siren', now transformed into a grief-stricken, half-crazed mourner:

> So, when of old, Sicilian shores along,
> Enchanting Syrens trill'd th' alluring song,
> Bound to the mast the charm'd Ulysses hears,
> And drinks the sweet tones with insatiate ears . . .
>
> Now leads Humanity the destin'd way,
> Where all the Loves in Otaheite stray.
> To bid the Arts disclose their wond'rous pow'rs,
> To bid the Virtues consecrate the bow'rs,
>
> She gives her Hero to its blooming plain. –
> Nor has he wand'red, has he bled in vain!

His lips persuasive charm the uncultur'd youth,
Teach Wisdom's lore, and point the path of Truth.

Gay Eden of the South, thy tribute pay,
And raise, in pomp of woe, thy COOK'S Morai [*marae*]!
Bid mild Omiah [Ma'i] bring his choicest stores,
The juicy fruit, and the luxuriant flow'rs;

Come, Oberea [Purea], hapless fair-one! come,
With piercing shrieks bewail thy Hero's doom! –
Loud the laments! – and long the Nymph shall stray
With wild unequal step round COOK's Morai![62]

In Tahiti, however, the people were perhaps more puzzled than grief-stricken. For a decade after Captain Cook's departure, no more tall ships with their spider-web rigging and billowing sails appeared over the horizon; and no more islanders sailed away to exotic, previously unimagined places. Some kin groups, particularly those who had gained most from their *taio* relationships with the European explorers, were left bereft; and in the case of Tu and his people at Pare-'Arue in Tahiti, exposed to the jealousies of their neighbours. Over the years, as iron tools rusted, fabrics tore and unravelled, beads and nails were lost and red feathers were no longer as highly prized as they had once been when they were few, obtained only after long, dangerous voyages, their memories of the Europeans faded. In many ways the islanders breathed a sigh of relief, because these ships had brought influxes of strangers who cut down their trees and took away quantities of pigs, chickens, plantains, breadfruit, fish, coconuts and other produce from the island. The sailors had slept with their women and left behind foul diseases; become drunk and riotous, fighting with local men; broken *tapu* restrictions; tried to escape from their ships to live among the islanders; and taken *ari'i* and their families hostage without good reason. Sometimes they had fired their cannons and muskets at the islanders, wreaking terrible havoc. It was certainly more peaceful now that these *pahi* (ships) from Peretani and Rima were no longer arriving, but at the same time life was less interesting and dramatic.

During this interval, however, Tu's people held fast to the memory of Captain Cook and the British, elevating James Cook to ancestral status. In July 1788, when the *Lady Penrhyn*, a British transport that had recently delivered a load of female convicts to the new penal colony in Botany Bay, anchored in Matavai Bay – the first European ship to arrive since Cook's departure – they received an ecstatic welcome. According to Lieutenant

John Watts, formerly a midshipman with Cook on board the *Resolution*, at dawn on 14 July when a messenger came out to the ship to invite Watts and Captain Sever ashore, a joyous crowd of 10,000 people stood on the beach. There were so many single and double canoes in the bay that as they rowed ashore, Sever and his companions could scarcely see the water. Tu, a very tall and muscular man, was waiting for them on the beach, attended by a number of other *ari'i*, and as Lieutenant Watts and Captain Sever landed, women slashed their foreheads with shark's teeth, mourning for those who had died since Cook's last visit to the island. A man stood beside Tu holding up Captain Cook's portrait, which the British commander had personally handed over as a gift to his *taio*. As he greeted Captain Sever, Tu took him as his bond friend; and when Sever invited him out to the ship, Tu sent Cook's portrait into the boat before he would come on board, repeating the same procedure when they arrived alongside the *Lady Penrhyn*. In the Great Cabin, Tu had Captain Cook's portrait fixed to the wall, and his attendants draped the entire ship with bark cloth, hanging it down the sides of the vessel and laying it over the quarterdeck, turning it into a great altar piled high with gifts – four large pigs, great piles of breadfruit, coconuts, chickens, bananas, *mahi* (fermented breadfruit) and mangoes.

And in October 1788 when Captain William Bligh arrived in Tahiti on the *Bounty*, sent to collect a cargo of breadfruit plants to feed black slaves on British plantations in the West Indies, once again Captain Cook's portrait was delivered to the ship, the envoy explaining that this was '*Tute te ari'i no Tahiti*' ('Cook, the high chief of Tahiti'). According to the messenger, when he gave Tu this portrait, Captain Cook had assured him that when his own son came to Tahiti, he must show it to him, and they would always be good friends. Bligh flung himself into the alliance that Captain Cook had initiated, telling the Tahitians that he was Cook's 'son', and that the great navigator was still alive in Britain. Like Cook, he forged a *taio* relationship with Tu, actively supporting him and his young son Pomare II against all challengers. Bligh stayed in Tahiti for five months, leaving his own men largely to their own devices while he spent time with Tu's family; and in return, Tu honoured Bligh on every possible occasion. During a Matahiti ceremony that was performed at the height of the Season of Plenty, for instance, Bligh was seated beside Cook's portrait, facing rows of male *'arioi* as a priest delivered a long oration to the portrait. Before wrapping his image and then Bligh himself in long lengths of bark cloth, the priest chanted:

> Hail, all hail Cook,
> Chief of Air, Earth and Water,

We acknowledge you Chief from the Beach to the Mountains,
Over Men, Trees & Cattle
Over the Birds of the Air and Fishes of the Sea![63]

Twisted plaits of coconut leaf, a ritual offering, were placed below
Cook's portrait and at Bligh's feet; and at the height of the ritual the male
'arioi stood and danced for them, exposing their genitals in a performance aimed at exciting the gods and enhancing the fertility of the island's
people and its resources.

In Tahiti, when the world began, the creator god Ta'aroa had mated
with a series of female goddesses, creating new forms of life. During each
epoch that followed, male and female powers came together and created
new kinds of beings. Sex was the sacred force that drove the cosmos, ensuring the continuity and well-being of descent lines and providing people
with key resources – pigs, chickens, breadfruit, fish, plantains, coconuts,
and so on. Whereas in England, a portrait of Cook held up by Britannia
had featured in the pantomime about Ma'i, illustrating the apotheosis of
this British explorer, in Tahiti, Webber's portrait of Cook was held up
during a ritual that activated the generative power of the gods, ensuring the fertility of the island. While in the pantomime, an angel heralded
Cook with her trumpet, in this ritual, men and women exposed themselves
to his portrait – celebrating imperial and Christian power on the one hand,
and the procreative power of the cosmos on the other.

At the same time that Bligh was forging his relationship with the
Pomare family, the Bounty's petty officers also took taio among the chiefs
and were given 'wives' from their families, the status of these women mir-
roring their own ranks on board the ship. As Bligh later argued, it was
largely the allure of these relationships (along with his own remarkable
capacity to hurt and alienate his men) that led to the infamous mutiny
on the Bounty. When they sailed away from Tahiti, his acting lieutenant Fletcher Christian left behind Maimiti (a high-born woman whom he
called 'Isabella' after a long-lost lover), while a number of the other mutineers also left 'wives' on the island. Almost all of the sailors had 'arioi
tattoos, some of them taking a large blue-black star on the left chest as
a sign that they were 'Knights of Tahiti', a brotherhood initiated during
Cook's second visit to the island. When they mutinied, they put eighteen
of their shipmates and Captain Bligh into the ship's launch; and as the
launch was cut loose, George Stewart performed a Tahitian dance on the
Bounty's deck while his comrades cried out 'Huzzay for Tahiti!'.

Myth tangled upon myth. Back in Britain, the mutiny on the Bounty and
its aftermath served only to confirm Tahiti's reputation as a mariner's idyll.

After making an extraordinary voyage in the launch, when Bligh reached Batavia he wrote to Sir Joseph Banks, blaming the mutiny squarely on the seductions of the island's women:

> It may be asked what could be the cause for such a Revolution. In Answer to which I have only to give a description of Otaheite, which has every allurement both to luxury and ease, and is the Paradise of the World.
>
> The Women are handsome, mild in their Manners and conversation, possessed of great sensibility, and have sufficient delicacy to make them admired and loved. I can only conjecture that [the mutineers] have Idealy assured themselves of a more happy life among the Otaheitans than they could possible have in England, which joined to some Female connections has most likely been the cause of the Whole business.[64]

And George Hamilton, the surgeon of the *Pandora*, the hell-hole of a ship that was sent to the Pacific to capture the mutineers, wrote after visiting the island in 1791:

> This may well be called the Cytheria of the southern hemisphere, not only from the beauty and elegance of the women, but their being so deeply versed in, and so passionately fond of the Eleusinian mysteries;[65] and what poetic fiction has painted of Eden, or Arcadia, is here realised, where the earth without tillage produces both food and cloathing, the trees loaded with the richest fruit, the carpet of nature spread with the most odiferous flowers, and the fair ones ever willing to fill your arms with love.
>
> It affords a happy instance of contradicting an opinion propagated by philosophers of a less bountiful soil, who maintain that every virtuous or charitable act a man commits, is from selfish or interested views. Here human nature appears in more amiable colours, and the soul of man, free from the gripping hand of want, acts with a liberality and bounty that does honour to his God.[66]

As one can see from these rapturous accounts, after two decades of contact by ships of different European nations – British, French and Spanish – the myth of 'Aphrodite's Island' had triumphantly survived, unscathed by experience.

The Angel of History

In her paper 'Artefacts of History', Marilyn Strathern remarks of the first meetings between Pacific peoples and Europeans:

> It has been something of a surprise for Europeans to realise that their advent in the Pacific was something less than a surprise . . . Their coming had been expected; they were previously known beings "returned" or manifest in new forms.

If the islanders seemed startled and even terrified when they saw the first Europeans, Strathern argues, this was as much as anything amazement at what they had conjured up; at their own power to produce these astonishing apparitions: 'Power they perhaps attributed to particular big men or neighbouring peoples. *Someone* must have produced them.' As she muses, in a world where ancestors can return among the living, summoned by chant or ritual, at any moment the past can spiral back into the present – time is recursive.[1] While in most Western accounts of these meetings, historical agency is assumed to rest with the Europeans and the islanders are depicted as the objects of European action, in the Pacific, the islanders assumed that they themselves had summoned up these spectres.

Indeed, Tupaia, Purea, Tu and their fellow islanders lived in this kind of world. From the time that Vaita had stood on the *marae* at Taputapuatea, wild-eyed and trembling, and prophesied that the 'glorious children of Tetumu' were coming, the people expected that something amazing would happen. The desecration of 'Oro's *marae* by the Borabora warriors had been so shocking that it disrupted the cosmos, breaching the barriers between Te Ao (the everyday world of light) and Te Po (the dark world of ancestors). Something extraordinary would burst through, and according to Vaita, these strange beings would have bodies different from the islanders, although they would also be the children of Tetumu. As for the sign by which they would be recognised, they were coming up in a 'canoe without an outrigger'.

When Captain Wallis's ship the *Dolphin* appeared off the coast of the island, the *'arioi* priests went out in their canoes to meet it. Gazing at it from a distance, they thought that it might be a floating island, propelled through the water by ancestral power. Or perhaps it was the canoe without an outrigger that Vaita had predicted. They boarded it and challenged these weird beings, summoning the power of Hiro (the ancestral explorer and god of thieves) and snatching iron and a gilded hat in the process. Later, when muskets flashed and crackled and a warrior fell back dead in his canoe, and cannons smoked and roared in Matavai Bay, knocking down breadfruit trees and killing many people, they were stunned by the power of the strangers. The marines in their scarlet coats, the red and yellow stripes on the side of the *Dolphin* seemed signs that 'Oro was among them, hurling bolts of thunder and lightning in his fury. His *marae* had been desecrated, and the Borabora warriors were still in possession of his sacred island. It is little wonder that the high priest Tupaia and many others thought that the strangers had come to help free Ra'iatea from the Borabora invaders, and restore the *mana* of Taputapuatea.

After the battles in Matavai Bay on the north coast of the island, the high chiefs and priests supposed that they had unleashed something terrible, and tried to propitiate the strangers. They gave them plantain branches (the *ata* or incarnation of human sacrifices), sacred pigs, dogs and bark cloth, and presented them with lovely young women. In Tahiti, everyone knew the story about how 'Oro's sisters had searched the island for a woman beautiful enough to wed their brother, and 'Oro's brothers had turned themselves into pigs and red feathers as a gift to celebrate the marriage. In addition, the islanders were accustomed to strip bare to the waist in the presence of the high chiefs and the gods; and when girls were offered to the *Dolphin*'s sailors, the old men removed their garments in a gesture of homage. The leading *'arioi* Purea forged a *taio* or bond friendship with Captain Wallis, encouraging her attendants to sleep with his sailors; and after his departure, a red pennant from the *Dolphin* was stitched into Te Ra'i-puatata, the red feather girdle that her high priest Tupaia had brought with an image of 'Oro from Taputapuatea, summoning the British gods in support of her son Teri'irere. Later, when Bougainville's ships arrived off Hitia'a, again the old people stripped the young women before offering them to the strangers; and when they went ashore, the French officers and the Prince of Nassau were invited to make love with these girls in front of curious spectators (as young *'arioi* sometimes did on ceremonial occasions).

Even when the Tahitians began to realise that the Europeans were human, they still regarded them as extraordinary, recruiting their leaders as *taio* and mingling their *varua* or spirits. When Captain Cook arrived on board the *Endeavour*, Purea and her high priest Tupaia, who had recently been defeated in a devastating attack during which the red feather girdle Te Ra'i-puatata and the image of 'Oro were captured, returned to Matavai Bay and renewed their alliance with the British. The aristocratic women began to stay away from the Europeans, however, sending their serv- ants or attendants instead to have sex with the sailors; and only William Monkhouse, the ship's surgeon who had acted as a priest on several occa- sions, was invited to the most private of the *'arioi* gatherings. Even the high-born young botanist Joseph Banks was excluded from these meet- ings, and when he slept with Purea at her invitation, by his own rueful confession she found the experience disappointing. The Tahitians were fanatical about personal hygiene, frequently changing their garments, bathing in the river several times a day and anointing their bodies with scented oil, whereas eighteenth-century Europeans (even gentlemen) were far from fastidious. During this early period, too, when they arrived on the island many of the sailors were suffering from scurvy, with its symptoms of black, ulcerated limbs, stinking breath and swollen, bleeding gums, and the Tahitian women must have found them repellent. Tupaia forged a bond friendship with Banks, however, giving him an *'arioi* tattoo and teaching Captain Cook some *'arioi* navigational lore; and when the *Endeavour* sailed from the island, Tupaia sailed with them. The high priest guided this 'canoe without an outrigger' from Huahine straight to Taputapuatea *marae*, thus fulfilling Vaita's prophecy; although he failed to persuade Cook to free his homeland from the Borabora invaders.

The first Spanish ships to arrive at southern Tahiti had Franciscan friars on board, inspired by apostolic zeal, and in striking contrast with the British and French, their crews were strictly forbidden to have sexual relations with local women. The islanders were at first puzzled and then impressed. Although they respected Boenechea, the Spanish commander, when the two Franciscan friars left on the island during his second visit objected to the sexually graphic dances performed by the *'arioi* and des- ecrated the local *marae*, they were incensed and did everything possible to drive them off the island. During the festival at Tautira when the two friars huddled in their mission, surrounded by hordes of *'arioi* who exhib- ited themselves at them, taunting them and calling them obscene names, it became obvious that the Spanish mission was doomed; although Máximo Rodríguez, the young *mestizo* marine who had learned Tahitian and forged close relationships with Tu and Vehiatua, joined in the *'arioi* festivities and was popular among them. When Máximo returned to Lima, he carried with him a sacred carved basalt bowl from 'Utu-'ai-mahurau *marae*, where the red feather girdle Te Ra'i-puatata and the image of 'Oro had been held since the attack on Mahaiatea.

During Captain Cook's third voyage when he returned to Tahiti, bringing Ma'i back from Britain and a cargo of red feathers from Tonga, the famed commander made an extraordinary impression. Ma'i's tales of the powers of King George III, along with the horses, fireworks, jack-in-a-box and other strange objects from 'Peretani' and the heaps of red feathers from Tonga, made the islanders marvel. Once again, high-born women flocked out to the ships, sleeping with the officers for red feathers, although afterwards these men did not see them again. After forging a *taio* relationship with Captain Cook, the young high chief Tu invited him to attend the offering of a human sacrifice at 'Utu-'ai-mahurau *marae*, where Tu wore Te Ra'i-puatata, the red feather girdle from Taputapuatea. Their bond friendship was sealed when Cook gave Tu a portrait of himself painted by John Webber; and Cook and Ma'i went on a rampage across Mo'orea, ostensibly because the people had stolen two goats, but in fact to punish the high chief Mahine for his attacks on Tu and his people.

If Captain Cook was changed by his experiences on the island, however, the fate of Tu and his lineage was utterly transformed. Almost annihilated on occasion, they rebounded with each successive British visit to the island. They came to treat Cook's portrait as an ancestor figure, wrapped in bark cloth and produced only on ritual occasions when his *mana* was required. As other Tahitians have often argued, it was because of the power of the British – Captains Cook, Sever and Bligh, the *Bounty* mutineers, Edwards, Vancouver and the London Missionary Society missionaries who followed them – that the Pomare dynasty gained a lasting pre-eminence on the island.

And as Marilyn Strathern has observed, if one acknowledges the recursive power of time in the Pacific, the narrative changes fundamentally, so that it does 'not look like our history at all'.[2] In Tahiti, it was as though the ancestors summoned the Europeans to work their will. Te Ra'i-puatata itself, the *maro 'ura* that is at the heart of so much of this history, stands as the sign of these invocations; with its squares of red and yellow feathers stitched to netting and pasted on bark cloth, with human sacrifices made to 'Oro each time that a new section was added. To the original feather girdle that Tupaia had brought from Taputapuatea, the red bunting from the *Dolphin* was stitched for Teri'irere's installation. When Tu was invested with the girdle at 'Utu-'ai-mahurau *marae*, another section was added, and a Union Jack given to him by Captain Cook was carried around the island as his banner. Later, when his son Pomare II was invested with Te Ra'i-puatata at Taraho'i, the family *marae* of the Pomares, with the help of the *Bounty* mutineers, the red feathers that Lieutenant Watts gave Tu's successor were added to a new section of the *maro 'ura*, along with red hair from Richard Skinner, one of the *Bounty* sailors.

If Tahitian ideas of history and ancestors shape this story, however, so do European mythic projections. In both cases, it is as though the Tahitians and the Europeans sent their visions flashing ahead of them, illuminating events before they could happen. Terra Australis Incognita, the Great Unknown Southern Continent, was the mirage that lured successive European ships into the Pacific, as the monarchs of different nations vied to discover this great land-mass, prophesied by the ancient geographers. In the end, as Captain Cook's ships painstakingly criss-crossed the Pacific, sailing through miles of this illusory continent, Terra Australis was erased from the maps of the world. The dreams of the Enlightenment, too, were potent, with the hope of discovering and naming new species and bringing 'progress' and 'improvement' to unenlightened peoples and places. There were also the musings of the *philosophes* about personal freedom, the corruptions of 'civilisation' and the innocence of a state of nature. In the case of the Spaniards, Manuel de Amat was touched by Enlightenment ideas, although the Spanish voyages were dominated by the missionary project of bringing the Virgin Mary and Christianity from South America to the islands of the Pacific.

For Tahiti, however, perhaps the most powerful of these enchantments was the Golden Age of Antiquity. Every educated European, it seems, who set foot in Tahiti, thought of Arcadia, the Elysian fields, and Greek and Roman gods and goddesses. From Banks to Bougainville and the Forsters, to George Hamilton, the surgeon on board that hell-ship *Pandora*, as they gazed at the tall, powerful chiefs, six feet four inches high in some cases, and the beautiful, bare-breasted girls draped in white bark cloth who were sent out to greet them, they saw Greek and Roman statues and paintings and thought of Homer and Virgil. The image of Hercules on the one hand, and of Aphrodite on the other – that gorgeous, capricious goddess of love – coupled with Enlightenment ideas about sexual freedom in a state of nature, became enduring myths of life on this island. These visions created an illusion of familiarity;[3] and neo-Hellenists like Joseph Banks and the Prince of Nassau felt a much closer affinity with the *'arioi* than did the Franciscan friars who accompanied Boenechea to Tahiti, or the London Missionary Society missionaries who later followed them to the island.

At the same time, the ordinary sailors on board the ships had little time for philosophical musings. After long months at sea, they were hungry for sex – and in Tahiti the girls were gorgeous and freely offered to them. The dreams that these men projected were those of the brothels, the maritime ports and the pleasures of popular festivals; or of courtship and family life back home in Europe (or in Peru, in the case of the Spanish). No doubt it was similar for many of the officers and gentlemen. For Banks, Bougainville and the Prince of Nassau (if not for the Forsters), for example, there were thoughts of masquerades, the 'Hellfire Club' or similar gatherings of men of a libertine inclination, and beguiling nights spent with the 'ladies of pleasure';[4] while for Captain Cook and the Forsters, there were the embodied habits of Quaker or Lutheran ideals, and in Cook's case, of domestic affection.

In the end, however, the dreams of 'Aphrodite's Island' and bare-breasted Polynesian maidens emerged out of the way that these traditions intermingled. Without the god 'Oro and the 'arioi, there would have been none of those sexually explicit dances and performances that so captivated and shocked the Europeans. As they gradually realised, adultery was not condoned in early Tahiti (although young people and the high chiefs had considerable sexual freedom, including – at least for men – the liberty to experiment with same-sex relationships); women usually covered their breasts, except when they were in the presence of ra'a or ancestral power; and young women and men, who were normally extremely modest, exposed their genitals only in certain kinds of sacred dances and rituals. When they were offered young girls, at first it was because the Europeans were associated with 'Oro himself; and later for their red feathers (used to communicate with the god), muskets and cannons (which thundered and flashed like the god) and iron. Tahitians and Europeans alike sent their ancestral fantasies flashing into the future, shaping how it happened.

As Walter Benjamin once famously wrote in his 'Theses on the Philosophy of History', in a vision curiously evocative of the winged creator god Ta'aroa and Tahiti's post-colonial experience:

> The past can be seized only as an image which flashes up at the instant when it can be recognized and is never seen again . . .
>
> A Klee painting named "Angelus Novus" shows an angel looking as though he is about to move away from something he is fixedly contemplating. His eyes are staring, his mouth is open, his wings are spread. This is how one pictures the angel of history.
>
> His face is turned toward the past . . . The angel would like to stay, awaken the dead, and make whole what has been smashed. But a storm is blowing in from Paradise; it has got caught in his wings with such a violence that the angel

can no longer close them. The storm irresistibly propels him into the future to which his back is turned, while the pile of debris before him grows skyward. This storm is what we call progress.[5]

In this apocalyptic revelation, one can hear echoes of Vaita's prophecy:

> The glorious children of Tetumu
> will come and see this forest at Taputapuatea.
> Their body is different, our body is different
> We are one species only from Tetumu.
>
> And this land will be taken by them
> The old rules will be destroyed
> And sacred birds of the land and the sea
> Will also arrive here, will come and lament
> Over that which this lopped tree has to teach
> They are coming up on a canoe without an outrigger.[6]

The Seasons in Tahiti

According to Teuira Henry, on the authority of King Pomare in 1818, there were two main seasons in Tahiti: the Season of Plenty or Matari'i-i-ni'a, which began when the Pleiades (Matari'i) first sparkled above the horizon at twilight, in the month of Tema on 20 November; and the Season of Scarcity or Matari'i-i-raro, which formally began on 20 May, when the Pleiades sank below the horizon (Henry, 1928, 332). During the Season of Plenty the ancestor gods were present on Tahiti, summoned by the priests and accompanied by the 'arioi; the Season of Scarcity was heralded by the departure of the gods, and the 'arioi no longer gathered.

According to Moerenhout in 1837, however, there were three main seasons of the year. The first of these was te tau, which lasted from mid-February to mid-June, the season of great abundance and festivities, especially at the beginning or towards the middle of May; the second, te tau poai, the season of dryness and rarity, lasted from July to November; and the third, te tau miti rahi, was the time of harvest and high tides; although most divided the year into only two seasons: te tau ahoune (tau 'ahune), season of rains, from October to April; and te tau poai, the dry season, from May to October (Moerenhout in Borden, ed., 1837, 395).

Moerenhout added that each season was celebrated by a festival heralded by the pa'i-atua ritual to renew the images of the gods – autumn by a harvest festival during March or April; summer by the Matahiti (First Fruits) festival held in December or January; winter by the festival held in June to farewell the gods and the 'arioi from the island; and spring by a festival held at the beginning of October to mark the return of the 'arioi after the spring equinox on 21 September, although this festival was quite minor because it occurred during the Season of Scarcity (Moerenhout in Borden, ed., 1837, 259–60).

William Ellis also claimed that there were three overlapping seasons in Tahiti: 'The first they called Tetau, autumn, or season of plenty, the harvest of breadfruit. It commenced with the month *Tetai*, December, and continued till Faahu [January to February]. This is not only the harvest, but the summer of the South Sea Islands. It is also the season of most frequent rain. The next was *Te tau miti rahi*, the season of high sea. This commences with *Tieri*, November, and continues until January. The third is the longest, and is called *Te Tau Poai*, the winter, or season of drought and scarcity. It generally commences in *Paroromua*, July, and continues till *Tema*, October.' (Ellis, 1859, I: 87.)

Taking King Pomare as our guide and trying to reconcile these accounts as far as possible, the main seasons and the thirteen lunar months of the year can be described as follows (see Moerenhout in Borden, ed., 259–60, 395; Ellis, 1859, I: 86–87; Henry 1928, 332–34).

A. MATARI'I-I-NI'A: THE SEASON OF PLENTY

According to King Pomare, the Season of Plenty or Matari'i–i–ni'a formally began on 20 November, when the Pleiades (Matari'i) first sparkles at twilight above the horizon near Orion's belt.

1. TETA'I – THE CRY

King Pomare gives Te-ta'i, abundance is coming, the breadfruit is growing, foodstuffs are carried from the interior to the sea. Ellis gives Te Tai, the whole or part of December, the *'uru* (breadfruit) nearly ripe. This was the beginning of summer, the rainy season and the harvest, a season of plenty known as *te tau*, which lasted until the month of Faahu. Moerenhout's calendar also includes *te tai*, November and December, when the *'arioi* left the mountains to return to the seashore. According to Moerenhout, the first fishing for the gods and then the *ari'i* took place in November and December, when the rainy season was already under way and the fishing for bonitos and scomber was opened. This was when the first fruits of the sea were offered to the gods, a very sacred time.

2. AVAREHU / O REHU – LEVELLING

According to King Pomare, when the harvest is coming in; between December and January. The Matahiti ceremony was held after the summer solstice (December 21) when the breadfruit ripened, and the first fruits of the land were offered to the gods. Henry adds that this festival also celebrated the return of the spirits and gods to the island, when deceased spirits became *'oromatua* or ancestors (Henry, 1928, 185–86). According to Moerenhout, the *para'a* Matahiti festival celebrating summer and the first fruits was held in December or January, when new canoes, mats, bark cloth and vast quantities of first fruits were brought to the *marae* by visiting groups, and the assembled people scrambled for these gifts. Afterwards there were feasts, dancing, mock combat and races. While Moerenhout's calendar includes the month Avarehou (Ava Rehu) in December (Moerenhout in Borden, ed., 1983, 395), Ellis calls this 'Avarehu', and points out that the new moon appears at about the time of the summer solstice in Tahiti, during the last ten days of December or the beginning of January.

3. FA'AHU-NUI – GREAT REPOSE
According to King Pomare, the sound sleep of plenty, between January and February (January and part of February, the season of plenty (Ellis)). Moerenhout's calendar includes a month he calls Faahi, in January or February, the season of abundance.

4. PIPIRI – PARSIMONY
According to King Pomare, when scarcity begins between February and March. The calendars of Moerenhout and Ellis include the month Pipiri, in February and part of March.

5. TA'A'OA – DEPARTING JOY
According to King Pomare, breadfruit is scarce, between March and April. Moerenhout, however, noted that the autumn harvest festival held in March or April was particularly brilliant, with feasts, foot and canoe races, and contests with spear and javelin; while according to the London Missionary Society records, in Matavai Bay the breadfruit remained plentiful from about the end of December to the middle of May (Oliver, 1974, I: 241). According to Wilder, the March to April harvest was the most important of the year (Wilder, Gerrit P., 1928, *The Breadfruit of Tahiti* (Honolulu, Bernice P. Bishop Museum Bulletin 50)). Moerenhout's calendar includes the month Taaoa, March and April, beginning of a new crop; Ellis includes Taaoa, March and part of April, in the season of scarcity. According to Johann Forster, the people began to make *mahi* or fermented breadfruit paste in March (Forster, Johann, in Thomas, Guest and Dettelbach, eds, 1996, 307).

6. AU-UNUUNU – SUSPENSION
According to King Pomare, the fisherman's paddles are put away, it is stormy; between April and May. The calendars of Moerenhout and Ellis include Au nounou and Aununu respectively, April and part of May, great abundance; Moerenhout, that the rainy season ends in May.

B. MATARI'I-I-RARO: THE SEASON OF SCARCITY

The Season of Scarcity or Matari'i-i-raro formally began on 20 May, marked by the setting of the Pleiades (Matari'i) below the horizon.

1. 'APA'APA – SEVERED IN TWAIN
According to King Pomare, the descent into the time of scarcity of food, the leaves of plants turn yellow then fall off, between May and June. The calendars of Moerenhout and Ellis include the month Apaapa in May and June. Moerenhout notes that the dry season began in May, and adds, the end of the year, they withdrew to the interior and went fishing no more; the god of abundance had withdrawn. According to Johann Forster, the period of scarcity lasted for four months (Forster, Johann in Thomas, Guest and Dettelbach, eds, 1996, 306).

2. PARORO-MUA – FIRST FALL
According to King Pomare, turmeric and wild ginger die out, between June and July. According to Ellis, *Te Tau Poai*, the winter, or season of drought and scarcity, began in Paroro Mua, and lasted until Tema. The ceremony to farewell the gods was held during this time, marking the season of mourning and the departure of the gods. The winter solstice is on 21 June, and the ceremony was held after the breadfruit season had ended. The calendars of Moerenhout and Ellis include Paroro Mua in June and July.

3. PARORO-MURI – AFTER FALL
According to King Pomare, the last of the fruit season, between July and August. The calendars of Moerenhout and Ellis include Pararo Mouri in July and August. According to Barrau, there was a smaller breadfruit harvest in late July to early August (Barrau, Jacques, 1971, *Plantes utiles de Tahiti* (Paris, Musée de l'Homme, dossier no. 8 de la Société des Oceanistes, 11)).

4. MURI-'AHA – PRAYER BEHIND
According to King Pomare, between August and September. Moerenhout gives Mouria ha, August and September; and Ellis gives Muriaha, the same months.

5. HIA'IA – CRAVINGS
According to King Pomare, descent into the greatest scarcity of food; between September and October. Moerenhout's calendar includes Iaia

in September and October; and Ellis gives Hiaia, September and part of October. According to Moerenhout, although a spring festival was held at the beginning of October to mark the return of the *'arioi* after the spring equinox on 21 September, this was relatively insignificant due to the scarcity of foodstuffs.

6. TEMA – THE CLEARING

According to King Pomare, when the crops are clean gone and the new crops are developing; the season for planting, between October and November. Moerenhout's calendar includes Tema, October and November, approach of a new crop, and he notes that the rainy season began in October. Ellis gives Tema, October and part of November, the season of scarcity, which he calls 'Avarehu'.

7. TE'ERI – SCARCITY

According to King Pomare, most of November, when the inflorescence of the breadfruit begins. Ellis gives Te'eri, the whole or part of November – the uru or young breadfruit begins to flower; and says that *Te tau miti rahi*, the season of high sea, begins in this month, and lasts until January. According to Beaglehole, there was a small harvest of breadfruit in November.

For a cross-Polynesian comparison of calendrical systems, see Kirch, Patrick and Green, Roger, 2001, *Hawaiki, Ancestral Polynesia: An Essay in Historical Anthropology* (Cambridge, Cambridge University Press), 260–73. For an excellent analysis of the Tahitian calendrical system, including the intricacies of reconciling thirteen lunar months with twelve calendar months, which explains some of the inconsistencies above, see Babadzan, 1993, 223–33.

Selected Bibliography

(See other sources cited in the notes.)

Adams, Henry Brook, 1910, *Tahiti: Memoirs of Arii Taimai* (Ridgewood, N.J., The Gregg Press).

Babadzan, Alain, 1993, *Les Dépouille des Dieux: Essai sur la religion tahitienne à l'époque de la découverte* (Paris, Maison de la science de l'homme).

———, 2003, 'The Gods Stripped Bare', in Chloë Colchester, ed., *Clothing the Pacific* (Oxford, Berg), 25–50.

Banks, Joseph in J.C. Beaglehole, ed., 1962, *The Endeavour Journal of Joseph Banks 1768–1771, I and II* (Sydney, The Trustees of the Public Library of New South Wales in Association with Angus and Robertson).

Baré, Jean-François, 2002, *Le Malentendu Pacifique: Des Premières Recontres entre Polynésiens et Anglais et ce qui s'ensuivant avec les Français jusqu'à nos jours* (Paris, Contemporary Publishing International).

Blanco, Francisco Mellén, 1986, *Manuscritos y documentos españoles para la historia de la isla de Pascua* (Madrid, Biblioteca CEHOPU).

Bougainville, Lewis de in John Reinhold Forster, ed., 1772, *A Voyage Round the World Performed by Order of His Most Christian Majesty, in the Years 1766, 1767, 1768, and 1769* (London, J. Nourse).

Bougainville, Louis-Antoine in John Dunmore, trans. and ed., 2002a, *The Pacific Journal of Louis-Antoine de Bougainville* (Cambridge, for the Hakluyt Society).

Burney, James in Beverley Hooper, ed., 1975, *With Captain James Cook in the Antarctic and Pacific: The Private Journal of James Burney, Second Lieutenant of the Adventure on Cook's Second Voyage 1772–1773* (Canberra, National Library of Australia).

Byron, John in Robert E. Gallagher, ed., 1964, *Byron's Journal of His Circumnavigation 1764–1766* (Cambridge, for the Hakluyt Society).

Cadousteau, Mai Ari'i, 1996, *Généalogies Commentées des Arii des Iles de la Société* (Pape'ete, Société des Études Océaniennes).

Camino, Mercedes, 2008, *Exploring the Explorers: Spaniards in Oceania 1519–1794* (Manchester, Manchester University Press).

Carter, Harold B., 1988, *Sir Joseph Banks* (London, British Museum (Natural History)).

Cock, Randolph, 1997, 'The Voyages of the *Dolphin* (1764–68) as Precursors of Cook's Voyages of Exploration', MA thesis, University of Exeter.

———, 1999, 'Precursors of Cook: The Voyages of the *Dolphin* 1764–68', *The Mariner's Mirror* 85/1, 30–52.

Cook, James in J.C. Beaglehole, ed., 1955, *The Journals of Captain James Cook on His Voyages of Discovery: Vol. I. The Voyage of the Endeavour 1768–1771* (Cambridge, for the Hakluyt Society).

——— in J.C. Beaglehole, ed., 1969, *The Journals of Captain James Cook on His Voyages of*

Discovery: Vol. II. The Voyage of the Resolution *and* Adventure *1772–1775* (Cambridge, for the Hakluyt Society).

——in Beaglehole, J.C. ed., 1967, *The Journals of Captain James Cook on His Voyages of Discovery: Vol. III. The Voyage of the* Resolution *and* Discovery *1776–1780*, 2 parts (Cambridge, for the Hakluyt Society).

Corney, Bolton Glanvill, ed., 1908, *The Voyage of Captain Don Felipe Gonzalez in the Ship of the Line San Lorenzo, with the Frigate Santa Rosalia in Company, to Easter Island in 1770–1, preceded by an Extract of Mynheer Jacob Roggeveen's Official Log of his discovery of and visit to Easter Island in 1722* (Cambridge, for the Hakluyt Society).

——, ed., 1913, *The Quest and Occupation of Tahiti by Emissaries of Spain during the Years 1772–1776, told in Despatches and other Contemporary Documents*, I, II and III (Cambridge, for the Hakluyt Society).

Davies, J., 1851, *A Tahitian and English Dictionary with Introductory Remarks on the Polynesian Language and a Short Grammar of the Tahitian Dialect* (London, London Missionary Society).

Dening, Greg, 1986, 'Possessing Tahiti', *Archaeology in Oceania* 21, 103–18.

Descola, Jean, 1968, *Daily Life in Colonial Peru* (London, George Allen and Unwin Ltd).

Di Piazza, Anne and Pearthree, Erik, 2007, 'A New Interpretation of Tupaia's Chart', *Journal of the Polynesian Society* 116/3, 321–40.

——, eds, 2008, *Canoes of the Grand Ocean* (Oxford, BAR International Series 1802).

Driessen, Hank, 1982, 'Outriggerless Canoes and Glorious Beings: Pre-contact Prophecies in the Society Islands', *Journal of Pacific History* XVII, pp. 3–28.

——, 1982, 'Dramatis Personae of Society Islanders, Cook's *Endeavour* Voyage 1769', *Journal of Pacific History* XVII, 227–31.

——, 1991, 'From Ta'aroa to 'Oro', PhD thesis, Australian National University.

——, 2005, 'Tupaia: The Trials and Tribulations of a Polynesian Priest', in Phyllis Herda, Michael Reilly and David Hilliard, eds., *Vision and Reality in Pacific Religion* (Christchurch, Macmillan Brown Centre for Pacific Studies), pp. 66–86.

Dunmore, John, 2002b, *Monsieur Baret: First Woman Around the World 1766–68* (Auckland, Heritage Press).

——, 2005, *Storms and Dreams: Louis de Bougainville, Soldier, Explorer, Statesman* (Auckland, Exisle Publishing Ltd).

Duyker, Edward, 1998, *Nature's Argonaut: Daniel Solander 1733–1782, Naturalist and Voyager with Cook and Banks* (Melbourne, The Miegunyah Press, Melbourne University Press).

Ellis, William, 1829, *Polynesian Researches during A Residence of nearly Eight Years in the Society and Sandwich Islands*, I and II (London, Henry G. Bohn).

Emory, Kenneth P., 1932, 'Traditional History of Maraes in the Society Islands', unpublished ms, Bishop Museum Archives.

——, 1938, 'The Tahitian Account of Creation by Mare', *Journal of the Polynesian Society* 47/186, 45–63.

Filihia, Meredith, 1996, ''Oro-dedicated Maro 'ura in Tahiti: Their Rise and Decline in the Early Post-European Contact Period', *Journal of Pacific History* 31/2, pp. 127–43.

Finney, B. R., 1999, 'The Sin at Awarua', *The Contemporary Pacific* 11, 1–33.

——, 2000, 'Nautical Cartography and Traditional Navigation in Oceania', in Woodward, D. and Lewis, G. Malcolm, eds, *Cartography in the Traditional African, American, Arctic, Australian and Pacific Societies*, Vol. II/3 (Chicago, University of Chicago Press), pp. 443–87.

Forster, George Adam, 1777, *A Voyage round the World in His Brittanic Majesty's Sloop, Resolution, Commanded by Captain James Cook, during the Years 1772, 3, 4 and 5*, I and II (London, B. White, J. Robson, P. Elmsly and G. Robinson).

Forster, Johann in Michael Hoare, ed., 1982, *The* Resolution *Journal of Johann Reinhold Forster 1772–1775*, I–IV (Cambridge, for the Hakluyt Society).

Gascoigne, John, 1994, *Joseph Banks and the English Enlightenment: Useful Knowledge and Polite Culture* (Cambridge, Cambridge University Press).

Gilbert, George in Christine Holmes, ed., 1982, *Captain Cook's Final Voyage: The Journal of Midshipman George Gilbert* (Partridge Green, Sussex, Caliban Books).

Green, Roger C. and Kaye, 1968, 'Religious Structures (*Marae*) of the Windward Society Islands: The Significance of Certain Historical Records', *New Zealand Journal of History* 2/2, 66–89.

Gunson, Niel, 1964, 'Great Women and Friendship Contract Rites in Pre-Christian Tahiti', *Journal of the Polynesian Society* 73, 53–69.

——, 1980, 'Cover's notes on the Tahitians, 1802', *Journal of Pacific History* 15/4, pp. 217–24.

——, 1987, 'Sacred Women Chiefs and Female "Headmen" in Polynesian History', *Journal of Pacific History* 22/3, 139–72.

——, 1992, 'Missionaries and the Unmentionable: Christian Propriety and the Expanded Tahitian Dictionary', in Tom Dutton, Malcolm Ross and Darrell Tryon, eds., *The Language Game: Papers in Memory of Donald C. Laycock* (Canberra, Dept of Linguistics, Research School of Pacific Studies, Australian National University).

Hammond, L. Davis, trans. and ed., 1970, *News from New Cythera: A Report of Bougainville's Voyage 1766–1769* (Minneapolis, University of Minnesota Press).

Handy, E.S., 1930, *History and Culture in the Society Islands* (Honolulu, Bernice P. Bishop Museum Bulletin 79).

Henare [Salmond], Amiria, 2005, *Museums, Anthropology and Imperial Exchange* (Cambridge, Cambridge University Press).

——, 2006, *Thinking through Things: Theorising Artefacts in Ethnographic Perspective* (London, University College London).

Henry, Teuira, 1893, 'The Genealogy of the Pomare Family of Tahiti, from the Papers of the Rev. J.M. Orsmond', *Journal of the Polynesian Society* 2/1, 25–42.

——, 1913, 'The Oldest Great Tahitian Maraes and the Last One built in Tahiti', *Journal of the Polynesian Society* 22, 25–27.

——, 1928, *Ancient Tahiti* (Honolulu, Hawai'i, Bernice P. Bishop Museum Bulletin 48).

Holmes, Christine, ed., 1984, *Captain Cook's Second Voyage: The Journals of Lieutenants Elliott and Pickersgill* (London, Caliban Books).

Howe, K.R., ed., 2006, *Waka Moana: Voyages of the Ancestors* (Auckland, David Bateman Ltd).

Lamb, Jonathan, 2001, *Preserving the Self in the South Seas 1680–1840* (Chicago, University of Chicago Press).

Lavaud, Commander, 1849, Documents ethnologiques sur les îles de la Société, National Library of Australis PMB70, part 4.

Lavaud, M., 1928, 'Hiro', *Bulletin de la Société d'Études Océaniennes*, II/5, 134–35.

——, 1928, 'La Création (Documents recuellis en 1849 par Mr. Lavaud)', *Bulletin de la Société d'Études Océaniennes*, III/4, 78–80.

Leverd, A., 1912, 'The Tahitian version of Tafa'i (or Tawhaki)', *Journal of the Polynesian Society* 21/1, 1–12.

McCormick, E.H., 1977, *Omai: Pacific Envoy* (Auckland, Auckland University Press, Oxford University Press).

Martin-Allenic, Jean Étienne, 1964, *Bougainville, navigateur et les découvertes de son temps*, I and II (Paris, Presses Universitaires de France).

Moerenhout, J.A., 1837, in Arthur R. Borden, Jr, trans. and ed., 1983, *Travels to The Islands of the Pacific Ocean* (Lanham, New York, University Press of America).

Morrison, James in Owen Rutter, ed., 1935, *The Journal of James Morrison* (London, Golden Cockerel Press).

Newbury, C.W., 1961, *The History of the Tahitian Mission 1799–1830* (Cambridge, for the Hakluyt Society).

Newell, Jenny, 2006, 'Paradise Exchanged: Tahitians, Europeans and the trade in nature', PhD thesis, Australian National University.

O'Brien, Patrick, 1988, *Joseph Banks: A Life* (London, Collins Harvill).

Oliver, Douglas, 1974, *Ancient Tahitian Society*, I, II and III (Canberra, Australian National University Press).

Orsmond, J.M., The Papers of Rev. J.M. Orsmond, Vol. 4, 'The 'Arioi War in Tahiti', National Library of Australia Mfm G7706, Mitchell Library A2608, Meredith Filihia transcript.

Parkinson, Sydney, 1773, *A Journal of a Voyage to the South Seas in His Majesty's Ship, The Endeavour* (London, for Stanfield Parkinson).

Riddle, Shane, 1999, 'Inscribing and Contextualising "Spanish Tahiti": A Comparative Study of Representations of an Eighteenth-Century Voyage', MA thesis, University of Auckland.

Robertson, George in Hugh Carrington, ed., 1948, *The Discovery of Tahiti: A Journal of the Second Voyage of H.M.S. Dolphin Round the World, Under the Command of Captain Wallis, R.N., In the Years 1766, 1767 and 1768, written by her master George Robertson* (Cambridge, for the Hakluyt Society).

—— in Oliver Warner, ed., 1955, *An Account of the Discovery of Tahiti, From the Journal of George Robertson, Master of H.M.S. Dolphin* (London, Folio Society).

Rosenzweig, Rachel, 2004, *Worshipping Aphrodite: Art and Cult in Classical Athens* (Ann Arbor, University of Michigan Press).

Rowe, Newton, 1955, *Voyage to the Amorous Islands: The Discovery of Tahiti* (London, Andre Deutsch).

Sahlins, Marshall, 1985, *Islands of History* (Chicago and London, University of Chicago Press).

Salmond, Anne, 1991, *Two Worlds: First Meetings Between Maori and Europeans 1642–1772* (Honolulu, University of Hawai'i Press; Auckland and London, Viking Press).

——, 1997, *Between Worlds: Early Exchanges Between Maori and Europeans 1773–1815* (Honolulu, University of Hawai'i Press; Auckland and London, Viking Press).

——, 2003, *The Trial of the Cannibal Dog: Captain Cook in the South Seas* (London, Penguin UK; Auckland, Penguin NZ), printed in North America as *The Trial of the Cannibal Dog: The Remarkable Story of Captain Cook's Encounters in the South Seas* (New Haven, Yale University Press).

——, 2005, 'Their Body is Different, Our Body is Different: European and Tahitian Navigators in the Eighteenth Century', *History and Anthropology* 16/2, 167–86.

Saura, Bruno, ed., 2000, *Histoire et traditions de Huahine et Borabora* (Pape'ete, Ministère de la Culture de Polynésie française).

——, ed., 2003, *La lignée royale des Tama-toa de Ra'iātea* (Pape'ete, Ministère de la Culture de Polynésie française).

——, ed., 2005, *Huahine aux temps anciens* (Pape'ete, Service de la Culture et du Patrimoine de Polynésie française).

Solander, Daniel in Edward Duyker and Per Tingbrand, eds., 1995, *Daniel Solander, Collected Correspondence 1753–1782* (Melbourne, The Miegunyah Press, Melbourne University Press).

Sparrman, Anders in Owen Rutter, ed., 1953, *A Voyage Round the World with Captain James Cook in HMS* Resolution (London, Robert Hale Limited).

Strathern, Marilyn, 1990, 'Artefacts of History: Events and the Interpretation of Images', in Jukka Siikala, ed., *Culture and History in the Pacific* (Helsinki, The Finnish Anthropological Society, Transactions No. 27), 25–43.

Taaroa, Marau, 1971, *Memoires de Marau Taaroa, Dernière Reine de Tahiti: Traduit par sa fille, la princesse Ariimanihinihi Takau Pomare* (Paris, Musée de l'Homme).

Taillemite, Étienne, 1977, *Bougainville et ses Compagnons autour du monde 1766–1769. Journaux de Navigation établis et commentés par Etienne Taillemite*, I and II (Paris, Imprimerie Nationale).

Tcherkézoff, Serge, 2004, '"First Contacts" in Polynesia: The Samoan Case (1722–1848)' (Canberra, for the Macmillan Brown Centre for Pacific Studies and the *Journal of Pacific History*).

——, 2004, *Tahiti – 1768: Jeunes filles en pleurs: La face cachée des premiers contacts et la naissance du mythe occidental* (Pape'ete, Au Vent des Iles).

Thomson, Rev. Richard, c. 1840, unpublished History of Tahiti, Alexander Turnbull Library Micro Ms Collection 2, Reel 169, London Missionary Society M660, Salmond transcript.

Trevenen, James in Christopher Lloyd and R.C. Anderson, 1959, eds, *A Memoir of James Trevenen* (London, Navy Records Society).

Turnbull, David, 2000, '(En-)countering Knowledge Traditions: The Story of Cook and Tupaia', *Humanities Research* 1 (Canberra, Australian National University).

——, 2001, 'Cook and Tupaia, a Tale of Cartographic Meconnaissance?', in M. Lincoln, ed., *Science and Exploration in the Pacific: European Voyages to the Southern Oceans in the Eighteenth Century* (Woodbridge, Suffolk, National Maritime Museum), 117–33.

Turnbull, John, 1810, *A Voyage Round the World in the Years 1800, 1801, 1802, 1803, and 1804* (Philadelphia, Benjamin and Thomas Kite).

Tyerman, Rev. Daniel and Bennet, George, 1831, *Journal of Voyages and Travels by the Rev. Daniel Tyerman and George Bennet deputed from the London Missionary Society to visit their various Stations in the South Sea Islands, China, India, &c. between the years 1821 and 1829, compiled from the original documents by James Montgomery* (London, Frederick Westley and A.H. Davis).

Williams, Glyndwr, 2003, 'Tupaia: Polynesian Warrior, Navigator, High Priest – and Artist', in Felicity A. Nussbaum, ed., *The Global Eighteenth Century* (Baltimore and London, John Hopkins University Press).

——, ed., 2004, *Captain Cook: Explorations and Reassessments* (Woodbridge, Suffolk, The Boydell Press).

Williams, John, 1838, *A Narrative of Missionary Enterprises in the South Sea Islands* (London, J. Snow).

Wilson, James, 1799, *Missionary Voyage to the Southern Pacific Ocean, Performed in the Years 1796, 1797, 1798 in the Ship* Duff, *commanded by Captain James Wilson* (London, T. Chapman).

Zimmerman, Henry in F.W. Howay, ed., 1929, *Zimmerman's Captain Cook* (Toronto, The Ryerson Press).

Notes

ACKNOWLEDGEMENTS

1. For works by Mercedes Camino and Amiria Salmond [Henare] from the Cross-cultural Voyaging project, see Camino, Mercedes, 2008, *Exploring the Explorers: Spaniards in Oceania 1519–1794* (Manchester, Manchester University Press) and Henare [Salmond], Amiria, 2005, *Museums, Anthropology and Imperial Exchange* (Cambridge, Cambridge University Press); 2006, *Thinking through Things: Theorising Artefacts in Ethnographic Perspective* (London, University College London); 2008, ed. with Rosanna Raymond, *Pasifika Styles: Artists inside the Museum* (Dunedin, Cambridge Museum of Archaeology and Anthropology and University of Otago Press).

INTRODUCTION: APHRODITE'S ISLAND

1. Bougainville, Louis-Antoine in John Dunmore, trans. and ed., 2002a, *The Pacific Journal of Louis-Antoine de Bougainville* (Cambridge, for the Hakluyt Society), 54.

2. Samuel Wallis visited Tahiti 19 June – 27 July 1767, arriving back in England on 20 May 1768. His discovery of Tahiti was first announced in Europe in 23–25 May of that year in *Lloyd's Evening Post and British Chronicle*, the report being reprinted in *The Gazetteer and New Daily Advertiser* on 26 and 27 May. The first extended account of the voyage was published in August 1768 when *The Gentleman's Magazine* printed a poem by the ship's barber, Rogers Richardson, describing the voyage and their arrival at Tahiti (*The Gentleman's Magazine and Historical Chronicle* (London, F. Newbery), XXXVIII, 390–91). Wallis's journal was first published (in an abbreviated version) along with those of Byron, Carteret and Cook by John Hawkesworth in 1773; while an 'epitome' of Wallis's voyage appeared in *The Gentleman's Magazine* in September–November of the same year (417–23; 484–94; 537–43).

Bougainville's voyage, on the other hand, received much more extensive publicity in the popular press in France and among intellectuals in Europe. In July 1769 a pamphlet reporting some observations from Tahiti was released in Paris – *News from New Cythera* (Hammond, L. Davis, trans. and ed., 1970, *News from New Cythera: A Report of Bougainville's Voyage 1766–1769* (Minneapolis, University of Minnesota Press)); and in November of that year his naturalist Commerson's rhapsodic letter about Tahiti was published by the *Mercure de France* newspaper, and made a sensation. Bougainville's own account of his voyage was presented to Louis XV in October 1769 and published in French in March or April 1771 in two issues totalling about 2500 copies; followed within two years by translations into English, Dutch and German, and an epitome of his voyage was published in *The Gentleman's Magazine* in February–March 1772 (59; 105–10).

Despite the fact that Wallis arrived at Tahiti ten months earlier than Bougainville, therefore, Bougainville's journal was published well before Wallis's, even in England, and had a much greater impact in popular and learned circles (see also Tcherkézoff's discussion of this point in

Tcherkézoff, Serge, 2004, *Tahiti – 1768: Jeunes filles en pleurs: La face cachée des premiers contacts et la naissance du mythe occidental* (Pape'ete, Au Vent des Iles), 109–13.

3. Bougainville, Lewis de in John Reinhold Forster, ed., 1772, *A Voyage Round the World Performed by Order of His Most Christian Majesty, in the Years 1766, 1767, 1768, and 1769* (London, J. Nourse), 218–19.

4. Fesche in Dunmore, ed., 2002a, 255.

5. Commerson quoted in Dunmore, John, 2002b, *Monsieur Baret: First Woman Around the World 1766–68* (Auckland, Heritage Press), 94.

6. Not all Europeans admired the classics, however. The London Missionary Society missionaries who later arrived in Tahiti, for instance, also referred to Greek mythology, but considered classical and Tahitian attitudes to sex alike to be depraved – for instance William Ellis in his classic work *Polynesian Researches*:

> No portion of the human race was ever perhaps sunk lower in brutal licentiousness and moral degradation, than this isolated people,
> > 'The Paphian Venus driven from the west,
> > In Polynesian groves long undisturbed,
> > Her shameful rites and orgies fould maintained,
> > The wandering voyager at Tahiti found
> > Another Daphne.'
> The veil of oblivion must be spread over this part of their character.

(Ellis, William, 1829, *Polynesian Researches during A Residence of nearly Eight Years in the Society and Sandwich Islands, Volumes I and II* (London, Henry G. Bohn), I: 97–98.)

7. See Art Gallery of New South Wales, 2000, *Les Sauvages de la Mer Pacifique* (Sydney, Australian Focus Series no. 7), 35; Watkin, David, 1967, 'Some Dufour Wallpapers: a neo-classical venture into the picturesque', *Apollo*, June 1967, 432–35; and Ringsmuth, Timothy, draft thesis paper, Australian National University, pers. comm.

8. Powell, Barry, 2004, *Classical Myth* (New Jersey, Pearson Prentice Hall), 83–84; also 177–80, 196–208, 408–11, 451–52. For an excellent discussion of the worship of Aphrodite, see Rosenzweig, Rachel, 2004, *Worshipping Aphrodite: Art and Cult in Classical Athens* (Ann Arbor, University of Michigan Press); and for an account of the iconography of Aphrodite/Venus in European art, see Bull, Malcolm, 2005, *The Mirror of the Gods: Classical Mythology in Renaissance Art* (London, Penguin).

9. Sahlins, Marshall, 1985, *Islands of History* (Chicago and London, University of Chicago Press), xi.

CHAPTER 1: THUNDER IN 'OPOA

1. Moerenhout, J.A., 1837, trans. Arthur R. Borden, Jr, 1983, *Travels to The Islands of the Pacific Ocean* (Lanham, New York, University Press of America), 210–11.

2. The Creation Chant recited to Rev. John Muggeridge Orsmond in 1822 by Paora'i of Borabora, and a later version by Vai'au, a high priest of Ra'iatea, and Pati'i, a high priest of Mo'orea in Henry, Teuira, 1928, *Ancient Tahiti* (Honolulu, Hawai'i, Bernice P. Bishop Museum Bulletin 48), 336–38. See also Pomare, Takau, ed., 1971, *Mémoires de Marau Taaroa, Dernière Reine de Tahiti, traduits par sa fille la Princesse Ariimanihinihi Takau Pomare* (Paris, Publications de la Société des Océanistes, Musée de l'Homme), 27: 47–50.

3. Lavaud, M., 1928, 'La Création (Documents recuellis en 1849 par Mr. Lavaud)', *Bulletin de la Société d'Études Océaniennes* III/4, 78–80.

4. Tetumu's phallus, Te Apo-i-ra'i (Curved Sky) – also known as Haruru-papa (Thunder-rock) – reached down to Te Papa Raharaha, or 'horizontal rock'; the first of their unions producing the red sands that clothed the earth (see Emory, Kenneth, 1938, 'The Tahitian Account of Creation by Mare', *Journal of the Polynesian Society* 47/186, 45–63; and Lavaud, 1928; see also Driessen, H.A.H., 1991, 'From Ta'aroa to 'Oro', PhD thesis, Australian National University, 128, 131; and

Eddowes, Mark, n.d., 'The Phenomena of the marae Taputapuatea in the 18th century Society Islands', unpublished manuscript, 2).

5. The Genealogies of the Gods, given by the same experts who dictated the Creation Chant, in Henry, 1928, 355–59, 369; see also the Handsome Shark of Ta'aroa, recited to Orsmond in 1833 by Tamara, high priest of Tahiti, and Pati'i high priest of Mo'orea, in ibid., 403–4. The sequence in which this and other stories recited by knowledgeable experts to Orsmond should be placed is uncertain, because unlike in New Zealand or Hawai'i, in Tahiti no cosmogonic genealogies appear to survive that link all of these ancestors and their feats together (Driessen, 1991, 114); although see Driessen's excellent discussion (ibid., 115–44) of the one surviving genealogy from the Society Islands (from Borabora) that goes back to the gods.

According to Oliver quoting Teuira Henry, the shark was an *ata* (incarnation) of Tane; the red-feathered duck and the frigate bird were *ata* of 'Oro; and the bird of paradise and the albatross were *ata* of Ta'aroa. (Oliver, Douglas, 1974, *Ancient Tahitian Society, Vols. I, II and III* (Canberra, Australian National University Press), I: 59.)

6. The Birth of the Heavenly Bodies, recited to Orsmond in 1818 at Borabora by Ruanui, a knowledgeable old woman in Henry, 1928, 359–63.

7. Ibid., 426. In Tahiti, a god could have many *ata* ('shadows' or incarnations) – animals, people or objects, and each was a part of the god. For an illuminating discussion of the multiple forms of the gods in Tahiti, see Tcherkézoff, Serge, 2004, '"First Contacts" in Polynesia: The Samoan Case (1722–1848)' (Canberra, for the Macmillan Brown Centre for Pacific Studies and the *Journal of Pacific History*), 109–53: 'Every "god" in the pantheon is a partial form of the beginning of the world and of the great demiurge, at the same time as it already contains the seeds of all human forms to come. Furthermore, these gods become manifest in the form of images.' (Tcherkézoff, 2004, 112.)

8. Ibid., 363.

9. The Birth of More Gods, recited in 1840 by Tamara and Pati'i, the same high priests, in ibid., 374–75.

10. The Creation of Man, recited in 1822 by Mahine, chief of Mai'ao; and in 1833 by Anani, a Tahitian chief, and Tamara, a high priest, in ibid., 402–3.

11. Ibid., 104.

12. Heralding of the Fish; The Departure of the Fish, recited to Orsmond in 1822 and 1824 by King Pomare II, Mahine, a chief, and Tamara, a priest; and Cutting the Sinews of the Fish in ibid., 433–43. See also Ellis, 1829, I: 167.

13. Rua and Hina Explore the Earth, recited to Orsmond in 1824 by Pape-au, a Tahitian scholar, and Sacred Canoe Song of Ru, recited in 1886 by Tetupaia, grandson of a chief of Motutapu, Tahiti, in Henry, 1928, 459–62.

14. Henry, Teuira, 1913, 'The Oldest Great Tahitian Maraes and the Last One built in Tahiti', *Journal of the Polynesian Society* 22, 25–27.

15. Moerenhout in Borden, ed., 1983, 226; Henry, 1928, 537–52. According to Henry, after one of his great voyages Hiro did not return home to Tahiti.

16. Fitzgerald, Robert, trans., 1984, Homer's *The Iliad* (Oxford, Oxford University Press); 1998, *The Odyssey* (New York, Farrar, Straus and Giroux); 1990, Virgil's *The Aeneid* (New York, Vintage Classics, Random House).

17. For Tafa'i's adventures, see Leverd, A., 1912, 'The Tahitian Version of Tafa'i (or Tawhaki)', *Journal of the Polynesian Society* 21/1, 1–12; and Henry, 1928, 440–42, 552–76. See also Babadzan's discussion of this story, and how it was reflected in funerary rituals and the investiture of high chiefs (Babadzan, Alain, 1993, *Les Dépouille des Dieux: Essai sur la religion tahitienne à l'époque de la découverte* (Paris, Maison de la science de l'homme), 145–90).

18. See for instance 'Ancestors of the Pomare family from Mare' in Henry, 1928, 265; and genealogies cited in Emory, Kenneth P., 1932, 'Traditional History of Maraes in the Society Islands', unpublished ms, Bishop Museum Archives.

19. See the missionary Jefferson in the Douglas Oliver missionary card index, card 34: 'His house is called yow-rey [*hau ra'i*] (clouds of heaven), his double canoe anooanooa [*anuanua*]

(the rainbow), his manner of riding on the shoulders of an attendant mahowta [*mahuta*] (flying), his torch Ooweera [*uira*] (lightning), a drum that is frequently beating for his amusement paateri [*patiri*] (thunder)'; and Ellis, 1829, III: 113–14.

20. Henry, 1928, 201, 338; Ellis, 1829, I: 244–46. According to Driessen, at Mt Mehani the god Tu-taho-roa guided souls either down to Apo'o-nui or Big Hole, the volcanic vent at the centre of the earth that served as the entrance to the Po; or up to Rohutu-no'ano'a. (Driessen, 1991, 104.)

21. Ellis, 1829, I: 397.

22. Henry, 1928, 564.

23. According to several accounts, Hiro (a famed sailor descended from 'Oro who was revered as the god of thieves) was responsible for taking a stone from the inland *marae* of Vaeara'i and building the *marae* named Taputapuatea at Cape Matahira-i-te-ra'i. His great-grandson Hoata'atama went to Borabora where he established a *marae* called Vai'otaha, instituting the chieftainship of the yellow feather girdle as a mark of his independence (Emory, 1932, 8–9, quoting de Bovis and Tyerman, Rev. Daniel and Bennet, George, 1831, *Journal of Voyages and Travels by the Rev. Daniel Tyerman and George Bennet deputed from the London Missionary Society to visit their various Stations in the South Sea Islands, China, India, &c. between the years 1821 and 1829, compiled from the original documents by James Montgomery* (London, Frederick Westley and A.H. Davis), 1831). For more about Hiro and his feats, see Lavaud, M., 1928, 'Hiro', *Bulletin de la Société d'Études Océaniennes* II/5, 134–35.

Henry gives a slightly different account, saying that when 'Oro was born, his father Ta'aroa gave him 'Opoa with its *marae* Feoro as his home. As 'Oro's *mana* grew, Feoro was renamed Vai'otaha (Water of the Man-o-War Bird), because the man-o-war bird was an *ata* of 'Oro. Later the *marae* was enlarged and renamed Taputapuatea. (Henry, 1928, 120–21.)

According to information given to de Bovis and genealogies cited by Emory, Hiro lived twenty-four generations before 1900; but according to Auna, the son of a former high priest at 'Opoa (Driessen, 1991, 166) quoted by Tyerman and Bennet, Hiro was a more recent god whose skull was kept at Taputapuatea well into historic times (Tyerman and Bennet, 1831, I: 255). Bruno Saura has resolved this apparent contradiction by pointing out that in fact there were two Hiro, one the 'god' of thieves, and the other the famed navigator (Saura, Bruno, 2008, pers. comm.).

24. Emory, 1932, 8.

25. Henry, 1928, 121.

26. Ellis, 1829, I: 341.

27. See also Pomare, ed., 1971, 51, the Creation Chant by Marau, as translated by Emory, 1932, 12: 'Ta'aroa cried out! My lower jaw I lay on *marae* Vai'otaha [in Borabora], My upper jaw on *marae* Mata'ire'a [in Huahine]. On Nu'u-te-vao-tapu I lay my belly [an ancient name for *marae* Vaeara'i in 'Opoa, where Ta'aroa entered the earth], On Nu'u-te-vao-tapu will I eat of my offerings.' (As corrected by Driessen, 1991, 105.) See also Tati Salmon's version of Marau, which gives the lower jaw as Ahuta'a-i-te-rai (that is Faretai); the upper jaw as Tahuea-i-te-turatura (that is To'erauroa, Huahine); the throat as Tetumu, at 'Opoa; the stomach as Haruru. (Emory, 1932, 13.)

28. Chant of Marae, recited by the priests Tamatera and Pati'i, the high priests of Tahiti and Mo'orea, in Henry, 1928, 150–51.

29. Hence *Taputapu* [intensely sacred] journeys + *Atea* [far-flung places]. Pers. comm., Romy Tavaeari'i, the orator for Taputapuatea, at a workshop in Mo'orea, September 2007.

30. Driessen, 1991, 130. According to Emory, 1932, 51, Tagi'ia-ariki of the Cook Islands was Ta'ihia, the son of Aua from Tautira, Tahiti. See also the story collected by the missionary Williams in Rarotonga in c. 1828, which recounts the tale of Tangiia, a chief of Fa'a'a in Tahiti who by cutting down a favourite breadfruit tree offended his brother Tutapu, who decided to kill him and all his family. Tangiia launched a large canoe and fled with his family and followers to Huahine, pursued by his brother; and then to Ra'iatea, Borabora and Maupiti. Out on the ocean he met Karika, a mighty warrior and navigator from the island of Manuka, and found Rarotonga, which was uninhabited. They forged an alliance, and when Tangiia's brother arrived to attack him, they defeated him (Williams, John, 1838, *A Narrative of Missionary Enterprises in*

the South Sea Islands (London, J. Snow), 195–98).

31. There was a sacred site called Taputapuatea at Whitianga (Mercury Bay), which was also the ancient name of Mokoia Island (Paul Tapsell, pers. comm. 2000) in the middle of Lake Rotorua. According to Judge Joe Williams of the Māori Land Court, there are many other sites with this name scattered around New Zealand, including one on Mangonui Bluff, and another in Tauranga; which suggests that if such sites had any association with the *'arioi* cult, it had spread at least throughout the northern North Island (pers. comm. 2002). There is also a *heiau*, or stone temple, called Kapukapuakea in the Hawaiian Islands.

The genealogical evidence suggests a number of migrations out of Tahiti to Hawai'i, the Cook Islands and New Zealand about thirty generations ago. According to Emory, the great-granddaughter of the creator god Ta'aroa married a man named Hiro 'from the sun, by the ship Te Ao Tea'. (*Aotea* is the name given to one of the migratory canoes that arrived in New Zealand.) According to Cook Island traditions, this Hiro was a great voyager, and his people were known as Te-tini-Oropa'a-ki-uta, Te-tini-Oropa'a-ki-tai (the multitude of Oropa'a from the land and the sea). A Puna'aui'a genealogy gives an ancestor named Te Rai-mavete, whose descendant Oropa'a lived twenty-nine generations ago. According to Hawaiian tradition, a chief Maweke who lived thirty-one generations ago led a colonising expedition to Hawai'i. His grandson Olopana married to Luukia in Kahiki. A Māori genealogy gives an ancestor Tu-koropanga who married Rukutia and lived in Tawhiti thirty generations ago; and during a visit by Tama-nui-a-rangi to Tu-te-koropanga, one party wore *Maro kura*. Emory concludes that all of these ancestors were part of an ancient diaspora from Tahiti, given that 'there can be no doubt that the Hawaiian Olopana and the Maori Tu-koropanga are the same individual, as both lived at the same time, and in the same foreign land, and had the same wife. There also can be little doubt that this man is one of the immediate family of the first Oropa'a at 29 generations on the main line of Puna'aui'a chiefs.' (Emory, 1932, 52–57.)

See also Salmon, Tati, 1910, 'On Ari'is in Tahiti', *Journal of the Polynesian Society* 19, 39–46, who discusses the voyage of Ta'ihia or Teri'i Vaetua in his canoe *Tainui*, when he was chased by his brother Tutapu who tried to kill him, and his expeditions on this canoe to the Tuamotu and Marquesas (and perhaps to New Zealand, as this canoe gives its name to the Tainui people); and Aromaitera'i's canoe *Matatua*, named after this chief's fighting stick 'Te raau-matamatua-e-tu-i-Mou'a-Tamaiti' (the stick of the godly eyes that stands on Mt Tamaiti), which sailed away from Tahiti and never returned – the founding canoe of the Matatua tribes in New Zealand.

32. Henry, 1928, 117.

33. Henry, Teuira, 1912, 'The Tahitian Version of the Names Ra'iatea and Taputapu-atea', *Journal of the Polynesian Society* 21, 77–78.

34. Henry, 1928, from Mrs John Platt, chieftainess of Ra'iatea, 116, 121–23; Emory, 1932, 7. Kenneth Emory in 'The Genealogy of Vaeara'i and Taputapuatea marae' recorded a text that has been translated by Eddowes: 'Paoa-uri and Paoa-tea were the men who put up this *marae* of Taputapuatea, and it was those two who planted the tree of Ta'imoana, from which was made the drum of chiefs, that of Ta'imoana. Ta'aroa-tahi-tumu was on top and Teteihiti was beneath, from whom was born Teanuanua.' (Eddowes, Mark, n.d., 'The Phenomena of the *marae* Taputapuatea in the 18th century Society Islands', 11.) In this paper Eddowes proposes the hypothesis that the *'arioi* cult was originally founded by 'Oro in Borabora, not Ra'iatea; and that the worship of 'Oro was introduced to Ra'iatea after the conquest of the island by the Borabora warriors. There are some early texts (including Orsmond, J.M., The Papers of Rev. J.M. Orsmond, Vol. 4, 'The 'Arioi War in Tahiti', National Library of Australia Mfm G7706, Mitchell Library A2608, Meredith Filihia transcript, 2) that support this supposition, but others place the worship of 'Oro on Ra'iatea well before the Borabora conquest. It seems impossible to disentangle this sequence of events, given the conflicting evidence.

35. Montgomery, 1832, quoted in Oliver, 1974, II: 666. See also Ellis, 1829, II: 313–16 for an account of a visit to 'Opoa.

36. Ellis, 1829, I: 238.

37. Orsmond, 'The 'Arioi War', trans. Ralph White, quoted in Oliver, 1974, II: 931.

38. Orsmond, 'The 'Arioi War', Filihia transcript, 8. Although Babadzan has mounted a persuasive argument that the *'arioi* were strongly associated with femininity and female powers (see Babadzan's discussion of the *'arioi* society, Babadzan, 1993, 253–76), I think that he overstates the case; because just as 'Oro was a god who controlled both fertility and war (whereas in ancient Maori and Hawaiian societies, these powers were divided between Rongo or Lono, the god of fertility, and Tu or Ku, the god of war), the *'arioi* were at once men and women, marshalling both male and female powers.

39. Much of the testimony about the *'arioi* cult collected by the early missionaries was censored and some was destroyed because they considered it pornographic. The missionary David Darling, for instance, eventually destroyed a history of the *'arioi* society that he had written; and an account of the *'arioi* written in Latin disappeared from the British Library (Gunson, Niel, 1992, 'Missionaries and the Unmentionable: Christian Propriety and the Expanded Tahitian Dictionary' in Tom Dutton, Malcolm Ross and Darrell Tryon, eds, *The Language Game: Papers in Memory of Donald C. Laycock* (Canberra), 602. Orsmond's *'arioi* manuscript transcribes much of the 'indecent' material only in Tahitian, presumably for the same reason.

40. See Orsmond, 'The 'Arioi War', Filihia transcript, 13: 'Their fleet that conveyed them from island to island was called a Mareva or a Auono.'

41. Ellis, 1829, I: 234.

42. Ellis, 1829 quoted in Oliver, 1974, II: 919.

43. Orsmond, Rev. John, 1850, Papers Vol. V, part of Tahitian dictionary, Mitchell Library, Sydney, A2609, Meredith Filihia transcript, 4 and 10, describes the *'Aha ta'ata* (or *'Aha mata-tini*) ritual for binding the sacrificial victim's head with this sacred sennit cord. *Mana* resided in the chief's head, and when it was bound in this way the *mana* of his entire lineage was 'entangled' or destroyed; while the *ure mau 'aha* ritual in which his penis was also bound destroyed the fertility of his lineage. See also Orsmond, 'The 'Arioi War', Filihia transcript, 51–53.

44. These drums were known as *pahu ra'a* or sacred drums, and could be eight feet tall (Ellis, 1829, I: 194–95). See also Henry, 1928, 124–25 and Oliver, 1974, I: 93.

45. Handy, E.S., 1930, *History and Culture in the Society Islands* (Honolulu, Hawai'i, Bernice P. Bishop Museum Bulletin 79), 89. According to Henry, 1928, 120, the white stone pillar at *marae* Taputapuatea is known as Te Papa-o-na-maha (the rock of the four), because four sacrificial victims were buried beneath it, one under each corner, or Te Papa-tea-i-ru'ea. Emory quotes a chant that mentions the stone pillar, calling it Te Papa-ua-mea-o-Ruea; while he gives the name of the 'coronation *marae*' beside it as Hauviri, and a coral slab lying in the lagoon in front of this as Te pua-pe-i-Hauviri (Emory, 1932, 11, 17; 14), and says that according to Tati Salmon, the white pillar of investiture was carried there by Hiro.

46. Henry, 1928, 95.

CHAPTER 2: THE GLORIOUS CHILDREN OF TETUMU

1. For accounts of the history of the period in Tahiti just before and after first contact with Europeans, see Orsmond, Rev. J.M., The Papers of Rev. J.M. Orsmond, Vol. 4, 'The 'Arioi War in Tahiti', National Library of Australia Mfm G7706, Mitchell Library A2608, Meredith Filihia transcript (although sadly a detailed history of Tahiti written by Orsmond has been lost, along with most of his original manuscripts; and my attempts to locate a Ralph White translation of the Tahitian sections in this manuscript were also unsuccessful); Moerenhout, J.A., 1837, trans. Arthur R. Borden, Jr, 1983, *Travels to The Islands of the Pacific Ocean* (Lanham, New York, University Press of America); Thomson, Rev. Richard, c. 1840, unpublished History of Tahiti, Alexander Turnbull Library Micro Ms Collection 2, Reel 169, London Missionary Society M660, Salmond transcript; Lavaud, Commander, 1849, Documents ethnologiques sur les îles de la Société, National Library of Australia PMB70, part 4; Ellis, William, 1859, *Polynesian Researches during A Residence of nearly Eight Years in the Society and Sandwich Islands, Volumes I and II* (London, Henry G. Bohn); Henry, Teuira, 1928, *Ancient Tahiti* (Honolulu, Hawai'i, Bernice P. Bishop Museum Bulletin 48); Adams, Henry Brook, 1910, *Tahiti: Memoirs of Arii Taimai* (Ridgewood, NJ, The Gregg Press); Taaroa, Marau, 1971, *Memoires de Marau Taaroa, Dernière Reine de*

Tahiti: Traduit par sa fille, la princesse Ariimanihinihi Takau Pomare (Paris, Musée de l'Homme); Oliver, Douglas, 1974, *Ancient Tahitian Society, Vols. I, II and III* (Canberra, Australian National University Press); Babadzan, Alain, 1993, *Les Dépouilles des Dieux: Essai sur la religion tahitienne à l'époque de la découverte* (Paris, Maison de la science de l'homme); Cadousteau, Mai Ari'i, 1996, *Généalogies Commentées des Arii des Iles de la Société* (Pape'ete, Société des Études Océaniennes); Saura, Bruno, ed., 2000, *Histoire et traditions de Huahine et Borabora* (Pape'ete, Ministère de la Culture de Polynésie Française); Baré, Jean-François, 2002, *Le Malentendu Pacifique: Des Premières Recontres entre Polynésiens et Anglais et ce qui s'ensuivant avec les Français jusqu'à nos jours* (Paris, Contemporary Publishing International); Saura, Bruno, ed., 2003, *La lignée royale des Tama-toa de Ra'iätea* (Pape'ete, Ministère de la Culture de Polynésie Française); Tcherkézoff, Serge, 2004, *Tahiti – 1768: Jeune filles en pleurs: La face cachée des premiers contacts et la naissance du mythe occidental* (Pape'ete, Au Vent des Iles, Editions Tahiti); Saura, Bruno, ed., 2005, *Huahine aux temps anciens* (Pape'ete, Service de la Culture et du Patrimoine de Polynésie Française); Driessen, Hank, 2005, 'Tupaia: The Trials and Tribulations of a Polynesian Priest' in Phyllis Herda, Michael Reilly and David Hilliard, eds, *Vision and Reality in Pacific Religion* (Christchurch, Macmillan Brown Centre for Pacific Studies).

2. For the story of 'Oro's rescue of the unsuccessful envoys, see Henry, 1928, 129.

3. Tamatoa I was more formally known as Tautu-ari'i-i-'Opoa. According to some accounts, his first wife Teha'ame'ame'a-i-Marae-te-hotu gave him three sons – Turi-ari'i-te-pou-tahi, or Tamatoa II, who had no children and sailed away to New Zealand (Saura, 2003, 9, 222; although in 1789 the *Bounty* mutineers found a chief named Tamatoa living on Tupua'i whose great-grandfather, a high chief from Ra'iatea, had been caught in a storm and driven to Tupua'i – presumably this man), and the twins Ari'i-rua and Rofa'i. Tamatoa I's second wife Te-ari'i-te-pou-anuanua gave him his last son, Te-ari'i-i-te-ua-na-tua, who became Tamatoa III. Tamatoa III's son by his legitimate wife Te nuhi-roro-o-Tevaito'a i Tainu'u, Tamatoa IV, was known as 'U'uru-ari'i (Saura, 2003, 9, 222), whom Cook met briefly at Ra'iatea in 1774.

According to other genealogies, Tamatoa I had three sons – Ari'ima'o, who married Te'e'eva and had Mau'a, Ari'i-rua and Rofa'i (Saura, 2003, 225; Henry, Teuira, 1893, 'The Genealogy of the Pomare Family of Tahiti, from the Papers of the Rev. J.M. Orsmond', *Journal of the Polynesian Society* 2/1, 25–42). Given that most of these genealogies give Turi-ari'i on the one hand and Ari'ima'o on the other as the elder brothers of Ari'i-rua and Rofa'i, it is likely that they were also brothers or half-brothers; and that Turi-ari'i was the eldest brother, as he was installed as Tamatoa II, a privilege never granted to Ari'ima'o as far as I can discern. See also Caillot's genealogy of the Tamatoas, which gives Ari'ima'o two older brothers; and Teuira Henry's genealogy (Saura, 2003, 226–29).

4. The introduction of the cult of 'Oro to Tahiti and the founding of Taputapuatea marae in Tautira is dated by Newbury to the early eighteenth century (Newbury, C.W., 1961, *The History of the Tahitian Mission 1799–1830* (Cambridge, for the Hakluyt Society), xxxvi); and by Filihia to about 1720 (Filihia, Meredith, 1996, "'Oro-dedicated Maro 'Ura in Tahiti: Their Rise and Decline in the Early Post-European Contact Period', *Journal of Pacific History* 31/2, 128.

Rev. Richard Thomson gives an excellent account of the introduction of the 'arioi cult to Tahiti in his unpublished History of Tahiti (Thomson, c. 1840, Salmond transcript, 9).

See also Orsmond, 'The 'Arioi War', Filihia transcript, 3–4 and Henry, 1928, 232–34 as dictated by Pomare II (drawn from Orsmond's account), which tells the rest of the story of Mahi. This identifies Tamatoa I as the high chief of Ra'iatea who sent Mahi to Tahiti, describes his three unsuccessful visits to the island and how he was finally befriended by Hua-atua of Afa'ahiti, a chief at Taravao, and his return trip to Ra'iatea, when Tamatoa I exchanged names with him and gave him rich gifts to support the introduction of the 'arioi cult to the island. According to Orsmond, like Thomson, the first 'arioi lodge was established at Afa'ahiti, Hua-atua's home.

5. Thomson, c. 1840, Salmond transcript, 8–9; see also Orsmond, Filihia transcript, 3. In trying to fix the timing of these events, one must note that all the historic sources agree that the cult of 'Oro was a relatively recent introduction to Tahiti. As noted above, according to Pomare II in 1840 (Henry, 1928, 232–33), Mahi was sent to Tahiti by Tamatoa I; while according to Thomson,

Taramanini, the other key player in these events, lived in the time of Pomare I's grandfather Tutaha, whose son Teu was alive when the first Europeans arrived at the island. Mau'a, a younger contemporary of Teu and the son of Ari'ima'o (Tamatoa I's son), was also alive at the time of the first European arrival in Tahiti. If these events occurred in about 1720, as Filihia has suggested (see fn. 4 above), it was almost certainly Tamatoa I, as Pomare II claimed in 1840 (rather than Tamatoa II, as Newbury has suggested in Newbury, 1961, fn. xxxvi), who was involved in the first introduction of the 'arioi cult to Tahiti. Although genealogies of the Pomare family from Mare (ibid., 247–49) say that Tamatoa I lived fourteen generations before this period, this probably reflects a general tendency to exaggerate the antiquity of significant events and leaders. For the difficulties associated with the numbering of ari'i in the Tamatoa line (Tamatoa I, II, III, IV etc.), see Saura, 2003, 6–9; for the list of gifts and other details of Mahi's visits to Tahiti, see Orsmond, 'The 'Arioi War', Filihia transcript, 3–4.

6. According to Tati Salmon, marae Vai'otaha in Tautira was established with a sacred stone from Borabora, brought to southern Tahiti by the renowned chief and navigator Ra'amauriri. When his grandson Ta'ihia (the Tangi'ia of Rarotonga) carried the god 'Oro to this marae, it was renamed Taputapuatea (Corney, Bolton Glanvill, ed., 1913, The Quest and Occupation of Tahiti by Emissaries of Spain during the Years 1772–1776, told in Despatches and other Contemporary Documents, Volumes I, II and III (Cambridge, for the Hakluyt Society), II: 127, cited in Emory, 1932, 102). According to Orsmond and Thomson, the first 'arioi lodge was established at Afa'ahiti (Orsmond, J.M, n.d., 'The 'Arioi War', Filihia transcript, 3–4 and Henry, 1928, 232–34).

7. Henry, 1928, 130, 232–34. See the account of these wrapped god-images or to'o in Babadzan, 1993, and 2003, 'The Gods Stripped Bare', in Chloë Colchester, ed., Clothing the Pacific (Oxford, Berg), 25–50, where he observes that the reason why the 'aito or piece of wood at the heart of each god-image had no particular shape was in order to reflect the original state of chaos before the creator god Ta'aroa gave form to the cosmos.

8. Thomson, c. 1840, Salmond transcript, 18.

9. Henry, 1928, 126.

10. Emory, 1932, 7.

11. Williams, 1838, 104. Williams had already heard the story of the great drum Ta'i-moana from an old priest in Ra'iatea, who told him that in earlier times when the islands of Ra'iatea and Rarotonga were close to each other, the people of Rarotonga sent Ta'i-moana with two priests as a gift to 'Oro at Taputapuatea. After they had presented the drum at the altar, the Raiateans killed them, and 'Oro was so incensed that he picked up Rarotonga and carried it far away (Williams, 1838, 57). Williams heard a great deal about Rarotonga from the people in Ra'iatea and vice versa, and was convinced that the two islands were in touch with each other by voyaging.

12. Finney, B.R., 1999, 'The Sin at Awarua', The Contemporary Pacific 11, 1–33.

13. See for instance Thomson, c. 1840, Salmond transcript, 11–15.

14. See Henry, Teuira, 1893, 'The Genealogy of the Pomare Family of Tahiti, from the Papers of the Rev. J.M. Orsmond', Journal of the Polynesian Society 2/1, 25–42.

15. Tupaia himself gave this information to James Magra during the Endeavour voyage (Marra, 1771, 62).

16. In Pomare, ed., 1971, Marau gives an interesting account of the origins of the maro 'ura or red feather girdle, saying that 'ura was the colour of Ta'aroa himself, who under the name Te Fatu slept with various female goddesses who gave birth to trees with red flowers, plants with red leaves, red bananas, red fish and a red-crested seabird. When he slept with Hehea, a high-born, beautiful young goddess, she gave birth to two bird children. One day, impatient for her caresses, one of these birds pecked her nose and drank her blood, and all his feathers became red. When her children flew away, leaving a packet of red feathers behind them, Hehea fastened these feathers to each end of Te Fatu's girdle, naming it Te ra'i-pua-tata; and this became the first of the sacred maro 'ura.

17. Ibid., 10. See also Oliver, 1974, III: 1199 for another version of this story.

18. Forster, George, quoted in Beaglehole, ed., 1969, xxx.

19. Wilson, James, 1799, Missionary Voyage to the Southern Pacific Ocean, Performed in the Years

1796, 1797, 1798 in the Ship Duff, *commanded by Captain James Wilson* (London, T. Chapman), xxxix.

20. According to William Ellis, the *rauti* were men of commanding person and military prowess who carried a small bunch of green *ti* leaves in their right hand during battle, in which their principal weapon, a small, sharp, serrated and barbed *airo fai* (or stingray barb) was hidden. (Ellis, 1829, I: 287–88.)

21. Henry, 1928, 15. Prior to this time, Tupaia was known as Parua (Forster, III: 524). Among other injuries, Tupaia was wounded through the back with a stingray barb, and perhaps his new name referred to this circumstance. For a recent discussion of Tupaia's biography, see Williams, Glyndwr, 2003, 'Tupaia: Polynesian Warrior, Navigator, High Priest – and Artist', in Felicity A. Nussbaum, ed., *The Global Eighteenth Century* (Baltimore and London, Johns Hopkins University Press), 38–51.

22. Driessen, Hank, 1982, 'Outriggerless canoes and glorious beings: pre-contact prophecies in the Society Islands', *Journal of Pacific History* XVII, 8–9; Tahitian text in Henry, 1928, 5. For variant versions of this story, see ibid., 4–6; 910.

23. For Tupaia's account of these battles as told to James Magra, one of Captain Cook's *Endeavour* crew, see Marra, James, 1771 (1967 facsimile), *A Journal of a Voyage Round the World in H.M.S. Endeavour* (Amsterdam, N. Israel), 61–64. See also Driessen's excellent and detailed account of these events (Driessen, 2005, 66–86).

24. Their full names were Tevahitua i Patea i Tooarai (Amo) and Te Vahine Airoro atua i Ahurai i Farepua (Purea) (Adams, 1910, 32, 38, 40).

25. Tupaia as told to James Marra (Marra, 1771, 63–64).

26. See Gallagher, Robert E., ed., 1964, *Byron's Journal of His Circumnavigation 1764–1766* (Cambridge, for the Hakluyt Society), 95–113.

27. By astute detective work, Hank Driessen has identified Ma'ua as the Mau'arua who sailed on the *Águila* to Lima in 1775 (Driessen, Hank, 2005, 'Tupaia: The Trials and Tribulations of a Polynesian Priest', in Phyllis Herda, Michael Reilly and David Hilliard, eds, *Vision and Reality in Pacific Religion* (Canberra, Pandanus Books), 81.

28. For an account of Teri'irere's genealogy and the background of Amo and Purea's ambitions, see Adams as told by Ari'i Taimai, 1910, 40–46.

29. Thomson, c. 1840, Salmond transcript, 27.

30. Henry, Teuira, 1928, *Ancient Tahiti* (Honolulu, Hawai'i, Bernice P. Bishop Museum Bulletin 48), 13. For accounts of human sacrifice in Tahiti, see Tyerman, Rev. Daniel and Bennet, George, 1831, *Journal of Voyages and Travels by the Rev. Daniel Tyerman and George Bennet deputed from the London Missionary Society to visit their various Stations in the South Sea Islands, China, India, &c. between the years 1821 and 1829, compiled from the original documents by James Montgomery* (London, Frederick Westley and A.H. Davis), 329–30; Ellis, William, 1859, *Polynesian Researches during A Residence of nearly Eight Years in the Society and Sandwich Islands, Volumes I, II, III and IV* (London, Henry G. Bohn), I: 316; and Oliver, Douglas, *Ancient Tahitian Society, Vols. I, II and III* (Canberra, Australian National University Press), 107–8.

31. For a discussion of how Europeans and their vessels were understood during 'first contacts' in Polynesia – as gods, goblins, ancestors on floating islands or sacred vessels, see Tcherkézoff, 2004, 128–30.

32. Carrington, Hugh, ed., 1948, *The Discovery of Tahiti: A Journal of the Second Voyage of H.M.S.* Dolphin *Round the World, Under the Command of Captain Wallis, R.N., In the Years 1766, 1767 and 1768, written by her master George Robertson* (Cambridge, for the Hakluyt Society), 135.

33. Gallagher, Robert E., 1964, *Byron's Journal of his Circumnavigation 1764–1766* (Cambridge, for the Hakluyt Society), 104.

34. For a report of this dialogue see the Prince of Masserano to the Marqués de Grimaldi, 10 June 1766, letter reproduced in Corney, ed., 1913, I: 27–28.

35. *Dolphin*'s Secret Instructions, PRO Adm 2/1332.

36. For published accounts of Wallis's voyage in the *Dolphin*, see Richardson, R., 1965, *A Poetical essay On The Dolphin Sailing Round The Globe in the years 1766, 1767, 1768 / by R. Richardson*

barber of the said ship, with an introduction by Miss Phyllis Mander Jones; and *Voyage du Dolphin autour du monde au cours des années 1766, 1767, 1768 / poème maritime par R. Richardson chirurgien à bord du-dit navire*, Avertissement au lecteur et traduction francaise par Denise Jean Simon (Paris, Editions Bibliophiles de la Société des Océanistes); 1955, *An Epistle From Oberea*, With Decorations By Ray Crooke (Ferntree Gully, Rams Skull Press) – original printed in London for J. Almon, 1774; 1809, *Struggles And Escapes Of Captain Wallis And His Crew* (London, printed for Thomas Tegg); Robertson, George in Hugh Carrington, ed., 1948, *The Discovery of Tahiti: A Journal of the Second Voyage of H.M.S.* Dolphin *Round the World, Under the Command of Captain Wallis, R.N., In the Years 1766, 1767 and 1768, written by her master George Robertson* (Cambridge, for the Hakluyt Society); Robertson, George in Oliver Warner, ed., 1955, *An Account of the Discovery of Tahiti, From the Journal of George Robertson, Master of H.M.S.* Dolphin (London, Folio Society); Rowe, Newton, 1955, *Voyage to the Amorous Islands: The Discovery of Tahiti* (London, Andre Deutsch); Pearson, W.H., 1969, 'European Intimidation and the Myth of Tahiti', *Journal of Pacific History* 4, 199–217.

For more recent accounts, see Dening, Greg, 1986, 'Possessing Tahiti', *Archaeology in Oceania* 21, 103–18; Cock, Randolph, 1999, 'Precursors of Cook: The Voyages of the *Dolphin* 1764–68, *The Mariner's Mirror* 85/1, 30–52; Cock, Randolph, 1997, 'The Voyages of the *Dolphin* (1764–68) as Precursors of Cook's Voyages of Exploration', MA thesis, University of Exeter.

For manuscript logs, journals and letters of Wallis's voyage, see Public Records Office, London: Mss Adm 2/1332, ff. 146–52 Secret Instructions for Captain Samuel Wallis, *Dolphin*; Adm 36/7580 Muster Roll *Dolphin*, Captain Samuel Wallis; Adm 33/440 Ship's Pay Books *Dolphin*, Captain Samuel Wallis; Adm 33/442–43 Treasurer's Paybook, *Dolphin*, Captain Samuel Wallis; Adm 55/35 Captain Wallis's Journal; Adm 1/2669–70, Adm 106/1150, 56, 65, 67, 69, 71, 73, 75, 222; Adm 106/1161/8–9; Adm 106/2895 Letters from Captain Wallis; Adm 51/4538/97–101 William Clarke (first lieutenant); Adm 51/4542/113–15 Tobias Furneaux (second lieutenant); Adm 51/4539/102–6 George Robertson (master); Adm 51/4540; Adm 51/4541/95–96 Francis Wilkinson; Adm 51/4541/107–8 William Luke; Adm 51/4541/123–24 Anonymous; Adm 51/4541/125 Benjamin Butler; Adm 51/4542/109–10 George Pinnock; Adm 51/4542/111–12 Henry Ibbot; Adm 4542/126–27 William Hambly; Adm 51/4543/115–16 Pender; Adm 51/4543/117–19 Samuel Horsnail; Adm 51/4543/128 Thomas Coles; Adm 51/4544/129 John Nichols; Adm 51/4541/123 Humphrey West; Adm 51/4539/124 Mr Douglas (carpenter); Adm 51/4544/131 Anonymous; Adm 51/4544/132 West; Adm 36/7580 Muster Roll of the *Dolphin*. British Library, London: Add Ms 15499 Wallis, Samuel, Rough Log, Holograph. National Maritime Museum, Greenwich: PGR 9 Papers re Samuel Wallis: Wallis, Captain Samuel, Rough Log of HMS *Dolphin* in three volumes, Colonel Willyams Carnarnton, Newquay, Cornwall, with sketches; Ms 78/161 Wallis, Captain Samuel, Xerox of Log kept by Samuel Wallis; JOD/57 Richard Pickersgill, Log, HMS *Dolphin*; FLI/8A Flinders, Matthew, Log: section on Crossing the Equator; Adm/B/178 Admiralty In-letters from the Navy Board Jan–Sept 1766; Adm/C/583 Victualling Board In-letters from the Admiralty Jul–Sept 1766; Adm/E/40 Sick and Hurt Board In-letters from the Admiralty Mar 1765 – Dec 1769; Adm/FP/9 Sick and Hurt Board Out-letters to the Admiralty Jan–Dec 1766. Mitchell Library, Sydney, Australia: Ms B1533 – B1534 Gore, John, master's mate, Logbook of HMS *Dolphin* August 21, 1766 – October, 1767; Ms Safe 1/98 Wallis, Samuel, 1768. Logbook and Sketchbook of Captain Samuel Wallis. National Library of Australia: Mfm M2013 Molineaux, Robert. Log of HMS *Dolphin*. Alexander Turnbull Library: qMs-2114, Wallis, Samuel, Journal (fair copy).

According to naval practice, while the ships were at sea the journals were kept in 'ship's time' (noon to noon), twelve hours ahead of civil time, with the date referring to the day of the second noon; and many of the *Dolphin*'s men were ill during their stay in Tahiti (including Captain Wallis). Their journal entries for Tahiti are thus often written after the events described, and the dates and details given for particular episodes are in disagreement. On the whole, I have relied on the excellent account given by George Robertson, the ship's master (who remained healthy throughout this visit), for the chronology of events during the *Dolphin*'s stay on the island. Throughout this book, ship's time is 'corrected' into civil time, so that the dates given for events at sea are consistent with the dates given for events on land.

37. Butler, Benjamin, A Plan of Port Royal Harbour in His Majesty King George 5's Island, Hydrographic Office, Somerset, Taunton, Pacific Folio 1, A191/8.

38. Robertson in Carrington, ed., 1948, 121:'Their was four double Canoes went from this little Town and one from the west end of the Island Joind them – the canoes appeard to be about thirty foot long and about four foot Broad and three or three and a half foot Deep – they are built out of several small planks which are sewed together, and pind or trimd to several small Timbers not unlyke the frame of our Boats – their Manner of Sailing is this they Bring two allongside of one Another and lays their Beam Across the two, one a Midships in which they Step their Mast and one fored and Another Aft – and the whole is well lashd to the Gunwals of both canoes, this prevents them from overseting when they Sail allong, they were lashd about three foot asunder, and the Mast stept in the Middle of the Midship beam which is suported with a pair of Shrouds and the halliards was belade closs aft, the Sail lookt lyke a topmast Steering sail with the Tack part Uppermost.'

39. Strictly speaking, this Vehiatua was probably Vehiatua III, but for convenience I have chosen to number the high chiefs in this lineage from the first holder of the title encountered by Europeans.

40. Lamb, Jonathan, 2001, *Preserving the Self in the South Seas 1680–1840* (Chicago, University of Chicago Press), 117–18.

41. Gunson, W.N, 1980, 'Cover's Notes on the Tahitians, 1802', *Journal of Pacific History* 15/4, 220.

42. According to James Morrison, one of the *Bounty* mutineers: 'If any Man is Caught in the act of Theft and is immediately put to Death, the Person who killd him is brought to No account for it. But if the Thief escapes & the Property is afterwards found on Him the Person whose property it is, may plunder him of His Goods and Chattels which the Thief always submits to, the Owner leaving with Him the property which he stole and taking all the rest, but should he absent himself, and take His goods off His land, the Person Injured may oblige the Thiefs land lord to deliver to Him the House & land which the Thief did posess till the damage is made good or ransom it with Hogs to the full satisfaction of the Party injured.' (Morrison in Rutter, ed., 1935, 192.) See also Ellis, 1829, III: 125–27 for an account of Tahitian attitudes towards theft.

43. Robertson in Carrington, ed., 1948, 139.

44. Clarke Journal, Adm 51/4538/97, 38.

45. The winter solstice in Tahiti at this time fell between 21–22 June. (Many thanks to Sarah Rusholme, Director and Duncan Hall, Chairman of the Carter Observatory, Wellington for checking this for me.)

46. Hiro was born at Ra'iatea, but when he was young he went to 'Uporu (now the district of Ha'apape in Tahiti), where his brothers had been admitted to the school of learning (or *fare hapi'ira'a*) known as Tapu-ata-i-te-ra'i, where their maternal grandfather Ana was the senior teacher. Although Hiro was too young to attend the school, he learned all the incantations and genealogies by sitting outside and listening while the students were being instructed. Afterwards he became one of its most accomplished scholars. Later Hiro decided to follow in the footsteps of Hiro, his eponymous ancestor and the god of thieves; and he also became a famous navigator and explorer who visited many islands. (Henry, 1928, 537–45, quoting the Raiatean scholars Ara-mou'a and Vara.) 'At Uporu is the school of learning of royal families, named Tapu-ata-i-te-ra'i (sacred cloud in the sky); there are the women teachers, Toa-te-manava of Ra'iatea and Mu-reo, reciter of heraldry . . . That school is attended by the children of the royal families of Tahiti and Ra'iatea, and other kindred people.' (Henry, 1928, 74–75.) According to Auna, Hiro was a recent god, whose skull was kept at 'Opoa (Montgomery, 1832, I: 186–87, quoted in Oliver, 1974, III: 1054).

47. In this period nails were sold at so many pence a hundred; so twenty-penny nails, which were three inches long, cost twenty pennies a hundred; ten-penny nails were two-and-a-quarter inches long and cost ten pennies a hundred; and so on.

48. *Dolphin*'s Secret Instructions, Adm 2/1322, ff. 73–77.

49. Parkinson, Sydney, 1773, *A Journal of a Voyage to the South Seas in His Majesty's Ship, The Endeavour* (London, for Stanfield Parkinson), 33.

50. As Driessen has pointed out, female genitals acted as an *ara* or pathway between the Po and the Ao, attracting sacredness back to the Po (Driessen, 1991, 57–58).

51. Butler, Benjamin, A Plan of Port Royal Harbour, Hydrographic Office, Taunton, Somerset, Pacific Folio 1, A191/8. For other charts of Tahiti from Wallis's voyage, see British Museum, George Pinnock, Add Ms 15499, 19 charts; Wallis, Samuel, Charts and Maps, Add Ms 21593; Hydrographic Office in Taunton, Robertson, George, 13 charts of Pacific Islands, A191 (2–7; 9–15).

52. Robertson in Carrington, ed., 1948, 150.

53. Ibid., 152.

54. Moerenhout in Borden, ed., 1983, 304–5; Ellis, 1829, I: 289.

55. Ellis reports that these banners, which were red, white or black, represented the gods carried into battle (Ellis, 1829, I: 285).

56. Wilkinson, Adm 51/4541/96, 48.

57. According to Teuira Henry, 'On the morning of the departure of the fleet, the enchantment ceremony, called the *pare-uru-va'a* or *papai-pauru-va'a* (striking to enchant canoe) was performed. With their colors – red, black, or white – flying, they approached the shore and formed in line, which was called '*ahara'a va'a* (making sennit of canoes). First came the god's canoe, with a priest presiding at the shrine of the gods. Next came the war canoes, which were sixty or ninety feet long, each having from one side to the other of the double hulls, a platform upon which the fighters stood, one or two *rauti* (war orators) and a *tarai-aro* (commander). The *tarai-aro* directed the maneuvering of his men and was always a man of quick perception and great experience. Last came the canoes with the provisions and other supplies.' (Henry, 1928, 316–17.)

58. Ellis, 1829, II: 486. According to Tyerman and Bennet, 'the sacred canoe always led the van of the rest, and the priests were accustomed to fight to the most desperate extremity in defence of their *palladium*, for while this was uncaptured the conflict might be maintained, but, as soon as it was lost, the party to which it belonged would fight no more. The moment the god fell into his adversary's hands, his divinity forsook him, and so did his adherents. Panic-struck, they fled in all directions.' (Tyerman and Bennet, 1831, I: 334.) For a description of the god-houses on such canoes, see Henry, 1928, 136.

59. Robertson in Carrington, ed., 1948, 156.

60. Gunson, 1980, 217–24; see also Driessen, Hank, 2005, 'Tupaia: The Trials and Tribulations of a Polynesian Priest' in Phyllis Herda, Michael Reilly and David Hilliard, eds, *Vision and Reality in Pacific Religion* (Christchurch, Macmillan Brown Centre for Pacific Studies), 74.

61. Ellis, 1829, I: 301–2. See also Thomson, Ms History of Tahiti, 32–37 for another early missionary account of the arrival of the *Dolphin*; and Moerenhout quoting Tati Salmon, I: 481.

CHAPTER 3: PUREA, 'QUEEN' OF TAHITI

1. Robertson in Carrington, ed., 1948, 158.

2. Mss Adm 2/1332, ff. 146–52 Secret Instructions for Captain Samuel Wallis, *Dolphin*.

3. According to Tyerman and Bennet, when a party desired peace they sent an ambassador with a flag of truce, a bunch of the sacred *miro* or a bunch of feathers fixed to a reed and called the *manu faiti* or proposal of peace. (Tyerman and Bennet, 1831, I: 329–30.)

4. Ibbot, Adm 51/4542/112, 119.

5. Babadzan and Tcherkézoff (see Babadzan, 1993, 294; Tcherkézoff, 2004, 309, 420) have both argued that '*arioi* killed their children at birth because the infants served as sacrifices to the gods; but this is probably mistaken. Rather, it seems likely that when '*arioi* had a child, much of their *mana* passed to the infant (especially a first-born or *tama aitu* – sacred child), and as a result they lost their *tapu* – their capacity to act as direct links to the ancestor gods; so their children were killed for this reason.

6. Teri'irere had inherited titles from Taputuara'i *marae* (the most ancient *marae* in Papara,

which stood in the small district known as Amo) and Teto'orara'i *marae*, founded with a stone from Taputuara'i. His title from Taputuara'i was Tu-i-te-ra'i-i-Taputuara'i; while his title from Teto'orara'i was Aromaitera'i-i-outu-rau-ma-To'oara'i (Oliver, II: 681).

7. Ellis, 1829, I: 318, II: 99–100.

8. Moerenhout in Borden, ed., 1983, 300.

9. Wilson, James, ed., 1799, *A Missionary Voyage to the South Pacific Ocean, Performed in the Years 1796, 1797, 1798, in the Ship* Duff, *Commanded by Captain James Wilson* (London, T. Chapman), 331–33.

10. Moerenhout in Borden, ed., 1983, 481. Moerenhout got much of his information from Tati Salmon, the high chief of Papara.

11. Robertson in Carrington, ed., 1948, 165.

12. Peace offerings began with the presentation of a plantain tree pulled up by the roots to the god at the *marae*, and then a flag of truce, or a bunch of sacred *miro* leaves, or a bunch of feathers (known as *manu faiti*) sent to the enemy party; followed by green boughs and two young dogs. See William Ellis for an excellent account of peace-making rituals in Tahiti (Ellis, 1829, I: 312–20).

13. Robertson in Carrington, ed., 1948, 166.

14. See Tcherkézoff, 2004, 7–8.

15. Robertson in Carrington, ed., 1948, 167.

16. See for instance Henderson, Tony, 1999, *Disorderly Women in Eighteenth Century London: Prostitution and Control in the Metropolis 1730–1830* (London and New York, Longman); Boucé, Paul-Gabriel, ed., 1982, *Sexuality in Eighteenth-Century Britain* (Manchester, Manchester University Press).

17. Tcherkézoff, 2004, 142–43, 428–43.

18. See Appendix I.

19. Ibbot, Adm 51/4542/112, 120.

20. See for instance Tyerman and Bennet, 1831, 246–48.

21. Adams, 1901, 12–14. See also Hervé, F., 1926, 'Légende des Teva (Papara)', *Bulletin de la Société d'Études Océaniennes* XV, 110–11; Cadousteau, G., 1980, *Bulletin de la Société d'Études Océaniennes* XVII/1, 727–32; and Lagayette, P., 1984, 'Les Teva et les Pomare', *Bulletin de la Société d'Études Océaniennes* No. 229, X/6, 1687–94.

22. Henry, 1928, 81.

23. See also Ellis, 1829, I: 167, 329 on the worship of sharks in Tahiti.

24. Handy, E.S. Craighill, 1971, *History and Culture in the Society Islands* (Honolulu, Hawai'i, Bernice P. Bishop Museum Bulletin 79), 31. See also Oliver, 1974, II: 684; Green, Roger C. and Kaye, 1968, 'Religious Structures (*Marae*) of the Windward Society Islands: The Significance of Certain Historical Records', *New Zealand Journal of History* 2/2, 66–89 for a detailed discussion of this *marae*. See also Babadzan, 1993, 75–88 for an insightful discussion of *ti'i* or ancestral figures in Tahiti, and their relationship with *tupu* or the principle of growth and fertility.

25. Robertson in Carrington, ed., 1948, 180.

26. Serge Tcherkézoff has shown that in a number of Polynesian societies including Samoa and Hawai'i, virgins were ritually deflowered by a high chief or clan orator, who were sacred enough to perform this function, removing their *tapu* and preparing them for marriage and child-bearing; and that their families often hoped that they would conceive in these unions, capturing some of the *mana* of these sacred individuals (Tcherkézoff, 2004, 428–43). There is little direct evidence of this for Tahiti, however; although Douglas Oliver reported a belief among Tahitian girls in the 1970s that they would contract *'ma'i fa'a'i'* [filled up sickness] if they did not engage in at least one act of intercourse within a few years after the onset of menstruation (Oliver, Douglas, 1981, *Two Tahitian Villages: A Study in Comparison* (Utah, Brigham Young University Press), 273–74). According to William Ellis, furthermore, nails were particularly prized to make into fish-hooks, and when the Tahitians first received nails from the *Dolphin*, they carried some to the altar of the *marae* as an offering to 'Oro and planted others in their gardens, hoping to see them grow (Ellis, 1829, I: 151).

27. Robertson in Carrington, ed., 1948, 186.

28. Quoted in Smith, Howard, 1975, 'The Introduction of Venereal Disease into Tahiti: a re-examination', *Journal of Pacific History*, 10: 41.

29. Wilkinson, Francis, Adm 51/4541/96, 51.

30. Henry, 1928, 157–77, quoting Pomare II, Mahine and other high chiefs and priests.

31. See Babadzan's insightful discussion of the *pa'i-atua* ritual and especially the wrapping of the *to'o*, which was called *urua* or 'entered, possessed' when it was fully wrapped again, in Babadzan, 2003, 30.

32. Henry, 1928, 172–73. [Translation adapted by Anne Salmond.]

33. Orsmond, John, n.d., 'The 'Arioi War', Mfm G7706, Mitchell Library, Sydney, Meredith Filihia transcript.

34. Or *tapairu* ('a young woman that lives delicately'): Orsmond, 'The 'Arioi War', Filihia transcript, 17; Davies, J., 1851, *A Tahitian and English Dictionary with Introductory Remarks on the Polynesian Language and a Short Grammar of the Tahitian Dialect* (London, London Missionary Society), 244, 250.

35. Wilson, James, 1799, *A Missionary Voyage to the Southern Pacific Ocean, Performed in the Years 1796, 1797, 1798, in the Ship Duff, commanded by Captain James Wilson* (London, T. Chapman), 142.

36. Robertson in Carrington, ed., 1948, 184.

37. In his manuscript 'The 'Arioi War', Orsmond distinguished between the large houses built by the *ari'i* and those built by the *'arioi* for their performances, saying that it was in the large houses of the *ari'i* that visitors were presented with feasts. The house where Purea was staying was thus presumably a house built by an *ari'i*, as she hosted feasts there (Orsmond, Filihia transcript, 11).

38. See Babadzan, 1993, 27–50, 75–88 for a comparative analysis of *ti'i* in the Society Islands, which establishes their role in protecting the fertility of people, plants and animals.

39. See Tcherkézoff, 2004, 159–61 for an excellent discussion of wrapping in bark cloth.

40. Moerenhout in Borden, ed., 1983, 263.

41. Henry, 1928, 319. See also Morrison in Rutter, ed., 1935, 175–76 for a contemporary description of the custom of adopting the killer of a close relative.

42. Robertson in Carrington, ed., 1948, 203.

43. See Orsmond, 'The 'Arioi War', Filihia transcript, 4, 6.

44. Oliver, 1974, II: 601–2.

45. This was probably the *'arioi* garment known as *tiputa pa'ave*, two ponchos impressed with figures from the *titi* and *pa'ave* plants dipped in red dye (Orsmond, 'The 'Arioi War', Filihia transcript, 12).

46. Robertson in Carrington, ed., 1948, 206.

47. Ibid., 209.

48. Ellis, 1829, I: 150–51.

49. Robertson in Carrington, ed., 1948, 212.

50. Henry, 1928, 388 and 336 (from a chant recited by Vaiau, a high priest of Borabora, and Pati'i, a high priest of Mo'orea).

51. Moerenhout in Borden, ed., 1983, 244; Ellis, 1829, I: 231–32.

52. Orsmond, 'The 'Arioi War', Filihia transcript, 5; Ellis, 1829, I: 77.

53. Ibid., I: 331–32.

54. There are two lists of artefacts collected by Wallis's men in the Pacific and sent by Wallis to the Admiralty in the National Archives (Adm 2670/2); and the second list includes a 'Canoe (Shovell)' from George's Island. This second list reads '[X] A Stick of Winter Bark, [X] a Canoe (Shovell) George's Island, & Tropick Birds Feathers, from Charlotte Island. [X] A Spontoon, [X] Drum, [X] Conques, [X] Flute, [X] Breast Plates, [X] Bow & [X] Casquet of Arrows, a Peice of Cloth, A Twig, & some rind, whereof it is made with, the Instrument they make it with. Instruments wherewith they mark their Backsides. [X] A Stone which they use to Bruize their Bread & other fruit with; [X] a piece of Rose wood, [X] Two Hatchetts, [X] A Fishing Nett, [X] Shark Hook & other Hooks from George's Island, some Tar from Osnaburg and Georges Island; [X] a Club from Wallis Island – sundry seeds from most places we were

at.' The Xs probably indicate that the items were checked off as they were received by the Admiralty.

55. I am very grateful to Joan Druett for guiding me to this third list of gifts in Wallis's own handwriting, at the back of the fair copy of his journal in the Alexander Turnbull Library (qMs-2114), which reads, 'An Account of what I delivered in at the Admiralty On my Arrival; A Wreath of Hair. One Hundred Pearls. Bunches of Feathers. Numbers of Fine Pearl Fish hooks. Fine Cloth, and Shells – these were presented to Her Majesty – Draughts and perspective & Views of all the places we Discovered, with a Map of the world & our Run prick'd off on it. A Logbook with all the Courses Steerd, Weather Remarks &c during the whole Voyage. A Book of all the Observations of Longitude as Observed by Mr. Maskelines Tables . . .' and a list of all the objects presented to the Admiralty as noted in the footnote above, with the comment, 'All the Foregoing were presented to the Museum, except the seeds, & they were given to divers People, particularly to the Princess Dowager of Wales's Gardner at Kew. Ld. Egmont Ld. Edwd Hawke, Sr. Charles Saunders . . . & many other Great Men, besides to the Physick Gardens at Oxford, Cambridge and Chelsea . . .' Many thanks also to the Manuscripts Librarian, Tim Lovell-Smith, for providing me with a copy at short notice.

56. Robertson in Carrington, ed., 1948, 227.

57. Ibid., 227.

58. See Williams, 1838, 551–52; Moerenhout in Borden, ed., 1983, 300; Henry, 1928, 188–89.

CHAPTER 4: HAPPY ISLAND OF CYTHERA

1. Robertson in Carrington, ed., 1948, 233.

2. Richardson, R., 1965, *A Poetical essay On The Dolphin Sailing Round The Globe in the years 1766, 1767, 1768 / by R. Richardson barber of the said ship*, with an introduction by Miss Phyllis Mander Jones; and *Voyage du Dolphin autour du monde au cours des années 1766, 1767, 1768 / poème maritime par R. Richardson chirurgien abord du-dit navire*, Avertissement au lecteur et traduction francaise par Denise Jean Simon (Paris, Editions Bibliophiles de la Société des Océanistes); Wallis, Samuel, Logbook and Sketchbook of Captain Samuel Wallis, Ms Safe 1/98, Mitchell Library, Sydney, attached to the end of the logbook.

3. Quoted in O'Brien, Patrick, 1997, *Joseph Banks: A Life* (London, The Harvill Press), 63.

4. 1768, *The Gentleman's Magazine* XXXVIII, 390.

5. Corney, ed., 1913, I: 139–42.

6. For Bougainville's life and career, see Dunmore, John, 2005, *Storms and Dreams: Louis de Bougainville, Soldier, Explorer, Statesman* (Auckland, Exisle Publishing Ltd); Kimbough, Mary, 1990, *Louis-Antoine de Bougainville 1729–1811: A Study in French Naval History and Politics* (Lewiston, The Edwin Mellen Press); Martin-Allenic, Jean Étienne, 1964, *Bougainville, navigateur et les découvertes de son temps*, I and II (Paris, Presses Universitaires de France).

7. See for instance quotes cited in Dunmore, 2005, 37, 40, 41, 48.

8. Rousseau, Jean-Jacques, 1761, *A Discourse upon the Origin and Foundation of the Inequality among Mankind* (London), 219–22.

9. De Brosses, Charles, 1756, *Histoire de Navigations aux Terres Australes, Vols. I and II* (Paris), I: 80.

10. Dunmore, 2005, 135.

11. For the published account of the voyage, see Bougainville, Louis-Antoine, Comte de, 1771, *Voyage autour du Monde, par la frégate du Roi La Boudeuse, et la flûte L'Étoile en 1766, 1767, 1768 & 1769* (Paris, Imprimerie de Le Breton); translated into English by Forster, Johann, 1772, *A Voyage Round the World Performed by Order of His Most Christian Majesty in the Years 1766, 1767, 1768, and 1769* (London, J. Nourse). For published logs and journals from Bougainville's Pacific voyage, see Taillemite, Étienne, 1977, *Bougainville et ses Compagnons autour du monde 1766–1769. Journaux de Navigation établis et commentés par Etienne Taillemite* (Paris, Imprimerie Nationale), I and II; Dunmore, John, ed. and trans., 2002a, *The Pacific Journal of Louis-Antoine de Bougainville 1767–1768* (Cambridge, for the Hakluyt Society); Saint-Germain, Louis-Antoine Starot de, clerk on *Boudeuse*, in Charles de la Roncière, 'Le routier inédit d'un compagnon de

Bougainville', *La Géographie* XXXV, 3, 217–50. See also Dunmore, John, 2002b, *Monsieur Baret: First Woman Around the World 1766–68* (Auckland, Heritage Press).

For manuscript logs and journals from Bougainville's Pacific voyage, see Archives National: Bougainville, Louis-Antoine de, Journal, Marine 4JJ 142, No. 17; Nassau-Siegen, Prince, passenger on *Boudeuse*, collection de la Maison du Roi, ref. 0 569 7 No. 28; MS C under reference BB4: 1001 no. 2; Duclos-Guyot, Pierre, commander of *Boudeuse*, personal file Marine C7: 207; Caro, Jean-Louis, second-in-command of *Étoile*, Marine C7: 53, Journal under reference 4JJ 1, No. 5. Affaires Etrangères: Nassau-Siegen, Prince, Memoires et documents de France 2115, ff. 128–75. Musée National d'Histoire Naturelle, Paris: Fesche, Charles-Felix-Pierre, volunteer junior officer on *Boudeuse*, Ms 1896–1898. Archives of Société de Geographie at Rochefort: Vivez, Francois, surgeon on *Étoile*, and another version in Municipal Library of Versailles, In-4 126. Bibliothèque du Musée d'Histoire Naturelle, Paris: Commerson, Philibert, naturalist on *Étoile*, Notebooks & Notes, Notes MS 2214. National Library of Australia, Canberra: La Giraudais, Chenard de, commander of *Étoile*, Mfm PMB 73.

12. Dunmore, 2002a, xxvii.
13. Ibid., xl.
14. For Baret's background and life see Dunmore, 2002b.
15. Quoted in Dunmore, 2002b, 55.
16. Ibid., liii.
17. Ibid., 48.
18. Vivez in Dunmore, ed. and trans., 2002a, 225.
19. There is difficulty in sorting out the chronology here, partly because of the difference between ship's time and civil time; and partly because many of the accounts were evidently written well after the event, and differ in the dates attributed to particular events. Here I have followed the sequence of events as given in Bougainville's shipboard journal. As mentioned earlier, throughout this work dates given in ship's time are 'corrected' and given in civil time, for consistency.
20. Caro in Dunmore, ed. and trans., 2002a, 203.
21. This was the *'arioi* garment known as *maro tai noa*, described by Orsmond as follows: 'The fibres of a creeping spreading vine – the leaves of an aromatic tree finely shredded.- the Banana stalk beat finely up. The coat of the cocoa nut leaves are used each separately for a girdle for the waist to cover the shameful parts all other parts are naked.' (Orsmond, 'The 'Arioi War', Filihia transcipt, 12.)
22. Vivez in Dunmore, ed. and trans., 2002a, 225.
23. Bougainville in ibid., 59.
24. Henry, 1928, 227: 'A comet was supposed to be a god forerunning war or sickness.' See also the missionary Davies, who reported that on an occasion when a fiery meteor flew across the island, the Tahitians cried out, *'He atua! He atua! [E atua! E atua!]'*, supposing this to be a god signalling some momentous event; and soon afterwards the high chief Tamatoa fell down in a fainting fit, and the people made prayers and offerings to appease the *atua* (Douglas Oliver Missionary card index, card 255).
25. Caro in Dunmore, ed. and trans., 2002a, 204.
26. Henry, 1928, 70–71.
27. Bougainville in Forster, trans., 1772, 218.
28. Commerson in Dunmore, ed. and trans., 2002a, 297.
29. Fesche in ibid., 255. See also Nassau-Siegen: 'One of these islanders, full of the confidence that innocence inspires, climbed on board with his wife. He asked for our friendship, the woman showing most willing all the perfection of a fine body, offered everything she had that could gain the heart of the newcomers, but the King's regulation, which no doubt had not foreseen such a circumstance, prevented us from responding to her civility on board', in ibid., 281; and Saint-Germain, 1921, translated by Isabel Ollivier: 'In answer to the inviting gestures of some Frenchmen, one of these island women climbed on board with an old man and several of her fellow countrywomen. These women were tall, well built, and had complexions of a pallor that

most Spanish women would not be ashamed of. Several Frenchmen, with appetites whipped to a pitch by forced abstinence for several months, crowded admiringly round. We were burning, but decency, the monster that so often battles with men's desires, kept our ardent impulses in check.' Dunmore has argued that the description of this episode in Bougainville's published journal is a fictional collage compiled from several similar encounters in Tahiti, but this seems unlikely given the convergence of a number of eyewitness accounts.

30. See Serge Tcherkézoff's brilliant commentary on this episode, and how the French explorers interpreted and reinterpreted what happened during this encounter in Tcherkézoff, 2004, 114–32.

31. Bougainville in Forster, trans., 1772, 219.

32. Nassau-Siegen in Dunmore, ed. and trans., 2002a, 282–83.

33. Tcherkézoff, 2004, 45–69, 217–23.

34. See Oliver, 1974, I: 157–58 for an account of the *ha'aporia* custom.

35. Bougainville in Forster, trans., 1772, 221.

36. Bougainville in Dunmore, ed. and trans., 2002a, 61.

37. Bougainville in ibid., 62.

38. Fesche in ibid., 256.

39. Nassau-Siegen in ibid., 283.

40. Ibid., 283. For an intriguing commentary on this episode, see Tcherkézoff, 2004, 133–38.

41. Moerenhout in Borden, ed., 1983, 395.

42. See for example Saura, 2000, 221, according to which Hiro-ari'i-e-tu-i-Mata-hira-i-te-ra'i by his second wife Na-mata-ari'i-i-'Opoa had a son, Tautu-ari'i-i-'Opoa or Tamatoa I.

43. As Tcherkézoff has argued using Samoan, Tongan, Maori and Marquesan parallels (Tcherkézoff, 2004, 184–97); although as I have discovered when drawing from Maori tradition, such parallels between Tahiti and other Polynesian societies (and perhaps particularly Western Polynesian societies) can be misleading.

44. Fesche in Bougainville in Dunmore, ed. and trans., 2002a, 259.

45. See Tcherkézoff's detailed discussion of how this Occidental myth was constructed (Tcherkézoff, 2004, 114–235).

46. Bougainville in Dunmore, ed. and trans., 2002a, 63.

47. Vivez in Dunmore, ed. and trans., 2002a, 232.

48. Nassau-Siegen in ibid., 284.

49. Vivez in ibid., 230.

50. Bougainville in Forster, trans., 1772, 228–29.

51. Tutaha was the younger brother of Teu, Tu's father (Emory, 1932, 185).

52. Two of the pieces of bark cloth are now held in Musée de Quai Branly, items 71.1928.30.1 and 2. My thanks to Jenny Newell for this information.

53. Fesche in Dunmore, ed. and trans., 2002a, 265.

54. Nassau-Siegen in ibid., 285.

55. Fesche in ibid., 265.

56. Ibid., 266.

57. Duclos-Guyot journal in Musée National d'Histoire Naturelle, Paris, Ms 2214, Book 1, ff. 145–60; the bark cloth is described on f. 151 and the sail on f. 155; translated by Isabel Ollivier.

58. Bougainville in Dunmore, ed. and trans., 2002a, 267.

59. Thomson, n.d., Salmond transcript, 22.

60. Cook in Beaglehole, ed., 1955, 98.

61. Bougainville in Dunmore, ed. and trans., 2002a, 74.

CHAPTER 5: AHUTORU AT THE OPÉRA

1. Ellis, 1829, I: 20–21. See also Turnbull, John, 1810, *A Voyage Round the World in the Years 1800, 1801, 1802, 1803, and 1804* (Philadelphia, Benjamin and Thomas Kite), 208–13, for an account of these visits to the '*Motu*'.

2. According to Morrison, when the chiefs drank '*ava* it almost immediately deprived them of

the use of their limbs and speech; they looked thoughtful and then fell over backwards, when their attendants massaged their limbs until they fell asleep; and several hours later they would wake up, fresh and ready for another drink. As he noted: 'After about a fortnights Constant use the Skin comes all over with a white scurf like the land scurvy and the Eyes grow red & firey and the Body lean and Meagre but on being left off for a few days the Scales fall off the Skin then becomes clear & smooth and they soon grow fat & wholesom to view.' (Morrison in Rutter, ed., 1935, 151.)

3. Bougainville in Forster, trans., 1772, 253.

4. Ibid., 262.

5. Bougainville in Dunmore, ed. and trans., 2002a, 82.

6. Vivez in ibid., 236–37.

7. Bougainville in ibid., 86.

8. Bougainville in Forster, trans., 1772, 276.

9. Bernard le Bovier de Fontenelle, in *Entretiens sur la Pluralité des Mondes* (*Conversations on the Plurality of Worlds*), published in 1686.

10. Bougainville in Forster, trans., 1772, 268.

11. Bougainville in Dunmore, ed. and trans., 2002a, 88.

12. Smith, Howard M., 1975, 'The Introduction of Venereal Disease into Tahiti: A Re-examination', *Journal of Pacific History* 10/1–2, 44. Smith also points out that while yaws, which is closely related to syphilis and gives immunity to it but is not sexually transmitted, had been long established on the island, this was not the case around Matavai Bay, where the humidity levels often dropped below the critical minimum required by yaws; and therefore many of the women there would not have been immune to syphilis.

13. Bougainville in Dunmore, ed. and trans., 2002a, 97.

14. Ibid., 102.

15. Ibid., 109.

16. Ibid., 108.

17. Ibid., 115.

18. Named Port Praslin by Bougainville, and now known as Kambotorosch.

19. Bougainville in Forster, trans., 1772, 335.

20. Bougainville in Dunmore, ed. and trans., 2002a, 135.

21. Ibid., 144.

22. Ibid., 150.

23. My thanks to Bruno Saura for this explanation.

24. Commerson's account was not the first description of life in Tahiti to be published in Europe. In July 1769 a pamphlet called *News from New Cythera* was published (Hammond, L. Davis, trans. and ed., 1970, *News from New Cythera: A Report of Bougainville's Voyage 1766–1769* (Minneapolis, University of Minnesota Press)), quickly followed by Bougainville's official account of the voyage; but the *Post-Scriptum* had the greater popular and philosophical appeal.

25. Both More's *Utopia* and Jean-Jacques Rousseau are quoted in the *Post-scriptum*; see Isabel Ollivier translation 2006.

26. For extended discussions of Utopias and fantasy voyages to the South Sea, see Cheek, 2003, *Sexual Antipodes: Enlightenment, Globalisation and the Placing of Sex* (Stanford, California, Stanford University Press); Fausett, David, 1993, *Writing the New World: Imaginary Voyages and Utopias of the Great Southern Land* (Syracuse, New York, Syracuse University Press); and Société des Études Océaniennes, 2004, *Utopies Insulaires* (Papeete, Bulletin de la Société des Études Océaniennes).This tradition also included Joseph Hall's imaginary voyage (1605) to an unknown continent with an island of hermaphrodites off the coast; Robert Burton's 'Utopia' on Terra Australis (1621); Francis Bacon's *New Atlantis* on a Pacific island (1621); and the *History of the Sevarites* (1675) by Denis Vairasse, in which a Dutch captain and his passengers were shipwrecked on a southern continent where mass marriage was practised, for instance.

27. Commerson in Dunmore, ed. and trans., 2002b, 94.

28. Commerson, trans. Isabel Ollivier, 2006.

29. Commerson notes, trans. Isabel Ollivier, 2006: 'Enoua erao piri piri. This was the refrain of a song sung by Poutaveri on the Ile de France, as if to say, cunnorum avara tellus [land miserly with pussy].'

30. Bougainville in Forster, trans., 1772, 469.

31. For descriptions of the Tahitian domed cosmos, see for instance Tyerman and Bennet, 1831, 287–88: 'The morning star, whether Jupiter or Venus, was called Horo poipoi [Horo po'ipo'i], or Tauroa [Taurua]. Having observed that the rest of the stars were fixed in their relative stations, they imagined that the sky was a substantial dome, the concave side (like a cocoa-nut cup turned upside down) being spread over the sea, and held in its place by the stars. When a strange ship arrived from a great distance they supposed it had come from under another inverted cone of sky, through a hole in the lower part of their own.'; and Ellis, 1829, III: 170–73: 'They imagined that the sea which surrounded their islands was a level plane, and that at the visible horizon, or some distance beyond it, the sky, or *rai*, joined the ocean, enclosing as with an arch, or hollow cone, the islands in the immediate vicinity. They were acquainted with other islands, such as Nuuhiva, or the Marquesas, Vaihi, or the Sandwich Islands, Tongatabu, or the Friendly Islands. The names of these occurred in their traditions or songs. Subsequently too, they had heard of Beritani, or Britain, Paniola, or Spain &c. but they imagined that each of these had a distinct atmosphere, and was enclosed in the same manner as they thought the heavens surrounded their own islands. Hence they spoke of foreigners as those who came from behind the sky, or from the other side of what they considered the sky of their part of the world.' Although some scholars have argued that this view of the Polynesian cosmos is a European fiction (Tent, Jan and Geraghty, Paul, 2001, 'Exploding Sky or Exploded Myth? The origin of Papalagi', *Journal of the Polynesian Society* 110, 2, 170–214), they ignore the fact that it is consistent with island traditions (for instance, that of the feathered creator god Ta'aroa in Tahiti who broke out of his shell, which was subsequently transformed into the domes of the sky) and with so many accounts from so many islands that it beggars belief to suppose that all those who collected them conspired together to deceive later generations. For a definitive rebuttal, see Tcherkézoff, Serge, 2004, *First Contacts in Polynesia: The Samoan Case (1722–1848): Western Misunderstandings about Sexuality and Divinity* (Canberra, Macmillan Brown Centre for Pacific Studies and the *Journal of Pacific History*), 109–53.

32. Mr de la Condamine's Remarks about the Polynesian Island brought to France from the Island of Tahiti by Mr de Bougainville, BN (François Mitterand) Res G 1.443, pièce 5, trans. Isabel Ollivier.

33. Pereire, Jacob Rodriguez, 'Vocabulaire Abrégé de la Langue de l'Ile Otahiti' in Bougainville, Louis-Antoine de, 1772, *Voyage autour du Monde* (Paris, Saillant et Nyon), 3 vols.

34. Diderot, Denis in Jean Stewart and Jonathan Kemp, trans., Jonathan Kemp, ed., 1979, *Diderot, Interpreter of Nature, Selected Writings* (Westport, Connecticut, Hyperion Press), 147.

35. Isherwood, Robert M., 1986, *Farce and Fantasy: Popular Entertainment in Eighteenth Century Paris* (New York, Oxford, Oxford University Press), 167–72.

36. De Bachaumont, Louis de, 1777, *Mémoires secrets* (London, John Adamson), 244, trans. Isabel Ollivier.

37. Bougainville in Forster, trans., 1772 describes Ahutoru's stay in Paris on 263–67. The Opéra House was burnt down in 1763, and in 1765 when Rev. William Cole was visiting Paris, the performances were held in a playhouse in the Tuileries while the Opéra was being rebuilt (Cole, Rev. William, ed. Francis Griffin Stokes, 1931, *A Journal of my Journey to Paris in the Year 1765* (London, Constable & Co.), 178.

38. Isherwood, 1986, see particularly chapters 3, The Opéra Comique, and 4, discussing the Comédie-Italienne which replaced it in 1762; and Thomas, A. Downing, 2002, *Aesthetics of Opera in the Ancien Régime* (Cambridge, Cambridge University Press).

39. Dixmérie, Nicolas Bricaire de la, 1989, *Le Sauvage de Taiti aux Français avec Un Envoi au Philosophe Ami des Sauvages* (Réédition de 1770; Papeete, Éditions Perspectives Maohi).

40. Diderot, 1979, 151–52.

41. In Delille, Jacques (Abbé), 1782, *Les Jardins, ou L'Art D'Embellir Les Paysages* (Paris, Valade

and Reims, Cazin), 45–46, 115–16 (a section of this lyrical poem concerns Ahutoru), trans. Isabel Ollivier.

42. Bougainville in Forster, trans., 1772, 266–67.

43. Poivre, 1773, in 'Extait d'une lettre de M. Poivre', *Supplément au Voyage de M. de Bougainville, ou Journal d'un Voyage Autour du Monde fait par MM. Banks et Solander, Anglais, en 1768, 1769, 1770, 1771* (Neuchatel, Imprimerie de la Société Typographique), 251–54.

44. For an account of Ahutoru in Mauritius, and the preparations for Marion's expedition, see Duyker, Edward, 1994, *An Officer of the Blue: Marc-Joseph Marion Dufresne, South Sea Explorer 1724–1772* (Melbourne, Melbourne University Press), 110–20. For contemporary accounts of Ahutoru and his adventures, see Perey, Lucien, 1905, *Charles de Lorraine et la cour de Bruxelles sous le régne de Marie-Thérèse* (Paris, Calmann-Lévy), 272–73; Fréron, M., 1771, 'Voyage auteur du monde par la Frégate du Roi *La Boudeuse* et la Flute *L'Étoile* en 1766, 1767, 1768 & 1769', *L'Année Littéraire* (Paris, Delalain Libraire) 6, Lettre III, 49–63; Brenellerie, Paul-Philippe, 1776, 'Aux manes de Louis XV, et des grands hommes qui ont réçu sous son régne', *Essai sur les progrès des Arts et de l'Esprit humain, sous le règne de Louis XV* (Deux Ponts, L'Imprimerie Ducale), I–II; Bauchaumont, Louis Petit de, 1777, *Mémoires Secrets, Pour Servir à l'Histoire de la Republique des Lettres en France, depuis 1762 jusqu'à nos Jours; ou Journal d'un observateur* (London, John Adamson), trans. Isabel Ollivier.

CHAPTER 6: A POLYNESIAN VENUS

1. Royal Society Archives: Manuscripts (General), Ms 633, quoted in Cook, Andrew S., 2004, 'James Cook and the Royal Society', in Glyndwr Williams, ed., 2004, *Captain Cook: Explorations and Reassessments* (Woodbridge, Suffolk, The Boydell Press), 46.

2. Douglas, James, 14th Earl of Morton, quoted in ibid., 48.

3. For accounts of James Cook's life, see Beaglehole, J.C., 1974, *The Life of Captain James Cook* (Cambridge, for the Hakluyt Society); Hough, Richard, 1995, *Captain James Cook: A Biography* (London, Hodder and Stoughton); Villiers, Alan, 1967, *Captain Cook, the Seamen's Seaman: A Study of the Great Discoverer* (London, Hodder and Stoughton); Rae, Julia, 1997, *Captain James Cook Endeavours* (London, Stepney Historical Trust).

For published logs and journals, see Beaglehole, J.C., ed., 1955, *The Journals of Captain James Cook on His Voyages of Discovery: Vol. I. The Voyage of the Endeavour 1768–1771* (Cambridge, for the Hakluyt Society); [Magra], John, 1967, *A Journal of a Voyage Round the World in H.M.S.* Endeavour (Amsterdam, N. Israel); Parkinson, Sydney, 1773, *A Journal of a Voyage to the South Seas in His Majesty's Ship, The* Endeavour (London, for Stanfield Parkinson); Banks, Joseph in J.C. Beaglehole, ed., 1962, *The* Endeavour *Journal of Joseph Banks 1768–1771, I and II* (Sydney, The Trustees of the Public Library of New South Wales in Association with Angus and Robertson).

For manuscript logs and journals, see Public Records Office, London: Cook, James PRO Adm 55/40; Hicks, Zachary Adm 51/4546/147–148; Molyneux, Robert Adm 51/4546/152, Adm 55/39; Pickersgill, Richard Adm 51/4547/140–141; Wilkinson, Francis Adm 51/4547/149–150; Forwood, Stephen Adm 51/4545/133; Bootie, James Adm 51/4546/134–135; Clerke, Charles Adm 51/4548/143–144; Anon., Adm 51/4547/153, Adm 51/4548/154, Adm 51/4548/155; Green, Charles Adm 51/4545/151. British Library: Ship's Log BM Add Ms 8959; BM Add Mss 27955, 27885; Monkhouse, W.B. Add Ms 27889. Mitchell Library, Sydney: Monkhouse, Jonathan, *Log*; Banks, Joseph, *Journal*. Auckland Public Library, Auckland: Banks, Joseph Grey Mss 47–75. Alexander Turnbull Library, Wellington: Hicks, Zachary, *Log*.

4. Mr Edward Young, quoted in O'Brien, Patrick, 1988, *Joseph Banks: A Life* (London, Collins Harvill), 23. For the life of Joseph Banks, and the part he played in the *Endeavour* expedition, the following works are also invaluable: Banks, R.E.R., Elliott, B. et al., 1993, *Sir Joseph Banks: A Global Perspective* (London, The Royal Botanic Gardens, Kew); Carter, Harold B., 1988, *Sir Joseph Banks* (London, British Museum (Natural History)); Gascoigne, John, 1994, *Joseph Banks and the English Enlightenment: Useful Knowledge and Polite Culture* (Cambridge, Cambridge University Press); Miller, David Philip, and Reill, Peter Hanns, eds, 1996, *Visions of Empire:*

Voyages, Botany, and Representations of Nature (Cambridge, Cambridge University Press).

5. Quoted in Miller and Reill, 1996, 156; for further discussion of plant sexuality in the Linnaean system, see Schiebinger, Londa in N. Jardine, J.A. Secord and E.C. Spary, 1996, *Cultures of Natural History* (Cambridge, Cambridge University Press), 163–77.

6. Gascoigne, 1994, 67–68; 61.

7. For Dr Daniel Solander and his role in the *Endeavour* voyage, see Solander, Daniel in Edward Duyker and Per Tingbrand, eds, 1995, *Daniel Solander, Collected Correspondence 1753–1782* (Melbourne, The Miegunyah Press, Melbourne University Press) and Duyker, Edward, 1998, *Nature's Argonaut: Daniel Solander 1733–1782, Naturalist and Voyager with Cook and Banks* (Melbourne, The Miegunyah Press, Melbourne University Press).

8. Douglas, James, 14th Earl of Morton, quoted in Beaglehole, 1955, 514–19.

9. Cook, quoted in Beaglehole, 1974, 471.

10. For the life of Charles Clerke, see Cowley, Gordon and Deacon, Les, 1997, *In the Wake of Captain Cook: The Life and Times of Captain Charles Clerke, R. N., 1741–1779* (Boston, Lincolnshire, Richard Kay).

11. Cook in Beaglehole, ed., 1955, 4.

12. Banks in Beaglehole, ed., 1962, I: 158.

13. Solander in Duyker and Tingbrand, eds., 1995, 277.

14. Solander in ibid., 274.

15. Banks in Beaglehole, ed., 1962, I: 207.

16. Cook in Beaglehole, ed., 1955, 44.

17. Cook in ibid., 45.

18. Banks in Beaglehole, ed., 1962, I: 239–40.

19. Their full names were Aro-mai-i-te-ra'i i ma To'ora'i and Teri'i Tu A'a i Ra'i.

20. For an excellent discussion of the rights associated with first-born women in senior chiefly families in Tahiti and Polynesia, see Gunson, Niel, 1964, 'Great Women and Friendship Contract Rites in Pre-Christian Tahiti', *Journal of the Polynesian Society* 73, 53–69; and 1987, 'Sacred Women Chiefs and Female "Headmen" in Polynesian History', *Journal of Pacific History* 22/3, 139–72.

21. Genealogy cited in Oliver, 1974, III: 1212; although as Bruno Saura has noted (Saura, 2003, 4), it is extremely difficult to establish the identity of Tetupaia's father and grandfather. Note that in the genealogy cited by Saura, Tu (or Pomare I) is known as Vaira'atoa (Saura, 2003, 225).

22. Saura, 2005, 115.

23. See Saura, 2003, 225; but see also the variant versions of the Tamatoa genealogy presented in this publication.

24. In Pomare, ed., 1971, 182–86, Marau gives a scathing account of how the first Vehiatua (formerly Teihe-moe-roa) got his name: after a beautiful young woman named Vehiatua visited his district from Ra'iatea, astonishing his people into shouts of admiration with her feats on a surfboard, Teihe-moe-roa was so outraged that his people should praise any other person in his hearing that he took her name on the spot, and thereafter his descendants were known as Vehiatua. Marau also describes an ancient war between this Vehiatua and the Teva ancestor Tavi. Marau blames Vehiatua's vanity for his daughter's breach of the *rahui* for Tavi's son, and the war that followed; but given her strong loyalty to her Papara ancestors, her account is far from neutral.

25. See Henry, 1928, 140.

26. The effectiveness of a *rahui* depended upon the *mana* of the *ari'i* who enacted it, because it was enforced by the power of their ancestor gods, who punished anyone who breached the ritual prohibition. A sign was put up – perhaps a breadfruit or coconut leaf, tied upside down to the trunk of a tree. The *rahui o te ara roa* or '*rahui* of the long road' lasted for perhaps six months to a year, in preparation for the festivals of birth, installation, marriage and death of an *ari'i*, and here the consumption of all the best foods, and the use of any new cloth, mats and canoes were reserved for the festival. This was inaugurated by a ritual at the *ari'i*'s *marae*, announced by messengers, and raised by a thanks-offering of the kinds of resources that had

been protected by the *rahui* (see Handy, 1930, 49).

27. This famous story is recounted by Arii Taimai in Adams, 1901, 42–46; see also Marau Ta'aroa's version in Pomare, ed., 1971, 204–10.

28. Ellis, 1829, I: 289, 293, 304–5, 310–11.

29. Henry, 1928, 312.

30. Oliver, 1974, I: 129; Morrison in Rutter, ed., 1935, 172.

31. Many thanks to Bruno Saura for this translation.

32. For accounts of Teri'irere's installation and the battle that prevented it, see Banks in Beaglehole 1962, I: 304–5; Tupaia as told to Marra, James, 1771 (1967 facsimile), *A Journal of a Voyage Round the World in H.M.S.* Endeavour (Amsterdam, N. Israel), 64; Thomson, Robert, n.d., *History of Tahiti*, London Missionary Society M660, Salmond transcript, 22–23; Ari'i Taimai as recounted in Adams, 1901, 57–61.

33. Adams, 1901, 59.

CHAPTER 7: CAPTAIN COOK IN ARCADIA

1. Parkinson, Sydney, 1773, 13.

2. Cook in Beaglehole, ed., 1955, 75.

3. Banks in Beaglehole, ed., 1962, I: 252.

4. The average male adult height in Britain at this time was approximately five feet five inches. Although I do not know Samuel Wallis's height, he was very ill during his visit to Tahiti and could scarcely walk; Bougainville was about five feet five inches tall.

5. Banks in Beaglehole, ed., 1962, I: 254.

6. Banks in Beaglehole, ed., 1962, I: 255.

7. Parkinson, 1773, 15.

8. Banks in Beaglehole, ed., 1962, I: 258.

9. A number of engravings were produced from Parkinson's sketches, many of which no longer survive in the original. The sketches may have been lost when they were sent to the engravers for the illicit posthumous publication of Parkinson's journal by his brother, Stanfield Parkinson, and for Hawkesworth's published version of Cook's journal.

10. Cook in Beaglehole, ed., 1955, 84.

11. Wilkinson in PRO Adm 51/4547/149, 251.

12. Molyneux in PRO Adm 55/39, 58.

13. Banks in Beaglehole, ed., 1962, I: 264.

14. Solander, 'Observations de Otaheite &c', School of Oriental and African Studies, London; published in Driessen, Hank, 1982, 'Dramatis Personae of Society Islanders, Cook's *Endeavour* Voyage 1769', *Journal of Pacific History* XVII, 227–31.

15. Parkinson, 1773, 21.

16. Banks in Beaglehole, ed., 1962, 266.

17. Cook in Beaglehole, ed., 1955, 554.

18. Banks in Beaglehole, ed., 1962, I: 276; see also Solander quoted in Driessen, 1982, 230.

19. Ellis noted that the collective baking of breadfruit was attended by 'debauchery', the people 'rioting, feasting and sleeping' until it was consumed; and that the breadfruit cooked in this way kept a long time, and was called *opio* (Ellis 1859, I: 41–42).

20. Moerenhout in Borden, ed., 1983, 259.

21. Banks in Beaglehole, ed., 1962, I: 270; Ellis, 1829, I: 204–9.

22. Ellis's description of the *taupiti* or *'Oro'a* ceremonial gathering, which featured wrestling and feasting, closely matches the journal accounts of this occasion.

CHAPTER 8: THE TRANSIT OF VENUS

1. See also Siena, Kevin, 2001, *Bulletin of Medical History* 75, 199–224 for eighteenth-century references to the 'Tomb of Venus' and the 'Garden of Venus' where these diseases were contracted.

2. Dr Rick Franklin, STD Clinic, Auckland Hospital, pers. comm.; Smith, Howard M., 1975,

'The Introduction of Venereal Disease into Tahiti: A Re-examination', *Journal of Pacific History* 10/1, 38–45.

3. Solander, Daniel, 'Observations de Otaheite &c', School of Oriental and African Studies, London; published in Driessen, Hank, 1982, 'Dramatis personae of Society Islanders, Cook's *Endeavour* Voyage 1769', *Journal of Pacific History* XVII, 227–31. As Parkinson noted: 'Most of our company procured temporary wives among the natives, with whom they occasionally cohabited' (Parkinson, 1784, 25).

4. Cook in Beaglehole, ed., 1955, 99.

5. Solander quoted in Driessen, 1982, 230–31.

6. Solander in Duyker, 1998, 140.

7. Cook in Beaglehole, ed., 1955, 98.

8. Banks in Beaglehole, ed., 1962, I: 287.

9. Molyneux in Beaglehole, ed., 1955, 556.

10. Banks in Beaglehole, ed., 1962, 375.

11. Molyneux in Beaglehole, ed., 1955, 555.

12. Ibid., 556.

13. Bark cloth was also laid on the ground when a woman entered a *marae*, for instance during the *uhi-a-'iri* ritual when a high chief's wife took her child to the family *marae* and it was washed in the living waters of Tane, removing some of the ritual restrictions on mother and child (Moerenhout, quoted in Oliver, 1974, I: 421). This prevented her female power from attacking the male power of the *marae*, from which women were normally excluded.

14. Orsmond, 'The 'Arioi War', Filihia transcript, 12: 'A tihi tomo [?] A dress that almost suffocated. it was wound quite round the female till she could hardly move & was unable to look save upwards. This the arioi took off. It was their perquisite. The female often fell and fainted beneath her load.' See also Henry, 1928, 239.

15. Banks in Beaglehole, ed., 1962, I: 275. Cook and Parkinson make it plain that on this occasion, after stripping off the bark cloth, the woman was entirely naked (Cook in Beaglehole, ed., 1955, 93; Parkinson, 1784, 27).

16. Morrison, one of the *Bounty* mutineers, describes this kind of ritual, which he calls an 'Ootdoo' [*Utu*] ceremony. The chief was accompanied by a priest who carried young plantain trees and a pig (although no pig was presented on this occasion, perhaps because they were so scarce at this time), and they stood about forty yards distant from the visiting chief. Tying a small bunch of red feathers to one of the plantain trees, the priest made a long speech of welcome and then walked to the visitor and laid the plantain at his feet. When the visiting chief picked up the red feather bunch and put it in his hair, he was presented with large quantities of cloth and pigs, and invited to a lavish feast. (Morrison, James in Owen Rutter, ed., *The Journal of James Morrison* (London, Golden Cockerel Press), 1935, 189–92.)

17. Tcherkézoff, 2004, 155–81 discusses wrapping and unwrapping, and how this was understood by early European visitors to Tahiti.

18. Molyneux in Beaglehole, ed., 1955, 557.

19. Cook in Beaglehole, ed., 1955, 94.

20. Ellis, 1829, III: 77.

21. Note that canoes from Nukutaveke clearly visited Tahiti (and were no doubt bartered with the local chiefs), which explains how Captain Wallis could have been presented with a canoe of this kind in Tahiti.

22. Banks in Beaglehole, ed., 1962, I: 279.

23. Hatchett, Charles, 'Banksiana written at the request of my Friend Dawson Turner Esq of Great Yarmouth', Banks Archive Project, Natural History Museum, London.

24. Molyneux in Beaglehole, ed., 1955, 559.

25. Solander in Driessen, 1982, 231.

26. Orsmond, 'The 'Arioi War', Filihia transcript, 5: 'Be on the alert let not the ceremony of the arioi be defiled. (If he went) he would be slain stricken by the club.'

27. Cook in Beaglehole, ed., 1955, 128.

28. Solander, 1772, 'Vocabulary of the Language of Taheite', MS 12023, School of Oriental and African Studies, London, which includes items such as 'to Fuck, Taimorhadi, Tamo, Io-hiahia, Tatue; To kiss with the tongue, mitte; to kiss or lick, Mi-ti te e ra hou; Sperm (semen masculinium), Ta-te-a, Tatea; Cock, Moa Tane, "a hen's husband"'.

29. Parkinson, 1773, 33.

30. Ibid.

31. See Morrison, 1935, 225, who described this dance as a *Ponara*: 'After they have Playd at this for some Hours they Kick the Ball to one side and both Partys strike up together, when each, to draw the Spectators to their exibition, produce two or three Young Wantons, who stripping of their lower Garments Cover them selves with a loose piece of Cloth and at particular parts of the Song they throw Open their Cloth and dance with their fore part Naked to the Company making many lewd gestures – however these are not merely the effects of Wantoness but Custom, and those who perform thus in Publick are Shy and Bashful in private, and seldom suffer any freedom to be taken by the Men on that account.'

32. Green, Roger C. and Kaye, 1968, 'Religious Structures (*Marae*) of the Windward Society Islands: The Significance of Certain Historical Records', *New Zealand Journal of History* 2/2, 66–89.

33. Cook in Beaglehole, ed., 1955, 96.

34. Ellis, 1829, I: 223–24 gives a vivid account of Tahitian surfing.

35. See ibid., II: 336–37 for a detailed description of this kind of ritual.

36. Henry, 1928, 359–63. Although Henry describes Tau'ura-nui as a male god, gender is not marked in Tahitian; and the other stories about Tau'ura-nui (for instance the account of Tafa'i's visit to the underworld) make it plain that this god was a woman.

37. Banks in Beaglehole, ed., 1962, I: 286.

38. Thomson, c. 1840, f. 38.

39. Oliver, 1974, I: 429.

40. Sir Joseph Banks to Dawson Turner, F.R.S., 1812, Letter, Fitzwilliam Museum, Cambridge, Banks Collection, MS 82, discovered by and quoted in Carter, Harold, 'Notes on the Drawings by an Unknown Artist from the Voyage of HMS *Endeavour*' in Margarette Lincoln, ed., 1998, *Science and Exploration in the Pacific: European Voyages to the Southern Oceans in the Eighteenth Century* (Woodbridge, Suffolk, The Boydell Press in association with the National Maritime Museum), 133–34.

41. Newell, Jenny, 2006, 'Paradise Exchanged: Tahitians, Europeans and the trade in nature', PhD thesis, Australian National University, 79.

42. See Parkinson's long and detailed account in Parkinson, 1773 of Tahitian methods for dyeing cloth – his descriptions of the use of 'taihinnoo' and 'e tau' leaves (37) and those from 'e pooa' (38) along with the figs of the 'mattee' tree (46) to make red dye or 'mattee'; the roots of 'e nono' (38) to dye bark cloth yellow; the juice of 'e peereepeeree' (40) to produce an 'indifferent' brown dye; the juice of its fruit and leaves of 'tamanno' (41) to give a pale yellow; the bark of 'e tootooe' to give a glossy substance to finish the cloth, and a black dye (44); and 'doodooe-awai' and 'oheparra' to dye cloth brown. See also his Tahitian vocabulary, which names different coloured bark cloths – white, buff, reddish and russet (56). Ellis, 1829, I: 182–83 also discusses Tahitian methods of dyeing.

43. Ellis, 1829, I: 262–67.

44. Parkinson, 1773, 25.

45. Moerenhout in Borden, ed., 1983, 219.

46. According to Teuira Henry, the young men and boys among the mourners for a member of the 'royal family' would pay an expert to paint their bodies in stripes and circles in red, white and black. Wearing only a small loincloth, they decorated their heads with fern fronds with bright berries and *fara* blossoms and behaved in a wild, bewildered fashion (*nevaneva*). The priest of the gods of mourning, Oviri-moe-aihere, Pautu-roa and Oviri-moe-aihere, led them up the mountainside to the *marae* of those gods, where they erected two sheds where they camped during the mourning rituals. The priest was elaborately dressed in a petticoat called the *tihi-*

parau; a waist girdle called a *moeho*; a turban of bark cloth decorated with snowy red-tipped tail feathers of the tropic bird; and the *parae* or mask of bright pearl shell. From the mask hung a bright crescent-shaped board decorated with mother-of-pearl chips threaded together, the *'ahu parau*; and from this hung pieces of yellow and black cloth called *pautu* or mourning cloth; with fronds of the *fare-rupe* fern hanging down behind. The priest led the way, jingling his *tete* or pearl-shell clappers and wielding the *paeho*, a sacred weapon about five feet long edged with shark's teeth which was ornamented with black feathers at the tip; while the *nevaneva* wielded spears with which they could kill anyone whom they encountered. (Henry, 1928, 293–94; also see Ellis, 1829, I: 412–14 for an account of this ritual.)

47. See Orsmond, 'The 'Arioi War', Filihia transcript, 6: 'A arioi would not run . . . from the mourners for the dead (who would cut and mangle any other person). The arioi passed on, the Mourners passed on. One would not molest another.' Babadzan, 1993, 145–90 gives a fascinating analysis of the mourning costume and its associations, although my analysis of Tepau's costume (which is based on the sketches by Spöring and Tupaia) differs in some details.

48. Banks in Beaglehole, ed., 1962, I: 289.

49. Ellis, 1829, I: 217–20 gives an excellent account of Tahitian archery. This pursuit, known as *te 'a*, was carried out on a triangular stone platform, with the archers dressed in particular costumes. Women were excluded from these contests. They shot their arrows between two white flags, and the aim was to shoot the arrow as far as possible. The archer knelt on one knee, drew back the string of the bow and when the head of the arrow touched the centre of the bow, it was released and flew with great force, the archer dropping the bow at the same time. Men holding white flags signalled by holding up the white flag for a shot that beat the others; and after the contest the archers had to change their costumes and bathe before eating or returning to their dwellings. (See also Handy, 1930, 58–59.)

50. Ellis, 1829, I: 235.

51. Banks in Beaglehole, ed., 1962, I: 290.

52. Cook in Beaglehole, ed., 1955, 101. Any sailor who stole (from the ship or the islanders) was immediately flogged; and the crew evidently regarded the injunction against shooting Tahitians who pilfered from them as an injustice.

53. Banks in Beaglehole, ed., 1962, I: 291.

54. Cook in Beaglehole, ed., 1955, 103.

55. Ellis, 1829, III: 101–6 gives an account of various ways in which Tahitians paid respect to their high chiefs.

56. Solander quoted in Driessen, 1982, 230.

57. Cook in Beaglehole, ed., 1955, 104.

CHAPTER 9: CIRCLING THE LAND

1. Intriguingly, three other islanders are named in the *Endeavour*'s muster book for this visit to Tahiti – 'Terrea', 'Nunahoe' and 'Tobia Tomita' – who were hired as 'Guides for the interior Parts of the Island & Pilots for the Coast & to assist in forming connections with the other Natives' (*Endeavour* Muster Book in Beaglehole, ed., 1955, 600).

2. Banks in Beaglehole, ed., 1962, I: 296.

3. Ibid., 297.

4. Henry, 1928, 86–87.

5. See Oliver, 1974, III: 1174.

6. James Morrison, the *Bounty* mutineer, noted that the breadfruit trees cropped earlier in the southern districts, where the rainfall was much higher (Morrison in Rutter, ed., 1935, 142).

7. Banks in Beaglehole, ed., 1962, I: 298.

8. Ibid., 346.

9. Ibid., 301.

10. Ibid., 303.

11. When Captain Wilson of the *Duff* visited this famous *marae* in 1797, he described it as being 270 feet long, 94 feet wide at the base and 50 feet high, and at the summit 180 feet long and 6 feet

wide. A flight of ten steps led to the summit, the bottom step being six feet high. The outer stones were of squared coral and rounded basalt laid with meticulous care, especially the *tiava* or cornerstones; and the *marae* is depicted in an engraving in the published *Voyage* (Wilson, James, 1799, *A Missionary Voyage to the Southern Pacific Ocean, performed in the Years 1796, 1797, 1798, in the ship Duff, commanded by Captain James Wilson* (London, T. Chapman), 211, 207).

12. A remarkable sketch of the tiered heavens by the Māori scholar Pei te Hurunui Jones, who was trained by priests from the Tainui school of learning (which he named as Rangiatea [or Ra'iatea]),is identical to the structure of Mahaiatea and similar *marae*, with each named tier representing one of the layered heavens.

13. Henry, Teuira, 1913, 'The Oldest Great Tahitian Maraes and the Last One Built in Tahiti', *Journal of the Polynesian Society* 22, 25–27. See also Babadzan, 1993, 42–50 for an excellent discussion of such images or *puna*.

14. Henry, 1928, 141. According to Henry: '[I]n 1865 its finely shaped stone steps were wanted by a planter for a stone bridge across the river of Taharu'u, between Papara and Atimaono. The planter influenced the French governor, De la Roncière, to force Mrs Ari'ita'imai Salmon (Chiefess of Papara) and her people to consent to the breaking down of the monument, which they regarded as too precious to destroy, and from those stones was erected a fine bridge. This, however, did not compensate the people long for their loss, as the river is subject to heavy freshets in the rainy season and soon destroyed the structure, and so both the marae and the bridge were lost.'

15. James Cook, Chart of King George's Island, British Library Add Ms 7085, f. 7.

16. Orsmond, 'The 'Arioi War in Tahiti', Filihia transcript, 51.

17. Ellis, 1829, I: 43.

18. Banks in Beaglehole, ed., 1962, I: 307.

19. Ibid., 310.

20. Ibid., 312.

21. Cook in Beaglehole, ed., 1955, 116.

22. Banks in Beaglehole, ed., 1962, I: 312.

23. Cook in Beaglehole, ed., 1955, 117.

24. Molyneux, Robert, Ship's Log, Adm 55/39, f. 61b.

CHAPTER 10: TUPAIA'S SHIP

1. Pickersgill in PRO Adm 51/4547/140, 36.

2. For an elegant, authoritative account of 'star paths' in the Pacific and how they worked, see Kursh, Charlotte O. and Kreps, Theodora C., 1974, 'Starpaths: Linear Constellations in Tropical Navigation', *Current Anthropology* 15/3, 334–37.

3. See for example Henry, Teuira, 1894, 'The Birth of New Lands, after the Creation of Havai'i (Ra'iatea)', *Journal of the Polynesian Society* 3/3, 136–39.

4. For accounts of Pacific navigation, see (in order of publication) Lewis, David, 1967, *Daughters of the Wind* (London, Gollancz); Lewis, David, 1972, *We, the Navigators* (Canberra, Australian National University Press); Levison, M., Ward, R.G. and Webb, J.W., 1973, *The Settlement of Polynesia: A Computer Simulation* (Canberra, Australian National University Press); Kursh, Charlotte O. and Kreps, Theodora C., 1974, 'Starpaths: Linear Constellations in Tropical Navigation', *Current Anthropology* 15/3, 334–37; Finney, B.R., ed., 1976, *Pacific Navigation and Voyaging* (Wellington, Polynesian Society); Lewis, David, 1978, *The Voyaging Stars: Secrets of the Pacific Island Navigators* (London, Collins); Gladwin, T., 1979, *East is a Big Bird: Navigation and Logic on Puluwat Atoll* (Cambridge, Mass., Harvard University Press); Finney, B.R., 1979, *Hokule'a: The Way to Tahiti* (New York, Dodd, Mead and Co.); Gell, A., 1985, 'How to Read a Map: Remarks on the Practical Logic of Navigation', *Man* 2/2, 271–86; Irwin, G., 1994, *Prehistoric Exploration and Colonisation of the Pacific* (Cambridge, Cambridge University Press); Taonui, R., 1994, 'Haerenga Waka: Polynesian origins, migrations and navigation', MA thesis, University of Auckland; Hutchins, E., 1995, *Cognition in the Wild* (Cambridge, MIT Press); Finney, B.R., 1999, 'The Sin at Awarua', *The Contemporary Pacific* 11, 1–33; Finney, B.R.,

2000, 'Nautical Cartography and Traditional Navigation in Oceania', in eds, D. Woodward and G.M. Lewis, *Cartography in the Traditional African, American, Arctic, Australian and Pacific Societies*, Vol. 3/2 (Chicago, University of Chicago Press); Salmond, Anne, 2005, 'Their Body is Different, Our Body is Different: European and Tahitian Navigators in the Eighteenth Century', *History and Anthropology* 16/2, 167–86; Howe, K. R., ed., 2006, *Waka Moana: Voyages of the Ancestors* (Auckland, David Bateman Ltd); Di Piazza, Anne and Pearthree, Erik, 2007, 'A New Interpretation of Tupaia's Chart', *Journal of the Polynesian Society* 116/3, 321–40; Di Piazza, Anne and Pearthree, Erik, eds, 2008, *Canoes of the Grand Ocean* (Oxford, BAR International Series 1802).

5. Although Cook's island list is inserted in his journal later in the voyage, it seems likely that Tupaia passed on much of this information before he left the island. After sailing from Tahiti, Cook wrote: 'These people have an extensive knowledge of the islands situated in these seas, Tupia as well as several others hath given us an account of upwards of seventy, but as the account they have given of their situation is so vague and uncertain I shall refar [refrain from] giving a list of them until I have learnt from Tupia the situation of each island with a little more certainty.' (Cook in Beaglehole, ed., 1955, 138.) For a detailed tabulation of the island lists given by Tupaia to Cook, Molyneux and in his chart, as well as those given by other island navigators to the Spanish explorers, see Salmond, Anne, 2008, 'Voyaging Exchanges: Tahitian Pilots and European Navigators', in di Piazza and Pearthree, eds. See also Dening, Greg, 1963, 'Geographical Knowledge of the Tahitians', in Jack Golson, ed., *Polynesian Navigation: A Symposium on Andrew Sharp's theory of Accidental Voyages* (Wellington, The Polynesian Society), 132–53.

6. Molyneux, Robert, Ship's Log, Adm 55/39, 62. Molyneux's island list is inserted after the entry for 13 July 1769, the day that the *Endeavour* sailed from Tahiti. See also Forster's island list, which includes descriptive material about a number of islands, in Forster, Johann in Thomas, Guest and Dettelbach, eds, 1996, 311–16.

7. Henry, 1928, 477 gives the names of Hiti-au-revareva, Hiti-tautau-atu, Hiti-poto, Hiti-uta, Hiti-ta'i and Hiti-marama as clans or islands encountered by Rata.

8. This chart can be found in the British Library at Add Ms 15508 no. 18.

9. Pickersgill, PRO Adm 51/4547/140, 36.

10. Parkinson, 1773, 67.

11. Henry, 1928, 393.

12. This wind was also known as the *Ahina-muri* or 'fire behind'; see definition and chant in Orsmond, Rev. John, 1850, Papers Vol. V, part of Tahitian dictionary, Mitchell Library, Sydney, A2609, Dr Meredith Filihia transcript, 32–33, 35.

13. Banks in Beaglehole, ed., 1962, I: 314.

14. Saura has identified this high-born chief as Mato, a son of Mau'arua (the son of Ari'i-ma'o and Te'e'eva who was exiled from Ra'iatea after the Borabora invasion; see Saura, 2003, 226, 228); and his senior wife as Fa'atuara'i. Although Cook thought that Ori was the paramount chief of the island, in fact this status belonged to his son Teri'itaria. According to Henry, Mato was a high priest of 'Opoa (Henry, 1928, 257).

15. Cook in Beaglehole, ed., 1955, 141.

16. See Henry, 1928 for this chant (re-translated by Anne Salmond), and an excellent description of these rituals.

17. Driessen, 1982, 232.

18. Magra, John, 1771, 61–65.

19. Banks in Beaglehole, ed., 1962, I: 316.

20. See Babadzan, 1993, 91–110 for a detailed discussion of *to'o* and the associated *pa'iatua* rituals, which occurred at the beginning of the seasonal festivities, when a new high chief was installed, a new 'national' *marae* was founded, or in the case of drought or some great calamity.

21. Orsmond, 1850, Filihia transcript, 5.

22. Parkinson, 1773, 69.

23. Orsmond, 1850, 10.

24. Banks in Beaglehole, ed., 1962, I: 320.

25. Ibid., 368.

26. Ibid., 323.

27. According to Henry, Ta'inu'u was the *marae* of the royal family of Rarotonga, who brought a *marae* stone from their own island, set up Ta'inu'u and intermarried with the royal family of 'Opoa (Henry, 1928, 121–22). See also the missionary Williams, who tells the story of a chief named Iouri who sailed from Ra'iatea to Rarotonga, returning with a woman who became the wife of Tamatoa, and also a quantity of *mahi* or preserved breadfruit, which he dedicated to the god 'Oro at Taputapuatea. As Williams noted: 'It became an object of ambition with every adventurous chief to discover other lands, and, on his return, to bring some article of value to his own island.' (Williams, 1838, 57–58.)

28. Solander quoted in Driessen, 1982, 232.

29. Banks in Beaglehole, ed., 1962, I: 324.

30. Ibid., 324.

31. Ellis, 1829, I: 299–300. See also Babadzan's discussion of the *fau*, which likens it to the *to'o* or god-image, which was also hollow, tall and decorated with feathers (Babadzan, 1993, 160–61).

32. The bodice or *tahema* worn by a *hura* dancer was often made of spotted cloth, while the *tihi* or ruff of white stiffened cloth, frequently edged with a scarlet border, was gathered around the waist, and the petticoat or *araitihi* was made of fine cloth (Ellis, 1829, I: 216).

33. Kaeppler, Adrienne, 1997, 'Polynesia and Micronesia', in Adrienne L. Kaeppler, Christian Kaufmann and Douglas Newton, eds., *Oceanic Art* (New York, Harry N. Abrams), 167.

34. Ellis gives an excellent account of the *hura*, where the chiefly female dancers were guided by a *ha'apii* or teacher, and the four male *fa'ata*, dressed in fringed mats, acted as clowns to entertain the spectators (Ellis, 1829, I: 215–17).

35. Magra, 1771, 61–65.

36. Banks in Beaglehole, ed., 1962, I: 327. Saura (Saura, 2005, 104) gives Puni's title as Te Iho-tu-mata-'aro'aro).

37. Ibid., 329.

38. Cook in Beaglehole, ed., 1955, 157.

39. Ibid., 156–57. See Appendix II.

40. Forster, Johann in Thomas, Guest and Dettelbach, eds, 1986, 309. According to Charles Barff, a long-time missionary on Huahine, the people of Huahine and their god Tane originally came from Manu'a, which he identified with Manu'a in the Samoan archipelago. (Driessen, 1991, 5–9.)

41. For the island list, see Appendix II. As for the chart, Cook stated firmly that this chart was 'Drawn by Tupia's own hands' (Cook in Beaglehole, ed., 1955, 293–94). On the other hand, Forster's account (which was hearsay) suggests that Tupaia dictated the name of each island, its bearing, and its size, and Cook translated this into a chart: 'Having soon perceived the meaning and use of charts, [Tupaia] gave directions for making one according to his account, and always pointed to that part of the heavens, where each isle was situated, mentioning at the same time that it was either larger or smaller than Taheitee, and likewise whether it was high or low, whether it was peopled or not, adding now and then some curious accounts relative to some of them' (Forster, Johann in Thomas, Guest and Dettelbach, eds, 1996, 310). There may thus have been two charts arising out of this collaboration – Tupaia's original, and Cook's translation of it. This is supported by the fact that the chart drawn by Cook marks islands with paired pinholes which are numbered in pencil, although two sets of pinholes are left blank (Di Piazza, Anne and Pearthree, Erik, 2007, 'A New Interpretation of Tupaia's Chart', *Journal of the Polynesian Society* 116/3, 321–40), suggesting that Cook's chart is an incomplete copy of an original.

42. Chart in BL Add Ms 21593.C.

43. Hale, Horatio, 1846, *Ethnology and Philology: United States Exploring Expedition 1838–42* (Philadelphia, Lea and Blanchard), 122.

44. See for example Thomas, N., 1997, *In Oceania: Visions, Artifacts, Histories* (Durham, Duke University Press), 4; Finney, B. in Woodward, D. and Lewis, G. Malcolm, eds, 2000, 'Nautical Cartography and Traditional Navigation in Oceania', *Cartography in the Traditional African,*

American, Arctic, Australian and Pacific Societies 3/2 (Chicago, University of Chicago Press); Turnbull, D., 2000, '(En-)countering Knowledge Traditions: The Story of Cook and Tupaia', Humanities Research 1 (Canberra, Australian National University); Turnbull, David, 2001, 'Cook and Tupaia, a Tale of Cartographic Meconnaissance?', in M. Lincoln, ed., Science and Exploration in the Pacific: European Voyages to the Southern Oceans in the Eighteenth Century (Woodbridge, Suffolk, National Maritime Museum), 117–33; Jolly, Margaret, 2007, 'Imagining Oceania: Indigenous and Foreign Representations of a Sea of Islands', The Contemporary Pacific 19/2, 508–45.

45. Di Piazza and Pearthree, 2007. See Appendix II.

46. Cook in Beaglehole, ed., 1955, fn. 120.

47. Ibid., 154.

48. Banks in Beaglehole, ed., 1962, I: 345.

49. Ibid., 383.

50. Ibid., 340.

51. See also Cook, ibid., 127: 'The young girls when ever they can collect 8 or 10 together dance a very indecent dance which they call Timorodee [te ai moro iti – simulated copulation? – although Saura cannot make sense of these words] singing most indecent songs and useing most indecent actions; . . . this exercise is however generaly left of, . . . for as soon as they have form'd a connection with man they are expected to leave of dancing Timorodee.'

52. Banks loaned 'Tupaia's Account of the South Sea Islanders' to Abbé José Francisco Correia de Serra to read during his exile in London in the early 1800s (letter from de Serra to Banks, returning the last sheet of this account on 7 April 1805, BL Add Ms 8099, f. 384). See also the version of the Tahitian creation myth recorded by James Cook in his holograph journal in the British Museum quoted in Carrington, A.H., 1939, Journal of the Polynesian Society 48, 30–31, which must have been dictated by Tupaia.

53. Ibid., 397–99.

54. Ibid., 399.

55. Williams, W.L., 1888, 'On the Visit of Captain Cook to Poverty Bay and Tolaga Bay', Transactions and Proceedings of the New Zealand Institute, XXI: 389–97 gives the story about the floating island, while the quote about the great bird is from Polack, Joel, 1838, New Zealand: Being a Narrative of Travels and Adventures, Vols. I and II (London, Bentley), I: 15.

56. Binney, Judith, 1995, Redemption Songs (Wellington, Bridget Williams Ltd), 11.

57. Harris, F., n.d., 11, typescript in Gisborne Museum and Art Gallery.

58. Colenso, William, 1851. My thanks to Patrick Parsons for supplying this quotation.

59. Banks in Beaglehole, ed., 1962, I: 420.

60. Polack, 1838, II: 135–36.

61. My grateful thanks to Dr Volker Harms of the Institute of Ethnology at the University of Tübingen, and Anke Sharrahs for allowing me to visit the poupou in Dresden. For an excellent account of the most likely European provenance of the carving, see Harms, Volker, 1996, 'A Maori Ancestor Panel which was brought to England from the first Voyage of Captain Cook (1768–1771), rediscovered in the Ethnographical Collection of Tübingen University', unpublished ms. Harms thinks that the noted geologist Ferdinand von Hochstetter, who had visited New Zealand in 1858–1859, and who later became director-general of the Imperial Museum in Vienna, must have purchased the artefact in England from a private collector or dealer, and brought it to Germany for display in his museum. After his death, it seems likely that his daughter Emma gave the carving to the Ethnographical Collection at Tübingen University.

62. See Polack, 1838, II: 135, who reported that according to the local high chief Te Kani: 'Tupia was a great favourite with our parents, so much so, that to gratify him, several children who were born in the village, during his sojourn among us, were named after him.'

63. Banks in Beaglehole, ed., 1962, I: 446–47.

64. Ibid., 455.

65. Pickersgill, Adm 51/4547/140–141, f. 61a.

66. Cook in Beaglehole, ed., 1955, 291.

67. Banks in Beaglehole, ed., 1962, II: 187.
68. Ibid., 191.
69. Cook in Beaglehole, ed., 1955, 442.

CHAPTER 11: THE VICEROY OF PERU

1. Corney, 1913, I: 28. For published accounts of this and the following Spanish voyages to Tahiti in 1772–75, see Corney, Bolton Glanvill, trans. and ed., 1913, *The Quest and Occupation of Tahiti by Emissaries of Spain, Vols, I, II and III* (Cambridge, for the Hakluyt Society).

For the manuscript accounts of this voyage, see Amat's Instructions to Amich and Bonamo, 30 March 1773, Archivo General de Indias (AGI), Lima 1035; Amat's instructions to Boenechea, Museo Naval, Madrid (MNM) Ms 412, 156–67; Boenechea, Domingo, 'Relación de la navegación que de orden del Excmo. Sr. Don Manuel de Amat . . . Don Domingo de Boenechea' (1773). Copies in AGI Lima 1035, and Biblioteca de la Real Academia de la Historia (Madrid) (BRAH). Printed by F. Barras in *España en la Polinesia Oriental*, trans. in Corney, ed., 1913, I: 284–345; 'Descripción de las isles del Occeano Pacifico, Por Dn. Domino de Boenechea, en los anos de 1772 y 1774', MNM Ms 476, trans. from original by Gwyn Fox; Hervé 1773, 'Noticia adquirida', AGI Lima 1035, trans. in Corney, ed., 1913, I: 351–59; Bonacorsi, Raymond (unsigned), 'Viaje a la isla de Otayty', contemporary copy in MNM Ms 208, ff. 101–36, trans. and printed by Corney, ed., 1913, II: 29–63; Anon., 'Las Noticias de Otahiti 1773', ms, AGI Lima 1035, Sevilla, trans. from original by Gwyn Fox; Amich, Friar Joseph, 'Diario . . .', held at AGI and RAH, first published in *El Viagero Universal* (1798), printed by Izaguirre (1925) and trans. by Corney, ed., 1913, II: 65–89.

For recent scholarship on these voyages, see Baquero, Mercedes Palau and Mouriz, Aranzazu Zabala, 1988, 'Spanish Expeditions to Tahiti' in Carlos Martinez Shaw, ed., *Spanish Pacific from Magellan to Malaspina* (Madrid, Ministerio de Asuntos Exteriores), 121–31; Riddle, Shane, 1999, MA thesis, University of Auckland, 'Inscribing and Contextualising "Spanish Tahiti": A Comparative Study of Representations of an Eighteenth-Century Voyage'; and Camino, Mercedes Maroto, 2008, *Exploring the Explorers: Spaniards in Oceania 1519–1784* (Manchester, University of Manchester Press).

2. For accounts of Manuel de Amat, the Viceroy of Peru, see Vicente Rodríguez Casado and Florentino Pérez Embid, eds, 1947, *Manuel de Amat y Junient, Viceroy of Peru 1761–76, Memoria de Gobierno* (Sevilla, Escuela de Estudios Hispano-Americanos de Sevilla), trans. Gwyn Fox; Descola, Jean, 1968, *Daily Life in Colonial Peru* (London, George Allen and Unwin Ltd).

3. For published accounts of this voyage, see Corney, Bolton Glanvill, ed., 1908, *The Voyage of Captain Don Felipe Gonzalez in the Ship of the Line San Lorenzo, with the Frigate Santa Rosalia in Company, to Easter Island in 1770–1, preceded by an Extract of Mynheer Jacob Roggeveen's Official Log of his discovery of and visit to Easter Island in 1722* (Cambridge, for the Hakluyt Society); and Blanco, Francisco Mellén, 1986, *Manuscritos y documentos españoles para la historia de la isla de Pascua* (Madrid, Biblioteca CEHOPU).

4. For the series of despatches and reports that form the basis of this paragraph, see Corney, ed., 1913, I: 1–240.

5. Clayton, L.A., 'Trade and Navigation in the Seventeenth Century Viceroyalty of Peru', *Journal of Latin American Studies* 7/1, 12.

6. Corney, ed., 1913, I: 267.

7. Arbesmann, Rudolph, 1945, 'The Contribution of the Franciscan College of Ocopa in Peru to the Geographical Exploration of South America', *The Americas*, 393–417; Amich, Jose, 1988, *Historia de Las Misiones Del Convento de Santa Rosa de Ocopa* (Iquitos, Peru, CETA).

8. Hall, Linda B., 2004, *Mary, Mother and Warrior: The Virgin in Spain and the Americas* (Austin, University of Texas Press).

9. For the history of Ocopa, see Arbesmann, Rudolph, n.d., 'The Contribution of the Franciscan College of Ocopa in Peru to the Geographical Exploration of South America', *The Americas* 1/4, 393–417; Heras, Fr Julián, O.F.M., *Comienzos de las misionas de Ocopa (Perú): Documentos Ineditos para su Historia (1724–43)* (Lima, Peru, Convento de los Descalzos); Pouncey, Lorene, 1968, 'The Library of the Convent of Ocopa', *Latin American Research Review* 13/3, 147–54. See also Brown,

Michael and Fernandez, Eduardo, 1991, *War of Shadows: The Struggle for Utopia in the Peruvian Amazon* (Berkeley, University of California Press); Iriate, Fr Lazaro, trans. Patricia Ross, 1982, *Franciscan History: The Three Orders of St. Francis of Assisi* (Chicago, Franciscan Herald Press).

10. For an account of many of these tensions, see Staving, Ward, 1999, *The World of Tupac Amaru: Conflict, Community and Identity in Colonial Peru* (Lincoln, University of Nebraska Press); and Griffiths, Nicholas, 1996, *The Cross and the Serpent: Religious Repression and Resurgence in Colonial Peru* (Norman, University of Oklahoma Press).

11. Martin, Luis, 1983, *Daughters of the Conquistadores: Women of the Viceroy of Peru* (Dallas, Southern Methodist University Press), 152.

12. For an account of La Perricholi and her affair with Manuel de Amat, see Villegas, Bertrand, 1999, *La Perricholi* (Buenos Aires, Ed. Sudamericana).

13. Ibid., 281.

14. Many thanks to Bruno Saura for correcting the name of this battle.

15. For accounts of these battles, see Forster, George Adam, 1777, *A Voyage round the World in His Brittanic Majesty's Sloop, Resolution, Commanded by Captain James Cook, during the Years 1772, 3, 4 and 5*, I and II (London, B. White, J. Robson, P. Elmsly and G. Robinson), II, 94–96; Cook, James, in Beaglehole, J.C., ed., 1967, *The Journals of Captain James Cook on His Voyages of Discovery*, Vol. III, 2 parts (Cambridge, for the Hakluyt Society), i: 205; Thomson, n.d., Salmond transcript, 27–33; Adams, Ch. VIII, 62–75, Ch. X, 88–97; Oliver, 1974, III: 1225–36.

16. Lescure, Rey, 1956, 'La mort de Vehi-atua', *Bulletin de la Société d'Études Océaniennes* X/2, 541.

17. See Morrison in Rutter, ed., 1935, 172.

18. Ta'aroa Manahune, Tu's paternal grandfather, married Tetuaehuri i Tai'arapu, the daughter of the Vehi-atua of that generation, thus forging a link between the Pare-'Arue and Tai'arapu lineages. (Corney, ed., 1913, II: xxxvii; Oliver, 1974, III: 1192.)

19. Lescure, 1956, 541. For an excellent unpublished account of this *ari'i*, see also Eddowes, Mark, n.d., 'Vehi-atua Teri'i ta'ata 'ura'ura: An *ari'i nui* of Vai-te-piha Tautira as described in the journals of the Spanish padres resident there from 1774–1775'.

20. Bonacorsi in Corney, ed., 1913, I: 45.

21. Ibid., 50.

22. Ibid., 59.

23. See also 'Description of the Isles of the Pacific Ocean, explored recently by order of His Majesty by Don Domingo de Boenechea, Captain of the frigate of the Royal Navy of His Majesty, named *Santa Maria Magdalena* (alias the *Águila*) in the years 1772–1774', trans. from original by Gwyn Fox, MNM Ms 476, 84–101.

24. Bonacorsi in Corney, ed., 1913, I: 50–51.

25. Moerenhout in Borden, ed., 1983, 260.

26. For various versions of Tu's ancestry, see Oliver, 1974, III: 1180–86. According to Ari'i Taimai, a chief from Paumotu entered the Taunoa channel, and was invited to be the guest of Maua-hiti, a chief of Pare; and after his death, Tu became his heir and successor. He married into the chief's family, and his grandson Ta'aroa Manahune married Tetuaehuri i Tai'arapu, and had Teu or Hapai, Tu's father. According to Marau, her daughter, the Tu family were descended from a chief who came from the Tuamotuan atoll of Fakarava. He was adopted by Maua-hiti, a chief of 'Arue, and married one of his daughters. Their son was Ta'aroa-Manahune, who married Tetuaehuri, daughter of Vehi-atua, and had Teu.

27. Henry, 1928, 75–76.

28. Bonacorsi in Corney, ed., 1913, I: 58.

29. Amich in ibid., 85.

30. Boenechea in ibid., 332.

31. Amich in ibid., 85.

32. Amich in ibid., 88.

33. Hervé in ibid., 350–59.

34. Ibid., 357.

CHAPTER 12: TUTE'S RETURN

1. Quoted in O'Brien, Patrick, 1988, *Joseph Banks: A Life* (London, Collins Harvill), 149.
2. *Town and Country Magazine: or, Universal Repository of Knowledge, Instruction and Entertainment*, September 1773, 457–58.
3. Scott-Waring, Major, 1774, *An Epistle from Oberea, Queen of Otaheite, to Joseph Banks Esq. Translated by T.Z.Q. Esq, Professor of the Otaheite language in Dublin* (London, printed for J. Almon), 5–6.
4. Quoted in Beaglehole, J.C., ed., 1969, *The Journals of Captain James Cook: The Voyage of* Resolution *and* Adventure, *1772–1775*, xxx.
5. Furneaux, Rupert, 1960, *Tobias Furneaux: Navigator* (London, Cassell), 3–7, 89. Tobias Furneaux's aunt, Anne Furneaux, had married a Samuel Wallis of a previous generation; Jack Rowe was first cousin to Tobias Furneaux's sister-in-law.
6. Elliott in Holmes, Christine, ed., 1984, *Captain Cook's Second Voyage: The Journals of Lieutenants Elliott and Pickersgill* (London, Caliban Books), 7–8.
7. Forster, Johann, ed. Michael Hoare, 1982, *The* Resolution *Journal of Johann Reinhold Forster 1772–1775, Volumes I–IV* (Cambridge, for the Hakluyt Society), II: 233.

For manuscript accounts of Cook's second voyage, see British Museum: Cook's Second Voyage Fragments, Add Ms 27889; South Sea Voyages Drawings and Prints, Add Ms 23920; Charts of Cook's Voyages, Add Ms 31360; Logbook of *Resolution*, Add Ms 27887; Logbook of *Resolution*, Add Ms 27956; James Cook's holograph *Resolution* Logbook, Add Ms 27886; Cook's draft *Resolution* Journal, Add Ms 27888; Charles Clerke's *Resolution* Logbook, Vol. I Add Ms 8951, Vol. II Add Ms 8952, Vol III. Add Ms 8953; Charts, Add Ms 31360; William Hodges's Views, Add Ms 15743; John Elliott's *Resolution* Memoirs, Add Ms 42714; Charts, Add Ms 15500; Cook's *Resolution* Journal, Eg Ms 2178; James Cook's *Resolution* Journal, Eg Ms 2177A and B. Public Record Office: James Cook's *Resolution* Journal (copy), Adm 55/108; James Cook's *Resolution* Letters, Adm 1/1610; Robert Cooper's *Resolution* Journal, Adm 55/104; Robert Cooper's *Resolution* Log, Adm 55/109; Charles Clerke's *Resolution* Log, Adm 55/103; Richard Pickersgill's *Resolution* Log, Adm 51/4553/5, /6; Joshua Gilbert's *Resolution* Log, Adm 55/107; Isaac Smith's *Resolution* Log, Adm 55/105; John Burr's *Resolution* Log, Adm 55/106; Thomas Willis's *Resolution* Journal, Adm 51/4554/199, /200, /201, /202; William Harvey's *Resolution* Journal, Adm 51/4553/185, /186, /187; Joseph Price's *Resolution* Log, Adm 51/4556/189; Joseph Price's *Resolution* Journal, Adm 51/4556/190; Anon. *Resolution* Log, Adm 51/4555/218; John Elliott's *Resolution* Log, Adm 51/4556/208; Alexander Hood's *Resolution* Log, Adm 51/4554/182, /183; Charles Loggie's *Resolution* Journal, Adm 51/4554/207; James Maxwell's *Resolution* Log, Adm 51/4555/206; Bowles Mitchel's *Resolution* Log, Adm 51/4555/194, /195; Tobias Furneaux's *Adventure* Log, Adm 55/1; Tobias Furneaux's Captain's Letters, Adm 1/1789; Arthur Kempe's *Adventure* Log, Adm 51/4520/1, /2, /3; James Burney's *Adventure* Journal, Adm 51/4523/2, /5, /6; Constable Love's *Adventure* Log, Adm 514520/7, /8; Henry Lightfoot's *Adventure* Log, Adm 51/4523/5; Anon. *Adventure* Journal, Adm 51/4524/17; Robert Browne's *Adventure* Journal, Adm 51/4521/9, /10; Thomas Dyke's *Adventure* Log, Adm 51/4521/12; John Falconer's *Adventure* Log, Adm 51/4524/1; William Hawkey's *Adventure* Log, Adm 51/4521/11; Richard Hergest's *Adventure* Journal, Adm 51/4522/13; John Wilby's *Adventure* Journal, Adm 51/4522/14. National Maritime Museum: James Cook's Journal copy; Richard Pickersgill's *Resolution* Journal, JOD/56. Royal Greenwich Observatory: William Wales's *Resolution* Logbook. National Library of Australia: letter to Cook from Sir Philip Stephens, 20 July 1776, Ms 688. Mitchell Library, Sydney: James Cook Log Leaves, Safe PH 17/2; Cook holograph fragments, Safe PH 17/2, 4, 12; William Wales Safe PH 18/4. Alexander Turnbull Library: Sandwich Family papers, WTU Ms Papers 841.

For published accounts see Forster, George, eds Nicholas Thomas and Oliver Berghof, 2000, I & II, *A Voyage Round the World* (Honolulu, University of Hawai'i Press); Forster, Johann, eds Nicholas Thomas, Harriet Guest and Michael Dettelbach, 1996, *Observations Made During a Voyage Round the World* (Honolulu, University of Hawai'i Press).

8. Cook in Beaglehole, ed., 1969, 175.

9. Ibid., 172.

10. Forster, George in Thomas and Berghof, eds, 2000, I: 127–28.

11. Sparrman, Anders in Owen Rutter, ed., 1953, *A Voyage Round the World with Captain James Cook in HMS* Resolution (London, Robert Hale Limited), 51.

12. Forster, George in Thomas and Berghof, eds, 2000, I: 148.

13. Ibid., 148–49.

14. Ibid., 150–51.

15. Marra, John, 1775, *Journal of the* Resolution's *Voyage in 1772, 1773, 1774, and 1775 on Discovery to the Southern Hemisphere* (London, F. Newbery), 45.

16. Forster, Johann, in Thomas, Guest and Dettelbach, eds, 1996, 244.

17. Henry, 1928, 236.

18. Wales in Beaglehole, ed., 1969, II: 796–97.

19. See Tcherkézoff, 2004, 116–19 for a discussion of this Polynesian custom.

20. Forster, George in Thomas and Berghof, eds, 2000, I: 165.

21. Ibid., 168.

22. Cook in Beaglehole, ed., 1969, 231.

23. Forster, Johann in Hoare, ed., 1982, II: 336 fn.

24. Pickersgill in Holmes, ed., 1984, 81.

25. Ibid., 81.

26. Sparrman in Rutter, ed., 1953, 62.

27. Forster, George in Thomas and Berghof, eds, 2000, I: 176.

28. Marra, 1775, 43.

29. Forster, George in Thomas and Berghof, eds, 2000, I: 176.

30. Cook in Beaglehole, ed., 1969, 206.

31. Marau, quoted in Handy, 1930, 41–42.

32. Forster, George in Thomas and Berghof, eds, 2000, I: 184–85.

33. Elliott in Holmes, ed., 1984, 31.

34. Jenny Newell tells me that one of these dancing belts with tassels is held in the British Museum (LMS.85).

35. Ellis, 1829, I: 76.

36. Elliott in Holmes, ed., 1984, 19.

CHAPTER 13: HITIHITI'S ODYSSEY

1. Ellis, 1829, I: 323, 336.

2. Cook in Beaglehole, ed., 1969, 220.

3. Ibid., 220.

4. Cook in Beaglehole, ed., 1969, 428 fn.

5. Forster, George in Thomas and Berghof, eds, 2000, I: 211. In his book on Huahine, Saura makes it plain that Omai's real name was Ma'i (Saura, 2005, 102).

6. Saura has identified 'Boba' as Tapoa, who married 'Aimata, the daughter of Pa Tane, Puni's brother (Saura, Bruno, *Huahine aux Temps Anciens* (Pape'ete, Cahiers du Patrimoine), 2005, fn. 102).

7. Forster, Johann in Thomas, Guest and Dettelbach, eds, 1996, 285; see Oliver, 1974, II: 931 for the translations.

8. See Appendix II.

9. See Monchoisy [pseud. d'Antoine Mativet], 1888, *La Nouvelle Cythère* (Paris, G. Charpentier et Cie), 211–13 for a rare account of the *huapipi* ceremony (which he calls *marama ra pori*), based on a lost manuscript from John Orsmond; which makes it plain that the ritual was associated with the initiation of new members of the society. See also Babadzan, 1993, 262–64.

10. Burney, James in Beverley Hooper, ed., 1975, *With Captain James Cook in the Antarctic and Pacific: The Private Journal of James Burney, Second Lieutenant of the Adventure on Cook's Second Voyage 1772–1773* (Canberra, National Library of Australia), 78.

11. Ibid., 226.

12. Cook in Beaglehole, ed., 1969, 236.

13. Sparrman in Rutter, ed., 1953, 92.

14. Forster, George in Thomas and Berghof, eds, 2000, I: 242.

15. Ibid., 249.

16. Forster, Johann in Hoare, ed., 1982, III: 405.

17. Cook in Beaglehole, ed., 1969, 286.

18. Sparrman in Rutter, ed., 1953, 111. Stalks of coconut leaves were used for counting and as mnemonic devices in the Society Islands (Ellis, 1829, I: 91).

19. Cook in Beaglehole, ed., 1969, 322.

20. Forster, George in Thomas and Berghof, eds, 2000, I: 315.

21. Ibid., 324

22. Ibid., 330.

23. My thanks to Bruno Saura for this term.

24. '*Qalis aut Nireus fuit, aut acqosâ, Raptus ab Idâ*' – 'Like Nireus, who was carried off from many-fountained Ida' (Horace, *Odes*, 3.20.15f).

25. See Appendix II.

CHAPTER 14: THE RED FEATHERS OF 'ORO

1. Forster, George in Thomas and Berghof, eds, 2000, I: 351.

2. Ibid., 351.

3. Ibid., 352.

4. Cook in Beaglehole, ed., 1969, 384.

5. After visiting this fleet, Johann Forster also went through a lengthy calculation to establish the likely population of Tahiti; and Cook's figure may have been based on Forster's estimate. According to Forster, because Atehuru, the largest district in Tahiti, could muster 159 war canoes with 70 smaller vessels; and 'Titaha' [Teataha], the smallest, could muster 44 war canoes with 20 or 30 smaller craft, the whole of northern Tahiti (or Te Porionu'u), which (according to what he had been told) had 24 districts at the time, could at the very least muster 1200 war canoes and 600 smaller canoes. Given an average (minimum) crew of 20 men on each war canoe (although some carried as many as 144 men), this gave a total of 24,000 men to crew the war canoes from northern Tahiti; while each small canoe had an average of 5 men on board, bringing the overall total to 27,000 men in the fleet for northern Tahiti. If each man had a wife and child, this came to 81,000 people. Doubling this figure for old men and women and additional children (given that some men had 8 children or more), he estimated that, in 1774, northern Tahiti had a population of about 160,000 people; while southern Tahiti, with its 20 districts, had about half that number, bringing the total population of the island to 240,000. (Forster, Johann, in Thomas, Guest and Dettelbach, eds, 2006, 148–49.) The difficulty with this calculation is that in fact there were many fewer districts in Tahiti, suggesting that the estimates were probably too high.

6. Probably the *fau* or war helmet given by Forster to the Ashmolean, which is now held in the Pitt-Rivers Museum in Oxford (1886.1.1637.1) – my thanks to Jenny Newell for this information.

7. Wales in Beaglehole, ed., 1969, 839.

8. Ibid., 836.

9. Forster, George in Thomas and Berghof, eds, 2000, I: 367.

10. Forster, Johann in Thomas, Guest and Dettelbach, eds, 2006, 149–50.

11. Ibid., 373.

12. Cook in Beaglehole, ed., 1969, 395.

13. Forster, George in Thomas and Berghof, eds, 2000, I: 376.

14. Cook in Beaglehole, ed., 1969, 398.

15. Ibid., 382.

16. Forster, Johann in Hoare, ed., 1982, III: 517.

17. Sparrman in Rutter, ed., 1953, 128.

18. Ibid.

19. Forster, George in Thomas and Berghof, eds, 2000, I: 389.

20. Forster, Johann in Thomas, Guest and Dettelbach, eds, 1996, 285. See also Oliver, 1974, I: 334–36.

21. Forster, Johann in Hoare, ed., 1982, III: 523.

22. Compare this with Johann Forster's description of the conditions on board a European ship in the tropics, where a putrid stench quickly spread below decks, impregnating the crew's hair and garments, especially for those who rarely or never washed or changed their clothing. (Forster, Johann in Thomas, Guest and Dettelbach, eds, 1996, 263–64.)

23. 'Nor are they unlike our grandees, who, from mere opulence, plunge into luxury and sensuality, and pursue the gratification of their brutish appetites; they like them roam over the fertile plains of their isle, in quest of youth and beauty, and employ all the arts and guiles known in civilized countries, in order to debauch the unwary young females.' (Forster, Johann in Thomas, Guest and Dettelbach, eds, 1996, 257.)

24. Forster, Johann in Thomas, Guest and Dettelbach, eds, 1996, 255.

25. Forster, George in Thomas and Berghof, eds, 2000, I: 402.

CHAPTER 15: THREE TAHITIANS IN LIMA

1. Green, R.C., 2005, 'Sweet Potato Transfers', in eds Chris Ballard, Paula Brown, R. Michael Bourke and Tracey Harwood, The Sweet Potato in Oceania: A Reappraisal (Pittsburgh, University of Pittsburgh Press), 60.

2. Storey, Alice, Ramirez, José Miguel, Quiroz, Daniel, Burley, David V., Addison, David J., Walter, Richard, Anderson, Atholl J., Hunt, Terry L., Athens, Stephen, Huynen, Leon and Matioso-Smith, Elizabeth, 2007, 'Radiocarbon and DNA evidence for a pre-Columbian introduction of Polynesian chickens', Proceedings of the National Academy of Sciences, online at www.pnas.orga/cgi/content/full/0703393104/DCI.

3. For life in Lima and Peru during this period, see Campbell, Leon G., 1972, 'A Colonial Establishment: Creole Domination of the Audencia of Lima during the Late Eighteenth Century', The Hispanic American Historical Review 52/1, 1–25; Campbell, Leon G., 1975, 'The Changing Racial and Administrative Structure of the Peruvian Military under the Later Bourbons', The Americas 32/1, 117–33; Campbell, Leon G., 1976, 'The Army of Peru and the Tupac Amaru Revolt, 1780–1783', The Hispanic American Historical Review 56/1, 31–57; Descola, Jean, 1968, Daily Life in Colonial Peru (London, George Allen and Unwin Ltd); Diggs, Irene, 1953, 'Colour in Colonial Spanish America', The Journal of Negro History 38/4, 403–27; Dobyns, Henry E. and Doughty, Paul L., 1976, Peru: A Cultural History (New York, Oxford University Press); Fisher, John, 1975, 'Silver Production in the Viceroyalty of Peru, 1776–1824', The Hispanic American Historical Review 55/1, 25–43; Hampe-Martinez, Teodoro, 1996, 'Recent works on the Inquisition and Peruvian Colonial Society 1570–1820', Latin American Research Review 31/2, 43–65; Mills, Kenneth, Idolatry and its Enemies: Colonial Andean Religion and Extirpation, 1640–1750 (Princeton, New Jersey, Princeton University Press); Rowe, John Howland, 1957, 'The Incas under Spanish Colonial Institutions', The Hispanic American Historical Review 37/2, 155–99; Staving, Ward, 1999, The World of Tupac Amaru: Conflict, Community and Identity in Colonial Peru (Lincoln, University of Nebraska Press).

4. Quoted in Descola, 1968, 52.

5. Amat y Junient, Manuel de, in Vicente Rodríguez Casado and Florentino Perez Embid, eds, 1947, Memoria de Gobierno (Sevilla, Publicationes de la Escuela de Estudios Hispano – Americanos de Sevilla), 193, trans. Gwyn Fox.

6. Radiguet, Max, 1859, Souvenirs de l'Amérique espagnole (Paris, Michel Levy Frères).

7. Descola, 1968, 109.

8. For accounts of La Perricholi, see Descola, 1968, 247–60; and Villegas, Bertrand, 1999, La Perricholi: A Queen for Lima (Buenos Aires, Ed. Sudamericana), trans. Gwyn Fox.

9. Amat in Casado and Embid, eds, 1947, trans. Gwyn Fox.

10. According to Mellén in his introduction to Rodríguez, Máximo, 1992, Españoles en Tahiti (Madrid, Historia 16), their godfathers at their baptism were José de Herrera, rector of the parish, and Don Antonio Amat y Rocaberti, lieutenant colonel of the fort of Callao; while at

their confirmation by the Archbishop of Lima, Diego Antonio Paradas, their sponsors were Don Balerio Gasols, captain of the Viceroy's guard, and the rector of the cathedral, Don José Aramburu y Morales.

11. Don Juan de Lángara y Huarte to the Secretary of State for the Navy, 13 November 1773, in Corney, ed., II: 360–63.

12. Amat's questions are given in Corney, ed., 1913, II: 21–28.

13. The manuscript records for the second Spanish voyage to Tahiti are as follows: Manuel de Amat, 'Instrucción que se le da al Capitán . . .', 1774, AGI Sevilla, Lima 1035; Joseph de Garmendia, 'Instrucción', 30 Decembre 1773, AGI Sevilla, Lima 1035; Boenechea, Domingo and Tomás Gayangos, 'Diario de la navegación que . . .' (1775), AGI Sevilla, Lima 1035, Ms copy in RAHM; Tomás Gayangos, 'Diario de la Navegación que para regresar desde la Isla de Amat . . .', Tomás Gayangos, letters re. Fray Gerónimo Clota and Fray Narciso Gonzalez, AGI Sevilla, Lima 1035; Andía y Varela, José, 'Relación del viaje . . .' (1774–75), MNM Ms 208, AGI Ms copy, Ms 208, fs. 2–100, and Ms 19, fs. 137–86; Rodríguez, Máximo, 'Relación diaria, que hizo el intérprete . . .', 1774–76, original in Royal Geographical Society, London, copy in MNM 705; Clota and Gonzalez letters and account at AGI Sevilla, Lima 1035, originals in BRAH; Pantoja y Arriaga, Juan, *Extracto del viaje* . . . (1775), BUS (Ms 330/117), copy in MNM Ms 2396, doc. 28, 1–74, trans. by Gwyn Fox; Pantoja y Arriaga, Juan, ed. Francisco Mellén Blanco, 1992, *Un diario inédito sobre la presencia española en Tahiti (1774–1775)* (Madrid, Revisita Española del Pacifico), trans. Gwyn Fox; Carta de Blas Barreda con Descripción de las islas del Océano Pacífico . . ., Ms copy in MNM Ms 476, fs. 83–102, trans. Gwyn Fox; *Noticia de algunas costumbres de los naturals de las neuvas isles o tierras de Quiros*, 1775, MNM Ms 476. It appears that the journals on this voyage were kept irregularly, because they often give different dates for the same events, making the task of reconstruction quite difficult in places.

14. If Hinoiatua was sixteen years old in 1774, he was born in 1758, the same year of birth that Oliver estimates for Tu's younger brother Ari'ipaea. (Oliver, 1974, III: 1184.) At one point, too, the Spaniards refer to Hinoi as Tu's half-brother, which strengthens the identification, because according to Marau in Adams (Adams, 1901, 113), Ari'ipaea was Tu's younger brother by Teu's second marriage (although the name of his mother is not given in this genealogy). The genealogical identification is made more difficult by the fact that Teu and Tetupaia had a daughter (Tu's sister) called Ari'ipaea-vahine (see for instance Saura, 2003, 225). I found no genealogies that refer to a half-brother or brother of Tu's named Hinoi, however. Ari'ipaea was later a leading *'arioi* priest and much given to the use of *'ava* (Oliver, 1974, I: 81–82). He was also known as Te-ari'i-fa'atau and Aroro (Oliver, 1974, III: 1184, 1190; Bligh, 1792, quoted in Oliver, 1974, II: 1041). The Spaniards refer throughout to Tu's two younger brothers, who are invariably identified elsewhere as Ari'ipaea and Vaetua.

15. Thomson, Rev. Richard, c. 1840, Salmond transcript, p. 54.

16. Henry, 1928, 198–99.

17. Ibid., 377.

CHAPTER 16: BOENECHEA'S BURIAL

1. Henry, 1928, 86–87.

2. Y Arriaga, Juan Pantoja in ed. Francisco Mellén Blanco, *Un diario inédito sobre la presencia española en Tahiti (1774–1775)*, trans. Gwyn Fox, 55.

3. Gayangos in Corney, ed. and trans., 1913, II: 128.

4. Oliver, 1974, I: 259–64. See also Handy, 1930, 49–50.

5. Y Varela in Corney, ed. and trans., 1913, II: 289.

6. Ibid., II: 258.

7. See Moerenhout in Borden, ed., 1983, 305–6 for a detailed description of the costume worn by the various warriors; also Ellis, 1829, I: 298–301.

8. Gayangos in Corney, ed. and trans., 1913, II: 138.

9. Y Varela in ibid., 260.

10. Rodríguez in ibid., III: 31.

11. Gayangos in ibid., II: 145.

12. Corney in ibid., II, footnote p. 163, where he says that the name is given variously in y Varela's journal as 'Mabarua', 'Mavarua' and 'Matarua', as well as the printed version 'Barbarua'. As mentioned earlier (Chapter 2, fn. 27), Driessen has identified this man with Mau'arua, the exiled paramount chief of Ra'iatea who had joined Tupaia at Papara.

13. Rodríguez in ibid., III: 35–36.

14. It is interesting that although Arriaga stated firmly that Vehiatua and Tu had gone to Vaiaotea, Gayangos says that they were both present on this occasion; while Máximo remarked that Tu was indisposed. It seems that Gayangos was eager to give as much authority as possible to the ceremony that acknowledged King Carlos III as the King of Tahiti; although as Corney notes, this declaration (unlike the one concluded with the chiefs in Easter Island) was not signed by any of the Tahitian leaders.

15. Thomson, c. 1840, Salmond transcript, 36.

16. Gayangos in Corney, ed. and trans., 1913, II: 173. Mau'arua's blood relationship with Tu was through Tetupaia, Tu's mother and the eldest child of Tamatoa III.

17. The Padres in ibid., II: 213–14.

18. Rodríguez in ibid., III: 43.

19. The Padres in ibid., II: 215.

20. Ibid., 261.

21. Ibid., 216–17.

22. Thomson, c. 1840, Salmond transcript, 37. Although the missionary Thomson translates *te ari'i no te maui* as 'the king of poison', as Bruno Saura points out, *maui* does not mean 'poison' in Tahitian.

23. Corney, ed. and trans., 1913, III: 48.

24. My thanks to Bruno Saura for this clarification.

25. See Salmond, Anne, in di Piazza and Pearthree, 2008.

26. Thanks to Bruno Saura for this translation.

27. This wind compass was also described by Rey-Lescure in 1957 in 'La Bousooule des Navigateurs Polynésiens', *Bulletin de la Société d'Études Océaniennes* X, 8, 720–23.

28. Ibid., II: 284–87.

29. Ibid., II: 287.

30. Amat, Manuel de, quoted in Vicente Rodríguez Casado and Florentino Pérez Embid, eds, 1947, *Manuel de Amat y Junient, Viceroy of Peru 1761–76, Memoria de Gobierno* (Sevilla, Escuela de Estudios Hispano-Americanos de Sevilla), trans. Gwyn Fox.

CHAPTER 17: MATIMO AND THE FRIARS

1. Corney, ed. and trans., 1913, III: 55.

2. Ibid., 60.

3. Tyerman and Bennet, 1831, I: 122.

4. Moerenhout in Borden, ed., 1983, I: 273.

5. Corney, ed. and trans., 1913, III: 69.

6. Ibid., 75.

7. The Padres in ibid., II: 323–24.

8. Rodríguez in ibid., III: 105.

9. Henry, 1928, 152–53.

10. See Oliver, 1974, I: 434–37.

11. The Padres in Corney, ed. and trans., 1913, II: 327.

12. Rodríguez, in ibid., III: 148.

13. Ibid., 148–49.

14. Ibid., 149. José Garanger has excavated a *marae* on this island, where parts of the *parae* or Chief Mourner's costume were discovered (Garanger, José, 1980, 'Prospections archéologiques de l'îlot Fenuaino et des vallées Airurua et Vaiote à Tahiti', *Journal de la Société des Océanistes* 66–67, 77–104).

15. Moerenhout in Borden, ed., 1983, 262.

16. Corney, ed. and trans., 1913, II: 332.

17. Moerenhout in Borden, ed., 1983, 258–59.

18. Henry, 1928, 164–65; see also Babadzan, 1993, 101–9 for a discussion of the *pa'iatua* ritual.

19. Henry, 1928, 158–59.

20. Rodríguez in Corney, ed. and trans., 1913, III: 175.

21. The Padres in ibid., II: 335.

22. Ibid., 336.

23. Ibid., 337.

24. Ellis, 1829, I: 349–50.

25. According to Ellis, at the funeral of her child a distraught mother might use a small cane with five or six shark's teeth fixed on opposite sides, or a short rod with two or three rows of shark's teeth fixed firmly in the wood. (Ellis, 1829, I: 407–8.)

26. Moerenhout in Borden, ed., 1983, 276–77. Although Babadzan has argued that this ritual combat involving neighbouring districts expressed the right of the junior and maternal lines of the high chiefs to veto the succession of a new *ari'i rahi* (Babadzan, 1993, 191–217), there is no particular evidence to support this in these early accounts.

27. Lescure, 1956, 538.

28. According to the missionary William Ellis, an eclipse of the moon was an evil omen, because the Tahitians supposed the planet was *natua* or being destroyed by some evil spirit. They went to the *marae* and prayed for its release; some imagined that the moon was being swallowed by the god. (Ellis, 1829, I: 331–32.) See also Davies in the Douglas Oliver Missionary Card Index, card 255: 'They suppose that an eclipse is a prodigy that portends war, the Death of a Chief or some such thing. They say the moon in the time of Eclipse is pressed and squeezed by some god and in danger of being devoured.'

29. De Lángara in Corney, ed. and trans., 1913, II: 381.

30. For accounts of this sacred *'umete*, see Corney, Bolton Glanvill, 1920, 'An Historic Stone Bowl', *Man* 20, 106–9; Blanco, Francisco Mellén, 2000, 'El "umete" de piedra del marae Taputapuatea de Puna'aui'a (Tahiti)', *Revista Española del Pacífico*, Publicaciones periódicas, 11.

CHAPTER 18: MA'I ON ICE SKATES

1. Ma'i and his adventures have inspired a number of works, the most authoritative of which is McCormick, E.H., 1977, *Omai: Pacific Envoy* (Auckland, Auckland University Press, Oxford University Press). See also Clark, Thomas Blake, 1969, *Omai: First Polynesian Ambassador to England* (Honolulu, University of Hawai'i Press); Alexander, Michael, 1977, *Omai: 'Noble Savage'*(London, Collins & Harvill Press); Anon., 2001, *Cook & Omai: The Cult of the South Seas* (Canberra, National Library of Australia in association with the Humanities Research Centre, Australian National University); Connaughton, Richard, 2005, *Omai: The Prince Who Never Was* (London, Timewell Press Ltd).

2. Bayly, William in Beaglehole, ed., 1969, fn. 281.

3. Burney in Hooper, Beverley, ed., 1975, *With Captain James Cook in the Antarctic and Pacific: The private journal of James Burney, Second Lieutenant of the* Adventure *on Cook's Second Voyage 1772–1773* (Canberra, National Library of Australia), 87.

4. Burney in Hooper, ed., 1975, 88.

5. Ibid., 89.

6. Ibid., 90.

7. Marra, 1775, 96.

8. Browne in Adm 51/4521/10: 48.

9. Notebook of the Revd J.E. Gambier, 11 August 1774, Kent Archives Office, Maidstone.

10. Burney, Fanny in Troide, Lars E., ed., 1990, *The Early Journals and Letters of Fanny Burney Vols. I and II* (Oxford, Clarendon Press), II: 41.

11. Hill, G.B., ed., 1934–50, *Boswell's Life of Johnson, Vols. I–VI* (Oxford, Clarendon Press), II: 247–48.

12. See for instance Anonymous, 1774, *An Epistle from Oberea, Queen of Otaheite, to Joseph Banks, Esq.* (London).

13. Anonymous, 1774, *An Epistle from Mr. Banks, Voyager, Monster-hunter and Amoroso, to Oberea, Queen of Otaheite* (London); attributed to John Scott-Waring. This was followed by 1774, *A Second Letter from Oberea, Queen of Otaheite, to Joseph Banks, Esq. Translated from the original, brought over by His Excellency Otaiparoo, Envoy Extraordinary and Plenipotentiary from the Queen of Otaheite, to the Court of Great Britain* (London); and 1774, *An Epistle (moral and philosophical) from an officer at Otaheite. To the Lady Gr*ˢ**ⁿ*ʳ. With Notes, Critical and Historical* (London); attributed to John Courtnay.

14. Banks, Joseph, 1773, 'Thoughts on the manners of Otaheite', in Beaglehole, ed., 1962, II: 330–34.

15. Cradock, J., 1828, *Literary and Miscellaneous Memoirs, Vols I–IV* (London, Nichols), I: 127–28.

16. Banks, Sarah Sophia, 'Memorandums', in Banks Papers, National Library of Australia, Canberra.

17. Many thanks to Jenny Newell for this information.

18. Ibid., 19–20.

19. Fanny Burney in Troide, ed., 1990, 61.

20. For an intriguing account of this controversy, see Fullagar, Kate, 'Reynolds' New Masterpiece: From Experiment in Savagery to Eighteenth Century Icon', in John Brewer, ed. (in press), *The Guises of Reason: Taste and Aesthetics 1650–1850* (New Haven, Yale University Press).

21. Anon., 1775, *An Historic Epistle, from Omiah to the Queen of Otaheite, Being his remarks on the English nation* (London).

22. Lord Sandwich to Banks, 29 December 1774, British Museum (Natural History).

23. During his career in London the Chevalier d'Eon was universally thought to be a woman who dressed and lived as a man. A fervent admirer of Jean-Jacques Rousseau, he was famous as a military hero, author and diplomat who had negotiated the Treaty of Paris. After his death it was discovered that in fact he was a man. (Kates, Gary, 1995, 'The Transgendered World of the Chevalier / Chevalière d'Eon', *The Journal of Modern History* 67/3, 558–94.)

24. Solander, Daniel in eds Edward Duyker and Per Tingbrand, 1995, *Daniel Solander, Collected Correspondence 1753–1782* (Melbourne, University of Melbourne Press), 347.

25. Cook in Beaglehole, ed., 1969, 682.

26. Elliott in Holmes, ed., 1984, 44.

27. Cook to Captain John Walker, 19 August 1774, in Beaglehole, ed., 1969, 960.

28. Coleman, George, 1830, *Random Records, Vols. I–III* (London), I: 152–56.

29. Sharp, Glanvill, 1786, *An English Alphabet* (London), 226–27.

30. Fanny Burney in Troide, ed., 1990, 194.

31. Boswell, James in ed. Charles Ryskamp, 1963, *Boswell: The Ominous Years, 1774–1776* (London, William Heinemann Ltd), 308–9.

32. Boswell, James, 1992, *The Life of Samuel Johnson* (New York, Alfred A. Knopf), 634.

33. Boswell in ibid., 659.

34. Boswell, quoted in Alexander, 1977, 107–8.

35. Cook, quoted by Johann Forster, in McCormick, 1977, 178.

36. Trevenen, James, eds Christopher Lloyd and R.C. Anderson, 1959, *A Memoir of James Trevenen* (London, Spottiswoode, Ballantyne and Co. Ltd, printed for the Naval Records Society), 36.

37. David Samwell to Matthew Gregson, 25 March 1776, in Cook in Beaglehole, ed., 1967, III: lxxxv.

38. 1776, *Omiah's Farewell, inscribed to the ladies of London* (London). On the same theme, see also 1776, *Seventeen hundred and seventy-seven, or a picture of the manners and customs of the age. In a poetical epistle from a lady of quality* (London); Fitzgerald, the Reverend Gerald, 1779, *The Injured Islanders: or, The Influence of Art upon the Happiness of Nature* (London); Perry, James, 1779, *Mimosa: or the Sensitive Plant* (London), dedicated to Banks and addressed to the Duchess

of Queensberry; and 1782, *A Letter from Omai to the Right Honourable the Earl of* ********, *Late --- Lord of the ---*., 'Translated from the Ulaietean tongue' (London).

CHAPTER 19: A BARE-CHESTED CAPTAIN

1. Samwell, David to Matthew Gregson, 22 October 1776, quoted in Beaglehole, J.C., 1967, *The Journals of Captain James Cook on His Voyages of Discovery*, Volume III, 2 parts (Cambridge, for the Hakluyt Society), ii: 1515.
2. Ibid., 1520.

For manuscript records of Cook's third Pacific voyage, see British Museum: James Cook's *Resolution* Journal, Egerton Ms 2177A, B, 2178–2179; James Burney's *Discovery* Journal, Add Ms 8955; John Webber's Drawings, Add Ms 15513; John Webber's Drawings, Add Ms 17277; George Gilbert's *Discovery* Journal, Add Ms 38530; David Samwell's *Discovery* Journal, Egerton Ms 2591; Thomas Edgar's *Discovery* Journal, Add Ms 37528; John Law's *Discovery* Journal, Add Ms 37327; Public Record Office: James Cook's *Resolution* Journal (copy), Adm 55/111; Charles Clerke's *Discovery* Log, Adm 55/22, /23; Charles Clerke's Log and Observations, Adm 51/4561/217; Adm 55/124; John Gore's *Resolution* Log, Adm 55/120, Adm 51/4532/49; James King's *Resolution* Log, Adm 55/116, Adm 55/122; James Burney's *Discovery* Journal, Adm 51/4528/45; John Williamson's *Resolution* Log, Adm 55/117; John Rickman's *Discovery* Log, Adm 51/4529/46; Thomas Edgar's *Discovery* Log, Adm 55/21, Adm 55/24; George Gilbert's *Resolution* Log, Adm 51/4559/213; William Lanyon's *Resolution* Log, Adm 51/4558/196–198; William Harvey's *Resolution* Log, Adm 55/110; William Charlton's *Resolution* Journal, Adm 51/4557/191–193; John Martin's *Discovery* Journal, Adm 51/4531/47; George Gilbert's *Resolution* Journal, Adm 51/4559/213–215; Mathew Paul's *Resolution* Log, Adm 51/4560/209; Nathaniel Portlock's *Discovery* Log, Adm 51/4531/67–69, Adm 51/4532/70; Edward Riou's *Discovery* Log, Adm 51/4529/41–44; William Shuttleworth's *Resolution* Journal, Adm 51/4561/210–211, Adm 51/4531/48; William Taylor's *Resolution* Log, Adm 51/4561/216; John Watts' *Resolution* Log, Adm 51/4559/212; Anonymous, Logs, Adm 51/4528/64; Adm 51/4530/65–66; 71–72; Adm 51/4561/220; Adm 51/4561/221; Adm 55/114, /123; William Bayly's *Discovery* Log and Journal, Adm 55/20; William Anderson's *Resolution* Journal, Adm 51/4560/203–204. Dixson Library, Library of New South Wales: James King's *Resolution* Log Ms; Henry Roberts' *Resolution* Log, Ms Q/51-51; William Griffin's Narrative; J. Dimsdell, Account of the Death and Remains of Capt. Cook – at Owhyhee recd from Joshua Lee Dimsdell Quarter Master of the Gunjara, Capt. James Barber, 1801, Ms Q 154; Mitchell Library: James Burney's *Discovery* Journal; Anonymous, 1781, Copy of Letter to Mrs Strachan of Spithead, 23 January 1781 (Safe 1/67); National Library of Australia: Alexander Home's *Discovery* notes and typescript (Ms 690); Anonymous, Account of the Death of Cook, 9–22 February 1779, by an Eyewitness; Alexander Turnbull Library: William Bayly's *Discovery* Journal; James Trevenen's *Resolution* notes.

For published accounts of Cook's last voyage see Cook in Beaglehole, ed., 1967; Ellis, William, 1782, *An Authentic Narrative of a Voyage performed by Captain Cook and Captain Clerke in His Majesty's Ships Resolution and Discovery, during the Years 1776, 1777, 1778, 1779, and 1780*, Vols. I and II (London, G. Robinson); Gilbert, George in Christine Holmes, ed., 1982, *Captain Cook's Final Voyage: The Journal of Midshipman George Gilbert* (Partridge Green, Sussex, Caliban Books); Home, George, 1838, *Memoirs of an Aristocrat* (London, Whittaker & Co.); Marra, John, 1775, *Journal of the Resolution's Voyage in 1771–1775* (Amsterdam, Biblitheca Australiana #15); Rickman, John, 1781 (1967 facsimile), *Journal of Captain Cook's Last Voyage to the Pacific Ocean* (Amsterdam, Biblitheca Australiana #16); Trevenen, James in Christopher Lloyd and R.C. Anderson, eds, 1959, *A Memoir of James Trevenen* (London, Navy Records Society); Zimmerman, Henry in F.W. Howay, ed., 1929, *Zimmerman's Captain Cook* (Toronto, The Ryerson Press).

3. Gore to Banks, 27 November 1776, in Beaglehole, ed., 1967, ii: 1522.
4. Cook in Beaglehole, ed., 1967, i: 59.
5. Samwell in ibid., ii: 995.
6. Burney quoted in ibid., i: 66.

7. Cook in ibid., i: 68.

8. Cook in ibid., i: 69.

9. King in ibid., i: 77 fn.

10. Gill, Reverend William Wyatt, 1880, *Historical Sketches of Savage Life in Polynesia* (Wellington, George Didsbury, Government Printer), 187.

11. Jukka Sikkala, pers. comm., 1999.

12. Williams, 1838, 104.

13. Burney in Adm 51/4528/45, 193.

14. King in Beaglehole, ed., 1967, ii: 1361–62.

15. Samwell in Beaglehole, ed., 1967, ii: 1021–22.

16. Williamson quoted in Beaglehole, ed., 1967, i: 151 fn.

CHAPTER 20: TUTE'S PORTRAIT

1. Cook in Beaglehole, ed., 1967, i: 186.

2. Ibid., 186.

3. Samwell in ibid., ii: 1379.

4. Gilbert in Holmes, ed., 1982, 42.

5. Cook in Beaglehole, ed., 1967, i: 187.

6. Bayly in ibid., i: fn. 182.

7. Samwell in ibid., ii: 1053.

8. King in ibid., ii: 1370.

9. Samwell in ibid., ii: 1055.

10. Samwell in Beaglehole, ed., 1967, ii: 1056.

11. Anderson in ibid., ii: 975.

12. Anderson in ibid., ii: 973–74.

13. Ibid., 224.

14. Williamson, Adm 55/117, 12 August 1777.

15. King in Beaglehole, ed., 1967, ii: 1373.

16. Cook in Beaglehole, ed., 1967, i: 193.

17. Rickman, 1781, *Journal of Captain Cook's Last Voyage to the Pacific Ocean on* Discovery (London, E. Newbury), 131–33.

18. Samwell in Beaglehole, ed., 1967, ii: 1059.

19. Rickman, 1781, 139.

20. Mahau was known variously as Teri'i-tapunui and Ari'i-tapunui; and he had no children. He married Auo, Tu's youngest sister, and was succeeded by his younger brother Ta'aroa-ari'i, who also had no male children. (Vancouver quoted by Oliver, 1974, III: 1206.)

21. Samwell in Beaglehole, ed., 1967, ii: 978.

22. The site of 'Utu-'ai-mahurau *marae* is shown on Map 2, facing xxvi in Davies, John in C.W. Newbury, ed., 1961, *The History of the Tahitian Mission 1799–1830* (Cambridge, for the Hakluyt Society). According to Henry (Henry, 1928, 78), it was located on a point of the same name in Pa'ea by To'ofaroa Pass (presumably the point now known as Teoneahu, by 'Irihonu Pass at Pa'ea). No doubt the image of 'Oro and Te Ra'i-puatata were taken there by To'ofa, the local *ari'i*, after the attack on Mahaiatea.

By the time that the first missionaries arrived at the island in 1797, 'Oro's main *marae* in Atehuru had shifted to Puna'aui'a, about a mile up the valley (or perhaps these were two linked sites – one coastal and one inland – that worked together in the worship of the war god). Its site is marked on Wilson's chart of the island, and Wilson gives a detailed description and an engraved image of this *marae*, which had a large platform for offerings that stood on sixteen wooden pillars, each eight feet high, and a number of *ti'i*. A house contained the 'ark' of 'Oro, which was only about four feet long and three feet wide; although the *atua* had been taken to a small *marae* beside the ocean, now usually referred to as Taputapuatea. The two god-images were brought and shown to Wilson the next day, bound in sennit and decorated with little bunches of red and yellow feathers (Wilson, 1799, description 211, engraving 208).

23. Henry, 1928, 78.

24. According to Oliver, this small stone platform was also known as the *ava'a* or 'god's bed', principally used as the place where the images of the gods were placed during *marae* rituals. During the investiture of a high chief, the chief might also stand here as he was invested with the *marae*'s highest title. Below some *ava'a* was a pit in which the discarded 'clothing' of the gods was placed after the *pa'i-atua* ritual, along with other ritual rubbish. (Oliver, 1974, I: 100.)

25. For a lengthy discussion, see Babadzan, 1993, 181–90.

26. Driessen, 1991, 111.

27. See Tcherkézoff for a discussion of the way in which chiefs, upon being installed with a title, became the temporary 'body' of the first ancestor to carry that title. (Tcherkézoff, 2004, 124–28.)

28. Both Cook and William Anderson, the surgeon, gave excellent descriptions of these rituals (Cook in Beaglehole, ed., 1967, i: 198–206; Anderson in ibid., ii: 980–86).

29. King in Beaglehole, ed., 1967, ii: 1375.

30. Bayly quoted in Beaglehole, ed., 1967, i: 210.

31. Griffin quoted in ibid., i: 210; Rickman, 1781, 140.

32. Ibid., 211.

33. Samwell in ibid., ii: 1066.

34. Orsmond, John, n.d., 'The 'Arioi War', Mfm G7706, Mitchell Library, Sydney, Meredith Filihia transcript, 9.

35. Home quoted in Beaglehole, ed., 1967, i: fn. 211.

36. Home, Alexander Home's *Discovery* notes and typescript, Ms 690, National Library of Australia, 1.

37. King in Beaglehole, ed., 1967, i: 214.

38. Moerenhout gives a detailed account of peace-making rituals on the island, although he states that human sacrifices were required to seal the peace on these occasions, and were brought to the *marae* in sacred canoes which were carried onto the *marae* without touching the ground. (Moerenhout in Borden, ed., 1983, 264–65.)

39. Home, Alexander Home's *Discovery* notes and typescript, Ms 690, National Library of Australia, 4.

40. King in Beaglehole, ed., 1967, ii: 1380.

41. Samwell in ibid., ii: 1055.

42. Home, Alexander Home's *Discovery* notes and typescript, Ms 690, National Library of Australia, 4.

43. Ibid., 4.

44. Trevenen in Lloyd and Anderson, eds, 1959, 27–28.

45. Trevenen in ibid., 21.

46. Gilbert in Holmes, ed., 1982, 46–47.

47. Zimmerman in Howay, ed., 1929, 57.

48. Williamson in Adm 55/117.

49. Home, Alexander Home's *Discovery* notes and typescript, Ms 690, National Library of Australia, 5.

50. Rickman, 1781, 160.

51. Samwell in Beaglehole, ed., 1967, ii: 1070.

52. Cook in Beaglehole, ed., 1967, i: 240–41.

53. Samwell in Beaglehole, ed., 1967, ii: 1073.

54. Home, Alexander Home's *Discovery* notes and typescript, Ms 690, National Library of Australia, 17.

55. Ibid.

56. Ibid.

57. Williamson quoted in Beaglehole, ed., 1967, i: fn. 251.

58. Ellis, 1782, I: 159–61.

59. Edgar in Beaglehole, ed., 1967, i: fn. 247.

60. Home, Alexander Home's *Discovery* notes and typescript, Ms 690, National Library of Australia, 13.

61. 'Christian', *Public Advertiser*.

62. Seward, Anna, 1780, *Elegy on Captain Cook. To which is added, an Ode on the Sun. By Miss Seward.* (London, printed for J. Dodsley).

63. Morrison, 1935, 86.

64. William Bligh to Sir Joseph Banks, Batavia, 13 October 1789 in Paul Brunton, ed., 1989, *Awake, Bold Bligh! William Bligh's letters describing the mutiny on HMS* Bounty (Sydney, Allen and Unwin), 35.

65. These fertility rituals dedicated to Demeter (the goddess of grain) and her daughter Persephone (the goddess of the annual renewal of life) were among the most sacred celebrations in ancient Greece. The participants took a vow of secrecy not to reveal what happened, but these rituals are thought to have featured ritual sex between the high priest and high priestess, and the offering of pigs.

66. Hamilton, George in Basil Thomas, ed., 1915, *Voyage of H.M.S* Pandora (London, Francis Edwards), 108–9.

CONCLUSION: THE ANGEL OF HISTORY

1. Strathern, Marilyn, 1990, 'Artefacts of History: Events and the Interpretation of Images', in Jukka Siikala, ed., *Culture and History in the Pacific* (Helsinki, The Finnish Anthropological Society, Transactions No. 27), 25–43.

2. Ibid., 28.

3. Although it must be said that these classical resonances were not entirely misleading. Aphrodite, for example, was not just the goddess of seduction and sexual passion, but a fertility goddess associated with the fecundity of plants and animals, worshipped in seasonal festivals. Among her female devotees were high-born young girls; and singers, musicians and dancers who performed acts of sexual intercourse dedicated to the goddess. Phallic imagery featured in her worship (and that of her companion Eros; and her son Priapus), reminiscent of Tetumu. Her followers, like the *taiato* among the *'arioi*, have often been described (and very likely misunderstood) as 'prostitutes' and 'whores'. (For these aspects of Aphrodite's worship, see for example Rosenzweig, 2004, 36–38, 45–55.)

4. Carter, Sophie, 1999, '"This Female Proteus": Representing Prostitution and Masquerade in Eighteenth Century English Popular Print Culture', *Oxford Art Journal* 22/1, 57–79; Maccubbin, Robert Purks, ed., 1985, *Tis Nature's Fault: Unauthorized Sexuality during the Enlightenment* (Cambridge, Cambridge University Press); Rousseau, G.S. and Porter, Roy, 1988, *Sexual Underworlds of the Enlightenment* (Chapel Hill, University of North Carolina Press).

5. Benjamin, Walter, in Hannah Arendt, ed., 1970, *Illuminations* (London, Jonathan Cape), 257–60.

6. Driessen, Hank, 1982, 'Outriggerless Canoes and Glorious Beings: Pre-contact Prophecies in the Society Islands', *Journal of Pacific History* XVII, 8–9; Tahitian text in Henry, 1928, 5 (for variant versions of this story, see ibid., 5, 9–10).

Index